Vietnam

a Lonely Planet travel survival kit

Robert Storey
Daniel Robinson

.ion

lished by
Lonely Planet Publications
Head Office: PO Box 617, Hawthorn, Vic 3122, Australia
Branches: 155 Filbert St, Suite 251, Oakland, CA 94607, USA
             10 Barley Mow Passage, Chiswick, London W4 4PH, UK
             71 bis rue du Cardinal Lemoine, 75005 Paris, France

Printed by
SNP Printing Pte Ltd, Singapore

Photographs by

Greg Alford	Glenn Beanland	Sara Jane Cleland
Lisa Croker	Richard Everist	Richard I'Anson
Brendan McCarthy	Karen O'Connor	John Perttula
Simon Rowe	Helen Savory	Robert Storey
Deanna Swaney	Genevieve Webb	Phil Weymouth
Tony Wheeler		

Front cover: Historic architecture, Hoi An (Sara Jane Cleland)
Title Page: Po Klong Garai Cham Towers, Phan Rang (Deanna Swaney)

First Published
February 1991

This Edition
November 1995

**Although the authors and publisher have tried to make the information as
accurate as possible, they accept no responsibility for any loss, injury or
inconvenience sustained by any person using this book.**

National Library of Australia Cataloguing in Publication Data

Storey, Robert
Vietnam.

3rd ed.
Includes index.
ISBN 0 86442 316 0.

1. Vietnam – Guidebooks. I. Robinson, Daniel. Vietnam.
II. Title. III. Title : Vietnam. (Series : Lonely Planet travel survival kit).

915.970444

text & maps © Lonely Planet 1995
photos © photographers as indicated 1995
climate charts compiled from information supplied by Patrick J Tyson, © Patrick J Tyson, 1995

Robert Storey

After graduating from the University of Nevada, Robert pursued a distinguished career as a slot machine repairman in a Las Vegas casino. He later worked for the government bureaucracy, though he is not quite sure what his job was. Seeking the meaning of life, he became a backpacker and drifted around Asia. Robert now lives in Taiwan, where he has devoted himself to such serious pursuits as writing books, studying Chinese, computer hacking and mountain climbing. He has written or contributed to several Lonely Planet guides, including *Ho Chi Minh City, Beijing, Mongolia, Indonesia, China, Taiwan, Korea* and *Hong Kong, Macau & Canton*.

Daniel Robinson

Daniel, researcher and writer of the first edition's Vietnam and Cambodia sections, grew up in the USA (the San Francisco Bay Area and Glen Ellyn, Illinois) and Israel. He has travelled extensively in the Middle East and South, South-East and East Asia. Daniel holds a BA in Near Eastern Studies from Princeton University. He has contributed to Lonely Planet's *Western Europe* shoestring series and is co-author of *France*. Daniel lives in Tel Aviv.

From the Authors

The first edition of this book was entitled *Vietnam, Laos & Cambodia – a travel survival kit.* Daniel Robinson did the Vietnam and Cambodia sections and Joe Cummings researched and wrote the Laos section. Laos and Cambodia have now been spun off to their own books, and this new update by Robert Storey deals exclusively with Vietnam.

For this edition, special thanks to Adrian Bloch, Mike Romano, Patrick Morris, Suzanne Grumet and Brigitte Wirtz. There are a number of Vietnamese people who served as guides, translators and travelling companions whom we'd love to thank. But sadly we feel it is more prudent to leave their names out of this book. However, we are especially grateful to them.

From the Publisher

This third edition of *Vietnam - a travel survival kit* was edited by Linda Suttie. Glenn Beanland was responsible for mapping, design and layout. Illustrations were done by Trudi Canavan and Ann Jeffree. Maliza Kruh, Trudi Canavan and Andrew Smith assisted with mapping. Paul Clifton designed and drew the colour map and Simon Bracken and Adam McCrow designed the cover. Proofing was done by Megan Fraser, Kristin Odijk and Greg Alford. The Vietnamese script was provided by Robert Storey and formatted by Dan Levin and Vicki Beale.

Sharon Wertheim compiled the index. Richard Everist and Andrea Webster supplied additional travel information for this update.

Special thanks goes to all the travellers who took the time to write to us about their experiences in Vietnam. Their names appear at the back of the book.

Warning & Request

A travel book is like a snapshot – it represents the way things were for a brief moment in time. Before the ink is dry on a new book, things change, and few places change more quickly than Vietnam. Prices go up, new hotels open, old ones degenerate, some burn down, others get renovated and renamed, bus routes change, bridges collapse and recommended travel agents get indicted for fraud.

Carry this book as a guide, not a gospel – since things go on changing we can't tell you exactly what to expect all the time. Hopefully this book will point you in a few of the right directions and save you some time and money while you're at it!

At Lonely Planet we get a steady stream of mail from travellers and it all helps – whether it's a few lines scribbled on the back of a used paper plate or a stack of neat typewritten pages spewing forth from our fax machine. We even get the occasional letter from local Vietnamese wanting to tell us about their country.

So if you find things aren't like they're described herein, don't get upset – get out your pen, typewriter or word processor and write to us. Your input will help make the next edition better. As usual, the writers of useful letters will score a free copy of the next edition, or another Lonely Planet guide if you prefer. We give away lots of books, but unfortunately not every letter-writer receives one.

Contents

Map Legend

BOUNDARIES

International Boundary
Regional Boundary

ROUTES

Freeway
Highway
Major Road
Unsealed Road or Track
City Road
City Street
Railway
Underground Railway
Tram
Walking Track
Walking Tour
Ferry Route
Cable Car or Chairlift

AREA FEATURES

Park, Gardens
National Park
Built-Up Area
Pedestrian Mall
Market
Cemetery
Reef
Beach or Desert
Mountain Ranges

HYDROGRAPHIC FEATURES

Coastline
River, Creek
Intermittent River or Creek
Lake, Intermittent Lake
Canal
Swamp

SYMBOLS

✪ CAPITAL		National Capital
◉ Capital		Regional Capital
◍ CITY		Major City
● City		City
● Town		Town
● Village		Village
■		Place to Stay
▼		Place to Eat
▮		Pub, Bar
✉	☎	Post Office, Telephone
❶	❸	Tourist Information, Bank
◒	🅿	Transport, Parking
🏛	⌂	Museum, Youth Hostel
🚐	▲	Caravan Park, Camping Ground
⛪	✚	Church, Cathedral
☪	✡	Mosque, Synagogue
卍	▲	Buddhist Temple, Temple

✚	★	Hospital, Police Station
✈	✝	Airport, Airfield
🛏	🐾	Swimming Pool, Beach
❖	🐘	Shopping Centre, Zoo
⚑	⛽	Golf Course, Petrol Station
←	A25	One Way Street, Route Number
	⸫	Archaeological Site or Ruins
🏛	🗼	Stately Home, Monument
🏯	◼	Castle, Tomb
⌒	⌂	Cave, Hut or Chalet
▲	☼	Mountain or Hill, Lookout
🗼	⚓	Lighthouse, Shipwreck
)(	◎	Pass, Spring
		Ancient or City Wall
		Rapids, Waterfalls
		Cliff or Escarpment, Tunnel
		Railway Station

Note: not all symbols displayed above appear in this book

Introduction

In the decades following World War II the name 'Vietnam' came to signify to many Westerners either a brutal jungle war or a spectacular failure of American power – or both. In the 1960s, bumper stickers in the USA demanded that America 'Stop the War!' and 'Bring Our Boys Home'. Once the war ended, most Americans wanted to forget it, but there have been countless reminders: half-a-dozen major motion pictures, several TV drama series, countless university courses and hundreds of books about Vietnam have captivated audiences around the globe. However, virtually all of this publicity and information concerns the American war in Indochina, not Vietnam the country. The real Vietnam, with its unique and rich civilisation, spectacular scenery and highly cultured and friendly people, has been largely ignored. While no doubt the Vietnam War continues to weigh heavily on the consciousness of all who can remember the fighting, the Vietnam of today is a country at peace.

After the fall of South Vietnam to Communist North Vietnamese forces in 1975, Vietnam was virtually isolated from the world. But towards the end of the 1980s, the Cold War thawed and the Hanoi government succeeded in reducing Vietnam's international isolation, in part by opening the country's doors to foreign visitors. Not long thereafter, the dramatic collapse of the Eastern Bloc and the ending of the Cambodian civil war greatly reduced tensions in Indochina.

Most visitors to Vietnam are overwhelmed by the sublime beauty of the country's natural setting. The Red River Delta in the north, the Mekong Delta in the south and almost the entire coastal strip are a patchwork of brilliant green rice paddies tended by peasant women in conical hats. Vietnam's 3451 km of coastline include countless kilometres of unspoiled beaches and a number of stunning lagoons; some sections are shaded by coconut palms and casuarinas, others bounded by seemingly endless expanses of sand dunes or rugged spurs of the Truong Son Mountains.

Between the two deltas, the coastal paddies lining the South China Sea give way to soaring mountains, some of whose slopes are cloaked with the richest of rainforests. Slightly farther from the littoral are the refreshingly cool plateaus of the Central Highlands, which are dotted with waterfalls. The area is home to dozens of distinct ethno-linguistic groups (hill tribes), more than almost any other country in Asia.

Visitors to Vietnam have their senses thrilled by all the sights, sounds, tastes and smells of a society born of over a century of contact between an ancient civilisation and the ways of the West. There's nothing quite

like grabbing a delicious lunch of local delicacies at a food stall deep inside a marketplace, surrounded by tropical fruit vendors and legions of curious youngsters. Or sitting by a waterfall in the Central Highlands, sipping soda water with lemon juice and watching newly wed couples on their honeymoon tiptoe up to the streambank in their 'Sunday finest'. Or being invited by a Buddhist monk to attend prayers at his pagoda conducted, according to ancient Mahayana rites, with chanting, drums and gongs.

One traveller writes:

Of the 30 or so countries I have been to, Vietnam is easily the most beautiful. I saw more shades of green than I knew existed. Rice fields manually tended from dawn to dusk were always in view, as were forest-covered mountains. I also frequently caught glimpses of pristine deserted beaches from the train window as we made our way along the coast...

Fiercely protective of their independence and sovereignty for 2000 years, the Vietnamese are also graciously welcoming of foreigners who come as their guests rather than as conquerors. No matter what side they or their parents were on during the war, the Vietnamese are, almost without exception, extremely friendly to Western visitors (including Americans) and supportive of more contact with the outside world. People who visit Vietnam during the first years of the country's renewed interaction within the West will play an important role in conveying to the Vietnamese the potentialities of such contact. And now that 'capitalism' is no longer a four-letter word, private Vietnamese businesses have mushroomed, adding an atmosphere of hustle and bustle to Ho Chi Minh City and other cities whose resurgent dynamism is reviving the Vietnamese economy.

The astonishing pace of economic development in East Asia has made many of these countries considerably more expensive, polluted and less enchanting than they used to be. Rice paddies have given way to industrial estates belching out black smoke, bicycles have been replaced by tour buses and thatched huts have been bulldozed to make way for five-star hotels and modern office towers.

Vietnam has not yet reached that level of development, and a visit to this country is almost like a journey back through time. Red tape kept foreign tourists and investors out for nearly two decades, but visiting has become considerably easier in the past couple of years and the tourist flood-gates have opened wide. Already, the short period of economic liberalisation and openness to outsiders have brought dramatic changes. Vietnam offers a rare opportunity to see a country of traditional charm and beauty taking the first hesitant steps into the modern world.

Facts about the Country

HISTORY

Visitors to Vietnam will notice that, invariably, the major streets of every city and town bear the same two dozen or so names. These are the names of Vietnam's greatest national heroes who, over the last 2000 years, have led the country in its repeated expulsions of foreign invaders and whose exploits have inspired subsequent generations of patriots.

Prehistory

The origins of the Vietnamese people are shrouded in legend. Recent archaeological finds indicate that the earliest human habitation of northern Vietnam goes back about 500,000 years. Mesolithic and Neolithic cultures existed in northern Vietnam 10,000 years ago; these groups may have engaged in primitive agriculture as early as 7000 BC. The sophisticated Bronze Age Dong Son culture emerged around the 13th century BC.

From the 1st to the 6th centuries AD, the south of what is now Vietnam was part of the Indianised kingdom of Funan, which produced notably refined art and architecture. The Funanese constructed an elaborate system of canals which were used for both transportation and the irrigation of wet rice agriculture. The principal port city of Funan was Oc-Eo in what is now Kien Giang Province. Archaeological excavations have yielded evidence of contact between Funan and China, Indonesia, India, Persia and even the Mediterranean. One of the most extraordinary artefacts found at Oc-Eo was a gold Roman medallion dated 152 AD and bearing the likeness of Antoninus Pius. In the mid-6th century, Funan was attacked by the pre-Angkorian kingdom of Chenla, which gradually absorbed the territory of Funan into its own.

The Hindu kingdom of Champa appeared around present-day Danang in the late 2nd century. Like Funan, it became Indianised (eg, the Chams adopted Hinduism, employed Sanskrit as a sacred language and borrowed a great deal from Indian art) by lively commercial relations with India and through the immigration of Indian literati and priests. By the 8th century, Champa had expanded southward to include what is now Nha Trang and Phan Rang. Champa was a semi-piratic country that lived in part from conducting raids along the entire Indochinese coast; as a result, it was in a constant state of war with the Vietnamese to the north and the Khmers to the west. Brilliant examples of Cham sculpture can be seen in the Cham Museum in Danang.

Chinese Rule (circa 200 BC to 938 AD)

When the Chinese conquered the Red River Delta in the 2nd century BC, they found a feudally organised society based on hunting, fishing and slash-and-burn agriculture; these proto-Vietnamese also carried on trade with other peoples in the area. Over the next few centuries, significant numbers of Chinese settlers, officials and scholars moved to the Red River Delta, taking over large tracts of land. The Chinese tried to impose a centralised state system on the Vietnamese and to forcibly Sinicise their culture, but local rulers made use of the benefits of Chinese civilisation to tenaciously resist these efforts.

The most famous act of resistance against the Chinese during this period was the Rebellion of the Trung Sisters (Hai Ba Trung). In 40 AD, the Chinese executed a high-ranking feudal lord. His widow and her sister, the Trung Sisters, rallied tribal chieftains, raised an army and led a revolt that compelled the Chinese governor to flee. The sisters then had themselves proclaimed queens of the newly independent Vietnamese entity. In 43 AD, however, the Chinese counterattacked and defeated the Vietnamese; rather than surrender, the Trung Sisters threw themselves into the Hat Giang River.

The early Vietnamese learned a great deal from the Chinese, including the use of the metal plough and domesticated beasts of burden and the construction of dikes and irrigation works. These innovations made possible the establishment of a culture based on rice growing, which remains the basis of the Vietnamese way of life to this day. As food became more plentiful, the population grew, forcing the Vietnamese to seek new lands on which to grow rice.

During this era, Vietnam was a key port of call on the sea route between China and India. The Vietnamese were introduced to Confucianism and Taoism by Chinese scholars who came to Vietnam as administrators and refugees. Indians sailing eastward brought Theravada (Hinayana) Buddhism to the Red River Delta while, simultaneously, Chinese travellers introduced Mahayana Buddhism. Buddhist monks carried with them the scientific and medical knowledge of the civilisations of India and China; as a result, Vietnamese Buddhists soon counted among their own great doctors, botanists and scholars.

There were major rebellions against Chinese rule – which was characterised by tyranny, forced labour and insatiable demands for tribute – in the 3rd and 6th centuries, but all (along with numerous minor revolts) were crushed. In 679, the Chinese named the country Annam, which means the Pacified South. But ever since this era, the collective memory of those early attempts to throw off the Chinese yoke has played an important role in shaping Vietnamese identity.

Independence from China (10th Century)

In the aftermath of the collapse of the Tang Dynasty in China in the early 10th century, the Vietnamese revolted against Chinese rule. In 938 AD, Ngo Quyen vanquished the Chinese armies at a battle on the Bach Dang River, ending 1000 years of Chinese rule. Ngo Quyen established an independent Vietnamese state, but it was not until 968 that Dinh Bo Linh ended the anarchy that followed Ngo Quyen's death and, following the custom of the times, reached an agreement with China: in return for recognition of their

de facto independence, the Vietnamese accepted Chinese sovereignty and agreed to pay triennial tribute.

The dynasty founded by Dinh Bo Linh survived only until 980, when Le Dai Hanh overthrew it, beginning what is known as the Early Le Dynasty (980-1009).

The dynasties of independent Vietnam were:

Ngo Dynasty	939-965
Dinh Dynasty	968-980
Early Le Dynasty	980-1009
Ly Dynasty	1010-1225
Tran Dynasty	1225-1400
Ho Dynasty	1400-1407
Post-Tran Dynasty	1407-1413
Chinese Rule	1414-1427
Later Le Dynasty (nominally until 1788)	1428-1524
Mac Dynasty	1527-1592
Trinh Lords of the North	1539-1787
Nguyen Lords of the South	1558-1778
Tay Son Dynasty	1788-1802
Nguyen Dynasty	1802-1945

Ly Dynasty (1010-1225)

From the 11th to the 13th centuries, the independence of the Vietnamese Kingdom (Dai Viet) was consolidated under the emperors of the Ly Dynasty, founded by Ly Thai To. They reorganised the administrative system, founded the nation's first university (the Temple of Literature in Hanoi), promoted agriculture and built the first embankments for flood control along the Red River. Confucian scholars fell out of official favour because of their close cultural links to China; at the same time, the early Ly monarchs, whose dynasty had come to power with Buddhist support, promoted Buddhism.

The Confucian philosophy of government and society, emphasising educational attainment, ritual performance and government authority, reasserted itself with the graduation of the first class from the Temple of Literature in 1075. Following years of study which emphasised classical education, these scholars went into government service, becoming what the West came to call mandarins. The outlines of the Vietnamese mandarinal system of government – according to which the state was run by a scholar class recruited in civil service examinations – date from this era.

During the Ly Dynasty, the Chinese, Khmers and Chams repeatedly attacked Vietnam but were repelled, most notably under the renowned strategist and tactician Ly Thuong Kiet (1030-1105), a military mandarin of royal blood who is still revered as a national hero.

Vietnamese conquests of Cham territory, which greatly increased the acreage under rice cultivation, were accompanied by an aggressive policy of colonisation that reproduced social structures dominant in the north in the newly settled territories. This process did not make allowances for the potential technological and cultural contributions of the Chams (and indeed destroyed Cham civilisation), but it did result in a chain of homogeneous villages that eventually stretched from the Chinese border to the Gulf of Thailand.

Tran Dynasty (1225-1400)

After years of civil strife, the Tran Dynasty overthrew the Ly Dynasty. The Tran increased the land under cultivation to feed the growing population and improved the dikes on the Red River.

After the dreaded Mongol warrior Kublai Khan completed his conquest of China in the mid-13th century, he demanded the right to cross Vietnamese territory on his way to attack Champa. The Vietnamese refused this demand but the Mongols – 500,000 of them – came anyway. The outnumbered Vietnamese under Tran Hung Dao attacked the invaders and forced them back to China, but the Mongols returned, this time with 300,000 men. Tran Hung Dao then lured them deep into Vietnamese territory; at high tide he attacked the Mongol fleet as it sailed on the Bach Dang River, ordering a tactical retreat of his forces to lure the Mongols into staying and fighting. The battle con-

tinued for many hours until low tide, when a sudden Vietnamese counteroffensive forced the Mongol boats back, impaling them on steel-tipped bamboo stakes set in the river bed the night before. The entire fleet was captured or sunk.

When the Tran Dynasty was overthrown in 1400 by Ho Qui Ly, both the Tran loyalists and the Chams (who had sacked Hanoi in 1371) encouraged Chinese intervention. The Chinese readily complied with the request and took control of Vietnam in 1407, imposing a regime characterised by heavy taxation and slave labour; Chinese culture and ways of doing things were forced on the population. The Chinese also took the national archives – and some of the country's intellectuals as well – to China, an irreparable loss to Vietnamese civilisation. Of this period, the great poet Nguyen Trai (1380-1442) would write:

Were the water of the Eastern Sea to be exhausted, the stain of their ignominy could not be washed away; all the bamboo of the Southern Mountains would not suffice to provide the paper for recording all their crimes.

Later Le Dynasty (1428-1524)

Le Loi was born into a large and prosperous family in the village of Lam Son in Thanh Hoa Province and earned a reputation for using his wealth to aid the poor. The ruling Chinese invited him to join the mandarinate but he refused. In 1418, Le Loi began to organise what came to be known as the Lam Son Uprising, travelling around the countryside to rally the people against the Chinese. Despite several defeats, he persisted in his efforts, earning the respect of the peasantry by ensuring that even when facing starvation his guerrilla troops did not pillage the land. After his victory in 1428, Le Loi declared himself Emperor Ly Thai To, thus beginning the Later Le Dynasty. To this day, Le Loi is revered as one of Vietnam's greatest national heroes.

After Le Loi's victory over the Chinese, Nguyen Trai, a scholar and Le Loi's companion in arms, wrote his famous *Great Proclamation*

(Binh Ngo Dai Cao), extraordinary for the compelling voice it gave to Vietnam's fierce spirit of independence:

Our people long ago established Vietnam as an independent nation with its own civilisation. We have our own mountains and our own rivers, our own customs and traditions, and these are different from those of the foreign country to the north...We have sometimes been weak and sometimes powerful, but at no time have we suffered from a lack of heroes.

The Later Le Dynasty ruled until 1524 and, nominally, up to 1788. Le Loi and his successors instituted a vast programme of agrarian reform and land redistribution. They also launched a campaign to take over Cham lands to the south. In the 15th century Laos was forced to recognise Vietnamese suzerainty.

Under the Le Dynasty, an attempt was made to break free of the cultural and intellectual domination of Chinese civilisation. In the realms of law, religion and literature, indigenous traditions were brought to the fore. The Vietnamese language gained favour among scholars – who had previously disdained it, preferring Chinese – and a number of outstanding works of literature were produced. Legal reforms gave women almost-equal rights in the domestic sphere, but two groups were excluded from full civil rights: slaves (many of them prisoners of war) and, oddly, actors. In the culture of the elite, however, Chinese language and traditions continued to hold sway, and neo-Confucianism remained dominant in the areas of social and political morality.

Trinh & Nguyen Lords

Throughout the 17th and 18th centuries, Vietnam was divided between the Trinh Lords, who ruled in the north under the titular kingship of the Later Le monarchs, and the Nguyen Lords, who controlled the south and also nominally recognised the Later Le Dynasty. The Trinh Lords repeatedly failed in attempts to take over areas under Nguyen control, in part because the Portuguese weaponry used by the Nguyen

was far superior to the Dutch armaments supplied to the Trinh. During this period the Nguyen extended Vietnamese control into the Khmer territories of the Mekong Delta, populating the area with Vietnamese settlers. Cambodia was forced to accept Vietnamese suzerainty in the mid-17th century.

Buddhism enjoyed the patronage and support of both the Trinh and the Nguyen, and pagodas were built all over the country. But by this time Vietnamese Buddhism was no longer doctrinally pure, having become intermingled with animism, ancestor-worship and popularised Taoism.

Early Contact with the West

According to Chinese records, the first Vietnamese contact with Europeans took place in 166 AD when travellers from the Rome of Marcus Aurelius arrived in the Red River Delta.

The first Portuguese sailors landed in Danang in 1516; they were followed by Dominican missionaries 11 years later. During the next few decades the Portuguese began to trade with Vietnam, setting up a commercial colony alongside those of the Japanese and Chinese at Faifo (present-day Hoi An near Danang).

Franciscan missionaries from the Philippines settled in central Vietnam in 1580, followed in 1615 by the Jesuits, who had just been expelled from Japan. In 1637, the Dutch were authorised to set up trading posts in the north, and one of the Le kings even took a Dutch woman as one of his six wives. The first English attempt to break into the Vietnamese market ended with the murder of an agent of the East India Company in Hanoi in 1613.

One of the most illustrious of the early missionaries was the brilliant French Jesuit Alexandre de Rhodes (1591-1660). He is most recognised for his work in devising *quoc ngu*, the Latin-based phonetic alphabet in which Vietnamese is written to this day. Over the course of his long career, de Rhodes flitted back and forth between Hanoi, Macau, Rome and Paris, seeking support and funding for his missionary activities and battling both Portuguese colonial opposition and the intractable Vatican bureaucracy. In 1645, he was sentenced to death for illegally entering Vietnam to proselytise but was expelled instead; two of the priests with him were beheaded.

By the late 17th century most of the European merchants were gone; trade with Vietnam had not proved particularly profitable. But the missionaries remained, and the Catholic Church eventually had a greater impact on Vietnam than on any country in Asia except the Philippines, which was ruled by the Spanish for 400 years. The Vietnamese – especially in the north – proved highly receptive to Catholicism, but mass conversions were hindered by the Catholic stand against polygamy and by the opposition of the Vatican to ancestor-worship. The Catholic emphasis on individual salvation undermined the established Confucian order, and wary officials of the mandarinate often restricted the activities of missionaries and persecuted their followers. But despite this friction, the imperial court retained a contingent of Jesuit scholars, astronomers, mathematicians and physicians.

The European missionaries did not hesitate to use secular means to help them achieve their goal – the conversion to Catholicism of all of Asia. Towards this end, French missionaries, who had supplanted the Portuguese by the 18th century, actively campaigned for a greater French political and military role in Vietnam.

Tay Son Rebellion (1771-1802)

In 1765, a rebellion against misgovernment broke out in the town of Tay Son near Qui Nhon. It was led by three brothers from a wealthy merchant family: Nguyen Nhac, Nguyen Hue and Nguyen Lu. By 1773, the Tay Son Rebels (as they came to be known) controlled the whole of central Vietnam, and in 1783 they captured Saigon and the rest of the south, killing the reigning prince and his family (as well as 10,000 Chinese residents of Cholon). Nguyen Lu became king of the south, and Nguyen Nhac became king of central Vietnam.

Prince Nguyen Anh, the only survivor of the defeated Nguyen clan, fled to Thailand and requested military assistance from the Thais. He also met the French Jesuit missionary Pigneau de Behaine (the Bishop of Adran), whom he eventually authorised to act as his intermediary in seeking assistance from the French. As a sign of good faith, Nguyen Anh sent his four-year-old son Canh with Pigneau de Behaine to France. The exotic entourage created quite a sensation when it arrived at Versailles in 1787, and Louis XVI authorised a military expedition. Louis XVI later changed his mind, but the bishop managed to convince French merchants in India to buy him two ships, weapons and supplies. With a force of 400 French deserters he had recruited, de Behaine set sail from Pondicherry, India, in June 1789.

Meanwhile, the Tay Son overthrew the Trinh Lords in the north and proclaimed allegiance to the Later Le Dynasty. The weak Le emperor, however, proved unable to retain his control of the country, but rather than calling on the Tay Son, he asked the Chinese for help. Taking advantage of the unstable situation, the Chinese sent 200,000 troops to Vietnam under the pretext of helping the emperor. In 1788, with popular sentiment on his side, one of the Tay Son brothers, Nguyen Hue, proclaimed himself Emperor Quang Trung and set out with his army to expel the Chinese. In 1789, Nguyen Hue's forces overwhelmingly defeated the Chinese army at Dong Da (near Hanoi) in one of the most celebrated military achievements in Vietnamese history.

In the south, Nguyen Anh, whose forces were trained by Pigneau de Behaine's young French adventurers, gradually pushed back the Tay Son. In 1802, Nguyen Anh proclaimed himself Emperor Gia Long, thus beginning the Nguyen Dynasty. When he captured Hanoi, his victory was complete, and for the first time in two centuries, Vietnam was united. Hué became the new national capital.

Nguyen Dynasty (1802-1945)

Emperors of the Nguyen Dynasty:

Gia Long	1802-1819
Minh Mang	1820-1840
Thieu Tri	1841-1847
Tu Duc	1848-1883
Duc Duc	1883
Hiep Hoa	1883
Kien Phuc	1883-1884
Ham Nghi	1884-1885
Dong Khanh	1885-1889
Thanh Thai	1889-1907
Duy Tan	1907-1916
Khai Dinh	1916-1925
Bao Dai	1925-1945

Emperor Gia Long (reigned 1802-19) initiated what historian David Marr has called 'a policy of massive reassertion of Confucian values and institutions' in order to consolidate the dynasty's shaky position by appealing to the conservative tendencies of the elite, who had felt threatened by the atmosphere of reform stirred up by the Tay Son Rebels.

Gia Long also began a large-scale programme of public works (dikes, canals, roads, ports, bridges, land reclamation) to rehabilitate the country, which had been devastated by almost three decades of warfare. The Mandarin Road linking the national capital, Hué, to both Hanoi and Saigon was constructed during this period, as was a string of star-shaped citadels – built according to the principles of the French military architect Vauban – in provincial capitals. All these projects imposed a heavy burden on the population in the forms of taxation, military conscription and *corvée* (forced labour).

Gia Long's son, Emperor Minh Mang (reigned 1820-40), worked to consolidate the state and establish a strong central government. Because of his background as a Confucian scholar, he emphasised the importance of traditional Confucian education which consisted of the memorisation and orthodox interpretation of the Confucian classics and texts of ancient Chinese history. As a result, education and spheres of activity dependent on it stagnated.

Minh Mang was profoundly hostile to Catholicism, which he saw as a threat to the Confucian state, and he extended this antipathy to all Western influences. Seven missionaries and an unknown number of Vietnamese Catholics were executed in the 1830s, inflaming passions among French

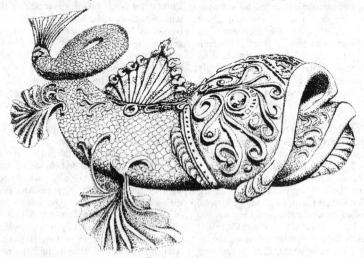

Dynastic sculpture, Hué

ROBERT STOREY

GREG ALFORD

KAREN O'CONNOR

BRENDAN McCARTHY

Vietnam in Focus

A
B
C
D

A Local transport, Vinh
B Po Nagar Cham Towers, Nha Trang
C Harvesting rice in the Mekong Delta
D Boat on the Perfume River, Hué

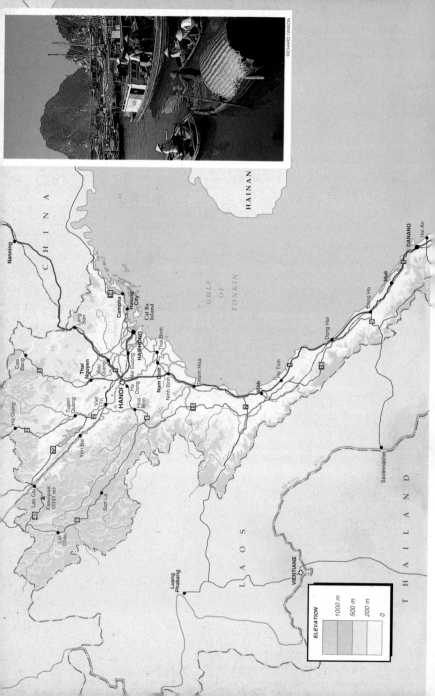

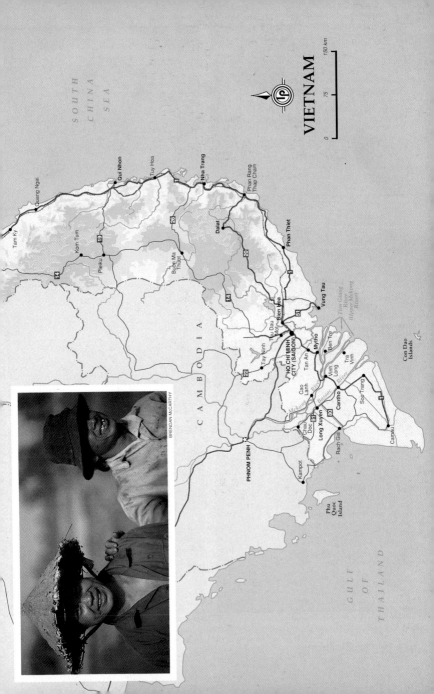

VIETNAM

SOUTH CHINA SEA

0   75   150 km

BRENDAN McCARTHY

Tam Ky
Quang Ngai
Kon Tum
Qui Nhon
Tuy Hoa
Pleiku
Buon Ma Thuot
Nha Trang
Dalat
Phan Rang
Thap Cham
Phan Thiet
Vung Tau
Bien Hoa
Thu Dau Mot
HO CHI MINH
CITY (SAIGON)
Tay Ninh
Mytho
Ben Tre
Tan An
Tra Vinh
Vinh
Long
Cao Lanh
Can Tho
Soc Trang
Chau Doc
Long Xuyen
Rach Gia
Camau
Con Dao
Islands
Kampot
PHNOM PENH
CAMBODIA
Tien Giang River
Upper Mekong River
Mekong River
Bassac River
Phu Quoc Island
GULF OF THAILAND

The People of Vietnam

Catholics who demanded that their government intervene in Vietnam.

Serious uprisings broke out in both the north and the south during this period, growing progressively more serious in the 1840s and 1850s. To make matters worse, the civil unrest in the deltas was accompanied by smallpox epidemics, tribal uprisings, drought, locusts and – most serious of all – repeated breaches in the Red River dikes, the result of government neglect.

The early Nguyen emperors continued the expansionist policies followed by preceding dynasties, pushing into Cambodia and westward into the mountains along a wide front. They seized huge areas of Lao territory and clashed with Thailand over control of the lands of the weak Khmer Empire.

The first half of the 19th century was marked by a great deal of literary activity. It was during this period that Nguyen Du (1765-1820), a poet, scholar, mandarin and diplomat, wrote one of Vietnam's literary masterpieces, *The Tale of Kieu (Kim Van Kieu)*.

Minh Mang was succeeded by Emperor Thieu Tri (reigned 1841-47), who expelled most of the foreign missionaries. He was followed by Emperor Tu Duc (reigned 1848-83), who continued to rule according to conservative Confucian precepts and in imitation of Qing practices in China. Both responded to rural unrest with repression.

French Rule (1859-1954)

Ever since Pigneau de Behaine's patronage of Nguyen Anh in the late 18th century and his son Canh's appearance at Versailles in 1787, certain segments of French society had retained an active interest in Indochina. But it was not until the Revolution of 1848 and the advent of the Second Empire that there arose a coalition of interests – Catholic, commercial, patriotic, strategic and idealistic (fans of the *mission civilisatrice*) – with sufficient influence to initiate large-scale, long-term colonial efforts. However, for the next four decades, the French colonial venture in Indochina was carried out haphazardly and without any preconceived plan. In fact, it was repeatedly on the verge of being discontinued altogether, and at times only the insubordinate and reckless actions of a few adventurers kept it going.

France's military activity in Vietnam began in 1847, when the French navy attacked Danang harbour in response to Thieu Tri's actions against Catholic missionaries. In 1858, a joint military force of 14 ships from France and the Spanish colony of the Philippines stormed Danang after the killing of several missionaries. As disease began to take a heavy toll and the expected support from Catholic Vietnamese failed to materialise, the force left a small garrison in Danang and followed the monsoon winds southward, seizing Saigon in early 1859. Huge quantities of Vietnamese cannon, firearms, swords, saltpetre, sulphur, shot and copper coins were seized; a fire set in rice storage granaries is said to have smouldered for three years.

The French victory in the 1861 Battle of Ky Hoa (Chi Hoa) marked the beginning of the end of formal, organised Vietnamese military action against the French in the south and the rise of popular guerrilla resistance led by the local scholar-gentry, who had refused en masse to collaborate with the French administration. This resistance took the form of ambushing French river craft, denying food supplies to French bases and assassinating collaborators.

In 1862, Tu Duc signed a treaty that gave the French the three eastern provinces of Cochinchina. In addition, missionaries were promised the freedom to proselytise everywhere in the country, several ports were opened to French and Spanish commerce, and Tu Duc undertook to pay a large indemnity. To raise the necessary cash he authorised the sale of opium in the north and sold the monopoly to the Chinese. Additionally, he debased the meritocratic mandarinate by putting low-ranking mandarinal posts up for sale.

The French offensive of 1867 broke the morale of the resistance, causing the scholar-gentry who had not been killed to flee the delta. Cochinchina became a French colony, and the peasantry assumed a position of non-violent resignation. At the same time, voices among the more educated classes of Vietnamese began to advocate cooperation with and subordination to the French in the interest of technical and economic development.

During this era, the Vietnamese might have been able to reduce the impact of the arrival of the European maritime powers and to retain their independence, but this would have required a degree of imagination and dynamism lacking in Hué. Indeed, until the mid-19th century, the imperial court at Hué, which was dominated by extreme Confucian conservatism, behaved almost as if Europe did not exist, though events such as the Opium War of 1839 in China should have served as a warning. In addition, resistance to colonialism was severely handicapped by an almost total lack of political and economic intelligence about France and the French.

The next major French action came in the years 1872 to 1874, when Jean Dupuis, a merchant seeking to supply salt and weapons to a Yunnanese general by sailing up the Red River, seized the Hanoi Citadel. Captain Francis Garnier, ostensibly dispatched to rein in Dupuis, instead took over where Dupuis left off. After capturing Hanoi, Garnier's gunboats proceeded to sail around the Red River Delta demanding tribute from provincial fortresses, an activity that ended only when Garnier was killed by the Black Flags (Co Den), a semi-autonomous army of Chinese, Vietnamese and hill-tribe troops who fought mostly for booty but resisted the French in part because of a strong antipathy toward Westerners.

These events threw the north into chaos: the Black Flags continued their piratic activities; local bands were organised to take vengeance on the Vietnamese – especially Catholics – who had helped the French; Chinese militias in the pay of both the French and the Nguyen emperors sprung up; Le Dynasty pretenders began asserting their claims; and the hill tribes revolted. As central government authority collapsed and all established order broke down, Tu Duc went so far as to petition for help from the Chinese

and to ask for support from the British and even the Americans.

In 1882, a French force under Captain Henri Rivière seized Hanoi, but further conquests were stubbornly resisted by both Chinese regulars and the Black Flags, especially the latter. The following year, Black Flags units ambushed Rivière at Cau Giay, killing him and 32 other Frenchmen, and triumphantly paraded his severed head from hamlet to hamlet.

Meanwhile, only a few weeks after the death of Tu Duc in 1883, the French attacked Hué and imposed a Treaty of Protectorate on the imperial court. There then began a tragicomic struggle for royal succession notable for its palace coups, mysteriously dead emperors and heavy-handed French diplomacy. Emperors Duc Duc and Hiep Hoa were succeeded by Kien Phuc (reigned 1883-84), who was followed by 14-year-old Emperor Ham Nghi (reigned 1884-85). By the time Ham Nghi and his advisers decided to relocate the court to the mountains and to lead resistance activities from there, the French had rounded up enough mandarin collaborators to give his French-picked successor, Emperor Dong Khanh (reigned 1885-89), sufficient legitimacy to survive.

Ham Nghi held out against the French until 1888 when he was betrayed, captured by the French and exiled to Algeria. Although the Indochinese Union (consisting of Cochinchina, Annam, Tonkin, Cambodia, Laos and the port of Qinzhouwan in China), proclaimed by the French in 1887, effectively ended the existence of an independent Vietnamese state, active resistance to colonialism continued in various parts of the country for the duration of French rule. The establishment of the Indochinese Union ended Vietnamese expansionism, and the Vietnamese were forced to give back lands taken from Cambodia and Laos.

Continuing in the tradition of centuries of Vietnamese dynasties, the French colonial authorities carried out ambitious public works, constructing the Saigon-Hanoi railway as well as ports, extensive irrigation and drainage systems, improved dikes, various public services and research institutes. To fund these activities, the government heavily taxed the peasants, devastating the traditional rural economy. The colonial administration also ran alcohol, salt and opium monopolies for the purpose of raising revenues. In Saigon, they produced a quick-burning type of opium which helped increase addiction and thus revenues.

And since colonialism was supposed to be a profitable proposition, French capital was invested for quick returns in anthracite coal, tin, tungsten and zinc mines and in tea, coffee and rubber plantations, all of which became notorious for the abysmal wages they paid and the subhuman treatment to which their Vietnamese workers were subjected. Out of the 45,000 indentured workers at one Michelin rubber plantation, 12,000 died of disease and malnutrition between 1917 and 1944.

As land, like capital, became concentrated in the hands of a tiny percentage of the population (in Cochinchina, 2.5% of the population came to own 45% of the land), a sub-proletariat of landless and uprooted peasants was formed. In the countryside these people were reduced to sharecropping, paying up to 60% of their crop in rents. Whereas the majority of Vietnamese peasants had owned their land before the arrival of the French, by the 1930s about 70% of them were landless. Because French policies impoverished the people of Indochina, the area never became an important market for French industry.

Vietnamese Anti-Colonialism

Throughout the colonial period, the vast majority of Vietnamese retained a strong desire to have their national independence restored. Seething nationalist aspirations often broke out into open defiance of the French, which took forms ranging from the publishing of patriotic periodicals and books to an attempt to poison the French garrison in Hanoi.

The imperial court in Hué, though corrupt, was a centre of nationalist feeling, a fact most evident in the game of musical thrones orchestrated by the French. Upon his death the subservient Dong Khanh was replaced by 10-year-old Emperor Thanh Thai (reigned 1889-1907), whose rule the French ended when he was discovered to have been plotting against them. He was deported to the Indian Ocean island of Réunion, where he remained until 1947.

His son and successor, Emperor Duy Tan (reigned 1907-16), was only in his teens in 1916 when he and the poet Tran Cao Van planned a general uprising in Hué that was discovered the day before it was scheduled to begin; Tran Cao Van was beheaded and Duy Tan was exiled to Réunion. Duy Tan was succeeded by the docile Emperor Khai Dinh (reigned 1916-25). On his death he was followed by his son, Emperor Bao Dai (reigned 1925-45), who at the time of his accession was 12 years old and in school in France.

Some Vietnamese nationalists (such as the scholar and patriot Phan Boi Chau, who rejected French rule but not Western ideas and technology) looked to Japan and China for support and political inspiration, especially after Japan's victory in the Russo-Japanese war of 1904-05 showed all of Asia that Western powers could be defeated. Sun Yatsen's 1911 revolution in China was also closely followed in Vietnamese nationalist circles.

The Viet Nam Quoc Dan Dang (VNQDD), a largely middle-class nationalist party modelled after the Chinese Kuomintang, was founded in 1927 by nationalist leaders including Nguyen Thai Hoc, who was guillotined along with 12 comrades in the savage French retribution for the abortive 1930 Yen Bai uprising.

Another source of nationalist agitation was among those Vietnamese who had spent time in France, where they were not hampered by the restrictions on political activity in force in the colonies. In addition, over 100,000 Vietnamese were sent to Europe as soldiers during WW I.

Ultimately, the most successful anti-colonialists proved to be the Communists, who were uniquely able to relate to the frustrations and aspirations of the population – especially the peasants – and to effectively channel and organise their demands for more equitable land distribution.

The institutional history of Vietnamese Communism – which in many ways is the political biography of Ho Chi Minh – is rather complicated. In brief, the first Marxist grouping in Indochina was the Vietnam Revolutionary Youth League (Viet Nam Cach Menh Thanh Nien Dong Chi Hoi), founded by Ho Chi Minh in Canton, China, in 1925. The Revolutionary Youth League was succeeded in February 1930 by the Vietnamese Communist Party (Dang Cong San Viet Nam), a union of three groups effected by Ho, which was renamed the Indochinese Communist Party (Dang Cong San Dong Duong) in October 1930. In 1941, Ho Chi Minh formed the League for the Independence of Vietnam (Viet Nam Doc Lap Dong Minh Hoi), better known as the Viet Minh, which resisted the Japanese occupation (and thus received Chinese and American aid) and carried out extensive political organising during WW II. Despite its broad nationalist programme and claims to the contrary, the Viet Minh was, from its inception, dominated by Ho's Communists.

Communist successes in the late 1920s included major strikes by urban workers. During the Nghe Tinh Uprising (1930-31), revolutionary committees (or soviets) took control of parts of Nghe An and Ha Tinh provinces (thus all the streets named 'Xo Viet Nghe Tinh'), but after an unprecedented wave of terror, the French managed to re-establish control. A 1940 uprising in the south was also brutally suppressed, seriously damaging the Party's infrastructure. French prisons, filled with arrested cadres, were turned by the captives into revolutionary 'universities' in which Marxist-Leninist theory was taught.

World War II

When France fell to Nazi Germany in 1940, the Indochinese government of Vichy-appointed Admiral Jean Decoux concluded an agreement to accept the presence of Jap-

anese troops in Vietnam. For their own convenience the Japanese, who sought to exploit the area's strategic location and its natural resources, left the French administration in charge of the day-to-day running of the country. The only group that did anything significant to resist the Japanese occupation was the Communist-dominated Viet Minh, which from 1944 received funding and arms from the US Office of Strategic Services (OSS), predecessor of the CIA. This affiliation offered the Viet Minh the hope of eventual US recognition of their demands for independence; it also proved useful to Ho in that it implied that he had the support of the Americans.

In March 1945, as a Viet Minh offensive was getting under way and Decoux's government was plotting to resist the Japanese – something they hadn't tried in the preceding $4\frac{1}{2}$ years – the Japanese overthrew Decoux, imprisoning both his troops and his administrators. Decoux's administration was replaced with a puppet regime – nominally independent within Japan's Greater East-Asian Co-Prosperity Sphere – led by Emperor Bao Dai, who abrogated the 1883 treaty that made Annam and Tonkin French protectorates. During the same period, Japanese rice requisitions and the Japanese policy of forcing farmers to plant industrial crops – combined with floods and breaches in the dikes – caused a horrific famine in which two million of northern Vietnam's 10 million people starved to death.

By the spring of 1945 the Viet Minh controlled large parts of the country, especially in the north. In mid-August – after the atomic bombing of Japan – Ho Chi Minh formed the National Liberation Committee and called for a general uprising, later known as the August Revolution (Cach Mang Thang Tam), to take advantage of the power vacuum. Almost immediately, the Viet Minh assumed complete control of the north. In central Vietnam, Emperor Bao Dai abdicated in favour of the new government (which later appointed him as its 'Supreme Adviser', whatever that means). In the south, the Viet Minh soon held power in a shaky coalition with non-Communist groups. On 2 September 1945, Ho Chi Minh – with American OSS agents at his side and borrowing liberally from the stirring prose of the American Declaration of Independence – declared the Democratic Republic of Vietnam independent at a rally in Hanoi's Ba Dinh Square. During this period, Ho wrote no fewer than eight letters to US President Truman and the State Department asking for US aid but did not receive replies.

A minor item on the agenda of the Potsdam Conference of 1945 was the procedure for disarming the Japanese occupation forces in Vietnam. It was decided that the Chinese Kuomintang (Nationalist Party) would accept the Japanese surrender north of the 16th parallel and the British would do the same south of that line.

When the British arrived in Saigon chaos reigned, with enraged French settlers beginning to take matters into their own hands and competing Vietnamese groups on the verge of civil war. With only 1800 British, Indian and Ghurka troops at his disposal, British General Gracey ordered the defeated Japanese troops (!) to help him restore order. He also released and armed 1400 imprisoned French paratroopers, who immediately went on a rampage around the city, overthrowing the Committee of the South government, breaking into Vietnamese homes and shops and indiscriminately clubbing men, women and children. The Viet Minh and allied groups responded by calling a general strike and by beginning a guerrilla campaign against the French. On 24 September, French General Jacques Philippe Leclerc arrived in Saigon, declaring, 'We have come to reclaim our inheritance'.

Meanwhile, in Hué, the imperial library was demolished (priceless documents were being used in the marketplace to wrap fish), and in the north 180,000 Chinese Kuomintang troops were fleeing the Chinese Communists, pillaging their way southward towards Hanoi. Ho tried to placate them, but as the months of Chinese occupation dragged on, he decided to accept a temporary return of the French in order to get rid of the anti-Communist Kuomintang, who, in addition to everything else, were supporting the Viet Minh's nationalist rivals. Most of the Kuomintang soldiers were packed off to Taiwan. The French were to stay for five years in return for recognising Vietnam as a free state within the French Union.

The British wanted out, the French wanted in, Ho Chi Minh wanted the Chinese to go and the Americans under President Truman were not as actively opposed to colonialism as they had been under President Roosevelt. So the French (ignoring the provisions of signed agreements) managed to regain control of Vietnam, at least in name. But when the French shelled Haiphong in November 1946 after an obscure customs dispute, killing hundreds of civilians, the patience of the Viet Minh ended. A few weeks later fighting broke out in Hanoi, marking the start of the Franco-Viet Minh War. Ho and his forces fled to the mountains, where they would remain for eight years.

Franco-Viet Minh War (1946-54)

In the face of Vietnamese determination that their country regain its independence, the French proved unable to reassert their control. Despite massive American aid and the existence of significant indigenous anti-Communist elements – who in 1949 rallied to support Bao Dai's 'Associated State' within the French Union – it was an unwinnable war. As Ho said to the French at the time: 'You can kill 10 of my men for every one I kill of yours, but even at those odds, you will lose and I will win'.

After eight years of fighting, the Viet Minh controlled much of Vietnam and neighbouring Laos. On 7 May 1954, after a 57-day siege, over 10,000 starving French troops surrendered to the Viet Minh at Dien Bien Phu – a catastrophic defeat that shattered the remaining public support for the war in France. The next day, the Geneva Conference opened to negotiate an end to the conflict; 2½ months later, the Geneva Accords were signed. The Geneva Accords provided for an exchange of prisoners, the temporary division of Vietnam into two zones at the Ben Hai River (near the 17th parallel), the free passage of people across the 17th parallel for a period of 300 days, and the holding of nationwide elections on 20 July 1956. In the course of the Franco-Viet Minh War, more than 35,000 men were killed and 48,000 wounded on the French side, but Vietnamese casualties were much greater.

South Vietnam

After the signing of the Geneva Accords, the South was ruled by a government led by Ngo Dinh Diem (pronounced 'zee-EM'), a fiercely anti-Communist Catholic whose brother had been killed by the Viet Minh in 1945. His power base was significantly strengthened by some 900,000 refugees – many of them Catholics – who fled the Communist North during the 300-day free-passage period.

In 1955 Diem, convinced that if elections were held Ho Chi Minh would win, refused – with US encouragement – to implement the Geneva Accords; instead, he held a referendum on his continued rule. Diem claimed to have won 98.2% of the vote in an election that was by all accounts rigged (in Saigon, he received a third more votes that there were registered voters!). After Diem declared himself president of the Republic of Vietnam, the new regime was recognised by France, the USA, Great Britain, Australia, New Zealand, Italy, Japan, Thailand and South Korea.

During the first few years of his rule, Diem consolidated power fairly effectively, defeating the Binh Xuyen crime syndicate and the private armies of the Hoa Hao and Caodai religious sects. During Diem's 1957 official visit to the USA, President Eisenhower called him the 'miracle man' of Asia. But as time went on Diem became increasingly tyrannical in dealing with dissent. Running the government became a family affair (Diem's much-hated sister-in-law became Vietnam's powerful 'first lady' while his father-in-law was appointed US ambassador).

Such blatant nepotism was offensive enough, but worse still, Diem's land-reform programme ended up reversing land redistribution effected by the Viet Minh in the '40s. The favouritism he showed to Catholics alienated many Buddhists. In the early 1960s, the South was rocked by anti-Diem unrest led by university students and Buddhist clergy, including several self-immolations by monks that shocked the world. When Diem used French contacts to explore negotiations with Hanoi, the USA threw its support behind a military coup; in November 1963, he was overthrown and killed. Diem was succeeded by a succession of military rulers who continued his repressive policies.

North Vietnam

The Geneva Accords allowed the leadership of the Democratic Republic of Vietnam to return to Hanoi and to assert control of all territory north of the 17th parallel. The new government immediately set out to eliminate elements of the population that threatened its power. A radical land-reform programme was implemented, providing about half a hectare of land to some 1.5 million peasants. Tens of thousands of 'landlords', some with only tiny holdings – and many of whom had been denounced to 'security committees' by envious neighbours – were arrested; hasty 'trials' resulted in 10,000 to 15,000 executions and the imprisonment of 50,000 to 100,000 people. In 1956, the Party, faced with serious rural unrest caused by the programme, recognised that the People's Agricultural Reform Tribunals had gotten out of hand and began a 'Campaign for the Rectification of Errors'.

On 12 December 1955 – shortly after Diem had declared the South a republic – the USA closed its consulate in Hanoi. It was not until 40 years later – in 1995 – that diplomatic ties were restored with Hanoi.

The Vietnam War

Though there were Communist-led guerrilla attacks on Diem's government during the mid-1950s, the real campaign to 'liberate' the South began in 1959 when Hanoi, responding to the demands of Southern cadres that they be allowed to resist the Diem regime, changed from a strategy of 'political struggle' to one of 'armed struggle'. Shortly thereafter, the Ho Chi Minh Trail, which had been in existence for several years, was expanded. In April 1960, universal military conscription was implemented in the North. Eight months later, Hanoi announced the formation of the National Liberation Front (NLF), whose platform called for a neutralisation of Vietnam, the withdrawal of all foreign troops and gradual reunification. In the South, the NLF came to be known derogatorily as the 'Viet Cong' or just the 'VC'; both are abbreviations for Viet Nam Cong San, which means 'Vietnamese Communist' (today, the words 'Viet Cong' and 'VC' are no longer considered pejoratives). American soldiers nicknamed the Viet Cong 'Charlie'.

When the NLF campaign got under way, the military situation of the Diem government rapidly deteriorated. To turn things around, the Strategic Hamlet Programme (Ap Chien Luoc) was begun in 1962. Following tactics employed successfully by the British in Malaya during the '50s, peasants were forcibly moved into fortified 'strategic hamlets' in order to deny the Viet Cong bases of support. The programme was widely criticised for incompetence and brutality, and many of the strategic hamlets were infiltrated by the VC and fell under their control. The Strategic Hamlets Programme was finally abandoned with the death of President Diem, but after the war ended the VC admitted that the programme had caused them very serious concern and that they had expended a major effort sabotaging it.

And it was no longer just a battle with the VC. In 1964, Hanoi began infiltrating regular North Vietnamese Army (NVA) units into the South. By early 1965, the Saigon government was in desperate straits; desertions from the Army of the Republic of Vietnam (ARVN), whose command was notorious for corruption and incompetence, had reached 2000 per month. It was losing 500 men and a district capital each week, yet since 1954, only one senior South Vietnamese army officer had been wounded. The

army was getting ready to evacuate Hué and Danang, and the Central Highlands seemed about to fall. The South Vietnamese general staff even prepared a plan to move its headquarters from Saigon to the Vung Tau Peninsula, which was easy to defend and was only minutes from ships that could spirit them out of the country. It was at this point that the USA committed its first combat troops.

Enter the Americans
The first Americans to set foot in Vietnam were the crew of the clipper ship *Franklin* under the command of Captain John White of Salem, Massachusetts, which docked at Saigon in 1820. Edmund Roberts, a New Englander selected by President Andrew Jackson, led the first official American mission to Vietnam in 1832. In 1845, the USS *Constitution* under Captain 'Mad Jack' Percival sent an armed party ashore at Hué to rescue a French bishop who was under sentence of death, taking several Vietnamese officials hostage. When this failed to convince Emperor Thieu Tri to free the bishop, Percival's men opened fire on a crowd of civilians. In the 1870s, Emperor Tu Duc sent a respected scholar, Bui Vien, to Washington in an attempt to garner international support to counter the French. Bui Vien met President Ulysses S Grant but, lacking the proper documents of accreditation, was sent back to Vietnam empty-handed.

The theory was rapidly gaining acceptance in the West that there was a worldwide Communist movement intent on overthrowing one government after another by waging various 'wars of liberation' (the 'Domino Theory', as it came to be known). The Domino Theory gained considerable support after the start of the Korean War in 1950, and the Americans saw France's colonial war in Indochina as an important part of the worldwide struggle to stop Communist expansion. By 1954, US military aid to the French war effort topped two billion dollars (and that's 1950s dollars). In 1950, 35 US soldiers arrived in Vietnam as part of the US Military Assistance Advisory Group (MAAG), ostensibly to instruct troops receiving US weapons on how to use them; there would be American soldiers on Vietnamese soil for the next 25 years.

The People's Republic of China established diplomatic relations with the Democratic Republic of Vietnam in 1950; shortly thereafter, the Soviet Union did the same. Only then did Washington recognise Bao Dai's French-backed government. The circumstances of this event are instructive: though Ho's government had been around since 1945, the USSR didn't get around to recognising it until the Communist Chinese did so, and the US State Department – which at the time was reverberating with recriminations over who was to blame for 'losing China' to Communism – recognised Bao Dai's government as a reaction to these events. From that point on, US policy in Indochina largely became a kneejerk reaction against whatever the Communists did.

When the last French troops left Vietnam in April 1956, the MAAG, now numbering several hundred men, assumed responsibility for training the South Vietnamese military; the transition couldn't have been neater. The first American troops to die in the Vietnam War were killed at Bien Hoa in 1959 at a time when about 700 US military personnel were in Vietnam.

As the military position of the South Vietnamese government continued to deteriorate, the Kennedy administration (1961-63) sent more and more military advisers to Vietnam. By the end of 1963, there were 16,300 US military personnel in the country.

The Vietnam War became a central issue in the American 1964 presidential election. The candidate for the Republican Party, Senator Barry Goldwater of Arizona, took the more aggressive stance – he warned that if elected he would tell Ho Chi Minh to stop the war 'or there won't be enough left of North Vietnam to grow rice on it'. Many Americans, with bitter memories of how Chinese troops came to the aid of North Korea during the Korean War, feared the same would happen again if the US invaded North Vietnam. The thought of a possible

nuclear confrontation with Russia could not be ruled out, either. With such horrors in mind, voters overwhelming supported Lyndon Baines Johnson.

Ironically, it was 'peace candidate' Johnson who rapidly escalated the American involvement in the war. A major turning-point in American strategy was precipitated by the August 1964 Tonkin Gulf Incidents, in which two American destroyers, the *Maddox* and the *Turner Joy*, claimed to have come under 'unprovoked' attack while sailing off the North Vietnamese coast. Subsequent research indicates that the first attack took place while the *Maddox* was in North Vietnamese territorial waters assisting a secret South Vietnamese commando raid and that the second attack simply never took place.

But on President Johnson's orders, carrier-based jets flew 64 sorties against the North, the first of thousands of such missions that would hit every single road and rail bridge in the country as well as 4000 of North Vietnam's 5788 villages. Two American aircraft were lost, and the pilot of one, Lieutenant Everett Alvarez, became the first American prisoner of war (POW) of the conflict; he would remain in captivity for eight years.

A few days later, an indignant (and misled) Congress almost unanimously passed (two Senators dissented) the Tonkin Gulf Resolution, which gave the President the power to 'take all necessary measures' to 'repel any armed attack against the forces of the United States and to prevent further aggression'. Only later was it established that the Johnson administration had in fact drafted the resolution before the 'attacks' had actually taken place. Until its repeal in 1970, the resolution was treated by US presidents as a blank cheque to do whatever they chose in Vietnam without congressional oversight.

As the military situation of the Saigon government reached a new nadir, the first US combat troops splashed ashore at Danang in March 1965, ostensibly to defend Danang air base. But once you had 'American boys' fighting and dying, you had to do everything necessary to protect and support them, including sending over more American boys. By December 1965, 184,300 American military personnel were in Vietnam, and American dead numbered 636. Twelve months later, the totals were 385,300 US troops in Vietnam and 6644 dead. By December 1967, 485,600 US soldiers were in-country and 16,021 had died. In 1967, with South Vietnamese and 'Free World Forces' counted in, there were 1.3 million men – one for every 15 people in South Vietnam – under arms for the Saigon government.

By 1966, the failed Strategic Hamlets Programme of earlier years was replaced with a policy of 'pacification', 'search and destroy' and 'free-fire zones'. Pacification meant building a pro-government civilian infrastructure of teachers, health-care workers and officials in each village, as well as soldiers to guard them and keep the VC away from the villagers. To protect the villages from VC raids, mobile 'search and destroy' units of soldiers moved around the country (often by helicopter) to hunt bands of VC guerrillas. In some cases, villagers were evacuated so the Americans could use heavy weapons like bombs, napalm, artillery and tanks in areas that were declared 'free-fire zones'. A relatively little publicised strategy was dubbed 'Operation Phoenix', a controversial programme run by the CIA aimed at eliminating VC cadres by assassination, capture or defection.

These strategies were only partially successful – US forces could control the countryside by day while the VC usually controlled it by night. The VC proved adept at infiltrating 'pacified' villages. Although lacking heavy weapons like tanks and aircraft, VC guerrillas still continued to inflict heavy casualties on US and ARVN troops in ambushes and by using mines and booby traps. Although free-fire zones were supposed to prevent civilian casualties, plenty of villagers were nevertheless shelled, bombed, strafed and napalmed to death – their surviving relatives often joined the Viet Cong.

The Turning Point

In January 1968, North Vietnamese troops launched a major attack at Khe Sanh (see the DMZ & Vicinity chapter for details). This battle, the single largest of the war, was in part a massive diversion for what was to come only a week later: the Tet Offensive.

The Tet Offensive of early 1968 marked a crucial turning point in the war. On the evening of 31 January, as the country celebrated the New Year, the Viet Cong launched a stunning offensive in over 100 cities and towns, including Saigon. As the TV cameras rolled, a VC commando team took over the courtyard of the downtown-Saigon US Embassy building.

The American forces had long been wanting to engage the VC in an open battle rather than a guerrilla war where the enemy couldn't be seen. The Tet Offensive provided the opportunity. Though taken by complete surprise (a major failure of US military intelligence), the South Vietnamese and Americans quickly counterattacked with massive firepower, bombing and shelling heavily populated cities as they had the open jungle. The effect was devastating on the VC but also on the civilian population. In Ben Tre, an American officer bitterly explained that 'we had to destroy the town in order to save it'.

The Tet Offensive killed about 1000 American soldiers and 2000 ARVN troops, but Viet Cong losses were more than 10 times higher at approximately 32,000 deaths. In addition, some 500 Americans and 10,000 North Vietnamese troops died at the battle of Khe Sanh a week before the Tet Offensive began. According to American estimates, 165,000 civilians also died in the three weeks following the start of the Tet Offensive; two million more became refugees.

The VC held the cities for only three or four days (with the exception of Hué, which they held for 25 days). The surviving VC then retreated to the jungles. The VC had hoped that their offensive would lead to a popular uprising against the Americans and that ARVN forces would desert or switch sides – this did not happen. General Westmoreland, commander of US forces in Vietnam, insisted that the uprising had been a failure and a decisive military blow to the Communists (and he was right – by their own admission, the VC never recovered from their high casualties). Westmoreland then asked for an additional 206,000 troops – he didn't get them and was replaced in July by General Creighton W Abrams.

Perhaps the VC lost the battle, but they were far from losing the war. After years of hearing that they were winning, many Americans – having watched the killing and chaos in Saigon on their nightly TV newscasts – stopped believing what they were being told by their government. While US generals were proclaiming a great victory, public tolerance of the war and its casualties reached the breaking point. For the VC, the Tet Offensive proved to be a big success after all – it made the cost of fighting the war (both in dollars and in lives) unbearable for the Americans.

Anti-war demonstrations rocked US campuses and spilled out into the streets. Seeing his political popularity plummet in the polls, President Lyndon Johnson decided not to stand for re-election.

Richard Nixon was elected president of the USA, in part because of a promise that he had a 'secret plan' to end the war. Many suspected that his secret plan would be a military invasion of North Vietnam, but it didn't turn out that way. The plan, later to be labelled the 'Nixon Doctrine', was unveiled in July 1969 and called on Asian nations to be more 'self-reliant' in defence matters and not expect the USA to become embroiled in future civil wars. Nixon's strategy called for 'Vietnamisation' – making the South Vietnamese military fight the war without American troops.

Nixon Doctrine or not, the first half of 1969 saw still greater escalation. In April, the number of US soldiers in Vietnam reached an all-time high of 543,400. By the end of 1969, US troop levels were down to 475,200; 40,024 Americans had been killed in action as had 110,176 ARVN troops. While the fighting raged, Nixon's chief negotiator, Henry Kissinger, pursued talks in Paris with his North Vietnamese counterpart Le Duc Tho.

In 1969, the USA began secretly bombing Cambodia. The following year, American ground forces were sent into Cambodia to extricate ARVN units whose fighting ability was still unable to match the enemy's. This new escalation infuriated previously quiescent elements of the American public, leading to bitter anti-war protests. The TV screens of America were almost daily filled with scenes of demonstrations, student strikes and even deadly acts of self-immolation. A peace demonstration at Kent State University in Ohio resulted in four protesters being shot dead by National Guard troops.

The rise of organisations like 'Vietnam Veterans Against the War' demonstrated that it wasn't just 'cowardly students fearing military conscription' who wanted the USA out of Vietnam. It was clear that the war was ripping the USA apart. Nor were the protests just confined to the USA – huge anti-American demonstrations in Western Europe were shaking the NATO alliance. There was even a Vietnamese peace movement – at great risk to themselves, idealistic young students in Saigon protested against the US presence in their country.

In 1971, excerpts from a scandalous top secret study of US involvement in Indochina were published in the *New York Times* after a legal battle which went to the US Supreme Court. The study, known as the 'Pentagon Papers', was commissioned by the US Defense Department and detailed how the military and former presidents had systematically lied to Congress and the American public. The Pentagon Papers infuriated the US public and caused anti-war sentiment to reach new heights. The *New York Times* obtained the study from one of its authors, Dr Daniel Ellsberg, who had turned against the war. Ellsberg was subsequently prosecuted for espionage, theft and conspiracy. A judge dismissed the charges after Nixon's notorious 'White House Plumbers' (so called because they were supposed to stop 'leaks') burgled the office of Ellsberg's psychiatrist to obtain evidence.

In the spring of 1972, the North Vietnamese launched an offensive across the 17th parallel; the USA responded with increased bombing of the North and mined seven North Vietnamese harbours. The 'Christmas Bombing' of Hanoi and Haiphong at the end of 1972 was meant to wrest concessions from North Vietnam at the negotiating table. Finally, Henry Kissinger and Le Duc Tho reached agreement. The Paris agreements, signed by the USA, North Vietnam, South Vietnam and the Viet Cong on 27 January 1973, provided for a cease-fire, the establishment of a National Council of Reconciliation and Concord, the total withdrawal of US combat forces and the release of 590 American POWs. The agreement made no mention of the approximately 200,000 North Vietnamese troops then in South Vietnam.

Richard Nixon was re-elected president in November 1972, shortly before the Paris peace agreements were signed. By 1973, he became hopelessly mired in the 'Watergate Scandal', resulting from illegal activities regarding his re-election campaign. The Pentagon Papers and Watergate contributed to such a high level of public distrust of the military and presidents that the US Congress passed a resolution prohibiting any further US military involvement in Indochina after 15 August 1973. Nixon resigned in disgrace in 1974 and was succeeded by Gerald Ford.

In total, 3.14 million Americans (including 7200 women) served in the US armed forces in Vietnam during the war. Officially, 58,183 Americans (including eight women) were killed in action or are listed as missing-in-action. The US losses were nearly double that of the Korean War. Pentagon figures indicate that by 1972, 3689 fixed-wing aircraft and 4857 helicopters had been lost and 15 million tonnes of ammunition had been expended. The direct cost of the war was officially put at US$165 billion, though its true cost to the economy was at least twice that. By comparison, the Korean War had cost America US$18 billion.

By the end of 1973, 223,748 South Vietnamese soldiers had been killed in action; North Vietnamese and Viet Cong fatalities were about one million. Approximately four million civilians – 10% of the population of Vietnam – were killed or injured during the war, many in the North due to the American bombing. Over 2200 Americans and 300,000 Vietnamese are still listed as missing-in-action.

As far as anyone knows, the Soviet Union and China – who supplied all the weapons to North Vietnam and the Viet Cong – did not suffer a single casualty.

Other Foreign Involvement

Australia, New Zealand, South Korea, Thailand and the Philippines sent military personnel to South Vietnam as part of what the Americans called the 'Free World Military Forces', whose purpose was to internationalise the American war effort and thus confer upon it legitimacy. The Koreans (who numbered nearly 50,000), Thais and Filipino forces were heavily subsidised by the Americans.

Australia's participation in the Vietnam War constituted the most significant commitment of Australian military forces overseas since the 1940s. At its peak strength, the Australian forces in Vietnam – which included army, navy and air force units – numbered 8300, two-thirds larger than the size of the Australian contingent in the Korean War. Overall, 46,852 Australian military personnel served in Vietnam, including 17,424 draftees; Australian casualties totalled 496 killed and 2398 wounded.

Most of New Zealand's contingent, which numbered 548 at its high point in 1968, operated as an integral part of the Australian Task Force, which was stationed near Baria (just north of Vung Tau).

The Australian foreign affairs establishment decided to commit Australian troops to the Vietnam War in order to encourage US military involvement in South-East Asia, thus, they argued, furthering Australia's defence interests by having the Americans play an active role in an area of great importance to Australia's long-term security. The first Australian troops in Vietnam were 30 guerrilla warfare specialists with experience in Malaya and Borneo sent to Vietnam in May 1962. Australia announced the commitment of combat units in April 1965, only a few weeks after the first American combat troops arrived in Danang. The last Australian combat troops withdrew in December 1971; the last advisers returned home a year later. The Australian and New Zealand forces preferred to operate independently of US units, in part because they felt that the Americans took unnecessary risks and were willing to sustain unacceptably high numbers of casualties.

Royal Thai army troops were stationed in Vietnam from 1967 to 1973; Thailand also allowed the US Air Force to base B-52s and fighter aircraft on its territory. The Philippines sent units for non-combat 'civic action' work. South Korea's soldiers, who operated in the South between 1965 and 1971, were noted for both their exceptional fighting ability and extreme brutality.

Taiwan's brief role was one of the most under-reported facts of the war because it was such an embarrassment. At that time, the USA still recognised Taiwan's ruling Kuomintang as the legitimate government of all China. Ever since 1949, when the Kuomintang troops were defeated by the Communists, Taiwan's President Chiang Kaishek had been promising to 'retake the mainland'. When US President Johnson asked Taiwan to supply around 20,000 troops, Chiang was happy to comply and some troops were immediately dispatched to Saigon. Chiang then rapidly tried to increase the number to 200,000! It soon became apparent that Chiang was planning to use Vietnam as a stepping stone to invade mainland China and draw the USA into his personal war against the Chinese Communists. The USA wanted no part of this and asked Chiang to withdraw his troops from South Vietnam – it was promptly done and the whole incident was hushed up.

It's not generally known that Spain's General Franco – whose regime was regarded by the USA as a bulwark against communism – supplied about 50 military personnel to the war effort. However, their role was noncombatant.

Fall of the South (1975)

Except for a small contingent of technicians and CIA agents, all US military personnel were out of Vietnam by 1973. The bombing of North Vietnam had ceased and the American POWs were released. But the guerrilla war was still on, the only difference being that the fighting had been thoroughly 'Vietnamised'. However, foreign powers continued to bankroll the war. America supplied the South Vietnamese military with weapons, ammunition and fuel while the USSR and China did the same for the North.

Although the USA had ended its combat role, anti-war organisations such as the Indochina Resource Center continued to lobby the US government to cut off all financial and military assistance to South Vietnam. They nearly succeeded – the US Senate came within two votes of doing just that. While the anti-war lobby failed to cut off all funding, they did succeed in having it greatly reduced. In 1975, America gave South Vietnam US$700 million in aid, less than half of what military experts estimated was needed. The South Vietnamese suddenly found that they were running desperately low on stocks of ammunition and fuel.

The North Vietnamese were quick to assess the situation. They continued a major military buildup with Soviet assistance, and in January 1975 the NVA launched a massive conventional ground attack across the 17th parallel using tanks and heavy artillery. The invasion – a blatant violation of the Paris agreements – panicked the South Vietnamese army and government, which in the past had always depended on the Americans. In March, the NVA quickly occupied a strategic section of the Central Highlands at Buon Ma Thuot. In the absence of US military support or advice, President Nguyen Van Thieu personally decided on a strategy of tactical withdrawal to more defensible positions. This proved to be a spectacular military blunder. Rather than stand and fight as expected, South Vietnamese troops were ordered to retreat from Central Highland bases at Pleiku and Kon Tum. The totally unplanned withdrawal was a disaster.

Retreating ARVN soldiers were intercepted and attacked by the well-disciplined North Vietnamese troops. The withdrawal became a rout as panicked ARVN soldiers deserted en masse in order to try to save their families.

Whole brigades of ARVN soldiers disintegrated and fled southward, joining the hundreds of thousands of civilians clogging National Highway 1. City after city – Buon Ma Thuot, Quang Tri, Hué, Danang, Qui Nhon, Tuy Hoa, Nha Trang – were simply abandoned by the defenders with hardly a shot fired. So quickly did the ARVN troops flee that the North Vietnamese army could barely keep up with them. The US Congress, fed up with the war and its drain on the treasury, refused to send emergency aid that President Nixon (who had resigned the previous year because of Watergate) had promised would be forthcoming in the event of such an invasion.

President Nguyen Van Thieu, in power since 1967, resigned on 21 April 1975 and fled the country, allegedly taking with him millions of dollars in ill-gotten wealth. He moved to Britain rather than the USA, and bitterly blamed the Americans for 'abandoning' his regime. For a while he lived in a stately London mansion called 'the White House', but later he sold it and has been keeping a very low profile. He is said to fear assassination and lives as a recluse.

Thieu's main political rival and former vice president, Nguyen Cao Ky, also fled Vietnam and has since been living in California. Unlike Thieu, he is outspoken and very willing to talk to reporters. He denies reports that he stole millions from Vietnam – he ran a California liquor store for a few years and filed for bankruptcy in 1984.

President Thieu was replaced by Vice President Tran Van Huong, who quit a week later, turning the presidency over to General Duong Van Minh, who surrendered on the morning of 30 April 1975 in Saigon's Independence Palace (now Reunification Palace) after only 43 hours in office.

The last Americans were evacuated to US ships stationed offshore, transported by helicopter from the US Embassy roof just a few hours before South Vietnam surrendered. Thus came to an end more than a decade of US military involvement. Throughout the entire episode, the USA had never declared war on North Vietnam.

The Americans weren't the only ones who left. As the South collapsed, 135,000 Vietnamese also fled the country; in the next five years, at least 545,000 of their compatriots would do the same. Those who left by sea would become known to the world as 'boat people'.

Since Reunification

The sudden success of the 1975 North Vietnamese offensive surprised the North almost as much as it did the South. As a result, Hanoi had not prepared specific plans to deal with integrating the two parts of the country, whose social and economic systems could hardly have been more different.

The North was faced with the legacy of a cruel and protracted war that had literally fractured the country; there was understandable bitterness (if not hatred) on both sides, and a mind-boggling array of problems. War damage extended from unmarked minefields to war-focussed, dysfunctional economies, from vast acreages of chemically poisoned countryside to millions of people who had been affected physically or mentally. The country was diplomatically isolated and its old allies were no longer willing or able to provide significant aid. Peace may have arrived, but in many ways the war was far from over.

Until the formal reunification of Vietnam in July 1976, the South was nominally ruled by a Provisional Revolutionary Government. Because the Communist Party did not really trust the Southern urban intelligentsia – even those of its members who had supported the Viet Cong – large numbers of Northern cadres were sent southward to manage the transition. This created resentment among Southerners who had worked against the Thieu government and then, after its overthrow, found themselves frozen out of positions of responsibility (even today, most of the officials and police in Saigon are from the North).

After months of debates, those in Hanoi who wanted to implement a rapid transition to socialism (including the collectivisation of agriculture) in the South gained the upper hand. Great efforts were made to deal with the South's social problems: millions of illiterates and unemployed, several hundred thousand prostitutes and drug addicts, and tens of thousands of people who made their living by criminal activities. Many of these people were encouraged to move to the newly collectivised farms in the countryside. This may have had some beneficial effects, but the results of the transition to socialism were mostly disastrous to the South's economy.

Reunification was accompanied by large-scale political repression. Despite repeated promises to the contrary, hundreds of thousands of people who had ties to the previous regime had their property and homes confiscated and were subsequently rounded up and imprisoned without trial in forced-labour camps euphemistically known as 're-education camps'. Tens of thousands of business people, intellectuals, artists, journalists, writers, trade-union leaders, Buddhist monks, Catholic priests and Protestant clergy – some of whom had opposed both Thieu and the war – were detained under horrendous conditions.

Some were able to buy themselves out, but most of the wealthy people simply had their bank accounts and property confiscated. While the majority of the detainees were released within a few years, some (declared to be 'obstinate and counterrevolutionary elements') were to spend the next decade or more in the camps. The purge and terrible economic conditions prompted hundreds of thousands of Southerners to flee their homeland by sea and overland through Cambodia.

The purge affected not only former opponents of the Communists, but also their families. Even today, the children of former 'counterrevolutionaries' can be discriminated against. One way this is done is to deny a *ho khau*, a sort of residence permit needed for attending school, seeking employment, owning farmland, a home or a business and so on.

Relations with China to the north and its Khmer Rouge allies to the west were rapidly deteriorating and war-weary Vietnam seemed beset by enemies.

An anti-capitalist campaign was launched in March 1978, during which private property and businesses were seized. Most of the victims were ethnic-Chinese – hundreds of thousands soon became refugees, and relations with China soured further. Meanwhile, repeated attacks on Vietnamese border villages by the Khmer Rouge forced Vietnam to respond. Vietnamese forces entered Cambodia at the end of 1978. They succeeded in driving the Khmer Rouge from power in early 1979 and set up a pro-Hanoi regime in Phnom Penh.

China viewed the attack on their Khmer Rouge allies as a serious provocation. In February 1979, Chinese forces invaded Vietnam and fought a brief, 17-day war before withdrawing (for details, see The North chapter).

Khmer Rouge forces, with support from China and Thailand, continued a costly guerrilla war against the Vietnamese on Cambodian soil for the next decade. Vietnam pulled its forces out of Cambodia in September 1989. The Cambodian civil war was officially settled in 1992 and United Nations peacekeeping forces were called in to monitor the peace agreement. Although Khmer Rouge units continue to violate the terms of the peace plan, Vietnam is no longer involved in the conflict. For the first time since WW II began, Vietnam is finally at peace.

Opening the Door

The recent liberalisation of foreign investment laws and the relaxation of visa regulations for tourists seem to be part of a general Vietnamese opening-up to the world.

Sweden, the first Western country to establish diplomatic relations with Hanoi, did so in 1969; since that time, most Western nations have followed suit. Even the USA, the last major holdout, decided in July 1995 to establish ties.

The Soviet Union began its first cautious opening to the West in 1984 with the appointment of Mikhail Gorbachev as Secretary

General of the Communist Party. Vietnam followed suit in 1986 by choosing reform-minded Nguyen Van Linh as General Secretary of the Vietnamese Communist Party. However, the dramatic changes in Eastern Europe and the USSR were not viewed with favour in Hanoi. The Vietnamese Communist Party denounced the participation of non-Communists in Eastern Bloc governments, calling the democratic revolutions 'a counterattack from imperialist circles' against socialism.

General Secretary Linh declared at the end of 1989 that 'we resolutely reject pluralism, a multiparty system and opposition parties'. But in February 1990, the government called for more openness and criticism. The response came swiftly, with an outpouring of news articles, editorials and letters from the public condemning corruption, inept leadership and the high living standards of senior officials while most people lived in extreme poverty. Taken aback by the harsh criticism, official control over literature, the arts and the media were tightened once again in a campaign against 'deviant ideological viewpoints'. An effort was made to blame public dissatisfaction on foreign imperialists. Interior Minister Mai Chi Tho wrote in the army's newspaper:

Through modern communications means and news-papers, letters and video tapes brought to Vietnam, they have conducted virulent attacks against Marxism-Leninism and the Party's leadership, blaming all socio-economic difficulties on the Communist Party in order to demand political pluralism, a multiparty system and bourgeois-type democracy.

At age 75, ailing Party Secretary General Nguyen Van Linh was replaced in June 1991 by Prime Minister Do Muoi (age 74). Regarded as a conservative, Muoi nevertheless vowed to continue the economic reforms started by Linh. At the same time, a major shake-up of the ruling Politburo and Central Committee of the Communist Party saw many members forcibly retired and replaced by younger, more liberal-minded leaders. The sudden collapse of the USSR just two

months later caused the government to reiterate its stand that political pluralism would not be tolerated, but at the same time economic reforms were speeded up.

Secretary General Do Muoi and Prime Minister Vo Van Kiet visited Beijing in November 1991 to heal Vietnam's 12-year rift with China. The visit was reciprocated in December 1992 when Chinese Prime Minister Li Peng visited Hanoi. Although it was all smiles and warm handshakes in front of the cameras, relations between Vietnam and China still remain tense. On the other hand, trade across the China-Vietnam border (both legal and otherwise) is booming.

Vietnam has also seen considerable easing of tensions with its old nemesis, the USA. In early 1994, the USA lifted its economic embargo, which had been in place against the old North Vietnam since the 1960s. With the embargo removed, Vietnam is now able to obtain loans from the International Monetary Fund (IMF), import high-tech goods and do business directly with American companies.

As of this writing full diplomatic relations with the USA are being restored. The exchange of ambassadors and the setting up of embassies and consulates should soon follow.

GEOGRAPHY

Vietnam stretches over 1600 km along the eastern coast of the Indochinese Peninsula (from 8°34' N to 23°22' N). The country's land area is 329,566 sq km including water, or 326,797 sq km of land surface. This makes it slightly larger than Italy and a bit smaller than Japan. Vietnam has 3451 km of coastline, and land borders of 1555 km with Laos, 1281 km with China and 982 km with Cambodia.

Vietnamese often describe their country as resembling a bamboo pole supporting a basket of rice on each end. The country is S-shaped, broad in the north and south and very narrow in the centre, where at one point it is only 50 km wide.

The country's two main cultivated areas are the Red River Delta (15,000 sq km) in the north and the Mekong Delta (60,000 sq km) in the south. Silt carried by the Red River and its tributaries, which are confined to their paths by 3000 km of dikes, has raised the level of the river beds above that of the surrounding plains. Breaches in the levees result in disastrous flooding. The Mekong Delta is very fertile where drainage is adequate. It was created by silt deposited by the Mekong River.

Three-quarters of the country consists of mountains and hills, the highest of which is 3143-metre-high Fansipan (also spelled Phan Si Pan) in the Hoang Lien Mountains in the far north-west of northern Vietnam. The Truong Son Mountains (Annamite Cordillera), which form the Central Highlands, run almost the full length of the country, along Vietnam's borders with Laos and Cambodia. Spurs of the Truong Son Mountains stretch eastward to the South China Sea, segmenting the fertile coastal plain.

The Vietnamese speak of their country as having three distinct geographical areas: Bac Bo (the north), Trung Bo (the central region) and Nam Bo (the south), which correspond to the former French administrative divisions of Tonkin (Nam Ky), Annam (Trung Ky) and Cochinchina (Bac Ky). Between 1954 and 1975, the country was divided at the Ben Hai River (the 17th parallel) into the Republic of Vietnam, with its capital at Saigon, and the Democratic Republic of Vietnam, which was governed from Hanoi.

Offshore Islands

Vietnam claims assorted offshore islands in the Gulf of Thailand and the South China Sea, including Phu Quoc Island off the Cambodian coast, the Tho Chu Islands south-west of Phu Quoc, the Con Dao Islands south-east of the Mekong Delta, the Paracel Islands (Quan Dao Hoang Xa) 300 km east of Danang and the Spratly Islands (Quan Dao Thruong Xa) 475 km south-east of Nha Trang.

Several of the Paracel Islands, which historically have been occupied only sporadically, were seized by the People's Republic of China in 1951. In the 1960s, a few of the

islands were occupied by the South Vietnamese, who were driven out by Chinese forces in 1964 – an action protested by both the Saigon and Hanoi governments.

The Spratlys, which consist of hundreds of tiny islets, are closer to Borneo than to Vietnam. They are claimed by virtually every country in the vicinity, including the Philippines, Malaysia, Indonesia, China, Taiwan and Vietnam. In 1988, Vietnam lost two ships and 70 sailors in a clash with China over the Spratlys. In mid-1992, Chinese military patrol boats reportedly opened fire on several occasions on Vietnamese cargo vessels leaving Hong Kong, bringing trade between Vietnam and Hong Kong to a near halt. The weak explanation was that China was trying to prevent smuggling.

Both archipelagos have little intrinsic value but the country that has sovereignty over them can claim huge areas of the South China Sea – reported to hold vast oil reserves – as its territorial waters. China pushed tensions to a new high in 1992 by signing contracts with a US company (Crestone Corporation) to explore for oil in the disputed areas. In June 1992, Chinese forces occupied one of the islets claimed by Vietnam.

CLIMATE

There are no good or bad seasons for visiting Vietnam. When one region is wet or cold or steamy hot, there is always somewhere else that is sunny and pleasantly warm.

Vietnam has a remarkably diverse climate because of its wide range of latitudes and altitudes. Although the entire country lies in the tropics and subtropics, local conditions vary from frosty winters in the far northern hills to the year-round sub-equatorial warmth of the Mekong Delta. Because about one-third of Vietnam is more than 500 metres above sea level, much of the country enjoys a subtropical or – above 2000 metres – even a temperate climate.

Vietnam lies in the South-East Asian monsoon zone. Its weather is determined by two monsoons, which set the rhythm of rural life. The winter monsoon comes from the north-east between October and March and

NGUYEN DYNASTY

Hué became the capital of Vietnam in 1802, when Nguyen Anh crowned himself Emperor Gia Long, thus founding the Nguyen Dynasty. Upon his accession, he began the construction of the Citadel, the Imperial Enclosure and the Forbidden Purple City. Gia Long instituted conservative Confucian values and began a large-scale programme of public works, including the construction of dikes, bridges, canals and the Mandarin Road linking Hué with both Saigon and Hanoi.

The early Nguyen emperors were hostile to Catholicism and Western influences. In keeping with their expansionist policies, they took over large areas of Cambodia and Laos. French colonial interest in Vietnam began in earnest in the 1840s, when the French responded to actions against Catholic missionaries. Following military defeat in 1862, Emperor Tu Duc signed a treaty that gave the French the three eastern provinces of Cochinchina, which became a French colony.

Upon the death of Tu Duc, the French attacked Hué and imposed a Treaty of Protectorate on the imperial court. From that time, the Nguyen Dynasty emperors ruled in name only. Anti-colonial resistance continued in Vietnam. In 1945, following Japanese occupation during World War II, the Communist Viet Minh gained power and Emperor Bao Dai abdicated. The capital was moved to Hanoi.

DEANNA SWANEY

Above: Ruins within the Imperial Enclosure, a legacy of the destruction of 1968.

Below Left: Thai Hoa Palace, once used for the emperor's official receptions.

Below Right: Thien Mu Pagoda, built in 1844, has become the unofficial symbol of Hué.

BRENDAN McCARTHY

SARA JANE CLELAND

KINGDOM OF CHAMPA

The kingdom of Champa flourished from the 2nd to the 15th centuries. It first appeared around present-day Danang and later spread south to what is now Nha Trang and Phan Rang. Champa became Indianised through commercial relations with India: the Chams adopted Hinduism, employed Sanskrit as a sacred language and borrowed from Indian art.

The Chams, who lacked enough land for agriculture along the mountainous coast, were semi-piratic and conducted attacks on passing trading ships. As a result, they were in a constant state of war with the Vietnamese to the north and the Khmers to the west. The Chams successfully threw off Khmer rule in the 12th century but were entirely absorbed by Vietnam in the 17th century.

The Chams are best known for the many brick sanctuaries (Cham towers) they constructed throughout the south. The greatest collection of Cham art is in the Cham Museum in Danang. The major Cham site is at My Son (near Danang), and other Cham ruins can be found in Nha Trang and Phan Rang-Thap Cham.

DEANNA SWANEY

Above Right: The 13th-century towers of Po Klong Garai in Phan Rang-Thap Cham.

Below Right: Detail of Po Klong Garai.

Below Left: Carving at the Cham Museum, Danang.

TONY WHEELER

GREG ALFORD

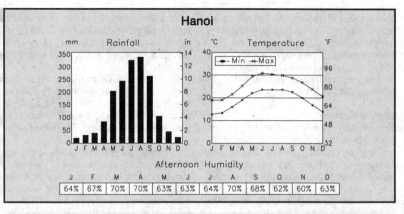

Hanoi

Rainfall / Temperature

Afternoon Humidity

J	F	M	A	M	J	J	A	S	O	N	D
64%	67%	70%	70%	63%	63%	64%	70%	68%	62%	60%	63%

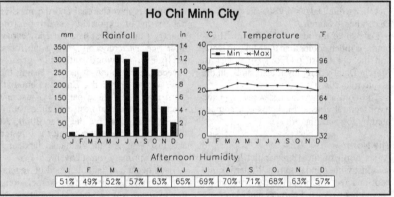

Ho Chi Minh City

Rainfall / Temperature

Afternoon Humidity

J	F	M	A	M	J	J	A	S	O	N	D
51%	49%	52%	57%	63%	65%	69%	70%	71%	68%	63%	57%

brings wet chilly winters to all areas north of Nha Trang, but dry and warm temperatures to the south. From April or May to October, the south-western monsoon blows, its winds laden with moisture picked up while crossing the Indian Ocean and the Gulf of Thailand. The south-western monsoon brings warm, humid weather to the whole country except those areas sheltered by mountains (such as the central coastal lowlands and the Red River Delta).

Between July and November, violent and unpredictable typhoons often develop over the ocean east of Vietnam, hitting central and northern Vietnam with devastating results.

Most of Vietnam receives about 2000 mm of rain annually, though parts of the Central Highlands get approximately 3300 mm of precipitation per annum.

The South

The south, whose climate is sub-equatorial, has two main seasons: the wet and the dry. The wet season lasts from May to November (June to August are the wettest months). During this time, there are heavy but short-lived downpours almost daily, usually in the afternoon. The dry season runs from December to April. Late February through May are hot and very humid, but things cool down slightly when the summer rainy season begins.

In Ho Chi Minh City, the average annual temperature is 27°C. In April, daily highs are usually in the low 30s. In January, the daily lows average 21°C. Average humidity is 80% and annual rainfall averages 1979 mm. The coldest temperature ever recorded in Ho Chi Minh City is 14°C.

Central Vietnam

The coastal lowlands are denied significant rainfall from the south-west monsoon (April or May to October) by the Truong Son Mountains, which are very wet during this period. Much of the coastal strip's precipitation is brought between December and February by the north-east monsoon. Nha Trang's dry season lasts from June to October while Dalat's dry season goes from December to March.

Dalat, like the rest of the Central Highlands, is much cooler than the Mekong Delta and the coastal strip. From November to March, Dalat's daily highs are usually in the low to mid-20s.

The cold and wet winter weather of the north-central coastal lowlands is accompanied by fog and fine drizzle.

The North

Areas north of the 18th parallel have two seasons: winter and summer. Winter is quite cool and wet and usually lasts from about November to April. February and March are marked by a persistent drizzling rain the Vietnamese call 'rain dust' *(crachin)*. The hot summers run from May to October. The north is subject to occasional devastating typhoons during the summer months.

FLORA & FAUNA
Flora

Originally, almost the whole of Vietnam was covered with dense forests. Since the arrival of the first human beings many millennia ago, Vietnam has been progressively denuded of forest cover. The first to lose their trees were coastal and low-lying areas, which were ideal for rice growing. Over the centuries, human exploitation has spread higher and higher into the hills and mountains, a process accelerated by the wars and population growth. While 44% of the original forest cover was extant in 1943, by 1976 only 29% remained and by 1983 only 24% was left.

The forests of Vietnam are estimated to contain 12,000 plant species, only 7000 of which have been identified and 2300 of which are known to be useful to humans for food, medicines, animal fodder, wood products and other purposes.

Currently, an estimated 2000 sq km are deforested every year because of slash-and-burn agriculture by Montagnards, forest fires (made all the fiercer by the dead wood of trees killed by the herbicide Agent Orange), relentless firewood collection, the processing of trees into charcoal and the massive harvesting of exportable hardwood (the country's third largest hard currency earner after rice and crude oil). Along the forest periphery, firewood gathering greatly exceeds regeneration capacity, causing the forest edge to recede. Environmentalists warn that unless these patterns of use are changed, Vietnam's forests will almost completely disappear by the year 2000. At present only 21% of the country is forested and just 8 to 9% of Vietnam's land area retains its primary forest cover.

Each hectare of land denuded of vegetation contributes to the flooding of areas downstream from water catchment areas, irreversible soil erosion (upland soils are especially fragile), the silting up of rivers, streams, lakes and reservoirs, and unpredictable climatic changes.

For many years, Vietnam has had an active reafforestation programme in which Ho Chi Minh himself is said to have taken a keen interest. However, only 36% of the 8720 sq km of trees planted between 1955 and 1979 were still forested at the end of the period. Currently, about 1600 sq km are planted with some 500 million trees each year. The Ministry of Education has made the planting and taking care of trees by pupils part of the curriculum. However, even at this rate, reafforestation is not keeping up with forest losses. There are plans to try to reafforest the

Ecocide

During the Vietnam War, the USA employed deliberate destruction of the environment (ecocide) as a military tactic on a scale unprecedented in the history of warfare. In an effort to deny bases of operation to the VC, 72 million litres of the herbicides known as Agent Orange, Agent White and Agent Blue were sprayed on 16% of South Vietnam's land area (including 10% of the inland forests and 36% of the mangrove forests). It is said that the deforestation caused by spraying these chemicals would have been enough to supply Vietnam's timber harvesters for 30 years. The most seriously affected regions were the provinces of Dong Nai, Song Be and Tay Ninh. Another environmentally disastrous method of defoliation employed by the military involved the use of enormous bulldozers called 'Rome plows' to rip up the jungle floor.

The 40 million litres of Agent Orange used contained 170 kg of dioxin (2,3,7,8-TCDD). Dioxin is the most toxic chemical known, highly carcinogenic and mutagenic. Today, more than 20 years after the spraying, dioxin is still present in the food chain though its concentrations are gradually diminishing. Researchers report elevated levels of dioxin in samples of human breast milk collected in affected areas, where about 7.5% of the population of the south now lives. Vietnamese refugees living in the USA who were exposed to Agent Orange have been showing unusually high rates of cancer. Ditto for American soldiers, who have filed a class action lawsuit against the US government to seek compensation.

In addition to the spraying, large tracts of forests, agricultural land, villages and even cemeteries were bulldozed, removing both the vegetation and topsoil. Flammable melaleuca forests were ignited with napalm. In mountain areas, landslides were deliberately created by bombing and by spraying acid on limestone hillsides. Elephants, useful for transport, were attacked from the air with bombs and napalm. By war's end, extensive areas had been taken over by tough weeds (known locally as 'American grass') that prevent young trees from receiving enough light to survive. The government estimates that 20,000 sq km of forest and farmland were lost as a direct result of the American war effort.

Overall, some 13 million tonnes of bombs – equivalent to 450 times the energy of the atomic bomb used on Hiroshima – were dropped on the region. This comes to 265 kg for every man, woman and child in Indochina. If the Americans had showered the people of Indochina with the money all those bombs cost (the war cost US$2000 per resident of Indochina), they might have won.

The long-term results of this onslaught have been devastating. The lush tropical forests have not grown back, fisheries (even those in coastal waters) remain depleted in both variety and productivity, wildlife populations have not recovered, cropland productivity is still below its prewar levels, and among the human population the incidence of various cancers and toxin-related diseases has greatly increased. The land is scarred by 25 million bomb craters up to 30 metres in diameter, many of which have filled up with water and become breeding grounds for malarial mosquitoes (though some of the craters have been converted into ponds for raising fish). ∎

bald midland hills, which have little or no agricultural value.

In 1992, Vietnam announced the banning of unprocessed timber exports. The Vietnamese press touted this as an attempt to prevent deforestation, but cynical foreign observers were less sure. The real reason, according to these sources, was so Vietnam could gain foreign investment to develop its own wood processing industry – 'value-added' wood exports are still allowed if the timber is first processed into paper, furniture, etc.

Some have found it suspicious that Australian aid in the field of forestry has been accompanied by the sudden appearance of large tracts of young eucalyptus trees in the Vietnamese countryside. Are we witnessing a form of ecological imperialism?

Fauna

Because Vietnam includes a wide range of habitats – ranging from equatorial lowlands to high, temperate plateaus and even alpine peaks – the country's wild fauna is enormously diverse. Vietnam is home to 273 species of mammals, 773 species of birds, 180 species of reptiles, 80 species of amphibians, hundreds of species of fish and thousands of kinds of invertebrates. Larger animals of special importance in conservation efforts include the elephant, rhinoceros, tiger, leopard, black bear, honey bear, snub-nosed monkey, douc langur (a monkey remarkable for its variegated colours), concolour gibbon, macaque, rhesus monkey, serow (a kind of mountain goat), flying squirrel, kouprey (a blackish-brown forest ox), banteng (a kind of wild ox), deer, peacock, pheasant, crocodile, python, cobra and turtle.

Tragically, Vietnam's wildlife is in a precipitous decline as forest habitats are destroyed and waterways become polluted. In addition, uncontrolled illegal hunting – many people in remote areas have access to weapons left over from the war – has exterminated the local populations of various animals, in some cases eliminating entire species from the country. Officially, the government has recognised 54 species of mammals and 60 species of birds as endangered. The tapir (a large perissodactyl ungulate) and the Sumatran rhinoceros are already extinct in Vietnam, and there are thought to be fewer than 20 koupreys and 20 to 30 Javan rhinoceroses left in the country.

It is encouraging that some wildlife seem to be returning to reafforested areas. For example, birds, fish and crustaceans have

Megamantiacus vuquangensis, a previously unknown species of deer discovered in 1994

reappeared in replanted mangrove swamps. But unless the government takes immediate remedial measures – including banning the sale and export of tiger skins and ivory – hundreds of species of mammals, birds and plants will become extinct within the next decade. Unfortunately, the impact of tourism could speed up the destruction of native species, as one traveller noted:

The locals sell colourful live coral dredged up from the sea floor, which of course goes white and dead in a few hours anyway. Coral reefs are becoming scarce enough without tourists depleting them further. OK, the local people need the money, but there are better ways to pass it over to them. If you want to take home souvenirs, try to find something else besides coral and rare seashells.

Vietnam seems to be one of the last remaining places in the world where zoologists are discovering previously unknown species of large mammals. None had been found for nearly 50 years until 1992, when a large goat-like animal (*Pseudoryx nghetinhesis*) was discovered at Vu Quang in northern Vietnam by John MacKinnon, who was working for the World Wildlife Fund – it was only the fourth large land mammal to be discovered in the 20th century. In 1994 a hitherto-unknown species of deer (*Megamantiacus vuquangensis*) was discovered near the same site. It is a very robust kind of barking deer, related to the muntjak. It is believed that both animals occur in border areas with Laos and Cambodia, from Nghe An to Dac Lac. However, travellers are advised not to try to see these rare animals in the wild, as they may put them in even greater peril – many local people believe that tourists want to buy skins and skulls. In general, travellers to Vietnam should not buy products made from wildlife.

Wildlife Books Useful books about Vietnam's wildlife are few and far between, and some of the better ones produced in the Vietnamese language are no longer in print. *A Guide to the Birds of Thailand* (Philip Round and Boonsong Lakagul, Saha Kam Bhaet Company, 1991) covers the majority, if not all, of Vietnam's birds. It's particularly relevant to the bird species in the southern and central regions of Vietnam. Slightly out of date and difficult to use, *A Field Guide to the Birds of South-East Asia* (Ben King, Martin Woodcock and Edward Dickinson, Collins, 1975) is still valuable because it gives thorough coverage to Vietnam. These two books are not available in Vietnam, but you should be able to find them in Bangkok (try Asia Books). If you're lucky, you may be able to pick up in an old Hanoi bookshop the two-volume *Chim Viet Nam* (Vietnamese Birds) by Vo Quy, a Vietnamese-language publication now out of print.

National Parks

Vietnam has several national parks, the main ones being Cat Ba, Ba Be Lake and Cuc Phuong national parks in the north; Bach Ma National Park in the centre; and Nam Cat Tien National Park in the south.

Cat Ba National Park is a beautiful island, and during the summer months attracts a steady flow of foreign travellers willing to make the boat journey. Ba Be Lake National Park features spectacular waterfalls and is accessible by rented jeep or motorbike from Hanoi. Cuc Phuong National Park is less visited and has suffered more ecological damage from logging and burning, but it is now protected. Bach Ma National Park near Hué is not developed and seldom visited, but has good potential. Nam Cat Tien National Park, in the Central Highlands of the south, is difficult to reach and sees few visitors.

In an attempt to prevent an ecological and hydrological catastrophe, the government has plans to set aside tens of thousands of sq km of forest land and to create 87 national parks and nature reserves. Thirty-seven reserves (including the national parks) have already received government approval. Ecologists hope that because tropical eco-systems have a high species diversity but low densities of individual species, reserve areas will be large enough to contain viable populations of each species. However, there are development interests which are not amen-

able to increasing the size of Vietnam's national parks and forest reserves – as in the West, even the best-laid plans can go awry.

Another problem is poaching, and this is one threat that travellers should take seriously. Poachers often carry guns, both for their illegal hunting activities and to drive away any potential witnesses or law enforcement authorities. They are also not above supplementing their income with armed robberies. Especially in areas near the Cambodian and Laotian borders, there is a fairly high chance of getting shot at if you go strolling in the jungle. The government discourages foreigners from visiting these remote nature reserves near the border, and scientists seeking permission to visit are usually obliged to take along a few AK-47-toting soldiers for protection. Of course, this doesn't apply to those parts of national parks which see a reasonable amount of tourist traffic.

GOVERNMENT

The Socialist Republic of Vietnam (SRV; Cong Hoa Xa Hoi Chu Nghia Viet Nam) came into existence in July 1976 as a unitary state comprising the Democratic Republic of Vietnam (DRV; North Vietnam) and the defeated Republic of Vietnam (RVN; South Vietnam). From April 1975 until the declaration of the SRV, the South had been ruled – at least in name – by a Provisional Revolutionary Government.

The SRV espouses a Marxist-Leninist political philosophy. Its political institutions have borrowed a great deal from the Soviet and Chinese models, but in many respects have developed to meet Vietnam's particular circumstances.

Flag & National Anthem

The flag of the Socialist Republic of Vietnam consists of a yellow star in the middle of a red field. Until 1976 this was the flag of the Hanoi-based Democratic Republic of Vietnam. The significance of the yellow star and red field are explained in the national anthem, *Marching to the Front (Tien Quan Ca)*, which reflects the martial history and outlook of the present government. The words are as follows:

Soldiers of Vietnam, we go forward
With the one will to save our Fatherland.
Our hurried steps are sounding on the long and arduous road.
Our flag, red with the blood of victory, bears the spirit of our country.
The distant rumbling of the guns mingles with our marching song.
The path to glory passes over the bodies of our foes.
Overcoming all hardships, together we build our resistance bases.
Ceaselessly for the people's cause we struggle,
Hastening to the battlefield!
Forward! All together advancing!
Our Vietnam is strong eternal.

Soldiers of Vietnam, we go forward,
The gold star of our flag in the wind
Leading our people, our native land, out of misery and suffering.
Let us join our efforts in the fight for the building of a new life.
Let us stand up and break our chains.
For too long we have swallowed our hatred.
Let us keep ready for all sacrifices and our life will be radiant.
Ceaselessly for the people's cause we struggle,
Hastening to the battlefield!
Forward! All together advancing!
Our Vietnam is strong eternal.

From 1973 to 1975, virtually every house in the South had either a South Vietnamese flag (three horizontal red stripes on a yellow field) or a National Liberation Front flag (a yellow star in the centre of a red and blue field split horizontally) painted near the door. The Paris agreements of 1973 gave equal status in the South to the South Vietnamese government and the Provisional Revolutionary Government (a group set up in 1969 by the Viet Cong). Because the areas under the control of each were noncontiguous and had no clear boundaries between them, the control of each village and neighbourhood was indicated by flags painted on roofs and near the doorways of every building. When the international observer force investigated alleged ceasefire violations, the flags provided instant, publicly acknowledged information on who was supposed to control the area.

When the Communists took over the South they painted over the old flags with flags of their own – first that of the National Liberation Front and then the SRV flag. Over the years, the flags of the SRV faded away or chipped off, revealing the NLF flags (which remind southerners of their forcible incorporation into a unitary state) and, underneath, the flags of the old Saigon regime. To this day, if you look carefully, you will see South Vietnamese flags painted on many buildings, bridges and other structures in south and central Vietnam. Is the government too poor to afford a new coat of paint, or is it that no one really cares about the old flags any more?

The Orwellian national slogan, which appears at the top of every official document, is *Doc Lap, Tu Do, Hanh Phuc*, which means 'Independence, Freedom, Happiness'. It's based on one of Ho Chi Minh's sayings.

The Communist Party

Vietnam's political system is dominated by the 1.8 million-member Communist Party (Dang Cong San Viet Nam), whose influence is felt at every level of the country's social and political life. Communist Party membership seems to be experiencing a slight upsurge after several years of decline in the early 1990s.

The leadership of the Party has been collective in style and structure ever since its founding by Ho Chi Minh in 1930. The Party's decentralised structure, though originally necessitated by the difficulty of communications between Party headquarters and its branches, has allowed local leaders considerable leeway for initiative. Unfortunately, this has also allowed the development of localised corruption, which Hanoi has had a difficult time controlling.

The official media has described a number of cases. In Thanh Hoa Province, local partychief Ha Trong Hoa turned his police force into a band of Mafia-style gangsters and ruled for years before Hanoi finally stepped in and ousted him. Pham Chi Tin, the son of a high-ranking Communist Party official, was arrested by the military in 1994 after his gang (the Nha Trang police force) terrorised local residents for years – Hanoi took action after he kidnapped a tourist from Hong Kong to extort money from the victim's family.

Relatively speaking, the policies of the Vietnamese Communist Party have been characterised by a flexible and non-doctrinaire approach.

The most powerful institution in the Party is the Political Bureau (Politburo), which has about a dozen members. It oversees the Party's day-to-day functioning and has the power to issue directives to the government. The Politburo is formally elected by the Central Committee, whose 125 or so full members and about 50 alternate members meet only once or twice a year.

Party Congresses, at which major policy changes are ratified after a long process of behind-the-scenes discussions and consultations, were held in 1935, 1951, 1960, 1976, 1982, 1986 and 1991. The last few Party Congresses have reflected intense intra-Party disagreements over the path Vietnamese Communism should take, with changing coalitions of conservatives and dogmatists squaring off against more pragmatic elements. The position of Party Chairman has been left vacant since Ho Chi Minh's death.

During the 1980s and early 1990s thousands of Party members were expelled, in part to reduce corruption (seen by a fed-up public as endemic) and in part to make room for more young people and workers. As in China, Vietnam has been ruled by a gerontocracy. At the time of writing, the average age of Politburo members is 65 years, down from 71 in 1990. Despite official rhetoric about the equality of women, females are under-represented in the Party, especially at the highest levels (there have been no female members of the Politburo since 1945).

Constitutions

The Socialist Republic of Vietnam and its Hanoi-based predecessor have had three constitutions. The 1946 Constitution, drafted by a committee headed by Ho Chi Minh, was designed to appeal to a broad spectrum of Vietnamese society while at the same time pre-empting criticism from abroad, especially from France and the USA (with this goal in mind, it contained material taken from the American Declaration of Independence).

The 1959 Constitution was drawn up after it became clear that the 1956 national elections, called for in the Geneva Accords of 1954, were not going to take place as scheduled. Three years of intense debate over the question of armed struggle in the South produced the 1959 Constitution, which made the goal of creating a Communist society, characterised by central planning and collective property ownership, explicit. Following the Chinese example on ethnic minorities policy, two 'autonomous regions', complete with their own zonal assemblies, administrations and militia forces, were created in northern and north-western North Vietnam.

After reunification in 1975, it was decided that the country again needed a new constitution. The 1980 Constitution was the result of four years of debate on how the south, with its radically different social and economic structure, should be absorbed. It reflects the victory of those who favoured rapid collectivisation. The 1980 Constitution, which borrows heavily from the 1977 Soviet Constitution, declared the Party to be 'the only force leading the State and society, and the main factor in determining all successes of the Vietnamese revolution'. Fearing the implications of creating a third minority autonomous region in the Central Highlands (where the government feared unrest by Montagnard insurgents backed, over the years, by France, the USA, China and Thailand), the two autonomous regions in the north were abolished.

Administration

The Vietnamese governmental structure administers the country but the main decision-making bodies are those of the Party, especially the Politburo, which can, independently of the government, issue decrees with the force of law. Party cadres dominate the higher echelons of government.

The unicameral National Assembly (Quoc Hoi) is Vietnam's highest legislative authority. Its 500 or so deputies, whose terms last five years, each represent 100,000 voters. The National Assembly's role is to rubber-stamp – usually unanimously – Politburo decisions and party-initiated legislation during its biannual sessions, which last about a week. Relative to the population, white-collar workers are over-represented in the National Assembly while peasants and women are greatly under-represented.

The Council of State functions as the country's collective presidency. Its members, who currently number 15, are elected by the National Assembly. The Council of State carries out the duties of the National Assembly when the latter is not in session. The Council of Ministers is also elected by the National Assembly. It functions as does a Western-style cabinet. Among its current members are the prime minister, nine deputy premiers, a secretary-general, 22 ministers with portfolio (Construction, Culture, Education, Finance, Information, Justice, Supply, Transport, etc), the heads of seven State Commissions (Planning, External Economic Relations, etc) and the directors of the State Bank and the Government Inspectorate. During the economic crises and reforms that began in 1975, cabinet shuffles have been frequent.

Though Hanoi has been promoting the idea that local governments play a greater role in planning, most such administrative units have been unable to come up with the requisite funds to make this possible. Indeed, even agricultural cooperatives, the regime's ideological backbone, have been unable to make ends meet without resorting to corruption and the black market. In the early 1980s, the provinces were allowed to establish their own import-export concerns, but when provisional governments showed a propensity to hoard foreign currency in order to buy goods from abroad, regulations allowing them to keep only part of their hard currency were implemented.

Elections

Candidates to the National Assembly and local People's Committees are elected to office. The voting age is 18. Everyone of voting age is required to vote, though proxy-voting is allowed (and is very common). This permits the government to boast that elections produce 100% voter participation, thus conferring legitimacy on the process.

Elections are held with great fanfare and it all appears very democratic on the surface. In practice, most Vietnamese are highly cynical about their 'democracy'. Only Party-approved candidates are permitted to run and opposition parties are prohibited. Some 'independents' have appeared on the slate in Ho Chi Minh City (and nowhere else), but they must also have the government's approval to run. During elections, the number of candidates running in a given constituency usually exceeds the number of contested seats by 20 to 30%.

The Military

The military does not seem to have any direct political role, even though virtually all of Vietnam's high-ranking politicians and officials came from the military.

The military has traditionally consumed something like half of the government's total budget, but this is now in the process of being reduced. This is forcing the military to find other means of finance, which even includes opening hotels and office buildings along with foreign joint ventures. Interestingly, while corruption can be a problem in dealing with some civilian Vietnamese officials, the military is widely believed to be relatively clean. Some foreign investors in Vietnam even go so far as to say the army makes a better joint-venture partner than almost any other government agency in the country.

Vietnam officially has universal conscription for males. According to the law, all men between the ages of 18 and 26 must serve two years in the military. But as in many other countries, draft dodging is a time-honoured tradition, and those with good political connections or money find ways to beat the system.

The Law

The French gave the Vietnamese the Napoleonic Code, much of which has not been repealed though these laws may conflict with later statutes. From about 1960 to 1975, South Vietnam modified much of its commercial code to resemble that of the USA. Since reunification, Soviet-style laws have been applied to the whole country, with devastating consequences for private property owners. The recent economic reforms have seen a flood of new property legislation, much of it the result of advice from the United Nations, the IMF and other international organisations. The rapid speed at which legislation is being enacted is a challenge for those who must interpret and enforce the law.

Political Divisions
Vietnam is divided into 50 provinces *(tinh)* which have a significant degree of autonomy. Thus, provinces vary widely in their approach to foreign investment, economic development, economic liberalisation, political reform, tourism, etc. Listed from north to south, Vietnam's provinces are:

Far North: Ha Giang, Tuyen Quang, Cao Bang, Lao Cai, Yen Bai, Lai Chau, Lang Son, Bac Thai, Son La, Vinh Phu, Ha Bac, Hoa Binh and Quang Ninh.

Red River Delta Area: Ha Tay, Hai Hung, Thai Binh, Nam Ha and Ninh Binh.

North-Central Vietnam: Thanh Hoa, Nghe An, Ha Tinh, Quang Binh, Quang Tri and Thua Thien-Hue.

South-Central Coast: Quang Nam-Danang, Quang Ngai, Binh Dinh, Phu Yen, Khanh Hoa, Ninh Thuan and Binh Thuan.

Central Highlands: Kon Tum, Gia Lai, Dac Lac (Dak Lak) and Lam Dong.

South: Song Be, Tay Ninh, Dong Nai, Ba Ria-Vung Tau, Long An, Dong Thap, An Giang, Tien Giang, Ben Tre, Vinh Long, Tra Vinh, Kien Giang, Cantho, Soc Trang and Minh Hai.

In addition, there are three independent municipalities: Greater Hanoi, Greater Ho Chi Minh City and Greater Haiphong.

The provinces and municipalities are divided into rural and urban districts. Rural districts are subdivided into village-level communes made up of hamlets while urban districts are divided into wards.

The government seems to have a hard time deciding how to carve the turkey. After reunification, the provincial structure of the south was completely reorganised. Then on 1 July 1989, several provinces that were joined after 1975 were split apart. Since then there have been even more splits. Don't be surprised if what you find on the ground differs from what your map says – even the Vietnamese have difficulty keeping up with the redrawing of political boundaries.

ECONOMY
Vietnam is one of the poorest countries in the world, with an estimated per capita income of US$300 per year and US$1.4 billion in hard currency debts (owed mainly to the IMF and Japan) it is unable to repay.

Debt forgiveness by Vietnam's creditors is unlikely, but the country's improving economy increases the possibility that it will all be paid off eventually. In 1994, Vietnam qualified for a new loan from the World Bank to repair National Highway 1 in the northern half of the country.

Despite its hard-working, educated workforce, the country's economy is beset by weak exports, a lack of raw materials for industry, chronic shortages of spare parts, a limited supply of consumer goods, unemployment, under-employment and, until recently, erratic runaway inflation (700% in 1986, 30% in 1989 and 50% in 1991). The economy was hurt by wartime infrastructure damage (not a single bridge in the North survived American air-raids, while in the South many bridges were blown up by the VC), but by the government's own admission the present economic fiasco is the result of ideologically driven policies followed after reunification plus corruption and the burden of heavy military spending.

Swords into Market Shares

The word is out – it's time to put away the guns and beat the swords into ploughshares. Yes, the Vietnam War is over, but the battle for market share is just beginning. And everyone wants a piece of the action. Joint-venture capitalists from Japan, Korea, Taiwan, France, Germany, England and Australia have been flocking to Vietnam since the beginning of the 1990s.

The most recent arrivals in town have been the Americans, and they bring with them several competitive advantages. As with the French, there is this strange nostalgia for doing business with those who were just yesterday Vietnam's enemy. Aside from that, the fact is that Vietnamese love anything American, be it Mickey Mouse or Michael Jackson. Long prohibited from doing business in Vietnam by a US-imposed embargo (lifted only in 1994), American companies are now beating a path to what they hope will be Asia's newest economic tiger.

The new American warriors don't wear green uniforms or carry M-16s. Rather, they come in pressed suits, carrying Gucci luggage and laptop computers. Their weapons of choice are cola drinks, Hollywood celluloid and compact disks. Their battle cry is 'Stocks, bonds and rock'n'roll!'.

Consumerism is now rampant in Vietnam, at least among the relatively affluent. Being called a member of the 'upper crust' (once defined as 'a lot of crumbs held together by dough') is no longer an insult. Making money is OK now. And so is spending it. It's this consumer boom that keeps foreign investors awake at night.

American companies have already splashed ashore. Computers sporting the label 'Intel Inside' are on display in newly opened hi-tech electronic shops. Chrysler has formed a joint venture to produce its gas-guzzling Jeep Cherokee in Vietnam. Motorola pagers can be heard beeping in the pockets and handbags of Saigon's well-to-do. Pepsi was the first American soft drink vendor to return to Vietnam, but Coke was not far behind.

American fast food should find a ready market among Vietnam's trendy urban elite. McDonald's, when it finally opens a branch in Saigon, will be an instant hit. That is, of course, if nobody clones the name first. Already, Ho Chi Minh City has two fake 7 Elevens.

The Americans, for their part, are displeased with the lack of protection for intellectual property rights. On the other hand, the Vietnamese government has so far refused anyone permission to capitalise on Ho Chi Minh's name. A proposal to open an American joint-venture called *Uncle Ho's Hamburgers* went up like a lead balloon. Nor were the Vietnamese persuaded when the American business reps pointed out that Ho Chi Minh does vaguely resemble Colonel Sanders. 'No' said the frowning Vietnamese, 'Ho Chi Minh was a general'. ■

Just how the average Vietnamese manages to survive economically is a mystery. Salaries in Ho Chi Minh City are in the neighbourhood of US$50 to US$80 per month, but elsewhere they're about half that. You simply can't survive on such wages unless you can grow your own food and build your own house (possible in the countryside but not in Ho Chi Minh City or Hanoi). So people scrounge on the side, finding some odd job they can do. In the case of women, some are forced to resort to part-time prostitution, while government officials and police may turn to corruption.

Until very recently, one of Vietnam's most valuable exports has been its people. Desperate for foreign currency, Vietnamese were given jobs that not even Russians would take – in Siberia, for instance. USSR-bound flights used to leave Hanoi full of excited young people, many of them young women, off to places like Novosibirsk where they earned US$500 per month, US$400 of which was paid to the Vietnamese government. Despite the harsh working conditions and low pay, competition for these dismal jobs was keen – one had to be of the right class background or have political connections. Many Vietnamese workers also went to the former East Germany, and when the Berlin Wall fell most of them fled to the West, where they continue to live and work, often illegally. Recently, many have become targets of abuse by Germany's notorious 'skinhead' gangs. Now that the Russian economy is in possibly worse condition than Vietnam's, interest in Siberian employment has fallen to zero.

Although Vietnam and Russia are still officially as close as lips and teeth, Vietnamese from all parts of the country seem to harbour an unreserved hostility towards the few remaining Russian experts in their country. This bitterness is an outgrowth of the widespread belief that Soviet economic policies are to blame for Vietnam's economy going straight down the toilet after reunification. The once ubiquitous posters of those two White guys, Marx and Lenin, served to underline the foreign origin of much of the Party's unpopular ideology, including collectivisation and centralised planning. Perhaps not surprisingly, the posters disappeared almost overnight when the Soviet Union also disappeared in 1991.

Economic Reforms

The Vietnamese are keenly aware that while their centrally planned economy has been stagnating (despite billions of roubles in Soviet aid), the free market economies of their capitalist neighbours (Thailand, Malaysia, Singapore, Hong Kong and Taiwan) have been flourishing. And whereas 25 years ago Bangkok and Saigon were economically comparable, today the former is one of Asia's boom towns while the latter has hardly changed. The Vietnamese also realise that the South-East Asian technological revolution is passing them by.

Vietnam's efforts to restructure the economy really got under way with the Sixth Party Congress held in December 1986. At that time, Nguyen Van Linh (a proponent of reform) was appointed General Secretary of the Communist Party. Recent reforms have cut state subsidies, allowed limited private enterprise, reduced centralised planning, rationalised exchange rates and liberalised foreign investment.

Immediately upon the legalisation of limited private enterprise, family businesses began popping up all over the country. But it is in the south, with its experience with capitalism, where the entrepreneurial skills and managerial dynamism needed to effect the reforms are to be found. With 'new thinking' in Hanoi now remaking the economic life of the whole country in the mould of the pre-reunification south, people have been

remarking that, in the end, the South won the war.

Vietnam's economy started growing in the late 1980s, reversing the trend of the previous decade when the country experienced precipitous negative economic growth. But official growth figures don't tell the whole story; there is a significant 'black economy' not recorded in the government's statistics. Indeed, the amount of smuggling going on across the Cambodian-Vietnamese border easily exceeds official trade between those two countries. Another fact the government doesn't like to admit is that the urban economy is improving much faster than that of rural areas, widening the already-significant gap in standards of living. The Vietnamese government fears what China is already experiencing – a mass exodus of rural residents into the already overcrowded cities.

Business people in Vietnam are generally optimistic. Ho Chi Minh City at least seems to be booming; every major hotel in Saigon and Cholon is filled with enthusiastic importers, investors, international lawyers and specialists of all stripes. Until recently, the situation was far gloomier in Hanoi, where titanic bureaucratic impediments were the norm. However, success tends to be contagious and now the north has also caught the capitalistic fever. Indeed, many investors consider the north to have even better long-term potential than the south because the north has more natural resources, lower wages, access to the Chinese border and a more reliable electricity supply. If the lid can be kept on corruption and bureaucracy (a big 'if'), the economic prospects for Vietnam appear bright.

Before 1991, Vietnam's major trading partners were the USSR and other members of Comecon (Council for Mutual Economic Assistance – the Eastern Bloc's equivalent to the European Community). Most of the trade with Comecon was on a barter basis; Vietnam traded its crude oil, wood and sugar cane for refined oil, machinery and weapons. Because the value of Vietnam's agricultural products was not nearly enough to pay for expensive value-added goods, the USSR had to subsidise the Vietnamese economy, leaving Vietnam with an enormous rouble-denominated debt.

The disintegration of Comecon and the USSR in 1991 could have brought complete economic collapse to Vietnam. Almost miraculously, this was avoided because Vietnam moved quickly to establish hard-currency trade relations with China, Hong Kong, Japan, Singapore, South Korea, Taiwan, Thailand and Western nations. This explains why Vietnamese officials have suddenly become so anxious to do business with the West. Many other former Eastern Bloc countries have not fared as well as Vietnam – their economies collapsed along with the USSR.

The transition from an isolated socialist barter economy to a free market, hard-currency trading economy is not complete and has not been easy. Many of Vietnam's manufactured goods (bicycles, shoes, even laundry detergent) are of such poor quality that they are practically unsaleable, especially in the face of competition from foreign goods. One of the first effects of free (or free-ish) trade with capitalist countries was to wipe out many state-run enterprises, leading to job lay-offs and increased unemployment. Even Vietnam's sugar-cane growers have been hurt – shoddy equipment at state-run sugar refineries produces such a low-quality product that imported refined sugar is taking over Vietnam's domestic market.

The Vietnamese government has responded with a number of 'temporary import bans' (protectionism). Such bans theoretically give a boost to struggling domestic industries but also lead to increased smuggling. But, slowly, the country is regaining its ability to compete in foreign markets; low wages and the strong Vietnamese work ethic (when given incentives) bodes well for Vietnam's export industries.

The more liberal rules have had a dramatic effect on foreign joint-venture operations – foreign investors have been tripping over themselves to get into the country. Foreign-owned trading companies have been proliferating like locusts. Some of the most successful joint ventures to date have involved hotels, though some of these 'investments' are clear cases of real-estate speculation (foreigners cannot buy land directly but businesses can with a Vietnamese partner). The leading foreign investors are Taiwanese, though many of their investments are little more than disguised land speculation. Other countries that have led the investment pack include Hong Kong, Australia and France. Now that foreign business people are taking an interest in Vietnam, prospects for developing highly competitive industries look certain if the reforms aren't derailed by politics.

Unfortunately, political meddling hasn't stopped completely. The bureaucracy is plagued by middle-level functionaries whose jobs are essentially worthless (or counterproductive) and should be eliminated. Such bureaucrats view the reforms as a serious threat and would like to see them fail, though on the other hand they are not averse to accepting bribes in exchange for the rubber stamps and permits which businesses need to operate. Recalcitrant bureaucrats or not, the reforms have already gained enough momentum that it's hard to imagine reversing them – putting the toothpaste back in the tube might well be impossible.

Foreign investors say that their biggest obstacles include the formidable Vietnamese bureaucracy, official incompetence and the ever-changing rules and regulations. On paper, intellectual property rights are protected, but enforcement is lax – patents, copyrights and trademarks are openly pirated. Tax rates and government fees are frequently revised. Some municipalities have forced foreign companies to hire employees from state employment agencies – and sometimes the only employees available are the 'spoiled brats' of cadres. Not surprisingly, such problems are worse in the north.

Privatisation of large state industries has not yet begun but is being considered. Likely candidates would be Vietnam Airlines, the banking industry, telecommunications, etc. Whether or not the generation of socialist leaders can bring themselves to put the state's prime assets on the auction block remains to be seen. At the present time, Vietnam has no stock market – establishing one would be a prerequisite to any privatisation moves. In 1995, the government promised to open a capital market by year's end, though initial trading will be only in government securities.

Vietnam joined ASEAN in July 1995, a step which observers say will greatly benefit Vietnam's economy.

Hanoi is intent on limiting Vietnam's restructuring *(doi moi)* to the economic sphere, keeping ideas such as pluralism and democracy from undermining the present power structure. Whether it is possible to have economic liberalisation without a concurrent liberalisation in the political sphere remains to be seen. Vietnam's role model at the moment is China, where economic liberalisation coupled with harsh political controls seems to be at least partially successful in reviving the economy. The role model of the former Soviet Union – where political liberalisation preceded economic restructuring – is pointed to as an example of the wrong way to reform.

Agriculture & Forestry

About 70% of Vietnam's people earn their living from agriculture. Vietnam's most important crop is rice. Other important food crops include sugar cane, maize, manioc, potatoes and sweet potatoes. Among Vietnam's cash crops are peanuts, soy beans, pepper, tobacco, coffee, tea, rubber, coconuts and mulberry leaves (to feed silkworms). About 21% of Vietnam's land area is used for agriculture.

Very little agricultural machinery (such as tractors) is in use. Because threshing equipment is in short supply, you often see piles of rice stalks placed in the middle of the highway. As passing vehicles drive over them, the rice is separated from the stalks. Rice and other crops are often dried in the sun at the side of the road.

Rice thresher, Central Vietnam

In 1978, collectivisation and natural disasters reduced food production, necessitating a cut in the food ration from 18 to 13 kg per person per month, a level two kg below the minimum subsistence level set by the UN. Urban residents had to stand in long lines to get their meagre ration of rice, a scene not uncommon in Russia, from which Vietnam borrowed many economic ideas. The massive 1979 exodus of boat people from Vietnam was inspired in part by a simple lack of food.

Agricultural policies have reversed course. Reforms allowing peasants to acquire small land holdings and more market-oriented policies have increased food production dramatically. The government has instructed officials to return land which was arbitrarily confiscated from peasants in southern Vietnam between 1978 and 1983. The new agricultural policies also emphasise family farming over state-run collectives.

Directly as a result of the reforms, Vietnam moved from being a rice importer in the mid-1980s to become the world's third-largest rice exporter in 1991 (after Thailand and the USA).

Because Vietnam's population is still growing at a rapid rate, however, the land available for agricultural use per capita continues to fall.

Fish, which constitutes the main source of protein in the diets of many Vietnamese, is the most important staple food after rice. Fishing employs 550,000 people.

Manufacturing

Following the traditions of their Soviet mentors, the Vietnamese placed great emphasis on heavy industry in the five-year plans of 1976-80 and 1981-85 – while sacrificing the production of quality consumer products. While cooking the books produced some impressive statistics on paper, many shoddy products failed to find a market. Shortages of fuel and capital, under-utilisation of industrial capacity, insufficient maintenance and inadequate standards all created production bottlenecks and led to shortages of essential items which no amount of creative accounting could hide. Recent smuggling from China has also put Vietnamese manufacturers at a disadvantage – the Chinese-made goods are simply better quality.

The economic reforms of the early 1990s has caused a number of foreign companies to consider locating facilities in Vietnam to take advantage of the cheaper labour. However, shifting regulations, bureaucracy and the high prices that foreigners are charged for basic services all have conspired to make most companies take a 'wait and see' attitude before committing major funds.

POPULATION

In 1994, Vietnam's population reached 73.6 million, making it the 12th most populous country in the world. Eighty-four percent of the population is ethnic-Vietnamese, 2% ethnic-Chinese and the rest Khmers, Chams and members of some 60 ethno-linguistic groups.

Vietnam has an overall population density of 225 persons per sq km, one of the world's highest for an agricultural country. Much of the Red River Delta has a population density of 1000 people per sq km or more. Overall life expectancy is 66 years and infant mortality is 48 per 1000. The current rate of population growth is 2.1% per year, and until recently ideology prevented effective family planning.

Unfortunately, the 15 years or so during which Vietnam encouraged large families will be a burden for quite some time to come. The country's population will likely double in the next century before zero population growth can be achieved. The task of reducing population growth in Vietnam is daunting. As elsewhere in the Third World, low education and low incomes tend to encourage large families. Unable to afford modern birth control techniques, most Vietnamese couples still rely on condoms, abortion or self-induced miscarriage to avoid unwanted births. Although the Vietnamese government now conducts educational campaigns to encourage family planning, there have as yet

---

Malthus vs Marx

Thomas Robert Malthus (1766-1834) was a political economist and the first to publish the theory that population growth would lead to mass poverty. The 'Malthusian Theory' had many critics, including the Pope. Another critic was Karl Marx (1818-83). Marx believed that more people meant more production, and he accused Malthus of being an apologist for the capitalists.

Not surprisingly, when the Vietnamese government adopted Marxism as an economic model, birth control was viewed as a capitalist plot to make Third World countries weak. In this regard, the Vietnamese were encouraged by their Soviet mentors – in the USSR, family planning was prohibited and 'hero mothers' were given rewards for having over 10 children. But when the USSR collapsed in 1991, the Vietnamese were forced to critically review their economic and social policies. The threat posed by runaway population growth was finally recognised and a family-planning programme was instituted. Couples are now encouraged to have no more than two children. ∎

---

been no attempts to adopt the harsh methods applied in China (forced abortions, etc).

PEOPLE
Ethnic-Vietnamese

The Vietnamese people (called 'Annamites' by the French) developed as a distinct ethnic group between 200 BC and 200 AD through the fusion of a people of Indonesian stock with Viet and Tai immigrants from the north and Chinese who arrived, along with Chinese rule, as of the 2nd century AD. Vietnamese civilisation was profoundly influenced by China and, via Champa and the Khmers, India, but the fact that the Vietnamese were never absorbed by China indicates that a strong local culture existed prior to the 1000 years of Chinese rule, which ended in 938 AD.

The Vietnamese have lived for thousands of years by growing rice and, as a result, have historically preferred to live in lowland areas suitable for rice growing. Over the past two millennia, they have slowly pushed southward along the narrow coastal strip, defeating the Chams in the 15th century and taking over the Mekong Delta from the Khmers in the 18th century. The Vietnamese have tended to view highland areas (and their inhabitants) with suspicion.

Vietnamese who have emigrated are known as Overseas Vietnamese (Viet Kieu). They are intensely disliked by the locals, who accuse them of being cowardly, arrogant, pampered, privileged and so on. These negative judgements are likely coloured by

jealousy. In the 1980s, returning Viet Kieu were often followed by the police and everyone they spoke to was questioned and harassed by the authorities. This has all changed. Indeed, official policy is now to welcome the Viet Kieu and encourage them to resettle in Vietnam. Many Viet Kieu are cynical about this. 'They don't want us back, just our money, professional skills and connections' is a comment you'll likely to hear in Overseas Vietnamese communities. The fact that the police still often shake down the Viet Kieu for money is not encouraging. The Vietnamese press frequently writes about the importance to the economy of receiving money transfers from relatives abroad.

Ethnic-Chinese

The ethnic-Chinese (Hoa) constitute the largest single minority group in Vietnam. Today, most of them live in the south, especially in and around Saigon's sister-city Cholon. Though the families of most of Vietnam's ethnic-Chinese have lived in Vietnam for generations, they have historically tried to maintain their separate Chinese identities, languages, school systems and even citizenships. The Chinese have organised themselves into communities, known as 'congregations' (bang), according to their ancestors' province of origin and dialect. Important congregations include Fujian (Phuoc Kien in Vietnamese), Cantonese (Quang Dong in Vietnamese or Guangdong in Chinese), Hainan (Hai Nam),

Chaozhou (Tieu Chau) and Hakka (Nuoc Hue in Vietnamese or Kejia in Mandarin Chinese).

During the 1950s, President Diem tried without much success to forcibly assimilate South Vietnam's ethnic-Chinese population. In the north, too, the ethnic-Chinese have resisted Vietnamisation.

The Chinese are well known for their entrepreneurial abilities – before the fall of South Vietnam in 1975, ethnic-Chinese controlled nearly half of the country's economic activity. Historical antipathies between China and Vietnam and the prominence of ethnic-Chinese in commerce have generated a great deal of animosity towards them. In March 1978, the Vietnamese Communists launched a campaign against 'bourgeois elements' (considered a euphemism for the ethnic-Chinese), which turned into open racial persecution. The campaign influenced China's decision to attack Vietnam in 1979 and caused about one-third of Vietnam's ethnic-Chinese to flee to China and the West. Vietnamese officials now admit that the anti-Chinese and anti-capitalist campaign was a tragic mistake which cost the country heavily.

Other Minorities

Vietnam has one of the most complex ethnolinguistic mixes in all of Asia. The country's 60 minority groups, many of whom are related to Thailand's hill tribes, live mostly in the Central Highlands and the mountainous regions of the north. The French called them *Montagnards* (which means 'highlanders'), a term they themselves still use when speaking English or French. The Vietnamese often refer to the hill-tribe people as *Moi*, a derogatory word meaning 'savages', which unfortunately reflects all-too-common popular attitudes. The present government prefers the term 'national minorities'.

Linguistically, the Montagnards can be divided into three main groups: those whose languages are of the Austro-Asian family (the Bru, Pacoh, Katu, Cua, Hre, Rengao, Sedang, Bahnar, M'nong, Maa and Stieng, who speak Mon-Khmer languages, and the Tai groups); the Malayo-Polynesian family (the Jarai, Hroi, Raday, Raglai, Chru and Chams); and the Sino-Tibetan family (the Hmong and Mien). Religiously, the minority groups are very diverse, practising ancestor-worship, animism and – as a result of proselytising in recent decades – Protestantism and Catholicism.

Some of the national minorities have lived in Vietnam for thousands of years while others have migrated into the region in the last few centuries. The areas inhabited by each group are often delimited by altitude, with later arrivals settling at higher elevations. Many of the groups have little in common with each other except a history of intertribal warfare.

Historically, the highland areas were allowed to remain virtually independent as long as their leaders recognised Vietnamese sovereignty and paid tribute and taxes. The

Montagnard woman, Central Highlands

1980 Constitution abolished two vast autonomous regions established for the ethnic minorities in the northern mountains in 1959. During the Vietnam War, both the Communists and the USA actively recruited fighters among the Montagnards of the Central Highlands.

Many of the hill tribes are semi-nomadic, living by slash-and-burn agriculture. Because such practices destroy the ever-dwindling forests, the government is trying to turn them to settled agriculture.

While there may be no official discrimination system, the Montagnards are at the bottom of the educational and economic ladder. Many are illiterate, marry early, have many children and die early. They tend to live in the mountainous regions, which are the most backwards economically. Those who live near the coast have fared better.

Chams Vietnam's 60,000 Chams are the remnant of the once-vigorous Indianised kingdom of Champa, which flourished from the 2nd to the 15th centuries and was destroyed as the Vietnamese expanded southward. Most of them live along the coast between Nha Trang and Phan Thiet and in the Mekong Delta province of An Giang.

Today, the Chams are best known for the many brick sanctuaries (known as 'Cham towers') they constructed all over the southern half of the country. The Cham language is of the Malayo-Polynesian (Austronesian) group. It can be written either in a traditional script of Indian origin or in a Latin-based script created by the French. Most of the Chams, who were profoundly influenced by both Hinduism and Buddhism, are now Muslims. There is a superb collection of Cham statues at the Cham Museum in Danang.

Khmers The Khmers (ethnic-Cambodians) numbers are estimated at about 700,000 and are concentrated in the south-western Mekong Delta. They practise Hinayana (Theravada) Buddhism.

Indians Almost all of South Vietnam's population of Indians, most of whose roots were in southern India, left in 1975. The remaining community in Saigon worship at the Mariamman Hindu Temple and the Central Mosque.

Amerasians One of the most tragic legacies of the Vietnam War is the plight of thousands of Amerasians, most of whom are now around age 20. Marriages and other less formal unions between American soldiers and Vietnamese women – as well as prostitution – were common during the war. But when the Americans were rotated home, all too often they abandoned their 'wives' and mistresses, leaving them to raise children who were half-Caucasian or half-Black in a society not particularly tolerant of such racial mixing.

After 1975, the Amerasians – living reminders of the American presence – were often mistreated by Vietnamese society and even abandoned by their mothers and other relatives. Many were forced to live on the street. When, in the early 1980s, it became known that the US government would resettle the Amerasians in the USA, Amerasian children were adopted by people eager to emigrate. After the adopted family arrived in America, many of these Amerasian children were subsequently dumped again and left to fend for themselves, creating a new social problem for the USA. At the end of the 1980s, the Orderly Departure Programme finally began to function as planned and the crowds of Amerasian street kids began to disappear from downtown Saigon.

Europeans Vietnam has a handful of ethnic-European citizens, most of whom are in fact racially mixed French-Vietnamese or French-Chinese.

Until about 1990, the only Caucasians most younger Vietnamese had ever seen were Russians. Unfortunately, the Russians have earned a reputation for being unfriendly and cheap. Should you be mistaken for a Russian, you may be snubbed.

Orderly Departure Programme

The Orderly Departure Programme (ODP), which is carried out under the auspices of the United Nations High Commission for Refugees (UNHCR), was designed to allow orderly resettlement in the West (mostly in the USA) of Vietnamese political refugees who otherwise might have tried to flee the country by land or sea. After years of stalling by Hanoi, the programme finally began functioning properly at the end of the 1980s, and thousands of Amerasians and their families were flown via Bangkok to the Philippines, where they underwent six months of English instruction before proceeding to the USA.

The ODP failed to stem the flow of refugees from the north. After the Vietnam-China border opened in 1990, many refugees simply took the train to China, from where they only had to take a short boat ride across the Pearl River to Hong Kong to be declared 'boat people'. As the refugee camps in Hong Kong swelled to the bursting point, the public's patience ran out. Most of Hong Kong's population have relatives in the Chinese mainland who would like to come to Hong Kong but are quickly deported if they manage to sneak in. Meanwhile, Vietnamese arriving literally by the boatload were being permitted to stay. 'Refugee fatigue' became the new buzzword in Hong Kong, and the public demanded that something be done.

Since all but a handful of the arrivals were declared to be economic migrants rather than political refugees, the Hong Kong government experimented with forcible repatriations in 1990. This prompted a vehement protest from the USA and the UNHCR. The Hong Kong government backed off temporarily but held negotiations with Vietnam and reached an agreement in October 1991 on a programme of combined voluntary and forced repatriation. Under the agreement, those willing to return would not be penalised by Vietnam and would receive a resettlement allowance of US$30 per month for several months to be paid by the UNHCR. Vietnam also had to agree to give refugees back their citizenship (the previous policy was to strip all refugees of their citizenship, thus rendering them stateless).

The voluntary repatriations didn't go quite as planned; some of the volunteers were back in Hong Kong a few months later seeking another resettlement allowance. In such cases, forcible repatriation swiftly followed. The programme has produced results – by the end of 1992 practically no new Vietnamese refugees had arrived in Hong Kong. Recent improvements in the Vietnamese economy may have also persuaded many prospective refugees to stay at home.

Nevertheless, Hong Kong's refugee problem has not entirely disappeared. Among the thousands of legitimate refugees were a small hardcore faction of misfits with a criminal past. The Vietnamese government doesn't want them back. Hong Kong certainly doesn't want them either, nor will any of the Western countries likely roll out the welcome mat. And so the worst of the refugees remain in the camps behind razor wire, preying on each other and staging occasionally violent protests over their grim situation.

China – which inherits Hong Kong and the refugee camps from Britain in 1997 – is demanding that the British find a solution quickly. China's critics note with some irony that the Vietnamese refugees might be the only ones willing to stay in Hong Kong after 1997 – the Hong Kongers themselves are fleeing, creating a 'refugee crisis' of a different sort. ■

EDUCATION

Compared with other desperately poor countries, Vietnam's population is very well educated. Vietnam's literacy rate is estimated at 82%, though official figures put it even higher (95%). Before the colonial period, the majority of the population possessed some degree of literacy, but by 1939 only 15% of school-age children were receiving any kind of instruction and 80% of the population was illiterate.

Today, almost all children receive primary education and 30 to 40% go on to secondary school, though a significant number of children are barred from enrolling in school because of their parents' political background. The country's 94 universities, technical colleges and other institutes enrol 30,000 students each year. Until recently, approximately 500 students per year went abroad for advanced training, mostly to the now defunct USSR and East Germany.

During the late 19th century, one of the few things that French colonial officials and Vietnamese nationalists agreed on was that the traditional Confucian educational system, on which the mandarinal civil service was based, was in desperate need of reform. Mandarinal examinations were held in Tonkin until WW I and in Annam until the war's end.

Many of Indochina's independence leaders were educated in elite French-language secondary schools such as the Lycée Albert Sarraut in Hanoi and the Lycée Chasseloup Laubat in Saigon.

ARTS
Film
One of Vietnam's first cinematographic efforts was a newsreel of Ho Chi Minh's 1945 proclamation of independence. After Dien Bien Phu, parts of the battle were restaged for the benefit of movie cameras.

Prior to reunification the South Vietnamese movie industry concentrated on producing sensational, low-budget flicks. Until recently, most North Vietnamese filmmaking efforts were dedicated to 'the mobilisation of the masses for economic reconstruction, the building of socialism and the struggle for national reunification'. Predictable themes included 'workers devoted to socialist industrialisation', 'old mothers who continuously risk their lives to help the people's army' and 'children who are ready to face any danger'.

The relaxation of ideological censorship of the arts has proceeded in fits and starts, but in the last few years, the gradual increase in artistic freedoms has affected film-making as well as other genres. But paranoia about the changes sweeping Eastern Europe has caused a return to greater government control of the arts.

Music & Dancing
Though heavily influenced by the Chinese and, in the south, the Indianised Cham and Khmer musical traditions, Vietnamese music has a high degree of originality in style and instrumentation. The traditional system of writing down music and the five-note (pentatonic) scale are of Chinese origin. Vietnamese choral music is unique in that the melody must correspond to the tones; it

cannot be rising during a word that has a falling tone.

There are three broad categories of Vietnamese music:

- Folk, which includes children's songs, love songs, work songs, festival songs, lullabies, lamentations and funeral songs. It is usually sung without instrumental accompaniment.
- Classical (or 'learned music'), which is rather rigid and formal. It was performed at the imperial court and for the entertainment of the mandarin elite. A traditional orchestra consists of 40 musicians. There are two main types of classical chamber music: Hat A Dao (from the north) and Ca Hue (from central Vietnam).
- Theatre, which includes singing, dancing and instrumentation (see the Theatre subsection for more information).

Each of Vietnam's ethno-linguistic minorities has its own musical and dance traditions, which often include colourful costumes and instruments such as reed flutes, lithophones (similar to xylophones), bamboo whistles, gongs and stringed instruments made from gourds. While in most hill tribes the majority of the dancers are women, a few Montagnard groups allow only the men to dance. A great deal of anthropological research has been carried out in recent years in order to preserve and revive minority traditions. At present, there are music conservatories teaching both traditional Vietnamese and Western classical music in Hanoi, Hué and Ho Chi Minh City.

Strange as it seems, most of the world's Vietnamese pop music is originally recorded in California by Overseas Vietnamese. One reason why Vietnam itself produces so few homegrown singers is because all music tapes are instantly pirated, thus depriving the singing stars of the revenue they would need to survive. As a result, only Overseas Vietnamese are economically secure enough to pursue a career in music.

Theatre & Puppetry

Vietnamese theatre integrates music, singing, recitation, declamation, dance and mime into a single artistic whole. There are five basic forms:

- Classical theatre is known as *Hat Tuong* in the north and *Hat Boi* ('songs with show dress') in the south. It is based on Chinese opera and was probably brought to Vietnam by the 13th-century Mongol invaders chased out by Tran Hung Dao. Hat Tuong is very formalistic, employing gestures and scenery similar to Chinese theatre. The accompanying orchestra, which is dominated by the drum, usually has six musicians. Often, the audience also has a drum so it too can comment on the on-stage action.

  Hat Tuong has a limited cast of typical characters who establish their identities using combinations of make-up and dress that the audience can readily recognise. For instance, red face-paint represents courage, loyalty and faithfulness. Traitors and cruel people have white faces. Lowlanders are given green faces; highlanders have black ones. Horizontal eyebrows represent honesty, erect eyebrows symbolise cruelty and lowered eyebrows belong to characters with a cowardly nature. A male character can express emotions (pensiveness, worry, anger, etc) by fingering his beard in various ways.

- Popular theatre (*Hat Cheo*) often engages in social protest through the medium of satire. The singing and declamation are in everyday language and include many proverbs and sayings. Many of the melodies are of peasant origin.

- Modern theatre (*Cai Luong*) originated in the south in the early 20th century and shows strong Western influences.

- Spoken drama (*Kich Noi* or *Kich*), whose roots are Western, appeared in the 1920s. It's popular among students and intellectuals.

- Conventional puppetry (*Roi Can*) and that uniquely Vietnamese art form, water puppetry (*Roi Nuoc*), draw their plots from the same legendary and historical sources as other forms of traditional theatre. It is thought that water puppetry developed when determined puppeteers in the Red River Delta managed to carry on with the show despite flooding.

These days, the various forms of Vietnamese theatre are performed by dozens of state-funded troupes and companies around the country. Water puppetry can be seen at several locations in Hanoi and Saigon.

Literature

Vietnamese literature can be divided into three types:

- Traditional oral literature (*Truyen Khau*), which was begun long before recorded history and includes legends, folk songs and proverbs.

- Sino-Vietnamese literature (*Han Viet*), which was written in Chinese characters (*chu nho*). It dates from 939 AD, when the first independent Vietnamese kingdom was established. Sino-Vietnamese literature was dominated by Confucian and Buddhist texts and was governed by strict rules of metre and verse.

- Modern Vietnamese literature (*Quoc Am*) includes anything recorded in *nom* characters or the Romanised *quoc ngu* script. The earliest extant text written in nom is the late-13th-century *Van Te Ca Sau (Ode to an Alligator)*. Literature written in quoc ngu has played an important role in Vietnamese nationalism.

Architecture

The Vietnamese have not been great builders like their neighbours the Khmers, who erected the monuments of Angkor in Cambodia, and the Chams, whose graceful brick towers, constructed using sophisticated masonry technology, grace many parts of the southern half of the country. For more information on Cham architecture, see Po Klong Garai under Phan Rang & Thap Cham in the South-Central Coast chapter, Po Nagar in the section on Nha Trang (in the same chapter) and My Son in the Danang chapter.

Most of what the Vietnamese have built has been made of wood and other materials that proved highly vulnerable in the tropical climate. Because almost all of the stone structures erected by the Vietnamese have been destroyed in countless feudal wars and invasions, very little pre-modern Vietnamese architecture is extant.

Plenty of pagodas and temples founded hundreds of years ago are still functioning but their physical plan has usually been rebuilt many times with little concern for making the upgraded structure an exact copy of the original. As a result, modern elements have been casually introduced into pagoda architecture, with neon haloes for statues of the Buddha only the most glaring example of this.

Because of the Vietnamese custom of ancestor-worship – and despite the massive dislocations of populations during the Vietnam War – many graves from previous centuries are still extant. These include temples erected in memory of high-ranking mandarins, members of the royal family and emperors.

Memorials for Vietnamese who died in the wars against the French, Americans and Chinese are usually marked by cement obelisks inscribed with the words *To Quoc Ghi Cong* ('The country will remember their exploits'). Many of the tombstones were erected over empty graves; most Viet Minh and Viet Cong dead were buried where they fell.

Sculpture

Vietnamese sculpture has traditionally centred on religious themes and functioned as an adjunct to architecture, especially that of pagodas, temples and tombs. Many inscribed stelae, erected hundreds of years ago to commemorate the founding of a

pagoda or important national events, can still be seen (eg, at Thien Mu Pagoda in Hué and the Temple of Literature in Hanoi).

The Cham civilisation produced spectacular carved sandstone figures for its Hindu and Buddhist sanctuaries. Cham sculpture was profoundly influenced by Indian art but, over the centuries, also incorporated Indonesian and Vietnamese elements. The largest single collection of Cham sculpture in the world is at the Cham Museum in Danang. For more information on Cham sculpture, see the Cham Museum section in the Quang Nam & Danang chapter.

Lacquerware

The art of making lacquerware was brought to Vietnam from China in the mid-15th century. Before that time, the Vietnamese used lacquer solely for practical purposes (such as making things watertight). During the 1930s, the Fine Arts School in Hanoi employed several Japanese teachers who introduced new styles and production methods. Their influence can still be seen in the noticeably Japanese elements in some Vietnamese lacquerware, especially that made in the north. Although a 1985 government publication declares that 'at present, lacquer painting deals boldly with realistic and revolutionary themes and forges unceasingly ahead', most of the lacquerware for sale is inlaid with mother-of-pearl and seems of traditional design.

Lacquer is a resin extracted from the *son* tree *(cay son)*. It is creamy white in raw form but is made black *(son then)* or brown *(canh dan*, 'cockroach wing') by mixing it with resin in an iron container for 40 hours. After the object to be lacquered (traditionally made of teak) has been treated with a fixative, 10 coats of lacquer are applied. Each coat must be dried for a week and then thoroughly sanded with pumice and cuttlebone before the next layer can be applied. A specially refined lacquer is used for the 11th and final coat, which is sanded with a fine coal powder and lime wash before the object is decorated. Designs may be added by engraving in low relief, by painting, or by inlaying mother-of-pearl, egg shell, silver or even gold.

Ceramics

The production of ceramics *(gom)* has a long history in Vietnam. In ancient times, ceramic objects were made by coating a wicker mould with clay and baking it. Later, ceramics production became very refined, and each dynastic period is known for its particular techniques and motifs.

For more information on Vietnamese folk art, you may want to refer to the book *Handicrafts* (published by Xunhasaba, Hanoi), number 62 in the English and French-language *Vietnamese Studies* series.

Painting

Traditional Painting done on frame-mounted silk dates from the 13th century. Silk-painting was at one time the preserve of scholar-calligraphers, who also painted scenes from nature. Before the advent of photography, realistic portraits for use in ancestor-worship were produced. Some of these – usually of former head monks – can still be seen in Buddhist pagodas.

Modern During this century, Vietnamese painting has been influenced by Western trends. Much of the recent work done in Vietnam has had political rather than aesthetic or artistic motives. According to an official account, the fighting of the Vietnam War provided painters with 'rich human material: People's Army combatants facing the jets, peasant and factory women in the militia who handled guns as well as they did their production work, young volunteers who repaired roads in record time...old mothers offering tea to anti-aircraft gunners...' There's lots of this stuff at the Fine Arts Museum in Hanoi.

The recent economic liberalisation has convinced many young artists to abandon the revolutionary themes and concentrate on producing commercially saleable paintings. Some have gone back to the traditional silk paintings, while others are experimenting with new subjects. There is a noticeable ten-

dency now to produce nude paintings, which might indicate either an attempt to appeal to Western tastes or an expression of long-suppressed kinky desires.

The cheaper stuff (US$10 to US$50) gets spun off to hotel gift shops and street markets. Supposedly, the higher standard works are put on display in one of two government-run art galleries: the Vietnamese Art Association, 511 Tran Hung Dao St, Hanoi; and the Ho Chi Minh City Association of Fine Arts (☎ 230025), 218 Nguyen Thi Minh Khai, District 1. Typical prices are in the US$30 to US$50 range, though the artists may ask 10 times that. It's important to know that there are quite a few forgeries around – just because you spot a painting by a 'famous Vietnamese artist' does not mean that it's an original, though it may still be an attractive work of art.

CULTURE

Traditions & Customs

Greetings The traditional Vietnamese form of greeting is to press your hands together in front of your body and to bow slightly. These days, the Western custom of shaking hands has taken over, but the traditional greeting is still sometimes used by Buddhist monks and nuns, to whom it is proper to respond in kind.

Name Cards Name cards are very popular in Vietnam, and like elsewhere in east Asia, exchanging business cards is an important part of even the smallest transaction or business contact. Get some printed before you arrive in Vietnam and hand them out like confetti. In Bangkok and Hong Kong, machines using the latest laser-printing technology can make inexpensive custom-designed business cards in 20 minutes. You need to put your occupation on your name card; if you don't have one, try 'backpacker'.

Face Having 'big face' is synonymous with prestige, and prestige is important in the Orient. All families, even poor ones, are expected to have big wedding parties and throw around money like water, in order to gain face. This is often ruinously expensive, but the fact that the wedding results in bankruptcy for the young couple is far less important than losing face.

Beauty Concepts The Vietnamese consider pale skin to be beautiful. On sunny days trendy Vietnamese women can often be seen strolling under the shade of an umbrella in order to keep from tanning. As in 19th-century Europe, peasants get tanned and those who can afford it do not. Women who work in the fields will go to great lengths to preserve their pale skin by wearing long-sleeved shirts, gloves, a conical hat and wrapping their face in a towel.

Women in Society Like in most parts of Asia, Vietnamese women are given plenty of hard work to do but little authority at the decision-making level. Vietnamese women proved to be highly successful as guerillas and brought plenty of grief to US soldiers. After the war, their contribution received plenty of lip-service but all important government posts were given to men. In the countryside, you'll see women doing such jobs as farm labour, crushing rocks at construction sites and carrying baskets weighing 60 kg or more. It's doubtful that most Western men are capable of such strenuous activity.

Vietnam's recent two-child-per-family policy does seem to be benefiting women, and more women are delaying marriage in order to get an education. University students are about 50% female, but it doesn't seem that their skills are put to much use after graduation.

One of the sadder ironies of Vietnam's recent opening to the capitalist West has been the influx of pimps posing as 'talent scouts'. Promises of lucrative jobs in developed countries are being dangled in front of naive Vietnamese women who discover only upon arrival abroad that the job is prostitution. With no money to return home, they usually have little choice but to submit. Japanese gangsters have been particularly active in this form of job recruitment.

Geomancy Geomancy is the art (or science if you prefer) of manipulating or judging the environment. If you want to build a house or find a suitable site for a grave then you call in a geomancer. The orientation of houses, communal meeting halls *(dinh)*, tombs and pagodas is determined by geomancers, which is why cemeteries have tombstones turned every which way. The location of an ancestor's grave is an especially serious matter – if the grave is in the wrong spot or facing the wrong way, then there is no telling what trouble the spirits might cause.

Businesses that are failing may call in a geomancer. Sometimes the solution is to move the door or a window. If this doesn't do the trick, it might be necessary to move an ancestor's grave. Distraught spirits may have to be placated with payments of cash (donated to a temple), especially if one wishes to erect a building or other structure which blocks the spirits' view.

The concept of geomancy is believed to have originated with the Chinese. Although the Communists (both Chinese and Vietnamese) have disparaged geomancy as superstition, it still has influence on people's behaviour.

Staring Squads This problem – if it can be called that – is likely to affect you only in rural areas. People in hip places like Saigon and Hanoi no longer take much notice of foreigners.

If you are in the hinterlands and doing something interesting (such as just standing there), many curious people – especially children – may gather round you to watch. When you get fed up with being the perennial centre of attention, hotel restaurants are a good place of refuge.

If you keep a diary or take notes, just about everyone will stick their nose into your notebook. Some people might even lift it out of your hands just to get a better look. On the other hand, other people get paranoid if you take notes, especially in the north.

Ong Tay & Ba Tay The main reason children shout *Ong Tay!* (Mr Westerner) and *Ba Tay!*

(Mrs Westerner) at Caucasians has something to do with people's motivations for tapping on aquarium fish tanks and catching the attention of primates at the zoo: they want to be recognised by an exotic being and to provoke some kind of reaction.

Often, children will unabashedly come up to you and pull the hair on your arms or legs (they want to test if it's real) or dare each other to touch your skin. Some travellers have been pinched or kicked without provocation, but this is rare.

In the recent past, you often heard the term *Lien Xo!* (Soviet Union) shouted at Westerners, all of whom were assumed to be Russians. This may have been partly to annoy the Russians residing in Vietnam, whose unpopularity was legendary. However, Russian tourists and technical advisers are far less common now than they used to be – few of them can afford a holiday in Vietnam any more and their technical skills are considered inferior to those available from the West. Therefore, Lien Xo is going out of fashion as an attention-getting phrase.

In the markets, vendors may try to woo you by calling you *Dong Chi!* (comrade) on the assumption that you will find this a kindred term of endearment.

If you are cycling, you may also hear people say '*Tay di xe dap*', which simply means 'Westerner travelling by bicycle'. While it may seem a strange form of address in the land of bicycles, it's perhaps understandable in a place where foreigners have in the past only been seen travelling first in Citroëns, then in jeeps, then in black Volgas and now in white Toyotas. But another explanation is that though the Vietnamese virtually all ride bicycles, they would never look back at one if they had the means to travel by motorbike or car. They simply do not believe that anyone, let alone a rich foreigner, would choose to travel by bicycle – there is obviously something wrong with such a person.

Showing Respect In face-conscious Asia, foreigners should pay double attention to showing respect (it's not a bad idea even at home). One expat in Vietnam had this to say on the matter:

The main reason I write is to ask you to clearly (in boldface if necessary) and strongly implore your readers to show a little respect for the locals. Fighting over and gloating about ripping off a cyclo driver for US$0.10 is a small 'victory' and a shameful thing to do. These people obviously need the money. If nothing else, travellers should at least be cordial and respectful – smile, it works wonders here. What I've seen recently here where I work has made me realise that imperialism is not yet dead. Because of the power of money, some foreigners act like they're inherently superior. The imperialist of old came with a gun and a uniform, the imperialist today comes with a camera.

Steve McNicholas

Taboos

Sweet Beggars A good way to anger adult Vietnamese is to offer sweets to a group of shy children you come across. You may have to practically force them to take it, but children know a good thing when they see it, and soon they may be tagging along behind tourists demanding gifts. US soldiers used to do this during the war, creating gangs of six-year-old beggars and causing a great deal of resentment.

If you want to feed a hungry child, give him or her something more substantial to eat – some French bread, for example, rather than junk food.

Deadly Chopsticks Leaving a pair of chopsticks sticking vertically in a rice bowl looks very similar to the incense sticks which are burned for the dead. This is a powerful death sign and is not appreciated anywhere in the Orient.

Mean Feet It's rude to let the bottoms of your feet point towards other people, except maybe close friends. When sitting on the floor, you should fold your legs into the lotus position so as to not be pointing your soles at others. And most importantly, never point the bottoms of your feet towards anything sacred, such as figures of Buddhas.

In formal situations, when sitting on a chair do not sit with your legs crossed.

Keep Your Hat in Hand As a form of respect to the elderly or other people regarded with respect (monks, etc), take off your hat and bow your head politely when addressing them.

Pity the Unmarried Telling the Vietnamese that you are single or divorced and enjoying a life without children will disturb them greatly. Not having a family is regarded as bad luck, and such people are to be pitied, not envied. Almost every Vietnamese will ask if you are married and have children. If you are young and single, simply say you are 'not yet married' and that will be accepted. If you are not so young (over 30) and unmarried, it's better to lie. Divorce is scandalous, and you'd be better off claiming that your former spouse died.

Avoiding Offence

Vernon Weitzel of the Australian National University sends these 10 tips for successfully dealing with Vietnamese officials, business people, etc:

- Always smile and be pleasant.
- Don't run around complaining about everything.
- If you want to criticise someone, do it in a joking manner to avoid confrontation.
- Expect delays – build them into your schedule.
- Never show anger – ever! Getting visibly upset is not only rude – it will cause you to lose face.
- Don't be competitive. Treating your interaction as a cooperative enterprise works much better.
- Don't act as though you deserve service from anyone. If you do, it's likely that you will be delayed.
- Don't be too inquisitive about personal matters.
- Sitting and sipping tea and the exchange of gifts (sharing cigarettes, for instance) are an important prelude to any business interaction.
- The mentality of officialdom is very Confucian. Expect astounding amounts of red tape.

Sport

The Vietnamese government emphasises gymnastics, which is a mandatory subject at all schools from the elementary level through university. Given the tropical climate and abundant water resources, swimming is popular. Other sports include tennis, badminton, table tennis and handball.

Thai Cuc Quyen

Thai cuc quyen, or slow motion shadow boxing, has in recent years become quite trendy in Western countries. It has been popular in Vietnam for centuries, but it originated in China, where it is known as *taijiquan*. It is basically a form of exercise, but it's also an art and is a form of martial arts related to Chinese *kung fu*. Kung fu differs from thai cuc quyen in that the former is performed at much higher speed and with the intention of doing bodily harm. Kung fu also often employs weapons. Thai cuc quyen is not a form of self-defence but the movements are similar to kung fu. There are different styles of thai cuc quyen.

Thai cuc quyen is very popular among old people, and also with young women who believe it will help keep their bodies beautiful. The movements are supposed to develop the breathing muscles, promote digestion and improve muscle tone.

A modern innovation is to perform thai cuc quyen movements to the thump of disco music. Westerners find it remarkable to see a large group performing their slow motion movements in the park at the crack of dawn to the steady beat of disco music supplied by a portable cassette tape player.

Thai cuc quyen and all manner of exercises are customarily done just as the sun rises, which means that if you want to see or participate in them, you have to get up early. In Saigon, the best place to see it is at Cong Vien Van Hoa Park, or else in the Cholon district because of its large ethnic-Chinese population. In Hanoi, look around Hoan Kiem Lake and at other parks. ■

RELIGION

Four great philosophies and religions have shaped the spiritual life of the Vietnamese people: Confucianism, Taoism, Buddhism and Christianity. Over the centuries, Confucianism, Taoism and Buddhism have fused with popular Chinese beliefs and ancient Vietnamese animism to form what is known collectively as the 'Triple Religion', or *Tam Giao*. Confucianism, more a system of social and political morality than a religion, took on many religious aspects. Taoism, which began as an esoteric philosophy for scholars, mixed with Buddhism among the peasants, and many Taoist elements became an intrinsic part of popular religion. If asked their religion the Vietnamese are likely to say that they are Buddhist, but when it comes to family or civic duties they are likely to follow Confucianism while turning to Taoist conceptions in understanding the nature of the cosmos.

Mahayana Buddhism

Mahayana Buddhism (Dai Thua or Bac Tong, which means 'From the North', ie, China; also known as the Greater Wheel school, Greater Vehicle school and Northern Buddhism) is the predominant religion in Vietnam. The largest Mahayana sect in the country is Zen (Dhyana; in Vietnamese, Thien), also known as the school of meditation. Dao Trang (the Pure Land school), the second-largest Mahayana sect in Vietnam, is practised mainly in the south.

Mahayana Buddhism differs from Theravada Buddhism in several important ways. Whereas the Theravadin strives to become a perfected saint (Arhat) ready for Nirvana, the Mahayanist ideal is that of the Bodhisattva, one who strives to perfect himself or herself in the necessary virtues (generosity, morality, patience, vigour, concentration and wisdom) but even after attaining perfection chooses to remain in the world in order to save others.

Mahayanists consider Gautama Buddha to be only one of the innumerable manifestations of the one ultimate Buddha. These countless Buddhas and Bodhisattvas, who are as numberless as the universes to which they minister, gave rise in popular Vietnamese religion – with its innumerable Taoist divinities and spirits – to a pantheon of deities and helpers whose aid can be sought through invocations and offerings.

Mahayana Buddhist pagodas in Vietnam usually include a number of elements. In front of the pagoda is a white statue of a standing Quan The Am Bo Tat (Avalokiteçvara Bodhisattva in Hindi, Guanyin in Chinese, Goddess of Mercy in English). A variation of the Goddess of Mercy shows her with multiple arms and sometimes multiple eyes and ears, permitting her to touch, see and hear all. This version of the Goddess of Mercy is called Chuan De (Qianshou Guanyin in Chinese).

Inside the main sanctuary are representations of the three Buddhas: A Di Da (pronounced 'AH-zee-dah'; Amitabha), the Buddha of the Past; Thich Ca Mau Ni (Sakyamuni, or Siddhartha Gautama), the Historical Buddha; and Di Lac (pronounced 'zee-lock'; Maitreya), the Buddha of the Future. Nearby are often statues of the eight Kim Cang (Genies of the Cardinal Directions), the La Han (Arhats) and various Bo Tat (bodhisattvas) such as Van Thu (Manjusri), Quan The Am Bo Tat (Avaloketeçvara) and Dia Tang (Ksitigartha). Sometimes, an altar is set aside for Taoist divinities such as Ngoc Hoang (the Emperor of Jade) and Thien Hau Thanh Mau (the Queen of Heaven), who is also known as Tuc Goi La Ba (the Goddess of the Sea and Protector of Fishermen and Sailors). Thien Hau is known as Tin Hau in Hong Kong and Matsu in Taiwan. Every pagoda has an altar for funerary tablets memorialising deceased Buddhist monks (who are often buried in stupas near the pagoda) and lay people.

The function of the Vietnamese Buddhist monk *(bonze)* is to minister to the spiritual and superstitious needs of the peasantry, but it is largely up to him whether he invokes the lore of Taoism or the philosophy of Buddhism. A monk may live reclusively on a remote hilltop or he may manage a pagoda on a busy city street. And he may choose to fulfil any number of functions: telling fortunes, making and selling talismans *(fu)*, advising where a house should be constructed, reciting incantations at funerals or even performing acupuncture.

History Theravada Buddhism was brought to Vietnam from India by pilgrims at the end of the 2nd century AD. Simultaneously, Chinese monks introduced Mahayana Buddhism. Buddhism did not become popular with the masses until many centuries later.

Buddhism received royal patronage during the 10th to 13th centuries. This backing included recognition of the Buddhist hierarchy, financial support for the construction of pagodas and other projects, and the active participation of the clergy in ruling the country. By the 11th century, Buddhism had filtered down to the villages. Buddhism was proclaimed the official state religion in the mid-12th century.

During the 13th and 14th centuries, Confucian scholars gradually replaced Vietnamese monks as advisers to the Tran Dynasty. The Confucians accused the Buddhists of shirking their responsibilities to family and country because of the Buddhist doctrine of withdrawal from worldly matters. The Chinese invasion of 1414 reinvigorated Confucianism while at the same time resulting in the destruction of many Buddhist pagodas and manuscripts. The Nguyen Lords (1558-1778), who ruled the southern part of the country, reversed this trend.

A revival of Vietnamese Buddhism began throughout the country in the 1920s, and Buddhist organisations were begun in various parts of the country. In the 1950s and '60s, attempts were made to unite the various streams of Buddhism in Vietnam. During the early 1960s, South Vietnamese Buddhist monks and lay people played an active role in opposing the regime of Ngo Dinh Diem.

Over the centuries, the Buddhist ideals and beliefs held by the educated elite touched only superficially the rural masses (90% of the population), whose traditions were transmitted orally and put to the test by daily observance. The common people were far less concerned with the philosophy of good government than they were with seeking aid from supernatural beings for problems of the here and now.

Gradually, the various Mahayana Buddhas and Bodhisattvas became mixed up with mysticism, animism, polytheism and Hindu Tantrism as well as the multiple divinities and ranks of deities of the Taoist pantheon. The Triple Religion flourished despite clerical attempts to maintain some semblance of Buddhist orthodoxy and doctrinal purity. Although most of the population has only a vague notion of Buddhist doctrines, they invite monks to participate in such life-cycle ceremonies as funerals. And Buddhist pagodas have come to be seen by many Vietnamese as a physical and spiritual refuge from an uncertain world.

After 1975, many monks, including some who actively opposed the South Vietnamese government and the war, were rounded up and sent to re-education camps. Temples were closed and the training of young monks was prohibited. In the last few years, most of these restrictions have been lifted and a religious revival of sorts is taking place.

Theravada Buddhism
Theravada Buddhism (Tieu Thua or Nam Tong, which means From the South; also known as Hinayana, the Lesser Wheel school, the Lesser Vehicle school and Southern Buddhism) came to Vietnam directly from India. It is practised mainly in the Mekong Delta region, mostly by ethnic-Khmers. The most important Theravada sect in Vietnam is the disciplinary school, Luat Tong.

Basically, the Theravada school of Buddhism is an earlier and, according to its followers, less corrupted form of Buddhism than the Mahayana schools found in most of East Asia and the Himalayan region. The Theravada school is called the 'Southern School' because it took the southern route from India, its place of origin, through South-East Asia (it came directly from India to Vietnam), while the 'Northern School'

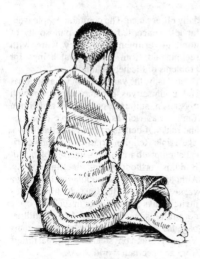

Monk in the Mekong Delta

proceeded north into Nepal, Tibet, China, Korea, Mongolia, Vietnam and Japan. Because the southern school tried to preserve or limit the Buddhist doctrines to only those canons codified in the early Buddhist era, the northern school gave Theravada Buddhism the name Hinayana, or Lesser Vehicle. They considered themselves Great Vehicle because they built upon the earlier teachings, 'expanding' the doctrine in such a way so as to respond more to the needs of lay people.

Confucianism

While it is more a religious philosophy than an organised religion, Confucianism (Nho Giao or Khong Giao) has been an important force in shaping Vietnam's social system and the everyday lives and beliefs of its people.

Confucius (in Vietnamese: Khong Tu) was born in China around 550 BC. He saw people as social beings formed by society yet capable of shaping their society. He believed that the individual exists in and for society and drew up a code of ethics to guide the individual in social interaction. This code laid down a person's specific obligations to family, society and the state. Central to Confucianism are an emphasis on duty and hierarchy.

According to Confucian philosophy, which was brought to Vietnam by the Chinese during their 1000-year rule (111 BC to 938 AD), the emperor alone, governing under the mandate of heaven, can intercede on behalf of the nation with the powers of heaven and earth. Only virtue, as acquired through education, gave one the right (the mandate of heaven) to wield political power. From this it followed that an absence of virtue would result in the withdrawal of this mandate, sanctioning rebellion against an unjust ruler. Natural disasters or defeat on the battlefield were often interpreted as a sign that the mandate of heaven had been withdrawn.

Confucian philosophy was in some senses democratic: because virtue could be acquired only through learning, education rather than birth made a person virtuous. Therefore, education had to be widespread. Until the beginning of this century, Confucian philosophy and texts formed the basis of Vietnam's educational system. Generation after generation of young people – in the villages as well as the cities – were taught their duties to family (including ancestorworship) and community and that each person had to know their place in the social hierarchy and behave accordingly.

A system of government-run civil service examinations selected from among the country's best students those who would join the non-hereditary ruling class, the mandarins. As a result, education was prized not only as the path to virtue but as a means to social and political advancement. This system helped create the respect for intellectual and literary accomplishment for which the Vietnamese are famous to this day.

The political institutions based on Confucianism finally degenerated and became discredited, as they did elsewhere in the Chinese-influenced world. Over the centuries, the philosophy became conservative and backward-looking. This reactionary trend became dominant in Vietnam in the 15th century, suiting despotic rulers who emphasised the divine right of kings rather than their responsibilities under the doctrine of the mandate of heaven.

Taoism

Taoism (Lao Giao or Dao Giao) originated in China and is based on the philosophy of Laotse (Thai Thuong Lao Quan). Laotse (literally The Old One) lived in the 6th century BC. Little is known about Laotse, and some question whether or not he really existed. He is believed to have been the custodian of the imperial archives for the Chinese government and Confucius is supposed to have consulted him.

It is doubtful that Laotse ever intended his philosophy to become a religion. Chang Ling has been credited with formally establishing the religion in 143 BC. Taoism later split into two divisions: the Cult of the Immortals and The Way of the Heavenly Teacher.

Understanding Taoism is not easy. The philosophy emphasises contemplation and simplicity of life. Its ideal is returning to the Tao (the Way – the essence of which all things are made). Only a small elite in China and Vietnam has ever been able to grasp Taoist philosophy, which is based on various correspondences (eg, the human body, the microcosmic replica of the macrocosm) and complimentary contradictions (am and duong, the Vietnamese equivalents of Yin and Yang). As a result, there are very few pure Taoist pagodas in Vietnam, yet much of Taoist ritualism has been absorbed into Chinese and Vietnamese Buddhism. You are most likely to notice the Taoist influence on temples in the form of dragons and demons which decorate the temple rooftops.

According to the Taoist cosmology, Ngoc Hoang, the Emperor of Jade (in Chinese: Yu Huang), whose abode is in heaven, rules over a world of divinities, genies, spirits and demons in which the forces of nature are incarnated as supernatural beings and great historical personages have become gods. It is this aspect of Taoism that has become assimilated into the daily lives of most Vietnamese as a collection of superstitions and mystical and animistic beliefs. Much of the sorcery and magic that are now part of popular Vietnamese religion have their origins in Taoism.

Ancestor-Worship

Vietnamese ancestor-worship, which is the ritual expression of filial piety (hieu), dates from long before the arrival of Confucianism or Buddhism. Some people consider it to be a religion unto itself.

The cult of the ancestors is based on the belief that the soul lives on after death and becomes the protector of its descendants. Because of the influence the spirits of one's ancestors exert on the living, it is considered not only shameful for them to be upset or restless but downright dangerous. A soul with no descendants is doomed to eternal wandering because it will not receive homage.

Traditionally, the Vietnamese venerate and honour the spirits of their ancestors regularly, especially on the anniversary of the ancestor's death when sacrifices are offered to both the god of the household and the spirit of the ancestors. To request intercession for success in business or on behalf of a sick child, sacrifices and prayers are offered to the ancestral spirits. The ancestors are informed on occasions of family joy or sorrow, such as weddings, success in an examination, or death. Important elements in the cult of the ancestor are the family altar, a plot of land whose income is set aside for the support of the ancestors, and the designation of a direct male descendent of the deceased to assume the obligation to carry on the cult.

Many pagodas have altars on which memorial tablets and photographs of the deceased are displayed. One may look at the young faces in the photographs and ponder the tragedy of so many people having had their lives cut short. Some visitors wonder if they died as a result of the wars. The real explanation is less tragic: most of the dead had passed on decades after the photos were taken, but rather than use a picture of an aged, infirm parent, survivors chose a more flattering (though slightly outdated) picture of the deceased in their prime.

Caodaism

Caodaism is an indigenous Vietnamese sect

that seeks to create the ideal religion by fusing the secular and religious philosophies of both East and West. It was founded in the early 1920s based on messages revealed in seances to Ngo Minh Chieu, the group's founder. The sect's colourful headquarters is in Tay Ninh, 96 km north-west of Ho Chi Minh City. There are currently about two million followers of Caodaism in Vietnam. For more information about Caodaism, see Tay Ninh in the Around Ho Chi Minh City chapter.

Hoa Hao Buddhist Sect

The Hoa Hao Buddhist sect (Phat Giao Hoa Hao) was founded in the Mekong Delta in 1939 by Huynh Phu So, a young man who had studied with the most famous of the region's occultists. After he was miraculously cured of sickliness, So began preaching a reformed Buddhism based on the common people and embodied in personal faith rather than elaborate rituals. His philosophy emphasised simplicity in worship and denied the necessity for intermediaries between human beings and the Supreme Being.

In 1940 the French, who called Huynh Phu So the 'mad monk', tried to silence him. When arresting him failed, they committed him to an insane asylum, where he soon converted the Vietnamese psychiatrist assigned to his case.

During WW II, the Hoa Hao Sect continued to grow and to build up a militia with weapons supplied by the Japanese. In 1947, after clashes between Hoa Hao forces and the Viet Minh, Huynh Phu So was assassinated by the Viet Minh, who thereby earned the animosity of what had by then become a powerful political and military force in the Mekong Delta, especially around Chau Doc. The military power of the Hoa Hao was broken in 1956 when one of its guerrilla commanders was captured by the Diem government and publicly guillotined. Subsequently, elements of the Hoa Hao army joined the Viet Cong.

There presently are thought to be about 1½ million followers of the Hoa Hao sect.

Catholicism

Catholicism was introduced into Vietnam in the 16th century by missionaries from Portugal, Spain and France. Particularly active during the 16th and 17th centuries were the French Jesuits and Portuguese Dominicans. Pope Alexander VII assigned the first bishops to Vietnam in 1659, and the first Vietnamese priests were ordained nine years later. According to some estimates, there were 800,000 Catholics in Vietnam by 1685. Over the next three centuries, Catholicism was discouraged and at times outlawed. The first known edict forbidding missionary activity was promulgated in 1533. Foreign missionaries and their followers were severely persecuted during the 17th and 18th centuries.

When the French began their efforts to turn Vietnam into a part of their empire, the treatment of Catholics was one of their most important pretexts for intervention. Under French rule the Catholic church was given preferential status and Catholicism flourished. Though it incorporated certain limited aspects of Vietnamese culture, Catholicism (unlike Buddhism, for instance) succeeded in retaining its doctrinal purity.

Today, Vietnam has the highest percentage of Catholics (8 to 10% of the population) in Asia outside the Philippines. Many of the 900,000 refugees who fled North Vietnam to the South in 1954 were Catholics, as was the then South Vietnamese President Ngo Dinh Diem. Since 1954 in the North and 1975 in the South, Catholics have faced severe restrictions on their religious activities, including strict limits on the ordination of priests and religious education. As in the former Soviet Union, all churches were viewed as being a capitalist institution and a rival centre of power which could subvert the government.

Since around 1990, the government has taken a more liberal line. There is no question that the Catholic religion is now making a comeback, though the old churches have become quite dilapidated and there is a shortage of trained clergy. Also, a lack of funds prevents many churches from doing necessary restoration work, but donations from both locals and Overseas Vietnamese is gradually solving this problem.

Protestantism

Protestantism was introduced to Vietnam in 1911. The majority of Vietnam's Protestants, who number about 200,000, are Montagnards living in the Central Highlands. The Protestants have been doubly unfortunate in that they were persecuted first by former South Vietnamese President Ngo Dinh Diem (who was a Catholic) and later by the Communists.

Until 1975, the most active Protestant group in South Vietnam was the Christian & Missionary Alliance, whose work went mostly unhindered after Diem's assassination in 1963. After reunification, many Protestant clergymen – especially those trained by American missionaries – were imprisoned. But since 1990, the government has mostly ignored the Protestant church.

Islam

Muslims – mostly ethnic-Khmers and Chams – constitute about 0.5% of Vietnam's population. There were small communities of Malaysian, Indonesian and south Indian Muslims in Saigon until 1975, when almost all of them fled. Today, Saigon's 5000 Muslims (including a handful of south Indians) congregate in about a dozen mosques, including the large Central Mosque in the city centre.

Arab traders reached China in the 7th century and may have stopped in Vietnam on the way, but the earliest evidence of an Islamic presence in Vietnam is a 10th-century pillar inscribed in Arabic which was found near the coastal town of Phan Rang. It appears that Islam spread among Cham refugees who fled to Cambodia after the destruction of their kingdom in 1471 but that these converts had little success in propagating Islam among their fellow Chams still in Vietnam.

The Vietnamese Chams consider themselves Muslims despite the fact that they have only a vague notion of Islamic theology and laws. Their communities have very few copies of the Koran and even their religious dignitaries can hardly read Arabic. Though Muslims the world over pray five times a day, the Chams pray only on Fridays and celebrate Ramadan (a month of dawn to dusk fasting) for only three days. Their worship services consist of the recitation of a few Arabic verses from the Koran in a corrupted form. Instead of performing ritual ablutions, they make motions as if they were drawing water from a well. Circumcision is symbolically performed on boys at age 15; the ceremony consists of a religious leader making the gestures of circumcision with a wooden knife. The Chams of Vietnam do not make the pilgrimage to Mecca and though they do not eat pork, they do drink alcohol. In addition, their Islam-based religious rituals exist side-by-side with animism and the worship of Hindu deities. The Chams have even taken the Arabic words of common Koranic expressions and made them into the names of deities.

Cham religious leaders wear a white robe and an elaborate turban with gold, red or brown tassels. Their ranks are indicated by the length of the tassels.

Hinduism

Champa was profoundly influenced by Hinduism and many of the Cham towers, built as Hindu sanctuaries, contain lingams (phallic symbols of Shiva) that are still worshipped by ethnic-Vietnamese and ethnic-Chinese alike. After the fall of Champa in the 15th century, most Chams who remained in Vietnam became Muslims but continued to practise various Brahmanic (high-cast Hindu) rituals and customs.

LANGUAGE

The Vietnamese language *(kinh)* is a fusion of Mon-Khmer, Tai and Chinese elements. From the monotonic Mon-Khmer languages, Vietnamese derived a significant percentage of its basic words. From the Tai languages, it adopted certain grammatical elements and tonality. Chinese gave Vietnamese most of its philosophical, literary, technical and governmental vocabulary as well as its traditional writing system.

From around 1980 to about 1987, anyone caught studying English was liable to get arrested. This was part of a general crackdown against people wanting to flee to the West. That attitude has changed and today the study of English is being pursued with a passion. The most widely spoken foreign languages in Vietnam are Chinese (Cantonese and Mandarin), English and French, more or less in that order. People in their 50s and older (who grew up during the colonial period) are much more likely to understand some French than southerners of the following generation, for whom English was indispensable for professional and commercial contacts with the Americans. Some southern Vietnamese men – former combat interpreters – speak a quaint form of English peppered with all sorts of charming southern-American expressions like 'ya'll come back' and 'it ain't worth didley-squat' and pronounced with a perceptible drawl. Apparently, they worked with Americans from the deep south, carefully studied their pronunciation and diligently learned every nuance.

Many of the Vietnamese who speak English – especially former South Vietnamese soldiers and officials – learned it while working with the Americans during the Vietnam War. After reunification, almost all of them spent periods of time ranging from a few months to 15 years in 're-education camps'. Many such former South Vietnamese soldiers and officials will be delighted to renew contact with Americans, with whose compatriots they spent so much time, often in very difficult circumstances, half-a-lifetime ago. Former long-term prisoners often have friends and acquaintances all over the country (you meet an awful lot of people in 10 or more years), constituting an 'old boys' network' of sorts.

These days, almost everyone has a desire to learn English. If you're looking to make contacts with English students, the best place is at the basic foodstalls around university areas. But at times you might find yourself looking to avoid such contacts, as one visitor commented:

At a sightseeing spot I was awaited by a group studying English in evening classes. They go in their spare time to tourist areas hoping to get a chance to talk with foreigners. Sometimes it gets a bit tiresome to cope with enthusiastic students having a very limited vocabulary, but I believe it is a must to be polite and never to be arrogant or rude. I observed that foreigners are often disrespectful towards Vietnamese, and that really annoyed me. Often the locals told me that foreigners are reluctant, evasive and also insulting when approached by Vietnamese students. I tried to explain to my counterparts that some travellers might be afraid when approached and surrounded by a group of strangers. I explained to them the paranoia caused by crime in the West, which they found surprising – they simply weren't aware of the problems of Western societies. When I told them openly of the negative aspects of my country, they immediately opened up to me too, telling off-the-record facts. Silly small talk is not what they are interested in, only the language barrier reduces conversations to that level. Better be prepared for questions about capitalistic societies: economics, law, the parliamentary system and so on.

Spoken Chinese (both Cantonese and Mandarin) is making a definite comeback after years of being repressed. The large number of free-spending tourists and investors from Taiwan and Hong Kong provides the chief motivation for studying Chinese. In addition, cross-border trade with mainland China has been increasing rapidly and those who can speak Chinese are well positioned to profit from it.

After reunification, the teaching of Russian was stressed all over the country. With the collapse of the USSR in 1991, all interest in studying Russian has ground to a screeching halt. Most Vietnamese who bothered to learn the language have either forgotten it or are in the process of forgetting.

Writing
For centuries, the Vietnamese language was written in standard Chinese characters (*chu nho*). Around the 13th century, the Vietnamese devised their own system of writing (*chu nom*, or just *nom*), which was derived by combining Chinese characters or using them for their phonetic significance only. Both writing systems were used simultaneously

WATER PUPPETRY

Water puppetry, or *Roi Nuoc*, is an art form unique to Vietnam, believed to have been first performed in the Red River Delta area in the 11th century. The performance takes place outdoors, with the surface of a lake or pool as the stage. The puppeteers, themselves immersed in about a metre of water behind a bamboo curtain, manipulate the wooden puppets via an apparatus hidden in the water. Visitors can see water puppetry at the Municipal Water Puppet Theatre on the shore of Hoan Kiem Lake in Hanoi or at the National Water Puppet Theatre eight km outside Hanoi. There is also a water puppet theatre at the Binh Quoi Tourist Village just outside Ho Chi Minh City, and there are occasional performances at the History Museum near the centre of the city.

RICHARD EVERIST

Above: A performance in Saigon.

Left: A wooden water puppet.

Below: Water puppetry, an art form unique to Vietnam.

PHIL WEYMOUTH

PHIL WEYMOUTH

VIETNAMESE FOLK ART

The art of lacquerware came to Vietnam from China in the 15th century, and Japanese art teachers in Hanoi earlier this century introduced Japanese elements. Lacquerware factories in Vietnam produce bowls, vases, boxes, statues, dinnerware and furniture. Mother-of-pearl inlay is often used for decoration. Vietnam also has a long history of ceramics production and, today, ceramics factories produce jars, vases, decorative pots and dinnerware. Travellers can tour lacquerware and ceramics factories, and this traditional folk art is on sale throughout the country.

GLENN BEANLAND

GLENN BEANLAND

Above: Laquerware vase with painted design.

Left: Laquerware jewellery box.

Below: Modern ceramic goods for sale in Saigon.

TONY WHEELER

until the 20th century: official business and scholarship was conducted in chu nho while chu nom was used for popular literature.

The Roman-based *quoc ngu* script, in wide use since World War I, was developed in the 17th century by Alexandre de Rhodes, a brilliant French Jesuit scholar who first preached in Vietnamese only six months after arriving in the country in 1627. By replacing nom characters with quoc ngu, Rhodes facilitated the propagation of the gospel to a wide audience. The use of quoc ngu served to undermine the position of mandarin officials, whose power was based on traditional scholarship written in chu nho and chu nom and largely inaccessible to the masses.

The Vietnamese treat every syllable as an independent word, so 'Saigon' gets spelled 'Sai Gon' and 'Vietnam' is written as 'Viet Nam'. Foreigners aren't too comfortable with this system – we prefer to read 'London' rather than 'Lon Don'. This leads to the notion that Vietnamese is a 'monosyllabic language', where every syllable represents an independent word. This idea appears to be a hangover from the Chinese writing system, where every syllable was represented by an independent character, and each character was treated as a meaningful word. In reality, Vietnamese appears to be polysyllabic, like English. However, writing systems do influence people's perceptions of their own language, so Vietnamese themselves may insist that their language is monosyllabic – it's a debate probably not worth pursuing.

Pronunciation & Tones

Most of the names of the letters of the quoc ngu alphabet are pronounced like the letters of the French alphabet. Dictionaries are alphabetised as in English except that each vowel/tone combination is treated as a different letter. The consonants of the Romanised Vietnamese alphabet are pronounced more or less as they are in English with a few exceptions, and Vietnamese makes no use of the Roman letters 'f', 'j', 'w' and 'z'.

c	Like a 'k' but with no aspiration.
đ	With a crossbar; like a hard 'd'.
d	Without a crossbar; like a 'z' in the north and a 'y' in the south.
gi-	Like a 'z' in the north and a 'y' in the south.
kh-	Like '-ch' in the German *buch*.
ng-	Like the '-nga-' in 'long ago'.
nh-	Like the Spanish 'ñ' (as in *mañana*).
ph-	Like an 'f'.
r	Like a 'z' in the north and an 'r' in the south.
s	Like an 's' in the north and 'sh' in the south.
tr-	Like 'ch-' in the north and 'tr-' in the south.
th-	Like a strongly aspirated 't'.
x	Like an 's'.
-ch	Like a 'k'.
-ng	Like '-ng' in 'long' but with the lips closed.
-nh	Like '-ng' in 'sing'.

The hardest part of studying Vietnamese for Westerners is learning to differentiate between the tones. There are six tones in spoken Vietnamese. Thus, every syllable in Vietnamese can be pronounced six different ways. Depending on the tones, the word *ma* can be read to mean phantom, mother, rice seedling, tomb, horse or but. *Ga* can mean railroad station and chicken as well as several other things.

The six tones of spoken Vietnamese are indicated with five diacritical marks in written form (the first tone is left unmarked). These should not be confused with the four other diacritical marks used to indicate special consonants (such as the 'd' with a cross through it).

Grammar

Vietnamese grammar is fairly straightforward, with a wide variety of sentence structures possible. The numbers and genders of nouns are generally not explicit nor are the tenses and moods of verbs. Instead, tool words (such as *cua*, which means 'belong to') and classifiers are used to show a word's relationship to its neighbours. Verbs are turned into nouns by adding *su*.

Questions are asked in the negative, as with *n'est-ce pas?* in French. When the Vietnamese ask 'Is it OK?' they say 'It is OK, is it not?' The answer 'no' means 'Not OK it is not,' which is the double-negative form of 'Yes, it is OK'. The answer 'yes', on the other hand, means 'Yes, it is not OK', or as we would say in English 'No, it is not OK'. The result is that when negative questions ('It's not OK, is it?') are posed to Vietnamese, great confusion often results.

Proper Names

Most Vietnamese names consist of a family name, a middle name and a given name, in that order. Thus, if Henry David Thoreau had been Vietnamese, he would have been named Thoreau David Henry. He would have been addressed as Mr Henry – people are called by their given name but to do so without the title Mr, Mrs or Miss is considered as expressing either great intimacy or arrogance of the sort a superior would use with his or her inferior.

In Vietnamese, Mr is *Ong* if the man is of your grandparents' generation, *Bac* if he is of your parents' age, *Chu* if he is younger than your parents and *Anh* if he is in his teens or early 20s. Mrs is *Ba* if the woman is of your grandparents' age and *Bac* if she is of your parents' generation or younger. Miss is *Chi* or *Em* unless the woman is very young, in which case *Co* might be more appropriate. Other titles of respect are Buddhist monk (*Thay*), Buddhist nun (*Ba*), Catholic priest (*Cha*) and Catholic nun (*Co*).

There are 300 or so family names in use in Vietnam, the most common of which is Nguyen (pronounced something like 'nwyen'). About half of all Vietnamese have the surname Nguyen! When women marry, they usually (but not always) take their husband's family name. The middle name may be purely ornamental, may indicate the sex of its bearer or may be used by all the male members of a given family. A person's given name is carefully chosen so that it forms a harmonious and meaningful ensemble with his or her family and middle names and with the names of other family members.

Pronouns

I
  tôi
you (to an older man)
  (các) ông
you (to an older woman)
  (các) bà
you (to a man your own age)
  (các) anh
you (to a woman your own age)
  (các) chi
you (to a woman, formal)
  (các) cô
you (to a younger person)
  (các) em
he
  cậu ấy/anh ấy (north)
  cậu đó/anh đó (south)
she
  chị ấy/cô ấy (north)
  chị đó/anh đó (south)
we
  chúng tôi
they
  họ
you (pl)
  quí vị

Useful Words & Phrases

come	*đến*
give	*cho*
fast	*nhanh* (north)
	mau (south)
slow	*chậm*
man	*nam*
woman	*nữ*
understand	*hiểu*
I don't understand.	*Tôi không hiểu.*
I need...	*Tôi cần...*
change money	*đổi tiền*

Greetings & Civilities

Hello.	*Xin chào.*
How are you?	*Có khoẻ không?*
Fine, thank you.	*Khoẻ, cám ơn.*
Good night.	*Chúc ngủ ngon.*
Excuse me.	*Xin lỗi.*
(often used before questions)	
Thank you.	*Cám ơn.*

Thank you very much.	*Cám ơn rất nhiều.*
Yes.	*Vâng.* (north)
	Dạ. (south)
No.	*Không.*

Small Talk

What is your name?	*Tên là gì?*
My name is...	*Tên tôi là...*
I like...	*Tôi thích...*
I don't like...	*Tôi không thích...*
I want...	*Tôi muốn...*
I don't want...	*Tôi không muốn...*

Getting Around

What time does the first bus depart?
Chuyến xe buýt sớm nhất chạy lúc mấy giờ?
What time does the last bus depart?
Chuyến xe buýt cuối cùng sẽ chạy lúc mấy giờ?
How many km is it to...
Cách xa bao nhiêu ki-lô-mét...
How many hours does the journey take?
Chuyến đi sẽ mất bao lâu?
Go.
Đi.
I want to go to...
Tôi muốn đi...
What time does it arrive?
Mấy giờ đến?
What time does it depart?
Xe chạy lúc mấy giờ?
hire an automobile
thuê xe hơi (north)
mướn xe hơi (south)

bus	*xe buýt*
bus station	*bến xe*
cyclo (pedicab)	*xe xích lô*
map	*bản đồ*
railway station	*ga xe lửa*
receipt	*biên lai*
sleeping berth	*giường ngủ*
timetable	*thời biểu*
train	*xe lửa*

Around Town

office	*văn phòng*
post office	*bưu điện*
restaurant	*nhà hàng*
telephone	*điện thoại*
tourism	*du lịch*

Accommodation

Where is there a (cheap) hotel?
Ở đâu có khách sạn (rẻ tiền)?
How much does a room cost?
Giá một phòng là bao nhiêu?
I would like a cheap room.
Tôi thích một phòng loại rẻ.
I need to leave at (5) o'clock tomorrow morning.
Tôi phải đi lúc (năm) giờ sáng mai.

hotel	*khách sạn*
guesthouse	*nhà khách*
air-conditioning	*máy lạnh*
bathroom	*phòng tắm*
blanket	*mền*
fan	*quạt máy*
hot water	*nước nóng*
laundry	*giặt ủi*
mosquito net	*mùng*
reception	*tiếp tân*
room	*phòng*
room key	*chìa khóa phòng*
1st-class room	*phòng loại 1*
2nd-class room	*phòng loại 2*
sheet	*ra trải giường*
toilet	*nhà vệ sinh*
toilet paper	*giấy vệ sinh*
towel	*khăn tắm*

Geographical Terms & Directions

street	*đường/phố*
boulevard	*đại lộ*
bridge	*cầu*
highway	*xa lộ*
island	*đảo*
mountain	*núi*
National Highway 1	*Quốc Lộ 1*
river	*sông*
square (in a city)	*công viên*
east	*đông*
north	*bắc*
south	*nam*
west	*tây*

Shopping

Don't have...
  Không có...
How much is this?
  Cái này giá bao nhiêu?
I want to pay in dong.
  Tôi muốn trả bằng tiền Việt Nam.

buy	*mua*
sell	*bán*
cheap	*rẻ tiền*
expensive	*đắt tiền* (north)
	mắc tiền (south)
really expensive	*rất đắt* (north)
	mắc qua (south)
market	*chợ*
mosquito coils	*hương đốt chống muỗi* (north)
	nhang chống muỗi (south)
insect repellent	*thuốc chống muỗi*
sanitary pads	*băng vệ sinh*

Times & Dates

evening	*chiều*
now	*bây giờ*
today	*hôm nay*
tomorrow	*ngày mai*
Monday	*Thứ hai*
Tuesday	*Thứ ba*
Wednesday	*Thứ tư*
Thursday	*Thứ năm*
Friday	*Thứ sáu*
Saturday	*Thứ bảy*
Sunday	*Chủ nhật*

Numbers

1	*một*
2	*hai*
3	*ba*
4	*bốn*
5	*năm*
6	*sáu*
7	*bảy*
8	*tám*
9	*chín*
10	*mười*
11	*mười một*
19	*mười chín*
20	*hai mươi*
21	*hai mươi mốt*
30	*ba mươi*
90	*chín mươi*
100	*một trăm*
200	*hai trăm*
900	*chín trăm*
1000	*một ngàn*
10,000	*mười ngàn*
1 million	*một triệu*
first	*thứ nhất*
second	*thứ hai*

Health

I'm sick.
  Tôi bị ốm. (north)
  Tôi bị đau. (south)
Please take me to the hospital.
  Làm ơn đưa tôi bệnh viện.
Please call a doctor.
  Làm ơn gọi bác sĩ.

dentist	*nha sĩ*
doctor	*bác sĩ*
hospital	*bệnh viện*
pharmacy	*nhà thuốc tây*
backache	*đau lưng*
diarrhoea	*tiêu chảy* (north)
	ỉa chảy (south)
dizziness	*chóng mặt*
fever	*cảm/cúm*
headache	*nhức đầu*
malaria	*sốt rét*
stomachache	*đau bụng*
toothache	*nhức răng*
vomiting	*ói/mửa*

Emergencies

Help!	*Cứu tôi với!*
Thief!	*Cướp, cắp!*
Pickpocket!	*Móc túi!*
police	*công an*
Immigration Police Office	*phòng quản lý người nước ngoài*

Books for Language Study

A number of pocket English-Vietnamese *(Anh-Viet)* and Vietnamese-English *(Viet-Anh)* dictionaries *(tu dien)* have been published in Vietnam over the years. You'd certainly be wise to buy these in Vietnam rather than in a Western country, where they will cost about 10 times more!

Among the best scholarly dictionaries are the 992-page *Tu Dien Viet-Anh (Vietnamese-English Dictionary)* (Hanoi University Press (Truong Dai Hoc Tong Hop Ha Noi Xuat Ban), Hanoi, 1986) by Bui Phung; and the massive 1960-page English-Vietnamese *Tu Dien Anh-Viet (Nha Xuat Ban Khoa Hoc Xa Hoi*, Hanoi, 1975).

If you do buy something in a Western country, check out Nguyen Dinh Hoa's *Essential English-Vietnamese Dictionary* (Charles E Tuttle Co, Rutland, Vt, and Tokyo, 1983) and *Essential Vietnamese-English Dictionary* (Charles E Tuttle Co, Rutland, Vt, and Tokyo, 1966).

A phrasebook can be very useful. Lonely Planet has the *Vietnamese Phrasebook*, which includes cultural tips, words and phrases, and a guide to pronunciation and grammar. There is also a forthcoming audio pack to help with pronunciation.

Speak Vietnamese (Hay Noi Tieng Viet; Foreign Languages Publishing House, Hanoi, 1982) gives phrases in Vietnamese, English, French and Russian and might prove useful in dealing with Russians and French people as well as the locals. A two-volume set for serious students of Vietnamese is *Introductory Vietnamese* and *An Intermediate Vietnamese Reader* (South-East Asia Program, Cornell University, Ithaca, NY, 1972) by Robert M Quinn.

Facts for the Visitor

VISAS & EMBASSIES

Arranging the necessary paperwork for a Vietnamese visa has become fairly straightforward, but it still tends to be expensive and time-consuming. Immigration authorities are sometimes a hassle to deal with upon arrival in Vietnam, but the biggest hassles of all have to do visa extensions.

In most cases you are better off getting your visa from a travel agent rather than from the Vietnamese embassy directly. This is because all visas issued by embassies will be stamped directly into your passport, while travel agencies will get it on a separate piece of paper *if you ask*. In most cases, having it on a separate paper will prove safer. The reason is because within Vietnam itself you will often be required to leave your visa with the hotel reception desk (they need it to register your presence with the police), or with a travel agency (to get a local travel permit), or with bureaucratic ministries of every sort. With so many hands shuttling your visa from one place to another, this valuable piece of paper could get lost. Replacing a lost visa will be a hassle but still *much* easier than replacing your entire passport.

The travel agency doing your visa needs a photocopy of your passport and two or three photos (the actual number differs in various countries). Do not leave your passport with the travel agency or it's likely the visa will be stamped into it despite whatever instructions to the contrary you may have given.

Bangkok has always been the most convenient place to get Vietnamese visas. Even travel agents in neighbouring countries send the paperwork by courier to Bangkok for processing because it's so much cheaper than dealing with their local Vietnamese embassies. In Bangkok, single-entry tourist visas cost US$40 at budget travel agencies. Many travel agencies offer package deals with visa and round-trip air ticket included (Bangkok-Saigon, returning Hanoi-Bangkok). The place to look for competitive prices is Khao San Rd in Bangkok.

Tourist Visas

Processing a visa application takes five working days in Bangkok (two days for an express visa), five days in Malaysia, five to 10 days in Hong Kong and 10 days in Taiwan. No one has yet to offer a satisfactory explanation of why it should take so much longer in some countries than in others.

Getting a Vietnamese visa in Cambodia is possible, but Bangkok seems to be a more efficient place to arrange this.

Visas are normally valid for 30 days from the date you specify, so you must let your travel agent know just when you plan to enter Vietnam. You must also decide on your port of entry (Ho Chi Minh City or Hanoi, but your visa can be stamped for both) because this will be written on the visa and cannot be changed later. Vietnamese visas also specify where you must exit the country, though this can be changed within Vietnam at the immigration police, Interior Ministry or the Foreign Ministry.

In the finest bureaucratic tradition, the Vietnamese require a special visa for entering overland from China. These visas cost double and take twice as long to issue as the normal tourist visas needed for entering Vietnam by air. Travellers who have tried to use a standard visa for entering Vietnam overland from China have fared poorly.

Theoretically, you can enter Vietnam with a sponsor's letter and get your visa stamped into your passport on arrival for US$25. This 'visa on arrival' process is fraught with risks and not recommended. Sometimes it works, but there have been many cases of travellers arriving with these letters, which were then arbitrarily rejected by the immigration authorities. In this case, travellers have had to do things like get a major government-owned hotel to sponsor them (this can be arranged at the airport, but you pay five-star hotel prices) or else be deported. Many airlines will not accept these sponsor's letters in lieu of a visa and deny you permission to board the aircraft. One traveller reports:

We couldn't get our visa upon arrival at Tan Son Nhat airport. We were forced to pay taxi fare and were brought to the First Chain Hotel (the officer called it the 'Police Hotel'). It cost us US$55 per night.

Buying your visa at the airport also requires you to have the right cash (US dollars only in the exact amount) because there is no place to change money before you pass through immigration.

You might think that after you've obtained your visa and landed in Vietnam that all is well. Unfortunately, you still have to pass Vietnamese immigration, and the people in charge of this have complete authority to decide on how long you can stay. While most people get through OK, the immigration staff may arbitrarily give you a shorter stay than what your visa calls for. Thus, your 30-day visa might only be validated for one week, or a three-month visa for just one month. No matter what it says on the front side of your visa, immediately after it's been stamped by the immigration officer, look on the back side and see how many days they've given you. If you've been given only a week, sometimes you can get it changed right at the airport or border checkpoint – otherwise, you will be forced to visit the immigration police and apply for an extension. It's been our experience that your physical appearance will play a part in the reception you receive from immigration – if you wear shorts, scruffy clothing, look dirty or unshaven, etc, then you can expect problems. You don't need to get all dressed up, but try to look 'respectable'.

Another issue – upon arrival you need to fill out an entry/exit form. This form asks, among other things, what hotel you will be staying at in Vietnam. Some travellers have left this blank in the belief that it didn't matter and, besides, how can they know in advance where they will stay? You'd best fill in something – immigration officials have

refused people entry for leaving this space blank. Your trusty Lonely Planet book can help here – look in the Places to Stay section and copy whatever name you like, because the authorities never check to make sure you actually stay there. And if you happened to have left this book in your checked luggage and thus don't have it at hand, you can always simply make up a likely-sounding name ('Saigon Hotel' or 'Hanoi Hotel' perhaps?).

Always have some photos with you because immigration police have been known to inexplicably give travellers more forms to fill out and attached photos are required. Of course, there is a photographer right there at the airport to serve you – for a substantial fee.

Business Visas

There are several advantages to having a business visa: such visas are usually valid for three months, can be issued for multiple-entry journeys and will look more impressive when you have to deal with bureaucratic authorities. Also, you are permitted to work if you have a business visa, though doing so will make you subject to taxes and other bureaucratic regulations which change from week to week.

Getting a business visa has now become fairly easy. The travel agencies which do tourist visas can also do business visas. The main drawback is cost – a business visa costs about four times what you'd pay for a tourist visa. Trying to obtain the visa yourself through a Vietnamese embassy will probably be more trouble than it's worth – you'd better let a travel agent handle it. However, remember the preceding warning – immigration officials may validate your visa for only one month upon arrival even though a business visa is good for three months.

There is another category of business visa, which remains valid for six months. To get these, you must apply in Vietnam. If approved, you must then go abroad (most travellers go to Phnom Penh or Vientiane) to pick up the visa from a Vietnamese embassy.

Student Visas

A student visa is something you usually arrange after arrival. It's acceptable to enter

Vietnam on a tourist visa, enrol in Vietnamese language courses and then apply at the immigration police for a change in status. Of course, you do have to pay tuition and are expected to attend class. A minimum of 10 hours of study per week is needed to qualify for student status.

Resident Visas

Only a few foreigners can qualify for a resident visa. Probably the easiest way to do this is to marry a local, though anyone contemplating doing this had best be prepared for mountains of paperwork. Spouses of Vietnamese nationals gain a few other advantages besides a resident visa – for example, they can own 50% of the couple's property (including real estate).

Residency visas currently cost US$170 for six months, plus US$170 for each extension.

Other Visas

Visas to Laos The Laotian Embassy in Hanoi is theoretically open Monday to Friday from 8 to 11 am and from 2 to 4.30 pm. There are also Laotian consulates in Ho Chi Minh City and Danang. Three photos and plane tickets are required for a five-day transit visa. It takes at least 24 hours to be issued a transit visa at the embassy, but some travellers have obtained the visa in just a few hours through travel agents in Ho Chi Minh City.

The Laotian Consulate in Ho Chi Minh City issues tourist visas valid for 15 days. Processing takes three days and costs US$25. The catch is that you have to book a tour, which you can do right in the consulate itself. Currently, they were asking US$115, which includes an air ticket, airport transfer and one night in the Vientiane Hotel. It works out slightly cheaper if you book at the Laotian Embassy in Hanoi.

If you're heading to Thailand after Laos, get your Thai visa in advance, because the Thai Embassy in Vientiane makes you wait three days.

Visas to Cambodia Visas for Cambodia are available on arrival at Phnom Penh Airport free of charge if you stay less than 15 days.

Vietnamese Embassies

Australia
6 Timbarra Crescent, O'Malley, Canberra, ACT 2603 (☎ 286-6059; fax 286-4534)
Belgium
Av de la Floride 130, 1180 Brussels (☎ 374 9370; fax 374 9376)
Cambodia
Son Ngoc Minh area (opposite 749 Achar Mean Blvd), Phnom Penh (☎ 25481)
Canada
695 Davidson Drive, Gloucester, Ottawa, Ontario K1J6L7 (☎ 744-0698; fax 744-1709)
China
32 Guangua Lu, Jianguomen Wai, Beijing (☎ 5321125; fax 532720)
Canton consulate (☎ 776 9555, ext 101, 604; fax 767 9000)
France
62-66 Rue de Boileau, Paris 16 (☎ 45 24 50 63; fax 45 24 39 48)
Germany
Konstantinstrasse 37, Bonn (☎ 357 0201)
India
17 Kautilya Marg Chanakyapury, Delhi (☎ 301 7714)
Indonesia
Jalan Teuku Umar 25, Jakarta (☎ 310 0358; fax 310 0359)
Italy
Piazza Barberini 12, 00187 Rome (☎ 475 5286)
Japan
50-11 Moto Yoyogi-cho, Shibuya-ku, Tokyo 151 (☎ 3466 3311)
Korea (South)
33-1 Hannam-dong, Yong-gu, Seoul (☎ 794 3570)
Laos
1 Thap Luang Rd, Vientiane (☎ 5578)
Malaysia
4 Pesiaran Stonor, Kuala Lumpur (☎ 484036; fax 483270)
Mongolia
Enkhe-Taivan Oudomjni 47, Ulan Bator (☎ 50465)
Myanmar (Burma)
30 Komin Kochin Rd, Yangon (☎ 50361)
Philippines
54 Victor Cruz, Malate, Metro Manila (☎ 500364, 508101)
Russia
Bolshaya Pirogovskaya ul 13, Moscow (☎ 245 0925)
Sweden
Örby Slottsväg 26, 125 36 Älvsj", Stockholm (☎ 861214; fax 8995173)
Thailand
83/1 Wireless Rd, Bangkok (☎ 251 7201)

UK
  12-14 Victoria Rd, London W8 5RD
  (☎ 937 1912; fax 937 6108)
USA
  Vietnamese Liaison Office, Washington DC
  (☎ (800) 874-5100). Visa processing is done by
  Travel Documents Inc, 734 15th St NW, Suite
  400, Washington, DC 20005 (☎ (202) 638-3800;
  fax 638-4674)

Visa Extensions

If you've got the dollars, they've got the rubber stamp. In Ho Chi Minh City and Hanoi, first-time visa extensions cost US$20 and subsequent ones are US$35. At least in those two cities, you should go to a travel agency to get this taken care of. Fronting up at the Immigration Police Office yourself usually doesn't work in Saigon or Hanoi, though in some other places it does. The procedure takes one or two days and one photo is needed. You can apply for your extension even several weeks before it's necessary. Official policy is that you are permitted two visa extensions, each one for the length of time of your original visa. So, that means a 30-day visa can be extended twice, permitting you 90 days in total before you leave the country. If you entered Vietnam on a 90-day visa, you should be able to extend twice for a total of 270 days.

So much for theory. In practice, you never know what is going to happen when you apply for an extension. Usually the first extension goes OK if you work through a reliable agent who has good connections. Then again, sometimes things inexplicably go wrong. And some Immigration Police Offices will refuse to do a second extension unless you also got your first extension from them, but other offices have no such rule. In fact, it seems that the immigration police don't know what the rules are and make them up as they go along. You hear numerous visa war stories in Vietnam, all of which reinforce our impression that the less you have to do with the bureaucracy, the better off you are.

In theory, you should be able to extend your visa in any provincial capital. In practice, it goes smoothest in certain cities catering to mass tourism. Hué and Vung Tau have a reputation for being good about visa extensions, while in Hanoi and Saigon success depends on the position of the moon and the stars. But even if you do everything by the book, you never know what official nonsense will come your way:

I got my visa extension in Vinh, which only cost US$2, but in Saigon I was later told that this was invalid. The police cancelled my first extension, forced me to buy a second one, plus I had to pay a US$10 fine for overstaying 13 days. I also lost three days dealing with the bureaucracy.

Gerhard Heinzel

The official word is that even if you do get your visa extension in some obscure backwater (such as Vinh) the airport immigration police will accept this and allow you to depart with no problems.

Re-entry Visas

If you wish to visit Cambodia, Laos or any other country, it is possible to do this and then re-enter Vietnam using your original single-entry Vietnamese visa. However, you must apply for a re-entry visa before departing Vietnam. If you do not have a re-entry visa, then you will have to go through the whole expensive and time-consuming procedure of applying for a new Vietnamese visa. Re-entry visas are easy enough to arrange in Hanoi or Ho Chi Minh City, but you will almost certainly have to ask a travel agent to do the paperwork for you. Travel agents charge about US$10 to US$20 for this service and can complete the procedure in one or two days. Although travellers can theoretically secure the re-entry visa without going through a travel agent, Vietnamese bureaucrats usually thwart such individual efforts.

Remember that your re-entry visa also must show the point where you intend to re-enter Vietnam. So if you fly from Vietnam to Cambodia and want to re-enter overland, your re-entry visa must so indicate. However, this can be amended by the Vietnamese Embassy in Cambodia if you didn't get it right the first time.

If you already have a valid multiple-entry visa for Vietnam, you do not need a re-entry visa.

Foreign Embassies in Vietnam

With the exception of visas for Laos and Cambodia, Hanoi's 37 embassies and Ho Chi Minh City's 13 consulates do very little visa business. For their addresses, see the Hanoi and Ho Chi Minh City chapters.

DOCUMENTS
Passport

A passport is essential, and if yours is within a few months of expiration, get a new one now – many countries will not issue a visa if your passport has less than six months of validity remaining. Make sure it has at least a few blank pages for visas and entry and exit stamps. It could be very inconvenient to run out of blank pages when you are too far away from an embassy to get a new passport issued or extra pages added.

Losing your passport is very bad news indeed. Getting a new one takes time and money. However, if you will be staying in Vietnam or any foreign country for a long period of time, it helps tremendously to register your passport with your embassy. This will eliminate the need to send faxes back to your home country to confirm that you really exist. It's wise to have a driver's licence, student card, ID card or some such thing with your photo on it – some embassies want this picture ID before issuing a replacement passport even if you've registered. Having an old expired passport is also very useful – as a backup ID and to give to hotels who demand your documents as 'security'.

If you're not able to register your passport, it certainly helps to at least have a separate record of your passport number, issue date and photocopy of the passport or birth certificate. While you're compiling that info, add the serial number of your travellers' cheques, details of health insurance and US$100 or so as emergency cash, and keep all that material separate from your passport and money (better hotels have a safe for valuables – that might be a good place to keep this stuff).

If you are a national of a country without diplomatic relations with Vietnam and lose your passport while in the country the situation is not good but still not hopeless. If the immigration police are unable to locate the passport, you will be issued documents allowing you to leave the country. You may be allowed to stay in Vietnam until your visa (the validity of which is on record with the police) expires.

Photocopies

The first thing you should do with both your passport and Vietnamese visa is photocopy them. The main reason for doing this is that in Vietnam you are almost certain to encounter various people who want to take your valuable documents away from you. This is particularly true of hotel clerks – they say they need your passport to register you with the police, though in many cases the only motive is to make sure you pay your hotel bill and don't steal the towels. Some hotels will accept photocopies, but most will not. Once you've handed over your passport and/or visa, this leaves you with no documentation at all. At least photocopies give you something to show to the authorities (the police, the railway ticket office, Vietnam Airlines, etc) while the hotel holds your original documents. And if worse comes to worse, photocopies are helpful if you need to replace the documents that the hotel or police manage to lose.

If police stop you on the street and ask to see your passport, give them the photocopy rather than the original, explaining that the hotel has your original. Trusting the police with your documents always puts you in a very vulnerable position.

Travel Permits

Formerly, foreigners had to have internal travel permits *(giay phep di lai)* to go anywhere outside the city in which they arrived. From 1975 to 1988, even citizens of Vietnam needed these permits to travel around their own country (to prevent them from fleeing). The central government changed the rules in 1993, so you no longer need an internal travel permit. There have been reports of some con artists, though, who will insist you still need one and will happily sell you a fake 'internal travel permit'.

Although internal travel permits have been abolished, uncertainty still prevails in small towns and villages. Unfortunately, the police in many places seem to make up their own rules as they go along, no matter what the Interior Ministry in Hanoi says. What this means is that some provincial governments are chasing foreign dollars by charging for local 'travel permits', which consist of a photocopied piece of paper with a policeman's signature on it. The bottom line is that you may have to inquire locally to see if a permit is required.

Information I obtained from Vietnam Tourism before departure clearly stated that since April 1993, there are no travel restrictions for tourists. This was confirmed by the immigration officer in Hanoi.

Nevertheless, I was 'apprehended' the day after my arrival in Thai Nguyen (some 80 km north of Hanoi) for failing to register with the local police. I was detained for some three hours before being allowed to leave (I paid no fine). The four or five police officers with interpreter were quite pleasant and friendly, and wished me a happy stay. It was explained, rightly or wrongly, that the easing of restrictions did not apply to independent travellers. More than likely, the police didn't even know what the regulations said but were happy to relieve their boredom and converse with a foreigner.

LR Hanson

Relieving boredom is one thing, extracting cash from foreigners is another. Some local provincial governments are demanding that you secure a permit on arrival to visit the surrounding area, pay a fee for this permit, hire a local guide and rent another car from the local government even if you've already arrived in an official government rental car! For example, if you visit Dalat in the Central Highlands, no permit is necessary. However, to visit the nearby Lat Village (12 km away), you need to get a permit from the Dalat police (US$7), hire a guide from Dalat Tourist and rent an official government car. The total cost for the privilege of visiting this tiny village comes to about US$25.

Besides the Lat Village, other places currently requiring permits include villages around Buon Ma Thuot, Pleiku, Hon Khoai Island, the canals on the Cambodian border (between Ha Tien and Chau Doc) and the DMZ. Additional information about obtaining these permits is provided in the relevant chapters.

However, don't be absolutely sure that the information in this book is correct, because the policies change. We are pleased to report that this tendency to require travel permits is diminishing. There seems to have been some strong pressure applied by Hanoi to stop this nonsense – the situation was totally out of control when we researched the previous edition of this book.

Driver's Licences
If you plan to be driving abroad get an International Driver's Licence from your local automobile association or motor vehicle department. In many countries, these are valid for one year only so there's no sense getting one far in advance of departure. However, some countries will issue International Driver's Licences valid for several years – it just depends on where you live. Make sure that your licence states that it is valid for motorcycles if you plan to drive one.

Health Certificates
Useful (though not essential) is an International Health Certificate to record any vaccinations you've had. These can also be issued in Vietnam.

Student ID Cards
Full-time students coming from the USA, Australia and Europe can often get some good discounts on international (not domestic) air tickets with the help of an International Student Identity Card (ISIC). To get this card, inquire at your campus. There is no place in Vietnam to get these cards. Youth cards are also available; for example, STA Travel in Australia issues STA Youth Cards to persons aged 13 to 26 years.

Miscellaneous
If you're travelling with your spouse, a photocopy of your marriage licence just might come in handy should you become involved

with the law, hospitals or other bureaucratic authorities.

If you're planning on working or studying in Vietnam, it could be helpful to have copies of transcripts, diplomas, letters of reference and other professional qualifications.

A collection of small photos for visas (about 10 should be sufficient) will be useful if you're planning on visiting several countries, but will also come in handy if you apply for visa extensions or other documents. Of course, these can be obtained in Vietnam and elsewhere. Visa photos must have a neutral background.

CUSTOMS

You are permitted to bring in duty-free 200 cigarettes, 50 cigars or 250 grams of tobacco; two litres of liquor; gifts worth up to US$50; and a reasonable quantity of luggage and personal effects. Items which you cannot bring in include opium, weapons, explosives and 'cultural materials unsuitable to Vietnamese society'.

Tourists can bring an unlimited amount of foreign currency into Vietnam, but they are required to declare it on their customs form upon arrival.

When entering Vietnam, visitors must also declare all precious metals (especially gold), jewellery, cameras and electronic devices in their possession. Customs is liable to tax you on gold bars, jewellery and diamonds – if you don't need this stuff, then don't bring it. Theoretically, declaring your goods means that when you leave, you will have no hassles taking these items out with you. It also means that you could be asked to show these items so that customs officials know you didn't sell them on the black market, though in practice you will seldom be troubled unless you bring in an unreasonable amount of goods or something of great value.

The import and export of Vietnamese currency and live animals is forbidden.

Most travellers have more trouble exiting the country than entering it. The great stumbling block seems to be what the authorities call 'cultural materials'. This includes video tapes, which must be screened in advance by 'experts' from the Department of Culture. This is to make sure that you haven't somehow snatched Ho Chi Minh's body and found a way to smuggle it out of the country on a video tape. A similar hassle occurs if you've bought antiques (or something which looks antique) unless you have an official export certificate:

When I was in the airport in Hanoi, a customs officer eyed two porcelain vases I had bought and told me that I should go to the Department of Culture in Hanoi to have them assessed or pay a fine of US$20. Of course, there was no representative of the Department of Culture at the airport to make such an evaluation, so getting them assessed would require me to miss my flight.

Anna Crawford Pinnerup

MONEY
Currency

The currency of Vietnam is the *dong* (abbreviated by a 'd' following the amount). Banknotes in denominations of 200d, 500d, 1000d, 2000d, 5000d, 10,000d, 20,000d and 50,000d are presently in circulation. It can be difficult to get change for the 50,000d notes in small backwaters, so keep a stack of small bills handy.

Now that Ho Chi Minh has been canonised, his picture appears on every banknote. There are no coins currently in use in Vietnam, though the dong used to be subdivided into 10 hao and 100 xu. All dong-denominated prices in this book are based on an exchange rate of US$1 to 11,053d.

In the recent past, many upmarket hotels and restaurants demanded payment in US dollars and would not accept Vietnamese currency. In 1994, the Vietnamese government banned this practice – with the notable exception of Vietnam Airlines, all businesses in Vietnam officially must now accept payment in dong only. In reality, many places still quote prices in dollars and will 'exchange' on the spot. Nevertheless, the new rules are good news for travellers – having to keep wads of dollars in small denomination bills is now a nuisance we no longer have to deal with.

Even though US dollars are now prohib-

Money for Nothing

The dong has certainly had a rocky history. In the days of French Indochina, it was known as the piastre. The partitioning of Vietnam in 1954 created separate versions of the dong for North and South Vietnam. In 1975, US$1 was equal to 450 dong in South Vietnam. In 1976, the communist Provisional Revolutionary Government (PRG) cancelled the South Vietnamese dong and issued its own PRG dong. The swap rate between the two dong was not set at 1:1, but rather at 500:1 in favour of the PRG dong. Furthermore, southerners were only permitted to exchange a maximum of 200 dong per family. This sudden demonetarisation of southern Vietnam instantly turned much of the affluent population into paupers and caused the swift collapse of the economy. Those with the foresight to have kept their wealth hidden in gold or jewellery escaped some of the hardships.

In 1977, both the North Vietnamese dong and the PRG dong were done away with and swapped for a 'reunification dong'. In the north the swap was 1:1, but in the south the ratio was 1:1.2. In this case the southerners got a slightly better deal than the northerners, though it was small compensation for the 500:1 loss of the previous year.

The last great attempt at currency swapping was in 1985. Realising that inflation was rapidly eroding the value of the dong, the government decided to solve the problem by reissuing a new dong at a swap ratio of 10:1 in favour of the new dong. This time each family was allowed only 2000 dong of the new banknotes, though on special application more could be obtained. Rather than controlling price increases as the government had hoped, the currency reissue ignited yet another new round of hyperinflation. These days, the old 20d notes are literally not worth the paper they're printed on. ■

ited for use as an unofficial currency, many prices (hotel rooms, air tickets, etc) are still quoted in US dollars. We also prefer to quote prices in US dollars in this book. There are two reasons for this. One is that rapid inflation causes dong prices to rise continually while the US dollar price remains fairly stable. The second reason is that dong prices are unwieldy. For example, a night at a mid-range hotel can easily cost over 300,000d, and buying a domestic air ticket from Hanoi to Ho Chi Minh City costs 1.65 million dong!

It's advisable to bring a small pocket calculator with you for converting currency, unless of course you are the sort of person who can nonchalantly multiply $33.50 times 11,053 (and add 10% tax) in your head.

During the Vietnam War, the Americans introduced Western banking practices – personal cheques were commonly used for large purchases, at least in Saigon. When the North took over, cheques, credit cards, South Vietnamese bank notes and South Vietnamese bank accounts became instantly worthless. As the Vietnamese dismantled the banking system, telegraphic transfers into Vietnam became practically impossible, though later a company called Cosevina was set up to allow Overseas Vietnamese to send money to their relatives.

That was then and this is now. Vietnam is now trying to rejoin the world's banking system. Capitalist-style monetary instruments like travellers' cheques, credit cards, telegraphic transfers and even letters of credit are all experiencing a revival. Domestic personal cheques have still not been re-introduced yet, but that should be coming soon.

Gold is also used extensively, especially for major transactions such as the sale of homes or cars. To pay with Vietnamese currency would require truckloads of dong.

It's a good idea to check that the dollars and travellers cheques you bring to Vietnam do not have anything scribbled on them or look too tattered, lest they be summarily rejected by uptight clerks. Ironically, some travellers have had problems changing dollars that looked 'too new' because the bank clerks often suspected that these were counterfeit!

Although you can at least theoretically convert French francs, German marks, pounds sterling, Japanese yen and other major currencies, the reality is that US dollars are still much preferred. Be sure to bring enough US dollars cash or travellers' cheques for your whole visit and to keep it safe, preferably in a money belt. Try not to keep the whole lot in one place (if the money belt goes then everything goes with it). Unless you borrow from a foreigner or get someone to wire money to you (which is only possible in Ho Chi Minh City and Hanoi), losing your cash could put you in a really bad situation. Of course, you could always try begging your embassy for help (if your country has one in Vietnam), but our experience has been that most embassy staff have little sympathy and will leave you twisting in the wind.

Exchange Rates

The dong has certainly experienced its ups and downs. Past attempts by the government to solve the country's debt problems with the printing press led to devastating inflation, and thus frequent devaluations. In 1991, the dong lost close to half its value. In 1992, the dong gained 35% against the US dollar, making it one of the best currency investments of the year! The surge in the dong's value was due to both shutting down the printing presses and the turnaround in Vietnam's chronic trade deficit – in 1992, the country experienced what is believed to be its first trade surplus since reunification.

Country	Unit		Dong
Australia	A$1	=	8140d
Canada	C$1	=	8158d
China	Y1	=	1294d
France	FFr1	=	2144d
Germany	DM1	=	7352d
Hong Kong	HK$1	=	1430d
Japan	¥1	=	113d
Malaysia	M$1	=	4306d
New Zealand	NZ$1	=	6740d
Philippines	P1	=	434d
Singapore	S$1	=	7498d
South Korea	W1	=	14d
Switzerland	SFr1	=	8826d
Taiwan	NT$1	=	423d
Thailand	B1	=	443d
UK	£1	=	17,754d
USA	US$1	=	11,053d

Changing Money

Foreign currency can be exchanged for dong in one of four ways: at the bank, through authorised exchange bureaus, at hotel reception desks and on the black market.

The best rates are offered by banks. Exchange bureaus are more convenient – they tend to be located just where you need them, and they stay open at times when banks are closed. Hotel reception counters often change money, but their exchange rates are usually the worst around.

Vietcombank is another name for the state-owned Bank for Foreign Trade of Vietnam (Ngan Hang Ngoai Thuong Viet Nam). Some other banks can change foreign currency and travellers' cheques, but Vietcombank is by far the best organised for this activity. Banking hours are normally from 8 am to 3 pm on weekdays, 8 am to noon on Saturdays and closed on Sundays and holidays. Most banks also close for 1½ hours during lunch.

Although changing money is feasible in some backwaters, you'll find it considerably easier in large cities like Hanoi, Ho Chi Minh City or Danang. Well-touristed mid-sized cities like Nha Trang, Hué, Vung Tau and Dalat also have functioning foreign exchange banks. Opportunities for changing money are pretty bleak in secluded hamlets like Long Hai and Sapa, despite the presence of tourists in those places. In such remote spots, your only hope is to do a private cash transaction (ie, black market).

Vietnam's 'black market' is almost a misnomer. Private individuals and some shops (particularly jewellery stores) will swap cash US dollars for dong and vice versa. While supposedly illegal, enforcement is virtually nonexistent. It's important to realise that black market exchange rates are *worse* than the official exchange rates. In other words, you don't gain anything by using the black market other than the convenience of changing money when and where you like.

If people approach you on the street with offers to change money at rates better than the official bank rate, then you can rest assured that you are being set up for a rip-off. Don't even think about trying it. Remember, if an offer sounds too good to be true, that's because it is.

You can reconvert reasonable amounts of dong back to dollars on departure without an official receipt, though just how one defines 'reasonable' is open to question. Most visitors have had no problem, but having an official receipt should settle any arguments if they arise. You cannot legally take the dong out with you.

The relatively low values of Vietnamese banknotes mean that almost any currency exchange will leave you with hundreds of banknotes to count. Notes are usually presented in brick-sized piles bound with rubber bands, but even so, counting them is a slow but necessary process. Changing US$100 will net you over 1.1 million dong – a large brick of 5000d notes, which will not fit in a money belt. You'll have to give some thought about just where you are going to keep these bricks as you cart them around the country.

It's not an uncommon experience to see foreigners rudely berate the Vietnamese bank staff when they dish out wads of 2000d or 5000d notes rather than the few crisp big ones. Of course, you can certainly ask (politely) for large denomination notes, but in many cases the small notes are the only ones they have.

Travellers' Cheques Travellers' cheques denominated in US dollars can be exchanged at Vietcombank for US dollars cash. A 2% commission is charged for this service. No commission is charged if you exchange travellers' cheques for dong.

If your cheques are denominated in other currencies besides US dollars, you may find that many banks are unwilling to accept them because they don't know the latest exchange rate. If you insist, the banks may exchange non-US-dollar cheques for dong but charge a hefty commission (perhaps 10%) to protect themselves from any possible exchange rate fluctuations.

Because there has been a sharp increase in the number of stolen travellers' cheques, Vietcombank will demand to see your original purchase receipt. If you don't have it, that could be a problem. In that case, the bank

staff *might* be willing to cash just one check for you if the amount isn't large. Save yourself a hassle and bring the receipt, but keep it separate from your original cheques. If you're stuck, try the foreign-run banks – they seem to be more easygoing though they often charge a 1% commission.

Credit Cards Visa, MasterCard and JCB cards are now accepted in all major cities and various touristy spots (Dalat, Halong Bay, etc). However, you will usually be charged a 3% commission every time you use a credit card to purchase something or pay a hotel bill.

Getting a cash advance from Visa, MasterCard and JCB is possible at Vietcombank in most cities. The fee for this is a 4% commission.

Telegraphic Transfers

It took the Vietnamese government a long time to realise that all those Vietnamese refugees living in the West are a potential gold mine because they like to send money home to their relatives still in Vietnam. Even after the government recognised the potential, before 1990 sending money to Vietnam from abroad was a painful process that took three weeks or longer and involved massive amounts of red tape. When the money finally arrived, the recipient was allowed to receive only dong, which quickly lost its value due to the 700% or so annual inflation rate. This has all changed.

Money can be cabled into Vietnam quickly and cheaply and the recipient can be paid in US dollars or Vietnamese dong. However, sending money by wire is fast only if the overseas office is a 'correspondent bank' with Vietcombank. The list of correspondent banks is not extensive, but is growing. If your home country does not have a correspondent bank, the transfer can be done via an intermediary bank (usually through New York City, the 'clearinghouse' for US dollars). Right now, only the branches of Vietcombank in Ho Chi Minh City and Hanoi are equipped to handle wire transfers. Money should be cabled to 'Vietcombank

Ho Chi Minh City' or 'Vietcombank Hanoi'. The cable needs to include the recipient's name and passport number. Vietcombank's telex number in Ho Chi Minh City is 811.234 VCB.VT or 811.235 VCB.VT.

Some correspondent banks which can cable money directly to Vietcombank are as follows:

Australia
　Commonwealth Bank Sydney (Australian and US dollars)
Canada
　Royal Bank of Canada (Canadian dollars only)
France
　BNP Paris (French francs), BFCE Paris (US dollars)
Germany
　BHF Frankfurt (Deutschmarks), Berliner Bank, Berlin (US dollars)
Hong Kong
　Hong Kong & Shanghai Banking Corporation (HK dollars), Peace Finance (US dollars)
Singapore
　BNP Singapore (Singapore dollars), UOB, BFCE Singapore (US dollars)
Switzerland
　Swiss Bank Corporation Zurich (US dollars and Swiss francs)
Taiwan
　Farmers Bank Taipei (US dollars)
Thailand
　Thai Military Bank, or Krung Thai Bank, Bangkok (US dollars)
UK
　Lloyds Bank, London (pounds sterling and US dollars)
USA
　Chase Manhattan Bank, Citibank, ABN Amro Bank (all in New York), Bank of America (California) (US dollars only)

Bank Accounts

Foreigners who spend much time in Vietnam working, doing business or just hanging around, can open bank accounts at Vietcombank. The accounts can be denominated in Vietnamese dong or US dollars. Both demand-deposit and time-deposit accounts are available and interest is paid.

Vietcombank can arrange letters of credit for those doing import and export business in Vietnam. It is even possible to borrow money from Vietcombank.

Costs

A survey taken in the early 1970s found that Ho Chi Minh City was the most expensive city in the world for travellers. Back then, it cost 63% more to visit Ho Chi Minh City than it did New York! This is not because Vietnamese people were receiving high wages, but simply because the Vietnamese government was ripping off people deemed to be 'capitalist tourists'.

Things have changed. The government has finally figured out that outrageous prices means no tourist business at all. Today, Vietnam is one of the best travel bargains in East Asia.

The cost of travelling in Vietnam depends on your tastes and susceptibility to luxuries. Ascetics can get by on US$10 a day, and for US$15 to US$20 a backpacker can live fairly well. Transport is likely to be the biggest expense if you rent a car, which many travellers wind up doing. If you choose to travel by bus or train, you can save a considerable sum but will also suffer some discomfort and lengthy delays – Vietnam's public transport is in very flimsy condition.

Foreigners are sometimes overcharged in restaurants – especially when unaccompanied by a Vietnamese – on the assumption that they cannot read either the menu or the bill. Such incidents are especially frequent in heavily touristed areas, such as downtown Saigon.

Tipping

Tipping according to a percentage of the bill is not expected in Vietnam but it is enormously appreciated. For someone making US$30 per month, 10% of the cost of your meal can equal half a day's wages. Government-run hotels and restaurants that specifically cater to tourists usually have an automatic 10% service charge. It's also not a bad idea to tip the person who cleans your room if you stay a couple of days in the same hotel – US$0.50 to US$1 should be enough. If you hire drivers and guides, also consider tipping them if they worked hard – after all, the time they spend on the road with you means time away from home and family.

If you spend any length of time in Vietnam, someone will almost certainly ask you for a tip. It might be the security guard at your hotel, a museum guide or a car park attendant. Some foreigners get upset at such requests, thinking that these people get a salary anyway and 'what right do they have to demand a tip?' But then ask yourself what you would do if you earned US$1 per day in a country where a soft drink costs US$0.25.

Men you deal with will also greatly appreciate small gifts such as a pack of cigarettes (women almost never smoke), but make sure it's a foreign brand of cigarettes. People will be insulted if you give Vietnamese cigarettes. The 555 brand (said to be Ho Chi Minh's favourite) is popular, as are most US brands. If you run out in Vietnam, don't worry – every street corner seems to have a little stand selling foreign cigarettes, sometimes for less than you paid duty-free!

It is considered proper to make a small donation at the end of a visit to a pagoda, especially if the monk has shown you around; most pagodas have contribution boxes for this purpose.

Bargaining

Always bargain in dong – then it is clear to everyone involved in the transaction what you are paying relative to what everything else in the country costs.

Remember, in Asia 'face' is important. Bargaining should be good-natured – smile, don't scream and argue. Many Westerners seem to take bargaining too seriously, and get offended if they don't get the goods for less than half the original asking price. In some cases you will be able to get a 50% discount, at other times only 10%, but by no means should you get angry during the bargaining process. And once the money is accepted, the deal is done – if you harbour hard feelings because you later find out that someone else got it cheaper, the only one you are hurting is yourself.

Consumer Taxes

On all goods you pay, the marked or stated price includes any relevant taxes. Only in some hotels and restaurants is there an additional 10% tax or service charge, and this should be made clear to you from the beginning (ask if not sure).

WHEN TO GO

Visitors should take into account that around Tet, the colourful Vietnamese New Year celebration which falls in late January or early February, flights into, out of and around the country are likely to be booked solid, and accommodation can be almost impossible to find. The New Year festival is more than just a one-day event – it goes on for at least a week. For at least a week before and two weeks after Tet you are likely to encounter some difficulties in booking hotels and flights; this applies also to the whole of eastern Asia.

WHAT TO BRING

Bring as little as possible. Many travellers try to bring everything and the kitchen sink. Keep in mind that you can and will buy things in Vietnam, so don't burden yourself with a lot of unnecessary junk.

Nevertheless, there are things you will want to bring from home. But the first thing to consider is what kind of bag you will use to carry all your goods.

Backpacks are the easiest type of bag to carry and a frameless or internal-frame pack is the easiest to manage on buses and trains. Packs that close with a zipper can usually be secured with a padlock. Of course, any pack can be slit open with a razor blade, but a padlock will usually prevent pilfering by hotel staff and baggage handlers at airports. A cable lock (or loop cable with lock) can be used to secure the backpack on buses and trains (pack snatchers are a serious problem).

A daypack can be handy. Leave your main luggage at the hotel or the left-luggage room in train stations. A beltpack is OK for maps, extra film and other miscellanea, but don't use it for valuables such as your travellers' cheques and passport, as it's an easy target for pickpockets.

If you don't want to use a backpack, a shoulder bag is much easier to carry than a suitcase. Some cleverly designed shoulder bags can also double as backpacks by re-arranging a few straps. Forget suitcases.

Inside? Lightweight and compact are two words that should be etched in your mind when you're deciding what to bring. Saw the handle off your toothbrush if you have to – anything to keep the weight down! You only need two sets of clothes – one to wear and one to wash. Dark coloured clothing is preferred because it doesn't show the dirt – white clothes will force you to do laundry daily. You will, no doubt, be buying clothes along the way – you can find some real bargains in Vietnam and neighbouring countries. However, don't believe sizes – 'large' in Asia is often equivalent to 'medium' in the West.

Nylon running or sports shoes are best – comfortable, washable and lightweight. Sandals are appropriate footwear in the tropical heat – even Ho Chi Minh wore them during his public appearances. Rubber thongs are somewhat less appropriate for formal occasions, but are nevertheless commonly worn in the south. In the north, many people will laugh at foreigners wearing rubber thongs (even if the laughers are wearing thongs themselves).

A Swiss army knife (even if not made in Switzerland) comes in handy, but you don't need one with 27 separate functions. Basically, you need one small sharp blade, a can opener and bottle opener – a built-in magnifying glass or backscratcher isn't necessary.

The secret of successful packing is plastic bags or nylon 'stuff bags' – they keep things not only separate and clean but also dry.

The following is a checklist of things you might consider packing. You can delete whatever you like from this list (though unlike on a computer, there will be no warning like 'Are you sure?'). If you do forget to bring some 'essential' item, most likely it can be bought in Vietnam, at least in Ho Chi Minh City and Hanoi.

Passport, visa, documents (vaccination certificate, diplomas, marriage licence photocopy, student ID card), money, money belt, air ticket, address book, name cards, extra visa photos, calculator (for currency conversions), Swiss army knife, camera and accessories, spare camera battery, colour slide film, video camera and blank tapes, radio, Walkman and rechargeable batteries, battery recharger (220 volt), reading material, padlock, cable lock (to secure luggage on trains), sunglasses, contact lens solution, alarm clock, leakproof water bottle, razor, razor blades, shaving cream, sewing kit, spoon, sunhat, sunscreen (UV lotion), toilet paper, tampons, toothbrush, toothpaste, dental floss, deodorant, shampoo, laundry detergent, underwear, socks, thongs, nail clipper, tweezers, mosquito repellent, insecticide, moist towelettes, vitamins, laxative, Lomotil, condoms, contraceptives, special medications you use and medical kit (see the Health section).

If you'll be doing any cycling, bring all necessary safety equipment (helmet, reflectors, mirrors, etc) as well as an inner tube repair kit.

A final thought: airlines do lose bags from time to time – you've got a much better chance of it not being yours if it is tagged with your name and address *inside* the bag as well as outside. Other tags can always fall off or be removed.

Clothing

Clothing is very cheap and abundant in Vietnam, so don't be concerned about bringing everything from abroad. The only problem might be in finding large Western sizes.

To the relief of backpackers, Vietnamese are less formal in dress than in many neighbouring countries (they can't afford the tailored suits and dresses yet). If you see a man walking around wearing a tie, he's more likely to be a Chinese businessman than a local.

Wearing short pants is generally considered rude in most parts of Vietnam, and this particularly applies to women. Until very recently, Vietnamese women never wore shorts in public, even when labouring in the rice paddies under the sweltering sun. But times are changing, especially in go-go Saigon, where Western trends are copied first before spreading around the country. Since about 1994, young women have started wearing shorts in Saigon and then in Hanoi, a fashion no doubt copied from Western tourists. At first the shorts were fairly conservative, but lately the styles have grown more bold. As for the Vietnamese men, short shorts are not on but the baggy Bermuda type have started to gain popularity. However, you are likely to see people wearing shorts only in major cities that see a lot of tourist traffic. Elsewhere, it is still regarded as indecent and that particularly applies to hill tribe areas such as the Central Highlands and far north.

For women, two-piece swimsuits are considered OK, but skimpy bikinis are pushing the limits. At hotel swimming pools frequented by foreigners, bikinis are now acceptable, though the locals may do a bit of staring. However, public beaches tend to be more conservative.

As for public nudity, it's just not acceptable anywhere in the country, not even beaches or hot springs resorts. It will be some years – if ever – before Vietnam can compete with the French Riviera or the Australian Sunshine Coast in this regard.

Footware Like the Chinese and Japanese, Vietnamese are obsessed with clean floors, and it's usual to remove shoes when entering somebody's home. If you are entering a 'shoes off' home, your host will provide a pair of slippers. Shoes must be removed inside most Buddhist temples, but this is not universal so watch what others do. If a bunch of shoes are piled up near the doorway, you should pay heed.

Definitely not recommended are the hill-climbing boots with 25 eyelets on each side. These may be great for mountain climbing, but you will regret them at every private home, temple and even mini-hotel where shoes should be removed. The often hot weather and need to take shoes off frequently would argue for wearing slip-off thongs or sandals. Just make sure that you buy a comfortable pair that you can walk in and which won't fall off when you ride on a motorbike.

One innovative type of sandal which you can easily purchase in Bangkok (but not yet in Vietnam) is fastened to your feet with Velcro straps, secure but easy to remove.

If you have particularly large feet, finding shoes to fit you could be difficult in Vietnam. For the average Western tourist, this will probably not be a problem.

TOURIST OFFICES
Local Tourist Offices
Vietnam's tourist offices are not like those found in capitalist countries. If you were to visit a government-run tourist office in Australia, Western Europe, Japan or decidedly free market Hong Kong, you'd get lots of free colourful, glossy brochures, maps and helpful advice on transport, places to stay, where to book tours and so on. Such tourist offices make no profit – indeed, they are big money losers, though they may be supported by a tax on travel agencies or hotels which benefit from the tourist office's services.

Vietnam's tourist offices operate on a different philosophy. They are government-owned enterprises whose primary interest is earning a profit. In fact, they are among the most profitable hard-currency cash cows the Vietnamese government has. Don't come here looking for freebies; even the colourful brochures and maps – when they have them – are for sale.

Vietnam Tourism (Tong Cong Ty Du Lich Viet Nam) and Ho Chi Minh City's Saigon Tourist (Cong Ty Du Lich Thanh Pho Ho Chi Minh) are the best examples of this genre. These large, state-run organisations are responsible for all aspects of a tourist's stay in Vietnam – arranging everything from visa extensions, accommodation, transport, guides and various kinds of tours, including to Cambodia.

Vietnam Tourism and Saigon Tourist can handle many of the bureaucratic headaches that come with travel in Vietnam, but they have neither the inclination nor indeed the staff to keep tabs on you. The local lowdown on both bodies and their functioning is listed in the Ho Chi Minh City and Hanoi chapters.

Every province has some sort of provincial tourism authority with which Vietnam Tourism coordinates its activities. As a result, if you book a tour to Danang with Vietnam Tourism, you'll have a Vietnam Tourism guide as well as a Quang Nam-Danang Province Tourism guide (in addition to a driver) – quite an entourage! Because every organisation in Vietnam – from the Foreign Ministry on down to the local taxi drivers – desperately wants US dollars, it is entirely possible to bypass Vietnam Tourism by working directly with either provincial tourism authorities or the budding free market travel agencies. Addresses of these organisations are listed under Information in the capital city of each province.

Overseas Reps

Vietnam's government tourist offices maintain representatives overseas at the following locations:

France
> Vietnam Tourism, 4 Rue Cherubini, 75002, Paris (☎ (01) 42 86 86 37; fax 42 60 43 32)
> Saigon Tourist, 24 Rue des Bernadins, 75005, Paris (☎ 40 51 03 02; fax 43 25 05 70)

Germany
> Saigon Tourist, 24 Dudenstrasse 78 W, 1000 Berlin 61 (☎ (030) 7865056; fax 7865596)

Japan
> Saigon Tourist, IDI 6th floor, Crystal Building, 1-2, Kanda Awaji-cho, Chiyoda-ku, Tokyo 101 (☎ (03) 3258-5931; fax 3253-6819)

Singapore
> Vietnam Tourism, 101 Upper Cross St, No 02-44 People's Park Centre, Singapore 0105 (☎ 532-3130; fax 532-2952; pager 601-3914)
> Saigon Tourist, 131 Tanglin Rd, Tudor Court, Singapore 1024 (☎ 735-1433; fax 735-1508)

USEFUL ORGANISATIONS
Chamber of Commerce

Vietcochamber, the Chamber of Commerce & Industry, is supposed to initiate and facilitate contacts between foreign business people and Vietnamese companies. They may also be able to help with receiving and extending business visas. Vietcochamber publishes a listing of government companies and how to contact them. They have offices in Ho Chi Minh City, Hanoi and Danang.

Non-governmental Organisations

There are various non-governmental churches, humanitarian aid organisations and the like working in Vietnam. One organisation, based in the USA, which helps the many amputees and war cripples in Vietnam is Vietnam Assistance for the Handicapped (☎ (703) 847-9582; fax 448-8207), PO Box 6554, McLean, VA 22106, USA.

Orderly Departure Programme

The Ho Chi Minh City offices of the Orderly Departure Programme (ODP) are at 184 Nguyen Thi Minh Khai St (Pasteur St), across Le Duan Blvd from Notre Dame Cathedral. This is a UN programme through which Vietnamese seeking to emigrate can do so without floating around the South China Sea in small boats.

Processing of emigration requests made via the ODP is a complex process and the vast majority of applications are now rejected. The waiting list just to get an interview assures that it will be years before every current application can be examined. Tourists are sometimes asked to help expedite the processing of ODP cases, many of which have been pending since the early 1980s. In most cases there is little to nothing you can do.

BUSINESS HOURS & HOLIDAYS

Vietnamese rise early (and consider sleeping in to be a sure indication of illness). Offices, museums and many shops open between 7 and 8 am (depending on the season – things open a tad earlier in the summer) and close between 4 and 5 pm. Lunch is taken very seriously, and virtually everything shuts down for 1½ hours between noon and 1.30 pm. Government workers tend to take longer breaks, so figure on getting nothing done from 11.30 am to 2 pm.

Most government offices are open on Saturday until noon. Sunday is a holiday. Most museums are closed on Mondays. Temples are usually open all day every day. Vietnamese tend to eat their meals by the clock regardless of whether or not they are hungry, and disrupting someone's meal schedule is considered very rude. This means, for example, that you don't visit people during lunch (unless invited). It also means that if you hire somebody for the whole day (a cyclo driver, a guide, etc) you must take a lunch break by noon and dinner by 5 pm. Delaying the lunch break until 1 pm will earn you a reputation as a sadistic employer.

Many small privately owned shops, restaurants and street stalls stay open seven days a week, often until late at night – they need the money.

Lunar Calendar

The Vietnamese lunar calendar closely resembles the Chinese one. Year 1 of the Vietnamese lunar calendar corresponds to 2637 BC, and each lunar month has 29 or 30 days, resulting in years with 355 days. Approximately every third year is a leap year; an extra month is added between the third and fourth months to keep the lunar year in sync with the solar year. If this weren't done, you'd end up having the seasons gradually rotate around the lunar year, playing havoc with all elements of life linked to the agricultural seasons. To find out the Gregorian (solar) date corresponding to a lunar date, check any Vietnamese or Chinese calendar.

Instead of dividing time into centuries, the Vietnamese calendar uses units of 60 years called *hoi*. Each hoi consists of six 10-year cycles *(can)* and five 12-year cycles *(ky)*. The name of each year in the cycle consists of the *can* name followed by the *ky* name, a system which never produces the same combination twice.

The 10 heavenly stems of the *can* cycle are as follows:

Giap	water in nature
At	water in the home
Binh	lighted fire
Dinh	latent fire
Mau	wood
Ky	wood prepared to burn
Canh	metal
Tan	wrought metal
Nham	virgin land
Quy	cultivated land

The 12 zodiacal stems of the *ky* are as follows:

Ty	rat
Suu	cow
Dan	tiger

Vietnamese Zodiac

If you want to know your sign in the Vietnamese zodiac, look up your year of birth in the following chart (future years included so you can know what's coming). However, it's a little more complicated than this because Vietnamese astrology goes by the lunar calendar. The Vietnamese Lunar New Year usually falls in late January or early February, so the first month will be included in the year before.

Rat	1924	1936	1948	1960	1972	1984	1996
Ox/Cow	1925	1937	1949	1961	1973	1985	1997
Tiger	1926	1938	1950	1962	1974	1986	1998
Rabbit	1927	1939	1951	1963	1975	1987	1999
Dragon	1928	1940	1952	1964	1976	1988	2000
Snake	1929	1941	1953	1965	1977	1989	2001
Horse	1930	1942	1954	1966	1978	1990	2002
Goat	1931	1943	1955	1967	1979	1991	2003
Monkey	1932	1944	1956	1968	1980	1992	2004
Rooster	1933	1945	1957	1969	1981	1993	2005
Dog	1934	1946	1958	1970	1982	1994	2006
Pig	1935	1947	1959	1971	1983	1995	2007

Mau	rabbit
Thin	dragon
Ty	snake
Ngo	horse
Mui	goat
Than	monkey
Dau	rooster
Tuat	dog
Hoi	pig

Public Holidays

Politics affects everything, including public holidays. As an indication of Vietnam's new openness, Christmas, New Year, Tet (the Lunar New Year) and Buddha's birthday have been added as holidays after a 15-year lapse. The following are Vietnam's public holidays:

1 January
New Year's Day (Tet Duong Lich)
1st to 7th days of the 1st moon (late January to mid-February)
Tet (Tet Nguyen Dan), the Vietnamese Lunar New Year
3 February
Anniversary of the Founding of the Vietnamese Communist Party (Thanh Lap Dang CSVN) The Vietnamese Communist Party was founded on this date in 1930.
30 April
Liberation Day (Saigon Giai Phong) The date on which Saigon surrendered is commemorated nationwide as Liberation Day. Many cities and provinces also commemorate the anniversary of the date in March or April of 1975 on which they were 'liberated' by the North Vietnamese Army.
1 May
International Workers' Day (Quoc Te Lao Dong) Also known as May Day, this falls back to back with Liberation Day giving everyone a two-day holiday.
19 May
Ho Chi Minh's Birthday (Sinh Nhat Bac Ho) Ho Chi Minh is said to have been born on this date in 1890 near Vinh, Nghe An Province.
8th day of the 4th moon (usually June)
Buddha's Birthday (Dan Sinh)
2 September
National Day (Quoc Khanh) This commemorates the proclamation in Hanoi of the Declaration of Independence of the Democratic Republic of Vietnam by Ho Chi Minh on 2 September 1945.
25 December
Christmas *(Giang Sinh)*

Until 1990, 3 September (the anniversary of Ho Chi Minh's death) was a public holiday. The holiday was eliminated when officials admitted that Ho actually died on 2 September 1969. The reason for reporting the date of his death as 3 September was so that it wouldn't coincide with National Day.

CULTURAL EVENTS

Special prayers are held at Vietnamese and Chinese pagodas on days when the moon is either full or just the thinnest sliver. Many Buddhists eat only vegetarian food on these days, which, according to the Chinese lunar calendar, fall on the 14th and 15th days of the month and on the last (29th or 30th) day of the month just ending and the 1st day of the new month.

The following major religious festivals are listed by lunar date:

1st to 7th days of the 1st moon
Tet (Tet Nguyen Dan), the Vietnamese New Year, is the most important festival of the year and falls in late January or early February. This public holiday is officially three days, but many people take off an entire week.

Tet is a time for family reunions, the payment of debts, the avoidance of arguments, special foods, new clothes, flowers and new beginnings. Great importance is attached to starting the year properly because it is believed that the first day and first week of the new year will determine one's fortunes for the rest of the year. Homes are decorated with sprigs of plum tree blossoms *(cay mai)*.

The first pre-Tet ceremony, *Le Tao Quan*, is designed to send the Spirit of the Hearth (Tao Quan) off to report to the Jade Emperor (Ngoc Hoang) in a positive frame of mind. A New Year's Tree (Cay Neu) is constructed to ward off evil spirits. Later, a sacrifice (Tat Nien) is offered to deceased family members. Finally, at midnight, the old year is ushered out and the new welcomed in with the ritual of *Giao Thua*, which is celebrated both in homes and in pagodas. Firecrackers were used until 1995 (when the government banned them) to commemorate the new year and welcome back the Spirit of the Hearth. Now only gongs and drums are used for this purpose. The first visitor of New Year's Day is considered very important and great care is taken to ensure that they be happy, wealthy and of high status. For this reason foreigners are likely to receive an invite!

A seasonal favourite is *banh chung*, which is sticky rice, yellow beans, pig fat and spices wrapped in leaves and boiled for half a day.

Visitors to Vietnam around Tet should take into account that flights into, out of and around the country are likely to be booked solid and accommodation impossible to find. Ditto for all of north-east Asia (China, Hong Kong, Macau, Taiwan and Korea).

5th day of the 3rd moon
Holiday of the Dead (Thanh Minh) People pay solemn visits to graves of deceased relatives – specially tidied up a few days before – and make offerings of food, flowers, joss sticks and votive papers.

8th day of the 4th moon
Buddha's Birth, Enlightenment & Death This day is celebrated at pagodas and temples, which, like many private homes, are festooned with lanterns. Processions are held in the evening.

5th day of the 5th moon
Summer Solstice Day (Doan Ngu) Offerings are made to spirits, ghosts and the God of Death to ward off epidemics. Human effigies are burned to satisfy the requirements of the God of Death for souls to staff his army.

15th day of the 7th moon
Wandering Souls Day (Trung Nguyen) This is the second-largest festival of the year. Offerings of food and gifts are made in homes and pagodas for the wandering souls of the forgotten dead.

15th day of the 8th moon
Mid-Autumn Festival (Trung Thu) This festival is celebrated with moon cakes of sticky rice filled with such things as lotus seeds, watermelon seeds, peanuts, the yolks of duck eggs, raisins and sugar. Colourful lanterns in the form of boats, unicorns, dragons, lobsters, carp, hares, toads, etc, are carried by children in an evening procession accompanied by drums and cymbals.

28th day of the 9th moon
Confucius' Birthday

POST & TELECOMMUNICATIONS

International postal service from Vietnam is not unreasonably priced when compared with most countries. However, international telecommunications charges are among the highest in the world – unless you have some matter of earthshaking importance, it's better to wait until you reach Hong Kong, Bangkok or Singapore to call the loved ones at home.

Post offices all over the country usually keep long hours, about 6 am to 8 pm, including weekends and public holidays (even Tet).

Postal Rates
Domestic letters cost 400d (less than US$0.04). To send a postcard to Europe costs US$0.55; to the USA it's US$0.45; to Australia, US$0.40; to east Asia (Hong Kong, Taiwan, etc), the rate is US$0.40.

Stamp values have had a difficult time keeping pace with inflation: until a few years ago, 50d stamps were the highest denomination available. Since there is no space on a 10-gram letter for many dozens of stamps (and all those stamps might weigh several tens of grams, necessitating additional postage, which would make the letter yet heavier, requiring more stamps, and so on), the post office began using postal meters, which were issued only to major post offices. Fortunately, inflation has slowed down considerably and larger-denomination stamps now make it possible to send letters with real stamps rather than a metered number.

International postal rates in Vietnam might not seem expensive to you, but just think about how the Vietnamese feel. The tariffs are so out of line with most salaries that locals *literally* cannot afford to send letters to their friends and relatives abroad. If you would like to correspond with a Vietnamese whom you meet during your visit, try leaving them enough stamps to cover postage for several letters, explaining that the stamps were extras you didn't use and would be of no value to you at home. A traveller writes:

Before leaving Vietnam I did buy US$15 of Vietnamese stamps. I now have many friends there and sending a letter to foreigners is amazingly expensive for them. So whenever I write to them, I include a few stamps in the envelope for their replies. They have told me that this was greatly appreciated.

Sending Mail
Items mailed from anywhere other than large towns and cities are likely to take over a month to arrive at their destinations. Airmail services from Ho Chi Minh City and Hanoi take approximately ten days to most Western countries provided the mail

readily passes 'security' (is not considered subversive).

Vietnamese stamps often have insufficient gum on them; use the paste provided in little pots at post offices. And make sure that the clerk cancels them *while you watch* so that someone for whom the stamps are worth a day's salary does not soak them off and throw your letters away.

Foreigners sending parcels out of Vietnam sometimes have had to deal with time-consuming inspections of the contents, but this is happening less often now. The most important thing is to keep the parcel small. If it's documents only, you should be OK. Sending out video tapes and the like can be problematic.

Express Mail Service (EMS) is available to most developed countries and a few less-developed ones. It's perhaps twice as fast to use EMS than to use regular airmail (taking as little as four days), but the big advantage is that the letter or small parcel will be registered. There is also domestic EMS between Ho Chi Minh City and Hanoi promising next-day delivery, and the service exists to some smaller cities such as Danang and Nha Trang. The domestic EMS rates are very reasonable: US$0.35 for a letter weighing under 20 grams.

Private Couriers DHL Worldwide Express offers express document delivery from the Ho Chi Minh City GPO (☎ 231525) and from their main office (☎ 446203, 444268; fax 445387) at 253 Hoang Van Thu St, Tan Binh District, Ho Chi Minh City. In Hanoi, DHL (☎ 236061, 267020) can be found at 49 Nguyen Thai Hoc St, Ba Dinh District. Other phone numbers for collection include: Cantho (☎ 25305), Dalat (☎ 25586), Danang (☎ 21327), Dong Nai (☎ 22046), Haiphong (☎ 42596), Nam Dinh (☎ 49382), Nha Trang (☎ 23989), Quang Ninh (☎ 25135) and Vung Tau (☎ 52343).

The main Federal Express office (☎ 290747; fax 290477) is at 1 Nguyen Hau St, District 1, Ho Chi Minh City. Outside of Ho Chi Minh City you can call Federal Express at their toll-free number (☎ (018) 290747).

United Parcel Service (☎ 243597; fax 243596) has a representative at the GPO, 2 Cong Xa Paris St, District 1, Ho Chi Minh City.

TNT Express Worldwide has its head office (☎ 446460, 446476, 446478; fax 446592) at 56 Truong Son St, Ward 2, Tan Binh District, Ho Chi Minh City.

Another alternative is Airborne Express (☎ 294310, 294315; fax 292961), with offices at two locations in Ho Chi Minh City: the GPO at 2 Cong Xa Paris St, and the main office (☎ 292976) at 80C Nguyen Du St, District 1.

The rates given below were quoted by Federal Express for document and parcel delivery (prices in US dollars). Other carriers can be expected to charge similar prices.

Document Service (International)							
Zone 1	Zone 2	Zone 3	Zone 4	Zone 5	Zone 6	Zone 7	Zone 8
Thailand	Japan	Australia	USA	UK	Spain	Brazil	Africa
34	39	42	48	49	54	56	60

Small Parcel Service (International)							
1st 500 g	40	47	48	53	54	60	66	71
Add 500 g	5	8	8	11	12.50	14	17	17

Domestic Service	
Major Cities	Other Cities
1st 500 g	20	30
Add 500 g	5	5

Freight Forwarders

Planning on shipping home Vietnamese furniture or a used car? Or will you move your entire household and belongings to Vietnam for a long stay? For this you need the services of a freight forwarder. One to contact is Sea & Air Freight International (SAFI), which has offices in both Saigon and Hanoi. The head office (☎ 241814; fax 231679) is at 3-5 Nguyen Hue St, District 1, Ho Chi Minh City. The Hanoi office (☎ 268171; fax 234937) is at 25A Phan Dinh Phung St, Ba Dinh District, Hanoi.

In Ho Chi Minh City, you could also contact Saigon Van (☎ 350396, 352676; fax 350397), 6E An Binh, District 5. This company is associated with the international Atlas Van Lines chain.

Receiving Mail

Every city, town, village and rural subdistrict in Vietnam has some sort of post office. All post offices are marked with the words 'Buu Dien'.

Mail delivery is at times stunningly fast and reliable, but for unknown reasons it can suddenly go haywire. From personal experience we've found that letters and parcels airmailed from Australia to Vietnam can be delivered in as little as four days or as long as 10 months! Prolonged delays are almost certainly due to the Vietnamese security apparatus inspecting any documents which have been deemed 'suspicious'.

Reliability is greatly enhanced if your envelope or package contains nothing that somebody would want to steal. Normal letters and postcards should be fine. Then again, we know one person who had all his New Year greeting cards confiscated (figure that one out). Thick envelopes are likely to be opened by censors and anything deemed 'subversive' will be removed. One of our correspondents in Saigon reports that his mail was opened recently and newspaper clippings about the Vietnamese economy were removed.

The poste restante windows work well at the GPOs in both Hanoi and Ho Chi Minh City. Elsewhere, it's far less certain. Foreign-ers now have to pay a US$0.04 service charge for each letter they pick up from poste restante.

Receiving even a small package from abroad can be a headache, and large ones will be a migraine. If you're lucky, customs will clear the package and the clerks at the post office will simply let you take it. If you're unlucky, customs will demand an inspection, at which you must be present. In that case, the post office will give you a written notice, which you take to the customs office along with your passport. In Ho Chi Minh City, the customs office for incoming parcels is in the rear of the GPO building. The procedure requires that you fill out numerous forms, pay some small fees (around US$1 in total), hand over your passport and hope that you eventually get it back along with the parcel. Your package will be opened in front of you and inspected, but don't think that's all there is to it. Your parcel then gets packed up again, and disappears into some other office along with your forms, passport and another fee. You take a seat in the waiting room, and after a few hours somebody will hopefully call your name. At that point, all your possessions should be returned to you, along with some more forms which you must get stamped before you can leave the building.

If you are particularly unlucky, customs may decide that you must pay import duty. If your parcel contains books, documents, video tapes, computer disks, or other 'dangerous' goods, it's possible that a further inspection will be required. This could take anywhere from a few days to a few weeks. Presumably, you will not have to spend the entire time in the waiting room while this is being done.

Telephone

International and domestic long-distance calls can be booked at many hotels, but this is expensive.

It's somewhat less expensive to book long-distance phone calls from the post office. For operator-assisted calls, you will be charged for three minutes even if you only talk for one minute, plus the rate per minute will be higher. As in most countries, the cheapest way to make a long-distance call is to dial direct.

International Calls Vietnam's international telephone service has improved in recent years but still leaves much to be desired. International calls from Vietnam are ridiculously expensive and, outside of major cities, unreliable. To be fair, the phone company has lowered rates slightly in the past two years, but international rates are easily two to five times higher than in Western countries. With the total monopoly enjoyed by the DGPT (Directorate General of Posts & Telecommunications), price decreases will come slowly and grudgingly.

Foreigners are not permitted to make international reverse-charge calls. However, Vietnamese nationals can. Why? Because the DGPT earns less from a reverse-charge call than from calls paid for in Vietnam. However, since most Vietnamese cannot possibly afford to pay for an international call, they are permitted to call collect to their overseas relatives (the assumption being that those relatives will probably send them money).

This means that if your credit cards or travellers' cheques are stolen, you will not be able to call collect to the issuing company to report the loss. At best this is a major nuisance – it could prove disastrous if you get robbed of all your cash and need to call abroad to get some help.

Calling from most countries to Vietnam will be about 50% cheaper than calling from Vietnam to abroad. So if you plan to talk more than a few minutes, it's best to make a very brief call abroad and ask the other party to call you back.

The cheapest and simplest way by far to make an international direct-dial (IDD) call is to buy a telephone card, known in Vietnam as a 'UniphoneKad'. They are on sale at the telephone company. UniphoneKads can only be used in special telephones, which are found mainly in Ho Chi Minh City, usually in the lobbies of major hotels. The cards are issued in four denominations: 30,000d

(US$2.72), 60,000d (US$5.45), 150,000d (US$10.90) and 300,000d (US$27.27). The 150,000 and 300,000d cards can be used to make both domestic and international calls, while the 30,000d and 60,000d cards will work only for domestic calls.

To make an IDD call, you must first dial the international prefix (00) followed by the country code, area code (if any) and the local number. Note that in many countries (Australia, for example), area codes start with a zero, but this zero must not be dialled when calling internationally. So to call Melbourne (area code 03) in Australia (country code 61) from Vietnam, you would dial 00-61-3-9123-4567. Some useful country codes include:

Australia-61, Belgium-32, Canada-1, Denmark-45, France-33, Germany-49, Hong Kong-852, Italy-39, Japan-81, Korea (South)-82, Malaysia-60, Netherlands-31, New Zealand-64, Norway-47, Philippines-63, Singapore-65, Spain-34, Sweden-46, Switzerland-41, Taiwan-886, Thailand-66, UK-44, USA-1, Vietnam-84

Calls are charged by one-minute increments; any fraction of a minute is charged as a full minute. From our own experience, we have found that international calls cost more than the advertised rate (perhaps there is some sort of hidden tax) – this applies even when you use a phone card. There is only a 10% discount for calls placed between 11 pm and 7 am. The full daytime rate for making IDD calls is as follows (prices in US dollars):

Country	1st min	Each additional min
Africa	5.20	4.00
Australia	3.80	2.95
Cambodia & Laos	3.10	2.60
Canada	3.90	3.00
China	3.80	2.95
Eastern Europe	3.90	3.00
Hong Kong	3.10	2.60
India	4.40	3.40
Indonesia	4.40	3.40
Ireland	4.50	3.70
Japan	3.90	3.00
Korea (South)	3.80	2.95
Malaysia	3.10	2.60

New Zealand	4.50	3.70
Philippines	4.40	3.40
Singapore	3.10	2.60
South America	5.20	4.00
Taiwan	3.80	2.95
Thailand	3.10	2.60
UK	4.40	3.40
USA	3.90	3.00
Western Europe	4.40	3.40

Domestic Calls Local calls can usually be made from any hotel or restaurant phone and are usually free.

Domestic direct-dialling is known as 'subscriber trunk dialling' (STD). To place an STD call, you must first dial the national trunk prefix (01) followed by the area code and local number. For example, to call Hanoi (area code 4), you would dial 01-4-123456. Area codes in Vietnam are assigned according to province. See the Provinces & Area Codes map for current area codes.

Ho Chi Minh City produces its own version of the Yellow Pages, in which you can look up services by subject. For example, to find the phone numbers of hotels look under *khach san*. You can find telephone books at most hotel reception desks, and you can also purchase these directories from the phone company offices.

Domestic long-distance calls are reasonably priced but will be cheapest if you dial direct. You can save up to 20% by calling at night (10 pm to 5 am).

An STD call between Hanoi and Ho Chi Minh City at the full daytime rate will cost US$0.45 per minute. An operator-assisted call would cost US$0.82 per minute but there is a three-minute minimum.

Fax, Telex & Telegraph

Most GPOs and many tourist hotels in Vietnam offer domestic and international fax, telegraph and telex services. Hotels are likely to charge more than the post office.

Fax machines are rapidly proliferating in Vietnam. Major hotels and many companies doing international business already have them. The main post offices in Ho Chi Minh City, Danang and Hanoi offer fax services

too. The cost for faxes is based on zone. The zones and rates (in US dollars) at the GPO are as follows:

Zone 1 – Laos, Cambodia, Hong Kong, Singapore, Malaysia
Zone 2 – China, Taiwan, Korea, Australia
Zone 3 – Eastern Europe, Japan, Canada, USA
Zone 4 – Western Europe, Philippines, India, Indonesia
Zone 5 – New Zealand, Pacific Islands, Ireland, Middle East, Africa, South America

Zone	1st page	Each extra
1	4.80	4.05
2	5.70	4.42
3	6.00	4.72
4	6.82	5.25
5	6.90	5.73

Telex is old technology which has become nearly extinct in the West due to fax machines and electronic mail. Vietnam still has telex machines, but they are dying off quickly and are used mainly by banks. Nevertheless, you can still easily send telexes from major post offices in Vietnam, though this service is useless if the person you need to reach does not have a telex number. Telex messages are charged by the minute, with a one-minute minimum. Given the slow transmission speed of telex (about 50 words per minute), you'd best keep the message short. As with fax, the cost for telex transmission is based on zone. See the foregoing fax information to understand the zone system. The rates (in US dollars) are as follows:

Zone	1 min	2 min	3 min	Each extra
1	2.60	4.70	6.80	2.10
2	2.90	5.30	7.70	2.40
3	3.10	5.70	8.30	2.60
4	3.40	6.30	9.20	2.90
5	4.00	7.50	11	3.50

The telegraph windows of major GPOs are open 24 hours a day seven days a week. Telegrams are charged by the word (including each word of the address) and there is a seven-word minimum charge. The cost per word varies from US$0.30 to US$0.60 depending on country of destination.

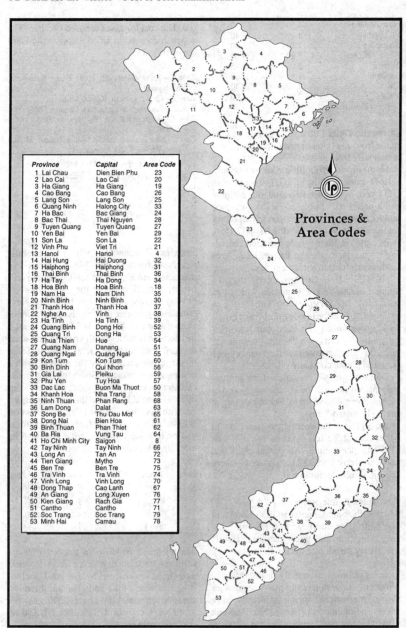

Province	Capital	Area Code
1 Lai Chau	Dien Bien Phu	23
2 Lao Cai	Lao Cai	20
3 Ha Giang	Ha Giang	19
4 Cao Bang	Cao Bang	26
5 Lang Son	Lang Son	25
6 Quang Ninh	Halong City	33
7 Ha Bac	Bac Giang	24
8 Bac Thai	Thai Nguyen	28
9 Tuyen Quang	Tuyen Quang	27
10 Yen Bai	Yen Bai	29
11 Son La	Son La	22
12 Vinh Phu	Viet Tri	21
13 Hanoi	Hanoi	4
14 Hai Hung	Hai Duong	32
15 Haiphong	Haiphong	31
16 Thai Binh	Thai Binh	36
17 Ha Tay	Ha Dong	34
18 Hoa Binh	Hoa Binh	18
19 Nam Ha	Nam Dinh	35
20 Ninh Binh	Ninh Binh	30
21 Thanh Hoa	Thanh Hoa	37
22 Nghe An	Vinh	38
23 Ha Tinh	Ha Tinh	39
24 Quang Binh	Dong Hoi	52
25 Quang Tri	Dong Ha	53
26 Thua Thien	Hue	54
27 Quang Nam	Danang	51
28 Quang Ngai	Quang Ngai	55
29 Kon Tum	Kon Tum	60
30 Binh Dinh	Qui Nhon	56
31 Gia Lai	Pleiku	59
32 Phu Yen	Tuy Hoa	57
33 Dac Lac	Buon Ma Thuot	50
34 Khanh Hoa	Nha Trang	58
35 Ninh Thuan	Phan Rang	68
36 Lam Dong	Dalat	63
37 Song Be	Thu Dau Mot	65
38 Dong Nai	Bien Hoa	61
39 Binh Thuan	Phan Thiet	62
40 Ba Ria	Vung Tau	64
41 Ho Chi Minh City	Saigon	8
42 Tay Ninh	Tay Ninh	66
43 Long An	Tan An	72
44 Tien Giang	Mytho	73
45 Ben Tre	Ben Tre	75
46 Tra Vinh	Tra Vinh	74
47 Vinh Long	Vinh Long	70
48 Dong Thap	Cao Lanh	67
49 An Giang	Long Xuyen	76
50 Kien Giang	Rach Gia	77
51 Cantho	Cantho	71
52 Soc Trang	Soc Trang	79
53 Minh Hai	Camau	78

Provinces & Area Codes

TIME

Vietnam, like Thailand, is seven hours ahead of GMT/UTC. Because it is so close to the equator, Vietnam does not have daylight-saving time (summer time). Thus, when it's noon in Hanoi or Ho Chi Minh City it is 10 pm the previous day in San Francisco, 1 am in New York, 5 am in London, 1 pm in Perth and 3 pm in Sydney. When the above-listed cities are on daylight-saving time, these times are one hour off.

ELECTRICITY

Electric current in Vietnam is mostly 220 volts at 50 Hertz (cycles), but often you'll still find 110 volts (also at 50 Hertz). Unfortunately, looking at the shape of the outlet on the wall gives no clue as to what voltage is flowing through the wires. In the south, most outlets are US-style flat pins. Despite the American-inspired design, the voltage is still likely to be 220 volts. In the north, most outlets are the Russian-inspired round pins and also *usually* carrying 220 volts. If the voltage is not marked on the socket try finding a lightbulb or appliance with the voltage written on it. All sockets are two-prong only – in no case will you find a third wire for ground (earth).

Much of the electrical wiring in Vietnam is improvised. Be especially careful in rural backwaters – exposed live wires are a fire hazard and offer opportunities to electrocute yourself.

In drought years, electricity outages increase sharply because hydroelectric power is used, and the situation is getting worse due to the increase in air-conditioners and power-hungry factories. There are plans to build a new power station in the Mekong Delta to alleviate this situation, but no one is sure just when that will occur. The north has long had considerable excess hydroelectric capacity, but consumerism has changed the picture and blackouts occasionally occur in summer when people start up the air-conditioners. A new power line opened in 1994 connecting the north and south has greatly alleviated the wintertime electricity shortages which formerly plagued Ho Chi Minh City.

In rural areas, power is usually supplied by diesel generators, which frequently are shut down and restarted. This means you should keep your torch (flashlight) handy. More seriously, it also means that there are probably frequent surges in the current. Sensitive electronic equipment should be shielded with a surge suppressor, or better yet, run on rechargeable batteries.

LAUNDRY

It is usually easy to find a hotel attendant who will get your laundry spotlessly clean (and perceptibly thinner) for the equivalent of a US dollar or two. Be sure that they have laundry detergent – in some of the poorer backwaters, people occasionally use friction alone to separate the dirt from the cloth (and often part of the cloth from the rest of the cloth). Allow at least a day and a half for washing and drying, especially in the wet season.

WEIGHTS & MEASURES

Vietnam uses the international metric system. For a metric conversion table, see the back of the book. In addition, there are two measurements for weight borrowed from the Chinese, the tael and the catty. A catty is 0.6 kg (1.32 pounds). There are 16 taels to the catty, so one tael is 37.5 grams (1.32 ounces). Gold is always sold by the tael.

Some Vietnamese words for measurements are:

gram	(same as English)
hectare	*hec-ta*
kg	(same as English)
km	*cay so*
litre	(same as English)
metre	*met*
metric	tonne *ton*
square metre	*met vuong*
tael	*luong*
catty	*can*

BOOKS & MAPS

A large number of English-language books about Vietnam have been published in the last three decades. They range from popular paperbacks to outstanding works of scholarship. Most focus on American involvement in Indochina (rather than on Vietnam itself), but quite a few also cover various aspects of Vietnamese culture, history, political development, etc. A sampling of the best are listed here.

People & Society

During the colonial period, French researchers wrote quite a number of works on Vietnam's cultural history and archaeology that remain unsurpassed. Several good ones on the Chams are *Les États Hinduisés d'Indochine et d'Indonésie* by Georges Coedes (Paris, 1928), *L'Art du Champa et Son Evolution* by Philippe Stern (Toulouse, 1942) and *Le Royaume du Champa* by Georges Maspero (Paris and Brussels, 1928). *Les Arts du Champa: Architecture et Sculpture* by Tran Ky Phuong, curator of the Cham Museum in Danang and Vietnam's foremost scholar of the Chams, was to be published in Paris in the early 1990s.

Cheap copies of *Vietnam, Civilisation & Culture* by Pierre Huard & Maurice Durand (Ecole Francaise d'Extreme-Orient) and *Ethnic Minorities in Vietnam* by Dang Nghiem Van, Chu Thai Son & Luu Hung (Foreign Language Publishing House, 1984) are readily available in Hanoi. Both give informative introductions to the diverse ethnic groups inhabiting Vietnam, though the latter book mixes ethnology with some silly propaganda. Also available in Hanoi is *Vietnam's Famous Ancient Pagodas* by Vo Van Tuong (Social Sciences Publishing House, 1992), with good colour photos and text in English, French, Chinese and Vietnamese.

Two collections of Vietnamese legends are *Land of Seagull and Fox* by Ruth Q Sun (Charles E Tuttle, Rutland, Vt, and Tokyo, 1967) and *Vietnamese Legends* by George F Schultz (Charles E Tuttle, Rutland, Vt, and Tokyo, 1965).

One of the most scholarly works on Caodaism is *Caodai Spiritism: A Study of Religion in Vietnamese Society* by Victor L Oliver (E J Brill, Leiden, 1976).

Vietnamese Studies is a series of books

published quarterly in both English and French by Xunhasaba (Hanoi). Each issue has a number of in-depth articles dealing with a particular subject, ranging from recent history to archaeology and ethnography. Histories and essays on political topics tend to be polemical.

Graham Greene's 1954 novel *The Quiet American*, which is set during the last days of French rule, is probably the most famous Western work of fiction on Vietnam. Much of the action takes place at Saigon's Continental Hotel and at the Caodai complex in Tay Ninh.

The Lover by Marguerite Duras is a fictional love story set in Saigon during the 1930s. The book has been made into a major motion picture.

Vietnam: Politics, Economics and Society by Melanie Beresford (Pinter Publishers, London and New York, 1988) gives a good overview of the aspects of post-reunification Vietnam mentioned in its title. You'll find out more than you ever wanted about life in the Red River Delta in *Hai Van: Life in a Vietnamese Commune* by François Houtard & Geneviève Lamercinier (Zed Books, London, 1984).

An excellent recent reference work is *Vietnam's Famous Ancient Pagodas (Viet nam Danh Lam Co Tu)*, which is written in Vietnamese, English, French and Chinese. The publisher is the Social Sciences Publishing House and you should be able to find copies in Hanoi and Ho Chi Minh City.

History

The Birth of Vietnam by Keith Weller Taylor (University of California Press, Berkeley, 1983) covers the country's early history.

The Vietnamese Gulag by Doan Van Toai (Simon & Schuster, New York, 1986) tells of one man's experiences in the post-reunification 're-education camps'.

An excellent little book by Ellen Hammer, *Vietnam: Yesterday and Today* (Holt, Rinehart & Winston, New York, 1966) is one of the few American works on Vietnam from the mid-'60s to have retained its usefulness. For a very readable account of Vietnamese history from prehistoric times until the fall of Saigon (with a focus on the American war) try Stanley Karnow's *Vietnam: A History* (Viking Press, New York, 1983), which was published as a companion volume to the American Public Broadcasting System series 'Vietnam: A Television History'. *The Socialist Republic of Vietnam* (Foreign Languages Publishing House, Hanoi, 1980) gives the pre-perestroika Hanoi line on Vietnam's history, economy, etc.

If you're having trouble keeping your dynasties, emperors and revolutionary patriots straight, Danny J Whitfield's solid *Historical and Cultural Dictionary of Vietnam* (Scarecrow Press, Metuchen, NJ, 1976) and William J Duiker's *Historical Dictionary of Vietnam* (Scarecrow Press, Metuchen, NJ and London, 1989) will be of great help. Duiker's book has a comprehensive bibliography in the back.

Vietnamese Nationalism *Vietnamese Anticolonialism 1885-1925* by David G Marr (University of California Press, Berkeley, Los Angeles and London, 1971) has become a classic in its field. *Tradition on Trial 1920-1945* (University of California Press, Berkeley, 1981) is another work by Marr, who is one of the most outstanding Western scholars of Vietnam (he is now at the Australian National University).

William J Duiker's *The Communist Road to Power in Vietnam* (Westview Press, Boulder, Colorado, 1981) and *The Rise of Nationalism in Vietnam 1900-1941* (Cornell University Press, Ithaca, NY, and London, 1976) trace the development of Vietnam's 20th-century anti-colonialist and nationalist movements.

A number of biographies of Ho Chi Minh have been written, including *Ho Chi Minh: A Political Biography* by Jean Lacouture (Random House, New York, 1968) and *Ho* by David Halberstam (Random House, New York, 1971).

Franco-Viet Minh War On this topic it's worth taking a look at Peter M Dunn's *The First Vietnam War* (C Hurst & Company,

London, 1985), or two works by Bernard B Fall: *Street Without Joy: Indochina at War 1946-54* (Stackpole Company, Harrisburg, Pa, 1961) and *Hell in a Very Small Place: The Siege of Dien Bien Phu* (Lippincott, Philadelphia, 1967).

American War The earliest days of US involvement in Indochina – when the OSS, predecessor of the CIA, was providing funding and weapons to Ho Chi Minh at the end of WW II – are recounted in *Why Vietnam?*, a riveting work by Archimedes L Patti (University of California Press, Berkeley, Los Angeles and London, 1980). Patti was the head of the OSS team in Vietnam and was at Ho Chi Minh's side when he declared Vietnam independent in 1945.

Three of the finest essays on the Vietnam War are collected in *The Real War* by Jonathan Schell (Pantheon Books, New York, 1987). An overview of the conflict is provided by George C Herring's *America's Longest War*, 2nd edition (Alfred A Knopf, New York, 1979 and 1986). *Fire in the Lake* by Frances Fitzgerald (Vintage Books, New York, 1972) is a superb history of American involvement in Vietnam; it received the Pulitzer Prize, the National Book Award and the Bancroft Prize for History.

A highly acclaimed biographical account of the US war effort is *A Bright Shining Lie: John Paul Vann and America in Vietnam* by Neil Sheehan (Random House, New York, 1988); it won both the Pulitzer Prize and the National Book Award. Another fine biography is Tim Bowden's *One Crowded Hour* (Angus & Robertson, 1988), which is the life of Australian film journalist Neil Davis. He shot some of the most famous footage of the war, including that of the North Vietnamese tank crashing through the gate of the Presidential Palace in Saigon in 1975.

Ellen J Hammer's *A Death in November* (E P Dutton, New York, 1987) tells of the US role in Diem's overthrow in 1963.

The Making of a Quagmire by David Halberstam (Ballantine Books, New York) is one of the best accounts of America's effort in the war during the early 1960s.

Two accounts of the fall of South Vietnam are *The Fall of Saigon* by David Butler (Simon & Schuster, New York, 1985) and *55 Days: The Fall of South Vietnam* by Alan Dawson (Prentice Hall, Englewood Cliffs, NJ, 1977).

Perhaps the best book about the fall of South Vietnam is *Decent Interval* by Frank Snepp. Except for pirated editions sold in Vietnam itself, it's out of print and for a very interesting reason. The author was the CIA's chief strategy analyst in Vietnam, but he broke his contract with the CIA by publishing this book (CIA agents are prohibited from publishing anything about their work). The US government sued Mr Snepp, and all the royalties which he earned from book sales were confiscated. Copies of the book can still be found in some public libraries though.

Highly recommended is *Brother Enemy* by Nayan Chanda (Asia Books, Macmillan, 1986). This is not actually a book about the war but about its immediate aftermath. Chanda was a correspondent for the *Far Eastern Economic Review* and was in Saigon when it fell.

An oft-cited analysis of where US military strategy in Vietnam went wrong is *On Strategy* by Colonel Harry G Summers Jr (Presidio Press, Novato, Calif, 1982, and Dell Publishing, New York, 1984). *The Pentagon Papers* (paperback version by Bantam Books, Toronto, New York and London, 1971), a massive, top-secret history of the US role in Indochina, was commissioned by Defence Secretary Robert McNamara in 1967 and published amid a great furore by the *New York Times* in 1971.

Australia Australia's involvement in the Vietnam War is covered in *Australia's Vietnam* (Allen & Unwin, Sydney, London and Boston, 1983), a collection of essays edited by Peter King; *Australia's War in Vietnam* by Frank Frost (Allen & Unwin, Sydney, London and Boston, 1987); Gregory Pemberton's *All the Way: Australia's Road to Vietnam* (Allen & Unwin, Sydney and Boston, 1987); *Desperate Praise: The Australians in Vietnam* by John J Coe (Artlook Books, Perth, 1982); and *Vietnam: The Australian Experience* (Time-Life Books of Australia, Sydney, 1987).

Soldiers' Experiences Some of the better books about what it was like to be an American soldier in Vietnam include: *Born on the Fourth of July* by Ron Kovic (Pocket Books, New York, 1976), which was made into a powerful movie; the journalist Michael Herr's superb *Dispatches* (Avon Books, New York, 1978); *Chickenhawk* by Robert Mason (Viking Press, New York, 1983, and Penguin Books, Middlesex, UK, 1984), a stunning autobiographical account of the helicopter war; *A Rumor of War* by Philip Caputo (Ballantine Books, New York, 1977); and *Nam* by Mark Baker (Berkley Books, New York, 1981). *A Piece of My Heart* by Keith Walker (Ballantine Books, New York, 1985) tells the stories of American women who served in Vietnam.

Two oral histories are: *Everything We Had* by Al Santoli (Ballantine Books, New York, 1981) and *Bloods: An Oral History of the Vietnam War by Black Veterans* by Wallace Terry (Ballantine Books, New York, 1984).

Some of the horror of the My Lai massacre of 1968 comes through in Lieutenant General W R Peers's *My Lai Inquiry* (W W Norton & Company, New York and London, 1979).

Chained Eagle by Everett Alvarez, Jr (Dell, 1989) is about the experiences of POWs. Alvarez was a US pilot who spent 8½ years as a prisoner in North Vietnam.

Brothers in Arms by William Broyles Jr (Avon Books, New York, 1986) is the story of the 1984 visit to Vietnam by an American journalist who served as an infantry lieutenant during the war.

Viet Cong Memoir by Truong Nhu Tang (Harcourt Brace Jovanovich, San Diego, 1985) is the autobiography of a VC cadre who later became disenchanted with post-1975 Vietnam.

One of the finest books about the war written by a Vietnamese is *The Sorrow of War* by Bao Ninh. The author fought for North Vietnam, but his book is by no means

THE AO DAI

The graceful national dress of Vietnamese women is known as the *ao dai* (pronounced 'ow-zai' in the north and 'ow-yai' in the south). It consists of a close-fitting blouse with long panels in the front and back that is worn over loose black or white trousers. One sees fewer and fewer women wearing ao dais these days, though they are still popular for formal occasions.

Traditionally, men have also worn ao dais. The male version is shorter and looser fitting. Before the end of dynastic rule, the colours of the brocade and embroidery indicated the rank of the wearer. Gold brocade accompanied by embroidered dragons was reserved for the emperor. High-ranking mandarins wore purple, while lower-ranking mandarins had to settle for blue.

Ao dais have been around a long time, and in the beginning they were anything but revealing. But in the past few years partially see-through ao dais have become all the rage – it's doubtful that even Western women would wear something so provocative. The see-through ao dais have even spread to the north.

Mourners usually wear either white or black ao dais (white is the traditional colour of mourning).

JOHN PERTTULA

Above: The familiar sight of women wearing ao dais riding bicycles.

Below: A more formal occasion.

HELEN SAVORY

VIETNAMESE FOOD

Two typical Vietnamese specialities are *chia gio* and *pho.*

Chia gio are similar to the spring rolls served in Chinese restaurants. They're made from rice paper softened in water and stuffed with a mixture of pork mince, mushrooms, prawns, noodles and bean shoots; sometimes egg yolk is also added. The rolls are deep-fried and served hot with *nuoc mam* (fish sauce), fresh lettuce leaves, mint and other fragrant herbs. To eat chia gio, grab one with your chopsticks, roll it up in a lettuce leaf along with the herbs and dip the whole thing in the nuoc mam.

Pho is Vietnam's most famous dish. It's a broth flavoured with aniseed star, ginger and pepper. The broth is poured into bowls containing cooked rice noodles and beef, chicken or pork slices, either cooked or raw. It is served hot enough to cook any raw meat and is garnished with coriander leaves.

GLENN BEANLAND

HELEN SAVORY

Above: Chia gio, Vietnamese spring rolls.

Left: Fresh fruit and spices used in Vietnamese cooking.

Below: Bowl of pho, the popular Vietnamese speciality.

GLENN BEANLAND

a piece of anti-American propaganda. On the contrary, he's cynical about the entire war and its avowed goals, and neither side comes out looking very good. The book won a literature prize in Vietnam in 1993 and English-language copies are available from bookstalls in Hanoi.

Travel Guides

We don't mean to toot our own horn, but you hold in your hands what is by far the most comprehensive travel guidebook to Vietnam on the market today. However, there are other books which can give you a different perspective.

Vietnam: Opening Doors to the World by Rick Graetz (Graetz Publications, 1989) is a full-colour coffee table book on Vietnam and its people today.

Another effort in this direction is *Ten Years After* by Tim Page. This impressive book boasts '12 months' worth of photos taken 10 years after the war'.

The *Vietnam Insight Guide* by Apa Publications of Singapore is a more portable coffee table book with much information about Vietnamese culture.

Guide to Vietnam by John R Jones (Bradt Publications, UK, 1989, and Hunter Publishing, Edison, NJ, 1989) does a better job conveying how things used to be rather than giving hands-on, how-to-travel information.

Barbara Cohen's *Vietnam Guidebook* (Houghton Mifflin Co, 1994) is aimed at Americans and includes many references to the war (the author served as a US Army psychiatrist during the war). As a travel guide, it is written for less-experienced travellers, including those in tour groups.

Murray Hiebert, the Hanoi correspondent for the *Far Eastern Economic Review*, has included a selection of his articles in his very interesting *Vietnam Notebook*.

A Dragon Apparent is about author Norman Lewis's fascinating journeys through Vietnam, Laos and Cambodia in 1950. This classic travelogue is now available as a reprint from Eland in London and Hippocrene in New York.

In 1974, Jeanne M Sales of the American Women's Association of Saigon wrote *Guide to Vietnam* without once mentioning the war! *Customs and Culture of Vietnam* by Ann Caddell Crawford (Charles E Tuttle, Rutland, Vt, and Tokyo, 1966) is getting very dated.

The classic guidebooks to Indochina were published by Claudius Madrolle before WW II. The English edition, *Indochina* (Société d'Éditions Géographiques, Maritimes et Coloniales, Paris, 1939), is a much condensed version of the outstanding two-volume set in French, *Indochine du Sud* and *Indochine du Nord*. The 2nd augmented edition of *Indochine du Sud* and the 3rd augmented edition of *Indochine du Nord* were published in 1939 by the Société d'Éditions Géographiques, Maritimes et Coloniales in Paris. Earlier editions of both books were published by Librairie Hachette, Paris, in the 1920s. The only place to find the Madrolle guides these days is in major university libraries and antiquarian bookshops.

Bookshops

Within Vietnam Due to strict censorship, book importers have a tough time getting their wares into the country. Consequently, you won't find many new imported English titles in Vietnam. On the other hand, the government regularly churns out foreign-language publications. Unfortunately, these are largely propaganda (such as laughable *Vietnam, A Long History* by Nguyen Khac Vien), or else exceedingly boring *(Investment Statistics*, etc). About the most interesting books you can get from the government are dictionaries.

If you need to read to preserve your sanity, then used books are your only salvation. Ho Chi Minh City and Hanoi both have several used-book shops, and the size and variety of what's on sale continues to expand. However, it's best to bring a bunch of books with you, because used-book shops like to trade rather than simply sell. Often they will swap books two-to-one, with no money changing hands. If you've got a stack of second-hand books you've been wondering what to do with, then wonder no longer.

Abroad Ironically, the best selection of books dealing with Vietnam are to be found outside the country. You should certainly have a look at the bookshops in your own country before leaving home, but Bangkok and Hong Kong book stores are also worth exploring.

Asia Books has three locations in Bangkok: 221 Sukhumvit Rd, between Soi 15 and Soi 17 (☎ 252-7277, 250-1822, 252-4373, 251-6042); 2nd Floor, Peninsula Plaza, Rajdamri Rd between the Erawan and Regent hotels (☎ 253-9786/7/8); and 3rd Floor, Landmark Plaza, Sukhumvit Rd between Soi 4 and Soi 6, open 10 am to 8 pm (☎ 252-5654/5).

In Hong Kong, check out Wanderlust Books (☎ 2523-2042), 30 Hollywood Rd, Central, Hong Kong Island. The store is on the corner of Hollywood Rd and Shelley St.

Maps

Urban orienteering is very easy in Vietnam. Vietnamese is written with a Latin-based

---

War of the Names

One of the primary battlegrounds for the hearts and minds of the Vietnamese people during the last four decades has been the naming of Vietnam's provinces, districts, cities, towns, streets and institutions. Some places have been known by three or more names since WW II, and in many cases more than one name is still used.

Urban locations have borne: (1) French names (often of the generals, administrators and martyrs who made French colonialism possible); (2) names commemorating the historical personages chosen for veneration by the South Vietnamese government; and (3) the alternative set of heroes selected by the Hanoi government. Buddhist pagodas have formal names as well as one or more popular monikers. Chinese pagodas bear various Chinese appellations – most of which also have Vietnamese equivalents – based on the titles and celestial ranks of those to whom they are consecrated. In the highlands, both Montagnard and Vietnamese names for mountains, villages, etc, are in use. The slight differences in vocabulary and pronunciation between the north, centre and south sometimes result in the use of different words and spellings (such as 'Pleiku' and 'Playcu').

When French control of Vietnam ended in 1954, almost all French names were replaced in both the North and the South. For example, Cap St Jacques became Vung Tau, Tourane was rechristened Danang and Rue Catinat in Saigon was renamed Tu Do (Freedom) St (since reunification it has been known as Dong Khoi (Uprising) St). In 1956, the names of some of the provinces and towns in the South were changed as part of an effort to erase from popular memory the Viet Minh's anti-French exploits, which were often known by the places where they took place. The village-based southern Communists, who by this time had gone underground, continued to use the old designations and boundaries in running their regional, district and village organisations. The peasants quickly adapted to this situation, using one set of names for where they lived when dealing with the Communists and a different set of names when talking to representatives of the South Vietnamese government.

Later, the US soldiers in Vietnam gave nicknames (such as China Beach near Danang) to places whose Vietnamese names they found inconvenient or difficult to remember or pronounce. This helped to make a very foreign land seem to them a bit more familiar.

After reunification, the first order of Saigon's provisional municipal Military Management Committee changed the name of the city to 'Ho Chi Minh City', a decision confirmed in Hanoi a year later. The new government immediately began changing street names considered inappropriate – a process which is still continuing – and renamed almost all the city's hotels, dropping English and French names in favour of Vietnamese ones. The only French names still in use are those of Albert Calmette (1893-1934; developer of a tuberculosis vaccine), Marie Curie (1867-1934; winner of the Nobel Prize for her research in radioactivity), Louis Pasteur (1822-95; chemist and bacteriologist) and Alexandre Yersin (1863-1943; discoverer of the plague bacillus).

All this renaming has had mixed results. Streets, districts and provinces are usually known by their new names. But most residents of Ho Chi Minh City still prefer to call the place Saigon, especially since Ho Chi Minh City is in fact a huge area that stretches from near Cambodia all the way to the South China Sea. And visitors will find that the old names of the city's hotels are making a comeback.

All this makes using anything but the latest street maps a risky proposition, though fortunately most of the important street-name changes were made before any of the maps currently on sale were published. ■

alphabet. You can at least read the street signs and maps, even if the pronunciation is incomprehensible! In addition, finding out where you are is easy: street signs are plentiful, and almost every shop and restaurant has the street name and number right on its sign. Street names are sometimes abbreviated on street signs with just the initials ('DBP' for 'Dien Bien Phu St', etc). Most street numbering is sequential with odd and even numbers on opposite sides of the street (although there are important exceptions in Ho Chi Minh City and Danang), but unfortunately, number 75 often can be three blocks down the street from number 76.

A few tips: many restaurants are named after their street addresses. For instance, 'Nha Hang 51 Nguyen Hue' *(nha hang* means restaurant) is at number 51 Nguyen Hue Blvd. If you are travelling by bus or car, a good way to get oriented is to look for the post office – the words following Buu Dien (post office) on the sign are the name of the district, town or village you're in.

Excellent maps of Ho Chi Minh City, Hanoi, Danang, Hué and a few other places are issued in slightly different forms every few years. Unfortunately, maps of smaller towns and cities are practically nonexistent – the government seems to treat these as military secrets.

If you will be travelling by road outside of the main cities and towns, it is worthwhile purchasing a map of the whole country.

MEDIA
Newspapers & Magazines
English-Language Most of Vietnam's English-language press is geared towards attracting the foreign investor and business traveller rather than peddling the news. While you may not be interested in knowing how many tons of bricks or fertiliser were produced last month, these publications can at least give you some idea of what's happening in Vietnam.

At the moment, the best magazine by far is the *Vietnam Economic Times*, which is published monthly. For subscription information, contact the magazine in Hanoi

(☎ 245253; fax 251888) or in Ho Chi Minh City (☎ 356717; fax 356716). Or contact the Vietnam Resource Group (☎ 222982; fax 222983), 92-96 Nguyen Hue Blvd, District 1, in Ho Chi Minh City. In the USA, subscriptions are available through the Vietnam Resource Group (☎ (202) 651-8007; fax 484-4899), 955 L'Enfant Plaza SW, No 4000, Washington DC 20024.

The best English-language newspaper is the *Vietnam Investment Review*, which is published weekly. Subscription and advertising information is available in Ho Chi Minh City (☎ 222440, 243111, 243112; fax 231699), 122 Nguyen Thi Minh Khai St, District 1, and Hanoi (☎ 235295, 250537, 250538, 250540; fax 257937), 175 Nguyen Thai Hoc St.

What's On in Saigon is produced monthly by expats living in Ho Chi Minh City. It gives a good rundown of the city's entertainment spots and includes some good articles of local interest. The magazine has the great advantage of being free – look for copies in hotel lobbies and expat pubs. For subscription information, call (☎ 357673) or write to PO Box 571, Central Post Office, Ho Chi Minh City.

The *Vietnam News* is published daily, but that's about the only good thing one can say for it. The blank space left over from the lack of news is filled in with harangues on the joys of Marxism-Leninism or the life and times of Ho Chi Minh. The advertisements are perhaps the most useful part of the newspaper.

Vietnamese-Language There are now about 135 periodicals published in Vietnam, all but 35 of them in Hanoi. Daily newspaper circulation is eight per 1000 people. *Nhan Dan* (The People), published in Hanoi, is the daily newspaper of the Communist Party of Vietnam. *Quan Doi Nhan Dan* (The People's Army), also published in Hanoi, is the daily paper of the army. *Saigon Giai Phong* (Liberated Saigon) is the daily of the Ho Chi Minh City section of the Vietnamese Communist Party and is published in both Vietnamese and Chinese. *Giai Phong Nhat Bao (Jiefang Ribao* in Chinese) is published daily in Chinese by the Fatherland Front. The recent liberalisation has yet to significantly reduce party and government control of the press.

Probably the most popular newspaper in Saigon is *Tuoi Tre* (Youth). Other popular newspapers in Saigon include the *Bao Cong An* (Security Police Newspaper) and *Bao Khoa Hoc* (Science Newspaper).

Radio & TV

The Voice of Vietnam broadcasts on short-wave, AM and FM for about 18 hours a day. The broadcasts are mostly music, but there are also news bulletins in Vietnamese, English, French and Russian. Don't worry if you miss one bulletin – you can always catch the next one since it doesn't change throughout the day. The broadcast programmes are printed daily in the *Vietnam News*.

The first broadcast of the Voice of Vietnam took place in 1945. During the Vietnam War, the Voice of Vietnam broadcast a great deal of propaganda programming to the South, including special English programmes for American GIs. From 1968 to 1976, the Voice of Vietnam used the transmitters of Radio Havana-Cuba to deliver its message direct to the American people.

Vietnamese domestic national radio broadcasts news and music programmes from 7 am until 11 pm. In Ho Chi Minh City, frequencies to try include 610 kHz and 820 kHz in the AM band and 78.5 MHz, 99.9 MHz and 103.3 MHz in the FM band.

Visitors interested in keeping up on events in the rest of the world – and in Vietnam itself – may want to bring along a small short-wave receiver. News, music and features programmes in a multitude of languages can easily be picked up, especially at night. Frequencies you might try for English-language broadcasts include:

Radio Australia
21,725 kHz, 21,525 kHz, 17,880 kHz, 17,750 kHz, 17,670 kHz, 17,630 kHz, 15,575 kHz, 15,170 kHz, 13,755 kHz, 11,910 kHz, 11,880 kHz, 9560 kHz, 9510 kHz. In the afternoons 21,725 kHz and 17,750 kHz are best, but in the evenings try 13,755 kHz.

BBC World Service
15,360 kHz (in the early morning); 15,280 kHz (during the day); and 15,310 kHz, 11,750 kHz, 9740 kHz and 6195 kHz (at night). Other frequencies to try include 11,955 kHz, 7145 kHz, 5975 kHz and 3915 kHz.

Voice of America
17,730 kHz and 15,215 kHz (in the morning); 11,755 kHz (in the evening); 6110 kHz, 9760 kHz and 15,760 kHz (at night).

Christian Science Monitor Radio
17,780 kHz (around noon).

Vietnamese TV began broadcasting in 1970 and it's fair to say that the content hasn't improved much since then. There is currently only one channel in Ho Chi Minh City. Broadcast hours are from Monday through Saturday from 9 to 11.30 am and from 7 to 11 pm. On Sunday there is an extra broadcast from 3 to 4 pm. English-language news comes on in the evenings as the last broadcast at sometime after 10 pm. Sometimes soccer or other sports come out at strange hours like 1.30 am.

Satellite TV is now widely available, though you're not likely to see it except in the large hotels catering to foreigners. Hong Kong's Star TV is most popular and features broadcasts in English, Chinese and other languages.

FILM & PHOTOGRAPHY
Airport X-Ray Machines

Efforts are being made to upgrade airport facilities, and the old 1950s x-ray machines have now been retired from Noi Bai Airport (Hanoi) and Tan Son Nhat Airport (Ho Chi Minh City). However, we cannot swear that you won't encounter these Soviet-made dental x-ray machines in some backwater like Phu Quoc Island or Pleiku.

Just to be sure, look for the words 'film-safe' written on the machine. If it doesn't say that, do *not* put your film into the machine no matter what the airport staff say. These antique machines will severely damage *any* film, whether it is exposed or unexposed and no matter how low the ASA or Din rating is. Prints made from irradiated negatives will come out all reddish (makes for colourful sunsets though) while slides get washed out.

Film & Developing

Fresh colour print film, imported in bulk, is widely available. Popular brands available in Vietnam include Kodak, Fuji and Konica. A 36-exposure 100 ASA roll of Kodacolor costs US$3.40; Konica costs US$2.60.

Western-made slide film can easily be bought in Hanoi and Ho Chi Minh City, but don't count on it elsewhere. In touristy resorts like Nha Trang and Halong Bay, look for slide film in hotel gift shops.

If you buy film in Vietnam, be sure to check the expiry date. This is especially important if the film has been stored in a warm environment, which is very likely. Many tourists travel around Vietnam by van or minibus – note that the metal floors of these vehicles get very hot, but you might not notice if the vehicle is air-conditioned. Many travellers have roasted their film by placing it in their backpacks and setting the backpack on the floor of the vehicle.

Photoprocessing shops have become ubiquitous in Ho Chi Minh City and other places where tourists congregate. Most of these places are equipped with the latest Japanese one-hour colour-printing equipment. Cost for developing is about US$0.50 per roll plus US$0.12 per 9x13-cm (3½x5-inch) print.

There are a handful of places which try to develop slide film in Vietnam, but equipment is basic and quality is not assured. Cost for processing is US$5 per roll, but most places do not mount the slides. However, you can buy the frames for around US$0.15 apiece and mount them yourself. The nearest places offering reliable slide processing and mounting are Thailand, Singapore and Hong Kong.

Lithium batteries for cameras are pretty easy to buy in Hanoi and Saigon these days, but you'd be wise to carry an extra when you're out in the hinterland.

Laminating

Plastic laminating is cheap and ubiquitous. Just look for the signs saying 'Ep Plastic'. It's particularly advisable to laminate photos intended as presents to protect them from Vietnam's tropical climate. Unlaminated photos deteriorate and go mouldy.

Photography Restrictions & Etiquette

The Vietnamese police usually don't care what you photograph, but on occasion they get pernickety. Obviously, don't photograph something that is militarily sensitive (airports, seaports, military bases, border checkpoints, soldiers and police accepting bribes, etc). Photography from aircraft is now permitted. Don't even think of trying to get a snapshot of Ho Chi Minh in his glass sarcophagus! Taking pictures inside pagodas and temples is usually all right, but as always it is better to ask permission from the monks.

Perhaps it would be wise for you to memorise the following message which appears on signs in various places: 'Cam Chup Hinh Va Quay Video', which means 'No Photography or Video Taping'.

Many of the touristy sites now charge a 'camera fee' of at least US$0.50, or a 'video fee' of US$2 to US$5.

Like their Japanese and Chinese counterparts, Vietnamese people have a near obsession with collecting hundreds (or thousands) of photos of themselves posing in front of something. The pose is always the same; a stiff, frontal shot, hands at the sides, etc. The result is that all of their photos look nearly identical. The purpose of the photos seems to be to prove that they've been to a particular place. Since many Vietnamese cannot afford their own camera, virtually every site of tourist potential has a legion of photographers always ready to snap a few pictures. Some photographers will get the film processed and mail it to their customers, while others will shoot a roll and hand it over unprocessed. Most Vietnamese cannot understand why Westerners shoot dozens of rolls of film without posing themselves in each and every frame. Furthermore, when Westerners show off their best photographs, Vietnamese look at them and say the photos are 'boring'.

Vietnamese aren't much different from Westerners when it comes to having their photos taken by strangers. In general they won't care, though a few might get upset. People will sometimes pose for you if you give a tip or buy something from them (like the old women selling bananas by the streetside, for example). For a small tip, we've even had soldiers pose for us in full battle dress, but be discreet when handing money to someone in uniform (they are not supposed to look like they are accepting bribes). Remember that monks are not photo models – ask permission and respect their wishes. Also, do not climb up into the lap of a Buddha statue to get that 'perfect gag photo' to show the folks back home.

One of the best things you can do for Vietnamese friends who don't own a camera is to take pictures of them or their families and send the photos to them after processing (or give them the roll of film and let them process it).

HEALTH

If you've heard of it, chances are someone in Vietnam's got it. It is important to realise, however, that the local population's susceptibility to many diseases is the result of poverty. Endemic deficiencies in immunisation, nutrition, sanitation and medical treatment are less likely to affect foreigners if they are careful.

Vietnam's economy has improved in recent years, which has brought with it some significant improvements to the medical situation. People were frequently malnourished before and therefore highly prone to disease – this is not a huge problem anymore. Also, immunisation programmes are helping to stop the spread of disease.

This having been said, serious problems persist. Malaria is endemic in some parts of the country and many cases go untreated for lack of the most basic medicines. Rural hospitals are short of vaccines and medical equipment (everything from scalpels to diagnostic gadgets). Many of the medicines that are available in rural pharmacies have been improperly stored and are way past their expiry dates. Doctors are even forced to reuse 'disposable' needles and syringes because replacements are simply not obtainable. Though foreigners with cold hard cash will receive the best treatment available, even bars of gold cannot buy you blood tests

and x-rays when the local health clinic doesn't even have a thermometer or aspirin. If you become seriously ill while in rural parts of Vietnam, get to Ho Chi Minh City quickly. If you need any type of surgery or other extensive treatment, don't hesitate to fly to Bangkok, Hong Kong or some other reasonably developed country as soon as possible.

Vietnam's children are the most seriously affected by this sad state of affairs and routinely die from eminently curable or preventable infectious diseases. Dysentery kills many children, simply because their parents (if they have parents) do not have access to oral rehydration salts or lack the knowledge of how to use them. Lack of sanitation spreads cholera and typhoid fever – again, children succumb most easily.

The Traveller's Health Guide by Dr Anthony C Turner (Roger Lascelles, London) or Staying Healthy in Asia, Africa and Latin America (Moon Publications) are guides to staying healthy while travelling and what to do if you fall ill. For the technically oriented, the classical medical reference is the Merck Manual, a weighty volume which covers virtually every illness known to humanity.

Children, particularly babies and unborn children, present their own peculiar problems when travelling. Lonely Planet's Travel with Children by Maureen Wheeler gives a rundown on health precautions to be taken with kids and advice on travel during pregnancy.

You can buy plenty of dangerous drugs across the counter in Vietnam without a prescription, but you should exercise restraint – some drugs, like steroids, can make you feel great and then kill you, especially if you have an infection. On any medicines you buy, take a look at expiry dates – drugs may not be of the same strength as in other countries or may have deteriorated due to age or poor storage conditions. Chinese shops often sell herbal medicines imported from China. If you need some special medication then take it with you.

The addresses and telephone numbers of the best medical facilities in Vietnam can be found in the Information section at the beginning of the chapters on Ho Chi Minh City and Hanoi. Those are the only two cities where you are likely to find health facilities that come close to meeting Western standards.

Resident foreigners can contact Asia Emergency Assistance in Ho Chi Minh City (☎ 298520) for information about their resident abroad programme. The cost is currently US$384. International SOS Assistance (Ho Chi Minh City ☎ 242866; Hanoi ☎ 226228) also has a different health scheme costing US$180 per year.

Pre-Departure Preparations

Your grandmother might have told you that 'an ounce of prevention is worth a pound of cure', though in these days of the metric system it's 'grams' and 'kilograms', respectively. No matter how you measure it, the advice is sound – you should practice preventive medicine. The best place to begin is with a trip to a doctor or public health clinic to update your vaccinations.

Vaccinations Various health authorities and other vaccination enthusiasts have recommended that travellers consider the following vaccines: rabies, hepatitis A, hepatitis B, BCG (tuberculosis), Japanese encephalitis, polio, typhoid, tetanus and diphtheria. Yellow fever is not endemic to Vietnam but you are required to have a yellow fever vaccination if you arrive in Vietnam within six days of leaving or transiting a yellow fever area. The cholera vaccine is not very effective and is contraindicated during pregnancy.

Plan ahead for getting your vaccinations: some of them require an initial shot followed by a booster, while some vaccinations should not be given together. Most travellers from Western countries will have been immunised against various diseases during childhood. But your doctor may still recommend booster shots against measles or polio, diseases still prevalent in many developing countries. If you are travelling with children, it's especially important to be sure that they've had all necessary vaccinations. The period of protection offered by vaccinations differs widely and some are contraindicated for pregnant women.

In some countries immunisations are available from airport or government health centres. Within Vietnam itself, vaccinations are difficult to come by and the few vaccines available are sometimes rendered ineffective because of age and mishandling.

You should have your vaccinations recorded in an International Health Certificate. This will serve as adequate proof of immunisation should you run into overzealous health authorities at the immigration queues.

Health Insurance Although you may have medical insurance in your own country, it is probably not valid in Vietnam. A travel insurance policy is a very good idea – to protect you against cancellation penalties on advance purchase flights, against medical costs through illness or injury, against theft or loss of possessions, and against the cost of additional air tickets if you get really sick and have to fly home. Read the small print carefully since it's easy to be caught out by exclusions.

If you undergo medical treatment, be sure to collect all receipts and copies of your medical report, in English if possible, for your insurance company. If you get robbed, you'll need a police report (good luck) if you want to collect from your insurance company.

If you purchase an International Student Identity Card (ISIC) or Teacher Card (ISTC), you may be automatically covered depending on which country you purchased the card in. Check with the student travel office to be sure. If you're neither a student or a teacher, but you're between the ages of 15 and 25, you can purchase an International Youth Identity Card (YIEE), which entitles you to the same benefits. Some student travel offices also sell insurance to people who don't hold these cards.

Medical Kit You should assemble some sort of basic first-aid kit. You won't want it to be too large and cumbersome for travelling, but some items which could be included are:

Anti-malarial tablets; Band-Aids, gauze bandage, plaster (adhesive tape); a thermometer; tweezers; scissors; sunscreen; insect repellent; multi-vitamins; water sterilisation tablets; ChapStick; antibiotic ointment; an antiseptic agent (Dettol or Betadine); any medication you're already taking; diarrhoea medication (Lomotil or Imodium); rehydration salts for treatment of severe diarrhoea; paracetamol (Panadol), ibuprofen or aspirin for pain and fever; antibiotics; anti-fungal powder; contraceptives (including condoms); antihistamine (Benadryl, Hismanal, etc) useful as a decongestant or for treating allergic reactions to insect stings.

Most of these medications are available in Vietnam at low cost, but it's still not a bad idea to come prepared. Bring a couple of syringes in case you need injections. Ask your doctor for a note explaining why they have been prescribed.

Ideally, antibiotics should be administered only under medical supervision and should never be taken indiscriminately. Overuse of antibiotics can weaken your body's ability to deal with infections naturally and can reduce the drug's efficacy on a future occasion. Take only the recommended dose as prescribed. It's important that once you start a course of antibiotics, you finish it even if the illness seems to be cured earlier. If you stop taking the antibiotics after one or two days, a complete relapse is more than likely. If you think you are experiencing a reaction to any antibiotic (a sudden rash is a warning sign), stop taking it immediately and consult a doctor.

Also, get your teeth checked and any necessary dental work done before you leave home. Always carry a spare pair of glasses or your prescription in case of loss or breakage.

Basic Rules

Food & Water In Ho Chi Minh City and Hanoi, tap water is not too 'bad (it's chlorinated) but it's still recommended that you boil it before drinking. In other parts of Vietnam, the water varies from pretty safe to downright dangerous. Especially after a typhoon and the subsequent flooding, there is a problem with sewers overflowing into reservoirs, thus contaminating the tap water used for drinking and bathing. Outbreaks of cholera and typhoid occur most often after floods so you must be particularly careful at such times – do not even brush your teeth with unboiled water after flooding.

Reputable brands of bottled water (both imported and domestic) or soft drinks are generally fine. Unfortunately, in some places bottles are refilled with tap water and resealed, and many travellers have suffered serious intestinal upsets (including dysentery) because of this. Take care with fruit juice, particularly if water may have been added. Milk should be treated with suspicion, as it is often unpasteurised. Boiled milk is fine if it is kept hygienically and yoghurt is always good.

Tea and coffee should both be OK since the water should have been boiled. You can also boil your own water if you carry an electric immersion coil and a large metal cup (plastic will melt). You can safely plug a 220-volt immersion coil into a 110-volt socket (not vice versa!), but the boiling time will be much longer. For emergency use, water purification tablets will help. Water is more effectively sterilised by iodine than by chlorine tablets, because iodine kills amoebic cysts. However, iodine is not safe for prolonged use, and also tastes horrible. Bringing water to a boil is sufficient to kill most bacteria, but 20 minutes of boiling is required to kill amoebic cysts. Fortunately, amoebic cysts are relatively rare and you should not be overly concerned about these. If you have nothing to boil or purify your water, you have to consider the risks of drinking possibly contaminated water against the risks of dehydrating – the first is possible, the second is definite.

It's a good idea to carry a water bottle with you. You are dehydrating if you find you are urinating infrequently or if your urine turns a deep yellow or orange; you may also find yourself getting headaches. Dehydration is a real problem if you go hiking in Vietnam – if you can't find water along the way or can't carry enough with you, then you will soon learn just how hot this place really is!

While boiling will kill nasty microbes, freezing will not. Since most small eateries in Vietnam lack refrigeration equipment, factory-frozen ice is delivered daily. In Ho Chi Minh City and Hanoi, the ice comes from a factory which has to meet certain standards of hygiene (the water is at least chlorinated), while in rural areas the ice could be made from river (sewer?) water. Another problem is that even clean ice often makes its way to its destination in a filthy sack carried on the bare backs of delivery men. The filthy outer layer may melt off, but then again it may not, though any thoughtful restaurant will at least wash the ice before cracking it into pieces. If you do not want to risk a possibly serious gut infection, avoid ice in rural backwaters – admittedly easier said than done in a hot tropical country.

When it comes to food, use your best judgement. Everything should be thoroughly cooked – you can get dysentery from salads and unpeeled fruit. Ice cream is usually OK if it is a reputable brand name, but beware of ice cream that has melted and been refrozen. Thoroughly cooked food is safest but not if it has been left to cool or if it has been reheated. Take great care with shellfish or fish and avoid undercooked meat.

Other Precautions Sunglasses not only give you that fashionable 'Hollywood look' but protect your eyes from the scorching Vietnamese sun. Amber and grey are said to be the two most effective colours for filtering out harmful ultraviolet rays.

Sunburn can be more than just uncomfortable. Among the undesirable effects of frying your hide are premature skin ageing and possible skin cancer in later years. Bring zinc cream for your nose and lips, sunscreen (UV) lotion and something to cover your head.

If you're sweating profusely, you're going to lose a lot of salt and that can lead to fatigue and muscle cramps. If necessary you can make it up by putting extra salt in your food (a teaspoon a day is plenty), but don't increase your salt intake unless you also increase your water intake. Soy sauce will also do the trick.

Take good care of all cuts and scratches. In this climate they take longer to heal and can easily get infected. Treat any cut with care; wash it out with sterilised water, preferably with an antiseptic (Betadine), keep it dry and keep an eye on it – they really can turn into tropical ulcers! It would be worth bringing an antibiotic cream with you. Cuts on your feet and ankles are particularly troublesome – a new pair of sandals can quickly give you a nasty abrasion which can be difficult to heal. Try not to scratch mosquito bites for the same reason.

The climate may be tropical, but you *can* catch a cold in Vietnam. One of the easiest ways is leaving a fan on at night when you go to sleep, and air-conditioners are even worse. You can also freeze by going up to mountainous areas without warm clothes. Antihistamines and decongestants can give symptomatic relief, but the way to cure a cold is to rest, drink lots of liquids, keep warm and wait it out.

Medical Problems & Treatment
Diarrhoea Diarrhoea is often due simply to a change of diet. A lot depends on what you're used to eating and whether or not you've got an iron gut. If you do get diarrhoea, the first thing to do is wait – it rarely lasts more than a few days.

Diarrhoea will cause you to dehydrate, which will make you feel much worse. The solution is not simply to drink water, since it will run right through you. You'll get much better results by mixing your water with oral rehydration salt, a combination of salts (both NaCl and KCl) and glucose. Dissolve the powder in *cool* water (never hot!) and drink, but don't use it if the powder is wet. The quantity of water is specified on the packet. Rehydration salts are also useful for treating heat exhaustion caused by excessive sweating.

If the diarrhoea persists, then the usual treatment is Lomotil or Imodium tablets. The maximum dose for Lomotil is two tablets three times a day. Both Lomotil and Imodium are prescription drugs in the West but are available over the counter in most

Asian countries. Anti-diarrhoeal drugs don't cure anything, but they slow down the digestive system so that the cramps go away and you don't have to go to the toilet all the time. Excessive use of these drugs is not advised, as they can cause dependency and other side effects. Furthermore, the diarrhoea serves one useful purpose – it helps the body expel unwanted bacteria.

Activated charcoal – while not actually considered a drug – can provide much relief from diarrhoea and is a time-honoured treatment.

Fruit juice, strong tea and coffee can aggravate diarrhoea – again, water with oral rehydration salts is the best drink. It will help tremendously if you stick to a light, fibre-free diet. Yoghurt or boiled eggs with salt are basic staples for diarrhoea patients. Later you may be able to tolerate rice porridge or plain white rice. Keep away from vegetables, fruits and greasy foods for a while. If you suddenly decide to pig out on a peperoni pizza with hot sauce, you'll be back to square one. If the diarrhoea persists for a week or more, it's probably not simple travellers' diarrhoea – it could be dysentery and it might be wise to see a doctor.

Allowing your diarrhoea problem to go untreated for weeks or months can lead to another illness called 'irritable bowel syndrome'. Basically, this means that the gut gets so irritated that the diarrhoea becomes self-perpetuating even though the original cause (bacteria) is gone. Curing irritable bowel syndrome can be a lengthy and difficult process, so it's best avoided by tackling the problem early.

Dysentery Many travellers claim to be suffering from 'dysentery' when all they've got is common, garden-variety diarrhoea. Dysentery causes diarrhoea, but it is worse – it's often accompanied by fever and blood and pus in the stool. The victim usually feels faint and totally lacking in energy and can barely eat or get out of bed. It's a real drag! Dysentery is classified into two categories, bacillary and amoebic.

Diarrhoea with blood or pus and fever is usually bacillary dysentery. It's quite common in Vietnam and many travellers fall prey to it. Since it's caused by bacteria infecting the gut, it can be treated with antibiotics. Norfloxacin 400 mg twice daily for three days or ciprofloxacin 500 mg twice daily for seven days is helpful. Or take erythromycin 250 mg three times daily or tetracycline 250 mg four times daily for about a week. A useful alternative is co-trimoxazole 160/800 mg (Bactrim, Septrin, Resprim) twice daily for five days. This is a sulpha drug and must not be used by people with a known sulpha allergy.

In most cases, bacillary dysentery will eventually clear up without treatment, but in some cases it's actually fatal, especially in children. Be sure to use water and rehydration salts (see previous section on Diarrhoea) to prevent dehydration.

Antibiotics are heavy artillery, so don't start swallowing them at the first sign of diarrhoea. The main problem is that antibiotics upset the balance of intestinal flora. The problem is more serious for women since this can lead to yeast infections, and tetracycline is also contraindicated in women who are pregnant or breastfeeding.

Diarrhoea with a copious, watery, brown foul-smelling stool but without fever is usually amoebic dysentery. This is a disease you should not neglect because it will not go away by itself. In addition, if you don't wipe out the amoebae while they are still in your intestine, they may migrate to the liver and other organs, causing abscesses, which could require surgery.

There are several ways to cure this disease. If you treat it promptly, the amoebae will still be restricted to the intestine.

The most sure-fire cure for amoebic dysentery is metronidazole (Flagyl), an anti-amoebic drug. It will wipe out amoebae no matter where they reside in the body, even in the liver and other organs. The dose is four 200 mg tablets (800 mg) three times daily for five days. Flagyl is also available in 400 mg tablets, so in that case you take two tablets per dose. An alternative to Flagyl is tinidazole (Fasigyn), taken as a two-gram daily dose for three days. If you take either drug, do not under any circumstances consume alcohol during treatment or for 48 hours afterwards.

Herbal medicine fanatics will be pleased to know that dried papaya seeds can actually cure amoebic dysentery, but only if it hasn't gone beyond the intestine. The dose is one heaping tablespoon daily for eight days. If you're really worried about catching amoebic dysentery, papaya seeds can be used as a preventive measure – one heaping tablespoon weekly is usually effective.

Remember that the seeds must be thoroughly dried and that they taste awful. Just because something is 'natural' doesn't mean it's harmless – papaya seeds can cause miscarriage in pregnant women and they may have other unknown side effects. Treat papaya seeds as you would any other medicine – with caution.

Giardiasis *Giardia lamblia* is a type of protozoan which causes severe diarrhoea, nausea and weakness but doesn't produce blood in the stool or cause fever. Giardiasis is very common throughout the world.

Although the symptoms are similar to amoebic dysentery, there are some important differences. On the positive side, giardiasis will not migrate to the liver and other organs – it stays in the intestine and therefore is much less likely to cause long-term health problems.

The bad news is that antibiotics and papaya seeds are no help whatsoever. It can only be cured with anti-amoebic drugs like Flagyl and Fasigyn – again, never drink alcohol while taking Flagyl or Fasigyn. Either can be used in a single-treatment dose. Without treatment, the symptoms may subside and you might feel fine for a while, but the illness will return again and again, making your life miserable.

Cholera Cholera tends to travel in epidemics (usually after floods) and outbreaks are generally widely reported, so you can often avoid such problem areas. This is a disease of poor sanitation, so if you've heard reports of cholera be especially careful about what you eat, drink and brush your teeth with.

Symptoms include a sudden onset of acute diarrhoea with 'rice water' stools, vomiting, muscular cramps, and extreme weakness. You need medical help – but treat for dehydration, which can be extreme, and if there is an appreciable delay in getting to hospital then begin taking tetracycline. The adult dose is 250 mg four times daily. It is not recommended for children eight years and under nor for pregnant women. An alternative drug is Ampicillin.

Cholera vaccination is not very effective and is no longer recommended by the World Health Organisation. If you get cholera, it's probably best to get on a plane to Bangkok – fast.

Typhoid Typhoid fever is another gut infection that travels the faecal-oral route – ie, contaminated water and food are responsible. Like cholera, epidemics can occur after floods because of sewage backing up into drinking water supplies.

Vaccination against typhoid is not totally effective and it is one of the most dangerous infections, so medical help must be sought.

In its early stages typhoid resembles many other illnesses: sufferers may feel like they have a bad cold or flu on the way, as early symptoms are a headache, a sore throat and a fever which rises a little each day until it is around 40°C or more. The victim's pulse is often slow relative to the degree of fever present and gets slower as the fever rises – unlike a normal fever where the pulse increases. There may also be vomiting, diarrhoea or constipation.

In the second week the high fever and slow pulse continue and a few pink spots may appear on the body; trembling, delirium, weakness, weight loss and dehydration are other symptoms. If there are no further complications, the fever and other symptoms will slowly dissipate during the third week. However you must get medical help before this because pneumonia (acute lung infection) or peritonitis (from a burst appendix) are common complications, and because typhoid is very infectious.

The fever should be treated by keeping the victim cool; dehydration should also be watched for. Chloramphenicol is the recommended antibiotic but there are fewer side affects with Ampicillin. The adult dose is two 250-mg capsules, four times a day. Children aged between eight and 12 years should have half the adult dose; younger children should have one-third the adult dose.

People who are allergic to penicillin should not be given Ampicillin.

Polio Polio is also a disease spread by insanitation and is found more frequently in hot climates. The effects on children can be especially devastating – they can be crippled for life. Fortunately, an excellent vaccination is available, but a booster every ten years is recommended by many doctors.

Tetanus Tetanus is due to a bacillus which usually enters the blood system through a cut, or as the result of a skin puncture by a rusty nail, wire, etc. It is worth being vaccinated against tetanus since there is more risk of contracting the disease in warm climates, where cuts take longer to heal. A tetanus booster shot should be given every five years.

Malaria The parasite that causes this disease is spread by the bite of the female *Anopheles* mosquito, though it can on rare occasion get passed by blood transfusion. Malaria has a nasty habit of recurring in later years – even if you're cured at the time – and it can kill you.

In the 1950s, the World Health Organisation launched a two-prong attack against malaria, spraying with the pesticide DDT and treating victims with the drug chloroquine. Meanwhile, research was begun to develop a malaria vaccine. Health authorities confidently predicted that by the year 2000, the malaria parasite would be extinct.

Unfortunately, mother nature has not cooperated. Rather than gracefully dropping dead, the mosquitoes developed resistance to DDT. The malaria parasite chipped in by developing resistance to chloroquine. And to add insult to injury, DDT was found to cause environmental damage, while long-term use of chloroquine is now known to be harmful to human health. It's become obvious that malaria is a moving target – as soon as one strategy is developed to attack the disease, the mosquitoes and the parasite mutate.

To further complicate the picture, there are four different types of malaria, though 95% of all cases are one of two varieties. The most serious of these two types is *P falciparum* malaria, which is widespread throughout Vietnam.

The illness usually develops 10 to 14 days after being bitten by the mosquito and symptoms consist of high fever with alternate shivering and sweating, intense headaches and usually nausea or vomiting. Without treatment the condition is fatal within two weeks in up to 25% of cases. It is this variety of malaria which is now showing widespread resistance to the most common anti-malarial drug, chloroquine. The problem is especially serious in the Mekong Delta and rice paddy areas.

P vivax malaria is the other main type and the two rarer types are similar to *vivax*. *P vivax* malaria may be severe, but is not dangerous to life. However, if not adequately treated, the illness will continue to recur, causing chronic ill-health.

Malaria is a risk year-round in most parts of Vietnam below 1200 metres. The locals have some natural immunity to malaria resulting from generations of exposure; foreigners from non-tropical countries have no such resistance. While it is not yet possible to be inoculated against malaria, limited protection is simple: either a daily or weekly tablet (the latter is more common). The tablets kill the parasites in your bloodstream before they have a chance to multiply and cause illness.

Newer drugs such as mefloquine (Lariam) and doxycycline (Vibramycin, Doryx) are often recommended for chloroquine and multidrug-resistant areas. Expert advice should be sought, as there are many factors to consider when deciding on the type of anti-malarial medication, including the area to be visited, the risk of exposure to malaria-carrying mosquitoes, your current medical condition and your age. It is also important to discuss the side-effect profile of the medication, so you can work out a suitable risk-benefit ratio. It is also very important to be sure of the correct dose of the medication prescribed to you. Some people have inadvertently taken weekly medication (chloroquine) on a daily basis, with disastrous effects.

The World Health Organisation advises pregnant women *not* to travel in malarial areas. Some anti-malarials may stay in your system for up to three months after the last dose is taken and may cause birth defects. So if you are pregnant or get pregnant within three months of taking anti-malarials, your unborn child could be endangered. It should also be noted that malaria *can* be passed from mother to child at birth.

A sensible precaution is to avoid being bitten in the first place. Most Vietnamese hotels are equipped with mosquito nets and you'd be wise to use them. In the evenings when mosquitoes are most active, cover bare skin, particularly the ankles. Use an insect repellent – any brand that contains the magic ingredient diethyl-toluamide ('deet') should work well. (Overuse of deet may be harmful, especially to children, but its use is considered preferable to being bitten by disease-transmitting mosquitoes.) Autan and Off! are two such popular brands widely available in Asia. The liquid form of this stuff sometimes comes in a leaky bottle, making for a rather messy backpack – you can avoid this hassle if you buy it in stick form. As an emergency substitute, 'green oil' (a Vietnamese cure-all sold in pharmacies) works well. Mosquito coils are effective, though the smoke thus produced irritates the lungs and eyes. There is also so-called 'electric mosquito incense' – cardboard pads soaked in insecticide which are heated up by a very small machine. These work well, fit easily into a backpack and are widely available in Vietnam, but they aren't much use if the electricity goes off. Having an electric fan blowing on you while you sleep is very effective at keeping the mossies away, but you might wind up with a cold instead.

Treating malaria is complicated and something you should not undertake yourself except in an emergency. Blood tests are needed to determine if you in fact have malaria rather than dengue fever (see next section), and the choice of drugs depends on how well you react to them (some people are allergic to quinine, for example). However, if you are far from hospitals and doctors, you may have no other choice than self-treatment, except to die. While you are discussing dosage for prevention of malaria with your doctor, it is advisable to ask about the dosage required for treatment, especially if your trip is through a high-risk area that would isolate you from medical care.

The most common drugs for self-treatment are Fansidar and mefloquine, but note that these drugs are not candy – allergic reactions can occur and are sometimes fatal. And even if you think you've cured yourself, you still need to get to a hospital and have blood tests – otherwise there is the strong possibility of relapse.

For prevention, the most common anti-malarial drugs are doxycycline, mefloquine and chloroquine, but new drugs are constantly under development. A lot of travellers are confused about what they should and should not be taking for malaria prevention – you should definitely consult a doctor before taking anything.

A brief rundown on common anti-malarial drugs follows (note that all doses are for adults):

Doxycycline This is a good preventative for the short-term (eight weeks or less) traveller. It is sometimes recommended for longer trips.

Doxycycline is a long-acting tetracycline (antibiotic). It is not recommended during pregnancy, breastfeeding or for children under age eight. Side effects include nausea, photosensitivity (severe sunburn) and vaginal yeast infections in women.

The preventative dose is 100 mg (one pill) daily. Treatment dose (with quinine) is 100 mg daily for 10 days. You should start taking doxycycline two days before you enter the malarial area and for 14 days after you leave.

Mefloquine This (or doxycycline) is the drug of choice for most travellers to areas with chloroquine-resistant *P falciparum* malaria. The dose is 250 mg (one tablet) once a week, on the same day, starting one week before entering the malarial area, while there and for two weeks after leaving the area.

It should not be taken by people who have a history of psychiatric disturbances or convulsions or those who require fine motor coordination, such as pilots and scuba divers. It is not recommended for use during pregnancy, and because the drug is eliminated slowly from the body, pregnancy should be avoided for three months after the last dose of mefloquine.

The most frequently reported side effects are dizziness and gastrointestinal disturbances, but these can be minimised by taking the tablet with the evening meal.

Mefloquine tablets can also be carried for self-treatment of presumed malaria. Their use in this way should be discussed with a doctor.

Chloroquine Once the most commonly prescribed drug for malaria prevention, chloroquine is now recommended only for those few remaining countries where the parasite is sensitive to the drug and this does not include Vietnam. However, it is the fallback option for travellers to chloroquine-resistant areas who may not be able to take the standard drug. It is still quite effective against *P vivax* malaria but virtually ineffective against *P falciparum*. Chloroquine is safe in pregnancy. Long-term use (over five years) of chloroquine has caused permanent retinal damage to the eyes in some people. Other side effects which have been reported include nausea, dizziness, headache, blurred vision, confusion, and itching, but such problems are rare.

Chloroquine tablets are available in at least two sizes, small (150 mg) and large (300 mg). Make sure you know which you have. The preventative dose is 300 mg weekly (either two small tablets or one large). You have to start taking the tablets two weeks before entering the malarial zone and continue taking them for about four to six weeks after you've left it.

Chloroquine can be used as a treatment for *P vivax*. Treatment dose is 600 mg initially, another 600 mg after eight hours and then 300 mg daily for two days.

Fansidar & Fansimef Fansimef is Fansidar with mefloquine added. Both are an effective treatment against *P falciparum* malaria but Fansidar is a poor drug against *P vivax*. Because of the risk of allergic reactions, they are best used as a treatment rather than as a preventative. Also, they are not recommended during pregnancy, especially during the last trimester. They should not be taken at all if there is a history of sulpha allergy.

For self-treatment, three tablets are taken in a single dose.

Quinine This is the drug of choice for treating severe and resistant *P falciparum* malaria. It should *only* be used as a treatment, not as a preventative.

Quinine is taken for at least seven days with tetracycline, doxycycline or Fansidar. The dose is 600 mg every eight hours. If taken alone, it should be continued for at least eight days (until blood slide is clear) or for 14 days if no blood test is available. It is safe in pregnancy, but should be used sparingly. Side effects include ringing in the ears, headache, nausea, decreased hearing, tremor and allergic reactions (sometimes severe).

There is some resistance to quinine and it is somewhat less effective against *P vivax* than chloroquine.

Qing Haosu (Artemesinine) This herbal medicine from China has generated much interest in medical circles recently. Qing haosu has been known since at least the 4th century when it was used to treat fevers, but only recently has its anti-malarial properties been established. It's important to note that just because this is a 'herbal medicine' it does not mean that it's harmless. Quinine – made from the bark of the cinchona tree – is also a herbal medicine but it is certainly not harmless. At the time of this writing, qing haosu was only available in China because studies have not yet been completed to determine the proper dose and possible side effects. Preliminary testing in animals suggests it is toxic to the foetus and therefore is not recommended during pregnancy.

Dengue Fever This is a mosquito-borne disease which resembles malaria, but is not fatal and doesn't recur once the illness has passed.

A high fever, severe headache and pains in the joints are the usual symptoms – the aches are so bad that the disease is also called breakbone fever. The fever usually lasts two to three days, then subsides, then comes back again and takes several weeks to pass. People who have had this disease say it feels like imminent death.

Despite the malaria-like symptoms, anti-malarial drugs have no effect whatsoever on dengue fever. Only the symptoms can be treated, usually with complete bed rest, aspirin, codeine and an intravenous drip. There is no means of prevention other than to avoid getting bitten by mosquitoes, but once you've had dengue fever, you're immune for about a year. The patient should be kept under a mosquito net until after the fever passes – otherwise there is the risk of infecting others.

Eye Infections Trachoma is a common eye infection which is easily spread by contaminated towels which are handed out by restaurants and even airlines. The best advice about wiping your face is to use disposable tissue paper or moist towelettes ('Wet Ones' or similar brands). If you think you have trachoma, you need to see a doctor – the disease can damage your vision if untreated. Trachoma is normally treated with antibiotic eye ointments for about four to six weeks. Be careful about diagnosing yourself – simple allergies can produce symptoms similar to eye infections, and in this case antibiotics can do more harm than good.

Sexually Transmitted Diseases South Vietnam was once famous for its legions of wartime prostitutes, but this supposedly came to an end in 1975. However, despite repeated declarations by the government that communism has eliminated such vices, prostitution is staging a comeback. Many of the private mini-hotels and a number of government-owned hotels have massage services that can provide more than just relief from aching muscles. As the country reopened to the outside world, the situation quickly got out of hand – by 1992, beach resorts like Vung Tau and Nha Trang were becoming famous for 'sex tours'. Finally, the national government in Hanoi took notice and ordered a crackdown.

At the time of this writing the situation was very much a mixed bag. The police in some places, like Saigon, have closed down places which were obviously fronts for prostitution, but this has only had the effect of driving the business underground. Barbershops, for example, often double as brothels. In other places, the local People's Committee owns the brothels and are too busy shovelling money into their own pockets to pay much heed to moral guidelines from Hanoi.

It's no secret that prostitutes often contract sexually transmitted diseases (STDs) and pass these on to their customers. During the war, prostitutes often tried to cure themselves of sexually transmitted diseases, but by under-medicating themselves with antibiotics, penicillin-resistant strains of gonorrhoea and syphilis were created. During the Vietnam War, American soldiers referred to these diseases as 'Vietnam Rose'.

While sexual abstinence is the only 100% preventative, using condoms is also effective. Gonorrhoea and syphilis are the most common of these diseases; sores, blisters or rashes around the genitals and discharges or pain when urinating are common symptoms. Symptoms may be less marked or not observed at all in women. Syphilis symptoms eventually disappear completely but the disease continues and can cause severe problems in later years, and if untreated can be fatal. There is no vaccine for gonorrhoea but there is one for syphilis. Both diseases can be treated with antibiotics.

There are numerous other sexually transmitted diseases, for most of which effective treatment is available. However, there is neither a cure nor a vaccine for herpes and AIDS. Using condoms is the most effective preventative.

AIDS *(SIDA* in Vietnamese) has recently become a major source of concern. The first case of HIV infection (the virus which causes AIDS) detected in Vietnam was found in a 14-year-old girl when she applied for the Orderly Departure Programme in 1990 (her application was rejected). Very little AIDS testing is going on because Vietnam has no money for it, but there are now conspicuous billboards around the country advocating the use of condoms.

AIDS can also be spread through infected blood transfusions; most developing countries cannot afford to screen blood for transfusions. It can also be spread by dirty needles – vaccinations, acupuncture, ear piercing and tattooing can potentially be as dangerous as intravenous drug abuse if the equipment is not clean. If you do need an injection it is a good idea to provide the doctor with a new needle and syringe.

Hepatitis A Hepatitis is a disease which affects the liver. There are several varieties, the most common being hepatitis A and B, but there is another strain called non-A non-

B. Hepatitis A occurs in countries with poor sanitation, of which Vietnam is definitely one. It's spread from person to person via infected food or water, or contaminated cooking and eating utensils. Salads which have been washed in infected water, or fruit which has been handled by an infected person, might carry the disease.

Symptoms appear 15 to 50 days after infection (generally around 25 days) and consist of fever, loss of appetite, nausea, depression, complete lack of energy, and pains around the bottom of your rib cage (the location of the liver). Your skin turns progressively yellow and the whites of your eyes change from white to yellow to orange.

The best way to detect hepatitis is to watch the colour of your urine, which will turn a deep orange no matter how much liquid you drink. If you haven't drunk much liquid and/or you're sweating a lot, don't jump to conclusions since you may just be dehydrated.

The severity of hepatitis A varies; it may last less than two weeks and give you only a few bad days, or it may last for several months and give you a few bad weeks. You could feel depleted of energy for several months afterwards. If you get hepatitis, rest and good food is the only cure; don't use alcohol or tobacco since that only gives your liver more work to do. It's important to keep up your food intake to assist recovery.

Havrix, a vaccine for hepatitis A, has recently been developed. It helps you develop antibodies and gives you lasting immunity.

Hepatitis B Hepatitis B is transmitted the same way the AIDS virus spreads: by sexual intercourse, by contaminated needles, by blood transfusion or during pregnancy from mother to foetus. Vietnamese 'health clinics' often reuse needles without proper sterilisation – no one knows how many people have been infected this way. Innocent use of needles – ear piercing, tattooing and acupuncture – can also spread the disease.

Although there is no treatment for hepatitis B, a cheap and effective vaccine is available; the only problem is that for long-lasting cover you need a six-month course. The immunisation schedule requires two injections at least a month apart followed by a third dose five months after the second. People who should receive a hepatitis B vaccination include anyone who anticipates contact with blood or other bodily secretions, either as a health-care worker or through sexual contact with the local population, particularly those who intend to stay in the country for a long period of time.

As for those 'health clinics', it might be wise to bring your own needle and syringe if you need injections or must have blood samples taken while in Vietnam.

Hepatitis C This is a recently defined virus. It is a concern because it seems to lead to liver disease more rapidly than hepatitis B.

The virus is spread by contact with blood - usually via contaminated transfusions or shared needles. Avoiding these is the only means of prevention, as there is no available vaccine.

Hepatitis D Often referred to as the 'Delta' virus, this infection occurs only in chronic carriers of hepatitis B. It is transmitted by blood and bodily fluids. Again, there is no vaccine for this virus, so avoidance is the best prevention. The risk to travellers is certainly limited.

Hepatitis E This is a very recently discovered virus, of which little is yet known. It appears to be rather common in developing countries, generally causing mild hepatitis, although it can be very serious in pregnant women.

Care with water supplies is the only current prevention, as there are no specific vaccines for this type of hepatitis. At present it doesn't appear to be too great a risk for travellers.

Japanese Encephalitis This illness was unheard of until the 1950s when US troops based in Okinawa (Japan) became infected. Later, cases starting showing up in Malaysia,

Indonesia, Thailand and Vietnam. Although still rare, the disease is spreading and health authorities fear that the world may yet see an epidemic. Recently, there have been outbreaks in the Mekong Delta and in District 4 of Ho Chi Minh City.

There is still much about Japanese encephalitis that is unknown. Estimates of the fatality rate range from 5% to 60%. What is certain is that if the disease infects the brain, the patient either dies or is left as a mental vegetable. Fortunately, not all cases reach the brain. Unfortunately, there is no treatment once you've been infected – all you can do is wait while the disease runs its course and hope for the best.

Mosquitoes transmit the bug that causes this illness. It's most likely to be a problem during the rainy season, and you should take care in the late afternoons and evenings, when mosquitoes are most active.

A very effective vaccine exists, but only one place in the world manufactures it – Kobe, Japan. As you may know, Kobe was devastated by an earthquake in early 1995. The factory which produces the vaccine was wrecked and there is now a worldwide shortage of this vital drug. This situation will no doubt be remedied in time, but no one can say just when.

You are not very likely to find the vaccine outside of tropical countries. Bangkok would be a logical place to get the vaccination. You can also get vaccinated at Travel Medical Consultancy (☎ 357644), 10 Nguyen Canh Chan St, District 1, Ho Chi Minh City. The big problem is the timing – you need three shots, each a week apart. You also should have a fourth jab after one year, and then every four years after that to maintain immunity.

The symptoms of Japanese encephalitis are sudden fever, chills and headache, followed by vomiting and delirium, a strong aversion to bright light, and sore joints and muscles. If it goes to the brain, convulsions, coma and death follow.

As with other mosquito-borne diseases, Japanese encephalitis can be prevented if you can avoid getting bitten by mosquitoes. See the Malaria section for some advice on how to do this.

Rabies Even if you're a devout dog lover, you aren't likely to go around petting the stray dogs you encounter in Vietnam. Third World dogs are not like the cute little fluffy creatures that play with children in the backyards of Western suburbia – they are often half-starved and badly mistreated and have been known to take a bite out of tourism.

Fido is likely to be even less friendly if infected with rabies. Although your chances of getting it is small, rabies is a disease worth guarding against. A vaccine is available but few people bother to get it. The vaccination requires three injections – one a week for three weeks – and is good for about two years. However, if you're bitten, the vaccine by itself is *not* sufficient to prevent rabies; it will only increase the time you have to get treatment, and you will require fewer injections if you've been vaccinated.

The rabies virus infects the saliva of the animal and is usually transferred when the rabid animal bites you and the virus passes through the wound into your body. It's important to realise that not only dogs carry rabies – any mammal which bites (like a rat) can transmit the virus. Also, if you have a scratch, cut or other break in the skin you could catch rabies if an infected animal licked that break in the skin. If you are bitten or licked by a possibly rabid animal, you should wash the wound thoroughly (but without scrubbing since this may push the infected saliva deeper into the your body) and then start on a series of injections which will prevent the disease from developing. Once it reaches the brain, rabies has a 100% fatality rate. New rabies vaccines have been developed which have fewer side effects than the older, animal-derived serums and vaccines.

The incubation period for rabies depends on where you're bitten. If on the head, face or neck then it's as little as 10 days, on the arms 40 days and on the legs 60 days. This allows plenty of time to be given the vaccine and for it to have a beneficial effect. With proper treatment administered quickly after being bitten, rabies will not develop.

Bilharzia Bilharzia (schistosomiasis) is not very common in Vietnam but occasional cases have been reported. Bilharzia is carried in water by minute worms. The larvae infect certain varieties of freshwater snails, found in rivers, streams, lakes and particularly behind dams or in irrigation ditches. The worms multiply and are eventually discharged into the water surrounding the snails.

They attach themselves to your intestines or bladder, where they produce large numbers of eggs. The worm enters through the skin, and the first symptom may be a tingling sensation and sometimes a light rash around the area where it entered. Weeks later, when the worm is busy producing eggs, a high fever may develop. A general feeling of being unwell may be the first symptom; once the disease is established, abdominal pain and blood in the urine are other signs.

Avoiding swimming or bathing in freshwater where bilharzia is present is the main method of preventing the disease. Even deep water can be infected. If you do get wet, dry off quickly and dry your clothes as well. Seek medical attention if you have been exposed to the disease and tell the doctor your suspicions, as bilharzia in the early stages can be confused with malaria or typhoid.

If you cannot get medical help immediately, praziquantel (Biltricide) is the recommended treatment. The recommended dose is 40 mg/kg in divided doses over one day. Niridazole is an alternative drug.

Prickly Heat & Fungus You can sweat profusely in tropical Vietnam; the sweat can't evaporate fast when the air itself is already moist, and before long you and your clothes are dripping in it. Prickly heat is a common problem for people from temperate climates. Small red blisters appear on the skin where your sweat glands have become swollen and blocked from the heavy workload. The problem is exacerbated because the sweat fails to evaporate. To prevent or cure it, wear clothes which are light and leave an air space between the material and the skin; don't wear synthetic clothes since they can't absorb the sweat; dry well after bathing and use calamine lotion or a zinc-oxide-based talcum powder. Anything that makes you sweat more – exercise, tea, coffee, alcohol – only makes the condition worse. You can also keep your skin dry with air-conditioning, electric fans or a trip to the cool mountains.

Fungal infections also occur more frequently in this sort of climate – travellers sometimes get patches of infection on the inside of the thigh (known as 'jock itch'). It itches like hell but is easy to clear up with an anti-fungal cream or powder. Powder is preferred because it doesn't make a sticky mess of your clothing, but best of all is to use both cream and powder.

Fungal ear infections usually result from swimming or washing in unclean water – Aquaear drops, available over-the-counter in Australia, are a preventative to be used before you enter or wash in the water. Some travellers carry a broad-spectrum antibiotic like Septrim to cure fungal infections. This is not a bad idea, although antibiotics can lower your resistance to other infections.

Athlete's foot is also a fungal infection, usually occurring between the toes. Wearing open-toed sandals will often solve the problem without further treatment because this permits the sweat to evaporate. It also helps to clean between the toes with warm soapy water and an old toothbrush.

Worms – Roundworm, Threadworm & Hookworm In warmer climates where hygiene standards are low there are many forms of worm infestation. Some are spread by infected meat, some by infected fish, some by infected water, and others by faecally infected earth or food.

If you get roundworm, threadworm or hookworm, treatment is straightforward. Mebendazole (a generic name which is marketed under many different labels) is most effective – you just take one pill which is good for three months. Children under six months old, nursing mothers and pregnant women should not take it without first consulting a doctor.

Ascaris, or roundworm, is the most common worm infestation that plagues foreigners. The eggs are usually ingested through vegetables that have been grown using human faeces as manure and which have not been properly washed; the eggs hatch in the stomach and then the larvae burrow through the intestines, enter the bloodstream and make their way through the liver to the heart, from where they work their way up to the lungs and the windpipe. They are then coughed up, swallowed and deposited in the intestines, where they mature and grow up to from 20 to 35 cm (eight to 14 inches) long. The most common symptoms of adult roundworm infestation are abdominal discomfort increasing to acute pain due to intestinal blockage.

Threadworm eggs, when swallowed, hatch in the stomach. The worms enter the intestine where they grow and mate; the mature female worms make their way through the bowel to the anus, where the depositing of their sticky eggs causes intense itching. One way to diagnose the presence of worms is to stretch a piece of adhesive tape over a flat stick, with the sticky area on the outside, and press it into the area around the anus. If there is an infestation you may be able to see worms and eggs on the tape – the mature worms look like little strands of cotton thread about 1.3 cm (half an inch) long.

Hookworms can be picked up by walking around with bare feet in soil littered with infected faeces. The eggs hatch in the soil and then the larvae enter the bloodstream by burrowing through the skin. Following much the same internal route as the roundworm, they reach the intestine and hook onto the lining. By feeding on the host's blood, hookworms can grow up to 1.3 cm (half an inch) long. The most common result of hookworm infestation is anaemia, although they can also do damage to the organs they come into contact with. The best prevention is to wear shoes unless on the beach. Even with shoes on, if you walk through muddy water there is a chance of getting it. Hookworms can also be absorbed by drinking infected water or eating uncooked and unwashed vegetables.

Cuts, Bites & Stings

Snakes Vietnam has several poisonous snakes, the most famous being the cobra. The small green-coloured bamboo snake is also highly venomous. Its habitat is not only bamboo trees, but also grass fields, and it can swim across small bodies of water. All sea snakes are poisonous and are readily identified by their flat tails, but sea snakes have small mouths and cannot bite humans easily.

Fortunately, snakes tend to avoid contact with creatures larger than themselves, which is good news for humans. On the other hand, snakes eat rats and will sometimes pursue their rodent delicacies right into people's homes. However, most snakebite victims are people who work in the fields and accidentally step on a snake. Be careful about walking through grass and undergrowth. Wearing boots gives a little more protection than running shoes.

A snake's head can bite even after it's been cut off. The biting reflex remains active for perhaps 45 minutes after the head has been severed. Keep this in mind if you go to a snake restaurant and want to play with a fresh cobra head.

Should you be so unfortunate as to get bitten, try to remain calm (sounds easier than it really is) and not run around. The conventional wisdom is to rest and allow the poison to be absorbed slowly. Tying a rag or towel around the limb to apply pressure slows down the poison, but the use of a tourniquet is not advisable because it can cut off circulation and cause gangrene. Cutting the skin and sucking out the poison has also been widely discredited. Immersion in cold water is also considered useless.

Treatment in a hospital with an antivenin would be ideal. However, getting the victim to a hospital is only half the battle – you will also need to identify the snake. In this particular case, it might be worthwhile to kill the snake and take its body along, but don't attempt that if it means getting bitten again. Try to transport the victim on a makeshift stretcher.

All this may sound discouraging, but the simple fact is that there is very little first-aid treatment you can give which will do much good. Fortunately, snakebite is rare and the vast majority of victims survive even without medical treatment.

Wasps & Bees Wasps, which are common in the tropics, are a more serious hazard than snakes because they are more aggressive and will chase humans when stirred up. They won't attack unless they feel threatened, but if they do attack, they usually do so en masse. This is not just uncomfortable, it can be fatal. If you're out hiking and see a wasp nest, the best advice is to move away quietly. A few brainless people like to see how skilful they are at throwing rocks at wasp nests – this is not recommended. Should you be attacked, the only sensible thing to do is run like hell.

It would take perhaps 100 wasp or bee stings to kill a normal adult, but a single sting can be fatal to someone who is allergic. In fact, death from wasp and bee stings is more common than death from snakebite. People who are allergic to wasp and bee stings are also allergic to bites by red ants. If you happen to have this sort of allergy, you'd be wise to throw an antihistamine such as epinephrine or Hismanal into your first-aid kit. Epinephrine is most effective when injected (though it can be taken in pill form), while Hismanal is preferred for long-term relief (just one pill per day). Both are prescription drugs in the West but can be bought over the counter in many Asian countries.

Agent Orange
Scientists have yet to conclusively prove a link between the residues of chemicals used by the USA during the war and spontaneous abortions, stillbirths, birth defects and other human health problems. However, the circumstantial evidence is certainly compelling. Tests have determined that the soil of southern Vietnam has one of the highest levels of dioxin in the world, whereas northern Vietnam, which was not defoliated, has one of the lowest levels of dioxin in the world. And statistics show that the rate of abnormal births is about four times as high in the south as in the north. Health professionals in

Vietnam are absolutely convinced that the abnormally high incidence of cancers and birth defects found in southern Vietnam is linked to the spraying of Agent Orange.

It is not clear what level of risk a visitor to Vietnam may face from these chemicals as a result of exposure to the food and water of the south. Dioxin is most concentrated in the tissues of water-born animals high on the food chain, such as shrimp and shellfish raised in the Mekong Delta. The risks of short-term low-level exposure are probably negligible. But women – especially those in the early months of pregnancy – may want to consider either postponing their visit or travelling only in the north. Or they may want to limit their intake of high-risk foods and consume only bottled drinks.

Those wishing to pursue this topic further might want to pay a visit to Tu Du Hospital on Nguyen Thi Minh Khai St in Ho Chi Minh City. Tragically, there are hundreds of dead deformed babies preserved in bottles here, each one marked with the date of birth. The gynaecologists at the hospital speak good English and will tell you all about it if you show genuine interest.

Traditional Medicine
There are a number of traditional medical treatments practised in Vietnam. Herbal medicine, much of it imported from China, is widely available and sometimes surprisingly effective. The Cholon district of Ho Chi Minh City is probably the best all around place in Vietnam to go looking for herbal treatments. As with Western medicine, it's best not to experiment yourself but to see a doctor. Traditional medicine doctors, also mostly ethnic-Chinese, can be readily found wherever a large Chinese community exists.

If you visit a traditional Chinese-Vietnamese doctor, you might be surprised by what he or she discovers about your body. For example, the doctor will almost certainly take your pulse and then may tell you that you have a slippery pulse or perhaps a thready pulse. Traditional doctors have identified more than 30 different kinds of pulses. A pulse could be empty, prison, leisurely, bowstring, irregular or even regularly irregular. The doctor may then examine your tongue to see if it is slippery, dry, pale, greasy, has a thick coating or maybe no coating at all. The doctor, having discovered that you have wet heat, as evidenced by a slippery pulse and a red greasy tongue, will prescribe the proper herbs for your condition.

One traditional treatment is called moxibustion. Various types of herbs, rolled into what looks like a ball of fluffy cotton, are held just near the skin and ignited. A slight variation of this method is to place the herb on a slice of ginger and then ignite it. The idea is to apply the maximum amount of heat possible without burning the patient. This heat treatment is supposed to be good for such diseases as arthritis.

Another technique employs suction cups made of bamboo placed on the patient's skin. A burning piece of alcohol-soaked cotton is briefly put inside the cup to drive out the air before it is applied. As the cup cools, a partial vacuum is produced, leaving a nasty-looking but harmless red circular mark on the skin. The mark goes away in a few days.

The rather horrible-looking red marks seen on the necks of Vietnamese (especially in the Mekong Delta region) are not from some disease. Rather, they are the result of the cure. The marks are made by pinching the skin or scraping it vigorously with a coin or spoon. This is supposed to bring blood to the surface – and indeed it does – producing nasty looking welts that eventually heal. This is a treatment for the common cold, fatigue, headaches and other ailments. Whether the cure hurts less than the disease is something one can only judge from experience.

Can you cure people by sticking needles into them? The adherents of acupuncture say you can, and they have some solid evidence to back them up. For example, some major surgical operations have been performed using acupuncture as the only anaesthetic (this works best on the head). In this case, a small electric current (from batteries) is passed through the needles.

Getting stuck with needles might not sound pleasant, but if done properly it doesn't hurt. Knowing just where to insert the needle is crucial. Acupuncturists have identified more than 2000 insertion points, but only about 150 are commonly used. The exact mechanism by which acupuncture works is not fully understood. Practitioners talk of energy channels or meridians which connect the needle insertion point to the particular organ, gland or joint being treated. The acupuncture point is sometimes quite far from the area of the body being treated.

Nonsterile acupuncture needles pose a genuine health risk in this era of the AIDS epidemic. You'd be wise to purchase your own if you wish to try this treatment.

Women's Health

Gynaecological Problems Poor diet, lowered resistance due to the use of antibiotics for stomach upsets and even contraceptive pills can lead to vaginal infections when travelling in hot climates. Keeping the genital area clean and wearing skirts or loose-fitting trousers and cotton underwear will help to prevent infections.

Yeast infections, characterised by a rash, itch and discharge, can be treated with a vinegar or even lemon-juice douche or with yoghurt. Nystatin suppositories are the usual medical prescription. Trichomonas is a more serious infection; symptoms are a discharge and a burning sensation when urinating. Male sexual partners must also be treated, and if a vinegar-water douche is not effective medical attention should be sought. Flagyl is the prescribed drug.

Pregnancy Most miscarriages occur during the first three months of pregnancy, so this is the most risky time to travel. The last three months should also be spent within reasonable distance of good medical care, as quite serious problems can develop at this time. Pregnant women should avoid alcohol and all unnecessary medication, but vaccinations should still be taken where possible. Additional care should be taken to prevent illness, and particular attention should be paid to diet and nutrition.

WOMEN TRAVELLERS

Like Thailand and other predominantly Buddhist countries, Vietnam is, in general, relatively free of serious hassles for women travellers. An important exception seems to be in or around cheap hotels where prostitution is a major part of the business.

The scarcity of public toilets seems to be a greater problem for women than for men. Vietnamese males can often be seen urinating in public, but this seems to be socially unacceptable for women. It is not very clear how Vietnamese women handle this situation.

DANGERS & ANNOYANCES
Theft

Vietnamese are convinced that their cities are very dangerous and full of criminals. Before reunification street crime was rampant in the South, especially in Saigon. Motorbike-borne thieves (called 'cowboys' by the Americans) would speed down major thoroughfares, ripping pedestrians' watches off their wrists. Pickpocketing and confidence tricks were also common. After the fall of Saigon, a few bold criminals even swindled the newly arrived North Vietnamese troops. When a few such outlaws were summarily shot, street crime almost disappeared overnight.

When the Vietnamese withdrawal from Cambodia was completed in 1989, the government accelerated its programme to cut military expenditures by discharging tens of thousands of soldiers from the army. Joining an already saturated job market without marketable skills and without government assistance in finding employment, many have been unable to earn a living. Some have turned to crime.

Another source of criminals are the disillusioned youths who have been discriminated against because their parents worked for the Americans during the war. The government has succeeded in creating an enormous new social problem for itself – not surprisingly some of the 'born bad' children are turning to criminal activities. This could explain why crime rates are highest in the south, especially in Ho Chi Minh City. Crime rates have risen precipitously in the past couple of years, and the criminals have not overlooked the lucrative tourism sector.

Especially watch out for drive-by thieves on motorbikes – they specialise in snatching handbags and cameras from tourists riding in cyclos. Some have become proficient at grabbing valuables from the open window of a car and speeding away with the loot. Foreigners have occasionally reported having their eyeglasses and hats snatched too.

Pickpocketing – often involving kids, women with babies and newspaper vendors – is also a serious problem, especially in tourist areas of Saigon, such as Dong Khoi and Pham Ngu Lao Sts.

The cute little children also wander right into cafes and restaurants where foreigners are eating, ostensibly to sell you a newspaper or postcards. In the process – and often with the help of another child accomplice – they can relieve you of your camera or handbag if you've set it down on an adjacent seat. If you must set things down while you're eating, at least take the precaution of fastening these items to your seat with a strap or chain. Remember, any luggage that you leave unattended for even a moment may grow legs and vanish.

We have had recent reports of people getting drugged and then robbed on long-distance public buses. The way it usually works is that a friendly fellow passenger offers you a free Coke, which turns out to be a chloral hydrate cocktail. You wake up hours later to find your valuables and newfound 'friend' gone. If you're very unlucky, you don't wake up at all because an overdose of chloral hydrate can easily be fatal.

Even assuming that you are too wise to accept gifts from strangers, there is at least one other way you can be drugged. One traveller we know well claims that his fellow passenger leaned across him to open a window, while an accomplice took advantage of the diversion to drop some drugs into his water bottle. The lesson seems to be that you should keep your water bottle where no one can easily get their hands on it.

Despite all this, you should not be overly paranoid. Although crime certainly exists and you need to be aware of it, theft in Vietnam does not seem to be any worse than elsewhere in the Third World (including 'Third World' cities in the West). Don't assume that everyone's a thief – most Vietnamese are very poor but reasonably honest.

And finally, there is the problem of your fellow travellers. It's a disgusting reality that some backpackers subsidise their journey by ripping off whomever they can, including other backpackers. This is most likely to happen if you stay in a dormitory, though in this regard Vietnam is relatively safe since dormitories are rare. Perhaps most disturbing of all are attempts by foreigners to rip off the Vietnamese. There have been reports of backpackers slipping out of restaurants without paying their bills, cheating their guides out of promised pay, etc. We know one fellow who deliberately short-changed his driver US$40 because the car's air-conditioner broke down on the last day of the trip. This is pretty sick.

To avoid theft, probably the best advice one can follow is to not bring anything valuable that you don't need. Expensive watches, jewellery and electronic gadgets invite theft, but do you really need these things while travelling?

Violence

Unlike in some Western cities, recreational homicide is not a popular sport in Vietnam. In general, violence against foreigners is extremely rare. Vietnamese thieves prefer to pick your pocket or grab your bag and then run away – knives, guns, sticks and other weapons are almost never used. However, there have been a few incidents involving guns, particularly on remote rural roads. One gang terrorised motorists in the Danang area for two years, stopping vehicles and robbing the passengers at gunpoint. After committing over 60 robberies, the gang was finally caught in mid-1994 and the thieves were sentenced to death.

Vietnamese newspapers have started reporting a recent upsurge in violent robberies. So far, the victims have been overwhelmingly Vietnamese – the thieves seem to be somewhat afraid to get involved with foreigners. That, of course, could change.

You do see a lot of street arguments between Vietnamese. Usually this takes the form of two young macho types threatening and pushing each other while their respective girlfriends try to separate them. The whole point of the threats and chest-thumping exercise is to save face, and there is seldom any bloodshed. The cause of these arguments usually has something to do with money, often the result of a minor motor vehicle accident and who should pay for the broken headlight or squashed chicken. Such macho posturing is likely to exclude foreigners. Indeed, the Vietnamese bend over backwards to be friendly towards foreigners – how they treat one another is a different matter.

'Prostitute' Vigilantes

An Asian woman accompanied by a Western male will automatically be labelled a 'Vietnamese whore'. The fact that the couple could be married (or just friends) doesn't seem to occur to anyone, nor does it seem to register that the woman might not be Vietnamese at all. If she's Asian then she's Vietnamese, and if she's with a Western male then she must be a prostitute. It will be difficult to convince most Vietnamese otherwise.

Women in this situation can expect daily verbal abuse, though it will be spoken entirely in Vietnamese, which means she may not realise that insults are being hurled at her if she doesn't speak the language. However, there will be no mistaking the hateful stares and obscene gestures. All this abuse will come from Vietnamese men (including teenagers) rather than Vietnamese women.

Verbal abuse is one thing, but there is the real possibility that the woman in question will become a target for occasional physical abuse too. Women labelled 'whores' have reported having had rocks thrown at them, being hit by sticks, being spit upon, etc. Fortunately, this is rarely a group activity – the vigilante is usually a sole low-life greased with a bit of alcohol. Cyclo drivers (always male) are some of the worst offenders, though teenage boys are fond of rock-throwing. Interestingly, all the abuse is directed at the woman – the Western male will be ignored unless he physically intervenes on his companion's behalf.

The Vietnamese government has made no attempt so far to educate the masses to stop this crude behaviour. For racially mixed couples wanting to visit Vietnam, no easy solution exists. Of course, public intimacy (holding hands, etc) is best avoided, but even just walking down the street together invites abuse. Four people travelling together are less likely to encounter trouble than just two, but this isn't guaranteed. In an actual confrontation, the woman should shout some abuse at the antagonist in any language *other* than Vietnamese – this might make the vigilante realise that he is confronting a foreigner rather than a 'Vietnamese whore'. If this revelation sinks in, he might suddenly apologise! The Western male might be tempted to physically bash a Vietnamese man who is insulting his Asian wife or girlfriend, but this could lead to a brawl with serious consequences. Before you hit anyone, remember that some of the spectators could be the man's brothers and they may retaliate.

Prostitute Scam

Of course, there are real prostitutes in Vietnam. What you might not be aware of is that there are fake ones too, as well as fake vigilantes. There have been persistent reports in the tourist zones (especially Dong Khoi St and Nguyen Hue Blvd in Saigon) of single male travellers being approached in the evening by women claiming to be prostitutes. Those foreigners foolish enough to even talk to these 'prostitutes' for a couple of minutes may suddenly be approached by a very angry, screaming 'husband' of the woman claiming that the foreigner is trying to rape his wife. He makes a big scene, a crowd gathers and he demands US$100 or so in 'compensation'.

Con artists are, of course, always seeking new tricks to separate naive tourists from their money. We can't warn you about every trick you might encounter, so perhaps the best advice we can give is to maintain a healthy scepticism and be prepared to argue when demands are made for your money.

The Police

The problem of police corruption has been acknowledged in official newspapers. To be fair, Vietnam is hardly unique in this sense. The conditions that plague many Third World police forces – very low pay and low levels of education and training– certainly exist in Vietnam.

If something does go wrong, or if something is stolen, the police often can't do much more than write a report for your insurance company. Unfortunately, even to get this limited help, some people have found it necessary to pay a 'tip' for this service. The tip can be anything from a pack of Marlboros to perhaps US$100.

In the last edition of this book, we reported that the police frequently stopped foreigners, asked to 'see their passports', and then refused to return these documents unless a considerable bribe was paid. We are now happy to say the government has cracked down hard on this practice. Hanoi has warned all provincial governments that any police caught shaking down foreign tourists will be fired and arrested. Unfortunately this has not eliminated the problem altogether.

Perhaps 10% of the hundreds of letters we receive from travellers contains some negative comment about the Vietnamese police – the following is typical:

The police seem to leave Westerners alone, but stopped and fined our cyclo driver after we were dropped off in Hué; sea police stopped and fined our boat captain near Cat Ba Island, visited our hotel in Hoi An and fined the manager and then woke us up at midnight to check our passports (the police were both drunk); money changed hands at street corners for 'traffic offences' quite openly.

Basically, the police first try to extort money from your Vietnamese drivers, guides and friends (should you be travelling with any). The police know that these people cannot afford to pay fines, but that you will probably fork out the cash. Fines are generally negotiable – the bidding may start at US$200 but can be reduced all the way down to US$5.

Certain places in Vietnam have acquired a particularly nasty reputation for this kind of scam. At the time of writing, we found that Dalat and Danang were the worst. Staying overnight in Dong Ha should also be avoided (the police confiscate passports from the hotels), though no one has reported problems just passing through. Dishonourable mention also goes to Hué and Haiphong, though the situation in those two cities is not quite as bad. More details are provided in the relevant chapters of this book.

With all this having been said, there is really no need for excessive paranoia. The Vietnamese police are a nuisance. You may have to pay, but you will usually not have to pay a lot. To avoid getting upset, you have to do as the Vietnamese do – think of 'fines' as a 'tax'.

Beggar Fatigue

Just as you're about to dig into the scrumptious Vietnamese meal you've ordered, you feel someone gently tugging on your shirt-sleeve. You turn around to deal with this latest 'annoyance' only to find it's a bony eight-year-old boy holding his three-year-old sister in his arms. The little girl has a distended stomach, her palm is stretched out to you and her hungry eyes fixed on your plate of steaming chicken, vegetables and rice.

This is the face of poverty. How do you deal with these situations? If you're like most of us, not very well. On occasion, we've given food to a small group of beggars and watched in horror as they fought over it.

Nevertheless, it's probably better to give food than to give money – little children are often forced by their parents to beg for money, but the cash is frequently used to support the parents' drinking and gambling habits rather than to feed the children or send them to school. Of course, that's if the kids have parents, which many of them don't.

So what can you do to help these street people, many of whom are malnourished and illiterate and have no future? Good question – we wish we knew. Give or refuse as you wish, and spare a moment to think of just how lucky you are.

I will always remember the beam of delight that came over the face of a hardbitten child beggar when I offered him a cake similar to the one I was eating.

Gordon Balderston

Undetonated Explosives

Four armies expended untold energy and resources for over three decades mining, booby-trapping, rocketing, strafing, mortaring, bombing and bombarding wide areas of Vietnam. When the fighting stopped most of this ordnance remained exactly where it had landed or been laid; American estimates at the time placed the quantity of unexploded ordnance at 150,000 tonnes. After the war only small areas were effectively cleared of mines and other explosives.

Since 1975, many thousands of Vietnamese have been maimed or killed by this leftover ordnance while clearing land for cultivation or ploughing their fields. While cities, cultivated areas and well-travelled rural roads and paths are safe for travel, straying away from these areas could land you in the middle of a minefield which, though known to the locals, may be completely unmarked.

Never touch any rockets, artillery shells, mortars, mines or other relics of the war you may come across. Such objects can remain lethal for decades. In Europe, people are still sometimes injured by ordnance left over from WW II and even WW I, and every few years you read about city blocks in London or Rotterdam being evacuated after an old bomb is discovered in someone's backyard.

Especially dangerous are white phosphorus artillery shells (known to the Americans as 'Willy Peter'), whose active ingredient does not deteriorate as quickly as do explosives. Upon contact with the air the white phosphorus contained in the shells ignites and burns intensely; if any of it gets on your body it will eat all the way through your hand, leg or torso unless scooped out with a razor blade – imagine that. This stuff terrifies even scrap-metal scavengers. If you want to find out more about it, just ask the doctors at any provincial hospital in an area that saw heavy fighting.

And don't climb inside bomb craters – you never know what undetonated explosive device is at the bottom.

Drugs

During the Vietnam War, US troops were known to partake of large quantities of noxious weeds, hashish and stronger recreational chemicals. After 1975, the loss of American customers plus the Communists' sophisticated police state apparatus and the country's extreme poverty suppressed domestic demand for drugs. However, the recent influx of foreign tourists, along with economic progress, has revived the drug trade. Besides domestic production, many drugs are smuggled in through Cambodia to Ho Chi Minh City, Vietnam's biggest consumer market.

Needless to say, the drug trade has its ugly side. There are many local heroin addicts in Ho Chi Minh City. In addition, there is corruption, and this can affect foreigners. The police are in a good position to extort money from the drug dealers, who in turn have good incentive to turn in Western customers – this satisfies the police, who can extort huge fines from foreigners. You should also be aware that there are many plain-clothes police in Vietnam – just because you don't see them doesn't mean they aren't there.

The drug export market has also been doing well, and Vietnam's reputation is such that customs officials at your next destination might vigorously search your luggage. In short, drug use in Vietnam is still a perilous activity and taking home samples is also a high-risk activity.

Cockroaches

While some travellers are amused by the antics of cockroaches, at least some people find them very disturbing. Vietnamese cockroaches are well fed and can grow to amazingly large size. Cockroach-infested hotel rooms are the norm in Vietnam, especially at the budget end of the scale.

Cockroaches are actually relatively easy to deal with if you come prepared. One way is to launch a chemical blitzkrieg against these beasties with insecticide, though such nerve-gas attacks might pose a hazard to your own health.

Boric acid (a white powder) is deadly poison to cockroaches if they so much as inhale the dust. This chemical is also very poisonous to humans if taken internally, but is harmless externally (mixed with water, boric acid is often used as eyewash). Sprinkling some boric acid powder in your hotel room under the bed (not in the bed!), in the corners, on the washroom floor and along other likely cockroach routes will have the desired effect. At first you might think there are more cockroaches than ever because the poison drives them out into the open, but after a few hours your room will be cockroach-free.

Boric acid can be purchased easily and cheaply in almost any pharmacy, both inside and outside Vietnam. Try to keep it in a reasonably sturdy container (not a plastic bag) – small, plastic jars are useful for this purpose. Some hazards: it's dangerous to keep around children, and some travellers report being harassed by customs because of boric acid's physical resemblance to cocaine!

Rats

Even cockroach enthusiasts are generally reluctant to share a hotel room with rats. If you encounter rats in Vietnam, they are not likely to be the cute, fluffy white creatures forced to smoke cigarettes and drink Diet Coke in Western medical experiments. Rather, they are the grey, decidedly less friendly variety.

Avoiding nocturnal visits by these creatures is fairly simple: don't keep any food in your hotel room.

Sea Creatures

If you spend your time swimming, snorkelling and scuba diving, you should be aware of various creatures which live in the sea that can be hazardous. It's a well-established fact that most nasty sea creatures live in warm water, so the farther south you are in Vietnam, the greater the risk of unpleasant encounters. The list of dangerous sea creatures found in Vietnam is extensive, and could include sharks, jellyfish, stonefish, scorpion fish, sea snakes and stingrays, to name a few. However, there is little cause for alarm – most of these creatures either avoid humans or humans avoid them, so the actual number of people injured or killed by sea animals is fairly small. Nonetheless, exercising some common sense is strongly advised.

Shark attacks mostly occur in deeper water – keeping to shallow spots decreases your chance of trouble. Sharks are attracted by bright colours like red, yellow and orange, so wearing a dark swimsuit is a reasonable precaution. Blood attracts sharks, so if you cut your foot you should get out of the water immediately.

Jellyfish tend to travel in groups, so avoiding them is usually not too difficult if you look before you leap into the sea. Make local inquiries – many places experience a 'jellyfish season' (usually summer). Stings from jellyfish are painful, but *usually* not fatal. However, some people experience allergic reactions, and certain species of tropical jellyfish are unusually dangerous. Dousing in vinegar (or urine in an emergency) will deactivate any stingers which have not 'fired'. Calamine lotion, antihistamines and analgesics may reduce the reaction and relieve the pain.

Stonefish, scorpion fish and stingrays tend to hang out in shallow water along the ocean floor and can be very difficult to see. Stepping on one can be bad news indeed. One way to protect yourself would be to wear shoes while wading in the sea, but most people won't do this. To treat a sting by a stonefish or scorpion fish, immerse the affected part in hot water (the hotter the better, but don't burn yourself!) and seek medical treatment.

All sea snakes are poisonous but are generally nonaggressive. Furthermore, their small fangs are placed towards the rear of the mouth and they would have a difficult time biting a large creature such as a human.

Noise

One thing that can be insidiously draining on your energy during a trip to Vietnam is noise. At night, there is often a competing cacophony from motorbikes, dance halls, cafes, video parlours, karaoke lounges, restaurants and so on; if your hotel is situated near any of the above (and it's unlikely to be in a totally noise-free zone), sleep may be difficult. In some places, such as Nha Trang, even the small carts of ice cream and snack vendors have a booming, distorted portable cassette player attached.

The Vietnamese themselves seem to be immune to the noise. Indeed, a cafe that doesn't have an eardrum-splitting cacophony emanating from a loudspeaker will have difficulty attracting customers. That is to say, 'Vietnamese customers'. The foreigners will flee as soon as the sound system is turned on. Those who stay long enough to finish a meal or a cup of coffee will walk away with their heads literally pounding.

Fortunately, most of the noise subsides around 10 or 11 pm, as few clubs stay open much later than that. Unfortunately, though, the Vietnamese are very early risers; most people are up and about from around 5 am onwards. This not only means that traffic noise starts early, but that you're likely to be woken up by the crackle of cafe speakers, followed by very loud (and often atrocious) local or foreign music. It's worth trying to get a hotel room at the back, so the effect of street noise is diminished (especially in Ho Chi Minh City with its motorcycle 'raceways'). Other than that, perhaps you could consider bringing a set of earplugs.

WORK

From 1975 to about 1990, Vietnam's foreign workers were basically technical specialists and military advisers from Eastern Europe and the now-defunct Soviet Union. The declining fortunes of the Eastern Bloc has caused most of these advisers to be withdrawn.

Vietnam's opening to capitalist countries has suddenly created all sorts of work opportunities for Westerners. However, don't come to Vietnam looking for big money. The most well-paid Westerners living in Vietnam are those working for official foreign organisations such as the United Nations and embassies, or else have been hired by private foreign companies attempting to set up joint-venture operations. People with certain high-technology skills may also find themselves much in demand and able to secure high pay and cushy benefits.

Nice work if you can get it, but such plum jobs are thin on the ground. Foreigners who look like Rambo have occasionally been approached by Vietnamese talent scouts wanting to recruit them to work as extras in war movies. But for the vast majority of travellers, the most readily available work opportunities will be teaching a foreign language.

English is by far the most popular foreign language with Vietnamese students. About 10% of foreign language students in Vietnam also want to learn French. There are also many Vietnamese who want to learn Chinese, but many ethnic Chinese live in Vietnam so there is little need to import foreign teachers. There is also some demand for teachers of Japanese, German, Spanish and Korean.

Government-run universities in Vietnam hire some foreign teachers. Pay is generally around US$2 per hour, but certain benefits like free housing and unlimited visa renewals are usually thrown in. Teaching at a university requires some commitment – you may have to sign a one-year contract, for example.

There is also a budding free market in private language centres and home tutoring, and this is where most newly arrived foreigners seek work. Pay in the private sector is slightly better than what the government offers – figure on US$3 to US$4 per hour depending on where in Vietnam you teach.

At private schools, free housing and other perks are usually not included. A business visa is required to be legally employed, and the school may not be in a good position to help you out with the authorities. One possible way around the visa hurdles is to sign up for Vietnamese language lessons at a university, but be aware that you may actually be expected to attend class and study.

Private tutoring pays even better, around US$5 per hour and more. In this case, you are in business for yourself. The authorities may or may not turn a blind eye to such activities.

Everyone who has become a foreign language teacher in Vietnam will have a different story to tell. There is no one way to do it. One experienced English teacher in Saigon gave this summation of his experience:

There are countless schools which are willing to hire you. Pay is around US$4 per hour in Saigon. They tell you a business visa is required for it to be legal, but some will let this slide. I don't advise signing a contract unless the school is *very* reputable (ie, other foreigners are working there and happy). Agreements mean nothing here. Your salary might be lowered without your consent, you might get underpaid (count the money in that envelope carefully) and you might find upon arriving for class that the director has decided that the lesson you have prepared has been replaced by another. Flakiness abounds on all fronts. The classes are huge (up to 60). You might find yourself yelling into a microphone, competing with the roar of traffic noises a few metres away and with the teachers shouting into microphones in the adjoining classrooms. Other than a few token nods to the Asian tradition of respecting teachers, the students are often uncooperative in these huge classes, talking to each other while you're lecturing, arriving late, leaving early, etc.

The answer, I find, is to teach privately. The students are much more motivated and respectful, especially if you keep the class size small. Still, there's the flakiness factor. Classes routinely cancel at the last minute with no reason given. Or a group of students might cancel out forever with no warning. Everything is subject to change at a moment's notice. Ask for payment two weeks in advance and things go much better, but they'll only agree if they know that you too are reliable and won't abscond. In other words, you have to work awhile to build up your reputation. You can make between US$5 and US$10 per hour depending on the number of students in your class and how affluent they are. I have a teaching certificate, but I hardly think it's mandatory – plenty of people find work without one.

The authorities must know what I've been doing all along, but they've never bothered me. I've been working on a tourist visa and have been getting away with it. Other teachers I know have obtained business visas through local companies, whom they basically bribed to exercise their pull with the authorities and say these teachers work for them as 'consultants'. The main hassle is finding a place to live. Landlords will tell you they're licensed to house foreigners, and then the cops will come by and kick you out a few days after you've moved in.

Finding teaching jobs is relatively easy in place like Saigon and Hanoi, but is sometimes possible in smaller towns that have universities. Pay in the smaller towns tends to be lower and work opportunities considerably scarcer. Looking for employment is a matter of asking around – jobs are rarely advertised. The longer you stay, the easier it is to find work – travellers hoping to land a quick job and depart two months later will probably be disappointed.

Now that the USA has re-established diplomatic relations with Vietnam, US citizens might be able to find volunteer work with the US Peace Corps. Citizens of the UK might want to contact the British Consul to find out about similar opportunities. Organisations like the International Red Cross might also be able to advise you.

Some Western journalists and photographers manage to make a living in Vietnam by selling their stories and pictures to Western news organisations. If you're lucky enough to land a full-time job with Reuters, that's great. However, most journalists and photojournalists are forced to work freelance and pay can vary from decent to dismal.

ACTIVITIES
Swimming, Snorkelling & Diving
With 3260 km of mostly tropical coastline, Vietnam would seem like Asia's answer to Queensland or the Spanish Riviera. Indeed, there are some excellent beaches, though not quite as many as you'd expect. Part of the reason is that the southern part of the country (which has the best tropical climate and highest population) is dominated by the huge Mekong Delta. While this region is lush, green and lovely, it's also very muddy and the beaches tend to be mangrove swamps. One of the few beach areas in this region is Ha Tien, right on the Cambodian border and facing the Gulf of Thailand.

The southernmost good beach on the east coast is Vung Tau, a very popular place just north of the Mekong Delta and very close to Ho Chi Minh City. Without a doubt, Nha Trang has emerged as Vietnam's premier beach resort in part because of its year-round lovely weather. Heading north towards Danang, you'll find numerous other good beaches, mostly undeveloped, but the weather becomes more seasonal – May to July is the best time, while during the winter powerful rip tides make swimming dangerous. North of Hué, the weather becomes truly awful, with frequent storms and typhoons. But in the far north near Haiphong, summers are usually fine and the beaches are often crowded.

Most Vietnamese people love the beach but have a respectful fear of the sea – they like to wade up to their knees but seldom dive in and go for a proper swim. Where you are most likely to see Vietnamese actually swimming is in rivers and public swimming pools. Surfing and windsurfing have only recently arrived on the scene, so far only in the Danang area. Such activities are sure to expand.

It is possible to hire snorkelling gear and scuba equipment at several beach resorts, particularly at Nha Trang. But some warnings are in order. Equipment is sometimes good, sometimes not. Half-empty tanks of air have been rented out. If a squall comes up, boat operators have occasionally been known to head for shore, leaving the hapless divers for lost! Of course, fatal diving accidents can and do occur in developed countries as well, but extra precautions should be taken in any poor country. Don't always assume that equipment and training is up to international standards.

Gambling
After being banned by the Communists for 14 years, gambling, that most bourgeois cap-

italist activity, is staging a comeback. Horse racing is once again popular in Saigon (see the Ho Chi Minh City chapter). Vietnam's first casino since liberation opened in 1994 at Do Son Beach near Haiphong. And in the back alleys of large cities, slot machines have popped up inside of karaoke clubs – these machines are now legal as 'entertainment devices'.

You can easily avoid the horse racing, casinos and slot machines if you don't want to play, but you'll have a hard time escaping the state lottery. Touts (mostly children) selling lottery tickets will approach you anytime and anywhere, and they are usually *very* persistent. If the kids seem miserable, it's not hard to understand – they get to keep only 12% of the face value of each ticket sold; 1% goes to the wholesaler and the other 87% goes to the government.

While your chances of winning are minuscule, hitting the jackpot in the state lottery can make you a dong multimillionaire. The smallest denomination lottery ticket is 1000d (less than US$0.10), while the largest prize is 25 million dong (somewhat less than US$2500).

The official state lottery has to compete against an illegal numbers game *(danh de)* reputed to offer better odds. Two of the most popular forms of illegal gambling are dominoes *(tu sat)* and cock fighting. Some of the ethnic Chinese living in the Cholon district of Ho Chi Minh City are said to be keen mahjong players.

Golf

Mark Twain once said that playing golf was 'a waste of a good walk', and apparently Ho Chi Minh agreed with him. When the French departed Vietnam, Ho Chi Minh's advisers declared golf to be a 'bourgeois practice'. In 1975, after the fall of South Vietnam, golf was banned and all courses were shut down and turned into farming cooperatives. However, times have changed – golf was rehabilitated in 1992 and now even government officials can be seen riding around in electric carts in hot pursuit of a little white ball.

Throughout the Far East, playing golf can win you considerable points in the 'face game' even if you never hit the ball. For maximum snob value, you need to join a country club, and the fees for this are outrageously high. In Vietnam, golf memberships start at around US$20,000 or so – Japanese travellers comment that this is incredibly cheap.

Most clubs (not all) will allow you to simply pay a steep guest fee for attacking a golfball with a No 5 iron. Chances are good that you'll have the course to yourself, since most of the members will be back at the club house drinking scotch. Nevertheless, some clubs will require that you at least be accompanied by a member before they permit you to play.

Places to pursue this activity include the environs of Ho Chi Minh City, Hanoi, Dalat and Vung Tau. See the relevant chapters for details.

Hash House Harriers

This is mainly for foreign residents of Hanoi and Ho Chi Minh City, so if you're just passing through you might not be enthusiastically welcomed. Hash House Harriers is a loosely-strung international club with branches all over the world. It appeals mainly to young people, or the young at heart. Activities typically include a weekend afternoon easy jogging session followed by a dinner and beer party, which can extend until the wee hours of the morning.

The Hanoi Hash is more active than the Ho Chi Minh City Hash. This may reflect the fact that the weather is cooler (thus better for running) in Hanoi or that there is a greater abundance of parks and other jogging spots around Hanoi. Or perhaps it has something to do with the large number of expat embassy staff stationed in Hanoi. Nevertheless, you can certainly find some fellow joggers in Ho Chi Minh City, and no shortage of places for nighttime drinking marathons.

The Hash is very informal. There is no club headquarters and no stable contact telephone or address. Nonetheless, finding the Hash is easy. Some embassy or consulate employees know about it; otherwise look for announcements in the *Vietnam Economic Times* and expat bars. See the Activities section in the Hanoi chapter of this book for information about the Hash in that city.

Language Courses

If you'd like to learn to speak Vietnamese, courses are now being offered in Ho Chi Minh City, Hanoi and elsewhere. To qualify for student visa status, you need to study at a bona fide university (as opposed to a private language centre or with a tutor). Universities require that you study 10 hours per week. Lessons usually last for two hours per day, for which you pay tuition of around US$5.

You should establish early on whether you want to study in northern or southern Vietnam, because the regional dialects are very different. Foreign students who learned Vietnamese in Hanoi and then moved to Saigon to find work (or vice versa) have often been dismayed to discover that they cannot communicate. But (get ready for this)

the majority of the teachers at universities in the south have been imported from the north, and will tell you that the northern dialect is the 'correct one'! So even if you study at a university in Saigon, you may find that you need to hire a local private tutor (cheap at any rate) to help rid you of a northern accent.

For information on specific language schools where you can study Vietnamese, see the Activities section in the chapters dealing with Hanoi and Ho Chi Minh City.

HIGHLIGHTS

Vietnam offers tremendous variety and can suit many different tastes – it's difficult to say just what places should be on the top of your list. Beach lovers will almost certainly want to check out Nha Trang. The splendid rock formations, sea cliffs and grottoes of Halong Bay in the north could easily rate as one of the wonders of the world. Similar and equally breathtaking scenery can be seen at the Perfume Pagoda and Hoa Lu. Cat Ba Island also gets rave reviews from all who make the effort to get here. The rugged over-

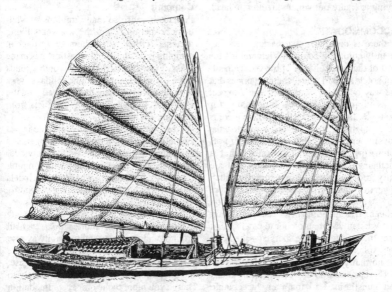

Junk at Halong Bay, Northern Vietnam

land trip to Sapa and Dien Bien Phu offers a glimpse of minority lifestyles in one of Vietnam's most wild and remote areas. The islands around Vinh Long give perhaps the best glimpse of rural Mekong Delta life. The Caodai Great Temple near Tay Ninh is a striking rococo structure. Dalat – with its parklike setting, waterfalls, ethnic minorities and cool mountain climate – also rates high.

History and architecture buffs will be attracted to Hué and Hoi An. For those fascinated by the Vietnam War and all its implications, what better place to pursue the topic than the old Demilitarised Zone (DMZ)?

And if you've had enough of seeing what Vietnam's landscape looks like, perhaps you'd like to see what's under it? There are few better places to do this than Phong Nha Cave.

Finally, one should not forget the cities. Freewheeling Saigon, with its dilapidated colonial elegance, outstanding food and bustling nightlife, is a laboratory for Vietnam's economic reforms. Hanoi, with its monuments, parks, lakes and tree-lined boulevards, is the beguiling seat of power in a country trying to figure out which direction to head.

ACCOMMODATION

If there is one thing that backpackers frequently complain about in Vietnam, it's the cost of the hotels. Many of the government-run hotels are bad value, charging prices that are way out of line with what you'd expect to find in Thailand or Indonesia, for example. In rural backwaters where there is no competition from the private sector, the government hotels can be an absolute rip-off (charging foreigners 10 times what a Vietnamese would pay for rooms that are truly grotty). Prices are generally much lower in urban areas or touristy places, where private hotels are numerous and competition is keen. The government's excuse is usually that Vietnamese are too poor to pay the high rates that foreigners are charged – this does not explain though why Overseas Vietnamese normally receive a 50% discount.

There are now regulations requiring hotels and guesthouses to maintain 'acceptable standards' before they can be approved to receive foreign guests (you'd never know it by some of the dumps around). So it is possible that you will front up to what seems like a perfectly serviceable hotel and be refused a room even if the place is empty. In that case, there is little point arguing. The hotel staff won't risk trouble with the police just to accommodate you, though they might refer you elsewhere.

Theoretically, these regulations are meant to protect foreign tourists from staying in dirty and dangerous places. In practice, the motive is often less honourable. In some places (Dalat comes to mind), foreigners are simply not allowed to stay in private hotels because these compete with the government-owned ones, even though the private hotels are often of a higher standard. Occasionally, this can create a real problem for you – if the approved hotels are all full and you can't stay in the unapproved ones, your only choice is to sleep in the street. The Vietnamese have a name for sleeping in the street – it's called staying in a 'thousand-star hotel'.

Camping

Perhaps because so many millions of Vietnamese spent much of the war years living in tents (either as soldiers or refugees), camping is not the popular pastime it is in the West. Even in Dalat, where youth groups often come for out-of-doors holidays, very little proper equipment can be hired (and the Dalat government prohibits foreigners from camping anyway).

However, some innovative private travel agencies in Saigon now offer organised camping trips for groups. As for individual travellers, the biggest problem with camping is finding a remote spot where curious locals won't gather around for a staring session.

Dormitories

While there are dormitories (nha tro) all around Vietnam (especially at railway and bus stations), most (but not all) of these are officially off limits to foreigners. In this case, the government's motives are not simply to charge you more money for accommodation – there is a significant chance of getting

SAIGON-HANOI RAILWAY

Construction of the 1726-km Saigon-Hanoi railway – the Transindochinois – was begun in 1899 and completed in 1936. During WW II, the Japanese made extensive use of the rail system, resulting in Viet Minh sabotage on the ground and US bombing from the air. After the war, efforts were made to repair the Transindochinois.

During the Franco-Viet Minh War, the Viet Minh engaged in massive sabotage against the rail system and managed to put into service 300 km of track in an area wholly under their control. The French responded with sabotage of their own.

In the late 1950s, the South, with US funding, reconstructed the track between Saigon and Hué, a distance of 1041 km. But between 1961 and 1964 alone, there were 795 VC attacks on the rail system, forcing the abandonment of large sections of track (including the Dalat spur). A major reconstruction effort was carried out between 1967 and 1969.

The North had repaired 1000 km of track by 1960, mostly between Hanoi and China. During the US air war against the North, the northern rail network was repeatedly bombed.

After reunification, the government immediately set about re-establishing the Hanoi-Saigon rail link as a symbol of Vietnamese unity. By the time the Reunification (Thong Nhat) Express Train was inaugurated on 31 December 1976, 1334 bridges, 27 tunnels, 158 stations and 1370 shunts (switches) had been repaired.

The rail link with Beijing was recently reopened and there is the possibility of reopening the entire 84-km Thap Cham-Dalat line – an eight-km stretch has been reopened as a tourist attraction.

SIMON ROWE

SIMON ROWE

Top Right: Traveller on the Saigon-Hanoi railway.

Middle Right: Railway station en route to Hanoi.

Below: Typical rural scenery on the Reunification Express.

SIMON ROWE

HO CHI MINH

Ho Chi Minh is the best known of some 50 aliases assumed over the course of his long career by Nguyen Tat Thanh (1890-1969), founder of the Vietnamese Communist Party and president of the Democratic Republic of Vietnam from 1946 until his death. The son of a fiercely nationalistic scholar-official of humble means, he was educated in the Quoc Hoc Secondary School in Hué before working briefly as a teacher in Phan Thiet. In 1911, he signed on as a cook's apprentice on a French ship, sailing to North America, Africa and Europe. He remained in Europe, where, while working as a gardener, snow sweeper, waiter, photo retoucher and stoker, his political consciousness began to develop.

After living briefly in London, Ho Chi Minh moved to Paris, where he adopted the name Nguyen Ai Quoc (Nguyen the Patriot). During this period, he mastered a number of languages (including English, French, German and Mandarin Chinese) and began to write about and debate the issue of Indochinese independence. During the 1919 Versailles Peace Conference, he tried to present an independence plan for Vietnam to US President Woodrow Wilson. Ho was a founding member of the French Communist Party, which was established in 1920. In 1923, he was summoned to Moscow for training by the Communist International, which later sent him to Guangzhou (Canton), where he founded the Revolutionary Youth League of Vietnam, a precursor to the Indochinese Communist Party and the Vietnamese Communist Party.

After spending time in a Hong Kong jail in the early '30s and more time in the USSR and China, Ho Chi Minh returned to Vietnam in 1941 for the first time in 30 years. That same year – at the age of 51 – he helped found the Viet Minh Front, the goal of which was the independence of Vietnam from French colonial rule and Japanese occupation. In 1942, he was arrested and held for a year by the Nationalist Chinese. As Japan prepared to surrender in August 1945, Ho Chi Minh led the August Revolution, which took control of much of the country; and it was he who composed Vietnam's Declaration of Independence (modelled in part on the American Declaration of Independence) and read it publicly very near the site of his mausoleum.

The return of the French shortly thereafter forced Ho Chi Minh and the Viet Minh to flee Hanoi and take up armed resistance. Ho spent eight years conducting a guerrilla war until the Viet Minh's victory against the French at Dien Bien Phu in 1954. He led North Vietnam until his death in September 1969 – he never lived to see the North's victory over the South. Ho Chi Minh is affectionately referred to as 'Uncle Ho' (Bac Ho) by his admirers.

Uncle Ho may have been the father of his country, but he wasn't the father of any children, at least none that are known. Like his erstwhile nemesis, South Vietnamese President Ngo Dinh Diem, Ho Chi Minh never married.

ROBERT STOREY

Toilet Paper Disposal

The issue of toilets and what to do with used toilet paper has caused some concern. As one traveller wrote:

We are still not sure about the toilet paper...in two hotels they have been angry with us for flushing the paper down the toilet. In other places it seems quite OK though.

In general, if you see a wastepaper basket next to the toilet, that is where you should throw the toilet paper. The problem is that in many hotels, the sewage system cannot handle toilet paper. This is especially true in old hotels, where the antiquated plumbing system was designed in the pre-toilet-paper era. Also, in rural areas there are no sewage treatment plants – the waste empties into an underground septic tank and toilet paper will really create a mess in there. For the sake of international relations, be considerate and throw the paper in the wastepaper basket.

Toilet paper is seldom provided in the toilets at bus and railway stations or in other public buildings, though hotels usually have it. You'd be wise to keep a stash of your own with you at all times while travelling around.

If you're wondering what poor Vietnamese do when they can't afford toilet paper (many actually cannot), the answer is simple: they use water and the left hand. There is often a bucket and water scoop next to the toilet for just such a purpose. Those who have been to other parts of South-East Asia should be well familiar with the procedure.

And while we're on this subject, another thing you need to be mentally prepared for is squat toilets. For the uninitiated, a squat toilet has no seat for you to sit on while reading the morning newspaper; it's a hole in the floor. The only way to flush it is to fill the conveniently placed bucket with water and pour it into the hole. While it takes some practice to get proficient at balancing yourself over a squat toilet, at least you don't need to worry if the toilet seat is clean. Furthermore, experts who study such things (scatologists?) claim that the squatting position is better for your digestive system.

Better hotels will have the more familiar Western-style sit-down toilets, but squat toilets still exist in cheaper hotels and in public places like restaurants, bus stations, etc. ■

robbed while sleeping in a Vietnamese dormitory. Even though budget travellers like to complain about this policy, it's one case where the Vietnamese government is really trying to protect you.

The concept of a relatively upmarket dormitory just for foreigners is just beginning to catch on. You are most likely to find these in private mini-hotels in areas frequented by budget travellers (Saigon's Pham Ngu Lao St pioneered the concept). Expect to see more such places in the future.

There is a third category, which might be labelled 'overflow dormitories'. The sudden tourist boom in Vietnam has left a few popular spots with a chronic shortage of hotel space (Hoi An is notorious). Rather than have foreigners sleeping in the streets, some local governments have seen fit to open special dormitories (foreigners only) on an emergency basis. However, this is a temporary measure, and whenever sufficient hotel space exists these dormitories will either be closed or placed off limits to foreigners again.

Hotels

Most hotels (khach san) and guesthouses (nha khach or nha nghi) are government-owned. There is also an increasing number of small private hotels, usually referred to as 'mini-hotels'.

There is some confusion over the terms 'singles', 'doubles, 'double occupancy' and 'twins', so let's set the record straight here. A 'single' is a room containing one bed, even if two persons sleep in it. If there are two beds in the room, that is a 'twin', even if only one person occupies the room. If two people stay in the same room, that is 'double occupancy' – in most cases, there is no extra charge for this. There is considerable confusion over the term 'doubles' – in some hotels this means twin beds, while in others it means double occupancy. More than a few travellers have paid extra for twin beds when what they really wanted was a single bed for two people. It's always a good idea to take a look at the room to make sure that you're getting what you wanted and are not paying extra for something you don't need.

Official policy is to insist that 'capitalist tourists' pay double what Vietnamese pay, but even so, the prices are still reasonable.

A few hotels might try to charge the foreigners' price for your Vietnamese guide and/or driver as long as they know that you're paying the bill. This is not on – if they stay in a separate room, they should be charged like any local tourist. Don't accept this nonsense from anyone.

During the festival of Tet (New Year), which usually falls in late January or early February, Vietnam's hotels are packed with domestic tourists and Overseas Vietnamese visiting relatives. Before, during and after the week-long festivities it is extremely difficult to find accommodation at any price.

The Vietnamese seem to be absolutely obsessed with air-conditioning, which has become a big prestige item. If you travel with guides, don't be surprised if they ask for an air-con room (which costs three times as much as a room with a fan) and then complain the next morning that they couldn't sleep because the room was too cold.

It is a good idea to keep all hotel receipts, especially if you are staying for more than a few days. Confusion, sometimes intentional, often arises over how many days you have paid for and how much you still owe. This is especially true of cheaper places with chaotic bookkeeping, since one shift at the front desk has no clue about what people from other shifts have and have not done.

For the definition purposes of this book, we define 'bottom-end' accommodation as costing less than US$25. From US$25 to US$50 would be 'mid-range' and anything over that is 'top-end'. But it's important to realise that many Vietnamese hotels offer a wide range of prices in the same building. For example, one popular hotel in Saigon has room prices running from US$12 to US$70. Cheap rooms are almost always on the top

floor because few hotels have lifts and most guests paying US$70 are not keen to walk up seven storeys or more.

If you arrive in Saigon or Hanoi and find your own hotel, you pay the going rate. If you make a prepaid booking in Bangkok or Hong Kong, you may well be charged up to 50% more.

The following are some of the more common hotel names and their translations:

Bong Sen	lotus
Cuu Long	nine dragons
Doc Lap	independence
Ha Long	descending dragon
Hoa Binh	peace
Huong Sen	lotus fragrance
Huu Nghi	friendship
Thang Long	ascending dragon
Thong Nhat	reunification
Tu Do	freedom

Hotel Security Hotel security can be a problem. Even though there may be a guard on each floor, the guards usually have keys to your room. Supposedly, they are responsible if anything gets stolen, but reports from travellers indicate that this often means nothing.

Many hotels post a small sign warning you not to leave cameras, passports and other valuables in your room. Many hotel rooms come equipped with a closet which can be locked – if so, use it and take the key with you. You would be very wise to bring a cable lock or loop cable with lock – this can be used to lock the closet and you won't have to worry about the employees having keys. If your room or the hotel's front desk has a safe, you can also make use of it. A few hotels have a place where you can attach a padlock to the outside of the door rather than a lock built into the door itself. At such hotels you will be provided with a padlock, but you'd be wise to bring your own, which means that you'll have the only key (don't lose it!). A combination lock might be more convenient, but make sure it's one that is not easily broken (the cheap ones can be pried apart with a screwdriver).

Police Registration Back in the old days when the Soviets told the Vietnamese how to run their country, all hotel guests had to deposit their passports and/or visas with the reception – the staff then had to take these valuable documents over to the police station and register the guests. And it was not uncommon for the police to then pay a visit to your hotel room and question you about why you were there, how long would you be staying, where did you come from and where were you going to next, etc. Your documents would be returned only upon your departure, and there was always the worry that they could be 'lost'.

The good news is that the national government no longer requires police registration of hotel guests. The bad news is that provincial governments make up their own rules. So, in Hanoi and Ho Chi Minh City, you do *not* need to leave your passport or visa with hotel reception, though most government-owned hotels want it anyway for 'security'. In Dalat, the police want to see your passport and visa *(both* are required here), but they will accept photocopies. The Danang police require that you deposit your original visa (no photocopies allowed), but you needn't show your passport.

In other words, these regulations are as clear as mud. Each city you visit will have its own rules, and these rules can change at the drop of a hat. On the positive side, the tendency of the past few years has been to make procedures easier and less bureaucratic for tourists. Hopefully, this is a trend that will continue. There is no question that most foreigners do not like to see their valuable documents passing through so many hands with the chance that something could get lost. We've had a few tense moments ourselves when the person on duty 'couldn't remember' where our passports were, or the person who did know had not shown up for work when we wanted to depart.

At many hotels, you will not be requested to pay in advance, but in that case they'll definitely want to hold your passport or visa as security. Before you depart, it is usual for the staff to check your room to make sure that

you don't have any kleptomaniac tendencies (are the towels and TV set still there?).

Rental

It's possible to arrange to stay in the homes of local people, but – depending on the local government – the family might have to register with the police all foreign visitors to their homes, including relatives. The police can – and often do – arbitrarily deny such registration requests and will force you to stay in a hotel or guesthouse licensed to accept foreigners.

Renting a medium-sized house in Ho Chi Minh City costs about US$20 per month for a Vietnamese family. Foreigners can rent cheaply directly from a family or landlord, but it's wise to report to the police that you are paying a bundle even if you are paying a pittance. The authorities are not happy with foreigners getting off cheaply. And remember, your living arrangements must receive the approval of the police – that approval can be revoked any time for no good reason.

FOOD

One of the delights of visiting Vietnam is the amazing cuisine – there are said to be nearly 500 different traditional Vietnamese dishes – which is, in general, superbly prepared and very reasonably priced. The Vietnamese are particularly fond of seafood, but they do equally well at preparing chicken, beef, pork and vegetable dishes. There is a wide assortment of dishes in Vietnamese cooking, and regional specialities add even more variety to the milieu.

The proper way to eat Vietnamese food is to take rice from the large shared dish and put it in your rice bowl. Using your chopsticks, take meat, fish or vegetables from the serving dishes and add them to your rice. Then, holding the rice bowl near your mouth, use your chopsticks to eat. Leaving the rice bowl on the table and conveying your food, precariously perched between chopsticks, all the way from the table to your mouth strikes Vietnamese as odd, though they will be more

Food vendor in Hanoi

amused than offended. When not eating, it is acceptable to set your chopsticks on flat across the top of your rice bowl. Sticking your chopsticks vertically into a rice bowl and leaving them there is very offensive (a classic Buddhist death sign).

Unlike the Western practice of each person getting their own individual plate of food, eating in most Asian countries is a communal affair. That is, various dishes are put out on the table to be shared by a small group. People often stick their individual chopsticks into the communal plate of food, which is not very sanitary but probably won't kill you. Using a serving spoon or 'serving chopsticks' solves this problem. Having three or four people to eat with you assures that you get to sample several different types of dishes. Once you get past the initial culture shock, this style of eating is much fun and very sociable – many foreigners come to prefer it over Western individualism. If you eat with a group of Vietnamese, you may find that some of your fellow diners pick out the best-looking pieces of food with their chopsticks and put it into your rice bowl. Some travellers find this disturbing, but you shouldn't – this is a way of honouring you as a distinguished guest.

The meat of some snakes and forest animals, prepared according to traditional recipes, is considered a delicacy by those who can afford it. Special restaurants around the country cater to this market, offering the fresh meat of such animals as cobras, deer, porcupines, bats, rats, turtles, wild pigs and pangolins (scaly animals similar to anteaters). Often, the animals to be eaten are kept alive in cages inside the restaurant until ordered by a customer. However, before you sink your teeth into one of these creatures, consider whether or not it could be a rare or endangered species. Despite laws prohibiting the shooting and trapping of endangered species, poaching is a problem and Vietnam lacks the funds required for strict enforcement. Price is a good guideline – that high-priced 'exotic' dish is probably very expensive because it's something very rare.

As in much of the Orient, dog meat can be found on the menu in a number of specialty restaurants. Not everyone is happy to see Fido fricasseed – in fact, the majority of Vietnamese do not eat dog. But dog meat is particularly popular in the north, especially during winter because it's believed to have tonic properties that ward off colds and flu. Dog meat costs more than beef or pork. This is not because dogs are an endangered species, but because dogs have to be raised on meat while cows eat grass and pigs eat anything. Because of its relatively high price, no restaurant is going to deliberately slip dog meat onto your plate as a means of cheating you. However, some foreigners have inadvertently eaten dog because they simply strolled into what looked like a good restaurant, pointed to somebody's plate and said 'I'll have that'. Most restaurants that serve dog have a sign indicating such, so you should learn to recognise the words in case you want to avoid (or seek out) such places. The words for 'dog meat' are *thit cho*.

Vegetarian Food

Because Buddhist monks of the Mahayana tradition are strict vegetarians (at least they are supposed to be), Vietnamese vegetarian cooking *(an chay)* has a long history and is an integral part of Vietnamese cuisine. In general, the focus of vegetarian cuisine in Vietnam has been on reproducing traditional dishes prepared with meat, chicken, seafood or egg without including these ingredients. Instead, tofu, mushrooms and raw, dried, cooked and fermented vegetables are used. Because it does not include many expensive ingredients, vegetarian food is unbelievably cheap.

On days when there is a full or sliver moon (the beginning and middle days of the lunar month), many Vietnamese and Chinese do not eat meat, chicken, seafood or eggs – or even *nuoc mam* (fermented fish sauce). On such days, some food stalls, especially in the marketplaces, serve vegetarian meals. To find out when the next full or sliver moon will be, consult any Vietnamese calendar.

Places to Eat

You'll never have to look very far for food in Vietnam – *nha hang* (restaurants) of one sort or another seem to be in every nook and cranny. There are a wide variety of places to eat, including curb-side food stands, road-side food stalls, high-volume government-run eateries catering to locals, Chinese restaurants, Western-style cafes, hotel restaurants (which are usually quite good though more expensive than most restaurants), pastry shops, restaurants serving traditional (rather than everyday) Vietnamese dishes, and restaurants that specialise in the exotic (cobra, etc).

Most places can rustle up something Western (such as a steak with chips) if you're desperate. For some inexplicable reason, tour groups are often served Western food unless the participants specifically request a Vietnamese menu. Occasionally, the Western food is truly awful – Vietnamese hamburgers are not an outstanding success, and the peanut butter often (not always) contains crunchy sugar granules that will jolt the fillings out of your teeth.

Unless you eat in exclusive hotels or aristocratic restaurants, food is very cheap. At the bottom of the barrel are street stalls, where a bowl of noodles costs around US$0.50. Very casual restaurants with bamboo and cardboard walls have meals costing perhaps US$1. Most cafes and decent restaurants can fill your stomach for US$1 to US$4. However, in classy restaurants the bill can add up fast, and be aware that the small dishes of snacks which appear on the table cost money if you indulge (and are charged per person!). And in many restaurants, the fresh hand towels might be charged too – say 'no thanks' if you object to paying US$0.10 for a hand wipe. Check the bill very carefully:

Overcharging seems to be standard practice when more than one person orders food or when many items are listed on the bill. I would say a good 50% of the time we were initially overcharged. After going over the menu and bill item by item and correcting with a pencil each problem and showing we didn't use the wash clothes or eat the appetiser nuts, the waitresses or waiters usually accepted our corrections.

Most Vietnamese restaurants do not have any prices on the menu at all. In this case, you must definitely ask the total price when you place your order. Vietnamese diners know this and will always ask, so don't be shy about speaking up. If you don't, be prepared for a shock when the bill finally comes.

Rice stalls along highways can be identified by signs reading 'Com' and noodle stalls are labelled 'Pho'. Your best bet for a late meal (after 8.30 pm) is usually a hotel restaurant.

To get the bill (check), politely catch the attention of the waiter or waitress and write in the air as if with a pen on an imaginary piece of paper.

Condiments

Nuoc mam (pronounced something like 'nuke mom') is a type of fermented fish sauce – instantly identifiable by its distinctive smell – without which no Vietnamese meal is complete. Though nuoc mam is to Vietnamese cuisine what soy sauce is to Japanese food, many hotel restaurants do not automatically serve it to foreigners, knowing that the odour may drive away their Western customers. Nuoc mam actually isn't bad once you get used to it, and some foreigners even go home with a few bottles in their luggage. The sauce is made by fermenting highly salted fish in large ceramic vats for four to 12 months.

If nuoc mam isn't strong enough for you, try *mam tom*, a powerful shrimp sauce which American soldiers sometimes called 'Viet Cong tear gas'.

Salt with chilli and lemon juice is often served as a condiment and most Westerners seem to like it.

On the other hand, monosodium glutamate (msg) gets mixed reviews from foreigners. It's salty and tasty, but some people have reported allergic reactions (the face gets flushed and hot). Others just don't like the sodium (also found in ordinary table salt), which can raise the blood pressure in sensitive individuals. While msg is used all over Vietnam, food in the north is positively buried in it.

Snacks

Vietnamese spring rolls are called *cha gio* (pronounced 'chow yau') in the south and *nem Sai Gon* or *nem ran* in the north. They are made of rice paper filled with minced pork, crab, vermicelli, *moc nhi* (a kind of edible fungus), onion, mushroom and eggs and then fried until the rice paper turns a crispy brown. *Nem rau* are vegetable spring rolls.

Banh cuon is a steamed rice pancake into which minced pork and moc nhi is rolled. It is served with a special sauce made from watered-down nuoc mam, vinegar, sugar, pepper, clove and garlic.

Oc nhoi is snail meat, pork, chopped green onion, nuoc mam and pepper rolled up in ginger leaves and cooked in snail shells.

Gio is lean pork seasoned and then pounded into paste before being packed into banana leaves and boiled.

Cha is pork paste fried in fat or broiled over hot coals. *Cha que* is cha prepared with cinnamon.

Chao tom is grilled sugar cane rolled in spiced shrimp paste.

Dua chua is bean sprout salad that tastes vaguely like Korean kimchi.

There are a number of Western-style snack foods. Excellent French bread is available everywhere fresh daily, especially in the morning. Imported French cheese spread can be bought from street stalls for around US$1.50 per box and sometimes salami is also available.

Soups & Noodles

Pho is the Vietnamese name for the noodle soup that is eaten at all hours of the day but is a special favourite for breakfast. It is prepared by quickly boiling noodles and placing them into a bowl along with greens (shallots, parsley) and shredded beef, chicken or pork. A broth made with boiled bones, prawns, ginger and nuoc mam is then poured into the bowl. Some people take their pho with chilli sauce or lemon.

Lau is fish and vegetable soup served in a bowl resembling a samovar with the top cut off. Live coals in the centre keep it hot.

Mien luon is vermicelli soup with eel seasoned with mushrooms, shallots, fried eggs and chicken.

Bun thang is rice noodles and shredded chicken with fried egg and prawns on top. It is served with broth made by boiling chicken, dried prawns and pig bones.

Xup rau is vegetable soup.

Canh kho hoa is a bitter soup said to be especially good for the health of people who have spent a lot of time in the sun.

The noodles served with Vietnamese soups are of three types: white rice noodles *(banh pho)*, clear noodles made from rice mixed with manioc powder *(mien)*, and yellow wheat noodles *(mi)*. Many noodle soups are available either with broth *(nuoc leo)* or without *(kho,* literally 'dry').

Main Dishes

The staple of Vietnamese cuisine is plain white rice dressed up with a plethora of vegetables, meat, fish and spices.

On menus, dishes are usually listed according to their main ingredient. For instance, all the chicken dishes appear together, as do all the beef dishes, and so on.

Cha ca is filleted fish slices broiled over charcoal. It is often served with noodles, green salad, roasted peanuts and a sauce made from nuoc mam, lemon and a special volatile oil.

Ech tam bot ran is frog meat soaked in a thin batter and fried in oil. It is usually served with a sauce made of watered-down nuoc mam, vinegar and pepper.

Rau xao hon hop is fried vegetables.

Bo bay mon are sugar-beef dishes.

Com tay cam is rice with mushrooms, chicken and finely sliced pork flavoured with ginger.

Desserts

Sweets *(do ngot)* and desserts *(do trang mieng)* you are likely to have an opportunity to sample include the following:

Banh chung, a traditional Tet favourite, is a square cake made from sticky rice and filled with beans, onion and pork and boiled in leaves for 10 hours.

Banh deo is a cake made of dried sticky rice flour mixed with a boiled sugar solution. It is filled with candied fruit, sesame seeds, fat, etc.

Banh dau xanh is mung bean cake. Served with hot tea it 'melts on your tongue'.

Mut (candied fruit or vegetables) is made with carrot, coconut, cumquat, gourd, ginger root, lotus seeds, tomato, etc.

Banh bao is a filled Chinese pastry that can most easily be described as looking like a woman's breast, complete with a reddish dot on top. Inside the sweet, doughy exterior is meat, onions and vegetables. *Banh bao* is often eaten dunked in soy sauce.

Banh it nhan dau, a traditional Vietnamese treat, is a gooey pastry made of pulverised sticky rice, beans and sugar. It is steamed (and sold) in a banana leaf folded into a triangular pyramid. You often see banh it nhan dau on sale at Mekong Delta ferry crossings. *Banh it nhan dua* is a variation made with coconut instead of beans.

Ice cream *(kem)* was introduced to Vietnam on a large scale by the Americans, who made ensuring a reliable supply of the stuff a top wartime priority. The US Army hired two American companies, Foremost Dairy and Meadowgold Dairies, to build dozens of ice cream factories all around the country. Inevitably, local people developed a taste for their product. Even 15 years after bona fide Foremost products ceased to be available in the Socialist Republic, the company's orange-and-white logo was prominently on display in shops selling ice cream. Recently, however, the government has been making an effort to purge the country of these obsolete signs because it wants to encourage these companies to return. Foremost did in fact return to Vietnam in 1994 to set up a new dairy.

Ice cream served in a baby coconut *(kem dua* or *kem trai dua)* deliciously mixes ice cream, candied fruit and the jelly-like meat of young coconut.

Ice cream stalls usually sell little jars or plastic cups of sweetened frozen yoghurt *(yaourt)*.

Fruit

Fruit *(qua* or *trai)* is available in Vietnam all year round, but many of the country's most interesting specialities have short seasons. Vietnamese bananas will fool you – the green bananas sold in the marketplace are usually ripe enough to eat, and in fact taste better than the yellow ones.

Avocado is often eaten in a glass with ice and sweetened with either sugar or condensed milk.

Cinnamon apple is also known in English as custard apple, sugar apple and sweetsop. It is ripe when very soft and the area around the stem turns blackish.

Mature coconuts are eaten only by children or as jam. For snacking, Vietnamese prefer the soft jelly-like meat and fresher milk of young coconuts.

Some useful survival terms for the food battleground include the following:

Breakfast

pancake	*bánh xèo ngọt*
banana pancake	*bánh chuối*
pineapple pancake	*bánh dứa* (north)
	bánh khóm (south)
papaya pancake	*bánh đu đủ*
orange pancake	*bánh cam*
plain pancake	*bánh không nhân*
bread	*bánh mì*
omelette	*trứng rán* (north)
	trứng chiên (south)
fried eggs	*trứng ốp la*
butter	*bơ*
butter & jam	*bơ - mứt*
jam	*mứt*
cheese	*phomát* (north)
	phomai (south)
butter & cheese	*bơ - phomát*
butter & honey	*bơ - mật ong*
sandwich	*săn huýt*

Lunch & Dinner

noodles & rice noodles
  mì - hủ tíu
beef noodle soup
  mì bò/phở bò (north)
  hủ tíu bò (south)
chicken noodle soup
  mì gà/phở gà (north)
  hủ tíu gà (south)
vegetarian noodle soup
  mì rau/mì chay
duck, bamboo-shoot noodle soup
  bún măng

potatoes
  khoai tây
french fries
  khoai rán (north)
  khoai chiên (south)
fried potato & tomato
  khoai xào cà chua
fried potato & butter
  khoai chiên bơ

fried dishes
  các món xào
fried noodles with chicken
  mì xào ga/hủ tíu xào gà

fried noodles with beef
  mì xào bò/hủ tíu xào bò
mixed fried noodles
  mì xào thập cẩm
mixed fries
  xào tổng hợp

chicken
  gà
roasted chicken
  gà quay/gà rô-ti
chicken salad
  gà xé phay
fried chicken in mushroom sauce
  gà sốt nấm
batter-fried chicken
  gà tẩm bột rán/chiên
fried chicken with lemon sauce
  gà rán/chiên sốt chanh
curried chicken
  gà cà-ri

pork
  lợn/heo
skewered grilled pork
  chả lợn xiên nướng/chả heo nướng
sweet & sour fried pork
  lợn xào chua ngọt/heo xào chua ngọt
roasted pork
  thịt lợn quay (north)
  heo quay (south)
grilled pork
  hịt tlợn nướng xả/heo nướng xả

beef
  thịt bò
beefsteak
  bít tết
skewered grilled beef
  bò xiên nướng
spicy beef
  bò xào sả ớt
fried beef with pineapple
  bò xào dứa (north)
  khóm (south)
fried beef with garlic
  bò xào tỏi
grilled beef with ginger
  bò nướng gừng

rare beef with vinegar
   bò nhúng giấm

hot pot (hot & sour soup)
   lẩu
beef hot pot
   lẩu bò
eel hot pot
   lẩu lươn
fish hot pot
   lẩu cá
combination hot pot
   lẩu thập cẩm

spring roll
   nem (north)
   chả gio (south)
meat spring rolls
   nem thịt (north)
   chả giò (south)
vegetarian spring rolls
   nem rau (north)
   chả giò chay (south)
sour spring rolls
   nem chua

pigeon
   chim bồ câu
roasted pigeon
   bồ câu quay
fried pigeon in mushroom sauce
   bồ câu xào nấm sốt

soup
   súp
chicken soup
   súp gà
eel soup
   súp lươn
combination soup
   súp thập cẩm
maize soup
   súp ngô (north)
   súp bắp (south)
vegetarian soup
   súp rau

fish
   cá
grilled fish with sugarcane
   chả cá bao mía
fried fish in tomato sauce
   cá rán/chiên sốt cà
sweet & sour fried fish
   cá sốt chua ngọt
fried fish with lemon
   cá rán/chiên chanh
fried fish with mushrooms
   cá xào hành nấm rơm
steamed fish with ginger
   cá hấp gừng
boiled fish
   cá luộc
grilled fish
   cá nướng
steamed fish in beer
   cá hấp bia

shrimp/prawns
   tôm
sweet & sour fried shrimp
   tôm xào chua ngọt
fried shrimp with mushrooms
   tôm xào nấm
grilled shrimp with sugarcane
   tôm bao mía (north)
   chạo tôm (south)
batter-fried shrimp
   tôm tẩm bột/tôm hỏa tiễn
steamed shrimp in beer
   tôm hấp bia

crab
   cua
salted fried crab
   cua rang muối
crab with chopped meat
   cua nhồi thịt
steamed crab in beer
   cua hấp bia

squid
   mực
fried squid
   mực chiên
fried squid with mushrooms
   mực xào nấm

fried squid with pineapple
mực xào dứa (north)
khóm (south)
squid in sweet & sour sauce
mực xào chua ngọt

eel
lươn
fried eel with chopped meat
lươn cuốn thịt rán/chiên
simmered eel
lươn om (north)
lươn um (south)
fried eel with mushrooms
lươn xào nấm

snail
ốc
spicy snail
ốc xào sả ớt
fried snail with pineapple
ốc xào dứa, khóm
fried snail with tofu & bananas
ốc xào đậu phu (đậu hủ) chuối xanh

vegetarian
các món chay
I'm a vegetarian.
Tôi là người ăn lạt. (north)
Tôi là người ăn chay. (south)
fried noodle with vegetable
mì/hủ tíu xào rau
vegetarian noodle soup
mì/hủ tíu nấu rau
fried vegetable
rau xào
boiled vegetable
rau luộc

vegetables
rau
fried vegetables
rau xào
boiled vegetables
rau luộc
sour vegetable
dưa góp (north)
dưa chua (south)
fried bean sprouts
giá xào

vegetable soup (large bowl)
canh rau
salad
rau sa lát
fried vegetable with mushrooms
rau cải xào nấm

tofu
đậu phụ/đậu hu
fried tofu with chopped meat
thịt nhồi đậu phụ/đậu hủ
fried tofu with tomato sauce
đậu phụ/đậu hủ sốt cà
fried tofu with vegetable
đậu phụ/đậu hủ xào

rice
cơm
steamed rice
cơm trắng
mixed fried rice
cơm rang thập cẩm (north)
cơm chiên (south)
rice porridge
cháo

specialities & exotica
đặc sản
lobster
con tôm hùm
frog
con ếch
oyster
con sò
bat
con dơi
cobra
rắn hổ
gecko
con tắc kè/kỳ nhông/kỳ đà
goat
con de
pangolin
con trúc/tê tê
porcupine
con nhím
python
con trăn
small hornless deer
con nai tơ

turtle
  con rùa
venison
  thịt nai
wild pig
  con heo rừng

Fruits

fruit	*trái cây*
apple	*trái táo* (north)
	bơm (south)
apricot	*trái lê*
avocado	*trái bơ*
banana	*trái chuối*
coconut	*trái dừa*
custard apple	*trái măng cầu*
durian	*trái sầu riêng*
grapes	*trái nho*
green dragon fruit	*trái thanh long*
guava	*trái ổi*
jackfruit	*trái mít*
jujube (Chinese date)	*trái táo ta*
persimmon	*trái hồng xiêm*
lemon	*trái chanh*
longan	*trái nhãn*
lychee	*trái vải*
mandarin orange	*trái quýt*
mangosteen	*trái măng cụt*
orange	*trái cam*
papaya	*trái đu đủ*
peach	*trái đào*
pineapple	*trái khóm/trái dứa*
plum	*trái mận/trái mơ*
pomelo	*trái bưởi*
rambutan	*trái chôm chôm*
starfruit	*trái khế*
strawberry	*trái dâu*
tangerine	*trái quýt*
three-seed cherry	*trái sê-ri*
water apple	*trái roi đường* (north)
	trái mận (south)
watermelon	*trái dưa hấu*
other dishes	*các món khác*
fruit salad	*sa lát hoa quả* (north)
	trái cây các loại (south)

yoghurt	*sữa chua* (north)
	da-ua (south)
mixed fruit cocktail	*cóc-tai hoa quả*

Condiments

pepper	*tiêu xay*
salt	*muối*
sugar	*đường*
ice	*đá*
hot pepper	*ớt trái*
fresh chillis	*ớt*
soy sauce	*xì dầu* (north)
	nước tương (south)
fish sauce	*nước mắm*

DRINKS
Nonalcoholic Drinks

Coffee Vietnamese coffee is fine stuff, but there is one qualifier – you'll need to dilute it with hot water. The Vietnamese prefer their coffee so strong and so sweet that it will turn your teeth inside out. Ditto for Ovaltine and Milo, which are regarded as desserts rather than drinks. Those restaurants which are accustomed to foreigners will be prepared with thermos bottles of hot water so you can dilute your coffee (or Ovaltine, etc) as you wish. However, restaurants which deal with a mostly Vietnamese clientele will likely be dumbfounded by your request for hot water. You'll also need to communicate the fact that you need a large glass – ultra-sweet coffee is traditionally served in a tiny cup, thus leaving you no room to add any water.

Rather than instant coffee, the Vietnamese prefer to brew it right at the table, French-style – a dripper with coffee grounds is placed over the cup and hot water poured in. If you prefer ice coffee, the same method is applied but with a glass of ice under the dripper.

Both the drippers and packaged coffee are favourite items with tourists looking for things to buy and take home.

Tea Vietnamese tea in the south is cheap but disappointing – the aroma is like perfume but the taste resembles the glue found on postal envelopes. Tea grown in the north is much better but much stronger – be prepared for a caffeine jolt. Excellent imported Chinese tea is found in some restaurants, but is considerably more expensive than the home-grown stuff. Both Vietnamese and Chinese teas are mainly of the green variety, and are available only in loose form. If you can't live without black tea, you'd better bring your own teabags.

Mineral Water The selection of mineral water *(nuoc suoi)* has been expanding rapidly ever since the Vietnamese realised that foreigners were willing to pay good money for water sealed in plastic bottles.

Imported mineral water is available for about US$1 per bottle. The Vietnamese brands are cheaper but quality varies. The Vietnamese-produced Vinh Hao carbonated mineral water is outstanding, especially when served with ice, lemon and sugar.

Coconut Milk There is nothing more refreshing on a hot day than fresh coconut milk *(nuoc dua)*. Coconut milk is as hygienic and safe to drink as the vessel it is served in is clean. The Vietnamese believe that coconut milk, like hot milk in Western culture, makes you tired. Athletes, for instance, never drink it before a competition.

The coconuts grown around the Ha Tien area in the Mekong Delta are a special variety with very tasty milk and delicious coconut flesh.

Soft Drinks Tri Beco is a domestic soft-drink manufacturer producing strawberry, lychee and other fruity-flavoured carbonated drinks. It's not overly sweet, which means it does a better job at quenching your thirst than some of the sugary imported brands. Tri Beco Coca (cola) is a touch watery compared with the Western stuff but not bad. In the north you'll find Feti cola, which is also OK.

Lemon soda *(so-da chanh)* is popular. An excellent domestic soft drink with a pleasant fruit flavour is called *nuoc khoang kim boi*; one bottle costs US$0.20.

Pepsi beat Coca-Cola into the Vietnamese market, a major coup. Sprite in cans is widely available but nothing yet in the way of diet drinks.

Alcohol
Beer Saigon Export (do they really export it?) and Saigon Lager are two local brands of beer costing about two-thirds the price of the imported brands in cans and half that in bottles. Other 100% Vietnamese brands include 333, Castel, Huda and Halida. Nameless regional beers, though watery and often flat, are available in bottles for less than the name brands. One traveller described such 'no-label beers' as being a cross between light beer and iced tea.

Memorise the words *bia hoi*, which means 'draft beer'. There are signs advertising it everywhere, and most cafes have it on the menu. Quality varies, but it is generally OK and very cheap (US$0.32 per litre!). Places that serve bia hoi usually also have good but cheap food.

There are a number of foreign brands which are brewed in Vietnam under licence. These include BGI, Carlsberg, Heineken and Vinagen.

Wine Vietnam produces over 50 varieties of wine *(ruou)*, many of them made from rice. The cheapest rice wines *(ruou de)* are used for cooking, not drinking, as you will find out to your displeasure if you drink them.

Another Vietnamese specialty is snake wine *(ruou ran)*. This is basically rice wine with a pickled snake floating in it. Snake meat is believed to possess tonic properties, and drinking snake wine is said to cure everything from night blindness to impotence. The more poisonous the snake, the better for your health.

A variation on the theme is to have the snake killed right at your table and the blood placed into a cup. You take some of the blood, dump it into a glass of rice wine and it's 'bottoms up'. This is believed to work as an aphrodisiac. While you're enjoying your wine with blood, the snake will be quickly spirited away to the kitchen, stir-fried with some vegetables and noodles and returned to you. As the Viet Cong used to say, 'make one thing serve two purposes'.

Champagne The Vietnamese will have to work on their techniques for distilling champagne. The presently available stuff tastes like it was drained from an old rusty radiator.

Hard Liquor Alcoholic beverages *(ruou manh)* from China are very cheap though vile. Russian vodka is one of the few things the former USSR has left to export. Locally produced Hanoi Vodka is also available.

Some useful terms for ordering Vietnamese drinks include the following:

Coffee

coffee
  cà phê
hot black coffee
  cà phê đen nóng
coffee with hot milk
  nâu nóng (north)
  cà phê sữa nóng (south)
iced black coffee
  cà phê đá
iced coffee with milk
  nâu đá (north)
  cà phê sữa đá (south)

Tea

tea
  chè (north)
  trà (south)
hot black tea
  chè đen nóng (north)
  trà nóng (south)
tea with hot milk
  chè đen sữa (north)
  trà pha sữa (south)
black tea with honey
  chè mật ong (north)
  trà pha mật (south)

Chocolate Drinks

chocolate - milk	*cacao - sữa*
hot chocolate	*cacao nóng*
iced chocolate	*cacao đá*
hot milk	*sữa nóng*
iced milk	*sữa đá*

Fruit Drinks

fruit juice	*nước quả/nước trái cây*
hot lemon juice	*chanh nóng*
iced lemon juice	*chanh đá*
hot orange juice	*cam nóng*
iced orange juice	*cam đá*
pure orange juice	*cam vắt*
fruit shake	*sinh to/trái cây xay*
banana shake	*nước chuối xay*
milk banana shake	*nước chuối sữa xay*
papaya shake	*nước đu đủ xay*
pineapple shake	*nước dứa* (north)
	khóm xay (south)
orange-banana shake	*nước cam/chuối xay*
mixed fruit shake	*sinh tố tổng hợp/ nước thập cẩm xay*
mango shake	*nước xoài xay*

Mineral Water

mineral water	*nước khoáng* (north)
	nước suối (south)
lemon mineral water	*khoáng chanh* (north)
	suối chanh (south)
big spring water	*nước suối chai lớn*
small spring water	*nước suối chai nhỏ*

Beer & Soft Drinks

beer	*bia*
Chinese beer	*bia Trung Quốc*
Halida beer	*bia Halida*
333 beer	*bia 333*
Tiger beer	*bia Tiger*
Tiger (large bottle)	*bia Tiger (chai to)*
Amstel beer	*bia Amstel*
Carlsberg beer	*bia Carlsberg*
San Miguel beer	*bia San Miguel*
Heineken beer	*bia Heineken*
BGI beer	*bia BGI*

tinned soft drinks	*thức uống đóng hộp*
Coke	*Coca Cola*
Pepsi	*Pepsi Cola*
7 Up	*7 Up*
tinned orange juice	*cam hộp*
soda water & lemon	*soda chanh*
soda water, lemon & sugar	*soda chanh đường*

TOBACCO

Vietnamese men smoke like chimneys, including those who have represented the country in the Olympic Games. The women almost never smoke, and for a woman to do so in public would indicate to most Vietnamese men that she's a prostitute.

As poor as Vietnam is, many men seem willing to spend their last dong on expensive imported cigarettes, especially American cigarettes. Imported brands like Marlboro, 555 and Dunhill sell for around US$1.10 if bought by the pack, or US$0.90 if bought by the carton. Jet is a very popular brand of cigarette made in Thailand and retails for about US$0.60. The infamous Puke cigarettes from China no longer seem to be available. There are some dirt cheap home-grown brands like Dien Bien Phu and Dalat costing around US$0.10 a pack, but these are without filters and have a very strong taste (rather like smoking old socks). There are also 'premium' domestic brands like Saigon and Cholon selling for US$0.55 a pack. Craven and Vinataba are produced in Vietnam under a joint-venture licence and cost around US$0.70 a pack. Cheapest of all is to buy tobacco and roll your own, but only a few older Vietnamese men do this – young people consider it terribly primitive.

Recently there has been a problem with counterfeit 'imported' cigarettes which look like the real thing, but smokers claim they can easily taste the difference.

Pipe tobacco and cigars also exist but have not proven popular. They can sometimes be purchased from street vendors near the tourist hotels.

ENTERTAINMENT

Cinemas

Movie theatres are common in nearly all major towns and cities. Many urban maps have cinemas (*rap* in Vietnamese) marked with a special symbol.

Films from the former Eastern Bloc are fading fast, being replaced with Western movies, which are either subtitled or dubbed. Vietnam now produces its own kung fu movies rather than importing all from China, Hong Kong and Taiwan. Love stories also are popular, but Vietnamese censors take a dim view of nudity and sex – murder and mayhem is OK.

Discos

Vietnam is one of the few places left where a major component of the nightlife is still ballroom dancing. Of course, these *soirées dansantes* have become more and more like discos in recent years, and the guests are likely to be affluent young people dressed in jeans and copies of the latest designer boot-legs from Bangkok, but the principle is the same. A place where dancing takes place is called a *vu truong* in Vietnamese; to dance is *khieu vu*.

After reunification, ballrooms and discos were denounced as imperialist dens of iniquity and were shut down by the authorities. Since around 1990 they have reopened, though certain forms of dancing (like Brazil's erotic dance, the lambada) remained banned. Young people unable to afford a night on the town often create impromptu discos with tape players and pirated rock music cassettes from the West. There are

---

Betelnut

One thing you'll undoubtedly find for sale at street stalls everywhere is betelnut. This is not a food – swallow it and you'll be sorry! The betelnut is in fact the seed of the the betel palm (beautiful trees, by the way) and is meant to be chewed. The seed is usually sold with a slit in it, mixed with lime and wrapped in a leaf. Like tobacco, it's strong stuff that you first can barely tolerate but eventually get addicted to. The first time you bite into betelnut, your whole face gets hot – chewers say it gives them a buzz. Like chewing tobacco, betelnut causes excessive salivation – the result is that betel chewers must constantly spit. The disgusting reddish-brown stains you see on sidewalks are not blood but betel-saliva juice. Years of constant chewing causes the teeth to become stained progressively browner, eventually becoming nearly black. ■

now even modern dance classes at public schools.

Karaoke

Some say it causes brain damage. Others say it's used by the government for brainwashing. Whatever it does, we do know that it originated in Japan and is rapidly spreading. And now karaoke has invaded Vietnam.

For those who haven't experienced karaoke, it's simply a system where you are supposed to sing along with a video. The words to the song are flashed on the bottom of the screen (a number of languages are possible) and participants are supplied with a microphone. Really fancy karaoke bars have superb audio systems and big screen videos, but no matter how good the equipment, it's not going to sound any better than the ability of the singer. And with a few exceptions, it usually sounds awful.

While it has not proven quite so popular with Westerners, karaoke is taking over Asia. At the moment, karaoke bars are permitted in hotels and restaurants but the Vietnamese government doesn't allow them elsewhere. To find karaoke, look for signs advertising 'KTV' ('Karaoke TV', the Japanese answer to MTV).

Pubs

During the Vietnam War, pubs staffed with legions of prostitutes were a major form of R&R ('rest & recreation') for American soldiers. After reunification, the pubs were shut down and the prostitutes were compelled to find other employment, like stoop labour in the rice paddies.

The pubs are back, at least in Saigon. Though these tend to be male-oriented businesses, there are a few places where women might feel comfortable having a drink. Such respectable pubs tend to be in the big tourist hotels. As time goes on, it's likely that some entrepreneurs will open places similar to British-style pubs with darts, food, live music and so on. Right now, such businesses are in their infancy.

Video Games

What the USA couldn't achieve with bombs and bullets is now being accomplished with a new, secret weapon. Video games are taking over Vietnam (though karaoke is giving it stiff competition). Never mind that people don't have enough to eat – almost everyone from well-heeled cadres to cyclo drivers and street beggars has a portable, hand-held video game commonly known as a 'game boy'. We've seen motorcycle drivers playing these games when they stop at traffic lights – some even try it while they're driving. We can only hope that these machines are banned from the cockpits of Vietnam Airlines flights.

For those who want the full effects of sound and colour, video-game parlours are just starting to spring up. Just how the government will cope with this latest imperialist assault upon the mental health of the Vietnamese people remains to be seen.

Video Parlours

Vietnam's opening to the outside world is creating massive headaches for the country's censors. Despite their best efforts, customs agents haven't been able to hold back the flood tide of video tapes which are smuggled into Vietnam. The pirating of video tapes has become big business and the tapes are sold or rented all over the country. Kung fu movies from Hong Kong and pornography from the West and Japan are much in demand. Ditto for the latest MTV (music and TV) tapes. Video movies about the Vietnam War are also enthusiastically sought after – some popular war movies include *Rambo, Apocalypse Now, Full Metal Jacket, Platoon, The Deer Hunter, Good Morning Vietnam, Born on the 4th of July, Air America* and *Heaven and Earth*.

Obviously, most Vietnamese cannot afford video equipment, but that hardly matters. Budding entrepreneurs have set up instant mini-theatres consisting of a video cassette recorder (VCR), a few chairs and curtains to keep out nonpaying onlookers. The admission price is very low, on the order of US$0.20. Some of these video parlours provide food and beverage services.

Spectator Sports

Football (soccer) is number one with spectators. Tennis has considerable snob appeal – trendy Vietnamese like to both watch and play. The Vietnamese are incredibly skilled at shuttlecock. Other favourites include volleyball and ping-pong.

THINGS TO BUY

As a general principal, try to find a shop that (1) does not cater particularly to tourists and (2) puts price tags on all its items. In touristy areas, items sold with no visible price tags must be bargained for – expect the vendor to start the bidding at two to five times the real price.

Handicrafts

Handicrafts available for purchase as souvenirs include lacquerware items, mother-of-pearl inlay, ceramics (including enormous elephants), colourful embroidered items (hangings, tablecloths, pillow cases, pyjamas and robes), greeting cards with silk paintings on the front, wood-block prints, oil paintings, watercolours, blinds made of hanging bamboo beads (many travellers like the replica of the Mona Lisa), reed mats (rushes are called *coi* in the north, *lac* in the south), Chinese-style carpets, jewellery and leatherwork.

Objects made of ivory and tortoise shell are on sale everywhere. Please remember that purchasing them directly contributes to the extinction of the world's endangered populations of elephants and sea turtles. And if that's not enough of an incentive to buy other souvenirs, maybe this is: ivory purchased in Vietnam might be confiscated by customs officials when you get home anyway.

Clothing

Ao dais are a popular item, especially for women. Ready-made ao dais cost about US$10 to US$20, while custom-tailored sets are notably more. Prices vary by the store and material used. If you want to buy custom-made clothing for your friends, you'll need their measurements: neck diameter, breast, waist, hip and length (from waist to hem). As a general rule, you get best results when you're right there and get measured by the tailor or seamstress.

Women all over the country wear conical hats, in part to keep the sun off their faces (though they also function like umbrellas in the rain). If you hold a well-made conical hat up to the light, you'll be able to see that between the layers of straw material are fine paper cuts. The best quality conical hats are produced in the Hué area.

T-shirts are ever popular items with travellers. A printed shirt costs around US$2 while an embroidered design will cost maybe US$3.50. Size XXL is about equivalent to medium in the West – if you are really large, forget it unless you want to have your shirts individually tailored.

Sandals are a practical item to take home, and cheap at around US$3.50. Finding large sizes to fit Western feet can be a problem, though. Make sure they are very comfortable before you purchase them – some tend to be poorly made and will give you blisters.

Stamps

Postage stamps already set in a collector's book are readily available either inside or near the GPO in major cities or at some hotel gift shops and book stores. You can even find stamps from the now-extinct South Vietnamese regime.

Gems

Vietnam produces some good gems, but there are plenty of fakes and flawed gems around. This doesn't mean that you shouldn't buy something if you think it's beautiful, but don't think that you'll find a cut diamond or polished ruby for a fraction of what you'd pay at home. Some travellers have actually thought that they could buy gems in Vietnam and sell them at home for a profit. Such business requires considerable expertise and good connections in the mining industry.

Music

Saigon and Hanoi both have an astounding collection of audio tapes for sale, most of which are pirated. The majority of Vietnamese hits were originally recorded by Overseas Vietnamese in California and bootlegged in Vietnam. There are also the latest Chinese music tapes from Hong Kong and Taiwan (mostly soft rock). Hard rock from the West is not as popular, but there is a small and devoted core of avant-garde types who like it.

CDs are not yet manufactured in Vietnam, though it seems like only a matter of time. Plenty are imported – about 80% are pirated copies from China and therefore very cheap. The official word is that this illegal practice will be 'cleaned up' by the authorities, but don't hold your breath waiting.

Electronics

Electronic goods sold in Vietnam are actually not such a great bargain and you'd be better off purchasing these in duty-free ports such as Hong Kong and Singapore. However, the prices charged in Vietnam are really not all that bad, mainly due to the black market (smuggling), which also results in 'duty-free' goods.

Only those items imported legally by an authorised agent will include a warranty card valid in Vietnam. Unfortunately, Vietnamese electronics which are not black market are often 'grey market' – that is, imported legally but by someone besides the authorised importer. This does not circumvent the need to pay import taxes, but it creates a tidy profit for the resellers because they avoid paying commissions to the authorised agent. However, as with smuggled goods, grey market items are usually sold without warranty, or at least no warranty which is valid in Vietnam. However, some electronic goods include an international warranty card, which presumably solves this problem.

War Souvenirs

In places frequented by tourists, it's easy to buy what looks like equipment left over from the Vietnam War. However, almost all of these items are reproductions and your chances of finding anything original is slim. Enterprising back-alley tailors turn out US military uniforms, and metalcraft shops have learned how to make helmets, bayonets and dog tags.

The 'Zippo' lighters seem to be the hottest-selling item. You can pay extra to get one that's been beat up to look like a war relic, or just buy a new shiny one for less money.

One thing you should think twice about purchasing are weapons and ammunition, *even if fake*. You may have several opportunities to buy old bullets and dud mortar shells, especially around the area of the old DMZ. Most of these items are either fake or deactivated, but you can occasionally find real bullets for sale with the gunpowder still inside. Real or not, it's illegal to carry ammunition on airlines and many countries will arrest you if any such goods are found in your luggage. Customs agents in Singapore are particularly strict and thorough, and travellers carrying souvenir ammunition and weapons have run into some serious problems there.

Old Cars

Assuming you are an automobile collector and have sufficient funds to support such an expensive habit, Vietnam is a worthwhile place to check out. During the war Saigon had a large population of resident US technical advisers, business people, journalists, diplomats, CIA agents, etc, many of whom bought imported American and European cars for personal use. When South Vietnam suddenly collapsed in 1975, the Americans had to flee abruptly, abandoning their vehicles in the process.

Ironically, Vietnam's severe poverty means that automobile owners take good care of their vehicles, since replacements are unaffordable. So if you're in the market for a 1965 Ford Mustang, an Austin-Healey convertible or an old De Soto, this is the place to look. Automobiles easily exceed the 20-kg luggage weight limit imposed by Vietnam Airlines, so you'll have to make arrangements to ship the vehicle home by sea freight, unless you want to attempt a land crossing into Cambodia. Good luck.

Getting There & Away

AIR
Vietnam Airlines

Vietnam's flag carrier is the government-owned Vietnam Airlines (Hang Khong Viet Nam). Long noted for shoddy service and unsafe aircraft, Vietnam Airlines has been working hard to spruce up its battered image. Safety standards have improved vastly now that the ageing Russian-built Tupolev aircraft have all been retired on all international routes (except those to China). Your flight is most likely to be on a French-built Airbus or US-made Boeings and Lockheed planes.

The majority of flights into and out of Vietnam are joint operations between Vietnam Airlines and foreign carriers. The air ticket you purchase might have the words 'Vietnam Airlines' printed on it, but you could find yourself flying on, for example, Cathay Pacific or THAI.

Refunds for tickets to Vietnam are possible but there is a US$40 cancellation charge and getting your money back – especially from Vietnam Airlines – could take several months. If you intend to fly into Ho Chi Minh City and fly out by way of Hanoi (or vice versa), you should get this specified on your ticket along with any other stopoffs. It is possible to get the airlines to allow a change of departure points after arrival in Vietnam; for example, a Ho Chi Minh City-Bangkok return ticket can be endorsed for a Hanoi-Bangkok return flight for a US$10 surcharge, but such a ticket will be of no use at all if you choose to stop over in Vientiane (Laos).

The 20-kg checked-luggage weight limit is strictly enforced, especially on Vietnam Airlines. On flights out of Vietnam, they can prevent you from leaving unless you pay the steep overweight fee.

At all Vietnam Airlines offices which book international flights, there is a computer link-up with the SITA international reservations system.

It is extremely difficult to get reservations for flights to or from Vietnam around Tet (the Lunar New Year), which can fall around late January to mid-February. If you will be in Vietnam during this period (which is a favourite time for family visits by Overseas Vietnamese) make reservations well in advance or you may find yourself marooned in Bangkok on the way in or stranded in Ho Chi Minh City on the way out. Travellers have reported that ticket scalpers and corrupt airline officials will come up with a seat (or jump you to the head of the waiting list) during Tet for a 'service charge' of US$100 or so.

Be aware that Vietnam is not the only country to celebrate the Lunar New Year – it's also *the* major holiday in Singapore, Hong Kong, Macau, China, Taiwan and Korea and is also celebrated by the sizeable Chinese minorities in Thailand and Malaysia. People from these countries hit the road at that time, with the result that airlines, trains and hotels are booked solid all over the Orient. The chaos begins about a week before the Lunar New Year and lasts until two weeks after it.

There are rather few discounts on flights going to Vietnam. Some travel agents booking flights to Vietnam offer a package deal with the visa and air ticket combined at a slight discount, but the savings isn't likely to be huge. The lack of discounts reflects the lack of cut-throat competition. Vietnam Airlines decides the official price, and all the airlines which have cooperative agreements with Vietnam Airlines must follow. Fortunately, the prices charged by Vietnam Airlines are not outrageous for the distances flown, though no doubt it would be cheaper if the airlines indulged in a cut-throat capitalist-style price war.

To give Vietnam Airlines some needed competition, Pacific Airlines (with Czech flight crews) started operations in 1992. At present, Pacific Airlines has a very limited flight schedule – the only domestic flight is Hanoi-Ho Chi Minh City. The only international routes flown by Pacific Airlines are Ho Chi Minh City-Taiwan (both Taipei and Kaohsiung airports). The airline has also announced plans to fly from Ho Chi Minh City to Bangkok, Paris, Moscow and Seoul. On domestic flights, Pacific Airlines charges the same prices as Vietnam Airlines, but there are reasonably good discounts on the flights to Taiwan. However, Pacific Airlines is said to be losing money and there is some question if it can even maintain current operations, let alone add new routes.

A few airlines do charter flights on demand to Vietnam – such flights might offer discount ticket possibilities.

Vietnam Airlines Overseas Offices
Australia
    61 Todman Ave, Kensington, Sydney 2033, NSW (☎ (02) 313-8943; fax 663-2505)
Cambodia
    537 Monivong Blvd, Phnom Penh (☎ 236 4460, 232 7426)
China
    Room 924, Garden Tower, Garden Hotel, 368 Huanshi E Rd, Guangzhou, 510064 (☎ (020) 328 7187, 333 8999, ext 924; fax 382 7187)
France
    24 Rue du Renard, Paris 75004 (☎ 44 54 39 00; fax 44 54 39 05)
Germany
    Berlin (☎ (30) 282 3262; fax 282 3686)
Hong Kong
    Room 1206B, Peregrine Tower, Lippo Centre, 89 Queensway, Admiralty, Hong Kong (☎ 2810-4896; fax 2869-8856)
Japan
    Osaka (☎ (06) 533-2689, 533-3318, 533-5781; fax 533-6234)
Korea (South)
    5th floor, No 5-2, Sunhwa Building, Sunhwa-dong, Chung-gu, Seoul (☎ 319 6648; fax 319 6649)
Laos
    141 Samsenthai Rd, Vientiane (☎ 4799; fax 6337)
Malaysia
    2.38-2nd floor, Wisma Stephens, 88 Jalan Raja Chulan 50200, Kuala Lumpur (☎ (03) 241 2416; fax 242 2801)
Philippines
    120 Ground floor, Anson, Arcade Building, Pasay Rd, Makati, Manila (☎ 843 4878; fax 812 5670)

Russia
    1 Tverskaia Lamskaia 30, Room 2, Moscow (☎ 250 0848; fax 251 0973)
Singapore
    15 Beach Rd, No 02-11 Beach Centre, Singapore 0718 (☎ 339 3552; fax 338 2982)
Taiwan
    Ground floor, 47 Jenai Rd, Section 2, Taipei (☎ (02) 393 0677; fax 395 6543)
    3rd floor, 54 Minsheng 1st Rd, Kaohsiung
Thailand
    578-580 Ploenchit Rd, Bangkok 10330 (☎ (02) 251 4242, 251 5439, 252 3895; fax 253 3459, 255 3978)

Pacific Airlines Overseas Offices
Taiwan
    7th floor, No 111, Sungchiang Rd, Taipei (☎ (02) 515 3177); 14-8 floor, No 56, Minsheng 1st Rd, Kaohsiung (☎ (07) 224 7217); CKS Airport (☎ (03) 393 1025)

Costs
When you're looking for bargain air fares, you have to go to a travel agent rather than directly to the airline, which can sell fares only at the full list price. But watch out – many discount tickets have restrictions (the journey must be completed in 60 days, no flights during holidays, and so on). It's important to ask the agent what restrictions, if any, apply to your ticket.

If you purchase a ticket and later want to make changes to your route or get a refund, you need to see the original travel agent. Airlines issue refunds only to the purchaser of a ticket – if you bought from a travel agent, then that agent is the purchaser, not you. Many travellers do in fact change their route half way through their trip, so think carefully about buying a ticket which is not easily refunded.

The one way in which you can get a significant discount on fares to Vietnam is to buy a group ticket. In theory, this means that you will arrive and depart with a tour group. In practice, you may never see the group or the tour guides. However, these tickets cannot be altered once issued – there are no changes permitted to arrival and departure dates, nor can you refund the unused portion of such tickets. Since many travellers do wind up extending their stay in Vietnam, buying such a ticket could be a false way to economise.

APEX (Advance Purchase Excursion) tickets are a variation on the theme. This doesn't require that you pretend to be with a group, but you are locked into a fairly rigid schedule. Such tickets must be purchased two or three weeks ahead of departure, may not permit stopovers and may have minimum and maximum stays as well as fixed departure and return dates. Unless you definitely must return at a certain time, it's best to purchase APEX tickets on a one-way basis only. There are stiff cancellation fees if you decide not to use your APEX ticket.

There are plenty of discount tickets which are valid for 12 months, allowing multiple stopovers with open dates. These tickets allow maximum flexibility. Unfortunately, few such tickets are available to Vietnam, but you can easily get such a ticket that will take you to Bangkok. And of course, getting from Bangkok to Vietnam should prove very easy and cheap.

Round-the-World (RTW) tickets are usually offered by an airline or combination of airlines, and let you take your time (six months to a year) moving from point to point on their routes for the price of one ticket. Sometimes this works out to be cheaper than buying all the tickets separately as you go along, but often it is actually more expensive. Overall, RTW tickets are not a bargain. The main restriction is that you have to keep moving in the same direction; a drawback is that because you are usually booking individual flights as you go, and can't switch carriers, you can get caught out by flight availabilities and have to spend more or less time in a place than you want.

Some airlines offer student discounts on their tickets of up to 25% to student card holders. Besides having an International Student Identity Card (ISIC), an official-looking letter from the school is also required by some airlines. Many airlines also require you to be age 26 or younger to qualify for a discount. These discounts are generally available only on ordinary economy-class fares. You wouldn't get one, for instance, on an APEX or an RTW ticket since these are already discounted.

Frequent flier deals can earn you a free air ticket or other goodies if you accumulate enough mileage with one airline. First, you must apply to the airline for a frequent flier account number (some airlines will issue these on the spot or by telephone if you call their head office). Every time you buy an air ticket and/or check in for your flight, you must inform the clerk of your frequent flier account number or else you won't get credit. Save your tickets and boarding passes, since it's not uncommon for the airlines to fail to give proper credit. You should receive monthly statements by post informing you how much mileage you've accumulated. Once you've accumulated sufficient mileage to qualify for freebies, you are supposed to receive vouchers by mail. Many airlines have 'black-out periods', or times when you cannot fly for free (Christmas and Tet are good examples). The worst thing about frequent-flier programs is that these tend to lock you into one airline, and that airline may not always have the cheapest fares or most convenient flight schedule.

Airlines usually carry babies up to two years of age at 10% of the adult fare; a few may carry them free of charge. Reputable international airlines usually provide nappies (diapers), tissues, talcum and all the other paraphernalia needed to keep babies clean, dry and half-happy. For children between the ages of four and 12 the fare on international flights is usually 50% of the regular fare or 67% of a discounted fare. These days most fares are likely to be discounted.

One thing to avoid are 'back-to-front' tickets. These are best explained by example. If you are living in Vietnam (where tickets are relatively expensive) and you want to fly to Bangkok (where tickets are somewhat cheaper), you can pay by check or credit card and have a friend or travel agent in Bangkok mail the ticket to you. The problem is that the airlines have computers and will know that the ticket was issued in Bangkok rather than Vietnam, and they will refuse to honour it.

Consumer groups have filed lawsuits over this practice with mixed results, but in most countries the law protects the airlines, not consumers. In short, the ticket is valid only starting from the country where it was issued. The only exception is if you pay the full fare, thus foregoing any possible discounts that Bangkok travel agents can offer.

Courier flights can be a bargain if you're fortunate enough to find one. The way it works is that an airfreight company takes over your entire checked baggage allowance. You are permitted to bring along a carry-on bag, but that's all. In return, you get a steeply discounted ticket. These arrangements usually have to be made a month or more in advance and are available only on certain routes. You aren't likely to find one to Vietnam, but you could possibly get one to Bangkok or Hong Kong. Another consideration – such tickets are sold for a fixed date and schedule changes can be difficult or impossible to make. Courier flights are occasionally advertised in the newspapers, or you can contact airfreight companies listed in the phone book.

To/From Australia

Australia is not a cheap place to fly out of, and air fares between Australia and Asia are absurdly expensive considering the distances flown. Air tickets purchased in Vietnam are actually cheaper than those bought in Australia. Ethnic-Vietnamese living in Australia are known to have the inside scoop on ticket discounts.

Among the cheapest regular tickets available in Australia are APEX tickets. The cost depends on your departure date from Australia. The year is divided into 'peak' (expensive), 'shoulder' (less expensive) and 'low' (relatively inexpensive) seasons; peak season is December to January.

It's possible to get reductions on the cost of APEX and other fares by going to the student travel offices and/or some of the travel agents in Australia that specialise in discounting.

The weekend travel sections of papers like *The Age* (Melbourne) or the *Sydney Morning Herald* are good sources of travel information. Also look at *Student Traveller*, a free newspaper published by Student Travel Australia (STA), the Australian-based student travel organisation, which now has offices worldwide. STA has offices all around Australia (check your phone directory) and you definitely do not have to be a student to use them.

Also well worth trying is the Flight Centre (☎ (03) 9670-0477), 386 Little Bourke St, Melbourne. They also have branches in Sydney (☎ (02) 233-2296) and Brisbane (☎ (07) 3229-9958).

Qantas and Vietnam Airlines offer joint service from Ho Chi Minh City to both Melbourne (9½ hours) and Sydney (eight hours). Rock-bottom excursion fares are US$600/1000 for one-way/return tickets.

To/From Cambodia

There are daily flights between Phnom Penh and Ho Chi Minh City (US$50 one way; US$100 return) on either Cambodia Airlines or Vietnam Airlines. There are flights between Phnom Penh and Hanoi (US$157 one way, US$314 return). There is a US$5 airport tax to fly out of Cambodia. Visas for Cambodia are available upon arrival at Phnom Penh Airport for free if you stay less than 15 days.

To/From Canada

Getting discount tickets in Canada is much the same as in the USA – go to the travel agents and shop around until you find a good deal.

CUTS is Canada's national student bureau and has offices in a number of Canadian cities, including Vancouver, Edmonton, Toronto and Ottawa – you don't necessarily have to be a student. There are a number of good agents in Vancouver for cheap tickets.

There are currently no direct flights between Canada and Vietnam. Most Canadian travellers transit at Hong Kong.

To/From China

China Southern Airlines and Vietnam Airlines fly the China-Vietnam route using fuel-guzzling Soviet-built Tupolev 134 aircraft. The only direct flight between Ho Chi Minh City and China is to Guangzhou (Canton). All other flights are via Hanoi. The Guangzhou-Hanoi flight (US$140 one way) takes 1½ hours; Guangzhou-Ho Chi Minh City (US$240 one way) takes 2½ hours. Return airfares cost exactly double.

The Beijing-Hanoi flight on China Southern Airlines stops at Nanning (capital of China's Guangxi Province) en route – you can board or exit the plane there. Unfortunately, this flight is a favourite of traders ('smugglers' as far as the authorities are concerned). This not only makes it difficult to get a ticket, but travellers arriving in Hanoi on this flight have reported vigorous baggage searches and numerous customs hassles. Going the other way, arrival in Nanning *might* be a little bit smoother, but don't count on it – Chinese customs agents are diligently on the lookout for drugs, and if you look like 'the type', expect a thorough going over.

To/From France
Vietnam Airlines cooperates with Air France. Flights between Paris and Ho Chi Minh City (usually via Dubai and sometimes Berlin) run three times weekly. One-way/return fares are US$830/1245. Paris-Hanoi fares are slightly cheaper at US$800/1200.

To/From Germany
Germany's Lufthansa and Vietnam Airlines offer joint service between Berlin and Ho Chi Minh City. There are two flights weekly which go via Dubai, and flying time is at least 14½ hours. Bottom-end one-way/-return fares are US$830/1245.

To/From Hong Kong
After Bangkok, Hong Kong is the second most popular point for departures to Vietnam. Hong Kong-Ho Chi Minh City flights run daily and require 2½ hours flying time. Hanoi-Hong Kong flights are also daily and take 1¾ hours.

A travel agent in Hong Kong specialising in discount air tickets and customised tours to Vietnam is Phoenix Services (☎ 2722-7378; fax 2369-8884) in Room B, 6th floor, Milton Mansion, 96 Nathan Rd, Tsimshatsui, Kowloon.

Hong Kong's flag carrier, Cathay Pacific, and Vietnam Airlines offer joint service between Hong Kong and Ho Chi Minh City (one-way/return US$291/436). There are also direct Hong Kong-Hanoi flights (US$264/396). The most popular ticket allows you to fly from Hong Kong to Ho Chi Minh City and return from Hanoi to Hong Kong.

To/From Indonesia
Vietnam Airlines does not fly to Indonesia, but Garuda Airlines does. A Jakarta-Ho Chi Minh City ticket costs US$437 each way. Round-trip excursion fares (good for 30 days) cost from US$705.

To/From Japan
Arranging visas and air tickets in Japan is so outrageously expensive and time-consuming that you might consider taking a boat to Korea instead and doing it from there. Even better is to go to Bangkok, but then that still puts you at the mercy of Japanese airline companies and the avaricious travel agents.

If you've got no choice and must fly from Japan, Vietnam Airlines flies between Osaka and Ho Chi Minh City three times weekly. At present, there are no direct flights from Tokyo, though that is expected to change. Osaka-Ho Chi Minh City flights take approximately 5½ hours. Japanese travel agents want US$150 to US$250 for a visa, which takes two to three weeks to process. Compare this with Bangkok, where cost is US$45 and processing time is five days.

Tickets purchased in Vietnam are cheaper than those available in Japan. Low-end prices in Vietnam for Ho Chi Minh City-Osaka one-way/return are US$500/800.

To/From Korea
Korean Air and Vietnam Airlines offer joint service between Seoul and Ho Chi Minh City daily except Tuesdays. Asiana Airlines also

flies to Vietnam. Flying time between Ho Chi Minh City and Seoul is 4¾ hours. The cheapest one-way/return fares are currently US$350/500.

Seoul is also a useful transit point connecting Vietnam to the USA.

To/From Laos
Lao Aviation and Vietnam Airlines offer joint service between Vientiane and Hanoi (US$80/160 one-way/return) or Vientiane and Ho Chi Minh City (US$170/340).

Visit Laos for free? It can be done if you are exiting Vietnam by air from Hanoi. An air ticket from Hanoi to Vientiane costs US$80; a Laos transit visa costs US$15, land transport (airport to hotel to boat) is US$5, the bus across the Mekong is US$1 and a train from Nong Khai to Bangkok costs US$16. The total is US$117, and compared to a straight Hanoi-Bangkok air ticket (US$176) you save US$59 – more than enough for food, shopping and other miscellaneous expenses!

To/From Malaysia
Malaysian Airline System (MAS) and Vietnam Airlines have joint service from Kuala Lumpur to Ho Chi Minh City (US$150/300 one-way/return). Flying time for Kuala Lumpur-Ho Chi Minh City is 1¾ hours. There are also Kuala Lumpur-Hanoi flights costing US$340/680 for one-way/return tickets.

To/From the Netherlands
Vietnam Airlines has a joint operation with KLM and flies Amsterdam-Ho Chi Minh City nonstop. The best prices you can hope to get on one-way/return tickets are currently US$825/1240.

To/From the Philippines
Philippine Airlines and Vietnam Airlines fly from Manila to Ho Chi Minh City. Economy one-way/return tickets start at US$185/280. Flying time from Manila to Ho Chi Minh City is 2½ hours.

To/From Russia
Aeroflot flies Ilyushin IL86s and IL62s from Moscow to Hanoi and Ho Chi Minh City with numerous stopoffs along the way. The whole hopscotch across Asia can take over 20 hours.

Vietnam Airlines flies twice weekly between Ho Chi Minh City and Moscow via Dubai. This airline uses Boeing 767s and the flight takes 14 hours. Tickets purchased in Russia cost more than those bought in Vietnam. The best prices you can get in Vietnam for one-way/return Ho Chi Minh City-Moscow tickets are US$640/1280.

To/From Singapore
Singapore Airlines and Vietnam Airlines offer daily joint service on the Ho Chi Minh City-Singapore route. Flight time between Singapore and Ho Chi Minh City is 1¾ hours. The one-way fare is US$213 and return fares are exactly double. Most flights from Singapore continue onwards to Hanoi. The Singapore-Hanoi one-way fare is US$330.

Vietnam Airlines now offers direct Vung Tau-Singapore flights.

To/From Taiwan
The large numbers of Taiwanese who visit Vietnam have made Taiwan a good embarkation point for Vietnam, with frequent flights now offered by four competing airlines. Flight time between Vietnam and Taiwan is around three hours. However, there are no diplomatic relations between Taiwan and Vietnam, so visa processing takes 10 days. For many travellers, this delay is unacceptably long.

Taiwan's China Airlines offers joint service with Vietnam Airlines between Ho Chi Minh City and the Taiwanese cities of Taipei and Kaohsiung. There are also Hanoi-Taipei flights twice weekly. The cheapest return fares are 90-day excursion tickets. At the bottom end, one-way/return fares are US$350/525.

Vietnam's Pacific Airlines offers the cheapest Ho Chi Minh City-Taipei service, at US$461 return. Be careful about purchasing tickets on this airline too far in advance because there have been reports questioning its long-term economic viability.

EVA Air claims to be Taiwan's luxury airline, but it charges luxury prices. There are some discounts on long routes such as Los Angeles-Taipei-Ho Chi Minh City. On a Taipei-Ho Chi Minh City excursion return ticket, figure around US$560.

Travel agents in Taiwan advertise return fares as low as US$423, but these are group tickets which must be booked well in advance and no changes are permitted.

A long-running discount travel agent with a good reputation is Jenny Su Travel (☎ (02) 594 7733, 596 2263; fax 592 0068), 10th floor, 27 Chungshan N Rd, Section 3, Taipei. An agent which has specialised in Vietnam tours is Hongyi Travel (☎ (02) 505 9212; fax 502 3763), 5/f-3, 129 Sungchiang Rd, Taipei.

To/From Thailand

Bangkok, only 80 minutes flying time from Ho Chi Minh City, has emerged as the main port of embarkation for air travel to Vietnam.

Thai Airways International (THAI), Air France and Vietnam Airlines offer Bangkok-Ho Chi Minh City service for US$150 one way; round-trip tickets cost exactly double.

There are daily flights from Bangkok to Ho Chi Minh City, and some of the flights continue on to Danang. There are also direct Bangkok-Hanoi flights (US$176 one-way).

Khao San Rd in Bangkok is budget travellers' headquarters and the place to look for bargain ticket deals. There are many agencies here milking the backpacker market, but one which has received frequent recommendations from travellers is Vista Travel Service (☎ 280 0348), 24/4 Khao San Rd. Another place that does all right for tickets and visas is Exotissimo Travel (☎ 253 5240; fax 254 7683).

To/From the USA

It's not advisable to send money (even checks) through the post unless the agent is very well established – some travellers have reported being ripped off by fly-by-night mail order ticket agents. Nor is it wise to hand over the full amount to Shady Deal Travel Services unless they can give you the

ticket straight away – most US travel agencies have computers that can spit out the ticket on the spot.

Council Travel is the largest student travel organisation, and, though you don't have to be a student to use them, they do have specially discounted student tickets. Council Travel has an extensive network in all major US cities and is listed in the telephone book. There are also Student Travel Network offices, which are associated with STA.

One of the cheapest and most reliable travel agents on the west coast is Overseas Tours (☎ (800) 222-5292), 475 El Camino Real, Room 206, Millbrae, CA 94030. Another good agent is Gateway Travel (☎ (214) 960-2000, (800) 878-2828; fax 490-6367), 4201 Spring Valley Rd, Suite 104, Dallas, TX 75244. Both of these places seem to be trustworthy for mail-order tickets.

China Airlines (of Taiwan, not China) currently offers the cheapest fares on US-Vietnam flights, all of which transit Taipei. Low-season San Francisco-Ho Chi Minh City one-way/return tickets cost US$464/837; New York-Ho Chi Minh City is US$573/1047.

Other possible but slightly pricier US-Vietnam tickets are available from EVA Air (also via Taipei), Cathay Pacific (via Hong Kong), THAI (via Bangkok) and Asiana (via Seoul).

At the time of this writing, no US air carriers were flying into Vietnam. However, this is expected to change shortly. Airlines to watch include Northwest and United.

To/From the UK

There are no direct flights between the UK and Vietnam, but cheap tickets are available on the London-Hong Kong run. From Hong Kong, it's easy enough to make onward arrangements to Vietnam by air or overland.

Air-ticket discounting is a long-running business in the UK and it's wide open. The various agents advertise their fares and there is nothing under-the-counter about it at all. However, do be careful about handing over large sums of cash to what might be fly-by-night operators who promise to deliver your ticket 'next week'.

To find out what's going, there are a number of magazines in Britain which have good information about flights and agents. These include: *Trailfinder*, free from the Trailfinders Travel Centre in Earl's Court, and *Time Out* or *City Limits*, London weekly entertainment guides widely available in the UK. Discount tickets are available almost exclusively in London.

LAND
To/From Cambodia
Land travel in Cambodia is not especially recommended due to attacks by the Khmer Rouge, but the situation fluctuates from being reasonably safe to exceedingly dicey. On the main highways where you have a troop escort, it should be OK, but safest of all is to fly. Make inquiries before proceeding.

The only frontier crossing between Cambodia and Vietnam open to Westerners is at Moc Bai, which connects Vietnam's Tay Ninh Province with Cambodia's Svay Rieng Province. Other border crossings which *might* open to foreigners in the future include the crossing between Kep in Kampot Province and Ha Tien in Kien Giang Province; between Kandal Province and Chau Doc in An Giang Province (by Mekong River ferry); and between Ratanakiri Province and Chu Nghe in Gia Lai Province, 65 km west of Pleiku.

Buses run every day between Phnom Penh and Ho Chi Minh City (via Moc Bai). The cost is US$5 or US$12 depending on whether you take the air-con coach or old De Soto rattletrap. In Vietnam, you purchase tickets from the Phnom Penh Bus Garage at 155 Nguyen Hue Blvd, Ho Chi Minh City, adjacent to the Rex Hotel, but the bus departs at 5 am from 145 Nguyen Du St. The biggest disadvantage of this bus is that you must wait for everybody to clear customs at the border, a procedure which can take hours.

There is a faster and cheaper way, though a bit more complicated. You can board one of the many bus tours heading for the Caodai Great Temple at Tay Ninh (as little as US$5). But instead of going to Tay Ninh, you get off sooner at Go Dau where the highway forks. There will be motorcycle taxis waiting here, and for as little as US$0.50 you can get a ride to the border crossing at Moc Bai. At the border you must walk across, and you will find air-conditioned share taxis waiting on the Cambodia side to take you to Phnom Penh for US$5 per person.

There are also share taxis direct from Saigon to Moc Bai border crossing, some costing as little as US$20 for three persons. In Saigon, Kim Café at 270-272 De Tham St, District 1, is one place to book these, but also check at other travel agencies.

To do this overland crossing, you will need a Cambodian visa (which takes seven working days to process) and a re-entry visa for Vietnam if you are going back to Vietnam rather than flying on to a third country. If you are entering or exiting Vietnam by this route, your Vietnamese visa (or re-entry visa) must indicate the Moc Bai crossing. If you forgot to do that in Saigon, amendments to Vietnamese re-entry visas can also be made at the Vietnamese Embassy in Phnom Penh.

Foreigners making the crossing at Moc Bai have reported attempts by Vietnamese customs agents to solicit bribes.

To/From Laos
We've waited for at least 20 years, but the big news in 1994 was that the Lao Bao border crossing between Vietnam and Laos has now opened. This makes it possible to drive between the southern Lao province of Savannakhet and central Vietnam via the border crossing at Lao Bao, which is on National Highway 9, 80 km west of Dong Ha. The road is in reasonably good condition, though it sees little traffic.

There is a cross-border bus running between Danang (Vietnam) and Savannakhet. In Vietnam, you can catch this bus in Danang, Dong Ha or Lao Bao. In Laos, the only place you are likely to board is Savannakhet. This bus is supposed to make its runs on Sunday, Tuesday and Thursday, but this schedule is hardly engraved in stone, and the bus probably won't run unless there are sufficient passengers. Dong Ha to

Savannakhet on this bus costs US$15 for foreigners. From the Vietnamese side, departure from Danang is at 4 am, from Dong Ha at 10 am, Lao Bao at 2 pm and arrival in Savannakhet at 7 pm. Border guards (both Lao and Vietnamese) have been know to ask for bribes.

There are also local buses which just go up to the border from the Vietnamese side, while on the Lao side the local 'bus' is a truck. It's cheaper to go by local bus rather than to take the cross-border express, but a lot more hassle. The bus from Dong Ha to Lao Bao costs US$1 to US$4 depending on whether it's 'deluxe' or 'standard'. These buses depart when full.

There is a restaurant on the Laotian side of the border, 500 metres back from the border post. You might be able to sleep in the restaurant if you ask real nice, but there are no hotels here. To say that the facilities around the border are primitive is an understatement.

A visa for Laos is needed, which can be obtained in Ho Chi Minh City, Hanoi or Danang. If you are departing or entering Vietnam via this route, your Vietnamese visa must indicate the Lao Bao border crossing. If you have a Vietnamese re-entry visa, it can be amended at the Vietnamese Embassy in Vientiane or even at the Vietnamese Consulate in Savannakhet.

On the Laotian side, the highway crosses the Ho Chi Minh Trail. This is one of the few places where you can actually get a look at it though there is not a whole lot to see.

To/From China

Vietnam's two land border crossings with China were closed for many years as a result of the 1979 Chinese invasion. The border has now reopened, a major boon to overland travellers.

The busiest border crossing is at Dong Dang (20 km north of Lang Son in north-east Vietnam), and the nearest major Chinese city to this border crossing is Nanning, capital of Guangxi Province. The crossing point is known in Vietnamese as Huu Nghi Quan (Friendship Gate). Vietnamese and Chinese traders can regularly be seen crossing this border, hauling tremendous quantities of 'personal luggage' in the hopes of avoiding import taxes. However, they are often intercepted by customs, who joyously rip open their luggage with knives and extort 'fines' or confiscate the goods.

There is a twice-weekly international train running between Beijing and Hanoi, which stops at Dong Dang, and you can board or exit the train at numerous stations in China. The entire Beijing-Hanoi run takes approximately 55 hours, including a three-hour delay (if you're lucky) at the border checkpoint. Schedules are subject to change, but at present train No 5 departs Beijing at 11.27 pm on Monday and Friday, arriving in Hanoi at 6.30 am on Thursday and Monday, respectively. Going the other way, train No 6 departs Hanoi at 11 pm on Tuesday and Friday, arriving in Beijing at 9.14 am on Friday and Monday, respectively. The complete schedule follows:

Station	To Hanoi Train No 5	To Beijing Train No 6
Beijing	11.27 pm	9.14 am
Shijiazhuang	2.54 am	5.58 am
Zhengzhou	7.53 am	12.53 am
Xinyang	11.50 am	8.53 pm
Hankou (Wuhan)	2.59 pm	5.35 pm
Wuchang (Wuhan)	3.34 pm	4.56 pm
Yueyang	6.47 pm	1.46 pm
Changsha	8.56 pm	11.42 am
Hengyang	11.49 pm	8.46 am
Lengshuitan	2.07 am	6.26 am
Guilin North	5.38 am	2.31 am
Guilin	5.59 am	2.12 am
Liuzhou	8.45 am	11.07 pm
Nanning	3.40 pm	6.20 pm
Pinxiang	10.04 pm	12.41 pm
Friendship Gate	10.00 pm*	8.00 am*
Dong Dang	1.00 am*	5.00 am*
Hanoi	6.30 am*	11.00 pm*

* Vietnamese Time

Before 1979, an 851-km metre-gauge railway, inaugurated in 1910, linked Hanoi with Kunming in Yunnan Province, crossing the border at Lao Cai in north-west Vietnam. The railway has not been resurrected, but you can cross on foot. The border town on the Chinese side is called Hekou.

Entering Vietnam overland requires a special visa. See the Visa section in the Facts for the Visitor chapter for details.

Exiting from Vietnam to China is much simpler. The Chinese don't require anything more than a standard tourist visa, and Chinese visas do not indicate entry or exit points. However, your Vietnamese visa must have the correct exit point marked on it, a change which can easily be made in Hanoi.

More details about crossing overland between Vietnam and China are included in the last chapter of this book (The North) under the Lang Son and Lao Cai sections.

SEA

Among fed-up Vietnamese nationals, unauthorised departure by sea has been very popular since 1975. Since about 1990, the numbers of boat people fleeing the country has been considerably reduced by the Orderly Departure Programme and the opening of the Chinese border, which provides a much safer and easier route.

For foreign tourists, there seem to be no options as yet to arrive or depart legally by sea. There is some talk of allowing luxury cruisers to dock at Vietnamese ports. Major port facilities in Vietnam include Haiphong, Danang, Vung Tau and Ho Chi Minh City – all frequent ports of call for freighters, especially from Singapore, Taiwan and Thailand.

Yachts and fishing boats that have shown up without authorisation in Vietnamese territorial waters have been seized and their crews imprisoned – sometimes for many months – until a satisfactory payment in hard currency gets delivered to the aggrieved authorities.

TOURS

Package tours are sold by a variety of agencies in Bangkok and elsewhere, but nearly all these tours, which usually follow one of a dozen or so set itineraries, are run by the omnipresent government tourism authorities, Vietnam Tourism and Saigon Tourist. You really could fly to Vietnam and make all the arrangements after arrival, so the only thing you gain by booking before arrival is maybe saving a little time. However, if your time is more precious than money, a pre-booked package tour could be right for you.

Tours booked outside Vietnam are not a total rip-off given what you get (visa, air tickets, tourist-class accommodation, food, transport, a guide, etc), but then again they're not inexpensive: they range in price from about US$480 for a three-day Saigon 'shopping tour' to over US$1,000 for a week-long trip that includes flying all around the country. An Australian travel agency advertises a 19-day excursion for US$1300 *not* including airfare. Doing the same things on your own can cost as little as US$15 a day (not including air fare).

Most agencies impose a surcharge for tours run for less than *two* people. In other words, a small group can purchase a virtually private tour. If you deal with a travel agent who deals directly with Vietnam, it should be possible to arrange for your itinerary to deviate significantly from the usual packages, but make sure to get any special arrangements *in writing* and to confirm them as soon as you arrive in Vietnam.

Companies in Bangkok selling their own versions of the standard tours often farm out the sale of their offerings to other travel agencies. The price may be pretty much the same if you purchase a tour on Khao San Rd rather than at one of the places listed in this section.

The following lists of travel agencies are by no means complete, nor can it be guaranteed that the agents listed here will necessarily offer you the best deal around. When purchasing a tour, remember the ancient Latin wisdom: *caveat emptor*, or 'buyer beware'.

East Asia

In East Asia, companies offering tours to Vietnam include:

Hong Kong
    Phoenix Services Agency, Room B, 6/F, Milton Mansion, 96 Nathan Rd, Tsimshatsui, Kowloon (☎ 2722-7378; fax 2369-8884)

Starlight Services Agency, David House, Room 1105, 8-20 Nanking St (one block N of Jordan Rd), Yaumatei, Kowloon (☎ 2332-5688; fax 2771-9698)

Friendship Travel, Room 604, 6/f, Mohan's Bldg, 14-16 Hankow Rd, Tsimshatsui, Kowloon (☎ 2312-1888; fax 2366-1623)

Japan

New Japan Tours, 1/F East Tokiwamatsu Bldg, 17-5 Higashi 1-Chome, Shibuya-Ku, Tokyo (☎ 3486-5110; fax 3486-5150)

SMI Indochina, 3F, 10 Sankyo Building, 1-2-7 Hamamatsu-Cho, Minatoku-Ku, Tokyo 105 (☎ 3437-1883; fax 3437-1983)

Philippines

Expertravel & Tours, 1971-1973 Mabini St, Malate, Manila (☎ (02) 509 360; fax 521 1785)

Far Travel, Asian Plaza, 1 De La Costa St, Salcedo Village, Makati (☎ (02) 816 4072; fax 815 6230

Robelle Tours & Travel, Ground floor L&S Bldg, 1414 Roxas Blvd, Ermita, Manila (☎ (02) 521 9168; fax 521 7358)

Singapore

Vietlink, 60 Eutong Sen St, No 01-17 Furama Hotel Shopping Centre, Singapore 0105 (☎ 538 2050; fax 538 6202)

Taiwan

Hong Yi Travel Service, 5F-3, 129 Sungchiang Rd, Taipei (☎ (02) 505 9212; fax 502 3763)

Zion Tours, 6F, 34 Minchuan W Rd, Taipei (☎ (02) 562 3233; fax 563 6224)

Thailand

Air People Tour & Travel Co Ltd, 2nd Floor, Regent House Bldg, 183 Rajdamri Rd, Bangkok 10500 (☎ (02) 254 3921; fax 255 3750)

Diethelm Travel, Kian Gwan Bldg II, 140/1 Wireless Rd, Bangkok 10500 (☎ (02) 255 9150/60/70; fax 256 0248/9). Diethelm tends to be much more expensive than other agencies.

SMI Travel Company, 578-580 Ploenchit Rd, Patumwan, Bangkok 10330 (☎ (02) 221 4614; fax 251 1785

Vietlink, 719-721, 2F Mahachai Rd, Burapha, Bangkok 10200 (☎ (02) 221 4614; fax 225 6389)

Australasia

Agencies in Australia and New Zealand offering tours to Vietnam include:

Australia

Orbitours, 3rd floor, 73 Walker St (PO box 834), North Sydney, NSW, 2060 (☎ (02) 9954-1399; fax 9954- 1655)

Peregrine, 5/38 York St, Sydney, NSW 2000 (☎ (02) 290-2770)

Prima Holidays Ltd,1st floor, 277 Flinders Lane, Melbourne, Vic 3000 (☎ (03) 9654-4211; fax 9654-7204)

Woollahra Travel, 227 Edgecliff Rd, Woollahra 2025, Sydney, NSW (☎ (02) 389-3399; fax 389-2404)

New Zealand

Destinations, 2nd floor, Premier Bldg, 4 Durham St, Auckland, New Zealand (☎ (09) 390 464)

North America

In North America you might try contacting:

California

South Sea Tour & Travel, 210 Post St, Suite 910, San Francisco, CA 94108 (☎ (415) 397-4644, (800) 546-7890; fax (415) 391-3752)

New York

VINA USA Travel Center, 373 Fifth Ave, New York, NY 10016 (☎ (212) 545-7474; fax 545-7698)

Texas

Que Huong Tours, 3555 W Walnut, Suite 203, Garland TX 75042 (☎ (214) 578-0219; fax 487-1356)

Washington, DC

The Global Spectrum, 1901 Pennsylvania Ave NW, Suite 204, Washington, DC 20006 (☎ (202) 293-2065, (800) 419-4446; fax (202) 296-0815)

British Columbia

Concord-Pacific Travel, Suite 921, 675 West Hastings St, Vancouver, BC V6B 1N2 (☎ (604) 669-1308; fax 266-1386)

Golden Star Travel, 879 East Hastings St, Vancouver, BC V6A 1R8 (☎ (604) 253-5265; fax 251-3277)

Quebec

Chama Gulf Asia Tours, 1111 Saint Urbain, Suite M08, Montreal, Quebec H2Z 1K8 (☎ (514) 395-4646; fax 395-4666)

New Asia Tours (Tour Nouvelle Asie), 1063 Blvd St Laurent, Montreal, Quebec H2Z 1J6 (☎ (514) 874-0266; fax 874-0251)

Saigon Tours, 3449 Str Denis No 1, Montreal, Quebec H2X 3L1 (☎ (514) 982-6168; fax 982-0820)

Europe

In western Europe, agencies booking tours to Vietnam include:

Belgium

Explotra Travel in Asia, Rue Leopold, 10-6000 Charleroi (☎ (07) 132 1515; fax 133 3603)

France

Consult Voyages, 16 Rue Laplace 75005, Paris (☎ 44 07 20 37)

Terres D'Aventure, 16 Rue Saint Victor 75005, Paris (☎ 43 29 94 50; fax 40 46 95 22)

Germany

New Asia Enterprise, Konrad-Wolf Str 99, 0-1092 Berlin (☎ 376 4690; fax 823 1621)

Sweden

Jade Travel, Olof Palmes Gata 16, 111 37 Stockholm (☎ (08) 119248; fax 214314)

Switzerland
> *Exotissimo*, 8 Ave du Mail, 1205 Geneva
> (☎ (022) 81 21 66; fax 81 21 71)
> *Artou*, 8 Rue de Rive, 1204 Geneva
> *Nayak*, Steinengrabes 42, CH-4001 Basel
> (☎ (061) 22 43 43)

UK
> *Indochina Travel*, 598-608 Chiswick High Rd,
> London W4 5RT (☎ (0181) 995 3883; fax 995 5346
> *Regent Holidays (UK) Ltd*, 15 John St, Bristol
> BS1 2HR (☎ (0117) 921 1711; fax 925 4866)

Adventure Tours

Cycling Vietnam's bad roads offer plenty of challenges to intrepid cyclists looking for adventure. One company catering to this market is *VeloAsia* (☎ (510) 524-3873; fax 524-4382; e-mail veloterra@aol.com), 1412 Martin Luther King Jr Way, Berkeley CA 94709, USA.

Rafting & Trekking A company which offers tours for intrepid trekkers, boaters and nature enthusiasts is Nonesuch Whitewater (☎ (707) 823-6603; fax 823-1954), 4004 Bones Rd, Sebastopol, CA 95472, USA.

Visits by US Vietnam Veterans

A growing number of US veterans of the Vietnam War are deciding to visit Vietnam. Many psychologists who deal with the long-term effects of the war believe that 'going back' to Vietnam can help groups of veterans confront the root causes of post-traumatic stress disorder (PTSD).

LEAVING VIETNAM

Be aware that Vietnamese visas specify from which point(s) – usually Ho Chi Minh City's Tan Son Nhat Airport and/or Hanoi's Noi Bai Airport – you are permitted to leave the country. If you intend to exit from some place not listed on your visa (such as to Cambodia via Moc Bai or China via 'Friendship Gate', make sure to have the immigration police or Foreign Ministry office add the additional border crossing to your visa.

Except at peak holiday times, it's not too difficult to get a flight out of the country, but it's wise to book your departure at least a few days in advance. At peak times everything might be chock-a-block and your only hope will be to upgrade to business or first class (and pay through the nose for it).

If you bought an air ticket with a definite departure date, it's essential to reconfirm after you've arrived in Vietnam or your seat will likely be given away to somebody else.

Travellers have reported things being pilfered from their luggage on departure, but some effort is being made to crack down on this.

Duty-Free Shopping

Like elsewhere in the world, Vietnam's airport duty-free shops offer the usual array of pricey souvenirs which cost much less if you buy them elsewhere. If you're bored while waiting for your flight, duty-free shops offer you a chance to browse and pig out on chocolate-coated macadamia nuts or drown your sorrows in a bottle of duty-free XO. One of the great ironies is that two years ago, we found the airport duty-free shops in Vietnam to be both cheap and filled with interesting locally produced goods. Now they have become expensive and most of what's on sale are the same items you can buy in Japanese-owned duty-free shops around the world. This is progress.

If you've got a nicotine habit, you can also get a duty-free fix at the airport, but prices for smuggled cigarettes on the streets of Saigon are nearly the same.

Departure Tax

The departure tax for international flights is now US$8. The tax is payable in either dong or US dollars.

Getting Around

AIR

Vietnam Airlines has a near monopoly on domestic flights, though upstart Pacific Airlines flies one route. Flights fill up fast on weekends and holidays, though you should be OK at other times. To be safe, make your booking a few days in advance. Many provincial destinations are included as a stopover on Hanoi-Ho Chi Minh City flights, such as Ho Chi Minh City-Hué-Hanoi runs.

In the past, purchasing a domestic air ticket literally required strong-arm tactics – you had to show up at the domestic booking office and dive into a struggling mass of elbows, hands and slithering bodies. If you were lucky, you'd emerge from the vortex an hour or so later with ticket in hand (though perhaps minus your wallet).

Thanks to a new computerised booking system, things have changed remarkably. Now you can even purchase air tickets through domestic travel agents, though it's usually quicker to go directly to the airline office yourself. Although the Vietnamese aren't real keen about standing in line, the crowds have been much reduced and you can usually conduct your business in 10 minutes or so.

You do need your passport and/or visa to make a booking on all domestic flights, and you will also need to show these documents at the check-in counter. Vietnamese nationals need to show their ID cards or they will not be permitted to board the aircraft.

Foreigners must pay for airline tickets with US dollars, though this will soon change. Vietnam Airlines does not usually accept other hard currencies, though travellers' cheques denominated in US dollars will be accepted and change given in cash US dollars. Vietnamese nationals are required to pay for their tickets in dong.

Vietnam Airlines has retired most of its Soviet-built aircraft and has purchased new Boeings and Airbuses. Some of these planes are on lease from foreign airlines, even including foreign flight crews! So don't be too surprised if your Vietnam Airlines domestic flight is on a Royal Brunei aircraft with a British pilot. Eventually, Vietnam Airlines will be fully Vietnamised, but the big problem is a shortage of funds. The airline is undergoing a major expansion, paid for with mostly borrowed money. Japanese banks are doing most of the financing, and some economists have questioned the viability of these enormous loans (expected to reach US$6 billion).

Charter flights on both planes and helicopters are possible. For information on arranging such private excursions, contact Vietnam Tourism. The price tag is likely to be in the thousands of US dollars.

Flights between Hanoi and Ho Chi Minh City do not fly over Laos and Cambodia even

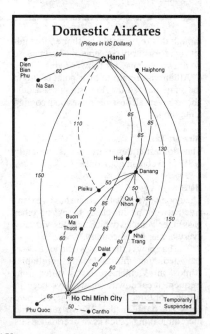

Domestic Airfares
(Prices in US Dollars)

159

Domestic Air Services

From	To	Frequency	Price
Danang	Buon Ma Thuot	6 Weekly	US$50
Danang	Haiphong	3 Weekly	US$85
Danang	Hanoi	3 Daily	US$85
Danang	Ho Chi Minh City	3 Daily	US$85
Danang	Nha Trang	4 Weekly	US$55
Danang	Pleiku	4 Weekly	US$50
Danang	Qui Nhon	3 Weekly	US$50
Hanoi	Danang	3 Daily	US$85
Hanoi	Dien Bien Phu	3 Weekly	US$60
Hanoi	Ho Chi Minh City	5 Daily	US$150
Hanoi	Hué	2 Daily	US$85
Hanoi	Na San (Son La)	1 Weekly	US$60
Hanoi	Nha Trang	1 Daily	US$130
Hanoi	Pleiku	Suspended	US$110
Ho Chi Minh City	Buon Ma Thuot	2 Daily	US$60
Ho Chi Minh City	Cantho	Suspended	US$50
Ho Chi Minh City	Dalat	3 Weekly	US$40
Ho Chi Minh City	Danang	3 Daily	US$85
Ho Chi Minh City	Haiphong	2 Daily	US$150
Ho Chi Minh City	Hanoi	5 Daily	US$150
Ho Chi Minh City	Hué	2 Daily	US$85
Ho Chi Minh City	Nha Trang	2 Daily	US$60
Ho Chi Minh City	Phu Quoc	5 Weekly	US$65
Ho Chi Minh City	Pleiku	1 Daily	US$60
Ho Chi Minh City	Qui Nhon	5 Weekly	US$60

though this route would be shorter. Regardless of any security concerns, the Vietnamese do not want to pay for flyover rights.

All aircraft return to their point of origin the same day, so the domestic air schedule above covers all possible routes both coming and going.

Airport Tax

The domestic departure tax is currently US$1, payable in dong only.

BUS

The good news is that Vietnam has an extensive network of dirt-cheap buses and other passenger vehicles which reaches virtually every corner of the country.

The bad news is that buses tend to be slow, crowded, uncomfortable and unreliable. Almost all Vietnamese buses suffer from frequent breakdowns (many have been in service for three to four decades, and spare parts are home-made). We've seen some incredible things, such as an overloaded bus driving backwards up a mountain pass because it didn't have a functioning low forward gear. The seats, often benches, are tiny and offer almost no leg room, let alone space for luggage (but most Vietnamese bring plenty of luggage anyway). You can purchase two tickets which, theoretically, entitles you to two seats – but you might have to defend your turf when the bus gets packed to overflowing!

Chronic overcrowding is the norm. Overloaded buses are often pulled over by the police but let go in exchange for a bribe. Many buses are literally standing room only – if you drop dead, you'll never hit the floor until the bus arrives at its destination. After an eight-hour ride, one foreigner put it succinctly when she said, 'I feel like a million dong'.

It's fair to say that riding the buses will give you ample opportunity to have 'personal contact' with the Vietnamese people. If you're looking to meet locals, what better way than to have a few sitting on your lap! As one reader says:

I enjoyed the bus-riding scene, the scenery and the conversations (gesturing) with people. Although I'd rate the conditions as terrible, the riding community suffered, slept and ate together.

Since around 1992, the government has introduced a system of renting the public buses to the drivers. The revenue from ticket sales has to be used by the driver to cover all expenses such as fuel, vehicle maintenance, etc. This recent capitalist-style reform might in time bring better service, but for now it often encourages speeding, overloading and a lack of anything but minimal vehicle maintenance.

Backpackers determined to pay the lowest possible price are advised not to buy tickets at the bus station. Rather, stand outside the station and wave down the bus – you can do a deal with the driver. You'll still pay twice what Vietnamese pay, but that's better than paying five times the going rate at the ticket office. However, drop by the bus station first to determine what the going rate is – it's helpful to know that in your negotiations with the bus driver.

Figuring out the bus system is anything but easy. Many cities have several bus stations, among which responsibilities are divided according to the location of the destination (whether it is north or south of the city) and the type of service being offered (local or intercity express or nonexpress).

Most intercity buses depart in the early morning. Often, a half-dozen vehicles to the same destination will leave at the same time, usually around 5.30 am. A few overnight runs have begun since curfew regulations were relaxed in 1989, but people are not especially fond of travelling all night long. Short-distance buses – which, like service taxis, depart when full (ie, jam-packed with people and luggage) – often operate throughout the day, but don't count on anything leaving after about 4 pm.

Don't be too trusting of bus drivers. Most are OK, but others are not. Travellers have had offers from bus drivers to bring them right to the front door of their hotel at no charge. Pulling up to the hotel entrance, the driver then suggests you go in and ask if they have a room. While you're doing this, the bus takes off with your luggage. Your luggage can also be pilfered at toilet stops unless you have a trusted friend watching it or you bring it to the toilet with you.

Classes

The appellation 'express' *(toc hanh)* is applied rather loosely in Vietnam. Genuine express buses are considerably faster than local buses, which drop off and pick up locals and their produce at each cluster of houses along the highway. But many express buses are the same decrepit vehicles used on local runs except that they stop less frequently. Unfortunately, they break down just as often, but somehow they do manage to limp along year after year, kept rolling by the sheer ingenuity and willpower of the driver/mechanic and the assistant. A good rule of thumb is that local buses average 15 to 25 km/h over the course of a journey. Express buses rarely exceed an average speed of 35 km/h. Real express runs – the minibus from Ho Chi Minh City to Vung Tau, for instance – can average 50 km/h or more.

However slow they may be, express buses do offer certain advantages. At ferries, they are usually given priority (as are cadre vehicles), which can save an hour or more at each crossing. And since they are marginally more expensive than regular buses, people lugging large parcels around the country to make a few dong reselling something are likely to consider their time and comfort less valuable than the cash.

Reservations

Buses normally leave early in the morning, so if you don't plan to bargain with the bus driver, show up at the bus station the day before departure and purchase a ticket.

Costs

Negligible, even though foreigners pay five times the going rate. Depending on class, figure around US$0.02 per km.

MINIBUS
There are two categories of minibus, public and chartered.

Public Minibuses
Public minibuses (actually privately owned) cater to the domestic market. They depart when full and will pick up as many passengers as possible along the route. They may also drive around town before departure, hunting for additional customers before actually heading out to the highway. Such minibuses will usually become ridiculously crowded as the journey progresses and are not comfortable by any means. The frequent stops to pick up and discharge passengers (and arrange their luggage and chickens) can make for a slow journey. In other words, public minibuses are really a small-scale version of the large public buses. You'll find these public minibuses congregate in the same general areas as the bus stations, though you can often arrange to have one pick you up at your hotel.

Chartered Minibuses
The majority of independent travellers in Vietnam choose this form of transport above all others. Chartered minibuses are just what the name implies. Some cater exclusively to foreigners, but well-heeled Vietnamese also travel this way.

This is the deluxe class – air-conditioning is *de rigueur* and you can be certain of having enough space to sit comfortably. Such luxury, of course, is something you must pay for – prices will be several times higher than what you'd pay on public buses. Nevertheless, it's still very cheap by any standard.

In places where tourists are numerous, there are bound to be people booking seats on chartered minibuses. Budget hotels and cafes are the best places to inquire about these vehicles.

TRAIN
The 2600-km Vietnamese railway system (Duong Sat Viet Nam) runs along the coast between Ho Chi Minh City and Hanoi and links the capital with Haiphong and points

north. While sometimes even slower than buses, the trains offer a more relaxing way to get around. Large-bodied Westerners will find that the trains offer more leg and body room than the jam-packed buses. And dilapidated as the tracks, rolling stock and engines may appear, the trains are more reliable than the country's ancient bus fleet. Furthermore, the railway authorities have been rapidly upgrading the facilities to accommodate foreign tourists – even air-conditioned sleeping berths are now obtainable on the express trains.

One key factor to take into account when deciding whether to go by train or bus should be the hour at which the train gets to where you want to go – trying to find a place to stay at 3 am is likely to be very frustrating.

Even the express trains in Vietnam are slow by developed-country standards, but conditions are improving as the tracks and equipment are now being upgraded. The quickest rail journey between Hanoi and Ho Chi Minh City takes 36 hours at an average speed of 48 km/h. The slowest express train on this route takes 44 hours, averaging 39 km/h for the 1726-km trip.

Then there are local trains, which do not make the complete journey but cover only part of the route, such as Ho Chi Minh City to Nha Trang. These local trains at times crawl along at 15 km/h. There are several reasons for the excruciating slowness. First of all, the track network is metre-gauge (except for 300 km in the north). Second, much of the track system is in poor condition, in part because of inadequate post-reunification repair of Viet Cong sabotage in the south and US bombing in the north. And third, there is only one track running between Ho Chi Minh City and Hanoi. Trains can pass each other only at those few points where a siding has been constructed. Each time trains go by each other, one of them has to stop on the prearranged sidetrack and wait for the oncoming train to arrive. If one is late, so is the other, and subsequent trains going in both directions may also be delayed.

Petty crime is a problem on Vietnamese

trains, especially if you travel in budget class, where your fellow passengers are likely to be desperately poor. While there don't seem to be organised pack-napping gangs as there are in India, the Vietnamese seem convinced that the young men and boys you see hanging out in the stations and on trains have only larceny on their minds. To protect your belongings, always keep your backpack or suitcase near you and lock or tie it to something, especially at night. If you must leave your pack for a moment, ask someone who looks responsible to keep an eye on it.

Thieves have become proficient at grabbing packs through the windows as trains pull out of stations. However, some trains are so slow that travellers have been known to jump off the train, run down the thief, recover the pack and hop back on board again!

Another hazard is that children frequently throw rocks at the train. Passengers have been severely injured this way, and many conductors will insist that you keep down the metal shield for just this reason. Unfortunately, these shields obstruct the view.

There is supposedly a 20-kg limit for luggage carried on Vietnamese trains. Enforcement isn't real strict, but if you have too much stuff you might have to send it in the freight car (hopefully on the same train) and pay a small extra charge. This is a hassle that you'll probably want to avoid. Bicycles can also be sent in the freight car. Just make sure that the train you are on *has* a freight car (most have) or your luggage will arrive later than you do.

Eating is no problem – there are vendors in every railway station who board the train and practically stuff food, drinks, cigarettes and lottery tickets into your pockets. However, the food that is supplied by the railway company (for free, as part of the cost of the ticket for some long journeys) could be better. It's not a bad idea to stock up on your favourite munchies before taking a long trip.

Schedules

Odd-numbered trains travel southward; even-numbered trains travel northward. The Reunification Express trains go between Ho Chi Minh City and Hanoi. Local rail services connect various cities along the coast. Small spur lines link Hanoi with Haiphong and points between the capital and the Chinese border.

One of the unfortunate things about the Reunification Express is that there is not yet a computerised booking system. This is no problem when you are purchasing tickets in Saigon or Hanoi, but a problem develops when you want to buy a ticket at some other point along the route. For example, many travellers want to board the Reunification Express in Nha Trang and take it to Hué, but the staff at Nha Trang railway station isn't always informed about empty seats and thus may not be able to sell you a ticket even when space is available. This is a problem that may be solved eventually.

At the time of this writing, there were two express trains daily departing Saigon and continuing all the way to Hanoi. The first departs Saigon Railway Station daily at 7.30 am. The second train departs Saigon on Monday, Wednesday and Saturday at 2.30 pm and on Tuesday, Thursday, Friday and Sunday at 3 pm.

In addition, there are local trains. One train departs Saigon daily at 4.50 pm and arrives in Nha Trang at 5.05 am. There is a local train to Hué departing Saigon every other day at 9.15 am. And there is a local train to Qui Nhon, departing Saigon every other day at 9.50 am.

The train schedule changes so frequently (about every six months) that there's little point in reproducing the whole thing here. The timetables for all trains are posted at major stations and you can copy these down. At one time, free photocopied timetables were also available at some stations but now seem to have vanished – perhaps the railway administration will get smart and start selling these.

It's important to realise that the train schedule is bare bones during Tet. For example, the Reunification Express is suspended for nine days starting four days before Tet and continuing four days after.

Various local trains run between cities along the coast. They are incredibly slow, partly because other trains are given priority in both equipment and switching and partly because most of them stop at every one-horse town on the way. Most offer only very basic hard-seat or half-seat cars and their condition is very poor.

The train was a zoo. The half-seat coach I was in had a centre aisle with benches on both sides arranged to face each other at a distance that allowed the knees of Vietnamese travellers to just miss each other. The other annoyance was that the constant traffic up and down the aisle required me to be continually moving my legs to unblock the path and allow the people to pass. Vendors of water and tea passed back and forth with ridiculous frequency. Constantly calling out their wares, they navigated the cluttered aisles in search of thirsty travellers whereby they would fill an aluminium Coke can that had had its top removed, leaving a jagged and rusted maw from which to drink. I preferred to purchase bottled water and carry it with me.

Both the train rides I took stopped about once an hour. During these stops the train cars would be besieged both from the exterior by vendors attempting to sell their goods to you through the open window and from the interior by the more persistent, who would add to the already crowded aisles (now filled with people getting on and off with their baggage). The variety of items to be purchased now ranged from whole cooked chickens to pieces of sugar cane to gnaw on.

The truly daring would climb onto the top of the train while it was stopped and then once we had started again and they believed it was safe, they would climb down and crawl through the open windows while the train was cruising along at its stately 40 to 50 km/h. They would then have someone above pass them their food and/or drink and we would now have more sellers to cope with. The unfortunate were the passengers whose window this new entrepreneur had decided to enter from. They would have to deal with a clambering soul who would come pouncing across the unsuspecting riders' laps. These travelling salespeople also had to deal with the train conductors, who carried electric shocking devices which they would use on someone that they caught sneaking on board. Often our aisle would fill with vendors who were being chased from one end to the other. When the conductor got too close, everyone would head for the windows paying little heed to the passengers they had to hastily crawl over in order to get to the windows and freedom.

On one winding bit of track, I leaned out the window and got a good look at the roof of the train. I saw about 30 people of all ages and genders milling about with their goods trying to find out from their comrades already in the train where the conductors were and which was the best window to climb back into.

David Fisher

Three rail lines link Hanoi with the other parts of northern Vietnam. One takes you east to the port city of Haiphong. A second heads north-east to the Chinese border at Lang Son and on to Beijing. A third goes north-west to the Chinese border at Lao Cai.

If you arrive early at a railway station in central Vietnam, you may be told that all tickets to Hanoi or Saigon are sold out. However, this may simply mean that there are no tickets *at the moment*, but more may become available later when Saigon and Hanoi phone through the details of unsold tickets. You do not have to pay a bribe to get these last-minute tickets – just hang out, be polite and persevere. Of course, not much can be done if all the seats are really sold out.

It's *very* important that you hang onto your ticket until you've exited the railway station at your final destination. Some travellers have discarded their tickets while leaving the train, only to find that the gatekeepers won't allow them to exit the station without a ticket. In this situation, you could be forced to purchase another ticket at the full price. The purpose of this system is to catch people who have sneaked aboard without paying.

Classes

There are six classes of train travel in Vietnam: half-seat, hard-seat, soft-seat, hard-berth, soft-berth and super-berth. Since it's all that the vast majority of Vietnamese can afford, half-seat and hard-seat are usually packed. Half-seat consists of a bench down the side of the train, which is anything but comfortable. Hard-seat is tolerable for day travel, but overnight it can be even less comfortable than the bus, where at least you are hemmed in and thus propped upright.

Hard-berth has three tiers of beds (six beds per compartment). Because the Vietnamese don't seem to like climbing up, the upper berth is cheapest, followed by the middle berth and finally the lower berth. The best bunk is the one in the middle because the bottom berth is invaded by seatless travellers during the day. There is no door to separate the compartment from the corridor.

Soft-seat carriages have vinyl-covered seats rather than the uncomfortable benches of hard-seat.

Soft-berth has two tiers (four beds per compartment) and all bunks are priced the same. These compartments have a door. Super-berth compartments have two beds in a room with a door, and on some trains you even get air-conditioning. At the present time, super-berth is available only on the fastest express trains.

Reservations

As with all forms of transport in Vietnam, the supply of train seats is insufficient to meet demand. Reservations for all trips – even short ones – should be made at least one day in advance. For sleeping berths, you may have to book passage three or more days before the date of travel. Bring your passport and visa when buying train tickets. Though such documents are rarely checked at bus stations, train personnel may ask to have a look at them.

In any given city, reservations can be made only for travel originating in that city. In Nha Trang, for instance, you can reserve a place to Danang but cannot book passage from Danang to Hué. For this reason – and because train stations are often far from the part of town with the hotels in it – it is a good idea to make reservations for onward travel as soon as you arrive in a city (provided the ticket office is open). Local information on rail services, train station hours, etc, is provided in the Getting There & Away listing under each city.

If you are unable to make reservations in advance, try showing up at the station half an hour before departure time. Station staff may make some sort of provision for you (after payment of an appropriate 'tip'), but be aware that because you are their guest, that provision may be the conductor's ordering some hapless Vietnamese to give up his or her seat.

If you are travelling with a bicycle (for which there is a small surcharge), it may be possible to get it out of checked baggage only at certain stations.

Costs

One disadvantage of rail travel is that, officially, foreigners and Overseas Vietnamese are supposed to pay a surcharge of around 400% over and above what Vietnamese pay. It works out to about US$100 for a Saigon-Hanoi ticket in a hard-sleeper compartment. This is compared with US$150 to fly the same route. Unlike with Vietnam Airlines, foreigners are expected to purchase rail tickets in dong rather than dollars.

Some foreigners have managed to pay local prices, but this is almost impossible to do unless you have an Asian face. Even with Asian features, you are supposed to show an ID when the ticket is purchased, though a Vietnamese could buy the ticket for you. The ticket clearly indicates whether you paid foreign or local prices, and the name of the purchaser is also written on the ticket. Most conductors will enforce the rules – if you have blond hair and a big nose, don't think that you're going to fool the conductors into believing you're Vietnamese, even if you do wear a conical hat.

One advantage the train has over flying is that tickets are priced by multiplying the length of the trip (in km) by the tariff for the class you are travelling in. In other words, you are not penalised for breaking your journey.

You might also combine train travel with cheaper modes of transport, taking the train only for the most scenic sections of your journey (say, between Danang and Hué), or only when the train schedule fits the times you wish to depart and arrive (you wouldn't want to arrive in Nam Dinh at 2 am no matter how cheap the ticket was).

The actual price you pay for a ticket depends on which train you take – the fastest trains are the most expensive. The first price table lists the cost for the Reunification Express trains taking 44 hours to make the

Reunification Express, Saigon-Hanoi 44 hours

Station	Distance from Saigon	Half Seat	Hard Seat	Soft Seat	High Berth	Mid Berth	Low Berth	Soft Berth
Muong Man	175 km	$3	$5	$6	$8	$9	$10	$10
Thap Cham	319 km	$5	$8	$10	$14	$16	$17	$18
Nha Trang	411 km	$6	$10	$13	$18	$20	$22	$23
Tuy Hoa	529 km	$7	$13	$16	$23	$26	$28	$29
Dieu Tri	631 km	$8	$15	$19	$27	$31	$34	$35
Quang Ngai	798 km	$10	$18	$24	$34	$38	$42	$44
Danang	935 km	$11	$21	$28	$40	$45	$50	$51
Hué	1038 km	$12	$24	$31	$45	$50	$55	$57
Dong Ha	1104 km	$13	$25	$33	$47	$53	$58	$61
Dong Hoi	1204 km	$14	$27	$36	$51	$57	$64	$66
Vinh	1407 km	$18	$35	$45	$65	$73	$81	$84
Thanh Hoa	1551 km	$19	$37	$48	$69	$77	$85	$88
Ninh Binh	1612 km	$19	$37	$49	$70	$79	$87	$90
Nam Dinh	1639 km	$20	$38	$50	$72	$80	$88	$92
Hanoi	1726 km	$20	$39	$51	$73	$82	$91	$94

Reunification Express, Saigon-Hanoi 36 Hours

Station	Distance from Saigon	Half Seat	Soft Seat	High Berth	Mid Berth	Low Berth	Soft Berth	Super Berth
Nha Trang	411 km	$9	$16	$22	$24	$26	$28	$31
Dieu Tri	631 km	$13	$24	$34	$37	$40	$43	$47
Danang	935 km	$18	$36	$50	$54	$59	$64	$69
Hué	1038 km	$20	$39	$55	$60	$65	$70	$77
Dong Hoi	1204 km	$23	$45	$64	$70	$76	$82	$89
Hanoi	1726 km	$33	$65	$91	$99	$108	$117	$127

Saigon-Hanoi run. The second table lists prices for the more expensive train, which takes 36 hours to do this route.

CAR

Renting a car or van with driver is a realistic option in Vietnam, even if you're a budget traveller. Divided among several people, the cost per day can be very reasonable.

In Vietnam they drive on the right-hand side of the road (usually). The police are known to be strict, though for a fee they may decide to forgive your transgressions.

Overall, the Vietnamese intercity road network of two-lane highways is fairly good, especially in the south (thanks to huge US war-time infrastructure investments). Though maintenance has been spotty and potholes are a problem in some places, highway travel is fast if you have a serviceable vehicle (a big *if*). Honking at all pedestrians and bicycles (to warn them of your approach) is considered a basic element of safe driving – larger trucks might as well have a permanent siren attached.

Black-market petrol *(xang)* is sold – along with oil *(dau)* – in soft drink bottles at little stalls along major roads and highways. In rural areas, you'll see the bottles stacked by the roadside next to a stall. In Saigon, it's not permitted to stack bottles of petrol by the roadside, so the vendor places a couple of bricks with a rolled-up newspaper stuck between in a vertical direction. In cities, this is the universal sign indicating petrol for sale. Be forewarned that black-market petrol is often mixed with kerosene (it's cheaper), which will likely cause you to have engine problems – use it in an emergency. If the vendor claims that bottled petrol costs the same as what you buy in a petrol station, that's a clear warning sign to stay away.

If travelling long distance by car, it's often necessary to find a hotel with a garage or fenced-in compound (many hotels are so equipped). There are also commercial non-hotel garages. Leaving an unattended car parked out on the street overnight is not wise.

The police hand out fines arbitrarily for all sorts of imagined offences. In some places, the police avoid making trouble when the vehicle carries foreigners (maybe to protect the country's image). In other spots, vehicles carrying foreigners are specifically targeted because the police hope to get more money. Most Vietnamese say that the police target vehicles which are new and expensive-looking on the theory that the drivers have more money. Aside from certain well-known trouble spots, some theorise that there are also specific times to avoid. One traveller writes:

The police are most likely to do their harassing (stopping cars to get a 'fine') between 7 am and 10 am. Danang seems to be the worst spot. One truck driver told us that the Saigon-Hanoi drive costs about US$50 in 'fines'.

Our own experience though is that you can get fined anytime. Between midnight and dawn, the army patrols major cities (including Saigon) and virtually all vehicles are stopped. These young soldiers tend to ask for money – if you want to argue with somebody toting an AK-47, more power to you.

Rental

Drive-them-yourself rental cars have yet to make their debut in Vietnam, but cars with drivers can be hired from a variety of sources. For details on exactly what is available, see each city's Getting There & Away and Getting Around sections.

Ho Chi Minh City has an especially wide selection of government bodies, state companies and private concerns that hire out vehicles. Vietnam Tourism will hire out new Japanese cars with drivers for US$0.35 per km (with a minimum per-day charge). The same service is offered by various competing agencies, including many provincial tourism authorities and newly formed private companies. Bargaining is entirely possible, and when you've completed negotiations a contract should be signed to prevent any later disputes.

Renting a van is another possibility. These can hold approximately eight to 12 passengers, so the cost per person works out to even less than a car. One advantage of vans is that they have high-clearance, a consideration on some of the dismal unsurfaced roads. With the exception of Russian-built or really old vehicles, most are equipped with air-conditioning. Since air-conditioned cars often cost more to rent, you might make your preferences known early when negotiating a price. Also, it's been our experience that not having an air-conditioner can be an advantage – Vietnamese drivers usually insist on keeping the air-conditioner at full-blast all day, even if it means wearing a winter coat in the tropical heat.

Many travellers have rented cars from private individuals – some have been satisfied and some have not. We've had no problems, but one person reports:

In Saigon there are many self-proclaimed guides with cars, offering very low prices. They have no insurance and are by law not permitted to transport tourists. As I heard from travellers, drivers were reckless, the vehicles were in lousy mechanical condition and there was often trouble with the police. I took such a private two-day tour from Hanoi to Halong Bay and I discourage travellers to do so. The driver was very inexperienced and the van was anything but safe. It's better to find companions and rent a car and driver from a reliable company.

New government regulations require that all cars carrying foreigners need a special permit (which simply means that the vehicle owner pays a special tax) and a licensed guide in the car at all times. While this might sound like a noble effort to protect foreigners, the result will certainly be an increase in prices. Bureaucracy is something you pay for.

Most drivers refuse to drive after dark in rural areas because the unlit highways often have huge potholes, occasional collapsed bridges and lots of bicycles and pedestrians who seem oblivious to the traffic.

Almost all cars are equipped with a cassette tape player. Bring some music tapes or buy them from the local markets, and hope your driver, guide and fellow passengers have the same taste in music as you do!

Buying a Car

Foreigners with resident certificates can purchase a car, but it would be almost madness to do so. Indeed, outside of Hanoi and Ho Chi Minh City, a foreigner driving a car will almost certainly be stopped by the police and the vehicle will be impounded.

Foreign companies can also purchase cars, though companies which do so also usually hire a Vietnamese driver rather than let their foreign employees drive themselves. Special licence plates are affixed to foreign-owned vehicles, and possibly this will be of some use in avoiding trouble with the police. On the other hand, the police may decide that a vehicle owned by a foreign company is a juicy target.

MOPED & MOTORCYCLE

Mopeds and motorcycles are ubiquitous in Vietnam and the number of these vehicles will continue to increase rapidly as the economy improves.

Travelling by motorbike can be good fun, but it can also be stressful – big trucks and buses come barrelling down the centre or wrong side of the highway as they please, lights flashing and air horns blaring. If you don't get creamed, you still have to breathe the obnoxious diesel fumes from these monsters. Obviously, the farther you get from civilisation, the easier to escape road hogs. However, the more rural the area, the worse the condition of the road. In the backwaters you can expect potholes the size of refrigerators.

Sunburn is another consideration – cover up exposed skin or wear sunblock lotion, because the cooling breeze prevents you from realising how badly burned you are getting until it's too late. Also consider the

opposite problem – occasional heavy rains. Especially during the monsoon season, rainsuits and ponchos should be carried. Fortunately, these are readily available at shops all over Vietnam.

Vietnam does not have an emergency rescue system or even a proper ambulance network – if something happens to you out on the road, you could be many hours from even rudimentary medical treatment.

It's wise to drive during daylight hours only. Many Vietnamese drivers do suicidal things like driving at night with the headlights turned off – they believe that this saves petrol (it doesn't).

The government has been talking about requiring the use of safety helmets. However, most Vietnamese disdain wearing them, in part because of the expense and also because of the tropical heat. You can purchase high-quality safety helmets in Saigon and Hanoi for US$50, or buy a low-quality 'eggshell' helmet for US$15. For the serious biker, bringing a helmet might be a good idea, but make sure it's something that you can tolerate wearing in hot weather. As a last resort, you might consider purchasing a slightly battered US Army helmet from the War Surplus Market – the bullet holes provide ventilation.

Road Rules

Basically, there aren't any. The biggest vehicle wins, by default. Be particularly careful about children in the road – Vietnamese parents make no effort to prevent their kids from playing hopscotch in the middle of a major highway. Many young boys seem to enjoy playing a game of 'chicken' – deliberately sticking their arms and legs in front of fast-approaching vehicles and withdrawing them at the last possible moment.

If you should be involved in an accident, be aware that calling the police is just about the worst thing you can do. The usual response of the police is to impound both vehicles regardless of who caused the accident, and then you must pay a substantial sum (around US$100 or more) to get the vehicle back. When Vietnamese have an accident, the usual response is for the two drivers to stand in the street and argue with each other for 30 minutes about whose fault it was. Whoever tires of the argument first hands over some money to pay for damages and it's all settled. As a foreigner, you're at a disadvantage in these negotiations. Perhaps it's best to feign some injury (to gain sympathy) but offer to pay for the other driver's minor damages. If none of this works and you are being asked to pay excessive damages, you could always say you want to call the police. As a foreigner, they might just believe you're crazy enough to do that and therefore the negotiations will likely be concluded quickly.

The legal definition of a moped is any motor-driven two-wheeled vehicle less than 100 cc, even if it doesn't have bicycle pedals. Motorcycles are two-wheeled vehicles with engines 100 cc and larger. In Vietnam, no driver's licence is needed to drive a moped, while to drive a motorcycle, you will need an international driver's licence endorsed for motorcycle operation. But expats remaining in the country over six months are expected to obtain a Vietnamese driver's licence. The Vietnamese licence will be valid only for the length of your visa! If you extend your visa, you need to extend your driver's licence too.

Technically, the maximum legal size for a motorcycle is 125 cc. There are indeed larger bikes around and you will no doubt see them, but to drive one the owner must join a motorcycle association and do voluntary public service work (riding in patriotic parades and sporting events, and so on). There is an awful lot of bureaucracy involved in owning such a bike, and riders can expect to be stopped by the police frequently to have their papers checked. Most people who own these road hogs are the sons of high-ranking officials – they apparently find loopholes in the regulations.

The major cities have parking lots *(giu xe)* for bicycles and motorbikes – usually just a roped-off section of sidewalk – which charge US$0.20 to guard your vehicle (bike theft is a major problem). When you pull up, a number will be chalked on the seat or stapled

to the handlebars and you'll be handed a reclaim chit. Without it, getting your wheels back may be a real hassle, especially if you come back after the workers have changed shifts. Outside of the designated parking lots, some travellers simply ask a stranger to watch their bikes – this may not always be such a good idea. One traveller reports:

> We asked some locals to watch our motorbike while we went to explore a beach in a nearby cove. When we returned, we found that our new 'friends' had removed some vital engine components and we had to buy these back from the very people who stole them.

Locals are required to have liability insurance on their motorbikes, but foreigners are not covered and there is currently no way to arrange this. If you want to insure yourself against injury, disfigurement or death, you'll need some sort of travel insurance with a foreign company (be sure that motorbike accidents are not excluded from your policy!). Travel insurance is something that must be arranged before you come to Vietnam. As for liability insurance, consider burning some incense at a local temple.

Rental

Renting a motorbike is now possible from a wide variety of sources – cafes, travel agencies, motorcycle shops, hotels, etc. If you don't want to drive yourself, many cyclo drivers are also willing to act as your personal motorbike chauffeur and guide for around US$5 per day. However, take care to find someone who you feel is competent and easy to get along with.

How much you pay for a motorbike depends on the engine size. Renting a 50-cc moped (the most popular model) is cheap at around US$5 to US$7 per day, usually with unlimited mileage. Large displacement bikes start from US$10 and there might be a distance charge in addition to the daily fee.

A minor complication is whether or not a deposit or some other security is required. Most motorbikes are not cheap, so leaving a deposit to cover its value would not be a trivial lump of cash. Some renters may prefer to hold your visa or passport as security until you return the bike. There have not been any huge problems with renters losing or refusing to return these items, though you are placing yourself in their hands. You should definitely sign some sort of agreement (preferably in English or another language you understand) clearly stating what you are renting, how much it costs, the extent of compensation you must pay if the bike is stolen, etc. People in the business of renting motorbikes are usually equipped with a standard rental agreement.

Most bikes have their rear-view mirrors removed or turned around so that they don't get broken in the handlebar-to-handlebar traffic. This might make sense in Saigon with its continuous close encounters, but you should have the mirrors properly installed if you're going out on the highway. It's rather important to know when a big truck is bearing down on you from behind.

Warning Beware of a motorcycle rental scam which some travellers have encountered in Ho Chi Minh City. What happens is that you rent a bike and the owner supplies you with an excellent lock and suggests you use it. What he doesn't tell you is that he has a key too, and somebody follows you and 'steals' the bike at the first opportunity. The thief, of course, is probably the owner's son. You then have to pay for a new bike or forfeit your passport, visa, deposit or whatever security you left. And the person who rented the bike to you still has it!

Buying a Bike
Except for bona-fide foreign residents, buying a motorcycle for touring Vietnam is illegal. However, there is an easy way around this rule and so far the authorities are turning a blind eye. The way it normally works is that you buy a bike but you register it in the name of a trusted Vietnamese friend. Some shops which sell motorcycles will let you keep the bike registered in the shop's name. This requires that you trust the shop owners, but in most cases this seems to work out OK. The big issue is what to do with the bike when

you are finished with it. If you return to the city where you originally purchased the bike, you can simply sell it back to the shop you bought it from (at a discount, of course). Another possible solution is to sell it to another foreigner travelling in the opposite direction – notice boards at the cafes in Saigon and Hanoi can be useful in this regard. If you're unlucky, you might have to simply scrap the bike. Given this possibility, it's best not to buy a very expensive motorbike in the first place.

Japanese-made motorbikes are the best available but by far the most expensive. Unless you can get an exceptionally good deal on a used Honda, the best alternative is to buy a Russian-made Minsk 125 cc, which sells brand-new for around US$550. Its quality is mediocre at best and it's a petrol pig, but it is a powerful bike and it's very easy to find spare parts and people who can do repairs (though repair shops frequently overcharge). The two-stroke engine burns oil like mad and the spark plugs frequently become oil-fouled, so always carry a spare spark plug and spark plug wrench.

There are some other bikes from Eastern Europe which are cheap but basically illegal to ride because the engine size is over 125 cc. One example is the Czech-made Jawa 350 cc, which can be bought second-hand for about US$200 to US$450. Another bike best avoided is the Russian-made Bocxog 175 cc, which can be bought used for US$150 to US$400.

BICYCLE
By far the best way to get around Vietnam's towns and cities is to do as the locals do: ride a bicycle. During rush hours, urban thoroughfares approach gridlock as rushing streams of cyclists force their way through intersections without the benefit of traffic lights. Riders are always crashing into each other and getting knocked down, but because bicycle traffic is so heavy, they are rarely going fast enough to be injured. Westerners on bicycles are often greeted enthusiastically by locals who may never have seen a foreigner pedalling around before.

Bicycles are utility vehicles in much of rural Vietnam. To see a bike carrying three pigs or 300 kg of vegetables is not unusual. One has to marvel at how they manage to load all these items on the bike and ride it without the whole thing tipping over.

Vietnam is also a good place for intercity cycling: much of the country is flat or only moderately hilly and the major roads are of a serviceable standard (especially those built by the Americans in the south, many of which have wide shoulders). Bicycles can be transported around the country on the top of buses or in train baggage compartments.

Groups of Western cyclists have begun touring Vietnam. The flat lands of the Mekong Delta region are one logical place for long-distance riding. The entire coastal route is also feasible, though some stretches of road are hilly and riddled with potholes.

Mountain bikes and 10-speed bikes can be bought at a very few speciality shops in Ho Chi Minh City, but you'll probably do better to bring your own if you plan to travel long distance by pedal power. Mountain bikes are definitely preferred – the occasional big pothole or unsealed road can be rough on a set of delicate rims. Basic cycling safety equipment is also not available in Vietnam, so such items as helmets, night lights, front and rear reflectors, leg reflectors and rear-view mirrors should be brought along. Another useful accessory to buy abroad is a pocket-size inner tube repair kit.

Hotels and some travel agencies are starting to get into the business of renting bicycles. The cost for this is around US$1 per day or US$0.20 per hour.

There are innumerable roadside bicycle repair stands in every city and town in Vietnam. Usually, they consist of no more than a pump, an upturned military helmet and a metal ammunition box filled with oily bolts and a few wrenches. In the south, the men who run these repair stands are mostly South Vietnamese army veterans who are denied other opportunities to make a living.

Pumping up a tyre costs US$0.05. Fixing a punctured inner tube should cost about US$0.50 depending on the size of the patch,

the time of day and the presence of competition. The mechanics employ a brilliant system that allows them to patch inner tubes without removing the wheel from the frame or even taking the tyre off the rim. The tyre and inner tube are taken half off the rim and the exposed inner tube is partially pumped up and wetted. As the air drains out of the hole, bubbles which are easily visible and audible are formed in the water. After the tyre is dried and sanded, rubber cement is used to glue on a patch.

Many travellers buy a cheap bicycle, use it during their visit and at the end either sell it or give it to a Vietnamese friend. Locally produced bicycles are available starting at about US$25 but are of truly inferior quality. A decent one-speed Chinese-made bicycle costs about US$75. A locally assembled three-speed bike made with imported (Chinese, Japanese and Taiwanese) parts costs about US$100. Older bikes used French parts but these are no longer being sold.

All Vietnamese-made bicycles have the same mixte frame, but the various models are equipped with different accessories. The best of the lot is the 'Corporate' (is that an appropriate name for a good socialist bicycle?), which goes for US$35. The 'Saigon' costs US$25. The bottom-of-the-line 'Huu Nghi' will set you back US$20.

The Vietnamese-made frame is serviceable but the locally produced moving parts (brakes, crank shaft, pedals and gears) should be avoided unless you enjoy frequent visits to bicycle repair shops.

The simplest place to buy a domestic bicycle is at government stores, but watch out for misaligned wheels, improperly assembled brakes, crooked bolts and worn threading. In general, private shops provide superior assembly work.

Although you will often see two Vietnamese riding on a single bike, this is generally *not* a good idea, as one traveller discovered:

I rented a bike in Saigon and had the splendid idea to carry my friend on the rear bike rack in order to return to the hotel. However, after only five metres, the rear wheel snapped! Back in the bicycle shop (by cyclo),

One for the Road

Cycling is often the best way to explore and experience a place, removing the barriers between you and native people common with other means of transportation. And nowhere is this more true than in Vietnam, a place dominated by two-wheel vehicles.

First and foremost, don't overpack! Besides quality bicycle parts and certain other essentials, almost anything forgotten can be bought cheaply in Saigon or Hanoi. But bring a tough bicycle – a mountain bike with tyres for the pavement and dirt is the best all-around choice. Pack spare parts such as spokes, tubes, pump, cables and a spare water bottle. Bring along some tools: spoke wrench and chain tool, or one of the new multi-function tools and a small bottle of chain lube. A bell is required equipment, the louder the better. Many cyclists find a rear-view mirror attached to a helmet or glasses useful. Padded gloves ease the shock from rough roads. For gifts, children like pens, and sharing pictures from home is always great at breaking the ice. Don't forget to deflate your tyres, as your bike will likely fly into Vietnam in an unpressurised cabin, which can lead to exploded tubes.

Don't feel driven to cycle the entire length of Vietnam. Some areas are definitely worth skipping if only to conserve energy for the better routes in the mountains. The Mekong has an enormous amount of traffic and narrow roads. The Central Highlands are sparsely trafficked with the bonus of cooler weather and excellent scenery. Skipping the ride from Hué to Hanoi may conserve your good impression of Vietnam. The area has notoriously bad roads and some areas curiously lacking the usual Vietnamese graciousness – thrown rocks are common.

Highway 1 can be unnerving, but rideable. Just remember that cyclists are at the bottom of the food chain. There are no traffic lines on the road and there are no traffic laws. You are supposed to get out of the way and drivers will expect you to in confrontations. Luckily the Vietnamese drivers honk constantly. Always ride far to the right and be prepared to bail out to the side of the road. Likewise, you should use your bell frequently. People do not look when crossing or turning unless they hear an engine or horn. An easy way to get killed cycling in Vietnam (or anywhere) is to wear earphones or ride at night. Rocks, holes, drying rice and coffee, darting children, chickens, dogs, water buffaloes all demand your undivided attention. Tired? Wave a truck down. Anyone with room will stop. Though money may not be demanded, some tip will be expected – a couple of dollars can take you a long way.

Bicycle theft is unlikely, but curious tinkering is not – gears are changed and cyclometers, water bottles and pouches can disappear. Keeping an eye on your things when suddenly surrounded by a hundred children can be difficult – keep important stuff tucked away. Solo travellers are always at a disadvantage, and this is especially true for women. Midday, amused harassment by beer-guzzling karaoke lounge lizards is not uncommon.

Unlike Bangkok, Saigon and Hanoi are still rideable cities, where bicycle and scooter traffic still dominate the wide, tree-lined boulevards. Although swarms of two-wheeled traffic crossing each other like schools of fish can be intimidating at first, it can soon become exhilarating. Sunday night cruising in Saigon is not to be missed. After nightfall, the city centre becomes packed with two-wheeling Vietnamese all dressed up going *di troi* – 'cruising'.

Patrick Morris, VeloAsia

I pretended an accident had occurred, so they charged me only $US3 extra. Conclusion: these cheap Chinese bikes can carry two local people, but apparently not two Westerners.

Thilo Shönfeld

HITCHING

Westerners have reported great success at hitching in Vietnam. In fact, the whole system of passenger transport in Vietnam is based on people standing along the highways and flagging down buses or trucks. To get a bus, truck or other vehicle to stop, stretch out your arm and gesture towards the ground with your whole hand. Drivers will expect to be paid for picking you up. Some Western travellers have had their offers to pay refused, but don't count on this. As long as you look like a foreigner (to many Vietnamese, foreigner = money) you rarely wait for more than a few passenger vehicles to pass before one stops.

One of the advantages of going from Hanoi to Saigon is that most people are doing just the opposite. Many folks pay for car rides heading north, so it's relatively easy to catch an empty car going south. I'd got to larger hotels, met the driver the night before and made a private deal (not with the driver's boss). I also tried standing by the roadside and flagging cars down. Some drivers knew what was going on and knew exactly how much to charge. But on certain stretches of highway, traffic of passenger vehicles was light indeed. The best advice in such cases is to start out early.

Ivan Kasimoff

The engines of most older trucks are equipped with an ingenious gravity-powered heat-dissipation system. When the vehicle's original radiator rusted out and became worthless, a drum was attached to the roof of the cab and connected to the engine by a hose routed via the driver's window, where a stop-cock was installed to allow him to control the flow. Cold water in the rooftop drum slowly drains into the engine; hot water squirts out the side of the truck from a little nozzle. When the drum is empty, the truck stops at any of the numerous water-filling stations that line major highways.

Licence Plates

You can learn a great deal about a vehicle by examining its licence plate. Whether you are in a confusing bus station looking for the right bus or hitchhiking and wish to avoid accidentally flagging down an army truck, the following information should prove useful.

First, there are the several types of licence plates. Vehicles with white numbers on a green field are owned by the government. Privately owned vehicles have black numbers on white. Diplomatic cars have the letters NG in red over green numbers on a white field. Other cars owned by foreigners begin with the letters NN and are green-on-white. Military plates have white numerals on red.

The first two numerals on a number plate are the two-digit code assigned to the vehicle's province of origin. Because the vast majority of vehicles in the country are controlled at the provincial level and used to link a given province with other parts of the country, there is usually a 50-50 chance that the vehicle is headed towards its home territory.

The two-digit number codes for most provinces (listed more or less north to south) are as follows:

13	Ha Bac
15	Greater Haiphong
17	Thai Binh
18	Nam Ha & Ninh Binh
20	Bac Thai
21	Lao Cai & Yen Bai
28	Hoa Binh
29	Greater Hanoi
36	Thanh Hoa
37	Nghe An
38	Ha Tinh
39/40	Quang Binh, Quang Tri & Thua Thien-Hué
43	Quang Nam-Danang
44	Quang Ngai & Binh Dinh
45	Phu Yen & Khanh Hoa
46	Kon Tum
47	Dac Lac
48	Binh Thuan
49	Lam Dong
50	Ho Chi Minh City (government)
51/55	Ho Chi Minh City (private)
60	Dong Nai
61	Song Be
62	Long An
63	Tien Giang
64	Vinh Long
65	Cantho
66	Dong Thap
67	An Giang
69	Minh Hai
70	Tay Ninh
71	Ben Tre
72	Ba Ria-Vung Tau

WALKING

You aren't likely to do much long-distance walking in the steamy tropical lowlands, which are dominated by dense vegetation, but some spots in the central highlands and the far north offer hiking possibilities. The biggest hazard is likely to be the police – check to make sure that you aren't entering a prohibited area.

One thing to be aware of in the south is that in equatorial regions, there is very little twilight – night comes on suddenly without warning. Therefore, you can't readily judge how many hours of daylight remain unless you have a watch. Pay attention to how long you'll need to get back to civilisation – otherwise, be prepared for an impromptu camping trip.

If you'd rather run, not walk, it's interesting to note that long-distance running has made its debut in Vietnam. At the end of the '80s, someone actually ran from Hanoi to Danang. No wonder the Vietnamese think that foreigners are mad.

BOAT

Vietnam has an enormous number of rivers that are at least partly navigable, the most important of which are the multi-branched Mekong River in the south and the Red River and its tributaries in the north. Both deltas are crisscrossed with waterways which can be crossed by boat. Vessels of all sorts can be hired in most riverine and seaside towns.

Travelling on a local bus

Some of the smaller rivercraft can accommodate only three or four people. Whenever you take such a small boat, it's wise to keep your camera in a plastic bag when not actually in use so as to protect it from being splashed by water.

LOCAL TRANSPORT
Bus

Vietnam has some of the worst local inner-city bus transport in Asia. There is a bare-bones bus system in Hanoi and Ho Chi Minh City, but in general, this is not a practical way to get around. Fortunately, there are many other options.

Taxi

Western-style taxis with meters have recently made their appearance in Ho Chi Minh City and Hanoi.

For sightseeing trips just around the Saigon or Hanoi areas, a car with driver can also be rented by the day or by the hour (renting by the day is cheaper). For definition purposes, a 'day' is eight hours or less with a total distance travelled of less than 100 km. Based on this formula, a car costs US$25 per day (or US$4 per hour) for a Russian-built vehicle; US$35 per day (US$5 per hour) for a small Japanese car; US$40 per day (US$6 per hour) for a larger late-model Japanese car; US$64 per day (US$8 per hour) for a limousine.

For details on exactly what is available in each city, see the Getting There & Away and Getting Around sections of each chapter. Ho Chi Minh City is particularly rich in options.

Cyclo

The cyclo, or pedicab (xich lo), short for the French cyclo-pousse, is the best invention since sliced bread. Cyclos offer an easy, cheap and aesthetic way to get around Vietnam's confusing, sprawling cities. Riding in one of these clever contraptions will also give you the moral superiority that comes with knowing you are being kind to the environment – certainly kinder than all those drivers on whining, smoke-spewing motorbikes.

Groups of cyclo drivers always hang out near major hotels and markets, and quite a number of them speak at least broken English (in the south, many of the cyclo drivers are former ARVN soldiers). The ones who speak English charge a little more than the ones who don't, but avoiding the language problem may be worth the minor added expense (we're talking peanuts). To make sure the driver understands where you want to go, it's useful to bring a city map with you, though some drivers cannot read maps either.

If you've wondered about the occasional cyclo driver who hangs out seeming to do nothing all day and showing little interest in finding customers, the answer is that you have probably observed an undercover policeman. If you stay in Vietnam long enough, you may even witness somebody being arrested by a 'cyclo driver'.

All cyclo drivers are male, though they vary in age from around 15 to perhaps 60 years old. Many of the younger ones are transients from the countryside, coming to Saigon and Hanoi to seek their fortune – with no place to live, they may even sleep in their cyclo. Most cyclo drivers rent their vehicles for US$1 per day. The more affluent cyclo drivers buy their own vehicle for US$200, but to do so requires that the owner have a residence permit for the place where the cyclo is to be driven – the transients from the countryside are thus excluded from vehicle ownership. Operating a cyclo is often a family business – a father-son team takes turns so the vehicle gets used 18 hours a day. But driving a cyclo is no way to get rich – average price charged is around US$0.20 per km. Bargaining is necessary; the drivers know that US$1 or its dong equivalent is nothing to most Westerners. If the cyclo drivers waiting outside the hotel want too much, flag down someone else less used to spendthrift tourists. Settle on a fare *before* going anywhere or you're likely to be asked for some outrageous quantity of dong at the trip's end.

Since 1995, the government has been requiring cyclo drivers to obtain a licence.

The requirements for this include passing an exam on traffic safety laws.

Have your money counted out and ready before getting on a cyclo. It also pays to have the exact money – drivers will sometimes claim they cannot make change for a 5000d note.

Cyclos are cheaper by time than by distance. A typical price is US$1 per hour. If this works out well, don't be surprised if the driver comes around your hotel the next morning to see if you want to hire him again.

Xe Lam

Xe Lams are tiny three-wheeled trucks used for short-haul passenger and freight transport (similar to the Indonesian *bajaj*). They tend to have whining two-stroke 'lawn mower' engines with no mufflers and emit copious quantities of blue exhaust smoke, but they get the job done.

Honda Om

The *Honda om* is an ordinary motorbike on which you ride seated behind the driver. Getting around this way with luggage is quite a challenge. There is no set procedure for finding a driver willing to transport you somewhere. You can either try to flag someone down (most drivers can always use some extra cash) or ask a Vietnamese to find a Honda om for you. The fare is a fraction more than a cyclo for short trips and about the same as a cyclo for longer distances.

Mekong Delta Special

Two forms of transport used mostly in the Mekong Delta are the *xe dap loi*, a wagon pulled by a bicycle, and the *xe Honda loi*, a wagon pulled by a motorbike.

Walking

If you don't want to wind up like a bug on a windshield, you need to pay attention to a few pedestrian survival rules, especially in motorbike-crazed Saigon. Foreigners frequently make the mistake of thinking that the best way to cross a busy Vietnamese street is to run quickly across it. Sometimes this works and sometimes it gets you creamed.

Most Saigonese cross the street slowly – very slowly – giving the motorbike drivers sufficient time to judge their position so they can pass to either side of you. They will *not* stop or even slow down, but they *will* try to avoid hitting you. Just don't make any sudden moves. Good luck.

TOURS

If you decide to rent a car with driver and guide, you'll have the opportunity to design your own itinerary for what amounts to a private tour for you and your companions. Seeing the country this way is almost like individual travel except that it's more luxurious and also offers you the opportunity to stop anywhere along the route for that once-in-a-lifetime photo.

The cost varies considerably. On the high end are tours booked through government travel agencies like Saigon Tourist and Vietnam Tourism. A tour booked with these agencies is about US$50 to US$60 a day for one person (and less each for two or more people because transport and lodging costs can be shared). Students receive a 15% discount, which they are more likely to get if they have an official-looking letter from their university registrar to show.

This price includes accommodation at a tourist-class hotel (which costs at least US$25 per night for a single anyway), a guide who will accompany you everywhere, a local guide in each province you visit, a driver and a car. Insist that your guides are fluent in a language you know well – this is often a serious problem with government guides. The cost of the car is computed on a per-km basis, but it varies depending on what type of vehicle you choose. A typical mid-sized Japanese car will cost US$0.35 per km, but they will often start the bidding by asking twice that much. Vans cost even more but can hold more people.

When you settle on your itinerary, make sure to get a written copy from the travel agency. If you later find that your guide feels like deviating from what you paid for, that piece of paper is your most effective leverage. If your guide asks for the itinerary, keep

the original and give him or her a photocopy, as there have been reports of guides taking tourists' itineraries and then running the tour their way. One traveller says:

Our guide was incredibly stubborn and arrogant, always thinking that he knew more than us. Whenever we tried to tell him something, he suddenly developed a hearing problem. But whenever he wasn't sure about something (like the location of a hotel, the name of a temple, etc), he asked to borrow our Lonely Planet book!

A tour booked with Vietnam Tourism, Saigon Tourist or any travel agency will likely be more expensive if you book it outside of Vietnam. However, large groups booking far in advance usually do get a discount.

Do-It-Yourself Tours

It's entirely possible to round up a small group of budget travellers, hire a guide and private car and arrange your own tour for much less than a travel agency would charge you.

Unfortunately, there is a strong possibility that privately arranged tours will soon no longer be allowed. Vietnam Tourism, Saigon Tourist and other government-owned companies have watched in dismay as foreign tourists have defected to less expensive private travel agencies. In late-1994, the government announced that it would 'take control' of foreign tourism.

Just what this means is unclear, but it's beginning to sound as if the government will nationalise the tourist industry. New regulations require that travel agencies, drivers and guides obtain special licences to work with foreign tourists. Obtaining such licences is proving difficult, except of course for government agencies, which can exempt themselves from the regulations. Fees of US$25,000 and up are being demanded for tourist licences, but even then, a private company must have a cooperative agreement with a government-owned travel agency in order to get a licence.

How this will affect individual travellers remains to be seen, but private companies we talked to expressed concern that they would either be driven out of business, or forced to raise prices drastically in order to pay off a state-owned company for the use of their licences. Looking at all this, you have to wonder if Vietnam isn't simply returning to where it was in 1989 when the state had a monopoly over tourism.

Our guess is that the state will attempt to reassert control, will make a complete mess of it and then backpedal. However it finally turns out, we are willing to predict that any attempt by the state to bureaucratise the tourist business will cause prices to rise.

Guides A good guide can be your translator and travelling companion and can save you as much money as he or she is costing you (by helping you pay local prices and by keeping you out of trouble with the police). A bad guide can ruin your trip. Interview your guide thoroughly before starting out – make sure that this is someone you can travel with. Agree on the price before beginning the journey; for a private guide, US$5 per day is a typical rate (this might increase in future) and it's proper to throw in a bonus at the end of your trip if your guide proved particularly helpful and saved you money.

A guide hired from a government-owned travel agency will cost you US$15 per day, of which perhaps only US$2 actually goes into the guide's pocket. Another problem with government guides is that they must be graduates from the government-owned Tourism School – we've found that many such guides are the spoiled-brat children of high-ranking officials who completely lack the concept of providing good service. Many of the best guides are former South Vietnamese soldiers, but of course they cannot gain admission to the government's Tourism School.

With private guides, you are also responsible for their travel expenses – with a guide hired from the government, you need to ask. If you can gather up a small group of travellers, the cost of hiring a guide can be shared among all of you. If you are travelling solo, your guide may be able to drive you around on a motorbike but you should pay for the petrol and parking fees. If the police stop you, do *not* say that this person is your guide since it is technically illegal for an unlicensed person to work as a guide – this person is 'just a friend'. If your guide gets fined, you of course should reimburse him or her – the cost of the 'fine' can usually be bargained down to US$5.

For the writing of this third edition, we found an able guide at the Kim Café in Saigon. The best time to look for guides seems to be in the morning – visit the cafes around 8 or 9 am. Otherwise, try the evenings – most of the best guides will be working during daytime hours.

For trips in and around big cities like Saigon and Hanoi, you will often find women working as guides. However, very few women are employed as guides on long-distance trips.

Ho Chi Minh City

When you arrive in Ho Chi Minh City, you'll see the hustle and bustle everywhere, and there is something invigorating about it all. Images of the exotic and mundane are everywhere. There are the street markets, where bargains are struck and deals are done. The sidewalk cafes, where stereo speakers fill the surrounding streets with a melodious thumping beat. The sleek new pubs, where tourists chat over beer, pretzels, coffee and croissants. A young female office worker manoeuvres her Honda through rush-hour traffic, long hair flowing, high heels working the brake pedal. The sweating Chinese businessman chats on his cellular phone, cursing his necktie in the tropical heat. A desperate beggar suddenly grabs your arm, rudely reminding you that this is still a Third World city despite the tinsel and trimmings.

The traffic roars. The jackhammers of progress pound the past into pulp to make way for the new. The city churns, ferments, bubbles and fumes. Yet within the teeming metropolis are the timeless traditions and beauty of an ancient culture. There are pagodas where monks pray and incense burns. Artists create their masterpieces on canvas or in carved wood. Puppeteers entertain children in the parks. In the back alleys where tourists seldom venture, acupuncturists poke needles into patients and students learn to play the violin. A seamstress carefully creates an *ao dai*, the graceful Vietnamese costume that could make the fashion designers of Paris envious.

Actually, Ho Chi Minh City is not so much a city as a large municipality covering an area of 2029 sq km stretching from the South China Sea almost to the Cambodian border. Most of this vast territory is overwhelmingly rural, dotted with villages and groups of houses set amid rice paddies. Rural regions make up about 90% of the land area of Ho Chi Minh City and hold around 25% of the municipality's population. The other 75% of the population is crammed into the remaining 10% that constitutes the urban centre.

The downtown section of Ho Chi Minh City, now officially called District 1, is still known as Saigon. In the south, most people use the terms 'Saigon' and 'Ho Chi Minh City' interchangeably. In the north, people toe the official line and almost everyone will 'correct' you if you say 'Saigon'. Since most government officials are from the north, you'd be wise to say 'Ho Chi Minh City' whenever dealing with them.

To the west of downtown is District 5, the huge Chinese neighbourhood called Cholon, which some people will tell you means 'Chinatown'. In fact, Cholon means 'Big Market', a good indication of the importance the Chinese have traditionally played in Vietnam's economy. Curiously, its Chinese name (Di An) means 'Embankment'. Whatever it's called, Cholon is decidedly less Chinese than it used to be, largely thanks to the anti-capitalist anti-Chinese campaign of 1978-79, which caused many ethnic Chinese to flee the country, taking with them their money and entrepreneurial skills. With Vietnam's recent opening to the outside world, many of these refugees are returning (with foreign passports) to explore investment possibilities, and Cholon's hotels are once again packed with Chinese-speaking business people.

Officially, Ho Chi Minh City claims a population of four million. In reality, perhaps six to seven million is the true figure. The wide discrepancy is explained by the fact that the government census takers only count those who have official residence permits, but probably one-third of the population lives here 'illegally'. Many of the illegal residents actually lived in Saigon prior to 1975 but their residence permits were transferred to rural re-education camps after liberation. Not surprisingly, these people (and now their children and grandchildren) have simply sneaked back into the city, though without a residence permit they cannot own property or a business. Furthermore, they are joined by an increasing number of rural peasants who come to Ho Chi Minh City to seek their fortune – many do not find the proverbial 'pot of gold at the end of the rainbow' and wind up sleeping on the pavement.

Still, Ho Chi Minh City accommodates them all. This is the industrial and commercial heart of Vietnam, accounting for 30% of the country's manufacturing output and 25% of its retail trade. It is to Ho Chi Minh City that the vast majority of foreign business people come to invest and trade. It is to Ho Chi Minh City that ambitious young people and bureaucrats – from the north and south – gravitate to make a go of it.

Explosive growth is making its mark, in new high-rise buildings, joint-venture hotels and colourful shops. The down side is the sharp increase in traffic, pollution and other urban ills. Yet the past shines through. Saigon's neoclassical and international-style buildings (and nearby sidewalk kiosks selling French rolls and croissants) give certain neighbourhoods a vaguely French atmosphere.

The Americans left their mark on the city too, at least in the form of some heavily fortified apartment blocks and government buildings. The former US embassy (soon to become the new US consulate) is a classic example of tropical post-modern mortar-proof architecture. The occasional balcony protected with iron bars or lined with barbed wire and broken glass make you wonder if the war is still on. Of course, there is a war going on, a war against crime. With so much poverty surrounding so much plenty, it's not hard to understand why.

While their rural compatriots are working from dawn to dusk in the country's rice paddies, Ho Chi Minh City's residents are working just as hard at the pursuits of urban people: selling vegetables, buying necessities, cutting business deals, commuting. The city hums and buzzes with commerce. All around you is living evidence of the tenacious will of human beings to survive and improve their lot. There is something reassuring about it, and perhaps something frightening too. It is here that the economic changes sweeping Vietnam – and their negative social implications – are most evident.

History

Saigon was captured by the French in 1859, becoming the capital of the French colony of Cochinchina a few years later. In 1950, Norman Lewis described Saigon as follows: 'its inspiration has been purely commercial and it is therefore without folly, fervour or much ostentation...a pleasant, colourless and characterless French provincial city'. The city served as the capital of the Republic of Vietnam (South Vietnam) from 1956 until 1975, when it fell to advancing North Vietnamese forces.

Cholon rose to prominence after Chinese merchants began settling there in 1778. Though Cholon still constitutes the largest ethnic-Chinese community in Vietnam, hundreds of thousands of Cholonese have fled the country since reunification because of anti-Chinese persecution by the government, most notably in the late '70s.

Orientation

Ho Chi Minh City is divided into 12 urban districts (quan, derived from French quartier) and six rural districts (huyen). The urban districts are numbered. District 1 corresponds to Saigon proper and District 5 is Cholon.

The centre of Saigon is the area around Nguyen Hue and Le Loi Blvds. The Rex Hotel (Ben Thanh Hotel), which is at the intersection of these two streets, is a convenient landmark. Nearby, at the intersection of Le Loi Blvd and Dong Khoi St, is the Municipal Theatre. Ben Thanh Market, which fronts a traffic roundabout at the southern end of Le Loi Blvd, is also a handy landmark. Dong Khoi St (known as Tu Do St before 1975 and as Rue Catinat under the French) stretches 1.1 km from the waterfront to Notre Dame Cathedral. On maps lacking a scale, you can use the known length of Dong Khoi St to estimate distances else-

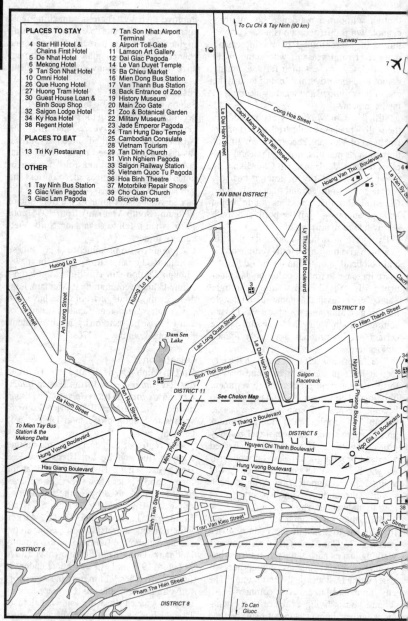

PLACES TO STAY

4 Star Hill Hotel & Chains First Hotel
5 De Nhat Hotel
6 Mekong Hotel
9 Tan Son Nhat Hotel
10 Omni Hotel
26 Que Huong Hotel
27 Huong Tram Hotel
30 Guest House Loan & Binh Soup Shop
32 Saigon Lodge Hotel
34 Ky Hoa Hotel
38 Regent Hotel

PLACES TO EAT

13 Tri Ky Restaurant

OTHER

1 Tay Ninh Bus Station
2 Giac Vien Pagoda
3 Giac Lam Pagoda
7 Tan Son Nhat Airport Terminal
8 Airport Toll-Gate
11 Lamson Art Gallery
12 Dai Giac Pagoda
14 Le Van Duyet Temple
15 Ba Chieu Market
16 Mien Dong Bus Station
17 Van Thanh Bus Station
18 Back Entrance of Zoo
19 History Museum
20 Main Zoo Gate
21 Zoo & Botanical Garden
22 Military Museum
23 Jade Emperor Pagoda
24 Tran Hung Dao Temple
25 Cambodian Consulate
28 Vietnam Tourism
29 Tan Dinh Church
31 Vinh Nghiem Pagoda
33 Saigon Railway Station
35 Vietnam Quoc Tu Pagoda
36 Hoa Binh Theatre
37 Motorbike Repair Shops
39 Cho Quan Church
40 Bicycle Shops

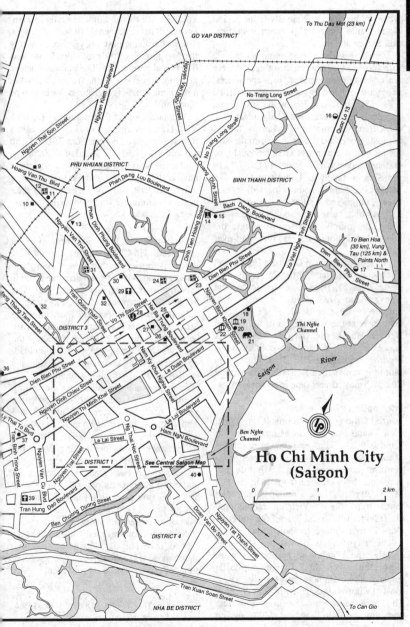

To Thu Dau Mot (23 km)

GO VAP DISTRICT

No Trang Long Street

16

Quoc Lo 13

PHU NHUAN DISTRICT

Nguyen Thai Son Street

Nguyen Kiem Boulevard

Nguyen Van Troi Street

Le Quang Dinh Street

No Trang Long Street

Hoang Van Thu Blvd

9

12   11

10

13

Phan Dang Luu Boulevard

BINH THANH DISTRICT

Phan Dinh Phung Boulevard

Bach Dang Boulevard

Dinh Tien Hoang Street

14   15

31

Tran Quoc Thao Street

30

29

32

24

23

Dien Bien Phu Street

Nguyen Binh Khiem Street

Xo Viet Nghe Tinh Street

Dien Bien Phu Street

To Bien Hoa (30 km), Vung Tau (125 km) & Points North

17

25

Vo Thi Sau Street

Hai Ba Trung Boulevard

27

26

28

Nam Ky Khoi Nghia Street

18

19

22   20

21

Thi Nghe Channel

DISTRICT 3

Mang Thang Tam Street

32

36

Dien Bien Phu Street

Le Duan Boulevard

Saigon

River

Nguyen Dinh Chieu Street

Nguyen Thi Minh Khai Street

Le Loi Boulevard

Ly Thai To Blvd

37

Tran Binh Trong Street

Nguyen Van Cu Blvd

Nguyen Trai Street

Ng Thai Hoc Street

Le Lai Street

Ham Nghi Boulevard

Ben Nghe Channel

DISTRICT 1

See Central Saigon Map

40

Ho Chi Minh City (Saigon)

0   1   2 km

39

Tran Hung Dao Boulevard

Ben Chuong Duong Street

Doan Van Bo Street

Nguyen Tat Thanh Street

DISTRICT 4

Tran Xuan Soan Street

NHA BE DISTRICT

To Can Gio

where in the city. Le Duan Blvd runs behind Notre Dame Cathedral between Reunification Palace and the Zoo.

Most streets have even numbers on one side and odd numbers on the other, but there are confusing exceptions. In some places, consecutive buildings are numbered 15A, 15B, 15C and so forth, while elsewhere, consecutive addresses read 15D, 17D, 19D, etc. Often, two numbering systems – the old confusing one and the new even-more-confusing one – are in use simultaneously, so that an address may read '1743/697'. In some cases (such as Lac Long Quan St, where Giac Lam Pagoda is located) several streets, numbered separately, have been run together under one name so that as you walk along, the numbers go from one into the hundreds (or thousands) and then start over again.

For fans of Graham Greene's 1954 novel *The Quiet American*, Rue Catinat is now Dong Khoi St; Blvd Charner has become Nguyen Hue Blvd; Blvd Bonnard is now known as Le Loi Blvd; Place François Garnier is at the intersection of Le Loi and Nguyen Hue Blvds; Blvd de la Somme is now Ham Nghi Blvd; Avenue Galliéni has become Tran Hung Dao Blvd; Quai de la Marne is now called Ben Van Don St; and Rue d'Ormay has become Mac Thi Buoi St.

Information

Tourist Offices Saigon Tourist (Cong Ty Du Lich Thanh Pho Ho Chi Minh) is Ho Chi Minh City's official government-run travel agency. Saigon Tourist owns or is a joint-venture partner in about 70 hotels and numerous high-class restaurants in Ho Chi Minh City, plus a car-rental agency and tourist traps like the Vietnam International Golf Club, the Chu Chi Tunnel site and Binh Quoi Tourist Village, to name a few.

The way Saigon Tourist got so big is simple: the hotels and restaurants were 'liberated' from their former capitalist (mostly ethnic-Chinese) owners after 1975, most of whom subsequently fled the country. The upper-level management of this state company are entirely former Viet Cong (no

kidding) and their attitude towards foreigners is still decidedly cool. To be fair, Saigon Tourist has in the past few years been wisely investing much of the profits back into new hotels and restaurants. The company keeps growing bigger – if Vietnam ever establishes a stock market, Saigon Tourist shares will be blue chip.

Vietnam Tourism (Tong Cong Ty Du Lich Viet Nam) is the national government's tourist agency and is open from 7.30 to 11.30 am and 1 to 4.30 pm Monday to Saturday. The senior staff of Vietnam Tourism seem to have a slightly better attitude than those at Saigon Tourist, but both agencies do their best to overcharge for their mediocre service.

Travel Agencies There are plenty of travel agencies in Ho Chi Minh City, mostly joint ventures between the government and private companies. These places can provide cars, book air tickets and extend your visa. Some of these places charge the same as Saigon Tourist and Vietnam Tourism, while others are much cheaper. Competition between the private agencies is keen – the price war has turned into a price bloodbath and you can often undercut Saigon Tourist's tariffs by 50% if you shop around.

From personal experience, we are willing to endorse Kim Café, Getra Tour Company, Thanh Thanh Travel Agency (Café 333) and Ann's Tourist. However, no matter what recommendations you get, chat with your fellow travellers before putting down the cash – management can change and good places can go bad. One place which we praised in the last edition of this book suddenly became exceedingly greedy and we can no longer recommend it. Such are the risks of giving endorsements.

A lineup of some agencies in Ho Chi Minh City follows. This list is by no means complete nor do we claim that all these agencies are good, so use it as a starting point:

Ann's Tourist
  58 Ton That Tung St, District 1 (☎ 332564, 334356; fax 323866)

Art Tourist
   63 Ly Tu Trong St, District 1 (☎ 230234; fax 293289)
Atlas Travel & Tours
   41 Nam Ky Khoi Nghia St, District 1 (☎ 210300, 224122; fax 298604)
Ben Thanh Tourist
   121 Nguyen Hue Blvd, District 1 (☎ 298597; fax 296269)
Cantho Tourist
   42 Cao Thant St, District 3 (☎ 330675; fax 358943); or contact Lotus Café at 197 Pham Ngu Lao St, District 1
CESAIS Tourism
   17 Pham Ngoc Thach St, District 3 (☎ 296750)
Cholon Tourist
   (Cong Ty Dich Vu Du Lich Cho Lon) 192-194 Su Van Hanh St, District 5 (☎ 359090; fax 355375)
Dong Thap Tourist
   16/1A Le Hong Phong St, District 10 (☎ 355826; fax 298540)
Eden Tourist
   104-106 Nguyen Hue Blvd, District 1 (☎ 293651; fax 230783)
Fiditourist
   195 Pham Ngu Lao St, District 1 (☎ 353018)
   71-73 Dong Khoi St, District 1 (☎ 296264)
Getra Tour Company
   86 Bui Vien St, District 1 (☎ 353021; fax 298540)
Hacotours
   8 Nguyen Binh Khiem St, District 1 (☎ 299360; fax 231302)
NHABEXIM
   31 Dong Khoi St, District 1 (☎ 298272)
OSC
   65 Nam Ky Khoi Nghia St, District 1 (☎ 296658; fax 290195)
Peace Tours
   (Cong Ty Du Lich Hoa Binh) 60 Vo Van Tan St, District 3 (☎ 290923; fax 294416)
Saigon Tourist
   49 Le Thanh Ton St, District 1 (☎ 298914; fax 224987)
Sao Viet Tour
   59 Dong Du St, District 1 (☎ 294561)
Thanh Thanh Travel Agency
   c/o Thanh Thanh 2 Hotel, 205 Pham Ngu Lao St, District 1 (☎ 360205)
   c/o Café 333, 217 Pham Ngu Lao St, District 1 (☎ 251550)
TNT
   9 Dong Khaoi St, District 1 (☎ 299363; fax 295832)
Vietlink Trading Travel & Tour Company
   411 Tran Hung Dao Blvd, District 5 (☎ 555849; fax 555852)

Vietnam Tourism
   234 Nam Ky Khoi Nghia St, District 3 (☎ 290776; fax 290775)
Vietnam Veteran Tourism
   97 Nguyen Dinh Chieu St, District 3 (☎ 241627; fax 248268)
Youth Tourist Company
   292 Dien Bien Phu St, District 3 (☎ 294580)
   c/o Kim Café, 270-272 De Tham St, District 1 (☎ 359859, fax 298540)

Money There is a bank at the airport, which gives an excellent exchange rate. The only problem is that the staff work banker's hours, which means it's closed when at least half of the flights arrive. For this reason, you'd be wise to have sufficient US dollar notes in small denominations to get yourself into the city.

Vietcombank (☎ 297245; fax 230310), also known as the Bank for Foreign Trade of Vietnam (Ngan Hang Ngoai Thuong Viet Nam), occupies two adjacent buildings at the intersection of Ben Chuong Duong and Pasteur Sts. The east building is the one that does foreign exchange, and it's worth a visit even if you don't change money – the ornate interior is absolutely stunning!

It's open from 7 to 11.30 am and 1.30 to 3.30 pm daily, except Saturday afternoons and the last day of the month. Besides US dollars, hard currencies which are currently acceptable (but this could change) include Australian dollars, British pounds sterling, Canadian dollars, Deutschmarks, French francs, Hong Kong dollars, Japanese yen, Singapore dollars, Swiss francs and Thai baht. Travellers' cheques denominated in US dollars can be changed for US dollars cash for a 2% commission. Especially on Mondays after holidays (like Tet), this bank can be very crowded with long waits.

There is a smaller branch of Vietcombank at 175 Dong Khoi St, opposite the Continental Hotel.

Sacombank at 211 Nguyen Thai Hoc St (at the intersection with Pham Ngu Lao St) is a popular place to change cash, travellers' cheques and to get advances on Visa cards. The bank is right in the centre of the budget travellers' zone.

Fiditourist, a private money changer, has a branch in budget travellers land at 195 Pham Ngu Lao St. The advantage of changing money here is the long hours – they stay open to 10 pm and work on weekends too.

There are several foreign-owned and joint-venture banks in Ho Chi Minh City with full-service branches. There are also a number of other foreign banks with representative offices in Saigon, but these banks are of little use to travellers. At the moment, the line-up of useful banks includes:

Bangkok Bank
117 Nguyen Hue Blvd, District 1 (☎ 223416; fax 223421)
Banque Française du Commerce Extérieur
11 Me Linh Square, District 1 (☎ 294144; fax 299126)
Banque Indosuez
39 Nguyen Cong Tru St, District 1 (☎ 296061; fax 296065)
Banque Nationale de Paris
2nd floor, State Bank Building, 1 Ton That Dam St, District 1 (☎ 299504; fax 299486)
Crédit Lyonnais
17 Ton Duc Thang St, District 1 (☎ 299226; fax 296465)
Firstvina Bank
3-5 Ho Tung Mau St (☎ 291566; fax 291583)
Indovina Bank
36 Ton That Dam St, District 1 (☎ 230130; fax 230131)
Thai Military Bank
11 Ben Chuong Duong St, District 1 (☎ 222218; fax 230045)
VID Public Bank
15A Ben Chuong Duong St, District 1 (☎ 223583; fax 223612)

You can get the bank rate at the officially sanctioned exchange windows in the jewellery shops at 71C Dong Khoi St (☎ 291522) and 112 Nguyen Hue Blvd (☎ 225693).

All the major tourist hotels can change money quickly, easily, legally and well after business hours. The catch is that they offer rates around 5% lower than the bank rate.

The men who accost you on the street offering great exchange rates are con artists.

Post & Telecommunications Saigon's French-style General Post Office (Buu Dien Thanh Pho Ho Chi Minh), with its glass canopy and iron frame, is at 2 Cong Xa Paris St, right next to Notre Dame Cathedral. The structure was built between 1886 and 1891 and is by far the largest post office in Vietnam.

The staff at the information desk (☎ 296555, 299615), which is to the left as you enter the building, speak English. Postal services are available daily from 7.30 am to 7.30 pm. To your right as you enter the building is poste restante, which is curiously labelled 'Delivery of Mail – Mail to Be Called For'. Pens, envelopes, aerograms, postcards and stamp collections are on sale at the counter to the right of the entrance and outside the GPO along Nguyen Du St.

Faxes can be sent to you at the GPO (fax 298540, 298546) and these will be delivered to your hotel for a small charge. In order for this to work, the fax should clearly indicate your name, hotel phone number and the address of the hotel (including your room number). The cost for receiving a fax is US$0.60.

A number of private carriers operate from the GPO, including DHL (☎ 231525; fax 445387), Federal Express (☎ 290747; fax 290477) and Airborne Express (☎ 294310, 294315; fax 292961). For rates, see the Post & Telecommunications section in the Facts for the Visitor chapter.

Postal, telex, telegram and fax services are available at counters run by the post office at the hotels Caravelle, Le Lai, Majestic, Palace and Rex.

The District 1 post office (☎ 299086), which serves downtown Saigon, is on Le Loi Blvd near its intersection with Pasteur St.

In Ho Chi Minh City, the following special phone numbers are available but don't be surprised if the person answering speaks only Vietnamese:

Ambulance	15
Directory Inquiries	16
Directory Information	108
Emergency	296485
Fire Brigade	14
International Calls	00 & 110
Interprovincial Calls	01 & 101
Police	13
Telex Service	296738
Traffic Police	296449

Consulates & Commercial Offices The addresses and telephone numbers of Ho Chi Minh City's foreign consulates and foreign commercial representatives are as follows:

Australia
    Landmark Building, 5B Ton Duc Thang St, District 1
    Trade Office: 4 Dong Khoi St, District 1 (☎ 299387)
Belgium
    236 Dien Bien Phu St, District 3 (☎ 294527)
Cambodia
    Consular: 124 Nguyen Dinh Chieu St, District 3 (☎ 295818)
    Trade Office: 180 Dien Bien Phu St, District 3 (☎ 296814)
Canada
    203 Dong Khoi St, No 303 (☎ 242000, ext 3320)
China
    39 Nguyen Thi Minh Khai St (☎ 292457, 292463)
Cuba
    45 Phung Khac Khoan St, District 1 (☎ 297350)
Czech
    176 Nguyen Van Thu St, District 1 (☎ 291475, 298277)
Denmark
    23 Phung Khac Khoan St, District 1 (☎ 230156)
France
    Consular: 27 Xo Viet Nghe Tinh St, District 3 (☎ 297231)
    Trade Office: 75 Tran Quoc Thao St, District 3 (☎ 296056)
Germany
    126 Nguyen Dinh Chieu St, District 3 (☎ 291967)
Hungary
    22 Phung Khac Khoan St, District 1 (☎ 290130)
India
    49 Tran Quoc Thao St, District 3 (☎ 294495, 294498)
Indonesia
    18 Phung Khac Khoan St, District 1 (☎ 223799)
Italy
    4 Dong Khoi St, District 1 (☎ 298721)
Japan
    13-17 Nguyen Hue Blvd, District 1 (☎ 225314)
Korea (South)
    107 Nguyen Du St, District 1 (☎ 225757)
Laos
    181 Hai Ba Trung St, District 3 (☎ 297667)
Malaysia
    53 Nguyen Dinh Chieu St, District 3 (☎ 299023)
Poland
    2 Tran Cao Van St, District 1 (☎ 290114)
Russia
    40 Ba Huyen Thanh Quan St, District 3 (☎ 292936, 292937)

Singapore
    5 Phung Khac Khoan St, District 1 (☎ 225173)
Switzerland
    270A Bach Dang Blvd, Binh Thanh District (☎ 442568)
Taiwan
    Trade Office: Taipei Economic & Cultural Office, 68 Tran Quoc Thao St, District 3
    Consular: ☎ 299348
    Commercial: ☎ 299349
Thailand
    Rex Hotel, Room 662 (☎ 293115)
UK
    261 Dien Bien Phu St, District 3 (☎ 298433)

Visa Extensions For what it's worth (and it's not worth much), the Immigration Police Office (Phong Quan Ly Nguoi Nuoc Ngoai; ☎ 392221) is at 254 Nguyen Trai St. It's open from 8 to 11 am and 1 to 4 pm. Most likely, you will be turned away and told to use the services of a private agency.

Hotels, cafes and travel agencies can arrange visa extensions – shop around for the best price but figure on around US\$20 for 30 days.

Bookshops Tiem Sach Bookstore, 20 Ho Huan Nghiep St, has a massive selection of mostly used English and French titles. The owner is an elderly ex-journalist. The shop is open daily from 8.30 am to 10 pm, and also functions as an ice cream parlour.

Hieu Sach Xuan Thu (☎ 224670) at 185 Dong Khoi St, District 1, is the best of the government-run book stores. You should at least manage to find a good dictionary or some maps here, as well as some more general books in English and French.

The best area to look for general map, book and stationery stuff is along the north side of Le Loi Blvd between the Rex Hotel and Nam Ky Khoi Nghia St (near the two Kem Bach Dang ice cream parlours). There are many small privately run shops and one large government book store here.

Libraries The address of the Municipal Library is 34 Ly Tu Trong St. Nearby at 69 Ly Tu Trong St is the General Sciences Library with a total of 500 seats in its reading rooms.

Maps Maps of Ho Chi Minh City and other Vietnamese cities are sold in downtown Saigon at sidewalk stands along Dong Khoi St, along Le Loi Blvd between Dong Khoi St and Nguyen Hue Blvd, and on Nguyen Hue Blvd between Le Loi Blvd and the Palace Hotel. These stalls have the best selection of maps in Vietnam; some of the maps sold here are impossible to find anywhere else in the country. If you think you will need any maps later in your trip, this is the place to get them. Maps of Ho Chi Minh City may also be on sale at the Rex Hotel gift shop.

If you are interested in the pre-1975 names of Ho Chi Minh City's streets, the map with the dark blue border and the inset of Ho Chi Minh City in the lower right-hand corner has an index of old and new names on the back. *Ten Truoc 1975* means 'Name before 1975'.

Photography Photoprocessing shops are ubiquitous, especially in areas frequented by foreigners (Pham Ngu Lao St, Nguyen Hue Blvd, etc). Both colour print and slide film can be bought easily and cheaply, but check expiry dates.

At the present time, colour-slide processing is not being done by anyone in Ho Chi Minh City. That is sure to change, but for now you'd be wise to take your slide film to Hong Kong, Thailand or wherever to get it processed.

Medical Facilities Travel Medical Consultancy (☎ 357644), 10 Nguyen Canh Chan St, District 1, is one of the newest medical facilities in Ho Chi Minh City. It's staffed by foreign doctors, and they can even perform surgery if necessary. This clinic is open during regular office hours, so you should go elsewhere if you have an emergency at night or on weekends.

Cho Ray Hospital (Benh Vien Cho Ray; ☎ 554137, 554138, 558074; 1000 beds), one of the best medical facilities in Vietnam, is at 201B Nguyen Chi Thanh Blvd, District 5 (Cholon). There is a section for foreigners on the 10th floor. About a third of the 200 doctors speak English. There are 24-hour

emergency facilities. Spending the night in the foreigners' ward would cost about US$25. The hospital was built in the 1970s before reunification and some of the equipment still dates from that period.

The Emergency Centre (☎ 225966, 291711, 292071), 125 Le Loi Blvd, District 1, operates 24 hours. Doctors speak English and French. A visit typically costs US$10.

The French Consulate operates a clinic (☎ 297231, 297235) at 27 Nguyen Thi Minh Khai St, District 3. You do not need to be a French national, and the doctor speaks English and French. Call for an appointment. This is *not* a 24-hour clinic and is closed on weekends.

Asia Emergency Assistance (☎ 298520; fax 298551), Hannam Office Building, 65 Nguyen Du St, District 1, has a medical services programme for resident expats. The payment of an annual fee buys you regular treatment, emergency medical care and evacuation 24 hours a day. You can also contact International SOS Assistance (☎ 242866) for information about their health plan and evacuation services.

The Pasteur Institute (☎ 230252), 167 Pasteur St, District 3, has the best facilities in Vietnam for doing medical tests. However, you need to be referred here first by a doctor.

The Cardiology Institute is a speciality clinic at 520 Nguyen Tri Phuong Blvd, District 10. Another specialised medical facility is Phu San (☎ 392722), 284 Cong Quynh St, District 1, which treats only women.

Binh Dan Hospital is said to have belonged to President Thieu during the days when he ruled South Vietnam. This hospital is still one of the best in Vietnam, but it's too far from the centre to be of much use to visitors. It's approximately 13 km north-west from the centre in the Tan Binh District.

Pharmacies are everywhere, some good but many not. One good one is at 678 Nguyen Dinh Chieu St, District 3. The owner there speaks excellent English and French and can even get unusual medicines not normally kept in stock (he makes a phone call and someone delivers the medicines by motorbike within a couple of hours).

Useful Organisations The Saigon branch of the Chamber of Commerce & Industry of Vietnam (Chi Nhanh Phong Thuong Mai Va Cng Nghiep, or Vietcochamber; ☎ 230331, 230339; fax 294472) is at 171 Vo Thi Sau St, District 3.

IMC (Investment & Management Consulting Corporation; ☎ 299062) offers various business services to investors and business people. The External Affairs Office of the Foreign Ministry (So Ngoai Vu; ☎ 223032, 224311) is at 6 Thai Van Lung St.

Aid Organisations Vietnam needs all the help it can get, and there are a number of international aid organisations filling that role. While most officially have their Vietnam branch headquarters in Hanoi, most maintain more staff in Ho Chi Minh City (which makes one wonder just where Vietnam's capital really is). They are:

FAO
> (UN Food & Agriculture Organisation; TC Luong Thuc Va Nong Nghiep) 2 Phung Khac Khoan St, District 1 (☎ 290781)

ICRC
> (International Committee of the Red Cross; UB Chu Thap Do Quoc Te) 79 Ba Huyen Thanh Quan St, District 3 (☎ 222965)

Rehabilitation Centre for Malnourished Children
> 38 Tu Xuong St, District 3 (☎ 290786, fax 222157)

UNDP
> (UN Development Programme; Chuong Trinh Cua LHQ Ve Phat Trien) 2 Phung Khac Khoan St, District 1 (☎ 295821, 295865)

UNHCR
> (UN High Commission for Refugees; Cao Uy LHQ Ve Nguoi Ti Nan) 257 Hoang Van Thu St, Tan Binh District (☎ 445895, 445896)

UNICEF
> (UN Children's Fund; Quy Nhi Dong LHQ) 2 Phung Khac Khoan St, District 1 (☎ 291006)

One of our more moving experiences was visiting an orphanage in Ho Chi Minh City. We brought used clothing with us that needed to be dropped off. We called all the major international aid organisations, but either they were unable to understand what I wanted or they didn't accept donations of clothing. The UNICEF people referred me to a newspaper, assuring me that this was definitely the place for me to drop off the goods. We loaded up the cyclo and were off to what we anticipated to be quite an adventure. As expected, the woman at the small streetside newspaper stand was completely dumbfounded as to why we wanted to give our things to her, but referred us to the Rehabilitation Centre for Malnourished Children at 38 Tu Xuong St, District 3. It's basically an orphanage for the malnourished, and we found this to be an excellent program doing excellent work. The doctor speaks fluent English as well as French. They issue receipts to avoid complications with customs due to 'missing baggage'.

Angelina Rauschenbach

Places of Worship – Ho Chi Minh City
The following places of worship are on the Ho Chi Minh City map.

Giac Lam Pagoda Giac Lam Pagoda dates from 1744 and is believed to be the oldest pagoda in Ho Chi Minh City. Because the last reconstruction here was in 1900, the architecture, layout and ornamentation have remained almost unaltered by the modernist renovations that have transformed so many other religious structures in Vietnam. Ten monks live at this Vietnamese Buddhist pagoda, which also incorporates aspects of Taoism and Confucianism. It is well worth the trip out here from downtown Saigon.

To the right of the gate to the pagoda compound are the ornate tombs of venerated monks. The *bo de* (bodhi, or pipal) tree in the front garden was the gift of a monk from Sri Lanka. Next to the tree is a regular feature of Vietnamese Buddhist temples, a gleaming white statue of Quan Am (Guanyin in Chinese, the Goddess of Mercy) standing on a lotus blossom, symbol of purity.

The roofline of the main building is decorated both inside and outside with unusual blue and white porcelain plates. Through the main entrance is a reception hall lined with funeral tablets and photos of the deceased. Roughly in the centre of the hall, near an old French chandelier, is a figure of 18-armed Chuan De, another form of the Goddess of Mercy. Note the carved hardwood columns, which bear gilded Vietnamese inscriptions written in nom characters, a form of writing in use before the adoption of the Latin-based *quoc ngu* alphabet. The wall to the left is covered with portraits of great monks from previous generations. Monks' names and biographical information about them are recorded on the vertical red tablets in gold *nom* characters. A box for donations sits nearby. Shoes should be removed when passing from the rough red floor tiles to the smaller, white-black-grey tiles.

On the other side of the wall from the monks' funeral tablets is the main sanctuary, which is filled with countless gilded figures. On the dais in the centre of the back row sits A Di Da (pronounced 'AH-zee-dah'), the Buddha of the Past (Amitabha). To his right is Kasyape and to his left Anand; both are disciples of the Thich Ca Buddha (the historical Buddha Sakyamuni, whose real name was Siddhartha Gautama). Directly in front of A Di Da is a statue of the Thich Ca Buddha, flanked by two guardians. In front of Thich Ca is the tiny figure of the Thich Ca Buddha as a child. As always, he is clothed in a yellow robe.

The fat laughing fellow, seated with five children climbing all over him, is Ameda. To his left is Ngoc Hoang, the Taoist Jade Emperor who presides over a world of innumerable supernatural beings. In the front row is a statue of the Thich Ca Buddha with four Bodhisattvas *(bo tat)*, two on each side. On the altars along the side walls of the sanctuary are various Bodhisattvas and the Judges of the Ten Regions of Hell. Each of the judges is holding a scroll resembling the handle of a fork.

The red and gold Christmas-tree-shaped object is a wooden altar bearing 49 lamps and 49 miniature statues of Bodhisattvas. People pray for sick relatives or ask for happiness by contributing kerosene for use in the lamps. Petitioners' names and those of ill family members are written on slips of paper, which are attached to the branches of the 'tree'.

The frame of the large bronze bell in the corner looks like a university bulletin board because petitioners have attached to it lists of names: the names of people seeking happiness and the names of the sick and the dead, placed there by their relatives. It is believed that when the bell is rung, the sound will resonate to the heavens above and the underground heavens below, carrying with it the attached supplications.

Prayers here consist of chanting to the accompaniment of drums, bells and gongs and follow a traditional rite seldom performed these days. Prayers are held daily from 4 to 5 am, 11 am to noon, 4 to 5 pm and 7 to 9 pm.

Giac Lam Pagoda is about three km from Cholon at 118 Lac Long Quan St in Tan Binh District. Beware: the numbering on Lac Long Quan St is extremely confused, starting over from one several times and at one point jumping to four digits. In many places, odd and even numbers are on the same side of the street.

The best way to get to Giac Lam Pagoda is to take Nguyen Chi Thanh Blvd or 3 Thang 2 Blvd to Le Dai Hanh St. Go north-westward on Le Dai Hanh St and turn right onto Lac Long Quan St. Walk 100 metres; the pagoda gate will be on your left. It is open to visitors from 6 am to 9 pm.

Giac Vien Pagoda Giac Vien Pagoda and Giac Lam Pagoda are similar architecturally. Both pagodas share the same atmosphere of scholarly serenity, though Giac Vien, which is right next to Dam Sen Lake in District 11, is in a more rural setting. Giac Vien Pagoda was founded by Hai Tinh Giac Vien about 200 years ago. It is said that the Emperor Gia Long, who died in 1819, used to worship at Giac Vien. Today, 10 monks live at the pagoda.

As you enter the pagoda, the first chamber is lined with funeral tablets. At the back of the second chamber is a statue of the pagoda's founder, Hai Tinh Giac Vien, holding a horse-tail swatch. Nearby are portraits of his successors as head monk and disciples. A donation box sits to the left of the statue. Opposite Hai Tinh Giac Vien is a representation of 18-armed Chuan De, who is flanked by two guardians.

The main sanctuary is on the other side of the wall behind Hai Tinh Giac Vien. A Di Da, the Buddha of the Past, is at the back of the dais. Directly in front of him is the Thich Ca Buddha, flanked by Thich Ca's disciples Anand (on the left) and Kasyape (on the right). To the right of Kasyape is the Ti Lu Buddha; to the left of Anand is the Nhien Dang Buddha. At the foot of the Thich Ca Buddha is a small figure of Thich Ca as a child. Fat, laughing Ameda is seated with children climbing all over him; far on either side of him are guardians, standing. In the front row of the dais is Thich Ca with two Bodhisattvas on each side.

In front of the dais is a fantastic brass incense basin with fierce dragon heads emerging from each side. On the altar to the left of the dais is Dai The Chi Bo Tat; on the altar to the right is Quan The Am Bo Tat (Avalokiteçvara), the Goddess of Mercy. The Guardian of the Pagoda is against the wall opposite the dais. Nearby is a 'Christmas tree' similar to the one in Giac Lam Pagoda. Lining the side walls are the Judges of the Ten Regions of Hell (holding scrolls) and 18 Bodhisattvas.

Prayers are held daily from 4 to 5 am, 8 to 10 am, 2 to 3 pm, 4 to 5 pm and 7 to 9 pm.

The pagoda is in a relatively poor part of the city. Because of the impossibly confusing numbering on Lac Long Quan St, the best way to get to Giac Vien Pagoda is to take Nguyen Chi Thanh Blvd or 3 Thang 2 Blvd to Le Dai Hanh St. Turn left (south-west) off Le Dai Han St on to Binh Thoi St and turn right (north) at Lac Long Quan St. The gate leading to the pagoda is at 247 Lac Long Quan St. From Lac Long Quan St there are signs pointing the way to the pagoda.

Pass through the gate and go several hundred metres down a pot-holed dirt road, turning left at the 'tee' and right at the fork. You will pass several impressive tombs of monks on the right before arriving at the pagoda itself. Giac Vien Pagoda is open from 7 am to 7 pm but come before dark as the electricity is often out.

Jade Emperor Pagoda The Jade Emperor Pagoda (known in Vietnamese as Phuoc Hai Tu and Chua Ngoc Hoang), built in 1909 by the Cantonese (Quang Dong) Congregation,

is truly a gem of a Chinese temple. It is one of the most spectacularly colourful pagodas in Ho Chi Minh City, filled with statues of phantasmal divinities and grotesque heroes. The pungent smoke of burning joss sticks fills the air, obscuring exquisite wood carvings decorated with gilded Chinese characters. The roof is covered with elaborate tilework. The statues, which represent characters from both the Buddhist and Taoist traditions, are made of reinforced papier-mâché.

As you enter the main doors of the building Mon Quan, the God of the Gate, stands to the right in an elaborately carved wooden case. Opposite him, in a similar case, is Tho Than (Tho Dia), the God of the Land. Straight on is an altar on which are placed, from left to right, figures of: Phat Mau Chuan De, mother of the five Buddhas of the cardinal directions; Dia Tang Vuong Bo Tat (Ksitigartha), the King of Hell; the Di Lac Buddha (Maitreya), the Buddha of the Future; Quan The Am Bo Tat; and a bas-relief portrait of the Thich Ca Buddha. Behind the altar, in a glass case, is the Duoc Su Buddha, also known as the Nhu Lai

ROBERT STOREY

Statues inside the Jade Emperor Pagoda

Buddha. The figure is said to be made of sandalwood.

To either side of the altar, against the walls, are two especially fierce and menacing figures. On the right (as you face the altar) is a four-metre-high statue of the general who defeated the Green Dragon. He is stepping on the vanquished dragon. On the left is the general who defeated the White Tiger, which is also getting stepped on.

The Taoist Jade Emperor, Ngoc Hoang, presides over the main sanctuary, draped in luxurious robes. He is flanked by the 'Four Big Diamonds' (Tu Dai Kim Cuong), his four guardians, so named because they are said to be as hard as diamonds. In front of the Jade Emperor stand six figures, three to each side. On the left is Bac Dau, the Taoist God of the Northern Polar Star and God of Longevity, flanked by his two guardians; and on the right is Nam Tao, the Taoist God of the Southern Polar Star and God of Happiness, also flanked by two guardians.

In the case to the right of the Jade Emperor is 18-armed Phat Mau Chuan De, mother of the five Buddhas of the north, south, east, west and centre. Two faces, affixed to her head behind each ear, look to either side. On the wall to the right of Phat Mau Chuan De, at a height of about four metres, is Dai Minh Vuong Quang, who was reincarnated as Sakyamuni, riding on the back of a phoenix. Below are the Tien Nhan, literally the 'godpersons'.

In the case to the left of the Jade Emperor sits Ong Bac De, a reincarnation of the Jade Emperor, holding a sword. One of his feet is resting on a turtle while the other rests on a snake. On the wall to the left of Ong Bac De, about four metres off the ground, is Thien Loi, the God of Lightning, who slays evil people. Below Thien Loi are the military commanders of Ong Bac De (on the lower step) and Thien Loi's guardians (on the upper step). At the top of the two carved pillars that separate the three alcoves are the Goddess of the Moon (on the left) and the God of the Sun (on the right).

Out the door on the left-hand side of the Jade Emperor's chamber is another room.

The semi-enclosed area to the right (as you enter) is presided over by Thanh Hoang, the Chief of Hell; to the left is his red horse. Of the six figures lining the walls, the two closest to Thanh Hoang are Am Quan, the God of Yin (on the left) and Duong Quan, the God of Yang (on the right). The other four figures, the Thuong Thien Phat Ac, are gods who dispense punishments for evil acts and rewards for good deeds. Thanh Hoang faces in the direction of the famous Hall of the Ten Hells. The carved wooden panels lining the walls graphically depict the varied torments awaiting evil people in each of the 10 regions of hell. At the top of each panel is one of the Ten Judges of Hell examining a book in which the deeds of the deceased are inscribed.

On the wall opposite Thanh Hoang is a bas-relief wood panel depicting Quan Am Thi Kinh, the Guardian Spirit of Mother and Child, standing on a lotus blossom, symbol of purity. Unjustly turned out of her home by her husband, Quan Am Thi Kinh disguised herself as a monk and went to live in a pagoda, where a young woman accused her of fathering her child. She accepted the blame – and the responsibility that went along with it – and again found herself out on the streets, this time with her 'son'. Much later, about to die, she returned to the monastery to confess her secret. When the Emperor of China heard of her story, he declared her the Guardian Spirit of Mother and Child.

It is believed that she has the power to bestow male offspring on those who fervently believe in her. On the panel, Quan Am Thi Kinh is shown holding her 'son'. To her left is Long Nu, a very young Buddha, who is her protector. To Quan Am Thi Kinh's right is Thien Tai, her guardian spirit, who knew the real story all along. Above her left shoulder is a bird bearing prayer beads.

To the right of the panel of Quan Am Thi Kinh is a panel depicting Dia Tang Vuong Bo Tat, the King of Hell.

On the other side of the wall is a fascinating little room in which the ceramic figures of 12 women, overrun with children and wearing colourful clothes, sit in two rows of six. Each of the women exemplifies a human characteristic, either good or bad (as in the case of the woman drinking alcohol from a jug). Each figure represents one year in the 12-year Chinese calendar. Presiding over the room is Kim Hoa Thanh Mau, the Chief of All Women.

To the right of the main chamber, stairs lead up to a 2nd-floor sanctuary and balcony.

The Jade Emperor Pagoda is at 73 Mai Thi Luu St in a part of Ho Chi Minh City known as Da Kao (or Da Cao). To get there, go to 20 Dien Bien Phu St and walk half a block north-westward (to the left as you head out of Saigon towards Thi Nghe Channel).

Dai Giac Pagoda This Vietnamese Buddhist pagoda is built in a style characteristic of pagodas constructed during the 1960s. In the courtyard, under the unfinished 10-level red-pink tower inlaid with porcelain shards, is an artificial cave made of volcanic rocks in which there is a gilded statue of the Goddess of Mercy. In the main sanctuary, the 2½-metre gilt Buddha has a green neon halo, while below, a smaller white reclining Buddha (in a glass case) has a blue neon halo.

Dai Giac Pagoda is at 112 Nguyen Van Troi St, 1.5 km towards the city centre from the gate to the airport.

Vinh Nghiem Pagoda Vinh Nghiem Pagoda, inaugurated in 1971, is noteworthy for its vast sanctuary and eight-storey tower, each level of which contains a statue of the Buddha. It was built with help from the Japan-Vietnam Friendship Association, which explains the presence of Japanese elements in its architecture. At the base of the tower (which is open only on holidays) is a store selling Buddhist ritual objects. Behind the sanctuary is a three-storey tower which serves as a repository for carefully labelled ceramic urns containing the ashes of people who have been cremated.

The pagoda is in District 3 at 339 Nam Ky Khoi Nghia St and is open from 7.30 to 11.30 am and 2 to 6 pm daily.

Le Van Duyet Temple This temple is dedicated to Marshal Le Van Duyet (pronounced 'Lee Van Zyet'), who is buried here with his wife. The Marshal, who lived from 1763 to 1831, was a southern Vietnamese general and viceroy who helped put down the Tay Son Rebellion and reunify Vietnam. When the Nguyen Dynasty came to power in 1802, he was elevated by Emperor Gia Long to the rank of marshal. Le Van Duyet fell into disfavour with Gia Long's successor, Minh Mang, who tried him posthumously and desecrated his grave. Emperor Thieu Tri, who succeeded Minh Mang, restored the tomb, fulfilling a prophecy of its destruction and restoration. Le Van Duyet was considered a great national hero in the South before 1975 but is disliked by the Communists because of his involvement in the expansion of French influence.

The temple itself was renovated in 1937 and has a distinctly modern feel to it. Since 1975, the government has done little to keep it from becoming dilapidated. Among the items on display are a portrait of Le Van Duyet, some of his personal effects (including European-style crystal goblets) and other antiques. There are two wonderful life-size horses on either side of the entrance to the third and last chamber, which is kept locked.

During celebrations of Tet and the 30th day of the 7th lunar month (the anniversary of Le Van Duyet's death), the tomb is thronged with pilgrims. Vietnamese used to come here to take oaths of good faith if they could not afford the services of a court of justice. The tropical fish are on sale to visitors. The caged birds are bought by pilgrims and freed to earn merit. The birds are often recaptured (and liberated again).

Le Van Duyet Temple is three km from the centre of Saigon in the Gia Dinh area at 131 Dinh Tien Hoang St (near where Phan Dang Luu Blvd becomes Bach Dang Blvd).

Tran Hung Dao Temple This small temple is dedicated to Tran Hung Dao, a Vietnamese national hero who in 1287 vanquished an invasion force, said to have numbered 300,000 men, which had been dispatched by the Mongol emperor Kublai Khan. The temple is at 36 Vo Thi Sau St, a block northeast of the telecommunications dishes that are between Dien Bien Phu St and Vo Thi Sau St.

The public park between the antenna dishes and Hai Ba Trung St was built in 1983 on the site of the Massiges Cemetery, burial place of French soldiers and settlers. The remains of French military personnel were exhumed and repatriated to France. Another site no longer in existence is the tomb of the 18th-century French missionary and diplomat, Pigneau de Béhaine, Bishop of Adran, which was completely destroyed after reunification.

The temple is open every weekday from 6 to 11 am and 2 to 6 pm.

Cho Quan Church Cho Quan Church, built by the French about 100 years ago, is one of the largest churches in Ho Chi Minh City. This is the only church we've seen in the city where the figure of Jesus on the altar has a neon halo. The view from the belfry is worth the steep climb.

The church is at 133 Tran Binh Trong St (between Tran Hung Dao Blvd and Nguyen Trai St), and is open daily from 4 to 7 am and 3 to 6 pm and Sundays from 4 to 9 am and 1.30 to 6 pm. Sunday masses are held in the morning at 5, 6.30 and 8.30 am, and also in the afternoon at 4.30 and 6 pm.

Places of Worship – Central Saigon
The following places are on the Central Saigon map.

Notre Dame Cathedral Notre Dame Cathedral, built between 1877 and 1883, is set in the heart of Saigon's government quarter. The cathedral faces down Dong Khoi St. Its neo-Romanesque form and two 40-metre-high square towers, tipped with iron spires, dominate the city's skyline. In front of the cathedral (in the centre of the square bounded by the GPO) is a statue of the Virgin Mary. If the front gates are locked, try the door on the side of the building that faces Reunification Palace.

Unusually, this cathedral has no stained glass windows. The glass was a casualty of fighting during WW II. A number of foreign travellers worship here, and the priests are allowed to add a short sermon in French or English to their longer presentations in Vietnamese. The 9.30 am Sunday Mass might be the best one for foreigners to attend.

There are several other interesting French-era churches around Saigon, including one at 289 Hai Ba Trung St.

Xa Loi Pagoda Xa Loi Vietnamese Buddhist Pagoda, built in 1956, is famed as the repository of a sacred relic of the Buddha.

In August 1963, truckloads of armed men under the command of President Ngo Dinh Diem's brother, Ngo Dinh Nhu, attacked Xa Loi Pagoda, which had become a centre of opposition to the Diem government. The pagoda was ransacked and 400 monks and nuns, including the country's 80-year-old Buddhist patriarch, were arrested. This raid and others elsewhere helped solidify opposition among Buddhists to the Diem regime, a crucial factor in the US decision to support the coup against Diem. This pagoda was also the site of several self-immolations by monks protesting against the Diem regime and the war.

Women enter the main hall of Xa Loi Pagoda by the staircase on the right as you come in the gate; men use the stairs on the left. The walls of the sanctuary are adorned with paintings depicting the Buddha's life.

Xa Loi Pagoda is in District 3 at 89 Ba Huyen Thanh Quan St, near Dien Bien Phu St. It is open daily from 7 to 11 am and from 2 to 5 pm. A monk preaches every Sunday morning from 8 to 10 am. On days of the full moon and new moon, special prayers are held from 7 to 9 am and from 7 to 8 pm.

Phung Son Tu Pagoda Phung Son Tu Pagoda, built by the Fujian Congregation in the mid-1940s, is more typical of Ho Chi Minh City's Chinese pagodas than is the Jade Emperor Pagoda. The interior is often hung with huge incense spirals that burn for hours. Worshippers include both ethnic-Chinese

Thich Quang Duc

Thich Quang Duc was a monk from Hué who travelled to Saigon and publicly burned himself to death in June 1963 to protest the policies of President Ngo Dinh Diem. A famous photograph of his act was printed on the front pages of newspapers around the world. His death soon inspired a number of other self-immolations.

Many Westerners were shocked less by the suicides than by the reaction of Tran Le Xuan (Madame Nhu, the president's notorious sister-in-law), who happily proclaimed the self-immolations a 'barbecue party' and said 'Let them burn, and we shall clap our hands'. Her statements greatly added to the already substantial public disgust with Diem's regime; the US press labelled Madame Nhu the 'Iron Butterfly' and 'Dragon Lady'. In November, both President Diem and his brother Ngo Dinh Nhu (Madame Nhu's husband) were assassinated by Diem's own military. Madame Nhu was outside the country at the time (fortunately for her) and was last reported to be living in Rome.

The Thich Quang Duc Memorial (Dai Ky Niem Thuong Toa Thich Quang Duc) is at the intersection of Nguyen Dinh Chieu and Cach Mang Thang Tam Sts, not far from the Xa Loi Pagoda. ■

and ethnic-Vietnamese. Phung Son Tu Pagoda is dedicated to Ong Bon, Guardian Spirit of Happiness and Virtue, whose statue is behind the main altar in the sanctuary. On the right-hand side of the main hall is the multi-armed Buddhist Goddess of Mercy.

This pagoda is only one km from downtown Saigon at 338 Nguyen Cong Tru St.

Mariamman Hindu Temple Mariamman Hindu Temple, the only Hindu temple still in use in Ho Chi Minh City, is a little piece of southern India in the centre of Saigon. Though there are only 50 to 60 Hindus in Ho Chi Minh City – all of them Tamils – this temple, known in Vietnamese as Chua Ba Mariamman, is also considered sacred by many ethnic-Vietnamese and ethnic-Chinese. Indeed, it is reputed to have miraculous powers. The temple was built at the end of the 19th century and dedicated to the Hindu goddess Mariamman.

The lion to the left of the entrance used to be carried around Saigon in a street procession every autumn. In the shrine in the middle of the temple are Mariamman flanked by her guardians, Maduraiveeran (to her left) and Pechiamman (to her right). In front of the figure of Mariamman are two lingams. Favourite offerings placed nearby include joss sticks, jasmine flowers, lilies and gladioli. The wooden stairs, on the left as you enter the building, lead to the roof, where you'll find two colourful towers covered with innumerable figures of lions, goddesses and guardians.

After reunification, the government took over the temple and turned part of it into a factory for joss sticks. Another section was occupied by a company producing seafood for export – the seafood was dried in the sun on the roof. The whole temple is to be returned to the local Hindu community.

Mariamman Temple is only three blocks from Ben Thanh Market at 45 Truong Dinh St. It is open from 7 am to 7 pm daily. Take off your shoes before stepping onto the slightly raised platform.

Saigon Central Mosque Built by South Indian Muslims in 1935 on the site of an earlier mosque, the Saigon Central Mosque is an immaculately clean and well-kept island of calm in the middle of bustling downtown Saigon. In front of the sparkling white and blue structure at 66 Dong Du St, with its four nonfunctional minarets, is a pool for ritual ablutions (washing), required by Islamic law before prayers. As with any mosque, take off your shoes before entering the sanctuary.

The simplicity of the mosque is in marked contrast to the exuberance of Chinese temple decorations and the rows of figures, elaborate ritual objects, in Buddhist pagodas. Islamic law strictly forbids using human or animal figures for decoration.

Only half-a-dozen Indian Muslims remain

in Saigon; most of the community fled in 1975. As a result, prayers – held five times a day – are sparsely attended except on Fridays, when several dozen worshippers (including many non-Indian Muslims) are present. The mass emigration also deprived the local Muslim community of much of its spiritual leadership, and very few Muslims knowledgeable in their tradition and Arabic, the language of the Koran, remain.

There are 12 other mosques serving the 5000 or so Muslims in Ho Chi Minh City.

Places of Worship – Cholon

The following places are on the Cholon map.

An Quang Pagoda The An Quang Pagoda gained some notoriety during the Vietnam War as the home of Thich Tri Quang, a politically powerful monk who led protests against the South Vietnamese government in 1963 and 1966. When the war ended, you would have expected the Communists to be grateful. Instead, he was first placed under house arrest and later thrown in solitary confinement for 16 months. Thich Tri Quang was eventually released and is said to still be living at An Quang Pagoda.

The An Quang Pagoda is on Su Van Hanh St near the intersection with Ba Hat St, District 10.

Tam Son Hoi Quan Pagoda This pagoda, known to the Vietnamese as Chua Ba Chua, was built by the Fujian Congregation in the 19th century and retains unmodified most of its original rich ornamentation. The pagoda is dedicated to Me Sanh, the Goddess of Fertility. Both men and women – but more of the latter – come here to pray for children. Tam Son Hoi Quan Pagoda is at 118 Trieu Quang Phuc St, which is very near 370 Tran Hung Dao B Blvd.

To the right of the covered courtyard is the deified general Quan Cong (in Chinese: Guangong) with a long black beard; he is flanked by two guardians, the mandarin general Chau Xuong on the left (holding a weapon) and the administrative mandarin

Quan Binh on the right. Next to Chau Xuong is Quan Cong's sacred red horse.

Behind the main altar (directly across the courtyard from the entrance) is the goddess Thien Hau, Goddess of the Sea and Protector of Fisherfolk and Sailors. To the right is an ornate case in which Me Sanh (the Goddess of Fertility; in white) sits surrounded by her daughters. In the case to the left of Thien Hau is Ong Bon, Guardian Spirit of Happiness and Virtue. In front of Thien Hau is Quan The Am Bo Tat enclosed in glass.

Across the courtyard from Quan Cong is a small room containing ossuary jars (in which the ashes of the deceased are reposited) and memorials in which the dead are represented by their photographs. Next to this chamber is a small room containing the papier-mâché head of a dragon of the type used by the Fujian Congregation for dragon dancing. There is a photograph of a dragon dance on the wall between Quan Cong's red horse and Me Sanh.

Thien Hau Pagoda Thien Hau Pagoda (also known as Ba Mieu, Pho Mieu and Chua Ba) was built by the Cantonese Congregation in the early 19th century. Of late it has become something of a showcase for tours operated by Saigon Tourist and Vietnam Tourism, which may explain the recent extensive renovations. This pagoda is one of the most active in Cholon.

The pagoda is dedicated to Thien Hau (also known as Tuc Goi La Ba), the Chinese Goddess of the Sea who protects fisherfolk, sailors, merchants and anyone else who travels by sea. It is said that Thien Hau can travel over the oceans on a mat and ride the clouds to wherever she pleases. Her mobility allows her to save people in trouble on the high seas.

Thien Hau is very popular in Hong Kong (where she's called Tin Hau) and in Taiwan (where her name is Matsu). This might explain why Thien Hau Pagoda is included on so many tour group agendas.

Though there are guardians to either side of the entrance, it is said that the real protectors of the pagoda are the two land turtles who live here. There are intricate ceramic friezes above the roofline of the interior courtyard. Near the huge braziers are two miniature wooden structures in which a small figure of Thien Hau is paraded around each year on the 23rd day of the 3rd lunar month. On the main dais are three figures of Thien Hau, one behind the other, each flanked by two servants or guardians. To the left of the dais is a bed for Thien Hau. To the right is a scale-model boat and on the far right is the Goddess Long Mau, Protector of Mothers and Newborns.

Thien Hau Pagoda is at 710 Nguyen Trai St and is open from 6 am to 5.30 pm.

Nghia An Hoi Quan Pagoda Nghia An Hoi Quan Pagoda, built by the Chaozhou Chinese Congregation, is noteworthy for its gilded woodwork. There is a carved wooden boat over the entrance and inside, to the left of the doorway, is an enormous representation of Quan Cong's red horse with its groom. To the right of the entrance is an elaborate altar on which a bearded Ong Bon stands holding a stick. Behind the main altar are three glass cases. In the centre is Quan Cong (Chinese: Guangong) and to either side are his assistants, the general Chau Xuong (on the left) and the administrative mandarin Quan Binh (on the right). To the right of Quan Binh is an especially elaborate case for Thien Hau.

Nghia An Hoi Quan Pagoda is at 678 Nguyen Trai St (not far from Thien Hau Pagoda) and is open from 4 am to 6 pm.

Cholon Mosque The clean lines and lack of ornamentation of the Cholon Mosque are in stark contrast to nearby Chinese and Vietnamese pagodas. In the courtyard is a pool for ritual ablutions. Note the tile *mihrab* (the niche in the wall indicating the direction of prayer, which is towards Mecca). The mosque was built by Tamil Muslims in 1932. Since 1975, the mosque has served the Malaysian and Indonesian Muslim communities.

Cholon Mosque is at 641 Nguyen Trai St and is open all day Friday and at prayer times on other days.

Quan Am Pagoda Quan Am Pagoda, at 12 Lao Tu St, one block off Chau Van Liem Blvd, was founded in 1816 by the Fujian Congregation. The temple is named for Quan The Am Bo Tat.

This is the most active pagoda in Cholon and the Chinese influence is obvious. The roof is decorated with fantastic scenes, rendered in ceramic, from traditional Chinese plays and stories. The tableaux include ships, houses, people and several ferocious dragons. The front doors are decorated with very old gold and lacquer panels. On the walls of the porch are murals in slight relief picturing scenes of China from the time of Quan Cong. There are elaborate wooden carvings on roof supports above the porch.

Behind the main altar is A Pho, the Holy Mother Celestial Empress, gilded and in rich raiment. In front of her, in a glass case, are three painted statues of Thich Ca Buddha, a standing gold Quan The Am Bo Tat, a seated laughing Ameda and, to the far left, a gold figure of Dia Tang Vuong Bo Tat.

In the courtyard behind the main sanctuary, in the pink tile altar, is another figure of A Pho. Quan The Am Bo Tat, dressed in white embroidered robes, stands nearby. To the left of the pink altar is her richly ornamented bed. To the right of the pink altar is Quan Cong flanked by his guardians, the general Chau Xuong (on the left) and the administrative mandarin Quan Binh (on the right). To the far right, in front of another pink altar, is the black-faced judge Bao Cong.

Phuoc An Hoi Quan Pagoda Phuoc An Hoi Quan Pagoda, built in 1902 by the Fujian Congregation, is one of the most beautifully ornamented pagodas in Ho Chi Minh City. Of special interest are the many small porcelain figures, the elaborate brass ritual objects and the fine wood carvings on the altars, walls, columns and hanging lanterns. From outside the building you can see the ceramic scenes, each containing innumerable small figurines, which decorate the roof. Phuoc An Hoi Quan Pagoda is at 184 Hung Vuong Blvd (near the intersection of Thuan Kieu St).

To the left of the entrance is a life-sized figure of the sacred horse of Quan Cong. Before leaving on a journey, people make offerings to the horse. They then pet the horse's mane before ringing the bell around its neck. Behind the main altar, with its stone and brass incense braziers, is Quan Cong, to whom the pagoda is dedicated. Behind the altar to the left is Ong Bon and two servants. The altar to the right is occupied by representations of Buddhist (rather than Taoist) personages. In the glass case are a plaster Thich Ca Buddha and two figures of the Goddess of Mercy, one made of porcelain and the other cast in brass.

Ong Bon Pagoda Ong Bon Pagoda (also known as Chua Ong Bon and Nhi Phu Hoi Quan) was built by the Fujian Congregation and is dedicated to Ong Bon, Guardian Spirit of Happiness and Virtue. The wooden altar is intricately carved and gilded.

As you enter the pagoda, there is a room to the right of the open-air courtyard. In it, behind the table, is a figure of Quan The Am Bo Tat in a glass case. Above the case is the head of a Thich Ca Buddha.

Directly across the courtyard from the pagoda entrance, against the wall, is Ong Bon, to whom people come to pray for general happiness and relief from financial difficulties. He faces a fine carved wooden altar. On the walls of this chamber are two rather indistinct murals of five tigers (to the left) and two dragons (to the right).

In the area on the other side of the wall with the mural of the dragons is a furnace for burning paper representations of the wealth people wish to bestow upon deceased family members. Diagonally opposite is Quan Cong flanked by his guardians Chau Xuong (to his right) and Quan Binh (to his left).

Ong Bon Pagoda is at 264 Hai Thuong Lai Ong Blvd, which runs parallel to Tran Hung Dao B Blvd, and is open from 5 am to 5 pm.

Ha Chuong Hoi Quan Pagoda Ha Chuong Hoi Quan Pagoda at 802 Nguyen Trai St is a typical Fujian pagoda. It is dedicated to Thien Hau Thanh Mau, who was born in Fujian.

The four carved stone pillars, wrapped in painted dragons, were made in China and brought to Vietnam by boat. There are interesting murals to either side of the main altar. Note the ceramic relief scenes on the roof.

This pagoda becomes extremely active during the Lantern Festival, a Chinese holiday held on the 15th day of the first lunar month (the first full moon of the new lunar year).

Cha Tam Church It is in Cha Tam Church that President Ngo Dinh Diem and his brother Ngo Dinh Nhu took refuge on 2 November 1963 after fleeing the Presidential Palace during a coup attempt. When their efforts to contact loyal military officers (of whom there were almost none) failed, Diem and Nhu agreed to surrender unconditionally and revealed where they were hiding.

The coup leaders sent an M-113 armoured personnel carrier to the church to pick them up (Diem seemed disappointed that a limousine befitting his rank had not been dispatched) and the two were taken into custody. But before the vehicle arrived in Saigon, the soldiers in the APC killed Diem and Nhu by shooting them at point-blank range and then repeatedly stabbing their bodies.

When news of the death of the brothers was broadcast on the radio, Saigon exploded into rejoicing. Portraits of the two were torn up and political prisoners, many of whom had been tortured, were set free. The city's nightclubs, closed because of the Ngos' conservative Catholic beliefs, reopened. Three weeks later, US president John F Kennedy was assassinated. Since Kennedy's administration supported the coup against Diem, some conspiracy theorists have speculated that Kennedy was killed by Diem's family in retaliation. Then again, there are theories that Kennedy was murdered by the Russians, the Cubans, left-wing radicals, right-wing radicals, the CIA and the Mafia.

Cha Tam Church, built around the turn of the century, is an attractive white and pastel-yellow structure. The statue in the tower is of François Xavier Tam Assou (1855-1934), a Chinese-born vicar apostolic of Saigon. (A vicar apostolic is a delegate of the pope who administers an ecclesiastical district in a missionary region.) Today, the church has a very active congregation of 3000 ethnic-Vietnamese and 2000 ethnic-Chinese.

Vietnamese-language masses are held daily from 5.30 to 6 am and on Sundays from 5.30 to 6.30 am, 8.30 to 9.30 am and 3.45 to 4.45 pm. Chinese-language masses are held from 5.30 to 6 pm every day and from 7 to 8 am and 5 to 6 pm on Sundays. Cha Tam Church is at 25 Hoc Lac St, at the western end of Tran Hung Dao B Blvd.

Khanh Van Nam Vien Pagoda Built between 1939 and 1942 by the Cantonese, Khanh Van Nam Vien Pagoda is said to be the only Taoist pagoda in all of Vietnam. This statement needs to be qualified since most Chinese practice a mixture of Taoism and Buddhism, rather than one or the other exclusively. The number of 'true' Taoists in Ho Chi Minh City is said to number only 4000, though you can take this figure with a grain of salt since most of the true Taoists are probably Buddhists too.

A few metres from the door is a statue of Hoang Linh Quan, chief guardian of the pagoda. There is a Yin and Yang symbol on the platform on which the incense braziers sit. Behind the main altar are four figures: Quan Cong (on the right) and Lu Tung Pan (on the left) represent Taoism; between the two of them is Van Xuong representing Confucianism; and behind Van Xuong is Quan The Am Bo Tat representing Buddhism.

In front of these figures is a glass case containing seven gods and one goddess, all of which are made of porcelain. In the altars to either side of the four figures are Hoa De (on the left), a famous doctor during the Han Dynasty, and Huynh Dai Tien (on the right), a disciple of Laotse.

Upstairs is a 150-cm-high statue of the founder of Taoism, Laotse (Vietnamese: Thai Thuong Lao Quan). Behind his head is a halo consisting of a round mirror with fluorescent lighting around the edge.

To the left of Laotse are two stone plaques with instructions for inhalation and exhalation exercises. The 80-year-old chief monk says that he has practised these exercises for the past 17 years and hasn't been sick a day. A schematic drawing represents the human organs as a scene from rural China. The diaphragm, agent of inhalation, is at the bottom. The stomach is represented by a peasant ploughing with a water buffalo. The kidney is marked by four Yin and Yang symbols, the liver is shown as a grove of trees and the heart is represented by a circle with a peasant standing in it, above which is a constellation. The tall pagoda represents the throat, and the broken rainbow is the mouth. At the top are mountains and a seated figure representing the brain and the imagination, respectively.

The pagoda operates a home at 46/14 Lo Sieu St for 30 elderly people who have no families. Each of the old folk, most of whom are women, have their own wood stove made of brick and can cook for themselves. Next door, also run by the pagoda, is a free medical clinic which offers Chinese herbal medicines (which are stored in the wooden drawers) and acupuncture treatments to the community. Before reunification, the pagoda ran (also free of charge) the school across the street.

The pagoda is open from 6.30 am to 5.30 pm every day and prayers are held from 8 to 9 am daily. To get there, turn off Nguyen Thi Nho St (which runs perpendicular to Hung Vuong Blvd) between numbers 269B and 271B; the address is 46/5 Lo Sieu St.

Phung Son Pagoda Phung Son Pagoda (also known as Phung Son Tu and Chua Go) is extremely rich in statuary made of hammered copper, bronze, wood and ceramic. Some are gilded while others, beautifully carved, are painted. This Vietnamese Buddhist pagoda was built between 1802 and 1820 on the site of structures from the Oc-Eo (Funan) period, which was contemporaneous with the early centuries of Christianity. In 1988, a Soviet archaeological team carried out a preliminary excavation and found the foundations of Funanese buildings, but work was stopped pending authorisation for a full-scale dig.

Phung Son Pagoda is in District 11 at 1408, 3 Thang 2 Blvd, near its intersection with Hung Vuong Blvd. Prayers are held three times a day from 4 to 5 am, 4 to 5 pm and 6 to 7 pm. The main entrances are kept locked most of the time because of problems with theft, but the side entrance (which is to the left as you approach the building) is open from 5 am to 7 pm.

Once upon a time, it was decided that Phung Son Pagoda should be moved to a different site. The pagoda's ritual objects – bells, drums, statues – were loaded onto the back of a white elephant for transport to the new location, but the elephant slipped because of the great weight and all the precious objects fell into a nearby pond. This event was interpreted as an omen that the pagoda should remain at its original location. All the articles were retrieved except for the bell, which locals say was heard ringing whenever there was a full or new moon until about a century ago.

The main dais, with its many levels, is dominated by a gilded A Di Da seated under a canopy flanked by long mobiles resembling human forms without heads. A Di Da is flanked by Quan The Am Bo Tat (on the left), and Dai The Chi Bo Tat (on the right). To the left of the main dais is an altar with a statue of Boddhi Dharma, the founder of Zen Buddhism, who brought Buddhism from India to China. The statue, which is made of Chinese ceramic, has a face with Indian features.

As you walk from the main sanctuary to the room with the open-air courtyard in the middle, you come to an altar with four statues on it, including a standing bronze Thich Ca Buddha of Thai origin. To the right is an altar on which there is a glass case containing a statue made of sandalwood. The statue is claimed to be Long Vuong (Dragon King), who brings rain. Around the pagoda building are a number of interesting monks' tombs.

Museums

War Crimes Museum Once known as the 'Museum of American War Crimes', the name has been changed so as not to offend the sensibilities of American tourists. However, the pamphlet handed out at reception pulls no punches; it's entitled 'Some Pictures of US Imperialist's Aggressive War Crimes in Vietnam'.

Whatever the current name, this has become the most popular museum in Saigon with Western tourists. Many of the atrocities documented in the museum were well publicised in the West, but it is one thing for US anti-war activists to protest against Pentagon policies and quite another for the victims of these military actions to tell their own story. But no matter what side of the political fence you stand on, the museum is well worth a visit – if for no other reason than to get a sobering reminder that war is anything but glorious.

In the yard of the museum, US armoured vehicles, artillery pieces, bombs and infantry weapons are on display. There is also a guillotine which the French used to deal with Viet Minh 'troublemakers'. Many of the photographs illustrating US atrocities are from US sources, including photos of the famous My Lai massacre. There is a model of the notorious tiger cages used by the South Vietnamese military to house VC prisoners on Con Son Island. There are also pictures of genetically deformed babies, their birth defects attributed to the widespread spraying of Agent Orange by the Americans. In an adjacent room are exhibits detailing 'counter-revolutionary war crimes' committed by saboteurs within Vietnam after the 1975 liberation. The counter-revolutionaries are portrayed as being allied with both US and Chinese imperialists.

The main objection to the museum comes from, not surprisingly, American tourists, many of whom complain that the museum is one-sided. There are some unnecessary crude comments placed under the photos, such as one of an American soldier picking up a horribly mangled body to show the photographer, and a caption saying 'this soldier seems satisfied'. And of course, there is official amnesia when it comes to the topic of the many thousands of people tortured and murdered by the VC.

Politically neutral war historians will perhaps be more disturbed by the lack of context and completeness of some of the photos and exhibits. It's surprising, for example, that there are no photos of Thich Quang Duc, the monk who burned himself to death to protest the war. Or photos of the Kent State students in the USA who were shot while protesting US policies. Hopefully, the museum will be expanded to include a larger slice of the war's history.

Despite these criticisms, there are few museums in the world which drive home the point so well that modern warfare is horribly brutal, and that many of the victims are civilians. Even those who adamantly supported the war will have a difficult time not being horrified by the photos of innocent children mangled by American bombing, napalming and artillery shells. There are also scenes of torture – it takes a strong stomach to look at these. You'll also have a rare chance to see some of the experimental weapons used in the Vietnam War which were at one time military secrets, an example being the 'flechette' (an artillery shell filled with thousands of tiny darts).

The War Crimes Museum (☎ 290325) is housed in the former US Information Service building at 28 Vo Van Tan St (at the intersection with Le Qui Don St). Opening hours are from 8 to 11.30 am and 2 to 5 pm daily. Explanations are written in Vietnamese, English and Chinese.

Revolutionary Museum Housed in a white neoclassical structure built in 1886 and once known as Gia Long Palace, the Revolutionary Museum (Bao Tang Cach Mang; ☎ 299741) is a singularly beautiful and amazing building. The museum displays artefacts from the various periods of the communist struggle for power in Vietnam. The photographs of anti-colonial activists executed by the French appear out of place in the gilded 19th-century ballrooms, but

---

Whitewashing Nature

Visitors to Ho Chi Minh City have often wondered why the lower half of all the trees are painted white. Theories posited by tourists have included: (1) the paint protects the trees from termites, (2) the paint protects the trees from Agent Orange, (3) it is some government official's idea of nouveau art and (4) it is an ancient Vietnamese tradition. It turns out that the mystery of the white trees has a much simpler explanation – the trees are painted white so people don't bump into them at night. ■

---

then again, the contrast helps you get a feel for the immense power and self-confident complacency of colonial France. There are photos of Vietnamese peace demonstrators in Saigon demanding that US troops get out, and a dramatic photo of the suicide of Thich Quang Duc, the monk who set himself on fire to protest the policies of President Ngo Dinh Diem.

The information plaques are in Vietnamese only, but some of the exhibits include documents in French or English and many others are self-explanatory if you know some basic Vietnamese history. Some of the guides speak English, and will often latch on to you in various rooms or on each floor and provide excellent if unrequested guided tours. There are donation boxes next to the visitors' books in various parts of the museum where you can leave a tip for the guides (US$1 to US$2 is appropriate). Most of the guides do fine work and get paid nothing for it.

The exhibition begins in the first room on the left (as you enter the building), which covers the period from 1859 to 1940. Upstairs, two more rooms are currently open. In the room to the left, is a *ghe* (a long, narrow rowboat) with a false bottom in which arms were smuggled. The weight of the contraband caused the boat to sit as low in the water as would any ordinary ghe. Nearby is a small diorama of the Cu Chi Tunnels. The adjoining room has examples of infantry weapons used by the VC and various captured South Vietnamese and

American medals, hats and plaques. A map shows Communist advances during the dramatic collapse of South Vietnam in early 1975. There are also photographs of the 'liberation' of Saigon.

Deep underneath the building is a network of reinforced concrete bunkers and fortified corridors. The system, branches of which stretch all the way to Reunification Palace, included living areas, a kitchen and a large meeting hall. In 1963, President Diem and his brother hid here immediately before fleeing to a Cholon church where they were captured (and, shortly thereafter, murdered). The network is not yet open to the public because most of the tunnels are flooded, but if you bring a torch, a museum guard may show you around.

In the garden behind the museum is a Soviet tank, an American Huey UH-1 helicopter and an anti-aircraft gun. In the garden fronting Nam Ky Khoi Nghia St is some more military hardware, including the American-built F-5E jet used by a renegade South Vietnamese air force pilot to bomb the Presidential Palace (now Reunification Palace) on 8 April 1975.

The Revolutionary Museum is at 65 Ly Tu Trong St (corner Nam Ky Khoi Nghia St), which is one block south-east of Reunification Palace. It is open from 8 to 11.30 am and 2 to 4.30 pm Tuesday to Sunday. The museum offices are at 114 Nam Ky Khoi Nghia St. Admission is free.

History Museum The History Museum (Vien Bao Tang Lich Su; ☎ 298146), built in 1929 by the Société des Études Indochinoises and once the National Museum of the Republic of Vietnam, is just inside the main entrance to the zoo, on Nguyen Binh Khiem St. Step inside the door and you're immediately confronted by a big statue of guess who? Also, the museum has an excellent collection of artefacts illustrating the evolution of the cultures of Vietnam, from the Bronze Age Dong Son civilisation (13th century BC to 1st century AD), to the Oc-Eo (Funan) civilisation (1st to 6th centuries AD), to the Chams, Khmers and Vietnamese.

There are many valuable relics taken from Cambodia's Angkor Wat.

At the back of the building on the 3rd floor is a research library (☎ 290268; open Monday to Saturday) with numerous books on Indochina from the French period.

Water puppet shows are performed here with advance booking, and cost US$1 per person.

The museum is open from 8 to 11.30 am and 1 to 4 pm, Tuesday to Sunday.

Uncle Ho's Museum for Mementos This oddly named museum (Khu luu niem Bac Ho; ☎ 291060) is in the old customs house at 1 Nguyen Tat Thanh St, just across Ben Nghe Channel from the quayside end of Ham Nghi Blvd. This place was (and still is) nicknamed the 'Dragon House' (Nha Rong) and was built in 1863. The tie between Ho Chi Minh (1890-1969) and the museum building is tenuous: 21-year-old Ho, having signed on as a stoker and galley-boy on a French freighter, left Vietnam from here in 1911, beginning 30 years of exile in France, the Soviet Union, China and elsewhere.

The museum houses many of Ho's personal effects, including some of his clothing (he was a man of informal dress), sandals, his beloved American-made Zenith radio and other memorabilia. The explanatory signs in the museum are in Vietnamese, but if you know much about Uncle Ho (Bac Ho), you should be able to follow most of the photographs and exhibits.

The museum is open on Tuesday, Wednesday, Thursday and Saturday from 8 to 11.30 am and 2 to 6 pm; on Sundays, it stays open until 8 pm. The museum is closed on Mondays and Fridays.

Military Museum The Military Museum is just across Nguyen Binh Khiem St (corner Le Duan Blvd) from the main gate of the zoo. US, Chinese and Soviet war matériel is on display, including a Cessna A-37 of the South Vietnamese air force and a US-built F-5E Tiger with the 20-mm nose gun still loaded. The tank on display is one of the tanks which broke into the grounds of what is now Reunification Palace on 30 April 1975.

Art Museum This classic yellow and white building with some modest Chinese influence houses one of the more interesting collections in Vietnam. If you are not interested in the collection, just enter the huge hall with its nice art nouveau windows and floors. The 1st floor seems to have housed the revolutionary art in former times. Those pieces are either in storage, thrown out or in some back rooms close to the toilet. Now you find on the 1st floor officially accepted contemporary art. Most of it is kitsch or desperate attempts to master abstract art, but occasionally something brilliant is displayed here. Most of the recent art is for sale and prices are fair.

The 2nd floor displays the old politically correct art. Some of this stuff is pretty crude – pictures of heroic figures waving red flags, children with rifles, a wounded soldier joining the Communist Party, innumerable tanks and weaponry, grotesque Americans and God-like reverence for Ho Chi Minh. Nevertheless, it's worth seeing because Vietnamese artists managed not to be as dull and conformist as their counterparts in eastern Europe. Once you've passed several paintings and sculptures of Uncle Ho, you will see that those artists who studied before 1975 managed to somehow transfer their own aesthetics into the world of prescribed subjects. Surprisingly, the Vietnamese Communists seem to have prescribed only the subjects but not the style. Most impressive are some drawings of prison riots in 1973. On the floor are some remarkable abstract paintings. Maybe the most striking fact in these politically correct paintings is that all Vietnamese heroes of great wars look a bit more European than Asian.

The 3rd floor displays a good collection of older art, mainly Oc-Eo (Funan) sculptures. Those Oc-Eo pieces strongly resemble the styles from ancient Greece and Egypt. You will also find here the best Cham pieces outside of Danang. Also interesting are the many pieces of Indian art, often of an elephant's head. There are some pieces which clearly originated in Angkor culture.

A cafe is in the garden in front of the museum and is a preferred spot for elderly gentlemen to exchange stamp collections and sip iced tea.

The Art Museum (Bao Tang My Thuat; ☎ 222577) is at 97A Pho Duc Chinh St in central Saigon. Opening hours are from 7.30 am to 4.30 pm Tuesday to Sunday. Admission is free.

Ton Duc Thang Museum This small, rarely visited museum (Bao Tang Ton Duc Thang; ☎ 294651) is dedicated to Ton Duc Thang, Ho Chi Minh's successor as President of Vietnam, who was born in Long Xuyen, An Giang Province, in 1888. He died in office in 1980. Photos illustrate his role in the Vietnamese Revolution, including the time he spent imprisoned on Con Dao Island. The explanations are in Vietnamese only.

The museum is along the waterfront at 5 Ton Duc Thang St, half a block north of the Tran Hung Dao statue at the foot of Hai Ba Trung St. It is open Tuesday to Sunday from 8 to 11 am and 2 to 6 pm.

Binh Soup Shop

It might seem strange to introduce a restaurant in the sightseeing section of this chapter rather than the Places to Eat section, but there is more to this shop than just the soup. The Binh Soup Shop was the secret headquarters of the Viet Cong in Saigon. It was from here that the VC planned the attack on the US Embassy and other places in Saigon during the Tet Offensive of 1968. One has to wonder how many American soldiers must have eaten here, unaware that the waiters and cooks were VC infiltrators.

The Binh Soup Shop is at 7 Ly Chinh Thang St, District 3. By the way, the soup isn't bad.

Markets

See the Things to Buy section at the end of this chapter for information on Ho Chi Minh City's bustling indoor markets. Even if you don't want to buy anything, these are a sight not to be missed.

Reunification Palace

It was towards this building – then known as Independence Palace or the Presidential Palace – that the first Communist tanks in Saigon rushed on the morning of 30 April 1975. After crashing through the wrought-iron gates in a dramatic scene recorded by a photo-journalist and shown around the world, a soldier ran into the building and up the stairs to unfurl a Viet Cong flag from the 4th-floor balcony. In an ornate 2nd-floor reception chamber, General Minh, who had become head of state only 43 hours earlier, waited with his improvised cabinet. 'I have been waiting since early this morning to transfer power to you', Minh said to the VC officer who entered the room. 'There is no question of your transferring power', replied the officer, 'you cannot give up what you do not have'.

Reunification Palace (Hoi Truong Thong Nhat) is one of the most fascinating things to see in Saigon, both because of its striking modern architecture and because of the eerie feeling you get, as you walk through the deserted halls, that from here ruled arrogant men wielding immense power who nevertheless became history's losers. The building, once the symbol of the Southern government, is preserved almost as it was on 30 April 1975, the day that the Republic of Vietnam, which hundreds of thousands of Vietnamese and 58,183 Americans died trying to save, ceased to exist. Some recent editions to the building include a statue of Ho Chi Minh and a video-viewing room, where you can watch the latest version of Vietnamese history in a variety of languages. The national anthem is played at the end of the tape and you are expected to stand up – it would be rude to refuse to do so.

Reunification Palace is open for visitors from 7.30 to 10 am and 1 to 4 pm daily except when official receptions or meetings are taking place. English and French-speaking guides are on duty during these hours. Each guide is assigned to a particular part of the palace, so you will have numerous guides as you move from room to room. The visitors' office and entrance is at 106 Nguyen Du St (☎ 290629). The entrance fee for foreigners is US$4 (free for Vietnamese).

In 1868 a residence for the French Governor General of Cochinchina was built on this site. The residence gradually expanded and became known as Norodom Palace. When the French departed, the palace became home for South Vietnamese President Ngo Dinh Diem. So hated was Diem that his own air force bombed the palace in 1962 in an unsuccessful attempt to kill him. Recognising that he had an image problem, the president ordered a new residence to be built on the same site but this time with a sizeable bomb shelter in the basement. The new mansion was designed by Paris-trained Vietnamese architect Ngo Viet Thu – work began in 1962 and was completed in 1966. Diem did not get to see his dream house because he was murdered by his own troops in 1963. The new building was named Independence Palace and was home for South Vietnamese President Nguyen Van Thieu until his hasty departure in 1975.

The building, both inside and out, is an outstanding example of 1960s architecture; it is much more interesting up close than you would expect from the street. Reunification Palace has an airy and open atmosphere and its spacious chambers are tastefully decorated with the finest modern Vietnamese art and craft. In its grandeur, the building feels worthy of a head of state.

The ground-floor room with the boat-shaped table was used for conferences. Upstairs, in the Presidential Receiving Room (the one with the red chairs in it, called in Vietnamese Phu Dau Rong, or the Dragon's Head Room), South Vietnam's president used to receive foreign delegations. The president sat behind the desk; the chairs with dragons carved into the arms were used by his assistants. The chair facing the desk was reserved for foreign ambassadors. Next door is a meeting room. The room with gold-coloured chairs and curtains was used by the vice president. For US$1, you can sit in the former president's chair and have your photo taken.

In the back of the structure is the area in which the president lived. Check out the model boats, horse-tails and severed elephants' feet. On the 3rd floor there is a card-playing room with a bar and a movie-screening chamber. The 3rd floor also boasts a terrace with a heliport – there is still a moribund helicopter parked here, but it costs US$1 admission to walk around on the helipad to take advantage of the photo opportunities. The 4th floor has a dance hall and casino.

Perhaps most interesting of all is the basement with its network of tunnels, telecommunications centre and war room (with the best map of Vietnam you'll ever see pasted to the wall). One tunnel stretches all the way to Gia Long Palace, which is now the Revolutionary Museum.

Former US Embassies

There are actually two former US embassies in Saigon: the one from whose roof the famous chaotic helicopter evacuation took place as the Communists took over the city in April 1975, and the building used before that one was built.

The older former US Embassy (Dai Su Quan My Truoc 1967) is an ugly fortress-like concrete structure at 39 Ham Nghi Blvd (corner Ho Tung Mau St). In 1967, the building was bombed by the VC. It now serves as a dormitory for young people studying banking.

The newer structure (Dai Su Quan My Tu 1967-75) – from which US policy was conducted during the last eight years of the Republic of Vietnam – is on the corner of Le Duan Blvd and Mac Dinh Chi St in the middle of what was (and still is) a neighbourhood of key government buildings. The main building, once the chancery, is encased in a concrete shield intended to protect it from bomb blasts as well as rocket and shell fire. There are round concrete pillboxes, protected with anti-grenade screens, at each corner of the compound.

The embassy building, which became a symbol of the overwhelming American presence in South Vietnam, was finished just in time to almost get taken over in the 1968 Tet Offensive. On TV, 50 million Americans watched chaotic scenes of dazed US soldiers and diplomats firing at the VC commando team which had attacked the embassy, leaving the grounds littered with US and Vietnamese dead. These images were devastating to US home-front support for the war.

The ignominious end of three decades of US involvement in Vietnam, also shown around the globe on TV, took place on the roof of the US embassy chancery building. As the last defences of Saigon fell to the North Vietnamese army and the city's capture became imminent, the Americans, as unprepared for the speed of the collapse of the South as everyone else (including the North Vietnamese), were forced to implement emergency evacuation plans. Thousands of Vietnamese desperate to escape the country (many of them had worked for the Americans and had been promised to be evacuated) congregated around the embassy and tried to get inside; US marine guards forced them back. Overhead, American helicopters (carrying both Americans and Vietnamese) shuttled to aircraft carriers waiting offshore. In the pre-dawn darkness of 30 April 1975, with most of the city already in Communist hands, US Ambassador Graham Martin, carrying the embassy's flag, climbed onto the roof of the building and boarded a helicopter. The end.

The compound was for a while occupied by the government-owned Oil Exploration Corporation, but they have now abandoned it. The official word is that the building is being reserved for the Americans to move back into now that full diplomatic relations have been restored between the USA and Vietnam. Of course, the former embassy will just be a US consulate – a new US embassy will be built in Hanoi.

Hotel de Ville

Saigon's gingerbread Hotel de Ville, one of the city's most prominent landmarks, was built between 1901 and 1908 after years of the sort of architectural controversy peculiar to the French. Situated at the north-western end of Nguyen Hue Blvd and facing towards the river, the white-on-pastel-yellow Hotel de Ville, with its ornate façade and elegant interior lit with crystal chandeliers, is now the somewhat incongruous home of the Ho Chi Minh City People's Committee. The building is now officially called the People's Committee Building, though few outside the government care to call it that. Whatever it's called, the building is not open to the public and requests by tourists to visit the interior are rudely rebuffed.

For gecko fans: at night, the exterior of the Hotel de Ville is usually covered with thousands of geckos feasting on insects.

French Colonial Architecture

Many of the buildings in Cholon are a distinctive mix of Chinese and French styles. Some of the most interesting structures in Cholon are to be found along Hung Vuong Blvd.

Zoo & Botanical Garden

The Zoo & Botanical Garden (Thao Cam Vien) is a pleasant place for a relaxing stroll under giant tropical trees which thrive amid the lakes, lawns and flower beds. Unfortunately, the zoo facilities are run-down, and the elephants in particular look like they'd be better off dead (many are close to it now). The other animals – which include crocodiles and big cats – seem to have it somewhat better.

The garden, founded in 1864, was one of the first projects undertaken by the French after they established Cochinchina as a colony. It was once one of the finest such gardens in Asia, but this is certainly no longer true. The emphasis now is on the fun fair, with kiddie rides, fun house, miniature train, house of mirrors, etc.

A rather gruesome form of amusement exists near the entrance to the zoo. There is a ride here where the animals upon which people sit are real! There are stuffed bears, deer and large cats following each other around the revolving platform. Some of them are looking a little tatty, but this no doubt creates employment for local taxidermists. At least these animals are dead (we hope).

The main gate of the zoo is on Nguyen Binh Khiem St at the intersection of Le Duan Blvd. There is another entrance on Nguyen Thi Minh Khai St near the bridge over Thi Nghe Channel.

The History Museum is next to the main gate. There are occasional water-puppet shows performed on a small island in one of the lakes – a small group can arrange a special showing.

Also just inside the main gate is the Temple of King Hung Vuong. The Hung kings are said to be the first rulers of the Vietnamese nation, having established their rule in the Red River region before being invaded by the Chinese.

Ice cream, fresh French bread and drinks are sold at a few places around the park, but food here is generally expensive and not too good. Just outside the main gate (along Nguyen Binh Khiem St) there are numerous food stalls selling excellent rice dishes, soup and drinks at reasonable prices.

Parks

Cong Vien Van Hoa Park Next to the old Cercle Sportif, an elite sporting club during the French period, the bench-lined walks of Cong Vien Van Hoa Park are shaded with avenues of enormous tropical trees.

This place still has an active sports club, although now you don't have to be French to visit. There are 11 tennis courts, a swimming pool and club house, which have a grand colonial feel about them. It's worth a look for the pool alone. There are Roman-style baths with a coffee shop overlooking the colonnaded pool.

The tennis courts are available for hire at a reasonable fee. Hourly tickets are on sale for use of the pool and you can even buy a bathing costume on the grounds if you don't have one. The antique dressing rooms are quaint but there are no lockers! Other facilities include a gymnasium, table tennis, weight lifting, wrestling mats and ballroom dancing classes.

In the morning, you can often see people here practicing the art of *thai cuc quyen*, or slow-motion shadow boxing.

Within the park is a small-scale model of the Cham towers in Nha Trang.

Cong Vien Van Hoa Park is adjacent to Reunification Palace. There are entrances across from 115 Nguyen Du St and on Nguyen Thi Minh Khai St.

Ho Ky Hoa Park Ho Ky Hoa Park, whose name means Lake and Gardens, is a children's amusement park in District 10 just off 3 Thang 2 Blvd. It is near the Hoa Binh Theatre and behind Vietnam Quoc Tu Pagoda. There are paddleboats, rowboats and sailboats for hire. Fishing is allowed in the lakes and a small swimming pool is open to the public for part of the year. The cafes are open year-round and there are also two arcades of Japanese video games. Within the park boundaries is a rather expensive hotel. Ho Ky Hoa Park is open from 7 am to 9.30 pm daily and is crowded on Sundays.

Binh Quoi Tourist Village

Built on a small peninsula in the Saigon River, the Binh Quoi Tourist Village (Lang Du Lich Binh Quoi; ☎ 991831) is a slick tourist trap operated by Saigon Tourist. Backpackers are not numerous, but upmarket tourists get brought out here by the busload and some city-weary locals also seem to like it.

The 'village' is essentially a park featuring boat rides, water-puppet shows, a restaurant, swimming pool, tennis courts, camping ground, guesthouse, bungalows and amusements for the kiddies. The park puts in a plug for Vietnam's ethnic minorities by staging traditional-style minority weddings accompanied by music. There are some alligators kept in an enclosure for viewing, but so far no alligator-wrestling shows. River cruises can be fun – the smaller cruise boats have 16 seats and the larger ones have 100 seats.

Next to the water puppet theatre, you can make bookings for the local nightlife. A sign in English advertises all sorts of fun-filled evening activities, as follows:

Saigon Tourist Brings You: 'Magical Evenings'. Sunset cruise, traditional show, dinner under the stars. Daily: Cruise & dinner show US$20 (5.30 to 9 pm); cultural show alone US$5 (7 to 8 pm).

Places to Stay The *Binh Quoi Bungalows* (☎ 991831, 991833; 50 rooms) is perhaps one of the better values around. Built on stilts above the water, the bungalows give you a little taste of traditional river life in the Mekong Delta, but with air-conditioning and tennis courts. The price range here is US$15 to US$35.

Getting There & Away Binh Quoi Tourist Village is eight km north from downtown Saigon in Binh Thanh district. The official address is 1147 Xo Viet Nghe Tinh St. You can get there by cyclo, motorbike or taxi. A much slower alternative is to charter a boat from the Floating Hotel area.

Orchid Farm

There are a number of orchid farms (Vuon Cay Kieng) in suburban Ho Chi Minh City, but most are concentrated in the Thu Duc District. These places raise more than orchids. The Artex Saigon Orchid Farm is the largest of all, with 50,000 plants representing 1000 varieties. It is primarily a commercial concern but visitors are welcome to stop by to relax in the luxurious garden.

The farm, founded in 1970, uses revenues from the sale of orchid flowers for its operating budget but makes its real profit selling orchid plants, which take six years to mature and are thus very expensive. In addition to varieties imported from overseas, the farm has a collection of orchids native to Vietnam. Ask to see the orange-yellow Cattleya orchid variety called Richard Nixon; they have another variety named for Joseph Stalin. The nurseries are at their most beautiful just before Tet when demand for all sorts of flowers and house plants reaches its peak. After Tet, the place is bare.

The Artex Saigon Orchid Farm is 15 km from Saigon in Thu Duc District, a rural part of Ho Chi Minh City, on the way to Bien Hoa. The official address is 5/81 Xa Lo Vong Dai, but this highway is better known as 'Xa Lo Dai Han', the 'Korean Highway', because it was built during the war by Koreans. At 'Km 14' on Xa Lo Dai Han there is a two-storey police post. Turn left (if heading out of Saigon toward Bien Hoa), continue 300 metres, and turn left again.

Saigon Racetrack

When South Vietnam was liberated in 1975, one of Hanoi's policies was to ban debauched capitalistic pastimes such as gambling. Horse race tracks – found mostly in the Saigon area – were shut down. However, the government's need for hard cash has caused a rethink. The Saigon Racetrack (Cau Lac Bo TDTT; ☎ 551205), which dates back to around 1900, was permitted to reopen in 1989.

Much of the credit for the reopening goes to Philip Chow, a Chinese-Vietnamese businessman who fled to Hong Kong as a youth but returned to Vietnam in 1987 after the government promised to launch capitalist-style reforms. After getting the racetrack up and running through his own hard work, Mr Chow was rewarded for his efforts by being sacked from his position. Government officials, sensing the opportunity to line their own pockets, saw no reason to keep an entrepreneur on the payroll.

Ever the optimist, Mr Chow approached the government with a proposal to reopen the Duc Hoa Thung Racetrack, 45 km from Saigon. Realising that this could draw some of the business away from their own state-run monopoly, government officials have adamantly refused.

Like the state lottery, the racetrack is extremely lucrative. But grumbling about just where the money is going has been coupled with widespread allegations about the drugging of horses. The minimum legal age for jockeys is 14 years; most look like they are about 10.

The overwhelming majority of gamblers are Vietnamese though there is no rule prohibiting foreigners. The maximum legal bet is currently US$2. High rollers can win a million dong (about US$92). Races are held Saturday and Sunday afternoons starting at 1 pm. Plans to introduce off-track betting have so far not materialised. However, illegal bookmaking (bets can be placed in gold!) offers one form of competition to the government-owned monopoly.

The Saigon Racetrack is in District 11 at 2 Le Dai Hanh St.

Pham Ngu Lao St

And now for something different. Pham Ngu Lao St, the hotel and restaurant centre for budget travellers, has nothing of interest for Western tourists beyond satisfying basic needs such as eating, drinking, socialising and sleeping. But it's a different story for the Vietnamese – Pham Ngu Lao is where they go to 'look at the hippies'. Yes it's true – Western backpackers have become a tourist attraction, much like the hill tribes of the Central Highlands. If you hang out here, remember to smile for the camera when the tour buses roll by.

Activities

Language Courses If you'd like to speak Vietnamese, courses are readily available in Ho Chi Minh City. Universities require that you study 10 hours per week. Lessons usually last for two hours per day, for which you pay tuition of around US$5. The regional dialects between northern and southern Vietnam are very different, and most foreigners who want to study in the south would prefer to learn the southern dialect. But (get ready for this) the majority of the teachers at universities in the south have been imported from the north, and will tell you that the northern dialect is the 'correct one'! So even if you study at a university in the south, you may find that you need to hire a local private tutor (cheap at any rate) to help rid you of a northern accent. The vast majority of foreign language students enrol at the General University of Ho Chi Minh City (Truong Dai Hoc Tong Hop) at 12

Binh Hoang, District 5. It's near the south-west corner of Nguyen Van Cu and Tran Phu Blvds.

Organised Tours

There are surprisingly few day tours available of Ho Chi Minh City itself, though no doubt Saigon Tourist can come up with something in exchange for a hefty fee.

On the other hand, there are heaps of tours to the outlying areas of Cu Chi, Tay Ninh and the Mekong Delta. Some of the tours are day trips and other are overnighters. The cheapest tours by far are available from cafes and agencies in the Pham Ngu Lao area.

The box below includes a list of tours which can be readily booked in the Pham Ngu Lao area. Realise that the prices quoted here are rock bottom. The reason why these tours are so cheap is that you'll be staying in the grottiest hotels and food is not included. You can, of course, upgrade your hotel room to something more luxurious but this will require that you pay more.

several such soldiers who managed to scrape together enough money to buy fish and produce at the market. To keep their purchases fresh, they put them in the Western-style toilet, an appliance completely foreign to them. Then, out of curiosity, one of the soldiers flushed the toilet and the fish and vegetables disappeared. They were outraged by this perfidious imperialist booby trap and bitterly cursed those responsible. We can't swear that this incident actually took place (or that it happened only once), but we do know that a great deal of damage was done to Saigon's hotels after reunification and that bathroom fixtures were especially targeted. Some of this damage has only recently been repaired.

The current tourist boom has created a shortage of hotel space, but this situation is improving rapidly – it seems like a new hotel or mini-hotel opens every week. There is considerable renovation work going on – old grotty dumps are getting new plumbing, safer electrical wiring and a badly needed facelift. On the downside, all this

Destination	3-4 People	6-8 People	8-10 People	10-15 People
Cu Chi and Tay Ninh	US$30/car	US$6/person	US$6/person	US$5/person
Mekong (1 day)	US$27/car	US$6/person	US$6/person	US$5/person
Mekong (2 days)	US$40/person	US$25/person	US$24/person	US$21/person
Mekong (3 days)	US$50/person	US$35/person	US$32/person	US$30/person
Mekong (6 days)	US$300/car	US$50/person	US$50/person	US$45/person
Hué (10 days)	US$480/car	US$80/person	US$80/person	US$70/person

Places to Stay

The oldest of Ho Chi Minh City's hotels were built early in the century under the French, the newest in the early 1970s to accommodate US military officials, Western business people and war correspondents. Some of the latter seem to have learned most of what they knew about Vietnam over drinks at hotel bars.

When the city surrendered in 1975 North Vietnamese soldiers, fresh from years in the field after having grown up in the Spartan North, were billeted in the emptied high-rise hotels. There is an oft-told story about

renovation comes at a price – it's getting harder and harder to find rooms for under US$10.

The rumour that the bankrupt floating hotel from Australia's Great Barrier Reef would come to the Saigon River turned out to be true! Will Saigon's Holiday Inn be finished on schedule (or ever)? Keep your ear to the ground.

Different categories of travellers have staked out their own turf. Budget travellers tend to congregate around Pham Ngu Lao St on the western end of District 1. Travellers with a little more cash to spare prefer the

7 WAR CRIMES 8-1130 2-5
51 REV MUSEUM 8-1130 2-4.30

Central Saigon

0   150   300 m

Streets and labels:

Dien Bien Phu Street
Cach Mang Thang Tam Street
Ba Huyen Thanh Quan Street
Ngo Thoi Nhiem Street
Truong Dinh Street
Nguyen Dinh Chieu Street
Vuon Chuoi Street
Vo Van Tan Street
Nguyen Dinh Chieu Street
Vo Van Tan Street
Cao Thang Street
Nguyen Thi Minh Khai Street
Suong N. Anh Street
Nguyen Du Street
Bui Thi Xuan Street
Le Thi Rieng Street
Luong H Khanh Street
Ton That Tung Street
Nguyen Trai Street
Pham Viet Chanh Street
Cong Quynh Street
Le Lai Street
Nguyen Thai Hoc Street
Nguyen Trai Street
Pham Ngu Lao Street
Do Dau Street
Bui Vien Street
Tran Hung Dao Boulevard
De Tham Street
Tran Binh Xu Street
Nguyen Cu Trinh Street
Co Bac Street
Nguyen Khac Nhu Street
Co Giang Street
Ho Hao Hon
Nguyen Canh Chan Street
To Cholon

Cong Vien Van Hoa Park

11   US EMBASSY   SING AIR 6 LELOI
                                                  BLVD
14   PALACE 7.30-10 1-4

Market 88 · 89.

PLACES TO STAY

3	Saigon Star Hotel
4	Bao Yen Hotel
5	Sol Chancery Hotel
6	International Hotel
8	Victory Hotel
15	Rang Dong Hotel
18	Hoang Yen Mini-Hotel
20	My Man Mini-Hotel
21	Thai Binh Hotel
24	Metropole Hotel
25	Miss Loi's Guest House
27	Guest House 70 & 72
28	Vien Dong Hotel
29	Hoang Vu Hotel
33	Prince (Hoang Tu) Hotel
35	A Chau Hotel
36	Palace Saigon Hotel
37	New World Hotel
39	Hoang Gia Hotel
42	Tao Dan Hotel
43	Embassy Hotel
44	Tan Loc Hotel
50	Norfolk Hotel
55	Rex Hotel
58	Continental Hotel
61	Caravelle Hotel
65	Orchid Hotel
67	Hotel 69 Hai Ba Trung
70	Saigon Hotel & Vung Tau Bus Stop
73	Kimdo Hotel
74	Century Saigon Hotel
75	Palace Hotel
76	Bong Sen Hotel & Mondial Hotel
81	Saigon Floating Hotel
84	Riverside Hotel
85	Dong Khoi Hotel
87	Majestic Hotel
95	Champagne Hotel
98	Van Canh Hotel
100	Rose 2 Hotel
101	Thai Binh Duong Hotel
102	Phong Phu Hotel

PLACES TO EAT

9	Nha Hang
16	Annie's Pizza
30	Lotus Cafe & Saigon Cafe
31	Kim Cafe & Madras House
32	Zen Vegetarian Restaurant
49	Kem Bach Dang (ice cream parlour)
54	Kem Bach Dang (ice cream parlour)
60	Q Bar
62	Le P'tit Bistrot de Saigon
63	Tex Mex
64	Ashoka
66	Camargue
69	Hien & Bob's Place
71	Augustin
77	Vietnam House
78	Apocalypse Now
82	Floating Restaurants
99	Tin Nghia Vegetarian Restaurant

OTHER

1	Xa Loi Pagoda
2	Thich Quang Duc Memorial
7	War Crimes Museum
10	French Consulate
11	Former US Embassy (1967-1975)
12	GPO
13	Notre Dame Cathedral
14	Reunification Palace
17	Ann's Tourist
19	Thai Binh Market
22	Immigration Police Office
23	Travel Medical Consultancy
26	Getra Tour Company
34	Sacombank
38	Bicycle Shops
40	Bus Stop (to Cambodia)
41	Mariamman Hindu Temple
45	Ben Thanh Market
46	Tran Nguyen Hai Statue
47	Saigon Intershop & Minimart
48	Government Bookshop
51	Revolutionary Museum
52	Hotel de Ville (People's Committee)
53	Phnom Penh Bus Garage
56	Vietnam Airlines
57	Saigon Tourist
59	Municipal Theatre
68	Saigon Central Mosque
72	Tax Department Store
79	Ton Duc Thang Museum
80	Me Linh Square & Tran Hung Dao Statue
83	Small Motorised Boats for Hire
86	Hieu Sach Xuan Thu Book Store
88	Huynh Thuc Khang Street Market
89	The Old Market
90	Ferries across Saigon River & to Mekong Delta
91	Pre-1967 US Embassy
92	Uncle Ho's Museum for Momentos
93	Vietcombank
94	An Duong Vuong Statue
96	Art Museum
97	Ben Thanh Bus Station
103	Phung Son Tu Pagoda

more upmarket hotels concentrated around Dong Khoi St at the eastern side of District 1. French travellers seems to have an affinity for District 3. Cholon attracts plenty of Hong Kongers and Taiwanese, but Western backpackers are rare despite the availability of cheap accommodation here – it seems that the herd instinct is too powerful a force to be resisted.

By international standards, prices for hotels in Ho Chi Minh City are still very reasonable. However, it's not going to be as cheap as Bangkok or Bali. There are a few grungy rooms available for US$5, but most travellers can expect to spend at least US$10. The highest priced rooms are currently at the New World Hotel – how does US$850 a night grab you?

Not all hotels in the city are permitted to receive foreign guests, but those which can will always display a sign in English including the words 'hotel' or 'guesthouse'.

Places to Stay – bottom end

Touts from private hotels hang around the airport looking for business. If you haven't got a clear idea of where you want to stay, you can at least talk to them. Cyclo drivers just outside the airport can also find you accommodation to suit any budget.

District 1 (Central Saigon) Pham Ngu Lao, De Tham and Bui Vien Sts form half a rectangle which is the heart of the budget traveller haven. These streets and the adjoining alleys are bespeckled with a treasure trove of cheap accommodation and cafes catering to the low-end market. Unfortunately, a major construction project will begin soon to redevelop the northern side of Pham Ngu Lao St into a luxury tourist area. The construction is estimated to take about four years and will generate a considerable amount of dust and noise. It's our prediction that the budget hotels and restaurants will quickly retreat from Pham Ngu Lao St one block south to Bui Vien St near the intersection with De Tham St. Indeed, there are already signs of this happening.

At 193 Pham Ngu Lao St is the huge *Prince Hotel* (☎ 322657; 66 rooms), otherwise known as the *Khach San Hoang Tu* in Vietnamese. Rooms here range from US$6 to US$11. The cheaper rooms are on the upper floors because there is no lift.

Close by is the decidedly smaller but very pleasant *Hotel 211* (☎ 352353) at 211 Pham Ngu Lao St. Singles/doubles cost US$8/12 with fan, or US$12/16 with air-con.

The first place in this neighbourhood to offer dormitory accommodation was *Thanh Thanh 2 Hotel* (☎ 324027; fax 251550) at 205 Pham Ngu Lao St. Dorm beds start at US$3.50 and regular rooms cost up to US$9.

The *Vien Dong Hotel*, 275A Pham Ngu Lao St (☎ 393001; fax 332812; 139 rooms), has budget rooms on the top floor costing US$12. However, on the lower floors it's considerably pricier at US$32 to US$70. The hotel boasts several amenities, including a busy karaoke (expensive), Star TV and a popular disco patronised by well-off young Vietnamese.

Next door at No 265A is the mammoth *Hoang Vu Hotel* (☎ 396522; 161 rooms). It's long been extremely popular with backpackers; singles are US$6 to US$13 and twins US$10 to US$15. Sadly, the building is slated for a major renovation with a corresponding increase in prices. Hopefully, the upper floors will still be kept cheap as at the Vien Dong.

At 325 Pham Ngu Lao St is the *Thai Binh Hotel* (☎ 399544; 28 rooms), perhaps the lowest of low-end hotels belonging to Saigon Tourist. There's no air-con here, but rooms have attached bath and range from US$5 to US$7.

Just around the corner is *My Man Mini-Hotel* (☎ 396544; 10 rooms). Yes, the name is both English and Vietnamese. Rooms with fan are US$10 to US$14, and with air-con it's US$14 to US$18. The address is officially 373/20 Pham Ngu Lao St, but it's actually down a tiny alley just behind the Thai Binh Market.

Just one block to the north-west of the Thai Binh Market at 83A Bui Thi Xuan St is the *Hoang Yen Mini-Hotel* (☎ 391348; fax 298540; 10 rooms). The owner speaks French but not much English. Singles/twins are US$16 to US$21 and the tariff includes breakfast.

South of Pham Ngu Lao on Bui Vien St are two very clean and very safe private hotels, *Guest House 70* (☎ 330569; eight rooms) and *Guest House 72* (☎ 330321; four rooms). The first charges US$8 to US$14 (add US$2 for air-con), and the latter costs US$7 to US$10.

An alternative to the Pham Ngu Lao area is a string of wonderful guesthouses on an alley connecting Co Giang and Co Bac Sts. The first hotel to appear here and probably still the best is *Miss Loi's Guest House* (☎ 352973), 178/20 Co Giang St. Room prices average US$8 to US$10 for a double. Many of Miss Loi's neighbours are jumping into this business and the area seems destined to develop into another budget travellers' haven.

The *A Chau Hotel* (☎ 331814; 8 rooms) is at 92B Le Lai St, one block west of the five-star New World Hotel. Singles/twins with fan cost US$7/10, while air-con twins are US$15.

The *Rang Dong Hotel* (☎ 398264; fax 393318; 127 rooms) at 81 Cach Mang Thang Tam St is new and nice, and fairly reasonably priced for this standard. Room rates range from US$15 to US$45.

Hidden behind the plush Embassy Hotel is the much cheaper *Tao Dan Hotel* (☎ 230299; 94 rooms), 35A Nguyen Trung Truc St. Long a favourite with Japanese backpackers, it boasts a wide range of rooms costing from US$12 to US$16 with fan, and US$20 to US$24 with air-con. There's a pleasant coffee shop on the ground floor.

A lot of backpackers also choose the *Van Canh Hotel* (☎ 294963; 33 rooms) at 184 Calmette St. All rooms have air-conditioning, though the very cheapest rooms are shared bath only. By way of compensation, breakfast is thrown in free. Rates for singles are US$5 to US$13; twins are US$7 to US$15.

Hotel 69 Hai Ba Trung (☎ 291513; 18 rooms) is, as its name suggests, at 69 Hai Ba Trung St. This small, pleasant place is conveniently near the centre. The tariff here ranges from US$22 to US$30.

The *Dong Khoi Hotel* (☎ 294046, 230163; 34 rooms) is at 12 Ngo Duc Ke St (corner Dong Khoi St). This charming building is notable for its spacious suites with 4.5-metre-high ceilings and French windows. The hotel is currently undergoing its second renovation, and most likely the prices will rise at least as high as the chandeliers.

District 3 This district seems to attract a large number of French travellers. Possibly this is because of the local architecture. Whatever the reason, if you speak French you'll have a chance to practice it here.

On the north side of Cong Vien Van Hoa Park at 9 Truong Dinh St is the *Bao Yen Hotel* (☎ 299848; 12 rooms). Rooms are a very reasonable US$12 to US$14 and all have air-conditioning.

One place which gets the thumbs up from

French travellers is the *Guest House Loan* (☎ 445313; 30 rooms). This place is also known as the *No 3 Ly Chinh Thang Hotel*, which is also its address. Prices are US$18 to US$25 and all rooms have air-con and hot water.

District 5 (Cholon) The *Phuong Hoang Hotel* (☎ 551888; fax 552228; 70 rooms) is in an eight-storey building at 411 Tran Hung Dao B Blvd. Also known as the Phoenix Hotel, this place is just off Chau Van Liem Blvd in the middle of downtown Cholon. Rooms with fan/air-con cost US$12/25.

Just up Chau Van Liem Blvd at Nos 111-117 is the *Truong Thanh Hotel* (☎ 556044; 81 rooms). It's definitely a budget place. Rooms with fan are US$5 to US$6, while air-con costs a modest US$13.

Half a block away, at 125 Chau Van Liem Blvd, is the *Thu Do Hotel* (☎ 559102; 70 rooms). It looks very much like a dump, a distinction it shares with the neighbouring Truong Thanh Hotel. Rooms cost a modest US$6 to US$8.

Across the street from the Phuong Huong Hotel, the *Song Kim Hotel* (☎ 559773; 33 rooms) is at 84-86 Chau Van Liem Blvd. It's a grungy and somewhat disreputable establishment with twins for US$5 with fan or US$8 with air-con. Reception is up a flight of stairs. You can do better than this for marginally more money.

The *Trung Mai Hotel* (☎ 552101, 554067; 142 rooms) is a six-storey establishment at 785 Nguyen Trai St, just off Chau Van Liem Blvd. It's definitely a 'lower end' hotel but should be OK for the night. Singles/twins with fan cost US$5/6 while air-con rooms are US$10/11.

The *Tan Da Hotel* (☎ 555711) is at 17-19 Tan Da St very close to the upmarket Arc En Ciel Hotel. This place is rather tacky and not overly friendly. Rooms with fan/air-con cost US$16/21. With air-con and refrigerator it's US$27.

The *Hoa Binh Hotel* (☎ 355133; 35 rooms) is a seven-floor building at 1115 Tran Hung Dao Blvd. The building is moderately tattered around the edges but is otherwise

OK. Like most places in Cholon, most of the guests are from Taiwan, Hong Kong and Singapore. Doubles with fan/air-con cost US$7/15.

The *Bat Dat Hotel* (☎ 555817, 555843; 117 rooms) at 238-244 Tran Hung Dao B Blvd is near the more well known Arc En Ciel Hotel. This place was a well-known cheapie before, but it is currently under renovation. We'd be willing to bet that it won't be a cheapie when it reopens. It was once famous for it's Chinese restaurant and should be again – check it out.

Places to Stay – middle & top end

District 1 Close to the very upmarket New World Hotel is the much cheaper *Palace Saigon Hotel* (☎ 331353; 10 rooms) at No 82 Le Lai St. There are also 16 additional rooms at their annexe (☎ 359421) at 108 Le Lai St. It's a fine place and reasonably good value at US$25 to US$35 for an air-con double.

The *Saigon Hotel* (☎ 299734; fax 291466; 100 rooms) is at 47 Dong Du St, across the street from the Saigon Central Mosque. Prices are mid-range with singles/twins from US$36/44 to US$69/79. The deluxe rooms come equipped with satellite TV.

The *Kimdo Hotel* (☎ 225914; fax 225913) on Nguyen Hue Blvd is another new and fancy pleasure-dome brought to you by Saigon Tourist. Rates for singles are US$119 to US$449, while twins cost US$134 to US$479, to which you must add a 10% tax. It's fair to say you get what you pay for at this place.

The *Thai Binh Duong Hotel* (☎ 322674) at 92 and 107 Ky Con St is a good middle-priced place with air-con rooms from US$20 to US$25. On the same street at No 105 is the *Phong Phu Hotel* (☎ 222020; fax 222020; 10 rooms), which costs US$25 to US$35.

Nearby at 141 Nguyen Thai Binh St is the *Rose 2 Hotel* (☎ 231573; fax 210070; 12 rooms). As their brochure says, the hotels has 'all comfortable and modern equipments'. All rooms have air-conditioning and cost US$25.

The *Champagne Hotel* (☎ 224922; fax 230776; 38 rooms), 129-133 Ham Nghi Blvd, is also known as the Que Huong Hotel. Singles are US$38 to US$48 and twins go for US$35 to US$45. If you stay three or more nights, you can get a 10% discount. There is a restaurant on the ground floor.

The *Orchid Hotel* (☎ 231809; fax 231811) is a relatively small place at 29A Don Dat St. The hotel has its own restaurant, coffee shop and karaoke lounge. Room prices start at US$40.

The *Bong Sen Hotel* (☎ 291516; fax 299744; 134 rooms) is affectionately called 'the BS' by travellers. It's at 117-119 Dong Khoi St and offers air-con singles/twins for US$27/36 to US$190, plus 10% surcharge. Formerly called the Miramar Hotel, the Bong Sen is also signposted as the Lotus Hotel, which is a translation of its Vietnamese name. There is a restaurant on the 8th floor.

The *Huong Sen Hotel* (☎ 291415; fax 290916; 50 rooms) is at 70 Dong Khoi St. Once known as the Astor Hotel, it's now an annexe of the nearby Bong Sen Hotel. This place charges US$35/50 to US$90 (plus 10% service) for singles/twins. The in-house restaurant is on the 6th floor.

The *Hoang Gia Hotel* (☎ 294846; fax 225346; 42 rooms) is at 12D Cach Mang Thang Tam St, just near the traffic circle. Recently refurbished, singles/twins go for US$30/35 and there are a few deluxe rooms for US$45. Breakfast is thrown in free and the hotel has a respectable restaurant.

The *Embassy Hotel* (☎ 291430; fax 295019) is a medium-sized place at 35 Nguyen Trung Truc St, not far from Reunification Palace. The hotel has its own restaurant, karaoke bar, live music in the evening and superb air-conditioning. Double rooms go for US$60 to US$100.

The classiest hotel in the city is unquestionably the venerable *Continental Hotel* (☎ 299201; fax 290936; 87 rooms), setting for much of the action in Graham Greene's novel *The Quiet American*. Situated just across the street from the Municipal Theatre at 132-134 Dong Khoi St, the hotel dates from the turn of the century and in the late '80s underwent a US$2.6 million renovation. The Continental, now run by Saigon Tourist, charges US$85 to US$170 for singles and US$105 to US$190 for twins (including breakfast and fruit). During the war, journalists used to sit on the terrace, known as the 'Continental Shelf', and sip beers, but it is now closed.

Another classic hotel in town is the *Rex Hotel* (Khach San Ben Thanh; ☎ 292185; fax 291469; 207 rooms). Its ambience of mellowed kitsch dates from the time it served as a hotel for US military officers. The Rex is at 141 Nguyen Hue Blvd (corner Le Loi Blvd). Singles cost from US$80 to US$760; twins are priced between US$90 and US$880. The Rex has, among other amenities, a large gift shop, tailor, unisex beauty parlour, photocopy machines, a postal counter with fax and telex services, massage service, acupuncture, a swimming pool on the 6th floor, an excellent restaurant on the 5th floor, a coffee shop on the ground floor and a beautiful view from the large 5th-floor veranda, which is decorated with caged birds and potted bushes shaped like animals. Reservations are advised. At the end of the day, the Rex is a great place to enjoy a sunset beer. But it won't come cheap. Expect to pay something like US$3.50.

The five-star *Saigon Floating Hotel* (☎ 290783; fax 290784; 201 rooms) was towed to the Saigon River from Australia's Great Barrier Reef (where it had gone spectacularly bankrupt) in 1989. Amenities offered by the Saigon Floating Hotel, which is moored at 1A Me Linh Square (on Ton Duc Thang St near the Tran Hung Dao Statue), include two restaurants, saunas, a gym, a tennis court, a swimming pool, meeting rooms, audio-visual equipment, satellite TV and a business centre with personal computers. Rooms are small but the price isn't; rates are between US$130 and US$425, plus 15% tax.

Another old favourite is the *Caravelle Hotel* (Khach San Doc Lap; ☎ 293704; fax 299902; 112 rooms) at 19-23 Lam Son Square (across the street from the Municipal

Theatre). Once owned by the Catholic Diocese of Saigon, the Caravelle is Saigon's most-French hotel, and this heritage is alive and well in the rude reception English-speakers may encounter (and in the form of the Air France office on the ground floor). Singles/twins with air-con cost from US$51/63 to US$180, but if it helps they throw in a free breakfast and basket of fruit. The hotel features two restaurants, a dance hall, massage services and a sauna.

The *Majestic Hotel* (Khach San Cuu Long; ☎ 295515; fax 291470; 115 rooms) is located along the Saigon River at 1 Dong Khoi St. It was once the city's most elegant and prestigious hotel. Singles/twins with breakfast range from US$35/47 to US$120/140, and Visa, MasterCard and JCB cards are accepted. Postal and telecommunications services are available in the lobby. There are restaurants on the street level and the 5th floor.

The *Palace Hotel* (Khach San Huu Nghi; ☎ 292860; fax 299872; 130 rooms) is at 56-64 Nguyen Hue Blvd. This hotel, whose Vietnamese name means 'friendship', offers superb views from the 14th-floor restaurant and 15th-floor terrace. Singles/twins cost from US$40/55 to US$120/140 with breakfast and tax included. The Palace has an imported-food shop, a dance hall, the Bamboo Bar and a small swimming pool on the 16th floor.

The *New World Hotel* (☎ 228888; fax 243694) is a five-star luxury tower at 76 Le Lai St. This Hong Kong joint venture is perhaps the most upmarket hotel in Vietnam. The clientele tends to be mainly Chinese-speaking tour groups from Hong Kong and Taiwan, but all with hard currency are welcome. Single/twin rooms start at US$175/185, while a presidential suite goes for a cool US$850. If it helps, they accept credit cards.

The *Norfolk Hotel* (☎ 295368; fax 293415) is at 117 Le Thanh Ton St. All rooms in this Australian joint-venture hotel boast satellite TV and a minibar. Singles/twins cost US$75/90 to US$150/165, plus 15% tax. The price includes breakfast.

Not far away is the *Tan Loc Hotel* (☎ 230028; fax 298360), 177 Le Thanh Ton St. This new place offers singles/twins for US$45/58 to US$86/100, plus 10% service charge. Visa and MasterCard are accepted.

The *Century Saigon Hotel* (☎ 230542; fax 292732; 109 rooms), 68A Nguyen Hue Blvd, is a Hong Kong joint venture. Rooms go for US$115 to US$200 plus 10% tax. You can book rooms from Century International offices abroad: Hong Kong (☎ 2598-8888); Australia (☎ (008) 021211 or (02) 261 5334); and USA (☎ (808) 955-9718).

The *Riverside Hotel* (☎ 224038; fax 251417; 75 rooms) is at 18 Ton Duc Thang St, very close to the Saigon Floating Hotel. This old colonial building has been renovated and now features a good restaurant and bar. Singles/twins cost US$45/60 to US$200/230 plus 15% tax.

The *Mondial Hotel* (☎ 296291; fax 296324) is at 109 Dong Khoi St, adjacent to the Bong Sen Hotel. Singles/twins range from US$56/86 to US$101/117.

Yet another new luxury hotel is the *Metropole Hotel* (☎ 322021; fax 322019; 94 rooms) at 148 Tran Hung Dao Blvd. Single/double rooms are US$86/95 to US$119/128. Suites are US$149. Long-term guests (a few days) can negotiate discounts.

District 3 Just behind the Lao Consulate is the *Huong Tram Hotel* (☎ 296086; fax 298540; 10 rooms) at 24/9 Pham Ngoc Thach St. This place is often filled with French travellers. Singles are US$30 and twins are US$43 to US$53. Breakfast is included in the tariff.

The *Que Huong Hotel* (☎ 294227; fax 290919; 48 rooms) – also known as the Liberty Hotel – is two blocks from the French Consulate at 167 Hai Ba Trung St. Singles/twins are priced from US$20/30 to US$30/40.

The *Victory Hotel* (☎ 294989; fax 299604), 14 Vo Van Tan St (one block north of Reunification Palace), is a brand-new place. Rates are from US$26 to US$50.

The *Saigon Star Hotel* (☎ 230260; fax 230255), 204 Nguyen Thi Minh Khai St, is

modern and luxurious. The hotel features the Venus Disco from 8 pm until 1 am, plus the Terrace Coffee Shop, a restaurant, a business centre and satellite TV. Room rates are US$89 to US$180, plus 15% tax and service charge.

On the road to the airport is the *Saigon Lodge Hotel* (☎ 230112; fax 251070), 215 Nam Ky Khoi Nghia St. This place boasts all the usual hotel amenities, plus satellite TV and halal Muslim food. Singles/twins are US$77/121 to US$88/143, or you can rent the 'penthouse' for US$300.

The *International Hotel* (☎ 290009; fax 290066), 19 Vo Van Tan St, District 3, is one of the newest in town. The standard is royal plush, and so are the prices: US$85 to US$165, plus 15% tax.

Another recent addition to the upmarket accommodation scene is *Sol Chancery Hotel* (☎ 299152; fax 251464) at 196 Nguyen Thi Minh Khai St. Rooms cost approximately US$110.

Tan Binh & Phu Nhuan Districts (Airport Area) The *Tan Son Nhat Hotel* (☎ 441039; fax 441324; 25 rooms) at 200 Hoang Van Thu Blvd has some truly stunning rooms. This place was built as a guesthouse for top South Vietnamese government officials. In 1975, the North Vietnamese army inherited it along with the nearby headquarters of the South Vietnamese army. Recently, the entrepreneurial spirit sweeping the south has infected even the army, which, hoping to earn some extra cash, renovated this place for use as a hotel. A ground-floor room used by South Vietnamese Prime Minister Tran Thien Khiem has been preserved exactly as it was in 1975, plastic fruit and all. There is a small swimming pool out the back. Room rates are relatively moderate at US$25 to US$50.

Almost within walking distance of the airport is the *Mekong Hotel* (☎ 441024; fax 444809), 261 Hoang Van Thu St. Singles/twins in this opulent place are US$35/40, while suites will set you back US$45. It's certainly one of the better deals near the airport.

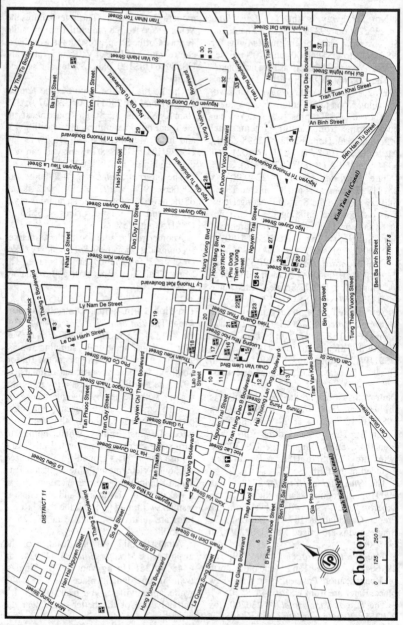

Cholon

DISTRICT 5

DISTRICT 8

DISTRICT 11

0   125   250 m

PLACES TO STAY

3	Phu Tho Hotel
4	Goldstar Hotel
10	Thu Do Hotel
11	Truong Thanh Hotel
12	Phuong Huang (Phoenix) Hotel
14	Song Kim Hotel
15	Trung Mai Hotel
25	Arc En Ciel (Rainbow) Hotel
26	Tan Da Hotel & Van Hoa Hotel
27	Bat Dat Hotel
29	Trung Uong Hotel
30	Cholon Hotel
31	Cholon Tourist Mini-Hotel
32	Caesar Hotel & Andong Market
33	Andong Hotel
34	Dong Khanh Hotel & Superstore
35	Hoa Binh Hotel
36	Tokyo Hotel
37	Hanh Long Hotel

OTHER

1	Phung Son Pagoda
2	Khanh Van Nam Vien Pagoda
5	An Quang Pagoda
6	Binh Tay Market
7	Cholon Bus Station
8	Cha Tam Church
9	Ong Bon Pagoda
13	Post Office
16	Ha Chuong Hoi Quan Pagoda
17	Quan Am Pagoda
18	Phuoc An Hoi Quan Pagoda
19	Cho Ray Hospital
20	Electronics Market
21	Thien Hau Pagoda
22	Nghia An Hoi Quan Pagoda
23	Tam Son Hoi Quan Pagoda
24	Cholon Mosque
28	Nha Sau Church

The *Omni Hotel* (☎ 449222; fax 449200; 248 rooms), 251 Nguyen Van Troi St, is perhaps the most posh accommodation in Ho Chi Minh City. This place has it all, everything from in-room safes to a florist and health club. The price for all this comfort is US$180 to US$300 per night.

The *Chains First Hotel* (☎ 441199; fax 444282; 132 rooms), 18 Hoang Viet St, boasts a coffee shop, gift shop, tennis courts, a sauna, massage services, three restaurants, a swimming pool, a business centre and free airport shuttle service. Singles/twins cost US$65/75 to US$125, plus 10% surcharge. The management throws in breakfast and a basket of fruit.

Just opposite the Chains First Hotel is the *De Nhat Hotel*, where room rates are US$35 to US$70. From the look of things, it's not worth it.

And right behind Chains First Hotel at 14 Hoang Viet is the considerably cheaper *Star Hill Hotel* (☎ 443625), which has air-conditioned twins for US$33 to US$44.

District 5 (Cholon) The *Arc En Ciel Hotel* (Khach San Thien Hong; ☎ 554435; fax 550332; 91 rooms) is also known as the Rainbow Hotel. A prime venue for tour groups from Hong Kong and Taiwan, it boasts everything a tour group would need, including the Volvo Disco Karaoke. Single/double rooms cost from US$44/55 to

US$55/66. Suites cost US$88. The hotel is at 52-56 Tan Da St (corner Tran Hung Dao B Blvd).

A near neighbour to the Arc En Ciel is the *Van Hoa Hotel* (☎ 554182; fax 563118), 36 Tan Da St. It looks like a good place and is priced at US$30 to US$45.

The *Hanh Long Hotel* (☎ 350251; fax 350742), 1027 Tran Hung Dao Blvd, is a new place. The name means 'happy dragon', but despite this and the location in Chinatown, the staff don't speak Chinese. Room prices range from US$50 to US$105.

The five-storey *Dong Khanh Hotel* (☎ 352410; 81 rooms) is the pride and joy of Saigon Tourist. At one time a budget hotel, it's been fully renovated into a spiffy pleasure palace. Even if you don't stay here, check out the supermarket next door. The hotel is at 2 Tran Hung Dao B Blvd. Singles/doubles cost from US$55/69 to US$129/157.

The five-storey *Tokyo Hotel* (Khach San Dong Kinh; ☎ 357558; fax 352505; 96 rooms), 106-108 Tran Tuan Khai St, has all the modern conveniences at nice prices plus friendly staff. Double rooms with air-con, telephone and refrigerator cost US$20 to US$41. The hotel boasts a gift shop, restaurant, dance hall and karaoke bar.

The *Regent Hotel* (☎ 353548; fax 357094), 700 Tran Hung Dao Blvd (see the Ho Chi Minh City map), is also called the

Hotel 700. The Regent is a joint venture between Vietnam Union and three Thai companies, and facilities are excellent. The price range here is US$40 to US$68.

The *Cholon Hotel* (☎ 357058; fax 355375; 24 rooms) at 170-174 Su Van Hanh St is superb value and popular with Taiwanese travellers. The desk clerks speak both English and Chinese, not to mention Vietnamese. Squeaky-clean singles/twins cost US$22/32 with breakfast part of the package deal.

Right next door is the privately owned *Cholon Tourist Mini-Hotel* (☎ 357100; fax 355375; 11 rooms) at 192-194 Su Van Hanh St. Like its neighbour, the hotel is of a high standard and caters to Taiwanese (but accepts anybody). Single/twin rooms cost US$22/28.

The *Trung Uong Hotel* (☎ 357952; fax 353432) at 200 Nguyen Tri Phuong Blvd is also known as the *Central Hotel*. It's often packed with Hong Kongers and Taiwanese. Rates for singles/doubles are US$28/42 to US$36/50.

The *Andong Hotel* (☎ 352001; 45 rooms) is at 9 An Duong Vuong Blvd right at the intersection with Tran Phu Blvd. It's a relatively new place and all rooms feature hot water, telephone, air-con and refrigerator. Doubles cost US$30 to US$38.

Right inside Andong Market is the *Caesar Hotel* (☎ 350677; fax 350106), a slick Taiwanese joint-venture operation. The official address is 34-36 An Puong Vuong St, District 5, but just ask taxis or cyclos to bring you to the market. The price range here is a breathtaking US$80 to US$150, plus 10% tax.

District 10 (North-West Area) The *Ky Hoa Hotel* (☎ 655036), 12-14 Ba Thang Hai St, is next to the amusement park by the same name. It's rather remote from the centre, but convenient if you like ferris wheels. Rooms in Building A go for US$70 to US$90. Cheaper accommodation in Building B costs from US$45 to US$60.

District 11 (West Area) About one km north of central Cholon is the *Phu Tho Hotel*

(☎ 551309; fax 551255) at 527 3 Thang 2 Blvd (see the Cholon map). The price range here is US$40 to US$50, with breakfast thrown in. There is a huge restaurant on the lowest three floors with built-in karaoke facilities.

The *Goldstar Hotel* (☎ 551646; fax 551644), 174-176 Le Dai Hanh St, is a spotlessly clean place where singles/doubles are US$30/40. All rooms have private bath, refrigerator and air-con, and the upper floors give a good view of the racetrack.

Places to Eat

Both Vietnamese and Western food are widely available in Ho Chi Minh City, and English menus are becoming more common. Central Saigon is the place to look for fine Western and Vietnamese food. Cholon's speciality is Chinese food.

Food Stalls Noodle soup is available all day long at street stalls and hole-in-the-wall shops everywhere. A large bowl of delicious beef noodles costs US$0.50 to US$1. Just look for the signs that say 'Pho'.

Sandwiches with a French look and a very Vietnamese taste are sold by street vendors. Fresh French baguettes are stuffed with something resembling pâté (don't ask) and cucumbers and seasoned with soy sauce. A sandwich costs between US$0.50 and US$1, depending on what is in it and whether you

A food vendor in Cholon

get overcharged. Sandwiches filled with imported French soft cheese cost a little more.

Markets always have a side selection of food items, often in the ground floor or basement. Clusters of food stalls can be found in the Thai Binh Market, Ben Thanh Market and Andong Market.

The best noodle soup that I had was in the Ben Thanh Market itself. The food stalls inside the market were clean, the food fresh and the soup very tasty. It's also a fun place to eat because you quickly become the centre of attention.

John Lumley-Holmes

Pham Ngu Lao & De Tham Pham Ngu Lao and De Tham Sts form the axis of Saigon's budget eatery haven. Western backpackers easily outnumber the Vietnamese here, and indeed the locals have trouble figuring out the menus ('banana muesli' does not translate well into Vietnamese).

A major construction project which is about to take place as we go to press will probably have a severe negative impact on Pham Ngu Lao's restaurants. It's our prediction that most of these places will move south to De Tham or Buu Vien Sts, but that remains to be seen.

A long-running hang-out for budget travellers is *Kim Café* (☎ 359859), 272 De Tham St. This is a very good place to meet people, arrange tours and get travel information.

Madras House (☎ 398122) at 268 De Tham St is right next to Kim Café. This place serves fine Indian vegetarian and non-vegetarian dishes. Highly recommended.

The *Lotus Café* at 197 Pham Ngu Lao St is possibly the best in the neighbourhood now. The friendly couple who run it prepare excellent Vietnamese and Western food at low prices.

The *Saigon Café* at 195 Pham Ngu Lao St (at the corner with De Tham St) is also worthy of a plug.

Sawadee at 252 De Tham St does excellent Thai food.

My Thanh Restaurant (☎ 357580) at 40 Bui Vien St is just around the corner from De Tham St. This place does splendid Chinese

food. You can eat at their outdoor tables or go upstairs, where there are air-conditioned rooms.

Dong Khoi St The *Givral Restaurant* (☎ 242750) at 169 Dong Khoi St (across the street from the Continental Hotel) has an excellent selection of cakes, home-made ice cream and yoghurt. This Japanese joint venture also does Kotobuki-style pastries. Aside from the junk food, there's French, Chinese, Vietnamese and Russian cuisine on the menu.

The *Liberty Restaurant* (☎ 299820), 80 Dong Khoi St, is a joint venture with Ben Thanh Tourist (Saigon District 1 government). Despite its government connections, it's a superb place (Saigon Tourist eat your heart out). It has a small but cheap and excellent Vietnamese menu, plus expensive Chinese and Western food. There is live music upstairs in the evening by a Vietnamese band. This place is also known as the *Tu Do Restaurant*.

The *Brodard Café* (☎ 223966), also known as *Nha Hang Dong Khoi*, is an oldie but goodie. Despite ongoing renovations, the decor is still vintage 1960s. This place is known for French food and prices are OK. Brodard is at 131 Dong Khoi St (corner Nguyen Thiep St).

The *Lemon Grass Restaurant* (☎ 298006) at 63 Dong Khoi St is a personal favourite, *the* place for power dining. You'd be hard-pressed to find anything bad on the menu, so if you can't decide what to order just pick something at random. The cuisine is mostly Vietnamese. Two women in traditional clothing play musical instruments and serenade you while you eat.

Homesick Korean travellers looking for a little *kimchi* and camaraderie come to the *Korean Food Restaurant* (☎ 223166) at 213B Dong Khoi St. The other competitor in this market is the *Seoul Restaurant* at 34 Ngo Duc Ke St, District 1.

Maxim's Dinner Theatre (☎ 296676) at 15 Dong Khoi St (next to the Majestic Hotel) is very much what the name implies; a restaurant with live musical performances. The menu includes Chinese and French food. If you look Western they give you the French menu, but ask for the Chinese menu, which is cheaper and more interesting. The sea slug and duck web has disappointed a few travellers, but the creme caramel, vanilla souffle and elderly waiter struggling to read the menu under dim light should not be missed. There is a very dark nightclub upstairs (free entry) with a live band playing '60s tunes. Maxim's is open from 11 am to 11 pm, but expect it to be empty until around dinnertime. Reservations are recommended on weekends and the place is sometimes closed due to wedding receptions. You can pay in dong or by credit card.

Gardenstadt (☎ 223623) at 34 Dong Khoi St is run by a German woman and a Swiss cook who dish up non-Vietnamese delicacies such as Pils vom Fass and Nürnberger Bratwürste. The food is excellent – figure on US$5 or more for a complete meal.

Vietnam House (☎ 291623), 93-95 Dong Khoi St, is on the corner of Mac Thi Buoi St. It's possibly the nicest combined bar and restaurant in Saigon. The cuisine is Vietnamese-style, and a standard dinner or lunch is US$8. But watch what you order, because it could easily be double that if you're not careful. In the 2nd-floor dining room, a traditional four-piece Vietnamese ensemble plays for dinner starting at 7.30 pm. The best part is the bar and lounge on the 1st floor. There is a young female pianist playing here from 5.30 pm until late at night. It's air-conditioned, and beer costs US$1.50 and is served up in a frozen glass with peanuts and shrimp crackers. The restaurant is open from 10 am until midnight.

The *Paloma Café* (☎ 295813) at 26 Dong Khoi St is a stylish place with wooden tables, white tablecloths, polished silverware, aggressive air-conditioning and waiters who need to be tipped. Judging from the crowd that packs in every night, they must be doing something right. This place stays open until nearly midnight.

Nha Hang Tan Nam (☎ 223407), 59-61 Dong Khoi St, is on the south side of the Lemon Grass Restaurant. This very up-market establishment boasts a fine garden restaurant in the rear courtyard. The bar is up front near the door. If you like to eat in plush surroundings, it would be hard to do better.

Augustin at 10 Nguyen Thiep St, just off Dong Khoi St, is a small, good-quality French bistro. There are all the traditional favourites, from onion soup on. Entrées range from US$2.50 to US$4, main courses from US$3.50 to US$7 (for the top-end seafood dishes).

Other Areas *Restaurant A, The Russian Restaurant* (☎ 359190) is the only place in Saigon that dishes up borscht and blintzes. The food is so good here that it's hard to believe it can be so bad in Moscow. The owner is a Russian-Vietnamese woman and the cook really is from Russia. You can find this unique restaurant at 361/8 Nguyen Dinh Chieu St, District 3. Prices are mid-range.

Annie's Pizza (☎ 392577) at 59 Cach Mang Thang Tam St, not far from the New World Hotel and a few blocks north of Pham Ngu Lao St, is renowned for its Aussie cuisine: the best pizza in town (with thin crust); toasted ham, cheese and tomato sandwiches; and genuine imported Four & Twenty pies you can have with mashed potato, peas and gravy (if you really must!). They'll also do home deliveries.

Down a side street just opposite the French Consulate, *Nha Hang* (☎ 225909), 11 Nguyen Vai Chien St, is renowned for its seafood. There's a pleasant outdoor eating area, and although it all looks a little frayed around the edges, it's moderately priced and attracts a large, mixed crowd of mobile phone-toting expats and local business people.

Not too much farther out, although it's a fair hike for a cyclo, especially if you start at Pham Ngu Lao St, *L'Etoile,* 180 Hai Ba Trung St (☎ 297939), is considered by many to have the best French cuisine in Vietnam. As usual, the best doesn't come cheap, and you could well end up paying up to US$30 per person – a large fortune in Vietnamese terms.

A new eating precinct is quickly developing to the east of Hai Ba Trung St, particularly along Le Thanh Ton and Thi Sach Sts. Patronised by locals, tourists and expats, the area is quieter and considerably more laid back than bright and bustling Dong Khoi St. There are a number of open air cafes along Thi Sach St that are crowded with Vietnamese family groups; and on Le Thanh Ton St there are some moderately priced restaurants (by Western standards) representing world cuisine from French to Indian and Mexican.

Ashoka (☎ 231372), 17A Le Thanh Ton St, is a remarkably good quality, genuine Indian restaurant with a tandoori oven. Although there are few apparent links between Indian and Vietnamese cooking, the Vietnamese waitresses look quite at home in the traditional Indian *kameez*, which isn't all that different from the ao dai. They serve all the standard dishes, and there are a good number of vegetarian selections. Expect to pay around US$10 per person.

Le P'tit Bistrot de Saigon (☎ 230219), 58 Le Thanh Ton St, is so French it's almost a dislocating experience to step through the door. The excellent food will not disappoint. Expect to pay from US$10 to US$15 per person depending on how much you drink.

Once again, it can be difficult to recall you're in Saigon once you've stepped through the doors of *Tex Mex* (☎ 295950) at 24 Le Thanh Ton St. There's everything you'd expect, including a relaxed atmosphere, a band, a pool table and chilli con carne.

On the corner of Cao Ba Quat (the eastern continuation of Le Loi Blvd, past the Municipal Theatre) and Thi Sach St, *Camargue* (☎ 243148) is in a restored villa and has an attractive open-air terrace. Favoured by well-off business people, it's an attractive, atmospheric spot with good-quality food. The menu has a variety of Western-style dishes. It's at the expensive end of the spectrum, and you could easily spend US$15 to US$20.

Floating Restaurants 'Never trust a restaurant that moves' is an old adage that you should consider breaking in Saigon. At the southern end of Dong Khoi St, at Bach Dang Quay, there are a number of large floating restaurants that provide an entertaining start to an evening. They make a short excursion up the Saigon River through the port area, and are surprisingly reasonable in price – you only pay for what you eat.

They're mostly patronised by Vietnamese family groups, and the most testing aspect of the experience is the music. The *Saigon* and *Ben Nghe* both have three decks and *two* loud, competing bands. The *Siren* (nearest the Saigon Floating Hotel) is less flashy, makes do with canned music at an acceptable volume and is used to Westerners. It's always cheaper to eat in a group sharing a number of dishes, but even by yourself you won't spend more than about US$12. The boats all leave around 8 pm and return by 9.30 pm, so you're not trapped for too long if you're not enjoying yourself.

Probably the most spectacular stretch of river, however, is the section where the boats actually tie up, where the river is bathed in neon light from huge signs towering above the shanties on the east side of the river. Nowhere is the brave new world of commercialism proclaimed more brashly. The Hammock Bar (see the Pubs section) is a good spot to catch the riverside breeze and reflect on the beauties of capitalism.

Vegetarian The ethnic-Vietnamese owners of the *Tin Nghia Vegetarian Restaurant* are strict Buddhists. This small, simple little establishment, which is about 200 metres from Ben Thanh Market at 9 Tran Hung Dao Blvd, serves an assortment of delicious traditional Vietnamese foods prepared without meat, chicken, fish or egg. Instead, tofu, mushrooms and vegetables are used. It is open from 7 am to 8 pm daily, but closes between 2 and 4 pm so the staff can take a rest. The prices here are incredibly cheap.

In Cholon, *Tiem Com Chay Thien Phat Duyen* is a small Chinese vegetarian restaurant about one km east of Chau Van Liem Blvd at 509 Nguyen Trai St. There are two Chinese vegetarian places, both called *Phat*

Huu Duyen, at 513 Nguyen Trai St and 116 Nguyen Tri Phuong St. *Tiem Com Chay Phat Huu Duyen*, also Chinese, is at 952 Tran Hung Dao Blvd (corner An Binh St, where Tran Hung Dao B Blvd begins); it is open from 7 am to 10 pm but is very expensive (by Vietnamese standards). Across An Binh St at 3 Tran Hung Dao B Blvd is another Chinese place, *Tiem Com Chay Van Phat Duyen*, which is open from 7 am to 9 pm. You can also check out the vegetarian restaurants at 45 Tran Hung Dao B Blvd and 523 Nguyen Trai St.

On the first and 15th days of the lunar month, food stalls around the city – especially in the markets – serve vegetarian versions of non-vegetarian Vietnamese dishes.

In the Pham Ngu Lao area, just off the main drag down a small side street (it's clearly signposted), is the *Zen Vegetarian Restaurant*. It's away from the traffic and has an excellent, good-value menu. There's a wide range of Vietnamese dishes (clearly described in English on the menu) as well as European standards and delicious fruit juices. It's a simple, friendly place and you can eat well for a dollar or two. The address is 175 Pham Ngu Lao St.

Exotica You can get your fill of snake, turtles, deer antlers and other exotic dishes at *Tri Ky Restaurant*, 82 Tran Huy Lieu St, Phu Nhuan District. Tran Huy Lieu St runs between Hoang Van Thu Blvd and Nguyen Van Troi St, the two major roads leading to Tan Son Nhat Airport.

Fried silkworms, fish spawn and other delectable treats are on the menu at a little restaurant at 79 Nguyen Dinh Chieu St, District 3.

Ice Cream The best ice cream (kem) in Ho Chi Minh City is served at the two shops called *Kem Bach Dang* (☎ 292707), which are on Le Loi Blvd on either side of Nguyen Thi Minh Khai St. Kem Bach Dang 1 is at 26 Le Loi Blvd and the other is at No 28. Both are under the same management and serve ice cream, hot and cold drinks and cakes for

very reasonable prices. A US$1.50 speciality is ice cream served in a baby coconut with candied fruit on top (kem trai dua).

Self-Catering Simple meals can easily be assembled from fruits, vegetables, French bread, croissants, cheese and other delectables sold in the city's markets and from street stalls. But avoid the unrefrigerated chocolate bars sold by street vendors – they taste like they were left behind by the Americans when they departed in 1975. Apparently, the chocolate gets repeatedly melted by the midday sun, rehardens at night and quickly becomes a ball of rancid mush.

The best bakery outside of Cholon is, according to many Saigonese, *Nhu Lan Bakery* at 66 Ham Nghi Blvd. You can buy oven-fresh bread here from morning till night.

Find yourself daydreaming about Kellogg's Frosties, Pringle's potato chips, Twinings tea or Campbell's soup? If you have an insatiable craving for plastic food, by far the best place to go in Ho Chi Minh City is the *Minimart* (☎ 298189, ext 44) on the 2nd floor of the Saigon Intershop, which is at 101 Nam Ky Khoi Nghia St (just off Le Loi Blvd). If this ultimate symbol of Western capitalism looks like it was transported lock, stock and barrel from Singapore, that's because it was. Considering that the cornucopia of goods are mostly imported, prices are amazingly reasonable. The Minimart is open from 9 am to 6 pm daily.

Besides the Minimart, there are several other options, though none quite as good. One is the supermarket next to the Saigon Hotel (opposite the mosque) at 35 Dong Du St. There is also a new supermarket at 41 Hai Ba Trung St, District 1. The government-owned *Agrimexco Supermarket* is at 85 Dong Khoi St, District 1.

There are at least two places in Saigon calling themselves *7 Eleven*, both of which are imposters. The better of the two is at 16 Nguyen Hue Blvd and carries imported foods (no Slurpies though). There is a real popcorn machine here, possibly the first in Vietnam.

The *Superstore* (☎ 357176) at 10-20 Tran Hung Dao Blvd, District 5, is in reality a small supermarket. It's just next to the Dong Khanh Hotel in Cholon. You can pick up all manner of goods here from frozen yoghurt to cheese puffs and peanut butter.

Le Chalet Suisse (☎ 293856) at 211A Dong Khoi St, District 1, is a small Swiss meat market on the ground floor. The bar and restaurant are upstairs.

The *Gourmet Shop* at the Omni Hotel, 251 Nguyen Van Troi St, Phu Nhuan District, is a treasure trove of rare items like cranberry sauce, French cheese, Sri Lankan tea and frozen cherry cheesecake.

Entertainment

Wartime Saigon was always known for its riotous nightlife. Liberation in 1975 put a real damper on evening activities, but the pubs and discos have recently staged a comeback. However, periodic 'crack-down clean-up' campaigns – allegedly to control drugs, prostitution and excessive noise – continue to keep Ho Chi Minh City's nightlife on the decidedly quiet side. Regulations introduced in 1995 require pubs and nightclubs to close by midnight. This doesn't mean that you need to retire to your hotel room by 9 pm for an evening of STAR TV, but if all-night revelry is what you need, consider a visit to Bangkok, Manila or Hong Kong.

Sunday Night Live Downtown Saigon is *the* place to be on Sunday and holiday nights. The streets are jam-packed with young Saigonese, in couples and groups, cruising the town on bicycles and motorbikes, out to see and be seen. The mass of slowly moving humanity is so thick on Dong Khoi St that you may have to wait until dawn to get across the street. It is utter chaos at intersections, where eight, 10 or more lanes of two-wheeled vehicles intersect without the benefit of traffic lights, safety helmets or sanity.

Near the Municipal Theatre, fashionably dressed young people take a break from cruising around to watch the endless proces-

sion, lining up along the street next to their cycles. The air is electric with the glances of lovers and animated conversations among friends. It is a sight not to be missed.

Pubs In the Pham Ngu Lao St area is the *Easy Rider Pub* (☎ 359338) at 193 Nguyen Thai Hoc St. This place opens at 11 am. Aside from the drinks, the house cuisine is American and French.

Not far away is *Bar Rolling Stones* at 177 Pham Ngu Lao St. This pub is known for its *loud* music.

Apocalypse Now, at the southern, riverside end of Thi Sach St, is extremely popular with a young Western crowd. On a good night it spills out on the street – and if ever a crowd could be said to spill, this is it. It's very noisy, very hectic and it can be great fun.

Nguyen Chat at 161 Pham Ngu Lao St is a Vietnamese place where you can sample local draft beer (bia hoi) for US$0.40 per litre. There are also plenty of cheap snacks here.

Buffalo Blues (☎ 222874), 72A Nguyen Du St, District 1, is a jazz bar with live music, billiards, darts and backgammon. It boasts the city's longest happy hour (2 pm to 8 pm) and dishes up fine meals, including excellent shepherd's pie.

Bavaria (☎ 222673), 20 Le Anh Xuan St, is a German restaurant and Bavarian-style pub.

Mogambo Café (☎ 251311), 20 Thi Sach St (at Hai Ba Trung St), is noted for its Polynesian decor. This place is a pub, cafe and guesthouse.

Hien & Bob's Place (☎ 230661), 43 Hai Ba Trung St (at Dong Du), District 1, advertises the coldest beer in town and American-style sandwiches. The interesting thing about this place is that Bob Shibley first came to Vietnam in 1969 as an American soldier. He is the first US veteran to have returned to open up a pub. Hien is his Vietnamese wife.

At 24 Mac Thi Buoi St is the legendary *Hard Rock Café*. The music here is mellower than the name suggests, but it's certainly a popular spot.

Next to the Hard Rock Café but even more

HO CHI MINH CITY

sedate is the *VSOP Club* (☎ 290520) at 56 Mac Thi Buoi St. This place touts its 'tropical cocktails' and 'famous cognacs'. Other refreshments on offer include brandy, coffee, cakes and sandwiches.

Saigon Headlines (☎ 225014), 7 Lam Son Square, District 1, is a really cool jazz bar and restaurant at the back of the Saigon Concert Hall. It serves the best Marguerita on the rocks this side of Hong Kong and has a good selection of international newspapers and magazines (hence the name). The atmosphere is relaxed but chic. It has an excellent band. It's open from 10 am until 2 am.

Built right into one side of the Municipal Theatre is the *Q Bar* (☎ 291299), a trendy place with murals on the walls and tables outside by a little garden. Expats tend to congregate here and swap yarns.

The slogan of the *River Bar* (☎ 293734) at 5-7 Ho Huan Nghiep St is 'a beat of Brazil, a beat of Africa, a lot of passion'. Personally, we thought the beer was expensive and warm. Nevertheless, good rattan furniture adds to the colourful atmosphere at this popular watering hole.

The *Press Club* at the corner of Hai Ba Trung St and Le Duan Blvd in District 1 is run by the Ho Chi Minh City Journalists' Association. It appeals to both expats and Vietnamese, and you don't need to be a journalist to go there.

The *Hammock Bar* is a converted junk with several pool tables and great views of the river and neon lights on the eastern bank. Moored in the Saigon River at Bach Dang Quay (the terminus of Ham Nghi Blvd), the boat can accommodate over 100 people on its two decks.

Stephanie's (☎ 258471), 14 Don Dat St, District 1, is a large bar with billiard tables upstairs.

Tiger Tavern (☎ 222738) at 227 Dong Khoi St seems to be an outlet for Singapore's most famous brew, Tiger Beer. Personally, we find this place a bit pricey and not too friendly, but expats do gather here. The pub is open daily from 11 am until midnight. The pub advertises live entertainment nightly from 6.30 to 9.30 pm featuring various performers (pianist, jazz band, etc). However, we've been in here during those hours and didn't see anything happening – perhaps we hit it on a bad day?

Dancing & Discos There is dancing with a live band at the *Rex Hotel*, 141 Nguyen Hue Blvd, nightly from 7.30 to 11 pm.

Cheers is the disco inside the Vien Dong Hotel at 257 Pham Ngu Lao St. This very popular place has both a Filipino band and taped music. Interestingly, when the band starts to play, everyone sits down to watch and listen – they get up to dance when the music tapes are played! Well, this is Vietnam. Besides the more open public dancing area, there are also plush private sitting rooms for the rich business types. Admission to Cheers costs US$8 and things get rolling from 8 pm onwards.

The *VIP Club* (☎ 229860, 231187), 2D Pham Ngoc Thach St, is a bar and disco with video game machines and billiard tables. There is also a karaoke room, but despite this the place has been very successful at cashing in on the Western expat crowd.

The *Starlight Nightclub* is on the 11th floor of the Century Saigon Hotel (☎ 231818, ext 46) at 68A Nguyen Hue Blvd, District 1. Here you'll find music of the '60s, '70s and '80s. It's open nightly from 7 pm until 2 am.

The Saigon Floating Hotel is where you'll find the *Down Under Disco*. Males must pay a cover charge of US$20, but females are permitted to enter for free. The excellent band (Filipino, not Vietnamese) really knows how to rock'n'roll.

The *Palace Hotel* at 56 Nguyen Hue Blvd, District 1, has a nightclub open from 8 to 11 pm. Ditto for the *Caravelle Hotel* at 19 Lam Son Square, District 1.

The *Superstar Disco Nightclub* (☎ 440242) is at 431/A/2 Hoang Van Thu St in the Tan Binh District. It's one of those brightly lit fancy clubs with staff able to speak a variety of languages such as English, Chinese, Korean, Japanese and Thai, not to mention Vietnamese. There is also a karaoke here. The club opens at 8 pm.

The *Venus Club* is in the Saigon Star

SIMON ROWE

RICHARD EVERIST

RICHARD I'ANSON

PHIL WEYMOUTH

PHIL WEYMOUTH

A	
B	C
D	E

Ho Chi Minh City (Saigon)

A The French-built Hotel de Ville
B Street vendor selling dried squid
C Traffic scene in central Saigon

D Boats delivering bananas to the
  Thi Nghe Market
E Housing along Ho Chi Minh City's canals

HELEN SAVORY

GLENN BEANLAND

SIMON ROWE

SIMON ROWE

Around Ho Chi Minh City

A	B
C	D

A The Caodai Great Temple at Tay Ninh
B Sunset at Bai Dua, Vung Tau
C A decorative door at the Caodai Great Temple, Tay Ninh
D The remains of an American tank, Cu Chi

Hotel, 204 Nguyen Thi Minh Khai St, District 3. It's notable for its disco and karaoke rooms.

The *Orient Club* (☎ 222547) at 104 Hai Ba Trung St, District 1, is another disco. You can find a disco-karaoke combination at the *Queen Bee* (☎ 229860) at 104 Nguyen Hue Blvd, District 1.

Close to the Dong Khoi Hotel (but not in it) is *Pub International* (☎ 295427), 32 Ngo Duc Ke St, District 1. The disco is upstairs.

It's a bit of a long trek out to *Shangri-La* (☎ 556831) at 1196 Ba Thang Hai St, District 11. But it turns out to be a pretty good discotheque and karaoke. There is also a health club here (gymnasium, etc), which will perhaps help you get in shape for the nighttime carousing.

Theatres The *Municipal Theatre* (Nha Hat Thanh Pho; ☎ 291249, 291584) is on Dong Khoi St between the Caravelle and Continental hotels. It was built in 1899 for use as a theatre but later served as the heavily fortified home of the South Vietnamese National Assembly.

Each week, the theatre offers a different programme, which may be Eastern European-style gymnastics, nightclub music or traditional Vietnamese theatre. There are performances at 8 pm nightly. Refreshments are sold during intermission; public toilets are in the basement.

The huge *Hoa Binh Theatre* complex (Nha Hat Hoa Binh, or the Peace Theatre) in District 10 often has several performances taking place simultaneously in its various halls, the largest of which seats 2400 people. The complex is at 14, 3 Thang 2 Blvd (next to the Vietnam Quoc Tu Pagoda). The ticket office (☎ 655199) is open from 7.30 am until the end of the evening show.

Evening performances, which begin at 7.30 pm, are usually held once or twice a week. Shows range from traditional and modern Vietnamese plays to Western pop music and circus acts. On Sunday mornings, there are marionette shows for children at 9 am in the 400-seat hall, and well-known Vietnamese pop singers begin performances in the large hall at 8.30 and 11 am.

Films are screened all day every day beginning at 8.30 am. Most of the films – from the Socialist countries, France, Hong Kong and the USA (Disney productions are a favourite) – are live-dubbed (someone reads a translation of the script over the PA system), leaving the original soundtrack at least partly audible. A weekly schedule of screenings is posted outside the building next to the ticket counter. Films cost US$0.20 (US$0.30 for a double feature).

The disco on the ground floor is open Tuesday to Sunday from 8 to 11 pm. Admission is US$1.25.

Conservatory of Music Both traditional Vietnamese and Western classical music are performed publicly at the *Conservatory of Music* (Nhac Vien Thanh Pho Ho Chi Minh; ☎ 396646), which is near Reunification Palace at 112 Nguyen Du St. Concerts are held at 7.30 pm each Monday and Friday evening during the two annual concert seasons, from March to May and from October to December. Tickets cost about US$0.25.

Students aged seven to 16 attend the Conservatory, which performs all the functions of a public school in addition to providing instruction in music. The music teachers here were trained in France, Britain and the USA as well as the former Eastern Bloc. The school is free but most of the students come from well-off families because only the well-to-do can afford musical instruments. There are two other conservatories of music in Vietnam, one in Hanoi and the other in Hué.

Cinemas Many Saigon maps have cinemas (*rap* in Vietnamese) marked with a special symbol. There are several cinemas downtown, including the *Rex Cinema* (☎ 292185) at 141 Nguyen Hue Blvd (next door to the Rex Hotel); another on Le Loi Blvd a block towards Ben Thanh Market from the Rex Hotel; and a third, *Rap Mang Non*, on Dong

Khoi St 100 metres up from the Municipal Theatre. *Rap Dong Khoi* is at 163 Dong Khoi St.

Culture Clubs These are really geared towards the domestic audience, but you might have some interest in seeing what sort of culture the government produces for the masses. Some venues for Vietnamese cultural entertainment include the *Youth House of Culture* at 4 Pham Ngoc Thach St; the *Children's House of Culture* at 4 Tu Xuong St; and the *Workers' Club* at 55B Xo Viet Nghe Tinh.

Things to Buy

Arts & Crafts In the last few years the free market in tourist junk has been booming – you can pick up a useful item like a lacquered turtle with a clock in its stomach or a ceramic Buddha that whistles the national anthem. And even if you're not the sort of person who needs a wind-up mechanical monkey that plays the cymbals, keep looking – Saigon is a good shopping city and there is sure to be something that catches your eye.

In the budget zone near Pham Ngu Lao St, we've personally gotten pretty good deals at the shop in the back of Getra Tour Company at 86 Bui Vien St. It's also productive to look at some of the stalls inside the Ben Thanh Market – you can find everything from lacquerware to conical hats.

Dong Khoi St is the centre for handicrafts, though the shop owners can be rapacious. Remember that the 'antiques' are almost certainly fakes, which is OK as long as you don't pay 'antique prices'.

One of the larger stores in this business is Culturimex (☎ 292574, 292896) at 50 Dong Khoi St, which sells ceramics, wood carvings, hand-painted greeting cards, copies of antiquities and other items you'd expect to find in a shop with a name like Culturimex.

Tu Do Art Gallery (☎ 231785), 142 Dong Khoi St, sells oil and lacquer paintings.

The Saigon Lacquerwares Factory (☎ 294183), at 139 Hai Ba Trung St, is the sort of place to which busloads of tourists are brought to do their souvenir shopping. The selection of lacquerware, ceramics, etc, is large but prices are high.

Just opposite the Omni Hotel (on the way to the airport) is Lamson Art Gallery (☎ 441361) at 106 Nguyen Van Troi St, Phu Nhuan District. This place sells exquisite but relatively expensive lacquerware, rattan, ceramics, wood carvings and more. You can watch the artisans create their masterpieces and it's certainly worth stopping by to have a look.

Oil paintings, watercolours and paintings on silk can be bought at Phuong Tranh Art Arcade, 151 Dong Du St (opposite the Caravelle Hotel). There is another art gallery, Thang Long, at 70 Nguyen Hue Blvd (next to the Century Saigon Hotel).

The Ho Chi Minh City Association of Fine Arts (☎ 230025), 218 Nguyen Thi Minh Khai St, District 1, is where aspiring young artists display their latest works. Typical prices for paintings are in the US$30 to US$50 range, but the artists may ask 10 times that.

Clothing At the budget end of the scale, T-shirts are available from vendors along Nguyen Hue Blvd in the centre, or De Tham St in the Pham Ngu Lao area. Expect to pay about US$2 for a printed T-shirt, or US$3 to US$5 for an embroidered one.

Vietsilk (☎ 291148), 21 Dong Khoi St, sells ready-made garments as well as embroidery and drawings on silk.

Women's ao dais (pronounced, in the south, 'ow-yai'), the flowing silk blouse slit up the sides and worn over pantaloons, are tailored at shops in and around Ben Thanh Market or the Saigon Intershop area. Behind Ben Thanh Market you can try a store called Italy, 11 Thu Khoa Huan St.

Thai Fashion at 92H Le Thanh Ton St, District 1, has ready-made women's fashions. You might want to check out nearby Down Under Fashions at 229 Le Thanh Ton St, District 1. Ditto for The He Moi at 87 Pasteur St, District 1.

Custom-made suits for men can be tailored at Cuu Long (☎ 296831), 175 Dong Khoi St.

There are numerous tailors' shops in Cholon and several in downtown Saigon; the Rex and Century Saigon hotels each have in-house tailors.

Coffee Vietnamese coffee is prime stuff and is amazingly cheap if you know where to buy it. The best grades are from Buon Ma Thuot and the beans are roasted in butter. Obviously, price varies according to quality and also with the seasons. You can buy whole beans or have them ground into powder at no extra charge.

The city's major markets are where you can find the best prices and widest selection. We scored some top-grade caffeine from Van Ly Huong at Stall No 905, Zone 3, in the Ben Thanh Market. This market is also the best place to find the peculiar coffee drippers used by the Vietnamese. Get a stainless steel one rather than aluminium – the latter is cheaper but a much bigger hassle to use. Also look in the market for a coffee grinder if you're buying whole beans rather than pre-ground ones.

War Surplus Market If you're in the market for a chic pair of combat boots and rusty dog tags, the place to go is Dan Sinh Market at 104 Nguyen Cong Tru St (next to Phung Son Tu Pagoda). The front part of the market is filled with stalls selling automobiles and motorbikes, but directly behind the pagoda building you can find reproductions of what appears to be second-hand military gear.

Stall after stall sells everything from gas masks and field stretchers to rain gear and mosquito nets. You can also find canteens, duffel bags, ponchos and boots. Anyone planning on spending time in Bosnia or New York City should consider picking up a second-hand flak jacket (demand has slumped since the Vietnam War ended, and the prices are now very competitive). On the other hand, exorbitant overcharging of foreigners looking for a poignant souvenir is common.

Tax Department Store The biggest department store in Ho Chi Minh City, Cua Hang Bach Hoa, is on the corner of Le Loi and Nguyen Hue Blvds. Built as the Grands Magasins Charner six decades ago, this three-storey emporium, which for years was run by the government and had a pathetic selection of goods, has been 'privatised', and floor space is now rented to individual shopowners. Items for sale include consumer electronics, blank and pirated cassette tapes, locally produced bicycles and parts, domestic alcoholic beverages, stationery, little globes of the world labelled in Vietnamese, sports equipment, cheap jewellery and clothing made of synthetic fibres.

Stamps & Coins As you enter the GPO, immediately to your right is a counter selling stationery, pens, etc, but also has some decent stamp collections. Also, as you face the entrance from the outside, to your right are a few stalls which also have stamp collections as well as other goods such as foreign coins and banknotes. You can even find old stuff from the former South Vietnamese regime. Prices are variable: about US$2 will get you a decent set of late-model stamps already mounted in a book, but the older and rarer collections cost more.

Perhaps the best place to look is Cotevina, the government corporation which issues Vietnamese stamps. There is a branch (☎ 22326, 91637) at 18 Dinh Tien Hoang St, District 1. The range is from 1960s stamps up to late-issued ones.

Many bookshops and antique shops along Dong Khoi St sell overpriced French Indochinese coins and banknotes and packets of Vietnamese stamps.

Street Markets The street market which runs along Huynh Thuc Khang and Ton That Dam Sts sells everything. The area used to be known as the Electronics Black Market until early 1989, when it was legalised. It's now generally called the Huynh Thuc Khang Street Market, though it doesn't have an official name.

You can still buy electronic goods of all sorts – from mosquito zappers to video cassette players – but the market has expanded

Vegetable seller at the Ben Thanh Market

enormously to include clothing, washing detergent, lacquerware, condoms, pirated cassettes, smuggled bottles of Johnny Walker, Chinese-made 'Swiss Army' knives and posters of national heroes, including Ho Chi Minh, Michael Jackson and Mickey Mouse.

Indoor Markets Ho Chi Minh City has a number of incredibly huge indoor markets selling all manner of goods. They are some of the best places to pick up the conical hats and ao dais for which Vietnam is famous.

Ben Thanh Market Ben Thanh Market (Cho Ben Thanh) and the surrounding streets are one of the city's liveliest, most bustling marketplaces. Everything commonly eaten, worn or used by the average resident of Saigon is available here: vegetables, fruits, meat, spices, biscuits, sweets, tobacco, clothing, hats, household items, hardware and so forth. The legendary slogan of US country stores applies equally well here: 'If we don't have it, you don't need it'. Nearby, food stalls sell inexpensive meals.

Ben Thanh Market is 700 metres southwest of the Rex Hotel at the intersection of Le Loi Blvd, Ham Nghi Blvd, Tran Hung Dao Blvd and Le Lai St. Known to the French as the Halles Centrales, it was built in 1914 of reinforced concrete and covers an area of 11 sq km; the central cupola is 28 metres in diameter. The main entrance, with its belfry and clock, has become a symbol of Saigon.

Opposite the belfry, in the centre of the traffic roundabout, is an equestrian statue of Tran Nguyen Hai, the first person in Vietnam to use courier pigeons. At the base, on a pillar, is a small white bust of Quach Thi Trang, a Buddhist woman killed during anti-government protests in 1963.

The Old Market Despite the name, this is not a place to find antiques. Rather, the Old Market is where you can most easily buy imported (black market?) foods, wines, etc. There is a problem using the Vietnamese name for this market (Cho Cu), because written or pronounced without the tones it means 'penis'. Your cyclo driver will no doubt be much amused if you say that this is what you're looking for. Perhaps directions would be better – the Old Market is on the north side of Ham Nghi Blvd between Ton That Dam and Ho Tung Mau Sts.

Binh Tay Market Binh Tay Market (Cho Binh Tay) is Cholon's main marketplace. Actually, it's technically not in Cholon proper, but about one block away in District 6 (Cholon is District 5). Much of the business here is wholesale. Binh Tay Market is on Hau Giang Blvd. It is about one km south-west of Chau Van Liem Blvd.

Andong Market Cholon's other indoor market, Andong, is very close to the intersection of Tran Phu and An Duong Vuong Blvds. This market is four storeys tall and is packed with shops. The 1st floor has heaps of clothing – imported designer jeans from Hong Kong, the latest pumps from Paris, Vietnamese ao dais – and everything else imaginable. The basement is a gourmet's delight of small restaurants – a perfect place to pig out on a shoestring.

Miscellaneous No bureaucracy, Communist or otherwise, can exist without the official stamps and seals that provide the *raison d'être* for legions of clerks. This need is catered to by the numerous shops strung out along the street just north of the New World Hotel (opposite side of the street and just west of Ben Thanh Market).

Most Vietnamese also own carved seals bearing their name (an old tradition borrowed from China). You can have one made too, but ask a local to help translate your name into Vietnamese. You might want to get your seal carved in Cholon using Chinese characters, since these are certainly more artistic (though less practical) than the Romanised script now used by the Vietnamese.

Getting There & Away

Upon arrival, be sure to check that you were given a full month on your visa (assuming, of course, that you were issued a one-month visa in the first place). Immigration officials have been know to arbitrarily give travellers only one week. One traveller reports:

Arriving at the airport in Ho Chi Minh City gave us our first taste of Vietnamese bureaucracy. Our airport official was intent at this desk, tapping information into a computer, rubber stamping and gazing at the screen and seemingly checking the information against that in my passport and on my entry/exit form. I got through after five minutes of this and waited for my partner. Out of curiosity I watched as the procedure was repeated, only this time I could see the computer screen. Official headings were displayed in English but no information about my partner was being registered on screen beside them despite some excellent mime that would suggest his life's history was being recorded in the computer. This performance continued throughout the line of new arrivals. We suppressed our laughter until well out of earshot.

Air Vietnam Airlines has direct international flights between Ho Chi Minh City and Amsterdam, Bangkok, Berlin, Dubai, Guangzhou (via Hanoi), Hong Kong, Kaohsiung, Kuala Lumpur, Los Angeles (via Taipei), Manila, Melbourne, Moscow, Osaka, Paris, Phnom Penh, Seoul, Singapore, Sydney, Taipei and Vientiane (via Hanoi).

The complete list of airline offices is as follows:

Aeroflot
    4B Le Loi Blvd, District 1 (☎ 293489)
Air France
    127 Tran Quoc Thao St, District 3 (☎ 293770)
Asiana
    141-143 Ham Nghi Blvd, District 1 (☎ 222665)
Cambodia Air
    343 Le Van St, Tan Binh District (☎ 440126)
Cathay Pacific
    49 Le Thanh Ton St, District 1 (☎ 223272)
China Airlines (Taiwan)
    132 Dong Khoi St (Continental Hotel), District 1
    (☎ 251387)
China Southern Airlines
    52B Pham Hong Thai St, District 1
    (☎ 291172, 298417)
EVA Air
    129 Dong Khoi St, District 1 (☎ 224488)
Garuda Indonesia
    106 Nguyen Hue Blvd (☎ 293644)
Korean Air
    141 Nguyen Hue Blvd, District 1 (☎ 296042)
KLM
    244 Pasteur St, District 3 (☎ 231990)
Lao Aviation
    39/3 Tran Nhat Duat St (☎ 442807)
Lufthansa
    132-134 Dong Khoi St (Continental Hotel), District 1 (☎ 298529)
Malaysian Airline System
    116 Nguyen Hue Blvd, District 1 (☎ 230695)
Pacific Airlines
    77 Le Thanh Ton St, District 1
    (☎ 231285, 290844)
Philippine Airlines
    4A Le Loi Blvd, District 1 (☎ 292113)
Qantas
    311 Dien Bien Phu St, District 3 (☎ 396194)·
Singapore Airlines
    6 Le Loi Blvd, District 1 (☎ 231583)
Thai International Airways
    65 Nguyen Du St, District 1 (☎ 223365)
Vietnam Airlines
    116 Nguyen Hue Blvd, District 1 (☎ 292118)
    15B Dinh Tien Hoang Rd (☎ 299910)

It is essential to reconfirm all reservations for flights out of the country. For more information on international air transport to and from Vietnam, see the Getting There & Away chapter.

Domestic flights from Ho Chi Minh City on Vietnam Airlines with one-way ticket prices are as follows:

Destination	Frequency	Price
Buon Ma Thuot	2 Daily	US$60
Cantho	Suspended	US$50
Dalat	3 Weekly	US$40
Danang	3 Daily	US$85
Haiphong	2 Daily	US$150
Hanoi	5 Daily	US$150
Hué	2 Daily	US$85
Nha Trang	2 Daily	US$60
Phu Quoc	5 Weekly	US$65
Pleiku	1 Daily	US$60
Qui Nhon	5 Weekly	US$60

Pacific Airlines also flies the Hanoi-Ho Chi Minh City route (once daily except Sundays) and charges the same price as Vietnam Airlines. For more information on domestic air transport, see the Getting Around chapter.

Visitors have reported pilfering from checked luggage, especially when leaving the country (the baggage handlers don't even leave a 'thank you' note).

Tan Son Nhat Airport (it was previously spelled Tan Son Nhut by southerners, but the northerners had the final say) was one of the three busiest airports in the world during the late 1960s. The runways are still lined with lichen-covered mortar-proof aircraft revetments and other military structures, some still showing war damage. The sagging aluminium hulks of US-built transport planes sit next to ageing Soviet helicopters and jets of the Vietnamese air force. The complex of the US Military Assistance Command (MACV), also known as 'Pentagon East', was blown up by the Americans on 29 April 1975, hours before Saigon surrendered to North Vietnamese troops.

Bus – Cholon Station Intercity buses depart from and arrive at a variety of stations around Ho Chi Minh City. Cholon Station is the most convenient place to get buses to Mytho and other Mekong Delta towns. The Cholon Bus Station is at the very western end of Tran Hung Dao B Blvd in District 5, close to the Binh Tay Market.

Bus – Mien Tay Station Less conveniently located than Cholon Bus Station, Mien Tay Bus Station nevertheless has even more

buses to points south of Ho Chi Minh City (basically the Mekong Delta). This enormous station (Ben Xe Mien Tay; ☎ 255955) is about 10 km west of Saigon in An Lac, a part of Binh Chanh District (Huyen Binh Chanh). There are buses from central Saigon to Mien Tay Bus Station from the Ben Thanh Bus Station (at the end of Ham Nghi Blvd near Ben Thanh Market). Express *(toc hanh)* buses are not quite as slow as regular buses.

Express buses and minibuses from Mien Tay Bus Station serve Bac Lieu (six hours), Camau (12 hours), Cantho ($3\frac{1}{2}$ hours), Chau Doc (six hours), Long Xuyen (five hours) and Rach Gia (six to seven hours).

These buses, which receive priority treatment at ferry crossings, all depart twice a day: at 4.30 am and at 3 pm. Tickets are sold from 3.30 am for the early buses and from noon for the afternoon runs. Express bus tickets are also on sale at 121 Chau Van Liem Blvd in Cholon; 142 Hung Vuong Blvd west of Cholon; and 638 Le Hong Phong St in District 10.

The following cities are served by non-express bus service from the Mien Tay Bus Station:

An Phu, Mytho, Bac Lieu, Ngoc Hien, Ben Tre, O Mon, Binh Minh Ferry, Phung Hiep, Camau (10 hrs), Rach Gia, Cang Long, Sa Dec, Cantho (five hrs), Soc Trang, Cao Lanh, Tam Binh, Cau Ke, Tam Nong, Cau Ngang, Tan Chau, Chau Doc, Tan Hiep, Chau Phu, Tay Ninh, Cho Moi, Thanh Tri, Duyen Hai, Thoai Son, Ha Tien, Thot Not, Ho Phong, Tieu Can, Hong Ngu, Tinh Bien, Long An, Tra Vinh, Long My, Thu Thua, Long Phu, Vam Cong, Long Xuyen, Vi Thanh, Moc Hoa, Vinh Chau, My Thuan, Vinh Long, My Xuyen.

Tickets for nonexpress buses are sold from 3.30 am to 4 pm at counters marked according to the province of destination. Nonexpress buses also leave from platforms arranged by province. At present, buses depart during daylight hours only. To guarantee a seat, you can make reservations a day in advance by asking someone who speaks Vietnamese to phone the station office (☎ 255955).

Bus – Mien Dong Station Buses to places north of Ho Chi Minh City leave from Mien Dong Bus Station (Ben Xe Mien Dong; ☎ 294056), which is in Binh Thanh District about five km from downtown Saigon on Quoc Lo 13 (National Highway 13). Quoc Lo 13 is the continuation of Xo Viet Nghe Tinh St. The station is just under two km north of the intersection of Xo Viet Nghe Tinh St and Dien Bien Phu St. The station's main gate is opposite 78 Quoc Lo 13 (according to the new numbering) and next to 229 Quoc Lo 13 (according to the old numbering). To get there, you can take a bus from Ben Thanh Bus Station near Ben Thanh Market.

There is express service from Mien Dong Bus Station to Buon Ma Thuot (15 hrs), Danang (26 hrs), Haiphong (53 hrs), Hanoi (49 hrs), Hué (29 hrs), Nam Dinh (47 hrs), Nha Trang (11 hrs), Pleiku (22 hrs), Quang Ngai (24 hrs), Qui Nhon (17 hrs), Tuy Hoa (12 hrs) and Vinh (42 hrs).

All the express buses leave daily between 5 and 5.30 am. To Nha Trang, there is also a daily bus at 5 pm. To buy express tickets, turn left as you enter the main gate of the station (which is on Quoc Lo 13) and go all the way to the end to a blue and white one-storey building. Tickets are sold between 4 am and 4 pm in the room marked Quay Ban Ve Xe Toc Hanh (Express Bus Ticket Counter). To make express bus reservations by telephone, have a Vietnamese-speaker call ☎ 294056.

Nonexpress buses from Mien Dong Bus Station serve:

Bao Loc, Lam Ha, Baria, Long Khanh, Ben Cat, Madagoui, Binh Long, Nha Trang, Bu Dang, Phan Rang, Buon Ma Thuot, Phan Ri, Cam Ranh, Phan Thiet, Dai Te, Phu Tuc, Dalat, Phuong Lam, Danang, Pleiku, Di Linh, Quang Ngai, Don Duong, Qui Nhon, Dong Xoai, Tan Dinh, Duc Linh, Tan Phu, Duc Trong, Tanh Linh, Gia Nghia, Tay Son, Ham Tan, Thu Dau Mot, Ham Thuan Nam, Tuy Hoa, Hué, Tuy Phong, Kien Duc, Vung Tau, Xuyen Moc.

Many of the nonexpress buses leave around 5.30 am. Tickets for short trips can be bought before departure. For long-distance buses, tickets should be purchased a day in advance.

The ticket windows, open from 5 am until the last seat on the last bus of the day is sold, are in a large open shed with a corrugated iron roof across from the express bus ticket counter. Tickets for many buses that leave from the Mien Dong Bus Station can also be purchased at the Mien Tay Bus Station in An Lac.

There are a number of restaurants just outside the station along Quoc Lo 13.

Bus – Van Thanh Station Vehicles departing from Van Thanh Bus Station (Ben Xe Van Thanh; ☎ 294839) serve destinations within a few hours of Ho Chi Minh City, mostly in Song Be and Dong Nai provinces. For travellers, most important are probably the buses to Dalat and Vung Tau.

Van Thanh Bus Station is in Binh Thanh District about 1.5 km east of the intersection of Dien Bien Phu and Xo Viet Nghe Tinh Sts, at 72 Dien Bien Phu St. As you head out of Saigon, go past where the numbers on Dien Bien Phu St climb up into the 600s. A cyclo ride from central Saigon should cost US$0.75.

An assortment of decrepit US vans, Daihatsu Hijets and Citroën Traction 15s leave Van Thanh Bus Station for Baria, Cho Lau, Ham Tan, Long Dien, Long Hai, Phu Cuong, Phu Giao, parts of Song Be Province, Vung Tau and Xuan Loc. Xe Lams go to Tay Ninh Bus Station in Tan Binh District. Vehicles leave when full. Van Thanh Bus Station is open from 6 am to about 6 pm.

Bus – Tay Ninh Station Buses to Tay Ninh, Cu Chi and points north-east of Ho Chi Minh City depart from the Tay Ninh Bus Station (Ben Xe Tay Ninh), which is in Tan Binh District. To get there, head all the way out on Cach Mang Thang Tam St. The station is about one km past where Cach Mang Thang Tam St merges with Le Dai Hanh St.

Bus – Vung Tau Just next to the Saigon Hotel and the mosque on Dong Du St is where you catch buses to Vung Tau. This is a bus stop, not an official bus station, so there is always the possibility that the location will be suddenly moved. In other words, inquire first.

Bus – Cambodia Details of the bus trip to Cambodia are provided in the general Getting There & Away chapter.

Train Saigon Railway Station (Ga Sai Gon; ☎ 230105) is in District 3 at 1 Nguyen Thong St. Trains from here serve cities along the coast north of Ho Chi Minh City. The ticket office is open from 7.15 to 11 am and 1 to 3 pm daily.

To get to the railway station, turn off Cach Mang Thang Tam St next to number 132/9. Go down the alley for about 100 metres and then follow the railway tracks to the left. Or you can go to the roundabout at the intersection of Cach Mang Tang Tam St and 3 Thang 2 Blvd and follow the disused railway tracks a few hundred metres. The tracks run down the middle of the alleyway that begins next to 252/1B Ly Chinh Thang St. A cyclo ride from the city centre to the station should cost US$0.50. The railway station is closed from noon until 1 pm for lunch.

The Reunification (Thong Nhat) Express Train connects Ho Chi Minh City with all the major towns along the coast from Phan Rang-Thap Cham to Hanoi. Schedules

An old car for hire

change, but at the time of this writing, there were two trains reunifying the country daily. There are also numerous local trains; useful ones go to Nha Trang, Qui Nhon and Hué.

Car Private drivers hang out in front of the Mondial Hotel. They ask about US$40 for a trip to Tay Ninh in an air-conditioned car.

Ann's Tourist (☎ 332564, 334356; fax 323866) at 58 Ton That Tung St, District 1, is good for car rentals. NHABEXIM (☎ 298272), 31 Dong Khoi St, District 1, is also OK. Youth Tourist Company, 292 Dien Bien Phu St, District 3 (or ask at Kim Café), has competitive prices.

Saigon Tourist and Vietnam Tourism charge double the going rate.

Cars with drivers can also be hired at the Phnom Penh Bus Garage, 155 Nguyen Hue Blvd, next to the Rex Hotel.

Major hotels can also arrange for cars; they charge US$30 to US$35 per day for distances under 100 km.

Boat Passenger and goods ferries to the Mekong Delta depart from a dock (☎ 297892) at the river end of Ham Nghi Blvd. There is daily service to the provinces of An Giang and Vinh Long and to the towns of Ben Tre (eight hours), Camau (30 hours; once every four days), Mytho (six hours; departs at 11 am) and Tan Chau. Buy your tickets on the boat. Simple food may be available on board. Be aware that these ancient vessels lack the most elementary safety gear, such as life jackets.

Getting Around
To/From the Airport Ho Chi Minh City's Tan Son Nhat International Airport is seven km from the centre of Saigon. The taxis for hire outside the customs hall will try to grossly overcharge, so bargain hard (a fair price into town is about US$7) or else take a metered taxi. Don't waste your time at the Tan Son Nhat Airport Taxi Booking Desk – the minimum fare is US$25 for a standard taxi, or US$50 for a limousine.

Cyclos (pedicabs) can be hailed outside the gate to the airport, which is a few hundred metres from the terminal building. A ride to central Saigon should cost about US$2. Motorbike 'taxis' hang out near the airport and typically ask US$3 to go downtown, though you may be able to bargain something better.

To get to the airport, you can ring up a taxi (see the following Taxi section for telephone numbers). Some of the cafes in the Pham Ngu Lao budget hotel area also do runs to the airport – these places even have sign-up sheets where you can book share taxis for US$2 per person. This, no doubt, will prove considerably cheaper than the limousine service available at the front desk of the Rex Hotel.

If you take a cyclo or motorbike to Tan Son Nhat, you may have to walk from the airport gate to the terminal. Private cars can bring you into the airport but must drop you off at the domestic terminal, only a one-minute walk from the international terminal.

Bus Few foreigners make use of the city buses, though they are safer than cyclos if less aesthetic. Now that Ho Chi Minh City's People's Committee has resolved to phase out cyclos, some money is finally being put into the heretofore badly neglected public transport system.

At present, there are only three bus routes, though more will undoubtedly be added. No decent bus map is available and bus stops are mostly unmarked, so it's worth summarising the three bus lines, which are as follows:

Saigon – Cholon Buses depart Central Saigon from opposite the Saigon Floating Hotel and continue along Tran Hung Dao Blvd to Binh Tay Market in Cholon, then return along the same route. The bus company running this route is an Australian joint venture – buses have air-conditioning and video movies, and the driver is well dressed! All this for US$0.20. Buy your ticket on board from the female attendant (sharply dressed in a blouse and skirt).

Mien Dong – Mien Tay Buses depart Mien Dong Bus Station (north-east Ho Chi Minh City), pass through Cholon and terminate at Mien Tay Bus Station in the western edge of town. The fare is US$0.40.

Van Thanh – Mien Tay Buses depart Van Thanh Bus Station (eastern Ho Chi Minh City), pass through Cholon and terminate at Mien Tay Bus Station (western Ho Chi Minh City). The fare is US$0.40.

Xe Lam Xe Lams (tiny three-wheelers, otherwise known as Lambrettas) connect the various bus stations. There is a useful Xe Lam stop on the north-west corner of Pham Ngu Lao and Nguyen Thai Hoc Sts, where you can catch a ride to the Mien Tay Bus Station. This station is where you get buses to the Mekong Delta.

Subway No, Ho Chi Minh City does not yet have a subway, nor is one under construction. However, foreign consultants have been called in and a feasibility study is under way. It's not likely that the subway will be completed within the lifespan of this book, or even during the next edition. Nevertheless, we want to be optimists. When the ribbon-cutting ceremony for the Ho Chi Minh City Metro finally happens, just remember that you read it here first.

Boat To see Ho Chi Minh City from the Saigon River, you can easily hire a motorised five-metre boat. Warning – there have been quite a few unpleasant incidents with bag snatching and pickpocketing at the docks at the base of Ham Nghi Blvd. It's better to go to the area just south of the Saigon Floating Hotel where you see the ships offering dinner cruises. Around that area, you'll always see someone hanging around looking to charter a boat – ask them to bring the boat to you, rather than you go to the boat (they can easily do this).

The price should US$5 per hour for a small boat, or US$10 to US$15 for a larger and faster craft. Interesting destinations for short trips include Cholon (along Ben Nghe Channel) and the zoo (along Thi Nghe Channel). Note that both channels are fascinating but filthy – raw sewage is discharged into the water. Foreigners regard the channels as a major tourist attraction, but the government considers them an eyesore and has already launched a programme to move local residents out. The channels will eventually be filled in, and the water will be diverted into underground sewer pipes. At that point, the only possible channel cruises will be by submarine.

For longer trips up the Saigon River, it would be worth chartering a fast speedboat from Saigon Tourist. Although these cost US$20 per hour, you'll save money when you consider that a cheap boat takes at least five times longer for the same journey. Splitting the cost among a small group of travellers makes a lot of economic sense, and it's always more fun to travel with others unless you prefer solitude. Although cruising the Saigon River can be interesting, it pales in comparison with the splendour of the canals in the Mekong Delta region (see the Mekong Delta chapter for details). One traveller reports:

We hired a small boat with driver and female guide for US$5 for an hour for two people and were able to go up the Cholon Channel and see life on the waterfront. The bridges are too low for regular tourist craft. It was extremely interesting to see how these stilt-house dwellers live. We were told that already when the water level is low 'pirate boys' board the boats demanding money, but we had no problems. We were able to take many interesting photographs.

But another traveller had a different attitude:

Boat trips through the Ben Nghe Channel to Cholon are a bit of a rip-off. The pieces of plastic and the waterplants in the very dirty water make the motor stop every two or three minutes. This forces the boat owner to stop and do a cleaning job, which takes much time. We spent 35 minutes drifting on five km of stinking water without any protection from the rain. There are certainly better places in Vietnam to do boat journeys, such as Cantho, Nha Trang, Hoi An and Hué, to name a few.

Gorrit Goslinga

Since you hire boats by the hour, some will go particularly slow because they know the meter is running. You might want to set a time limit from the outset.

Ferries across the Saigon River leave from a dock at the foot of Ham Nghi Blvd. They run every half hour or so from 4.30 am to 10.30 pm.

Car If, in this age of compact and subcompact automobiles, you have ever wondered how it was that US teenagers of the 1950s were supposed to have been sexually initiated in the back seat of a car, experiencing Ho Chi Minh City's boat-like 'wedding taxis' will put to rest forever your logistical confusion. These huge US cars date from the late '50s and early '60s, and many come complete with tail fins and impressive chrome fenders. They are now used mostly to add a touch of class to Vietnamese weddings, but they can also be hired for excursions in and around Ho Chi Minh City.

Hop Tac Xa Xe Du Lich (Tourist Car Corporation; ☎ 290600), opposite Vietcombank and across the street from 43 Ben Chuong Duong St (corner Nam Ky Khoi Nghia St), is easy to spot: dozens of the old classics are lined up next to the dispatcher's booth. Make reservations the day before your departure. Always specify exactly where you want to go and the times you expect to depart and return *before* you sign anything or hand over any money. The usual deposit is between one-quarter and one-third of the total; the balance should be paid at the end of the trip.

Taxi Metered taxis occasionally cruise the streets, but it's much easier to find one if you ring up their dispatcher. Generally, you'll only have to wait a few minutes before the vehicle arrives. Vina Taxi (☎ 442170) operates cabs yellow in colour. Airport Taxi (☎ 446666) has white vehicles, and they will drive you anywhere around town, not just to the airport. Flagfall is US$0.75 and cost per km also runs US$0.75

There is a taxi stand on Le Loi Blvd in front of the Rex Hotel. There is another taxi stand along the median strip in the middle of Ham Nghi Blvd by No 54. Again, check if there is a meter; if not, set the fare before starting out.

In Cholon, there are always a few ancient Renault 4 taxis sitting next to the entrance to the Pham Ngoc Thach Hospital at 120 Hung

Vuong Blvd. They are there to transport sick people too ill to walk or ride in a cyclo, but healthy people who can pay are also welcome to use them. These Renault 4s break down frequently and are not recommended for travel outside the city.

Motorbike If you're convinced of your immortality, you can rent a motorbike and really earn your 'I Survived Saigon' T-shirt. Many say that this is the fastest and easiest way to get around Ho Chi Minh City, and that's probably true as long as you don't crash into anything.

Motorbike rentals are ubiquitous in places where tourists congregate. The Pham Ngu Lao St area is as good as any to satisfy this need. Ask at the cafes or else talk to a cyclo driver for ideas on where to find rentals.

For motorbike repairs, also try the area around the intersection of Hung Vuong Blvd and Tran Binh Trong St.

A 50-cc motorbike can be rented for US$5 to US$10 per day. Before renting one, make sure it's rideable.

Honda Om A quick (if precarious) way around town is to ride on the back of a motorbike (Honda om). You can either try to flag someone down (most drivers can always use whatever extra cash they can get) or ask a Vietnamese to find a Honda om for you. The accepted rate is comparable to what cyclos charge.

Cyclo Cyclos (pedicabs) can be hailed along major thoroughfares almost any time of the day or night. In Saigon, many of the drivers are former South Vietnamese army soldiers, and quite a few of them know at least basic English while others are quite fluent. Each of them has a story of war, 're-education', persecution and poverty to tell.

There are a number of major streets on which cyclos are prohibited to ride. As a result, your driver must often take a circuitous route to avoid these trouble spots since the police will not hesitate to fine them. For the same reason, the driver may not be able to drop you off at the exact address you want

A cyclo driver taking a break

though he will bring you to the nearest side street. Many travellers have gotten angry at their cyclo drivers for this, but try to have some sympathy since it is not their fault.

Short hops around the city centre should cost about US$0.50; central Saigon to central Cholon costs about US$1. Overcharging is common, so negotiate a price beforehand and have the exact change ready. Renting a cyclo for US$1 per hour is a fine idea if you will be doing much touring.

Enjoy cyclos while you can – the government of Ho Chi Minh City intends to phase them out. In an effort to prevent the cyclo population from expanding, the municipal government no longer registers new cyclos. However, enterprising locals have started manufacturing fake licence plates in an effort to thwart the ban on new vehicles. One effect of these 'pirate cyclos' *(xe bo trong)* is that if the driver gives you a bad time and you copy down his licence number to report him to the police, the number may turn out to be a dud.

Bicycle A bicycle is a good, slow way to get around the city and see things if you're an experienced cyclist and can manage the chaotic traffic. Bikes can be rented from a number of places: the Prince Hotel (☎ 322657) at 187 Pham Ngu Lao St; from a stand opposite the Rex Hotel; SGT Travel Service (☎ 298914), 49 Le Thanh Ton St; The Youth Centre (☎ 294345), 1 Pham Ngoc Thach St; Eden Tourist Office (☎ 295417), 114 Nguyen Hue Blvd.

The best place in Ho Chi Minh City to buy a decent (ie, 'imported') bicycle is at Federal Bike Shop (☎ 332899) with stores at three locations: 139H Nguyen Trai St, 158B Vo Thi Sau St and 156 Pham Hong Thai St. Cheaper deals may be found at some of the shops around 288 Le Thanh Ton St (corner Cach Mang Thang Tam St). You can also buy bike components: Czech and French frames, Chinese derailleurs, headlamps, etc. A decent bicycle with foreign components costs about US$100. In Cholon, you might try the bicycle shops on Ngo Gia Tu Blvd just south-west of Ly Thai To Blvd (near An Quang Pagoda). In District 4 there are bicycle

parts shops along Nguyen Tat Thanh St just south of the Ho Chi Minh Museum.

For cheap and poorly assembled domestic bicycles and parts, try the ground floor of Cua Hang Bach Hoa (Tax Department Store) on the corner of Nguyen Hue and Le Loi Blvds. Vikotrade Company at 35 Le Loi Blvd (across the street from the Rex Hotel) also has locally made components.

For on-the-spot bicycle repairs, look for an upturned army helmet and a hand pump sitting next to the curb. There is a cluster of bicycle repair shops around 23 Phan Dang Luu Blvd.

Bicycle parking lots in Ho Chi Minh City are usually just roped-off sections of a sidewalk. For US$0.10 you can leave your bicycle knowing that it will be there when you get back (bicycle theft is a big problem). When you pull up, your bicycle will have a number written on the seat in chalk or stapled to the handlebars. You will be given a reclaim chit (don't lose it!). If you come back and your bicycle is gone, the parking lot is supposedly required to replace it.

Around Ho Chi Minh City

CU CHI TUNNELS

The town of Cu Chi had about 80,000 residents during the Vietnam War but has now become a district of greater Ho Chi Minh City with a population of 200,000. At first glance, there is little evidence here to indicate the heavy fighting, bombing and destruction that went on in Cu Chi during the war. To see what went on, you have to dig deeper – underground.

The tunnel network of Cu Chi became legendary during the 1960s for its role in facilitating Viet Cong control of a large rural area only 30 to 40 km from Saigon. At its height, the tunnel system stretched from the South Vietnamese capital to the Cambodian border; in the district of Cu Chi alone, there were over 250 km of tunnels. The network, parts of which were several storeys deep, included innumerable trap doors, specially constructed living areas, storage facilities, weapons factories, field hospitals, command centres and kitchens.

The tunnels made possible communication and coordination between Viet Cong-controlled enclaves isolated from each other by South Vietnamese and American land and air operations. They also allowed the guerrillas to mount surprise attacks wherever the tunnels went – even within the perimeters of the US military base at Dong Du – and to disappear into hidden trapdoors without a trace. After ground operations against the tunnels claimed large numbers of casualties and proved ineffective, the Americans resorted to massive firepower, eventually turning Cu Chi's 420 sq km into what writers Tom Mangold and John Peny-

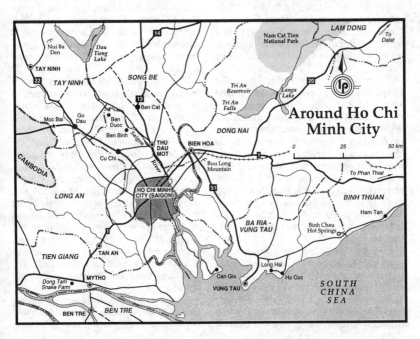

Around Ho Chi Minh City

237

cate have called 'the most bombed, shelled, gassed, defoliated and generally devastated area in the history of warfare'.

Today, Cu Chi has become a pilgrimage site for Vietnamese school children and Party cadres. Parts of this remarkable tunnel network – enlarged and upgraded versions of the real thing – are open to the public. The unadulterated tunnels, though not actually closed to tourists, are hard to get to and are rarely visited. There are numerous war cemeteries all around Cu Chi, though tour groups don't usually stop at these except on special request.

History

The tunnels of Cu Chi were built over a period of 2½ decades beginning in the late 1940s. They were the improvised response of a poorly equipped peasant army to its enemy's high-tech ordnance, helicopters, artillery, bombers and chemical weapons.

The Viet Minh built the first dugouts and tunnels in the hard, red earth of Cu Chi – ideal for the construction of tunnels – during the war against the French. The excavations were used mostly for communication between villages and to evade French army sweeps of the area.

When the National Liberation Front (Viet Cong) insurgency began in earnest around 1960, the old Viet Minh tunnels were repaired and new extensions excavated. Within a few years the system assumed enormous strategic importance, and most of Cu Chi District and nearby areas came under firm Viet Cong control. In addition, Cu Chi was used as a base for infiltrating intelligence agents and sabotage teams into Saigon itself. The stunning attacks in the South Vietnamese capital itself during the 1968 Tet Offensive were planned and launched from Cu Chi.

In early 1963, the Diem government implemented the botched 'strategic hamlet' programme, under which fortified encampments, surrounded by rows of sharp bamboo spikes, were built to house people relocated from Communist-controlled areas. The first 'strategic hamlet' was in Ben Cat District,

next door to Cu Chi. Not only was the programme carried out with incredible incompetence and cruelty, alienating the peasantry, but the Viet Cong launched a major (successful) effort to defeat it – the Viet Cong was able to tunnel into the hamlets and control them from within. By the end of 1963, the first showpiece hamlet had been overrun.

The series of setbacks and defeats suffered by the South Vietnamese government forces in the Cu Chi area helped make a complete Viet Cong victory by the end of 1965 seem a distinct possibility. Indeed, in the early months of that year, the guerrillas boldly held a victory parade in the middle of Cu Chi town. Viet Cong strength in and around Cu Chi was one of the reasons the Johnson administration decided to involve American combat troops in the war.

To deal with the threat posed by Viet Cong control of an area so near the South Vietnamese capital, one of the Americans' first actions was to establish a large base camp in Cu Chi District. Unknowingly, they built it right on top of an existing tunnel network. It took months for the 25th Division to figure out why they kept getting shot at in their tents at night.

The Americans and Australians tried to 'pacify' the area around Cu Chi that came to be known as the 'Iron Triangle' by a variety of methods. They launched large-scale ground operations involving tens of thousands of troops but failed to locate the tunnels. To deny the Viet Cong cover and supplies, rice paddies were defoliated, huge swathes of jungle bulldozed and villages evacuated and razed. The Americans also sprayed chemical defoliants on the area from the air and then, a few-months later, ignited the tinder-dry vegetation with gasoline and napalm. But the intense heat interacted with the wet tropical air in such a way as to create cloudbursts that extinguished the fires. The Viet Cong remained safe and sound in their tunnels.

Unable to win this battle with chemicals, the US Army began sending men down into the tunnels. These 'tunnel rats', who were often involved in underground fire fights, sustained appallingly high casualty rates.

When the Americans began using Alsatians trained to use their keen sense of smell to locate trapdoors and guerrillas, the Viet Cong put out pepper to distract the dogs. They also began washing with American toilet soap, which gave off a scent the canines identified as friendly. Captured American uniforms, which had the familiar smell of bodies nourished on American-style food, were put out to confuse the dogs further. Most importantly, the dogs were not able to spot booby traps. So many dogs were killed or maimed that their horrified army handlers refused to send them into the tunnels.

The Americans declared Cu Chi a free-fire zone: minimal authorisation was needed to shoot at anything in the area, random artillery was fired into the area at night and pilots were told to drop unused bombs and napalm there before returning to base. But the Viet Cong stayed put. Finally, in the late 1960s, the Americans carpet-bombed the whole area with B-52s, destroying most of the tunnels along with everything else around. But it was too late; the USA was already on its way out of the war. The tunnels had served their purpose.

The Viet Cong guerrillas serving in the tunnels lived in extremely difficult conditions and suffered horrific casualties. Only about 6000 of the 16,000 cadres who fought in the tunnels survived the war. In addition, uncounted thousands of civilians in the area, relatives of many of the guerrillas, were killed. Their tenacity despite the bombings, the pressures of living underground for weeks and months at a time and the deaths of countless friends and comrades is difficult to comprehend.

The villages of Cu Chi have been presented with numerous honorific awards, decorations and citations by the government, and many have been declared 'heroic villages'. Since 1975, new hamlets have been established and the population of the area has more than doubled to 200,000, but chemical defoliants remain in the soil and water and crop yields are still poor.

For more details, you might want to take a look at *The Tunnels of Cu Chi* by Tom Mangold & John Penycate (Random House, New York, 1985).

The Tunnels

Over the years the Viet Cong, learning by trial and error, developed simple but effective techniques to make their tunnels difficult to detect or disable. Wooden trapdoors were camouflaged with earth and branches; some were booby-trapped. Hidden underwater entrances from rivers were constructed. To cook, they used 'Dien Bien Phu kitchens', which exhausted the smoke through vents many metres away from the cooking site. Trapdoors were installed throughout the network to prevent tear gas, smoke or water from moving from one part of the system to another. Some sections were even equipped with electric lighting.

Presently, two of the tunnel sites are open to visitors. One is near the village of Ben Binh and the other is at Ben Duoc.

The Tunnels at Ben Binh

This small, renovated section of the tunnel system is near the village of Ben Binh. In one of the classrooms of the visitors' centre, a large map shows the extent of the network (the area shown is in the north-western corner of Greater Ho Chi Minh City). The tunnels are marked in red. Viet Cong bases are shown in light grey. The light blue lines are rivers (the Saigon River is at the top). Fortified villages held by South Vietnamese and American forces are marked in grey. Blue dots represent the American and South Vietnamese military posts that were supposed to ensure the security of nearby villages. The dark blue area in the centre is the base of the American 25th Infantry Division. Most pre-arranged tours do not take you to this former base, but it is not off limits and if you have your own guide and driver you can easily arrange a visit.

To the right of the large map are two cross-section diagrams of the tunnels. The bottom diagram is a reproduction of one used by General William Westmoreland, the commander of American forces in Vietnam from 1964 to 1968. For once, the Americans seemed to have had their intelligence information right (though the tunnels did not pass under rivers nor did the guerrillas wear headgear underground).

The section of the tunnel system presently open to visitors is a few hundred metres south of the visitors' centre. It snakes up and down through various chambers along its 50-metre length. The unlit tunnels are about 1.2 metres high and 80 cm across. A knocked-out M-48 tank and a bomb crater are near the exit, which is in a reafforested eucalyptus grove.

Entry to the tunnel site, which is now controlled by Saigon Tourist, costs US$2 for foreigners but is free for Vietnamese nationals.

The Tunnels at Ben Duoc

These are not the genuine tunnels but a full-fledged reconstruction for the benefit of tourists. The emphasis here is more on the fun fare, and tourists are given the chance to imagine what it was like to be a guerilla. At this site there is even the opportunity to fire an M-16, AK-47 or Russian carbine rifle. This costs US$1 per bullet, but may be the only opportunity you'll ever get. It's recommended that you wear hearing protection.

Admission to the tunnels at Ben Duoc is US$3.

Cu Chi War History Museum

This museum is not actually at the tunnel sites but, rather, just off the main highway in the central area of the town of Cu Chi. Sad to say, the Cu Chi War History Museum (Nha Truyen Thong Huyen Cu Chi) is rather disappointing and gets few visitors.

It's a small museum, and almost all explanations are in Vietnamese. Indeed, we found only one English explanation, a placard attached to a canoe which read:

Mr Nguyen Van Tranh's boat. He now is living in hamlet Mui Con, Phuoc Hiep village. During the wars against the French colonialists and the American imperialists, he was using this boat for transporting food and weapons as well as carrying revolutionary cadres to and fro.

There is a collection of some gruesome photos showing severely wounded or dead civilians after being attacked by American bombs or burned with napalm. A painting on the wall shows American soldiers armed with rifles being attacked by Vietnamese peasants armed only with sticks. A sign near the photos formerly read (in Vietnamese) 'American conquest and crimes', but this was changed in 1995 to read 'Enemy conquest and crimes'. Apparently, some effort is being made to tone down the rhetoric in anticipation of receiving more American visitors.

One wall of the museum contains a long list of names, all Viet Cong guerillas killed in the Cu Chi area. An adjacent room of the museum displays recent photos of prosperous farms and factories, an effort to show the benefits of Vietnam's economic reforms. There is also an odd collection of pottery and lacquerware with no explanations attached. In the lobby near the entrance is a statue of Ho Chi Minh with his right arm raised, waving hello.

Admission to the Cu Chi War History Museum costs US$1 for foreigners.

Getting There & Away

Cu Chi is a district which covers a large area, parts of which are as close as 30 km to Saigon. The Cu Chi War History Museum is the closest place to the city, but the actual tunnels that exist now are about 65 km from central Saigon by highway. However, there is a backroad which cuts the commute down to 35 km, though it means driving on bumpy dirt roads.

Bus Buses from Ho Chi Minh City to Tay Ninh leave from the Tay Ninh Bus Station (Ben Xe Tay Ninh) in Tan Binh District and Mien Tay Bus Station in An Lac. All buses to Tay Ninh pass though Cu Chi town, but getting from the town of Cu Chi to the tunnels by public transport is difficult.

Taxi Hiring a taxi in Saigon and just driving out to Cu Chi is not all that expensive, especially if the cost is split by several people. If you want to visit the 'real' tunnels rather than those open to the public, make this clear to your driver before you cut a deal. A non-English-speaking guide can be hired at the visitors' centre. For details on hiring vehicles in Saigon, see the Getting There & Away and Getting Around sections in the Ho Chi Minh City chapter.

A visit to the Cu Chi tunnel complex can easily be combined with a stop at the headquarters of the Caodai sect in Tay Ninh. A taxi for an all-day excursion to both should cost about US$40.

Tours Some of the cafes on Pham Ngu Lao St run combined full-day tours to the Cu Chi Tunnels and Caodai Temple for as little as US$5. Organised tours run by Saigon Tourist and Vietnam Tourism often visit the Cu Chi Tunnels, but these are no bargain. Private travel agents can also make arrangements.

TAY NINH

Tay Ninh town, capital of Tay Ninh Province, serves as the headquarters of one of Vietnam's most interesting indigenous religions, Caodaism. The Caodai Great Temple at the sect's Holy See is one of the most striking structures in all of Asia. Built between 1933 and 1955, it is a rococo extravaganza combining the architectural idiosyncrasies of a French church, a Chinese pagoda, the Tiger Balm Gardens and Madame Tussaud's Wax Museum.

Tay Ninh Province, which is north-west of Ho Chi Minh City, is bordered by Cambodia on three sides. The area's dominant geographic feature is Nui Ba Den (Black Lady Mountain), which towers 850 metres above the surrounding plains. Tay Ninh Province's eastern border is formed by the Saigon River. The Vam Co River flows from Cambodia through the western part of the province.

Because of the once-vaunted political and military power of the Caodai, this region was the scene of prolonged heavy fighting during the Franco-Viet Minh War. Tay Ninh Province served as a major terminus of the Ho Chi

Minh Trail during the Vietnam War. In 1969, the Viet Cong captured Tay Ninh town and held it for several days.

During the period of tension between Cambodia and Vietnam in the late-1970s, the Khmer Rouge launched a number of cross-border raids into Tay Ninh Province, during which horrific atrocities were committed against the civilian population. Several grisly cemeteries around Tay Ninh are stark reminders of these atrocities.

Information
Tourist Office Tay Ninh Tourist (☎ 22376) is presently in the Hoa Binh Hotel on 30/4 St. However, the office is supposed to move just across the street when a new building is completed, though no word yet on just when that might be. The staff here have plans to introduce tours to nearby Dau Tieng Reservoir, complete with boat trips and optional waterskiing.

Interestingly, they currently offer tours across the border 17 km into Cambodia to the hamlet of Chang Riet. The destination here is the Southern Central Department Base (Can Cu Trung Uong Cuc Mien Nam), an old Viet Cong base 62 km north-west of Tay Ninh. It was intentionally located inside Cambodia to avoid attacks by South Vietnamese troops. It served as Communist Party headquarters for the southern command from 1973 to 1975. Unfortunately, these tours are currently only open to domestic tourists. Possibly foreigners will be allowed in the future if certain bureaucratic visa hurdles can be overcome.

The Caodai Religion
Caodaism (Dai Dao Tam Ky Pho Do) is the product of an attempt to create the ideal religion through the fusion of the secular and religious philosophies of the East and West. The result is a colourful and eclectic potpourri that includes bits and pieces of most of the religious philosophies known in Vietnam during the early 20th century: Buddhism, Confucianism, Taoism, native Vietnamese spiritism, Christianity and Islam.

The term 'Caodai', which literally means 'high tower or palace', is used to refer to God. The religion is called 'Caodaism'; its adherents are the 'Caodais'. The hierarchy of the sect, whose priesthood is non-professional, is partly based on the structure of the Roman Catholic Church.

History Caodaism was founded by the mystic Ngo Minh Chieu (also known as Ngo Van Chieu; born 1878), a civil servant who once served as district chief of Phu Quoc Island. He was widely read in Eastern and Western religious works and became active in seances, at which his presence was said to greatly improve the quality of communication with the spirits. Around 1919 he began to receive a series of revelations from Caodai in which the tenets of Caodai doctrine were set forth.

Caodaism was officially founded as a religion in a ceremony held in 1926. Within a year, the group had 26,000 followers. Many of the sect's early followers were Vietnamese members of the French colonial administration. By the mid-1950s, one in eight southern Vietnamese was a Caodai, and the sect was famous worldwide for its imaginative garishness. But in 1954, British author Graham Greene, who had once considered converting to Caodaism, wrote in *The Times* of London: 'What on my first two visits has seemed gay and bizarre (was) now like a game that had gone on too long'.

By the mid-'50s, the Caodai had established a virtually independent feudal state in Tay Ninh Province, and they retained enormous influence in the affairs of Tay Ninh Province for the next two decades. They also played a significant political and military role in South Vietnam from 1926 to 1956, when most of the 25,000-strong Caodai army, which had been given support by the Japanese and later the French, was incorporated into the South Vietnamese army. During the Franco-Viet Minh War, Caodai munitions factories specialised in making mortar tubes out of automobile exhaust pipes.

Because they had refused to support the Viet Cong during the Vietnam War – and despite the fact that they had been barely tolerated by the Saigon government – the Caodai feared the worst after reunification. Indeed, all Caodai lands were confiscated by the new Communist government and four members of the sect were executed in 1979, but in 1985, the Holy See and some 400 temples were returned to Caodai control.

Caodaism is strongest in Tay Ninh Province and the Mekong Delta, but Caodai temples can be found throughout southern and central Vietnam. Today, there are an estimated three million followers of Caodaism. Vietnamese who fled abroad after the Communists came to power have spread the Caodai religion to Western countries, though their numbers are not large.

Philosophy Much of Caodai doctrine is drawn from Mahayana Buddhism mixed with Taoist and Confucian elements (Vietnam's 'Triple Religion'). Caodai ethics are based on the Buddhist ideal of 'the good person' but incorporate traditional Vietnamese taboos and sanctions as well.

The ultimate goal of the disciple of Caodaism is to escape the cycle of reincarnation. This can be achieved by the performance of certain human duties, including first and foremost following the prohibitions against killing, lying, luxurious living, sensuality and stealing.

The main tenets of Caodaism include believing in one God, the existence of the soul and the use of mediums to communicate with the spiritual world. Caodai practices include priestly celibacy, vegetarianism, communications with spirits through seances, reverence for the dead, maintenance of the cult of ancestors, fervent proselytising and sessions of meditative self-cultivation.

Following the Chinese duality of Yin and Yang, there are two principal deities, the Mother Goddess, who is female, and God, who is male. There is a debate among the Caodai as to which deity was the primary source of creation.

According to Caodaism, history is divided into three major periods of divine revelation. During the first period, God's truth was revealed to humanity through Laotse and figures associated with Buddhism, Confucianism and Taoism. The human agents of revelation during the second period were Buddha (Sakyamuni), Mohammed, Confucius, Jesus and Moses. The Caodai believe that their messages were corrupted because of the human frailty of the messengers and their disciples. They also believe that these revelations were limited in scope, intended to be applicable only during a specific age to the people of the area in which the messengers lived.

Caodaism sees itself as the product of the 'Third Alliance Between God and Man', the third and final revelation. Disciples believe that Caodaism avoids the failures of the first two periods because it is based on divine truth as communicated through spirits, which serve as messengers of salvation and instructors of doctrine. Spirits who have been in touch with the Caodai include deceased Caodai leaders, patriots, heroes, philosophers, poets, political leaders and warriors as well as ordinary people. Among the contacted spirits who lived as Westerners are Joan of Arc, René Descartes, William Shakespeare (who hasn't been heard from since 1935), Victor Hugo, Louis Pasteur and Vladimir Ilyich Lenin. Because of his frequent appearances to Caodai mediums at the Phnom Penh mission, Victor Hugo was posthumously named the chief spirit of foreign missionary works.

Communication with the spirits is carried on in Vietnamese, Chinese, French and English. The methods of receiving messages from the spirits illustrate the influence of both East Asian and Western spiritism on Caodai seance rites. Sometimes, a medium holds a pen or Chinese calligraphy brush. In the 1920s, a 66-cm-long wooden staff known as a *corbeille à bec* was used. Medium(s) held one end while a crayon attached to the other wrote out the spirits' messages. The Caodai also use what is known as *pneumatographie*, in which a blank slip of paper is sealed in an envelope and hung above the altar. When the envelope is taken down, there is a message on the paper.

Most of the sacred literature of Caodaism consists of messages communicated to Caodai leaders during seances held between 1925 and 1929. Since 1927, only the official seances held at Tay Ninh have been considered reliable and divinely ordained by the Caodai hierarchy, though dissident groups continued to hold seances which produced communications contradicting accepted doctrine.

The Caodai consider vegetarianism to be of service to humanity because it does not involve harming fellow beings during the process of their spiritual evolution. They also see vegetarianism as a form of self-purification. There are several different vegetarian regimens followed by Caodai disciples. The least rigorous involves eating vegetarian food six days a month. Priests must be full-time vegetarians.

The clergy (except at the highest levels) is open to both men and women, though when male and female officials of equal rank are serving in the same area, male clergy are in charge. Female officials wear white robes and are addressed with the title *Huong*, which means 'perfume'. Male clergy are addressed as *Thanh*, which means 'pure'. Caodai temples are constructed so that male and female disciples enter on opposite sides; women worship on the left, men on the right.

All Caodai temples observe four daily ceremonies, which are held at 6 am, noon, 6 pm and midnight. These rituals, during which dignitaries wear ceremonial dress and hats, include offerings of incense, tea, alcohol, fruit and flowers. All Caodai altars have above them the 'divine eye', which became the religion's official symbol after Ngo Minh Chieu saw it in a vision he had while on Phu Quoc Island.

Caodai Holy See

The Caodai Holy See, founded in 1926, is four km east of Tay Ninh in the village of

Long Hoa. Guests should wear modest and respectful attire (no shorts or tank tops). The complex includes the Great Temple, administrative offices, residences for officials and adepts, and a hospital of traditional Vietnamese herbal medicine to which people from all over the south travel for treatment. After reunification, the government 'borrowed' parts of the complex for its own use (and perhaps to keep an eye on the sect).

Prayers are conducted in the Great Temple every day at 6 am, noon, 6 pm and midnight, though they may be suspended during Tet. It's worth visiting during prayer sessions (the one at noon is most popular with tour groups from Saigon, but take care not to disturb the worshippers. Only a few hundred priests participate in weekday prayers, but on festivals several thousand priests, dressed in special white garments, may attend. The Caodai clergy have no objection to your photographing temple objects, but you cannot photograph people without their permission, which is seldom granted. However, you can photograph the prayer sessions from the upstairs balcony, an apparent concession to the troops of tourists who come here every day.

Above the front portico of the Great Temple is the 'divine eye', the supreme symbol of Caodaism. Americans often comment that it looks as if it were copied from the back of a US$1 bill. Lay women enter the Great Temple through a door at the base of the tower on the left. Once inside, they walk around the outside of the colonnaded hall in a clockwise direction. Men enter on the right and circumambulate the hall in a counter-clockwise direction. Shoes and hats must be removed upon entering the building. The area in the centre of the sanctuary (between the pillars) is reserved for Caodai priests.

A mural in the front entry hall depicts the three signatories of the 'Third Alliance Between God and Man'. The Chinese statesman and revolutionary leader Dr Sun Yatsen (1866-1925) holds an inkstone while Vietnamese poet Nguyen Binh Khiem (1492-1587) and Victor Hugo (1802-85), French poet and author, write 'God and Humanity' and 'Love and Justice' in Chinese and French. Victor Hugo uses a quill pen; Nguyen Binh Khiem writes with a brush. Nearby signs in English, French and German each give a slightly different version of the fundamentals of Caodaism.

The Great Temple is built on nine levels, which represent the nine steps to heaven. Each level is marked by a pair of columns. At the far end of the sanctuary, eight plaster columns entwined with multicoloured dragons support a dome representing – as does the rest of the ceiling – the heavens. Under the dome is a giant star-speckled blue globe with the 'divine eye' on it.

The largest of the seven chairs in front of the globe is reserved for the Caodai pope, a position that has remained unfilled since 1933. The next three chairs are for the three men responsible for the religion's law books. The remaining chairs are for the leaders of the three branches of Caodaism, which are represented by the colours yellow, blue and red.

On both sides of the area between the columns are two pulpits similar in design to the *minbars* found in mosques. During festivals, the pulpits are used by officials to address the assembled worshippers. The upstairs balconies are used if there is an overflow crowd downstairs.

Up near the altar are barely discernible portraits of six figures important to Caoda-

Great Temple at the Caodai Holy See, Tay Ninh

ism: Sakyamuni (founder of Buddhism), Ly Thai Bach (Li Taibai, a fairy from Chinese mythology), Khuong Tu Nha (Jiang Taigong, a Chinese saint), Lao Tu (Laotse, the founder of Taoism), Quan Cong (Guangong, Chinese God of War) and Quan Am (Guanyin, the Goddess of Mercy).

Long Hoa Market

Long Hoa Market is several kilometres south of the Caodai Holy See complex. Open every day from 5 am to about 6 pm, this large market sells meat, food staples, clothing and pretty much everything else you would expect to find in a rural marketplace. Before reunification, the Caodai sect had the right to collect taxes from the merchants here.

Places to Stay

The main place in town accepting foreigners is the *Hoa Binh Hotel* (☎ 22376, 22383; 57 rooms) on 30/4 St. Rooms with fan only are US$6, but most rooms have air-con and are priced from US$8 to US$18. The hotel is five km from the Caodai Temple.

The other alternative is the *Anh Dao Hotel* on 30/4 St, 500 metres west of the Hoa Binh Hotel. There are 14 double rooms here priced from US$8 to US$16.

Places to Eat

Nha Hang Diem Thuy (☎ 27318) on 30/4 St is a great restaurant with low prices. Giant crayfish (tom can) are one of their specialities and, though not cheap, cost only one-third of what you'd pay in Saigon.

One km north of the Tay Ninh market near the river is the *Hoang Yen Restaurant*, considered by locals to be the best in town. Right on the river next to the bridge is the government-owned *Festival Restaurant*, which has great ambience, though the food is not spectacular.

Getting There & Away

Bus Buses from Ho Chi Minh City to Tay Ninh leave from the Tay Ninh Bus Station (Ben Xe Tay Ninh) in Tan Binh District and Mien Tay Bus Station in An Lac.

Tay Ninh is 96 km from Ho Chi Minh City

on National Highway 22 (Quoc Lo 22). The road passes through Trang Bang, where a famous news photo of a young naked girl, severely burned, screaming and running, was taken during an American napalm attack. There are several Caodai temples along National Route 22, including one, under construction in 1975, that was heavily damaged by the Viet Cong.

Taxi An easy way to get to Tay Ninh is by taxi, perhaps on a day trip that includes a stop in Cu Chi. An all-day round trip by taxi should cost about US$40.

NUI BA DEN

Nui Ba Den (Black Lady Mountain), 15 km north-east of Tay Ninh town, rises 850 metres above the rice paddies of the surrounding countryside. Over the centuries, Nui Ba Den has served as a shrine for various peoples of the area, including the Khmer, Chams, Vietnamese and Chinese. There are several cave-temples on the mountain. The summits of Nui Ba Den are much cooler than the rest of Tay Ninh Province, most of which is only a few dozen metres above sea level.

Nui Ba Den was used as a staging ground by both the Viet Minh and the Viet Cong and was the scene of fierce fighting during the French and American wars. At one time, there was a US Army fire base and relay station at the summit of the mountain, which was defoliated and heavily bombed by American aircraft.

The name Black Lady Mountain is derived from the legend of Huong, a young woman who married her true love despite the advances of a wealthy mandarin. While her husband was away doing military service, she would visit a magical statue of Buddha at the summit of the mountain. One day, Huong was attacked by kidnappers but, preferring death to dishonour, threw herself off a cliff. She reappeared in the visions of a monk living on the mountain, who told her story.

The hike from the base of the mountain to the main temple complex and back takes about 1½ hour. Although steep in parts, it's not a difficult walk – plenty of elderly women in sandals make the journey to worship at the temple. At the base of the mountain, you'll have to fend off the usual crowd of very persistent kids selling tourist junk, lottery tickets and chewing gum – they'll pursue you up the mountain but you can easily outpace them if you wear running shoes and don't carry a heavy bag. Things are much more relaxed around the temple complex where there are only a few stands selling snacks and drinks and the vendors are not pushy.

If you need more exercise, a walk to the summit of the peak and back takes about six hours.

Visiting during a holiday or festival is a bad idea. Aside from the crowds, at such times the main gate is closed. This forces vehicles to park two km away from the trailhead, which means you've got an additional four-km walk added to the return trip. This extra walking eats up a good deal of extra time, making it difficult to complete the trip if you're coming from Saigon and returning the same night.

Places to Stay

About 500 metres past the main entrance gate are eight A-frame bungalows, where double rooms can be rented for US$6 to US$10.

ONE PILLAR PAGODA

The official name of this interesting place is Nam Thien Nhat Tru, but everyone calls it the One Pillar Pagoda of Thu Duc (Chua Mot Cot Thu Duc).

The One Pillar Pagoda of Thu Duc is modelled after Hanoi's One Pillar Pagoda, though the two structures do not look identical. Hanoi's original pagoda was built in the 9th century, but was destroyed by the French and rebuilt by the Vietnamese in 1954. Ho Chi Minh City's version was constructed in 1958.

When Vietnam was partitioned in 1954, Buddhist monks and Catholic priests wisely fled south so that they could avoid persecution and continue practicing their religion.

One monk from Hanoi who came south in 1954 was Thich Tri Dung. Shortly after arrival in Saigon, Thich petitioned the South Vietnamese government for permission to construct a replica of Hanoi's famous One Pillar Pagoda. However, President Ngo Dinh Diem was a Catholic with little tolerance for Buddhist clergy, and he denied permission. Nevertheless, Thich and his supporters raised the funds and built the pagoda in defiance of the president's orders. At one point, the government ordered the monks to tear down the temple, but they refused even though they were threatened with imprisonment for not complying. Faced with significant opposition, the government's dispute with the monks reached a stand-off. However, the president's attempts to harass and intimidate the monks in a country that was 90% Buddhist did not go down well, and ultimately contributed to Diem's assassination by his own troops in 1963.

In the current politically correct atmosphere, Vietnamese history books say that this pagoda served as a base for Viet Cong guerillas who disguised themselves as clergy. This is stretching the truth. At this pagoda and others, the Viet Cong cadres did pose as poor peasants from the countryside willing to donate their labour to Buddhism. This provided them with a convenient cover so that they could live in Saigon and conduct secret activities (political indoctrination meetings, smuggling weapons, planting bombs, etc) at night. While most monks then (and now) were divorced from politics, it's doubtful that they had any idea just to what extent they were being used by the Viet Cong.

During the war, the One Pillar Pagoda of Thu Duc was in possession of an extremely valuable plaque said to weigh 612 kg. After liberation, the government took it for 'safekeeping' and brought it to Hanoi. However, none of the monks alive today could say just where it is. There is speculation that the government sold it to overseas collectors, but this cannot be confirmed. Certainly, it belongs in a museum.

The One Pillar Pagoda (☎ 960780) is in

the Thu Duc District, about 15 km east of central Saigon. The official address is 1/91 Nguyen Du St. Tours to the pagoda are rare, so most likely you'll have to visit by rented motorbike or car.

CAN GIO
The only beach within the municipality of Ho Chi Minh City is at Can Gio, a swampy island where the Saigon River meets the sea. The island was created by silt washing downstream, with the result that the beach consists of hard-packed mud rather than the fluffy white sand that sun worshippers crave. Furthermore, the beach sits in an exposed position and is lashed by strong winds. For these reasons, Can Gio gets few visitors and the beach remains entirely undeveloped.

Before you scratch Can Gio off your list of places to visit, it's worth noting that the island does have a wild beauty of its own. Unlike the rest of Ho Chi Minh City, overpopulation is hardly a problem here. The lack of human inhabitants is chiefly because the island lacks any fresh water supply.

The land here is only about two metres above sea level and the island is basically one big mangrove swamp. The salty mud makes most forms of agriculture impossible, but aquaculture is another matter. The most profitable business here is shrimp farming. Also, the hard-packed mud beach teems with clams and other sea life, which island residents dig up to sell or eat themselves. There is also a small salt industry – sea water is diverted into shallow ponds and is left to evaporate until a white layer of salt can be harvested. Can Gio also has a small port where fishing boats can dock, but the shallow water prevents any large ships from dropping anchor here.

From about 1945 through 1954, Can Gio was controlled by Bay Vien, a general who also controlled a casino in Cholon. He was something of an independent warlord and gangster, but former President Ngo Dinh Diem persuaded Bay Vien to join forces with the South Vietnamese government. Not long thereafter, Bay Vien was murdered by an unknown assailant.

Can Gio Market
Can Gio does have a large market, made conspicuous by some rather powerful odours. Seafood and salt are definitely the local specialties. The vegetables, rice and fruit are all imported by boat from Saigon.

Caodai Temple
Though much smaller than the Caodai Great Temple at Tay Ninh, Can Gio can boast a Caodai Temple of its own. The temple is near the market and is easy to find. We didn't see anybody around, and it seems that you can just walk inside and photograph as you please. Of course, if you encounter any worshippers, be respectful and don't photograph them without at least asking first.

War Memorial & Cemetery
Adjacent to the shrimp hatchery is a large and conspicuous cemetery and war memorial (Nghia Trang Liet Si Rung Sac). Like all such sites in Vietnam, the praise for bravery and patriotism goes entirely to the winning side and there is nothing said about the losers. Indeed, all of the former war cemeteries containing remains of South Vietnamese soldiers were bulldozed after liberation, a fact which still causes much bitterness.

The War Memorial & Cemetery is two km from Can Gio Market.

Shrimp Hatchery
Cofidec (Coastal Fishery Development Corporation, or Cty Phat Trien Kinh Te Duyen Hai in Vietnamese) is a large company which has sewn up much of the shrimp-breeding industry in Can Gio. This is a joint venture with the Philippines and appears to be very well organised. Two types of shrimp – black tiger and white shrimp – are bred here. One building houses a small plant where the shrimp are cleaned, packed and frozen before being shipped off to Saigon.

Cofidec has its operational headquarters close to the War Memorial in Can Gio, but the shrimp-breeding ponds stretch out for several kilometres along the beachfront.

The staff at Cofidec are friendly and not opposed to your poking around a bit, but please don't interfere with their operations. Foreigners will continue to be welcomed here only if they tread lightly. This is private property, and the management could easily put up 'no trespassing' signs if travellers don't behave themselves. Some of the staff speak English, and if you approach them positively they may be willing to show you around a bit and explain their operation.

The Beach

The southern side of the island faces the sea, creating a beachfront nearly 10 km long. Unfortunately, a good deal of it is inaccessible because it's been fenced off by shrimp farmers and clam diggers. Nevertheless, there is a point about four km west of the Can Gio Market where a dirt road turns off the main highway to Saigon and leads to the beach. The road can be distinguished by having some telephone poles and wires alongside it. At the beach, you'll find a small collection of buildings belonging to Cofidec and a forlorn shack selling food and drinks.

The surface of the beach is as hard as concrete, and it is possible to drive a motorbike on it. However, this is not recommended as it damages the local ecology. While the beach may seem dead at first glance, it swarms with life just below the surface as the breathing holes in the mud suggest. You can hear the crunch of tiny clam shells as you stroll along the surface. The water here is extremely shallow and you can walk far from shore, but take care – you can be sure that there is a good deal of inhospitable and well-armed sea life in these shallow waters. Stingrays, stone fish and sea urchins are just some of the xenophobic local residents who can and will retaliate if you step on them.

The hills of the Vung Tau Peninsula are easily visible on a clear day. You should also be able to the see offshore oil-drilling platforms which belong to Vietsovpetro.

Places to Stay

Most visitors do Can Gio as a day trip, and for good reason – the one hotel in town has only four rooms, is overpriced and is a dump. In fact, the *Duyen Hai Hotel* (Khach San Duyen Hai; ☎ 740246) is usually full and you need to call ahead for a reservation if you intend to stay. Vietnamese pay US$2, and when we asked the price for foreigners the manager seemed unsure. After thinking about it for a while, he decided on US$10. Personally, we thought that US$2 was too expensive for this shack, so maybe you should try bargaining.

The hotel does have a fresh-water tank, which means you don't have to bathe with sea water. The water is brought in from Saigon by ship, so perhaps this partially justifies the price charged for this downmarket accommodation. Toilets are a long walk from the main building. In fact, the toilets are built on stilts over a canal, which might just reduce your enthusiasm for eating Can Gio clams.

The hotel is about four km from the main beach area.

Places to Eat

There are a few stalls around the market near the fishing port, but one look at the level of sanitation can eliminate your appetite without the need to eat anything at all!

That having been said, Can Gio boasts one remarkably good restaurant with an extensive menu. In fact, it's so good that Saigonese in the know come to Can Gio for no other reason than to eat here. The place you want is the *Duyen Hai Restaurant*, which is a stone's throw from the Duyen Hai Hotel. Unlike the hotel, the restaurant is good value.

There is one solitary food and drink stall next to the beach. Basically, all they have on the menu is Coca-Cola and instant noodles, but it beats starving. It might be prudent to bring some bottled water with you on the off chance that this food stall is closed.

Getting There & Away

Motorbike & Car Can Gio is about 60 km from central Saigon, and the fastest way to make the journey is by motorbike. Travel time is approximately three hours.

Cars can also make the journey, but this is much slower. The reason is that you need to make two ferry crossings. The large ferries which can accommodate cars are infrequent. By contrast, small boats make these crossings every few minutes, shuttling passengers and motorbikes. These small boats are so cheap that you could even charter one if need be.

The first ferry crossing is 15 km from Saigon at Cat Lai, a former US Navy base. Small ferry boats cost about US$0.20 for a motorbike and two passengers. Cars must wait for the large ferry, which runs about once every 30 minutes, and there is usually a long queue of vehicles.

The second ferry, which is less frequent, is 35 km from Saigon and connects the two tiny villages of Dan Xay (closer to Saigon) with Hao Vo (on Can Gio Island). Motorbike riders can take a small ferry which costs around US$0.35 and runs about once every 10 to 15 minutes. The car ferry is much less frequent, but there is a posted schedule:

Ferry Departure Times

Dan Xay	Hao Vo
5 am	5.15 am
7	7.15
8.30	8.45
10	10.15
11.30	11.45
1 pm	1.15 pm
2.30	2.45
4	4.15
5.30	5.45
7	

The road is paved up to the first ferry at Cat Lai – after that, it's a dirt surface but gets regular maintenance and is in good nick. Once you get past the first ferry, there is very little traffic and both sides of the road are lined with lush mangrove forests.

Boat There is one boat daily between Can Gio and Saigon. From either direction, the boat departs at approximately 5 to 6 am and takes six hours for the journey.

There is also a small boat between Can Gio and Vung Tau. Departures from Can Gio are at 5 am, arriving in Vung Tau at 8 am. The boat departs Vung Tau at about noon, arriving in Can Gio three hours later. Occasionally, there is a later boat leaving Can Gio at around 2 pm, but you need to inquire because it doesn't run daily.

In Can Gio, you catch boats at the shipyards, which are built on an inlet two km west of the Can Gio Market. In Saigon, you get the boat at Thu Thiem, the pier on the opposite shore of the Saigon River from the Floating Hotel. In Vung Tau, you catch the boats from the beachfront market area opposite the Grand Hotel.

BUU LONG MOUNTAIN

Various tourist pamphlets and even local residents of Saigon will tell you that Buu Long Mountain is the 'Halong Bay of the south'. Seeing how Halong Bay is northern Vietnam's top scenic drawing card, you might be forgiven for thinking that Buu Long Mountain must be nothing short of stunningly beautiful.

Indubitably, we were stunned when we visited Buu Long Mountain. Mostly, we were stunned that anyone would waste the time and admission fee to visit this place. Residents of Saigon indeed have a vivid imagination to call this another Halong Bay. Residents of Halong Bay ought to consider filing a defamation lawsuit against whoever invented that silly tourist slogan and wrote those pamphlets.

Nevertheless, if you're bored and want to enjoy some perverse sort of comic relief, it does no harm to visit Buu Long Mountain. The summit towers a big 60 metres above the car park. During the five-minute walk to the top, beggars and vendors will follow half a metre behind you the entire way. Your followers might try to steer you off-course to visit the 'English-speaking monk', who will charge you a fee for speaking English to him.

The top of the mountain is marked by a pagoda. From this vantage point, you can look down and clearly see Dragon Lake (Long An). The shoreline is dressed up with a few pavilions and decorative souvenir stands. To reach the lake, you have to descend the mountain and pass through another gate, where you pay an additional admission fee. And for a small extra charge, you can paddle a boat around the slimy green waters in pursuit of the dragon which is said to live at the bottom of the lake. Although we didn't spot the dragon, we did find the boat ride an excellent way to escape the lottery ticket and postcard vendors.

Buu Long Mountain is 32 km from central Saigon. It's two km off the main highway after crossing the bridge that marks the border between Ho Chi Minh City and Dong Nai province. The admission fee is US$0.30, plus there is an extra charge for bringing in a camera. Considering how little there is to see here, you might as well leave the camera at home. There are a few refreshment shops here where you can buy cold drinks and noodles.

TRI AN FALLS

The Tri An Falls are a cascade on the Be River (Song Be), eight metres high and 30 metres wide. They are especially awesome in late autumn, when the river's flow is at its greatest. Tri An Falls are in Song Be Province, 36 km from Bien Hoa and 68 km from Saigon (via Thu Dau Mot).

TRI AN DAM & RESERVOIR

Farther upstream from Tri An Falls is Tri An Reservoir (Ho Tri An). This large artificial lake is created by Tri An Dam. Completed in the early 1980s with Soviet assistance, the dam and its adjoining hydroelectric station supplies the lion's share of Ho Chi Minh City's electric power.

The reservoir, dam and hydroelectric station are off limits to tourists for security reasons. The area is not much of a tourist attraction anyway because during the dry season, the water level drops dramatically leaving an ugly 'bathtub' ring around the reservoir. Probably the main interest this place offers to outsiders could be to foreign investors – the hydroelectric station is severely overtaxed by the surging demand for electricity and the Vietnamese are reportedly looking for foreign partners to provide some sort of solution. Should you happen to be in the electrical engineering business, the

Vietnamese would probably like to hear from you.

If you are seriously contemplating a visit to Tri An Dam and Reservoir, be sure that you have official permission.

VUNG TAU

Vung Tau, known under the French as Cap Saint Jacques (it was so named by Portuguese mariners in honour of their patron saint), is a beach resort on the South China Sea, 128 km south-east of Saigon. Vung Tau's beaches are not Vietnam's nicest by any stretch of the imagination, but they are easily reached from Ho Chi Minh City and have thus been a favourite of the Saigonese since French colonists first began coming here around 1890. Seaside areas near Vung Tau are dotted with the villas of the pre-1975 elite, now converted to guesthouses and villas for the post-1975 elite.

In addition to sunning on the seashore and sipping sodas in nearby cafes, visitors to this city of 100,000 can cycle around or climb up the Vung Tau Peninsula's two mountains. There are also a number of interesting religious sites around town, including several pagodas and a huge standing figure of Jesus blessing the South China Sea.

Vung Tau was once the headquarters of Vietsovpetro, a joint Soviet-Vietnamese company that operated oil rigs about 60 km offshore. Soviet expats used to live in a large compound bordering Front Beach, occupying the most desirable neighbourhood in the city. The Russian Compound (whose entrances were, until 1989, sealed by roadblocks) was the area between Quang Trung St, Hoang Dieu St, Le Loi Blvd and Bacu St. Perhaps because of the strategic importance of oil exploration, Vung Tau was once famous for its elaborate secret police apparatus. With the collapse of the Soviet Union and waning Russian influence, the compound fences have come down and the area has given way to new hotels catering to well-heeled Western tourists. However, the oil venture continues and Russian workers with their families can still be seen around town. There are also plenty of former Hanoi

AROUND HO CHI MINH CITY

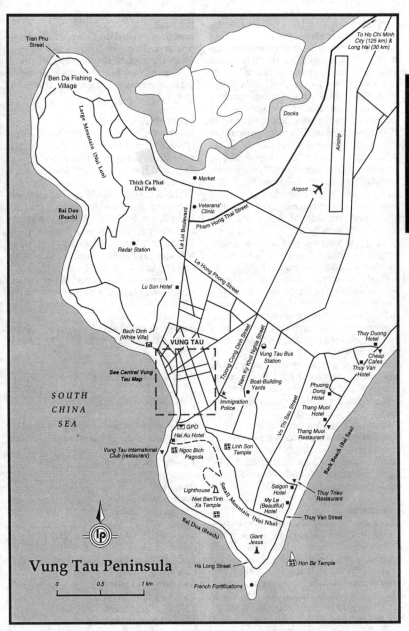

Vung Tau Peninsula

0   0.5   1 km

residents, brought in years ago for supervision of the oil fields.

Vung Tau became briefly known to the world in 1973, when the last American combat troops in Vietnam departed from here by ship. However, a small contingent of American advisers, diplomats and CIA agents remained in Vietnam for another two years – their moment on the world's centre stage came in 1975 during the rooftop helicopter evacuation from the US Embassy in Saigon.

The local fishing fleet is quite active, though many Vietnamese fleeing their homeland by sea set sail from Vung Tau, taking many of the town's fishing trawlers with them. Vietnamese navy boats on patrol offshore ensure that the rest of the fleet comes home each day.

Vung Tau has long been competing with Saigon to attract foreign 'sex tours' to Vietnam – massage parlours are ubiquitous, but there has been a recent effort to make it less visible so as to enhance the community's 'family image'. Despite claims of innocence and virginal purity by government officials, high-ranking cadres are said to be the most frequent customers, though all with hard cash are welcome.

Another negative – watch out for kids around the kiosks along Front Beach. Some may try to pick your pockets or snatch a bag.

Vung Tau is heavily commercialised and seems to be getting more so all the time. Despite this and a few other negative points, you'd still have a hard time not enjoying the place – plenty of sand, sun, surf, good food, draft beer and even a few budding discos. It's a party town and – for traffic-weary Saigonese – a welcome change of pace.

Orientation

The triangular Vung Tau Peninsula juts into the South China Sea near the mouth of the Saigon River. There are four main beach areas. On the central-west portion of the peninsula is Front Beach (Bai Truoc), the most commercialised but reasonably scenic. The south-west area is Bai Dua Beach, which is too rocky for swimming but OK to look at. Back Beach (Bai Sau), on the eastern side of

the peninsula, is the largest beach but the least scenic. Bai Dau Beach, in the north-west area, is the most laid-back and scenic of Vung Tau's beaches but has very little sand.

Much of Vung Tau's industry is located on the northern coast. The airport is also in this area.

Information

Tourist Office Ba Ria-Vung Tau Tourism (☎ 47467; fax 59860) is the official provincial tourism authority for Ba Ria-Vung Tau Province. The office is at 40/5 Thu Khoa Huan St.

The foregoing should not be confused with Vung Tau Tourism (Cong Ty Du Lich Vung Tau; ☎ 52314) at 18 Thuy Van St.

Oil Service Company & Tourism (Cong Ty Du Lich Phuc Vu Dau Khi Viet Nam; ☎ 52405; fax 52834) – better known by it's acronym OSC – owns 10 hotels in Vung Tau and is involved in a wide range of tourist-related businesses. The office is at 2 Le Loi Blvd.

Money Vietcombank (Ngan Hang Ngoai Thuong Viet Nam; ☎ 59874) is at 27-29 Tran Hung Dao Blvd.

Post & Telecommunications The GPO (☎ 52377, 52689, 52141) is at 4 Ha Long St at the southern end of Front Beach.

Immigration Police The immigration police operate out of the police station on Truong Cong Dinh St near the intersection with Ly Thuong Kiet St.

Beaches

Back Beach The main bathing area on the peninsula is Back Beach (Bai Sau, also known as Thuy Van Beach), an eight-km-long stretch of sun, sand and tourists. Unfortunately, it's also the ugliest stretch of beach in Vung Tau, largely thanks to crass commercialisation. The northern section of Back Beach is a little better because the palm trees have been left standing, but elsewhere it's basically concrete, car parks and cafes. The surf here can be dangerous.

Front Beach Front Beach (Bai Truoc, also called Thuy Duong Beach) borders the centre of town. The trees make it reasonably attractive, though the beach itself has become rocky and eroded. Shaded Quang Trung St, lined with kiosks, runs along Front Beach. Early in the morning, local fishing boats moor here to unload the night's catch and clean the nets. The workers row themselves between boats or to the beach in *thung chai*, gigantic round wicker baskets sealed with pitch.

Bai Dau Bai Dau, a quiet coconut-palm-lined beach, is probably the most scenic spot in the Vung Tau area because it hasn't been overdeveloped (yet). The beach stretches around a small bay nestled beneath the verdant western slopes of the Large Mountain. The only real problem with Bai Dau is that there isn't a lot of sand – it's a rocky beach with only a few small sandy coves where you can go bathing. Nevertheless, Bai Dau's many cheap guesthouses attract low-budget backpackers, and it would be our first choice for a relaxing holiday in Vung Tau.

Bai Dau is three km from the city centre along Tran Phu St. The best way to get there is by bicycle or motorbike – there is no public transport and the road is too rough and hilly to be negotiated by cyclos.

On a clear day you can look out from Bai Dau and see a low-lying palm-fringed island in the distance. That is Can Gio, an island at the mouth of the Mekong Delta which is within the municipal boundaries of Ho Chi Minh City. There is a once-daily boat from Vung Tau's Front Beach to Can Gio. See the Can Gio section for details.

Bai Dua Bai Dua (Roches Noires Beach) is a small, rocky beach about two km south of the town centre on Ha Long St. This is a great place to watch the sun setting over the South China Sea.

Pagodas & Temples
Hon Ba Temple Hon Ba Temple (Chua Hon Ba) is on a tiny island just south of Back Beach. It can be reached on foot at low tide.

Niet Ban Tinh Xa One of the largest Buddhist temples in Vietnam, Niet Ban Tinh Xa is on the western side of Small Mountain. Built in 1971, it is famous for its 5000-kg bronze bell, a huge reclining Buddha and intricate mosaic work.

Thich Ca Phat Dai Park
A must-see site for domestic tourists, Thich Ca Phat Dai is a hillside park of monumental Buddhist statuary built in the early 1960s. Inside the main gate and to the right is a row of small souvenir kiosks selling, among other things, inexpensive items made of sea-shells and coral. Above the kiosks, shaded paths lead to several large white cement Buddhas, a giant lotus blossom and many smaller figures of people and animals. A couple of path-side refreshment stalls sell cold drinks. There are several restaurants near the main gate.

Thich Ca Phat Dai, which is open from 6 am to 6 pm, is on the eastern side of the Large Mountain at 25 Tran Phu St. To get there from the town centre, take Le Loi Blvd north almost to the end and turn left onto Tran Phu St.

Lighthouse
The 360-degree view of the entire hammer-head-shaped peninsula from the lighthouse (*hai dang*) is truly spectacular, especially at sunset. The lighthouse was built in 1910 and sits atop Small Mountain (Nui Nho; elevation 197 metres). The concrete passage from the tower to the building next to it was constructed by the French because of Viet Minh attacks.

The narrow paved road up Small Mountain to the lighthouse intersects Ha Long St 150 metres south-west of the GPO. The grade is quite mild and could even be bicycled. There is also a dirt road (which gets muddy during the wet season) to the lighthouse from near Back Beach.

Giant Jesus
An enormous Rio de Janeiro-style figure of Jesus (Thanh Gioc) with arms outstretched gazes across the South China Sea from the southern end of Small Mountain.

The Giant Jesus, 30 metres high, was constructed in 1974 on the site of a lighthouse built by the French a century before. The statue can be reached on foot by a path that heads up the hill from a point just south of Back Beach. The path circles around to approach the figure from the back.

Unfortunately, Jesus is literally in a precarious position these days. Small Mountain continues to get smaller – the demand for rock and sand to build new hotels and highways is causing the southern slope of the mountain to be dug up and carted away. The digging has continued almost right up to the base of the statue's feet, and there is the real possibility that a bad typhoon could send the whole structure toppling into the sea. Local Christians are reportedly unhappy at the prospect of their statue being made to walk on water, and have protested the matter – so far to no avail.

Bach Dinh
Bach Dinh (White Villa, or Villa Blanche) is a former royal residence set amid frangipanis and bougainvilleas on a lushly forested hillside overlooking the sea. It is an ideal place to sit, relax and contemplate.

Bach Dinh was built in 1909 as a retreat for French governor Paul Doumer. It later became a summer palace for Vietnamese royalty. King Thanh Thai was kept here for a while under house arrest before being shipped off to the French island of Reunion to perform hard prison labour. In the late 1960s to the early '70s, the building was a part-time playground for South Vietnamese President Thieu.

The mansion itself is emphatically French in its ornamentation, which includes colourful mosaics and Roman-style busts set into the exterior walls. Inside, there is an exhibit of old Chinese (Qing Dynasty) pottery salvaged from an 18th-century shipwreck near Con Dao Island. There are also lots of 'new antiques' on sale in the villa's gift shop.

The main entrance to the park surrounding Bach Dinh is just north of Front Beach at 12 Tran Phu St. It is open from 6 am to 9 pm. The admission price is US$1.20 for foreign-ers. If you want to take photos it will cost you an additional US$0.20, and to use a video the 'service charge' is US$1.20.

There are a couple of cafes near the main gate, though they seem to do less than robust business.

Veterans' Clinic
The Veterans' Clinic (☎ 57348, 52573), officially called the Huu Nghi (Friendship) Clinic, was built in early 1989 by a group of American veterans of the Vietnam War working alongside war vets from the other side. Its construction marked a milestone in post-1975 cooperation between Americans and Vietnamese. Though the California-based Veterans' Vietnam Restoration Project, which initiated and funded the undertaking, was shamelessly overcharged by the local People's Committee, the clinic was completed and is now used for both obstetrics and general medicine. Hundreds of babies are delivered here each year. The clinic also welcomes sick travellers with hard currency.

The Veterans' Clinic is 1.5 km north of the centre of town. To get there, go 100 metres down an alley across the street from 99 Le Loi Blvd. The clinic entrance, marked by a plaque, is on the right.

Boat-Building Yards
New wooden fishing craft are built at a location which, oddly enough, is over a kilometre from the nearest water. The boat yards are on Nam Ky Khoi Nghia St, 500 metres south of Vung Tau Bus Station.

Golf Course
A Taiwanese joint venture is constructing a golf course in Vung Tau. It is not known when it will be open.

Small Mountain Circuit
The six-km circuit around Small Mountain (Nui Nho), known to the French as *le tour de la Petite Corniche*, begins at the GPO and continues on Ha Long St along the rocky coastline. A road leads up the hill to the lighthouse, 150 metres south of the GPO.

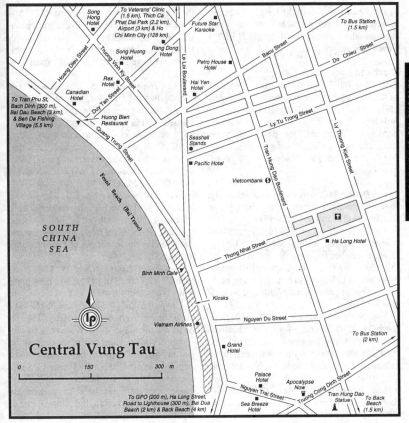

Central Vung Tau

SOUTH CHINA SEA

Song Hong Hotel

To Veterans' Clinic (1.5 km), Thich Ca Phat Dai Park (2.2 km), Airport (3 km) & Ho Chi Minh City (128 km)

Future Star Karaoke

To Bus Station (1.5 km)

Song Huong Hotel

Rang Dong Hotel

Petro House Hotel

Bacu Street

Do Chieu Street

Hoang Dieu Street

Truong Vinh Ky Street

Le Loi Boulevard

Rex Hotel

Canadian Hotel

Hai Yen Hotel

Duy Tan Street

To Tran Phu St, Bach Dinh (300 m), Bai Dau Beach (3 km), & Ben Da Fishing Village (5.5 km)

Huong Bien Restaurant

Quang Trung Street

Front Beach (Bai Truoc)

Ly Tu Trong Street

Ly Thuong Kiet Street

Seashell Stands

Pacific Hotel

Vietcombank

Tran Hung Dao Boulevard

Ha Long Hotel

Thong Nhat Street

Binh Minh Cafe

Kiosks

Nguyen Du Street

Vietnam Airlines

To Bus Station (2 km)

Grand Hotel

Palace Hotel

Apocalypse Now

Truong Cong Dinh Street

0   150   300 m

Nguyen Trai Street

Sea Breeze Hotel

Tran Hung Dao Statue

To Back Beach (1.5 km)

To GPO (200 m), Ha Long Street, Road to Lighthouse (300 m), Bai Dua Beach (2 km) & Back Beach (4 km)

Ha Long St passes Ngoc Bich Pagoda (which is built in the style of Hanoi's famous One Pillar Pagoda), Bai Dua Beach and a number of villas before reaching the tip of the Vung Tau Peninsula. The promontory here, reached through a traditional gate, was once guarded by French naval guns whose reinforced concrete emplacements remain, slowly crumbling in the salt air.

Phan Boi Chau St goes from the southern end of Back Beach into town along the eastern base of Small Mountain, passing century-old Linh Son Temple, which contains a Buddha of pre-Angkorian Khmer origin.

Large Mountain Circuit

The 10-km circuit around the Large Mountain (Nui Lon; elevation 520 metres) passes seaside villas, Bai Dau Beach, the homes of poor families living in old French fortifications and a number of quarries where boulders blown out of the hillside by dynamite are made into gravel by workers using sledgehammers. Blasting sometimes closes the road for a few hours. At the northern tip of the Large Mountain is Ben Da fishing village with its large church; from here a road leads up and along the spine of the hill to the old radar installation (rada).

On the eastern side of the Large Mountain, which faces tidal marshes and the giant cranes of the Vietsovpetro docks, is Thich Ca Phat Dai statuary park.

Places to Stay

The Vung Tau Peninsula has quite a number of hotels and guesthouses, both in town and at Back Beach, Bai Dau and Bai Dua. During holidays, Vung Tau's hotels are usually booked out. Rumours about new hotels to be built are always circulating – will Club Med's much-heralded resort ever be built? Stay tuned.

Front Beach This part of town is definitely moving upmarket. If you need a cheap place to stay, first take a look at Bai Dau.

The *Lu Son Hotel* (☎ 52576; 65 rooms) is a large, airy place north of town at 27 Le Loi Blvd. It's rather far from the beach, and for this reason it's somewhat cheaper than many other places in Vung Tau of similar standard. Double rooms with private bath and air-con cost US$15.

The *Song Huong Hotel* (☎ 52491; 33 rooms) is at 10 Truong Vinh Ky St. This was once a dormitory for Soviet expats but has seen some recent renovation and steep price increases to match. Singles/doubles are US$30/45.

The *Rang Dong Hotel* (☎ 52133; 84 rooms) is at 5 Duy Tan St just off Le Loi Blvd. This large place was also once a dormitory for Soviet expats and looks the worse for wear. Rooms are reasonably priced at US$10 to US$20. The hotel has its own restaurant and owns a tennis court across the street from the main building.

The *Ha Long Hotel* (☎ 52175) is an older place at 45 Thong Nhat St across the street from the church. It was once cheap, but was under renovation at the time of our visit and prices will no doubt be ramped upwards. Express buses to Saigon used to depart from here, and that will probably be the case once again after the renovation is completed.

The *Song Hong Hotel* (☎ 52137; 39 rooms) is at 12 Hoang Dieu St (corner Truong Vinh Ky St). Doubles with air-con-

ditioning and private bath cost US$16 to US$30. Although it looks like a good place, the staff at the front desk were notably unfriendly at the time of our visit, and other travellers have reported similar experiences here.

The *Grand Hotel* (☎ 52469; fax 59878; 60 rooms) has a grand location at 26 Quang Trung St, just opposite the beachfront. Owned by the Oil Services Company, the hotel is proud of its souvenir shop, steam bath, disco and Thai massage facilities. Singles with fan and private bath are US$15, while singles/doubles with air-con are US$20/30 and US$30/40.

The *Hai Yen Hotel* (☎ 52571; 23 rooms) at 8 Le Loi Blvd advertises its restaurant, cafe, dancehall, steam bath and Thai massage. Massage or not, it's a fairly pleasant place to stay with friendly management. Doubles range from US$25 to US$40.

The *Petro House Hotel* (☎ 52462; 57 rooms), 89 Tran Hung Dao, is a new place with rooms starting at US$25.

The *Rex Hotel* (☎ 52135; fax 59862) is a nine-storey high-rise at 1 Duy Tan St. Although the name seems more than coincidental, it's no relation to the very upmarket Rex in Saigon. All rooms have air-con and a terrace and cost US$30, US$35 and US$45, but travellers give the place the thumbs down due to surly staff. The hotel has two restaurants, tennis courts and a nightclub, but tends to be noisy with echo-chamber hallways. Someone described it as 'Soviet prison architecture'.

It's a long way from Canada, but the *Canadian Hotel* (☎ 59852; fax 59851) flies the red maple leaf at 48 Quang Trung St. The hotel's glossy pamphlet promises that it is 'where the sun-kissed beaches and cool sea breeze bring you into the exciting world of deep crystal blue sea'. The hotel is very classy and very thoroughly air-conditioned and costs US$45 to US$90.

The *Palace Hotel* (☎ 52265; fax 59878; 105 rooms), also known as the *Hoa Binh Hotel*, is a fancy place owned by the Oil Services Company. The hotel is on Nguyen Trai St, 100 metres off Quang Trung St.

RICHARD I'ANSON

KAREN O'CONNOR

SARA JANE CLELAND

KAREN O'CONNOR

Mekong Delta

A	
B	D
C	

A A hive of activity on the Mekong River, Mytho
B Ducks and chickens bound for the market
C Cantho floating market
D Boat on the Mekong River, Cantho

SARA JANE CLELAND

GREG ALFORD

ROBERT STOREY

Mekong Delta
Top: Local corner shop on the Mekong River's backwaters
Middle: Boat operator on the Mekong River, Cantho
Bottom: Bat Pagoda, near Soc Trang

Rooms cost between US$35 and US$70. The hotel advertises, among other things, 'gentle receptionists'.

The *Sea Breeze Hotel*, or *Hanh Phoc Hotel* (☎ 52392; fax 59856; 36 rooms), which also serves as an office for express buses to Saigon, is at 11 Nguyen Trai St. There are two categories of rooms, normal (US$40) and special (US$60). The normal rooms look just as nice and seem a much better deal. This hotel is an Australian joint venture.

The Czech joint-venture *Pacific Hotel* (☎ 52279; 53 rooms), 4 Le Loi Blvd (corner Ly Tu Trong St), is a clean and modern place. Room rates depend on whether or not you get a sea view. The price range here is US$23 to US$33.

The *Hai Au Hotel* (☎ 52178; 64 rooms) is at 100 Ha Long St on the southern end of Front Beach near the GPO. Taiwanese tour groups congregate here, and it's a fancy place with tour group amenities, including a swimming pool, private beach, barber shop, post office, disco bar and business centre. Rooms cost from US$35 to US$55 and credit cards are accepted.

Back Beach Perhaps the most beautiful place to stay in otherwise ugly Back Beach is the *Thang Muoi Hotel* (☎ 52665, 52645; 93 rooms) at 4-6 Thuy Van St. The Thanh Muoi is an old hotel featuring single-storey buildings set on quiet, spacious grounds with trees. Apparently, many tourists prefer the 'modern' high rises of the newer hotels, with the result that the Thanh Muoi is relatively cheap. Doubles cost between US$11 and US$23. The hotel's restaurant is air-conditioned.

One of the cheapest in this neighbourhood is the *Saigon Hotel* at 72 Thuy Van St, adjacent to the pricier Beautiful Hotel. Rooms are large and complete with terrace and private bath. The price range here is US$10 to US$35.

The *Beautiful Hotel* (Khach San My Le; ☎ 53174; fax 53177; 100 rooms) isn't bad, though 'beautiful' doesn't apply to the price. Rooms cost US$32 to US$55. The hotel is at the southern end of Back Beach; the official address is 100 Thuy Van St.

The *Phuong Dong Hotel* (☎ 52593; 45 rooms) at 2 Thuy Van St is one of the most impressive hotels in the Vung Tau area. It was built to cater mostly to Hong Kongers, Taiwanese and Singaporeans, as evidenced by the massive karaoke facilities. Rooms cost US$30 to US$40.

The *Thuy Duong Hotel* (☎ 52635; nine rooms) is a small but attractive place at the northern end of Thuy Van St. Also known as the Weeping Willow Hotel, all rooms have air-con and hot water. The tariff is between US$25 and US$50.

Close to the foregoing is the *Thuy Van Hotel* with 93 rooms. Rates here are US$18 to US$32.

Bai Dau There are dozens of guesthouses *(nha nghi)* in former private villas along Bai Dau. This is the cheapest neighbourhood in the Vung Tau area, though no longer dirt-cheap as it once was. This relative cheapness is not because Bai Dau is an unattractive place (indeed, the opposite), but the lack of a white-sand beach and other tourist amusements makes this a relative backwater. If it's touristland you want, head to Back Beach.

Most of the guesthouses have rooms with fans and communal bathrooms and cost US$10 or less, but several upmarket places have now added air-con and private baths. A few of the guesthouses do meals, but most don't. However, there are plenty of cheap restaurants offering fine sea views.

Nha Nghi My Tho, with its rooftop terrace overlooking the beach, is at 47 Tran Phu St. A light, airy room with ceiling fan and beach view will cost you US$6 per person. You may have to bargain for meals to get the Vietnamese price.

Nha Nghi 128 is at 128 Tran Phu St. Rooms for four cost US$7. It's rather dilapidated-looking.

Nha Nghi 29 is right on the seafront. It's a large good-looking place and can be recommended. Rooms with air-con cost US$20.

Nha Nghi Doan 28 is at 126 Tran Phu St.

It's also a large hotel with air-con rooms and private bath. Doubles cost US$25.

Nha Nghi DK 142 also has relatively high-standard air-con rooms with private bath for US$25.

Thuy Tien Hotel at 96 Tran Phu is a place to avoid! Two years ago rooms here cost US$7, but this has been raised to US$100! No renovation work has been done on the hotel's eight rooms to justify this increase. This is now the most expensive hotel in Vung Tau.

Bai Dua Among the villas-turned-guesthouses at Bai Dua are *Nha Nghi 50 Ha Long* at 50 Ha Long St, *Nha Nghi Dro* at 88B Ha Long St and, at 48 Ha Long St, *Nha Nghi 48 Ha Long*, which charges foreigners US$20 for a triple with air-con. Their cheapest double goes for US$15.

Places to Eat

For excellent seafood, try *Huong Bien Restaurant*, which is along Front Beach at 47 Quang Trung St. There are several places to eat nearby and quite a few more along Tran Hung Dao Blvd. Hotels with excellent restaurants include the *Palace*, *Pacific* and the *Grand*, as the following comments testify:

The attractive terrace restaurant at the Palace Hotel does excellent food – better fried rice than we ever had in Hong Kong! The fried eel is highly recommended. A couple of dishes with rice and a few beers cost us US$8. Very limited choice of wine though – expensive white (US$25) or cheap but dodgy-looking red with a label all in some Eastern European language we couldn't read. But all in all, a great place to eat.

Sarah Clifford

I ate at Stanislav's Czech Restaurant in the Pacific Hotel. The restaurant was empty every time I went in, but the food was cheap and delicious. The schnitzel and potato salad (US$0.90) was fantastic. So was the baked fish, caviar sandwiches and potato cream soup, which each cost less than US$1.

At the southern end of Back Beach is the excellent *Thuy Trieu Restaurant*, which does a mean salad and splendid seafood, yet charges low prices. The largest restaurant along Back Beach is the *Thang Muoi Restaurant* (☎ 52515) at 7-9 Thuy Van St. An upmarket Taiwanese restaurant called *Paradise* was under construction at the time of this writing at the north-east part of Back Beach.

At Bai Dau, you might try the seaside restaurant run by An Giang Tourism at 41 Tran Phu St, which is across the street from 114 Tran Phu St.

At Bai Dua, there are restaurants at 88 Ha Long St and 126 Ha Long St.

Entertainment

Apocalypse Now is a raging bar and cafe at 438 Truong Cong Dinh St.

The *Grand Hotel* has a disco and karaoke lounge which operate from 7 pm until midnight.

The *Future Star Karaoke* (☎ 52805), 93 Tran Hung Dao Blvd, is a Taiwanese joint venture which was once a hotel. Apparently, there is more money to be made catering to those aspiring to be future stars.

The *Rex Hotel* (☎ 59559) also operates a karaoke thing on the ground floor.

Things to Buy

Colourful seashells and various items made out of shells (purses, plant hangers, necklaces, etc) can be bought for US$0.10 and up at the intersection of Le Loi Blvd and Ly Tu Trong St (across the street from the Pacific Hotel). Other souvenir shops are located along Front Beach and at the Thich Ca Phat Dai statuary park.

The government Tourist Shop at the intersection of Le Loi Blvd and Quang Trung St and other such shops in major hotels carry imported goods.

Getting There & Away

Air There are (sometimes) chartered helicopter flights available from Vung Tau to the Con Dao Islands.

The most interesting news is that since 1995 there are international flights operating between Vung Tau and Singapore. The planes are small 40-seater jets and the round-trip airfare is US$280.

Bus The most convenient minibuses to Vung Tau depart from in front of the Saigon Hotel on Dong Du St near the Saigon Central Mosque. Departures are approximately once every 15 minutes between 6 am and 6 pm. The 128-km trip takes two hours and costs US$2. To return from Vung Tau, you catch these minibuses at the petrol station.

Buses to Vung Tau also leave from the Mien Dong Bus Station and the Van Thanh Bus Station. There are also buses direct from Vung Tau to Dalat, Nha Trang and Hanoi.

Vung Tau Bus Station (Ben Xe Khach Vung Tau) is about 1.5 km from the city centre at 52 Nam Ky Khoi Nghia St. To get there from Front Beach, take either Bacu St or Truong Cong Dinh St to Le Hong Phong St. Turn right and then turn right again onto Nam Ky Khoi Nghia St. There are non-express buses from here to Baria, Bien Hoa, Saigon, Long Khanh, Mytho and Tay Ninh. An express bus to Ho Chi Minh City leaves at 6 am, 9 am and 3 pm.

Express buses and minibuses to Ho Chi Minh City also depart from the Sea Breeze Hotel in Vung Tau.

Taxi For a day trip to Vung Tau, you might consider hiring a taxi or 'marriage taxi'. Information on hiring vehicles in Saigon appears in the Getting There & Away section of the Ho Chi Minh City chapter.

Boat It may be possible to get from Vung Tau to the Con Dao Archipelago by boat, but don't count on it.

Yachties who have shown up in Vung Tau without the necessary authorisations have been imprisoned and had their boats seized.

Getting Around
The best way to get around the Vung Tau Peninsula is by bicycle. These are available for hire from some hotels for around US$1 per day.

CON DAO ISLANDS
The Con Dao Archipelago is a group of 14 islands and islets 180 km (97 nautical miles) south of Vung Tau. The largest island in the

group, whose total land area is 20 sq km, is partly forested Con Son Island, which is ringed with bays, bathing beaches and coral reefs. Con Son Island is also known by its Europeanised Malay name, Poulo Condore (Pulau Kundur), which means Island of the Squashes. Local products include teak and pine wood from the islands' forests, fruits (cashews, grapes, coconuts and mangoes), pearls, sea turtles, lobster and coral.

Occupied at various times by the Khmers, Malays and Vietnamese, Con Son also served as an early base for European commercial ventures in the region. The British East India Company maintained a fortified trading post here from 1702 to 1705, an experiment which ended when the English on the island were massacred in a revolt by the Makassar soldiers they had recruited on the Indonesian island of Sulawesi.

Under the French, Con Son was used as a prison for opponents of French colonialism, earning a fearsome reputation for the routine mistreatment and torture of prisoners. In 1954, the prison was taken over by the South Vietnamese government, which continued to take advantage of its remoteness to hold opponents of the government (including students) in horrifying conditions. The island's Revolutionary Museum has exhibits on Vietnamese resistance to the French, Communist opposition to the Republic of Vietnam and the treatment of political prisoners held on the island. A ditch in which Communist Party members were dunked in cow's urine is open to the public.

There has been talk of building a casino and giving Con Dao duty-free status. At the present time, Con Dao sees few foreign visitors other than the occasional tour group interested in the island's history as a horrific prison.

Getting There & Away
Air Vietnam Airlines flies chartered helicopters from Vung Tau to Con Son Island.

Boat The 215-km route between Vung Tau and Con Dao takes about 12 hours on a ship operated by the Vietnamese navy. Civilians

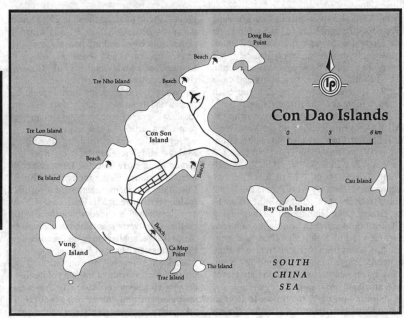

Con Dao Islands

can get permission to do this boat journey provided that there is a reasonably large group making the trip. The place to inquire about this is OSC at 2 Le Loi Blvd in Vung Tau.

LONG HAI

Commercialised tourism has turned Vung Tau into something of a circus, and many travellers crave a less-developed seaside retreat. As a result, backpackers are increasingly heading to Long Hai, 30 km north-east of Vung Tau. The southern end of the beach here is where fishing boats moor, and therefore not too clean. However, the northern end is quite all right, with a reasonable amount of white sand and palm trees.

There are a couple of drawbacks to staying here. The first is that accommodation is basic, though that is also one of the attractions. If you need a room with hot water and shag carpeting, you'd better stay in Vung Tau. Restaurants also tend towards the

downmarket side, but there is a certain charm to the makeshift beach huts set up by the locals.

Perhaps the biggest drawback is the noise in the evening. Forget about sitting on your hotel's porch listening to the waves roll in. That sinister plot by hearing-aid manufacturers – karaoke – has taken Long Hai by storm. Your eardrums will be pounded all evening until about 11 pm or so, and some of the real enthusiasts fire up their evil noise machines in the morning too. There is no use complaining about this – it comes with the territory. If you're deaf, you should love Long Hai. If you're not, you will be by the time you leave.

Places to Stay

There are currently only two hotels in Long Hai, but this is expected to change quickly. Currently the largest hotel on offer is the *Long Hai Hotel* (☎ 68010; 25 rooms). It's difficult to recommend this place – rooms cost US$20 to US$25, the beach next to the hotel is dirty and the 'massage service' looks rather kinky.

The preferred place to stay is the *Military Guest House* (☎ 68002; 28 rooms) at the north end of the beach. The main building has 17 rooms priced from US$8 to US$20. There are also two beach houses (recommended!) where rooms cost only US$5.

Getting There & Away
Public transport is a little difficult, mainly because there isn't any. You can rent a motorbike in Vung Tau or Saigon and drive yourself. If you can afford to rent a car and round up a group to share the cost, so much the better.

The Military Guest House in Long Hai rents out a boat (US$30 per hour) which can hold five persons and can make the run to Vung Tau. This seems like an expensive way to go, and there is always the problem of how you are to arrange this boat when you're starting out from Vung Tau. This same guesthouse also has its own minibus for hire, if that's any help.

Most likely, Long Hai's popularity will continue to grow. As this happens, no doubt enterprising locals will start offering minibus service. Ask around the cafes in Saigon for the latest transport news.

HO COC BEACH
A short drive to the north of Long Hai is the remote but beautiful Ho Coc Beach. It's still a very undeveloped area, though this will no doubt change. The *Ho Coc Guest Houses* consists of one bungalow with five rooms. It's the only place to stay at Ho Coc and you might have it to yourself. To get there, you'll need a car or a motorbike because no public transport is available.

BINH CHAU HOT SPRINGS
About 50 km north of Long Hai is Binh Chau Hot Springs (Suoi Nuoc Nong Binh Chau). There is a small resort here, but tacky commercialisation is blessedly absent. The resort is in a compound six km north of the village of Binh Chau, and foreigners have to pay an admission fee of US$0.20.

Massage and acupuncture are on offer. Locals may also offer to take you on a hunting expedition (for a fee) to help exterminate any remaining wildlife in the area. From the looks of things, they've already done a good job – the only wildlife we encountered were the swarms of noisy cicadas buzzing away in the trees.

The resort consists of a hotel and adjoining restaurant. To see the actual hot springs, you have to walk down a wooden path. Be sure that you don't stray from the path, as the earthen crust is thin here and you could conceivably fall through into an underground pool of scalding water! The hottest spring here reaches 82°C, which is warm enough to boil eggs. Indeed, you'll find a small spring where bamboo baskets have been laid aside for just this purpose. If you don't happen to have any eggs in your pockets, inquire back at the hotel's restaurant.

Places to Stay
If you want to spend the night, the only choice on offer is the *Binh Chau Hotel*. There are 16 rooms in the main hotel building costing US$10 to US$15. The hotel also has bungalows for rent costing just US$8, but the toilet is outside.

Getting There & Away
Until recently, the road to Binh Chau consisted primarily of mud and potholes. This changed in the early 1990s when the Australian government donated funds to build a new highway. You might question why Binh Chau was so favoured (do Canberra officials have an irresistible urge to visit hot springs?) but you can't complain about the road. Indeed, it's one of the best roads in Vietnam, but it's a pity that it just sort of dead ends at Binh Chau and doesn't connect up to National Highway 1. Perhaps some other benevolent government will step in and donate the cash so that the highway can continue all the way up to the massage parlours of Nha Trang.

Good highway or not, there is no public transport. You'll need a motorbike or rented car. If you choose the latter, perhaps you can find some travellers to share the expense. If you drive this highway, be forewarned that there are several crucial intersections where you need to make turns and none of these are signposted.

HAM TAN

Ham Tan is the new name for this place, but many locals still call it by its former name, Binh Tuy. Basically, it's a pleasantly secluded beach 30 km north of Binh Chau Hot Springs. There is a small hotel here, but it's safe to say that visitors of any sort are not frequent.

Unfortunately, Ham Tan is not the easiest place to reach unless you have access to a helicopter. The already-mentioned road which the Aussies so generously built for the residents of Binh Chau peters out im-

mediately after the hot-springs resort. If you don't want to visit Ham Tan, you might still want to take a look at the old highway just to praise your good fortune at not having to drive on it. Potholes are the size of bomb craters, and indeed you might get to wondering if the Americans didn't build this road from the air using B-52s. A motorbike should be able to make the journey, and a few adventurous travellers have even done it on mountain bikes. Any vehicle with four wheels attempting this trip should have four-wheel drive and/or high clearance. If it's been raining recently, expect a sea of mud.

If you do make it to Ham Tan, it's only another 30 km to National Highway 1. However, that road also will give bikers an opportunity to test their motocross skills. Good luck.

Mekong Delta

Pancake flat but lusciously green and beautiful, the Mekong Delta is the southernmost region of Vietnam. It was formed by sediment deposited by the Mekong River, a process which continues today; silt deposits extend the delta's shoreline at the mouths of the river by as much as 79 metres per year. The river is so large that it has two daily tides – indeed, at low tide in the dry season boats cannot even move through the shallow canals.

The land of the Mekong Delta is renowned for its richness; almost half of the region's total land area is under cultivation. The area is known as Vietnam's 'breadbasket', though 'ricebasket' would be a more appropriate term. The Mekong Delta produces enough rice to feed the entire country with a sizeable surplus left over. When the government introduced collectivised farming to the delta in 1975, production fell way down and there were food shortages in Ho Chi Minh City. However, farmers in the delta easily grew enough to feed themselves, even if they didn't bother to send it to market. People from Saigon would head down to the delta to buy sacks of black-market rice to take home, but the police set up checkpoints and confiscated rice from anyone carrying more than 10 kg to 'prevent profiteering'. All this ended in 1986, and farmers in this region have propelled Vietnam forward to become the world's third largest rice exporter.

Other food products from the delta include coconut, sugar cane, various fruits and fish. Although this area is primarily rural, it is one of the most densely populated regions in Vietnam – nearly every hectare is intensively farmed. An exception is the sparsely inhabited mangrove swamps around Camau in Minh Hai Province, where the land is not very productive.

The Mekong River, one of the great rivers of the world, is known to the Vietnamese as Song Cuu Long, River of the Nine Dragons. The Mekong originates high in the Tibetan plateau, flowing 4500 km through China, between Myanmar and Laos, through Laos, along the Lao-Thai border, and through Cambodia and Vietnam on its way to the South China Sea. At Phnom Penh, the Mekong splits into two main branches: the Hau Giang (the Lower River, also called the Bassac River), which flows via Chau Doc, Long Xuyen and Cantho to the sea; and the Tien Giang (Upper River), which splits into several branches at Vinh Long and empties into the sea at six points.

The level of the Mekong begins to rise around the end of May and reaches its highest point in September; its flow ranges from 1900 to 38,000 cubic metres per second depending on the season. A tributary of the river which empties into the Mekong at Phnom Penh drains Cambodia's Tonlé Sap Lake. When the Mekong is at flood stage, this tributary reverses its flow and drains *into* Tonlé Sap, thereby somewhat reducing the danger of serious flooding in the Mekong Delta. Unfortunately, deforestation in Cambodia is upsetting the whole delicate balancing act, resulting in more floods in Vietnam's portion of the Mekong River basin.

Living on a flood plain presents some technical challenges. Lacking any high ground to escape flooding, many delta residents build their houses on bamboo stilts to avoid the rising waters. Many roads get submerged or turn to muck during floods – all-weather roads have to be built on raised embankments, but this is expensive. The traditional solution has been to build canals and travel by boat. There are thousands of canals in the Mekong Delta – keeping them properly dredged and navigable is a constant but essential chore.

Estuarine crocodiles are found in the southern parts of the delta rivers, particularly near the Hau Giang (Bassac) River area. These creatures can be dangerous and travellers are advised to keep a healthy distance from them.

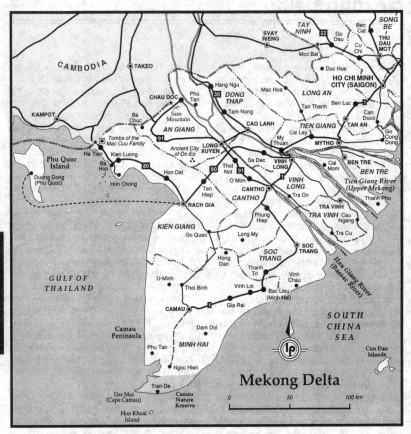

Mekong Delta

The Mekong Delta was once part of the Khmer kingdom and was the last region of modern-day Vietnam to be annexed and settled by the Vietnamese. The Cambodians, mindful that they controlled the area until the 18th century, still call the delta 'Lower Cambodia'. The Khmer Rouge tried to follow up on this claim by pulling nighttime raids on Vietnamese villages and massacring the inhabitants. This led the Vietnamese army to invade Cambodia in 1979 and oust the Khmer Rouge from power. Most of the current inhabitants of the Mekong Delta are ethnic-Vietnamese, but there are significant populations of ethnic-Chinese and Khmer as well as a few Chams.

Many travellers heading to the delta go by public bus (cheap but rough) or by rented motorbike (good fun, though you can get lost in the maze of roads). The other way is by minibus tour. There are quite a few of these on offer, including many inexpensive ones which can be booked at the budget cafes frequented by travellers in Pham Ngu Lao St. However, before you book anything, do a little bit of comparative shopping. Cheapest is not always best – the cost depends in large part on how far from Saigon the tour goes.

Search and Destroy

Only one major battle occurred in the Mekong Delta (in 1972 at Cai Lay, 20 km from Mytho). Aside from that, all fighting in the delta during the Vietnam War was confined to small-scale ambushes. Unfortunately for the Americans, the lush jungles, tall grass and mangrove swamps provided perfect camouflage for the Viet Cong. The high civilian population density made it impossible for the Americans to use indiscriminate bombing, so it was necessary to send in ground-level 'search and destroy missions'. From the air, helicopter gunshops raked the grasslands and jungles with machine-gun fire. On the water, US forces used high-speed military boats to patrol the hundreds of canals crisscrossing the delta in an effort to intercept guerillas travelling by canoe to their sanctuaries.

For their part, the Viet Cong responded with booby traps, nighttime raids, assassinations of 'uncooperative elements' and mines planted in the canals – essentially, the Communists controlled much of the delta at night. Both the Communists and the ARVN conscripted young men from the delta into their respective armies – it wasn't unusual for brothers to be fighting on opposite sides, often against their will. Desertions from both sides were high.

Caught in the crossfire, local villagers sensibly fled. By 1975, 40% of Saigon's population was from the Mekong Delta region.

Agent Orange was used to clear the mangrove forests of the delta in an effort to deny the guerillas sanctuary. Ironically, spraying the mangroves with defoliants may have backfired on the Americans. Obtaining food and supplies was one of the biggest headaches for the VC. Spraying the mangroves with Agent Orange caused the leaves of the plants to die, fall off and decay, providing a source of nutrition for shrimp, which in turn were harvested by the VC. This provided the guerillas with a major short-term gain – the VC ate the shrimp and sold the surplus in the local markets to buy other needed supplies. ■

This is not to say that you need to book a pricey tour with Saigon Tourist, but sometimes 'rock bottom' means just that and all you will get is a brief glance at the delta region. Obviously, the more days you spend and the more distance travelled, the greater the cost. The standard of accommodation will be another factor.

MYTHO

Mytho, the capital of Tien Giang Province, is a quiet city of 90,000 easily reached from Saigon yet very near some of the most beautiful rural areas of the Mekong Delta.

Mytho was founded in the 1680s by Chinese refugees fleeing Taiwan for political reasons. The economy of the area is based on fishing and the cultivation of rice, coconuts, bananas, mangoes, longans and citrus fruit.

Orientation

Mytho, which sprawls along the bank of the northernmost branch of the Mekong River, is laid out in a fairly regular grid pattern. The bus station, Ben Xe Khach Tien Giang, is several km west of town. Coming from the station, you enter Mytho on Ap Bac St. Ap Bac St turns into Nguyen Trai St, which is oriented west-east. The main north-south thoroughfare in town (and the widest street in the city) is Hung Vuong Blvd.

Information

Tourist Office Tien Giang Tourism (Cong Ty Du Lich Tien Giang; ☎ 72154, 72105) is the official tourism authority for Tien Giang Province. The office is on the riverfront at the corner of Rach Gam and Trung Trac Sts.

Warning If you're just passing through and only stopping in Mytho to sleep or eat, then you shouldn't have any problems at all with the authorities.

The big trouble begins if you decide to take an 'unauthorised' boat trip. Tien Giang Tourism belongs to the government, which means it belongs to the People's Committee. Mytho's People's Committee hasn't heard about the economic reforms sweeping the country and continues to run its tourist industry as a State-owned monopoly. Since boat trips are *the* major attraction in Mytho, the government wishes to monopolise this business. Tien Giang Tourism charges approximately five times the going rate for its mediocre boat journeys, and travellers who have attempted to hire private boats have been arrested and fined.

Police patrol boats set up checkpoints at various strategic spots. The private boat operators have tried to evade the police by sending travellers to a remote spot via cyclo, then picking them up with a boat and taking them for a boat tour. This usually works, but the authorities have gotten wise to the scheme and now send plainclothes police by motorbike to patrol.

Given this ridiculous situation, Mytho has become much less attractive to travellers and many potential visitors are skipping the town entirely. Most tourists now head for Cantho, were boat trips are cheap and plentiful.

There is always the possibility that things

will change for the better, so ask around at some of the cafes in Saigon or else in Mytho itself to see what the latest story is. With that optimistic thought in mind, consider visiting some of the following places...

Island of the Coconut Monk

Until his imprisonment by the Communists for anti-government activities and the consequent dispersion of his flock, the Coconut Monk (Ong Dao Dua) led a small community on Phung Island (Con Phung), a few kilometres from Mytho. In its heyday, the island was dominated by a fantastic open-air sanctuary that looked like a cross between a cheaply built copy of Disneyland and the Tiger Balm Gardens of Singapore. The dragon-enwrapped columns and the multi-platformed tower with its huge metal globe must have once been brightly painted, but these days the whole place is faded, rickety and silent. With a bit of imagination, though, you can picture how it all must have appeared as the Coconut Monk presided over his congregation, flanked by elephant tusks and seated on a richly ornamented throne.

The Coconut Monk, so named because it is said that he once ate only coconuts for three years, was born Nguyen Thanh Nam (though he later adopted Western name order, preferring to be called Nam Nguyen Thanh) in 1909 in what is now Ben Tre Province. He studied chemistry and physics in France at Lyons, Caen and Rouen from 1928 until 1935, when he returned to Vietnam, married and had a daughter.

In 1945 the Coconut Monk left his family to pursue a monastic life. For three years, he sat on a stone slab under a flagpole and meditated day and night. He was repeatedly imprisoned by successive South Vietnamese governments, who were infuriated by his philosophy of bringing about the country's reunification through peaceful means. The monk died in 1990.

The Coconut Monk founded a religion, Tinh Do Cu Si, which was a mixture of Buddhism and Christianity. Representations of Jesus and the Buddha appeared together, as did the Virgin Mary and eminent Buddhist

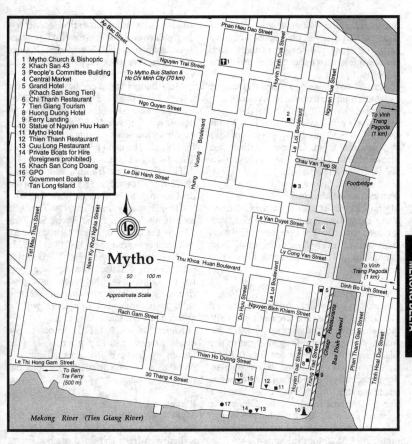

Mytho

1 Mytho Church & Bishopric
2 Khach San 43
3 People's Committee Building
4 Central Market
5 Grand Hotel
   (Khach San Song Tien)
6 Chi Thanh Restaurant
7 Tien Giang Tourism
8 Huong Duong Hotel
9 Ferry Landing
10 Statue of Nguyen Huu Huan
11 Mytho Hotel
12 Thien Thanh Restaurant
13 Cuu Long Restaurant
14 Private Boats for Hire
   (foreigners prohibited)
15 Khach San Cong Doang
16 GPO
17 Government Boats to
   Tan Long Island

0 50 100 m
Approximate Scale

Mekong River (Tien Giang River)

MEKONG DELTA

women. He employed both the cross and
Buddhist symbols.

The Coconut Monk's complex is visible
from the car ferry that runs from near Mytho
to Ben Tre Province. The plaques on the
3½-metre-high porcelain jar (created in
1972) tell all about the Coconut Monk. In
recent years, the island has been evolving
into a tourist trap and is becoming less interesting.

The Mytho police will not permit you to
visit this island using a private motorboat
(only US$3 per hour), so you will have to
hire one for at least US$20. Another possi-

bility is to hire a boat from Ben Tre Province,
which is just across the river. In fact, Phung
Island is in Ben Tre Province, which means
that the Mytho police really don't have juris-
diction here. However, the Mytho police can
grab you going to and from the island even
if they can't come onto the island itself. If
you do first cross the river to Ben Tre Province, you can easily get a boat from there to
Phung Island without the Mytho police being
able to do anything.

Mytho Church & Bishopric
Mytho Church, a solid pastel-yellow build-

ing at 32 Hung Vuong Blvd (corner of Nguyen Trai St), was built about a century ago. The stone plaques set in the church walls express *merci* and *cam on* to Fatima and other figures.

Today, two priests, two sisters and several assistants minister to much of Mytho's Catholic population of 7000. The church is open to visitors every day from 4.30 to 6.30 am and 2.30 to 6.30 pm. Daily masses are held at 5 am and 5 pm. On Sunday, there are masses at 5 am, 7 am and 5 pm and catechism classes in the late afternoon.

Mytho Central Market

Mytho Central Market is an area of town along Trung Trac St and Nguyen Hue St that is closed to traffic. The streets are filled with stalls selling everything from fresh food (along Trung Trac St) and bulk tobacco to boat propellers.

Tan Long Island

The well-known longan *(nhan)* orchards of Tan Long Island are pleasant to walk through, and there is a small restaurant on the island. The lush, palm-fringed shores of the island are lined with wooden fishing boats similar to those used by the 'boat people' to flee the country. Some of the residents of the island are shipwrights. Tan Long Island is a five-minute boat trip from the dock at the southern end of Le Loi Blvd, but the obligatory government-owned boats charge a minimum US$20 for the journey.

Vinh Trang Pagoda

Vinh Trang Pagoda is a beautiful and well-maintained sanctuary. The charitable monks here provide a home to orphaned, handicapped and other needy children.

The pagoda is about one km from the city centre at 60A Nguyen Trung Truc St. To get there, take the bridge across the river (at Nguyen Trai St). The entrance to the sanctuary is on the right-hand side of the building as you approach it from the ornate gate.

Places to Stay

Because the police have been chasing away tourists, the accommodation scene has deteriorated noticeably in the past few years. There are now actually fewer hotels in town than there were when we published the previous edition of this book!

Most budget travellers now stay at the *Khach San Cong Doang* (☎ 74324). Good river views are one of the attractions here. A double with fan costs US$7, or you can have a room with air-conditioning and refrigerator for US$15. The hotel is on the corner of 30 Thang 4 St and Le Loi Blvd.

The five-storey *Huong Duong Hotel* (☎ 72011; 20 rooms) at 33 Trung Trac St has doubles for US$13. Overall, it's not bad.

The eight-storey *Grand Hotel* (☎ 72009; 35 rooms), also known as the *Khach San Song Tien*, is the largest in town. All rooms have air-conditioning and go for US$13 to US$25.

The run-down *Mytho Hotel* (24 rooms) at 67, 30 Thang 4 St used to accept foreigners but no longer does. This place has a good river view and definite renovation potential, so it is possible that foreigners will be allowed in the future.

Khach San 43 (☎ 72126; 16 rooms) is a clean, modern and airy place at 43 Ngo Quyen St. However, the government now prohibits foreigners from staying here, but this could change.

Places to Eat

Mytho is known for a special vermicelli soup, *hu tieu My Tho*, which is richly garnished with fresh and dried seafood, pork, chicken and fresh herbs. It is served either with broth or dry (with broth on the side).

There are numerous excellent small and cheap restaurants along Trung Trac St between the statue of Nguyen Huu Huan (a 19th-century anti-colonial fighter) on 30 Thang 4 St and the Thu Khoa Huan Blvd bridge. A good one to try here is *Chi Thanh Restaurant*.

Thien Thanh Restaurant is at 65, 30 Thang 4 St. Across the street, next to the Tan Long Island ferry dock, is *Cuu Long Restaurant*, which has river views but mediocre food.

The *Grand Hotel* has a decent restaurant. *Khach San 43* also has a restaurant.

Getting There & Away

Bus Mytho is served by nonexpress buses leaving Ho Chi Minh City from Mien Tay Bus Station in An Lac.

The Mytho Bus Station (Ben Xe Khach Tien Giang) is several kilometres west of town; it is open from 4 am to about 5 pm. To get there from the city centre, take Ap Bac St westward and continue on to National Highway 1.

Buses to Ho Chi Minh City leave when full from the early morning until about 5 pm; the trip takes 1½ hours. There is daily bus service to Cantho (five hours; departs at 4 am and 9 pm), Chau Doc (leaves at 4 am), Phu Hoa (departs at 6 pm), Tay Ninh (six hours; departs at 5 am) and Vung Tau (five hours; leaves at 5 am). There are also buses to Ba Beo, Bac My Thuan, Cai Be, Cai Lay, Go Cong Dong, Go Cong Tay, Hau My Bac, Phu My, Tan An and Vinh Kim. There is no express bus service from Mytho.

Car By car, the drive from Ho Chi Minh City to Mytho on National Highway 1 (Quoc Lo 1) takes about 90 minutes.

Road distances from Mytho are: 16 km to Ben Tre, 104 km to Cantho, 70 km to Ho Chi Minh City and 66 km to Vinh Long.

Boat A passenger ferry to Mytho leaves Ho Chi Minh City daily at 11 am from the dock at the end of Ham Nghi Blvd. The trip should take about six hours if you're lucky. The cost for foreigners is US$5.

The car ferry to Ben Tre Province from Mytho leaves from a station (Ben Pha Rach Mieu) about one km west of the city centre near 2/10A Le Thi Hong Gam St (Le Thi Hong Gam St is the western continuation of 30 Thang 4 St). The ferry operates from 4 am to 10 pm and runs at least once an hour. Ten-person trucks shuttle between the ferry terminal and the bus station.

Getting Around

Assuming that the police change their attitude, motorised seven-metre boats can be hired at an unmarked ferry landing on Trung Trac St at the eastern end of Thien

Elderly man in Mytho

Ho Duong St; ferry boats to points across the river also dock here. Wooden rowboats to Tan Long Island leave from the pier at the southern end of Le Loi St next to Cuu Long Restaurant.

AROUND MYTHO
Dong Tam Snake Farm

There is a snake farm at Dong Tam, which is about 10 km from Mytho towards Vinh Long. Most of the snakes raised here are pythons and cobras. The snakes are raised for a variety of purposes: for eating, for their skins and for the purpose of producing snake anti-venoms. The king cobras are raised only for exhibit – they are extremely aggressive and are even capable of spitting poison – do not get too close to their cages. The regular cobras are kept in an open pit and will generally ignore you if you ignore them, but will strike if provoked. On the other hand, the pythons are docile enough to be taken out of their cages and 'played with' if you dare, but the larger ones are capable of strangling a human.

Dong Tam also has a collection of mutant turtles and fish on exhibit. The cause of their genetic deformities is almost certainly from the spraying of Agent Orange during the war, which was particularly intensive in forested parts of the Mekong Delta.

Other creatures kept on exhibit here include deer, monkeys, bears, crocodiles, owls, canaries and various other birds.

The Snake Farm is operated by the Vietnamese military for profit. It's definitely open to the public and taking photos is even encouraged. At your request, the staff will be all too happy to drape you with a large python to create that perfect photo for the loved ones back home.

The technology for raising the animals is somewhat primitive, as are the housing facilities for the reptiles. It's certainly a sharp contrast to Bangkok's slick Snake Institute. Nevertheless, Dong Tam Snake Farm is an interesting place to visit. Admission costs US$1.

BEN TRE

The picturesque province of Ben Tre is just south of Mytho. The entire province consists of several large islands in the mouth of the Mekong River, but the area gets few visitors because it's off the main highways. The provincial capital is also called Ben Tre and is a friendly sort of place with a few old buildings near the mighty Mekong River.

Information
Tourist Office Ben Tre Tourism (☎ 29618) is the local tourist office.

Vien Minh Pagoda
Located right in the centre of Ben Tre town, this is the head office of the Buddhist Association of Ben Tre Province. Though the history of the pagoda is vague, the local monks say it is over 100 years old. The original structure was made of wood, but it was torn down to make way for the present building. Reconstruction took place from 1951 to 1958, this time using bricks and concrete.

A feature of this pagoda is a large white statue of Quan The Am Bo Tat (the Goddess of Mercy) in the front courtyard. The Chinese calligraphy which dresses up this pagoda was done by an old monk who has now passed away. None of the current monks can read Chinese, though some of the local worshippers can.

Truc Giang Lake
Truc Giang Lake, a small but pleasant lake fronting the Dong Khoi Hotel, is a place to play around in paddleboats. The surrounding park is rather too small for doing much strolling.

Island of the Coconut Monk
This island is actually in Ben Tre Province, and the Ben Tre cops do not care if you hire a small private boat (unlike in Mytho where you must go on an expensive government cruise). Private boats can be had for US$3 per hour. For more information, see the Mytho section.

Nguyen Dinh Chieu Temple
This temple is dedicated to Nguyen Dinh Chieu, a local scholar. It's about a one-hour drive from the town of Ben Tre. It's a very charming temple, excellent for photography.

Bird Sanctuary
The locals make much of the Bird Sanctuary (Vam Ho), which is 36 km from Ben Tre town. Storks nest here, but access is difficult enough that most travellers won't bother.

Places to Stay
There are three hotels in town which can accommodate foreigners. Bottom of the barrel is the *Hung Vuong Hotel* (☎ 22408) at 166 Hung Vuong St. Rooms with fan are US$5 to US$7. Air-con ups the tab to US$15 for a double.

Next in the pecking order is the *Ben Tre Hotel* (☎ 22223) at 226/3 Tran Quoc Tuan St. Rooms with fan cost US$6, while air-con ranges from US$12 to US$15.

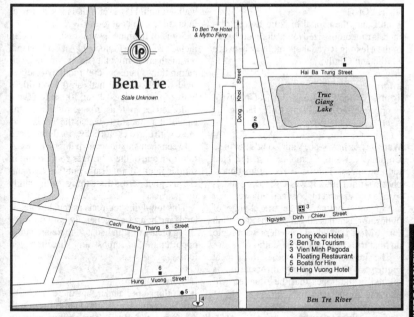

Ben Tre

Scale Unknown

*To Ben Tre Hotel
& Mytho Ferry*

Dong Khoi Street

Hai Ba Trung Street

*Truc
Giang
Lake*

Nguyen Dinh Chieu Street

Cach Mang Thang 8 Street

Hung Vuong Street

Ben Tre River

1 Dong Khoi Hotel
2 Ben Tre Tourism
3 Vien Minh Pagoda
4 Floating Restaurant
5 Boats for Hire
6 Hung Vuong Hotel

MEKONG DELTA

Ben Tre's plushest accommodation can be found at the *Dong Khoi Hotel* (☎ 22240; 35 rooms), 16 Hai Ba Trung St. All rooms have air-conditioning. Singles cost US$26 to US$33, while twins are US$28 to US$35. Even if you don't stay here, take a peek at the hotel's gift shop – the souvenir spoons, chopsticks and ashtrays made of coconut wood may not be the most durable but they certainly are beautiful.

Places to Eat
The *Dong Khoi Hotel* has the spiffiest restaurant in town. On Saturday night, a band entertains the guests.

The *Floating Restaurant* is anchored on the south side of town near the boat pier. We can't vouch for the food, but you can't beat the atmosphere.

Getting There & Away
Seeing how this is an island province, cross-ing the Mekong River is a prerequisite for reaching Ben Tre. However, this ferry crossing is particularly slow – figure on at least an hour each way.

Slow as it is, the Mytho-Ben Tre crossing is the fastest of the lot. There are other possible ferry crossings farther south that can get you to Vinh Long, but these are so slow and unreliable that you shouldn't count on them. Ferry crossings are quicker if you're travelling by motorcycle (as opposed to a car) since there are numerous small boats which can take you across the river.

Getting Around
Boat Ben Tre Tourism has a high-speed boat for rent, though it's not cheap at US$31 per hour. Like most speedboats, it can hold only five persons – all you need to do is bring a pair of waterskis. Slower and larger boats can also be rented here, but other bargains can be negotiated at the public pier.

VINH LONG

Vinh Long, the capital of Vinh Long Province, is a medium-sized town along the banks of the Mekong River about midway between Mytho and Cantho.

Information

Tourist Office Cuu Long Tourist (☎ 23616) is opposite the Hoa Nang Café, facing the river.

Warning As in Mytho, Vinh Long's People's Committee wants to monopolise the boat tour business. This is a recent metamorphosis – until 1995 it was OK to hire locals to take you around by boat and this was very cheap and popular. Since the change of policy, tourism has all but collapsed in Vinh Long. Most individual travellers wanting to do boat trips now head for Cantho.

The situation could change, so make local inquiries. The following information is offered in the hopes that the situation will return to normal.

Mekong River Islands

What makes a trip to Vinh Long worthwhile is not the town itself but the beautiful small islands in the river. The islands are totally given over to agriculture, especially the raising of tropical fruits, which are shipped to markets in Ho Chi Minh City.

A trip to the islands requires that you charter a boat. If you book through the government tourist office, small boats cost US$30 per hour, of which just US$1 per hour goes to the boat owner. If you negotiate directly with the boat owners, you can cut the price to something like US$1.50 to US$3 per hour. Unfortunately, this is currently not permitted. Tours booked with the government tourist office include an English or French-speaking Vietnamese guide – something of an asset since you can't count on the boat owners speaking anything but Vietnamese. Having a guide will allow you to get the full benefit of the trip.

One way to partially bypass the government monopoly is to take the public ferry (US$0.10) to one of the islands and then

walk around. However, this is not nearly as interesting as a boat tour.

Some of the more popular islands to visit include Binh Hoa Phuoc and An Binh Island, but there are many others. One of the fascinating things here are the 'monkey bridges' *(cau khi)*. These are makeshift footbridges built of uneven logs about 30 cm to 80 cm wide and as high as 20 metres above the canals. It's amazing to watch the locals cross these with bicycles and heavy loads balanced between their shoulders on bamboo poles. A fall from one of these bridges could result in serious injury if not death, but the Vietnamese just glide across these things with a smile on their face.

This low-lying region is as much water as land, and houses are generally built on stilts. Bring plenty of film because there are photo opportunities in almost any direction you look.

Military Museum

It's nothing spectacular, but there is a Military Museum (Bao Tang Quan Su) close to the Cuu Long Hotel. The various military museums in Saigon and Hanoi are significantly better.

Van Thanh Mieu Temple

A big surprise in Vinh Long is the large and beautiful Van Thanh Mieu Temple by the river. As Vietnamese temples go, it's unusual in a number of respects. To begin with, it's a Confucian temple, and these are very rare in southern Vietnam. Another oddity is that, while the rear hall is dedicated to Confucius, the front hall was built in honour of local hero Phan Thanh Gian.

Van Thanh Mieu Temple is sometimes called Phan Thanh Gian Temple by the locals. A plaque outside the temple entrance briefly tells his story. Phan Thanh Gian led an uprising in 1930 against the French. When it became obvious that his revolt was doomed, Phan killed himself rather than be captured by the colonial army. No one is quite certain when the hall honouring Phan was built, but it seems to have been after 1975.

The rear hall of the large and spacious

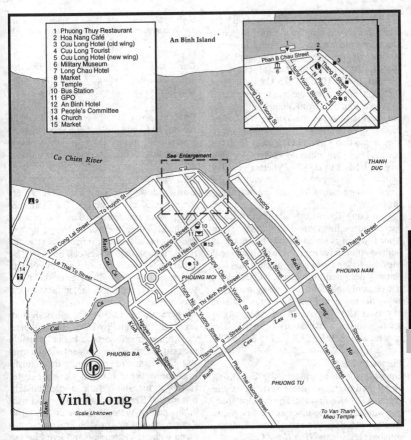

1 Phuong Thuy Restaurant
2 Hoa Nang Café
3 Cuu Long Hotel (old wing)
4 Cuu Long Tourist
5 Cuu Long Hotel (new wing)
6 Military Museum
7 Long Chau Hotel
8 Market
9 Temple
10 Bus Station
11 GPO
12 An Binh Hotel
13 People's Committee
14 Church
15 Market

An Binh Island

Phan B Chau Street

1 Thang 5 Street

Hung Vuong Street

C Lang St

N Pret St

Co Chien River

See Enlargement

THANH DUC

To Huynh St

Tran Cong Lai Street

Rach Cai Ca

Le Thai To Street

3 Thang 2 Street

Hoang Thai Hieu Street

Nguyen Hue Street

Nguyen Thi Minh Khai St

Hung Vuong St

Hung Dao Vuong Street

PHUONG MOI

Truong

Tan

Rach

30 Thang 4 Street

30 Thang 4 Street

PHUONG NAM

Bau

Long Street

Ho

Tran Phu Street

PHUONG BA

Nguyen Du Street

Kinh Phu Te

2 Thang

Rach

Pham Thai Buong Street

Cau

9 – Street

Lau

15

PHUONG TU

Vinh Long

Scale Unknown

To Van Thanh
Mieu Temple

MEKONG DELTA

grounds is dedicated to Confucius, whose portrait hangs above the altar. The building was designed very much in the Confucian style and looks like it was lifted straight out of China. The Confucian Hall was built in 1866.

Van Thanh Mieu Temple is several kilometres south-east of the centre along Tran Phu St. Don't confuse it with the much smaller Quoc Cong Pagoda on Tran Phu St, which you will pass along the way.

Places to Stay
The *Long Chau Hotel* (☎ 23611; 15 rooms),

1, 1 Thang 5 St, is where most backpackers wind up staying. A room with toilet outside is US$6, or you can have a room with attached bath and fan for US$8 to US$10. Air-con rooms are US$12.

The *Cuu Long Hotel* (24 rooms) has two branches right on the riverfront. The main branch is at 501, 1 Thang 5 St. A room with fan costs US$12, or you can have it with air-con for US$30 to US$35. This hotel can book boat trips, arrange traditional massage, rent cars, etc.

The *An Binh Hotel* (☎ 23190; 40 rooms), 3 Hoang Thai Hieu St, is nice enough, but not favoured by Westerners because it's far from the scenic riverfront. Still, if you're stuck for a place to stay, you could do worse. Rooms with fan and outside toilet are US$5. Rooms with attached toilet and air-con raises the tariff to US$10 to US$15. Other facilities include tennis courts and massage service.

About four km from Vinh Long (on the way to the ferry) is the *Truong An Tourist Villas* (☎ 23161). It's an excellent place to stay if you don't mind being away from the town. There are bungalows here for rent costing US$22 to US$28. Whether you stay or not, it's lovely to sit in the cafe by the riverside and enjoy the parklike surroundings.

Cuu Long Tourist can arrange for you to spend the night in the *Farm House* (Ngu Vuon), which is on an island. The house is built on stilts above the river in the traditional Mekong River Delta style, but this one was actually designed for tourists. Nevertheless, it's certainly peaceful and many travellers enjoy the place, but you have to be the sort of person who likes isolation. Commuting to town involves a mandatory boat trip. The cost for all this is US$12, US$15 or US$20.

Places to Eat

Opposite the new wing of the Cuu Long Hotel and right on the riverfront is the *Phuong Thuy Restaurant*. The food isn't bad, but what makes the place is the fine view. Another place for good river views and reasonable meals is the *Hoa Nang Café*.

However, if great food at cheap prices is more important than scenery, check out the *Vinh Long Market*. This is also a great place to try some delicious fruit, everything from bananas to mangos and papayas.

Getting There & Away

Bus Buses to Vinh Long leave Ho Chi Minh City from Cholon Bus Station in District 5, and from Mien Tay Bus Station in An Lac. Nonexpress buses take four hours. You can also get there from Mytho. A reader reports:

In Mytho, I was told that there were no more buses that day to Vinh Long, but *not* that there are plenty of buses to My Thuan. My Thuan is at the ferry head, and from there to Vinh Long is only a ferry hop and a moped ride away.

Car Vinh Long is just off National Highway 1, 66 km from Mytho, 98 km from Cantho and 136 km from Ho Chi Minh City.

Boat It is possible to go from Vinh Long all the way to Chau Doc, but you should have a Vietnamese guide along if you want to attempt this.

TRA VINH

Bordered by the Tien and Hau rivers (branches of the Mekong), Tra Vinh's location on a peninsula makes it somewhat isolated. Getting there is a straight up and back trip because no car ferries here cross the rivers, though motorbikes can be ferried by small boats. Western tourists are few, though Japanese travellers discovered the place several years ago. There are, in fact, several very worthwhile things to see here.

There are about 300,000 ethnic-Khmer people in Tra Vinh Province. At first glance, the Khmers might seem to be an 'invisible minority' – they all speak fluent Vietnamese, and there is nothing outwardly distinguishing about their clothing or lifestyle. However, digging a little deeper quickly reveals that Khmer culture is alive and well in this part of Vietnam. There are over 140 Khmer pagodas in Tra Vinh Province, compared with 50 Vietnamese and five Chinese pagodas. The pagodas have organised schools to teach the Khmer language – most of the locals in Tra Vinh can read and write Khmer at least as well as Vietnamese.

Vietnam's Khmer minority are almost all believers in Theravada Buddhism. If you've visited monasteries in Cambodia, you may have observed that Khmer monks are not involved in growing food and rely on donations from the strictly religious locals. Here in Tra Vinh, Vietnamese guides will proudly point out the rice harvest by the monks as one of the accomplishments of liberation. To the Vietnamese, non-working monks were viewed as 'parasites'. The

Khmers don't necessarily see it the same way and still continue to donate funds to the monasteries surreptitiously.

Between the ages of 15 and 20, most boys set aside a few months or years to live as monks (they decide themselves on the length of service). Khmer monks can eat meat, though they cannot kill animals.

There is also a small but active Chinese community in Tra Vinh, one of the few remaining in the Mekong Delta region. Most of the Overseas Chinese fled this part of Vietnam during the years of persecution in 1978 and 1979.

Information

Tourist Office The Tra Vinh Tourist Company (☎ 62491, 62042; fax 63769) is in the Cuu Long Hotel. The staff can book trips to various sites around the province – they seem fond of the pomelo orchards (Vuon Buoi) though the boat trips should prove more interesting.

Ong Pagoda

The Ong Pagoda (Chua Ong, also known as Chua Tau) is a very ornate, brightly painted building at the corner of Dien Bien Phu and Tran Phu Sts. Unusual for the Mekong Delta region, this is a 100% Chinese pagoda and is still a very active place of worship. The red-faced god on the altar is the deified general Quan Cong (in Chinese: Guangong, Guandi or Guanyu). Quan Cong is believed to offer protection against war and is based on an historical figure, a soldier of the 3rd century. You can read more about him in the Chinese classic *The Romance of the Three Kingdoms*.

The Ong Pagoda was founded in 1556 by the Fujian Chinese Congregation but has been rebuilt a number of times. Recent visitors from Taiwan and Hong Kong have contributed money for the pagoda's restoration, which is why it is currently in such fine shape.

Ong Met Pagoda

The chief reason for visiting this large Khmer pagoda is that it's the most acces-

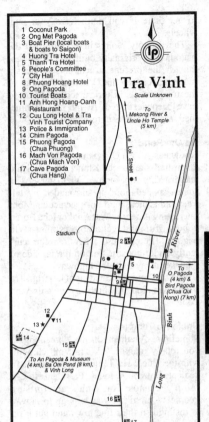

sible, being right in the centre of town. Next door is a French-era Catholic church. The monks at Ong Met Pagoda (Chua Ong Met) are friendly and happy to show you the interior.

Chim Pagoda

An interesting monastery, Chim Pagoda (Chua Chim) sees few visitors because you have to twist and wind your way along dirt roads to find it. It's actually just one km off the main highway to Vinh Long in the southwest part of town. Having a local take you there on a motorbike is probably the best way to get there if you don't have your own wheels.

The friendly monks here claim that the pagoda was originally built 500 years ago, though the present structure is obviously much newer than that. Unfortunately, all of the monastery's historical records seem to have been destroyed. At the present time, there are 17 monks in residence here.

Ba Om Pond

Known as Ao Ba Om (Square Lake), this is a spiritual site for the Khmers and a picnic and drinking spot for local Vietnamese. The square-shaped pond is surrounded by tall trees and is pleasant if not spectacular. More interesting is nearby Wat Angkor Icha Borei, a beautiful and venerable Khmer-style pagoda. There is also a new museum currently under construction on the far side of the lake (away from the highway).

Ba Om Pond is located eight km from Tra Vinh town along the highway towards Vinh Long.

Uncle Ho Temple

Sometimes Vietnam throws something at you totally unexpected. Tra Vinh chips in with the Uncle Ho Temple (Den Tho Bac), dedicated of course to late President Ho Chi Minh. Perhaps Tra Vinh's enterprising People's Committee was looking for a way to distinguish their fine town and put it on

the tourist circuit. If so, it looks as though they have succeeded. Although no monks have yet taken up residence, 'worshippers' continue to flock here (Communist Party brass arrive regularly in chauffeur-driven limousines). A locally produced tourist pamphlet calls the temple the 'Pride of Tra Vinh's inhabitants'. Ho himself would no doubt be horrified.

The Uncle Ho Temple is located within the Long Duc commune, five km from Tra Vinh town.

An Pagoda & Museum

Four km south-west of Tra Vinh town is the An Pagoda (Chua An) and Khmer Minority People's Museum.

Boat Trips

The narrow Long Binh River meanders southwards from Tra Vinh town for over 10 km before reaching a spillway. The spillway was built to prevent seawater from intruding at high tide. Otherwise, the salt water would contaminate the river and kill the crops.

It is possible to hire boats from the pier on the east side of town to take you downstream to the spillway. Of course, the Tra Vinh Tourist Company can also book you onto these trips, which typically take about 1½ hours by speedboat, more for a slower boat.

Tours can also be arranged to Oyster Island (Con Ngao), an offshore mud-flat that

Buffalo near Tra Vinh

supports a small contingent of oyster farmers. Tra Vinh Tourist Company offers trips for US$100 per boat regardless of group size, though you should be able to negotiate something cheaper.

Places to Stay
The *Huong Tra Hotel* (☎ 62433; 12 rooms), 67 Ly Thuong Kiet St, is Tra Vinh's bottom-end place. Rooms with shared toilet cost just US$3.50, but an air-con room with attached bath goes for US$7.

Slightly fancier is the *Phuong Hoang Hotel* (☎ 62270) at 1 Le Thanh Ton St. All rooms have attached bathroom. Rooms with fan only are US$3.50 to US$4.50, while air-con doubles are US$6 to US$9.

The *Cuu Long Hotel* (☎ 62615) at 999 Nguyen Thi Minh Khai St offers reasonable accommodation at US$12 to US$24.

The *Thanh Tra Hotel* (☎ 63621, 63622; fax 63769), 1 Pham Thai Buong St, is where most of the tour groups put up for the night. However, there are also some budget rooms, and rates range from US$8 to US$32.

Getting There & Away
Tra Vinh is 68 km from Vinh Long and 205 km from Ho Chi Minh City. Either Vinh Long or Cantho would be logical places to catch buses to Tra Vinh.

AROUND TRA VINH
Chua Co
Chua Co is a particularly interesting Khmer monastery because the grounds form a bird sanctuary. Several types of storks and ibises arrive here in large numbers just before sunset to spend the night. Of course, there are many nests here and you must take care not to disturb them.

Chua Co is 45 km from Tra Vinh.

Luu Cu Site
Some ancient ruins are to be found at Luu Cu, south of Tra Vinh near the shores of the Hau River. The site is protected and there is still some archaeological excavation going on here.

SA DEC
The former capital of Dong Thap Province, Sa Dec gained some small fame as the setting for *The Lover*, a movie based on the novel by Marguerite Duras. Among the Vietnamese, Sa Dec is famous for the many nurseries cultivating flowers and bonsai trees. The flowers are picked almost daily and transported fresh to shops in Ho Chi Minh City. The nurseries are a major sightseeing attraction for domestic tourists, not just foreigners.

Groups doing a whirlwind tour of the Mekong River Delta often make a lunch stop here and drop in on the nurseries. However, Sa Dec isn't a huge attraction. It used to be better when there were rice noodle factories here (which you could visit), but for some reason this industry suddenly vanished in 1994.

Hung Tu Pagoda
The Hung Tu Pagoda (Chua Co Hung Tu) is of classic Chinese design. A bright white statue of Quan Am (Guanyin in Chinese, the Goddess of Mercy) standing on a pedestal adorns the grounds. Don't confuse this place with the adjacent Buu Quang Pagoda, which is somewhat less glamorous.

Nurseries
The nurseries *(vuon hoa)* operate all year round, though they get stripped bare of their flowers just before Tet. You're welcome to have a look around, but not to pick any flowers unless you plan on buying them. Photography is certainly permitted – indeed, the flower farmers are very used to it.

The nurseries don't belong to one person. There are many small operators here, each with a different speciality. The most famous garden here is called the Tu Ton Rose Garden (Vuon Hong Tu Ton), which has over 500 different kinds of roses in 50 different shades and colours. The busiest time here is Tet, but that's actually not a good time to visit – the garden is nearly empty then because the roses get shipped off to markets elsewhere.

Uncle Ho Statue
We're not being facetious – yes, they really

MEKONG DELTA

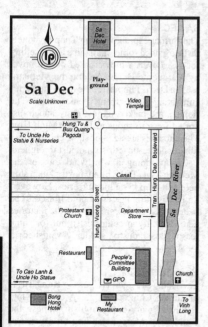

Sa Dec

Scale Unknown

Sa Dec Hotel

Playground

Video Temple

Hung Tu & Buu Quang Pagoda

To Uncle Ho Statue & Nurseries

Canal

Tran Hung Dao Boulevard

Sa Dec River

Hung Vuong Street

Protestant Church

Department Store

Restaurant

To Cao Lanh & Uncle Ho Statue

People's Committee Building

GPO

Church

Bong Hong Hotel

My Restaurant

To Vinh Long

call it 'Uncle Ho Statue' (Tuong Bac Ho) in Vietnamese. Ho Chi Minh didn't live in Sa Dec, but his father did. To commemorate this bit of historical consequence, a large statue of Ho Chi Minh (but not his father!?) has been erected a few kilometres to the west of town. You'll need a motorbike to get out there as it's probably too far for cyclos unless you have a lot of time and patience. The statue is along the route to the nurseries, so you can take in both sights on the same journey.

Places to Stay
Not many foreigners overnight in Sa Dec because nearby Cao Lanh, Long Xuyen and Vinh Long all tend to siphon off the tourists. Still, Sa Dec is a pleasant if not very exciting place to spend an evening.

The main tourist accommodation is the *Sa Dec Hotel* (☎ 61430; 38 rooms). All rooms have attached bath. With a fan it costs US$10, and with air-con you pay US$15 to US$25.

The cheapest place to stay is the *Bong Hong Hotel* (☎ 61301; 15 rooms). A room with fan and attached toilet cost US$6. The management is friendly.

Places to Eat
Both hotels do acceptable meals, but the *Bong Hong Hotel* seems to be the better of the two. In the centre of town is the *My Restaurant* (the name means 'American Restaurant'), which has become the hot spot for backpackers.

Getting There & Away
Sa Dec is in Dong Thap Province, midway between Vinh Long and Long Xuyen.

CAO LANH
Cao Lanh is a new town carved from the jungles and swamps of the Mekong Delta region. Its up and coming status has much to do with its designation as the provincial capital of Dong Thap Province.

Information
Dong Thap Tourist Company (☎ 51343, 51547), 2 Doc Binh Kieu St, deserves kudos for being helpful. This is the best place to inquire about boat tours of the surrounding area.

War Memorial
The War Memorial (Dai Liet Si) off Highway 30 on the east end of town is Cao Lanh's most prominent landmark. This masterpiece of socialist sculpture boasts a clamshell-shaped building displaying a large Vietnamese star alongside a hammer and sickle. In front of this are several large concrete statues of victorious peasants and soldiers brandishing weapons and upraised fists. The surrounding grounds are decked out with the graves of 3112 fallen comrades who fought for the winning side.

Construction of the War Memorial began in 1977 and finished in 1984. There is no admission fee.

Nguyen Sinh Sac Gravesite
Aside from the 3112 graves at the War

MEKONG DELTA

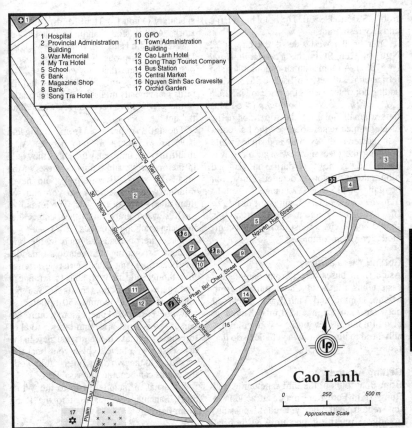

1 Hospital
2 Provincial Administration Building
3 War Memorial
4 My Tra Hotel
5 School
6 Bank
7 Magazine Shop
8 Bank
9 Song Tra Hotel
10 GPO
11 Town Administration Building
12 Cao Lanh Hotel
13 Dong Thap Tourist Company
14 Bus Station
15 Central Market
16 Nguyen Sinh Sac Gravesite
17 Orchid Garden

Cao Lanh

0   250   500 m

Approximate Scale

MEKONG DELTA

Memorial, another significant tomb is that of Nguyen Sinh Sac (1862-1929). Mr Nguyen's contribution to Vietnamese history was being the father of Ho Chi Minh. His large tomb (Lang Cu Nguyen Sinh Sac) occupies one hectare, about one km to the south-west of central Cao Lanh.

Although there are various plaques (in Vietnamese) and tourist pamphlets exhorting Nguyen Sinh Sac as a great revolutionary, there is little evidence to suggest that he was involved in the anti-colonial struggle against the French. Needless to say, the revolutionary credentials of his son are without question.

Water Skiing

Enterprising Dong Thap Tourist Company owns a speedboat and a pair of waterskis, which they are willing to rent out at US$25 per hour. Waterskiing on the local canals or even the Mekong River itself should provide an interesting diversion from the standard museum and bird-watching tours.

Places to Stay

Currently Cao Lanh's largest hotel is the *My Tra Hotel* (☎ 51469; 21 rooms). It's on the east side of town on Highway 30, opposite the War Memorial. Room prices here range from US$15 to US$30. The hotel has a large and airy restaurant.

Over on the west side of the city at 72 Nguyen Hue St is the *Cao Lanh Hotel* (☎ 51061). A room with air-conditioning and refrigerator will set you back US$15, while adding hot water pushes the price to US$20.

Dong Thap Tourist Company (☎ 51343) runs a small hotel on the top floor of its office. A nice feature here are the balconies – sit outside in the evening and sip tea while enjoying the pleasant view. The place was undergoing a renovation during our visit and room rates were not yet decided, but should be in the US$15 to US$20 range.

In the centre of Cao Lanh is the *Song Tra Hotel*. Currently under construction, this should be the city's most upmarket accommodation when completed.

Getting There & Away

Aside from buses direct from Saigon, the easiest bus routes to Cao Lanh are from Mytho, Cantho and Vinh Long. The road between Cao Lanh and Long Xuyen is beautiful but has few buses – you will probably need to hire your own vehicle to do that route.

Getting Around

Boat Boat tours of the bird sanctuaries and Rung Tram Forest are major attractions in this region. Although you could possibly arrange something privately with boat owners, you'll probably find it easier to deal with Dong Thap Tourist. Fortunately, their rates are reasonable. There are too many different combinations of boat sizes and possible destinations to list them all, but a group of 15 persons would be charged about US$2 per person for a half-day tour with all transport included. A group of five might pay US$5 each for the same thing. You may not be travelling with 14 companions, but it's not difficult to round up other foreigners at the few hotels in town where everyone stays.

AROUND CAO LANH
White Stork Sanctuary

To the north-east of Cao Lanh is a bird sanctuary (Vuon Co Thap Muoi) for white storks. A white stork standing on the back of a water buffalo is the symbol of the Mekong Delta, and you probably have more chance of seeing it here than anywhere else. The sanctuary covers only two hectares, but the birds seem mostly undisturbed by the nearby farmers (who have been sternly warned not to hunt the storks).

The storks are protected from hunting and have grown accustomed to people. As a result, they are fairly easy to spot as they feed in the mangrove and bamboo forests in the area. The storks live in pairs and never migrate with the seasons, so you can see them at any time of the year. The birds live on freshwater crabs and other tidbits that they can catch in the canals.

There are no roads as such to the bird sanctuary, so getting there requires a mandatory boat trip. Dong Thap Tourist can arrange this, though you may be able to arrange it elsewhere. A speedboat costs US$25 per hour, and the ride requires 50 minutes. A slow boat costs US$4 per person, requires 20 persons to get that price and takes a total of three hours to make the return journey. In the dry season, you have to plan your boat trip according to the two daily tides – at low tide the canals can become impassable.

It's usual to include a trip to the White Stork Sanctuary with a visit to the Rung Tram Forest.

Rung Tram Forest

South-east of Cao Lanh and accessible by boat tour is the 46-hectare Rung Tram Forest near My Long village. The area is one vast swamp with a beautiful thick canopy of tall trees and vines. It's one of the last natural forests left in the Mekong Delta, and by now probably would have been turned into a rice paddy were it not for its historical significance. During the Vietnam War, the Viet Cong had a base here called Xeo Quit, where top-brass VC lived in underground bunkers. But don't mistake this for another Cu Chi Tunnels – it's very different.

Only about 10 VC were here at any given time. They were all generals who directed the war from Xeo Quit, just two km from a US military base. The Americans never realised that the VC generals were living right under their noses. Of course, they were suspicious about that patch of forest, and periodically dropped some bombs on it just to reassure themselves, but the Viet Cong remained safe in their underground bunkers.

The location of the base was so secret that the wives of the generals didn't even know its location. The wives did occasionally pay their husbands a conjugal visit, but this had to be arranged at another special bunker.

When the American military departed Vietnam in 1973, the Viet Cong grew bolder and put the base above ground. Attempts by the South Vietnamese military to attack were thwarted – while the South was running out of funding and ammunition that the Americans had promised would be forthcoming, the VC was able to build up its forces in the Mekong Delta and challenge the Saigon regime openly.

Access to the area is by boat, and most visitors combine this with a trip to the White Stork Sanctuary. A speedboat from Cao Lanh to the Rung Tram Forest takes only 10 minutes, but a slow boat will require at least 30 minutes.

Beware of the very mean red ants here – they are huge, fast and they bite. If you are allergic to red-ant bites (many people are), you probably should not visit.

Tam Nong Nature Reserve

Due north of Cao Lanh is the Tam Nong Nature Reserve (Tram Chim Tam Nong), notable for its large number of cranes. Over 220 species of birds have been identified within the reserve, but ornithologists will be particularly interested in the rare red herons which nest here from approximately December to June. From July to November, the birds go on holiday in Cambodia, so you've got to schedule your visit to coordinate with the birds' travel itinerary if you want to see them. Also, the birds are early risers – early morning is the best time to see them, though you might get a glimpse when they return home in the evening. During the day, the birds are of course engaged in the important matter of eating.

Seeing these birds requires a fair amount of commitment (time, effort and money), so it's really a special interest tour. Because you'll need to be up at the crack of dawn, staying in Cao Lanh doesn't work out too well – you would have to head out at 4.30 am and travel in the dark over an unlit dirt road to the town of Tam Nong.

Tam Nong is a sleepy town 45 km from Cao Lanh. The one-way drive takes 1½ hours by car, though in future it may be reduced to one hour when the currently abysmal road gets resurfaced. It is also possible to get there by boat. A speedboat requires only one hour, but costs US$25 per hour to rent. A slow boat which costs US$4 per person can be arranged from Dong Thap Tourist, but it takes four hours for the one-way journey and requires 20 people to make it economically viable. From the guesthouse in Tam Nong, it takes another hour by small boat (at US$15 per hour) to reach the area where the red herons live and another hour to return. To this, add whatever time you spend (perhaps an hour) staring at your feathered friends through binoculars, and then the requisite one to four hours to return to Cao Lanh depending on your mode of transport. This is not advisable, so you really need to stay at the government guesthouse in Tam Nong, which is much closer to where the birds are.

There are actually two guesthouses in Tam Nong, though the one usually open to foreigners is inconveniently far from town (about two km). The guesthouse has 10 rooms, which cost US$6/10 for fan/air-con doubles. The toilets are outside. We found the guesthouse quite OK except that it was absolutely overrun with thousands of bugs and the staff had no insecticide. Fortunately, we scored a can of bug killer in town (not easy to find!) and proceeded to commit entomological genocide. If you're going to stay here, you may want to stock up on toxic chemicals in Cao Lanh. Go up to the roof of the guesthouse for some great views.

Tam Nong shuts down early – if you want

to eat dinner in town, make arrangements before 5 pm. Meals can be served later if you book in advance, but of course you will have to pay extra for the late-night service. There are heaps of mosquitoes here in the evening, so come prepared with insect repellent. If you don't have any, the local pharmacy can sell you the cure-all green oil which works as an acceptable substitute.

CANTHO

Cantho (population 150,000), capital of Cantho Province, is the political, economic, cultural and transportation centre of the Mekong Delta. Rice-husking mills are a major local industry.

This friendly, bustling city is connected to most other population centres in the Mekong Delta by a system of rivers and canals. These waterways are the major tourist drawcard in Cantho – travellers come here to do economical boat trips. Unlike in Mytho and Vinh Long, Cantho's People's Committee has so far not attempted to monopolise the boat tour business and so prices have remained low.

Orientation

Nguyen Trai St links Cantho's bus station, north-west of the centre, with Hoa Binh Blvd, a wide avenue with a centre strip. Hoa Binh Blvd becomes 30 Thang 4 Blvd at Nguyen An Ninh St. Hai Ba Trung St runs along the Cantho River waterfront. Phan Dinh Phung St, the main commercial thoroughfare, is two blocks inland from Hai Ba Trung St.

Information

Tourist Office Cantho Tourist (Cong Ty Du Lich Can Tho; ☎ 21853; fax 22719) is the provincial tourism authority; the office is at 20 Hai Ba Trung St.

Money Vietcombank (Ngan Hang Ngoai Thuong Viet Nam; ☎ 20445) is at 7 Hoa Binh Blvd.

Post & Telecommunications The GPO is a five-storey building near the fountain.

Emergency The general hospital is on the corner of Chau Van Liem St and Hoa Binh Blvd.

Munirangsyaram Pagoda

The ornamentation of Munirangsyaram Pagoda, located at 36 Hoa Binh Blvd, is typical of Khmer Hinayana Buddhist pagodas, lacking the multiple Bodhisattvas and Taoist spirits common in Vietnamese Mahayana pagodas. In the upstairs sanctuary, a 1½-metre-high representation of Siddhartha Gautama, the historical Buddha, sits under a *potthe* (bodhi) tree. Built in 1946, Munirangsyaram Pagoda serves the Khmer community of Cantho, which numbers about 2000. The two Khmer monks, one in his 70s and the other in his 20s, hold prayers at 5 am and 6 pm every day.

Quan Thanh De Pagoda

This small Chinese pagoda, also known as Minh Huong Hoi Quan, was built by the Cantonese Congregation about 70 years ago. Cantho previously had a large ethnic-Chinese population, but most fled after the anti-Chinese persecutions of 1978-79.

Quan Thanh De Pagoda is on Le Minh Ngu On St between Nguyen Hue B and Nguyen Trai Sts and is open from 5 am to 8 pm. On the main dais are Quan Cong and his guardians, the general Chau Xuong and the administrative mandarin Quan Binh. To the left of the dais is Ong Bon, Guardian Spirit of Happiness and Virtue. Thien Hau, the Goddess of the Sea, is to the other side of the dais.

Central Market

The Central Market is strung out along Hai Ba Trung St. The main market building is at the intersection of Hai Ba Trung St and Nam Ky Khoi Nghia St.

Ho Chi Minh Museum

This is the only museum in the Mekong Delta devoted to Ho Chi Minh. It's a bit of a mystery why it was built here, as Ho Chi Minh never lived in Cantho. If you are willing to overlook that small sticking point,

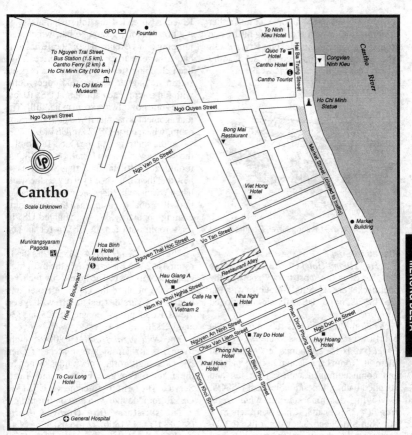

Cantho
Scale Unknown

there is no reason not to visit this large museum, which only opened its doors in 1995. It's near the GPO on Hoa Binh Blvd.

University of Cantho
Cantho University, founded in 1966, is on 30 Thang 4 Blvd.

Nearby Rural Areas
Rural areas of Cantho Province, renowned for their durian, mangosteen and orange orchards, can easily be reached from Cantho by boat or bicycle.

Boat Rides
The most interesting thing to do in Cantho is take a boat ride. The cost for this is very reasonable, around US$1.50 per hour for a small paddle boat which can carry two or three passengers. You won't have to look hard for the boats – they will be looking for you. Just wander by the docks across from the Quoc Te Hotel and you'll have plenty of offers. Most of the boats are operated by women. Bring your camera, though keep it in a plastic bag when you're not actually shooting because it's easy to get splashed by the wake of motorised boats.

MEKONG DELTA

Larger boats with motors can go farther afield, and it's worth considering hiring one to make a tour of the Mekong River itself. The paddleboats only go on the Cantho River, because the current is weaker.

Boat on the Mekong River, Cantho

Places to Stay

The *Huy Hoang Hotel* (☎ 25833) at 35 Ngo Duc Ke St is the most trendy spot for the backpacker crowd. Singles/doubles with fan are US$7/9, or pay US$9 for air-conditioned comfort.

When the foregoing is full, much of the overflow crowd migrates to the *Phong Nha Hotel* (☎ 21615; 20 rooms) at 79 Chau Van Liem St. Rooms are clean if not spectacular, and come equipped with ceiling fan and attached bath. Singles/doubles cost US$4/5.

Moving downmarket, the *Khai Hoan Hotel* (☎ 35261) at 83 Chau Van Liem St is dirty but dirt-cheap. They don't like to take foreigners, but they might accept you. Otherwise, you'll be referred to a 'decent hotel'. Rooms cost US$4.

The *Tay Do Hotel* (☎ 21009; 25 rooms) on Chau Van Liem St offers doubles with fan and outside toilet for US$5. You get plenty of dirt for your money.

The *Hoa Binh Hotel* (☎ 20536) at 5 Hoa Binh Blvd is a reasonably well-appointed place which also tries to milk the foreign market. Service is sloppy, but rooms are OK. A small single with fan and private bath costs US$8, while air-con doubles are US$12 and US$14. A triple air-con room costs US$21.

The *Quoc Te Hotel* (☎ 22079; 32 rooms) at 12 Hai Ba Trung St is along the Cantho River. Also called the International Hotel, it's notable for its karaoke bar, which gets jumping on weekends. The Quoc Te has long had a large market share, but prices have been climbing steadily and backpackers are starting to migrate elsewhere. Budget rooms with fan and private bath start at US$10, but these somehow always seem to be 'full'. The management is happier if you take an air-con room, which costs US$23 to US$43.

On the south side of the Quoc Te Hotel is the all new *Cantho Hotel* (☎ 22218; 20 rooms) at 14-16 Hai Ba Trung St. It was so new that the paint wasn't yet dry on the walls when we visited. Prices are very reasonable, but will probably go up when the place starts gaining popularity. We were quoted US$10 for a room with fan, or US$14 for air-con rooms.

The *Ninh Kieu Hotel* (☎ 24583, 25285; 31 rooms) at 2 Hai Ba Trung St is the most high class place in town. The hotel is by the river just to the north of the Quoc Te Hotel, and boasts a riverside restaurant with good views. Room prices here are US$25, US$30 and US$36.

The *Nha Nghi Hotel* (☎ 20049; eight rooms) is a sharp-looking place at 1 Dien Bien Phu St. It's brand-new and is owned by the Cantho Province Finance and Tariff Service. The tariff for foreigners is US$15 to US$20 for a double with air-conditioning.

The six-storey *Hau Giang A Hotel* (☎ 21851; fax 21806; 32 rooms) at 34 Nam Ky Khoi Nghia St is also very pleasant and attracts many foreigners – even the lobby has air-conditioning. All this luxury costs US$23 to US$40 a night.

The *Hau Giang B Hotel* (☎ 21950; 25 rooms), 27 Chau Van Liem St, is a branch of the foregoing. Fan rooms are US$8 to US$9, and air-conditioning raises it to US$12.

The *Viet Hong Hotel* (☎ 25831) at 55 Phan Dinh Phung St was once a well-worn cheapie but was closed for renovation during our visit. We anticipate that prices will be renovated too when it reopens.

The *Cuu Long Hotel* (80 rooms), 52 Quang Trung St, is at the intersection with Hoa Binh Blvd. Rooms in this enormous place cost US$8 to US$10 with fan only. Air-con rooms are US$20 to US$25.

Places to Eat
Along the Cantho River waterfront there are several restaurants serving Mekong Delta specialities such as fish, snake, frog and turtle.

The *Quoc Te Hotel* (☎ 22079) operates two restaurants; both have English menus but the staff speak limited English. The upstairs air-conditioned restaurant is great value – the menu includes deep-fried snake, turtle soup and some of the largest prawns you'll ever see.

Restaurant Alley is an appropriate name for Nam Ky Khoi Nghia St between Dien Bien Phu and Phan Dinh Phung Sts. There are about a dozen restaurants lining both sides of the street, all of them good. Mobile stands selling soup and French-roll sandwiches are often set up on Hoa Binh Blvd near the GPO.

Congvien Ninh Kieu is a waterside cafe across the street from the Quoc Te Hotel.

Entertainment
All upmarket hotels have the requisite karaoke bars. The one in the *Quoc Te Hotel* deserves special mention, since it doubles as a disco. Entrance is free to hotel residents but costs US$0.80 for others.

Getting There & Away
Air Flights between Cantho and Ho Chi Minh City run on what might best be described as an on-again off-again basis. At the time of this writing, they were off yet again but expected to resume. Vietnam Airlines seems to have no information on when this might come to pass. So at present, Cantho's airport is being used for military aircraft only.

Even flakier are the flights to Phu Quoc Island from Cantho. It's worth asking about this though.

Bus Buses to Cantho leave Ho Chi Minh City from Mien Tay Bus Station in An Lac. Nonexpress buses take five hours; the express bus, which has priority at ferry crossings, takes about 3½ hours.

The main bus station in Cantho is several kilometres out of town at the intersection of Nguyen Trai and Tran Phu Sts. There is another bus depot near the intersection of 30 Thang 4 Blvd and Mau Than St.

Car By car, the ride from Ho Chi Minh City to Cantho along National Highway 1 usually takes about four hours. There are two ferry crossings between Ho Chi Minh City and Cantho, the first at Vinh Long and the second at Cantho itself. The Cantho ferry runs from 4 am to 2 am. Fruit, soft drinks and other food are sold where vehicles wait for the ferries.

To get from Hoa Binh Blvd in Cantho to the ferry crossing, take Nguyen Trai St to the bus station and turn right onto Tran Phu St.

Road distances from Cantho are as follows:

Camau	179 km
Chau Doc	117 km
Ho Chi Minh City	168 km
Long Xuyen	62 km
Mytho	104 km
Rach Gia	116 km
Sa Dec	51 km
Soc Trang	63 km
Vinh Long	34 km

Getting Around
To/From the Airport Cantho Airport is 10 km from the centre along the road leading to Rach Gia. Transport by motorbike will of course be cheaper than by taxi.

Xe Honda Loi Unique to the Mekong Delta, these makeshift vehicles are the main form of transport around Cantho. A *xe Honda loi* is essentially a two-wheeled wagon attached to the rear of a motorbike, creating what resembles a motorised cyclo. Of course, it also differs from a cyclo in that there are four wheels touching the ground rather than two. Fares around town should be about US$1, but more for trips to outlying areas.

MEKONG DELTA

LONG XUYEN

Long Xuyen, the capital of An Giang Province, has a population of about 100,000. It was once a stronghold of the Hoa Hao sect, founded in 1939, which emphasises simplicity in worship and does not believe in temples or intermediaries between humans and the Supreme Being. Until 1956, the Hoa Hao had an army and constituted a major military force in this region.

Today, Long Xuyen is the most prosperous town in the Mekong Delta. There are a few sights around town, but for travellers its value is mainly as a useful transit point with good accommodation and food.

Orientation

Tran Hung Dao St runs north from the bus station and then continues on towards Chau Doc. Nguyen Hue St and Hai Ba Trung St, which are perpendicular to each other, are both wide, divided avenues.

Information

Tourist Office The office of An Giang Tourist Company (☎ 52086) – the government-owned official tourist authority for An Giang Province – is at 83-85 Nguyen Hue B St.

Tourism Services Company (Xi Nghiep Dich Vu Du Lich; ☎ 52277) at 93 Nguyen Trai St runs tours to Cambodia and may be able to provide other services, such as car rental.

Money Vietcombank (☎ 53589) is at 1 Hung Vuong St.

Post & Telecommunications The GPO is at 11 Ngo Gia Tu St.

Long Xuyen Catholic Church

Long Xuyen Catholic Church, an impressive modern structure with a 50-metre-high bell tower, is one of the largest churches in the Mekong Delta. It was constructed between 1966 and 1973 and can seat 1000 worshippers. The church is on the triangular block created by Tran Hung Dao, Hung Vuong and Nguyen Hue A Sts and is open for visitors

from 4 am to 8 pm. Masses are held daily from 4.30 to 5.30 am and 6 to 7 pm; on Sunday, there are masses from 5 to 6.30 am, 3.30 to 5 pm and 6 to 7.30 pm.

Long Xuyen Protestant Church

Long Xuyen Protestant Church is a small modern structure at 4 Hung Vuong St. Prayers are held on Sunday from 10 am to noon.

Cho Moi District

Cho Moi District, across the river from Long Xuyen, is known for its rich groves of banana, durian, guava, jackfruit, longan, mango, mangosteen and plum. The women here are said to be the most beautiful in the Mekong Delta. Cho Moi District can be reached by ferry from the Cho Moi (An Hoa) Ferry Terminal at the foot of Nguyen Hue St.

Places to Stay

The *Binh Dan Hotel* (12 rooms), 12 Nguyen An Ninh St, is a basic dump that even the cockroaches try to avoid. You enter the hotel through a long, dark and grim corridor. If none of this deters you, rooms are very cheap at US$2.50.

The *Phat Thanh Hotel* (14 rooms) is on the same block at 2 Nguyen An Ninh St. It's also a dump but marginally better than the Binh Dan Hotel. Rooms with fan and private bath are US$4.

The *Thien Huong Hotel* (nine rooms) is nearby at 4 Nguyen An Ninh St. Like the preceding, it's also awful but cheap at US$3 for a double with electric fan.

Most backpackers prefer the *Song Hau Hotel* (☎ 52308; 20 rooms), 10 Hai Ba Trung St. Rooms here are decent and still moderately priced at US$8 with electric fan and US$10 with air-con. All rooms come equipped with attached bath.

The *Kim Tinh Hotel* (☎ 53137) at 39-41-43 Nguyen Trai St is a reasonably good alternative. Double rooms with fan/air-con cost US$5/6. The best feature of this hotel is its restaurant.

The *Thai Binh Hotel* (☎ 52184, 52345; 24 rooms) is at 12 Nguyen Hue A St. Living

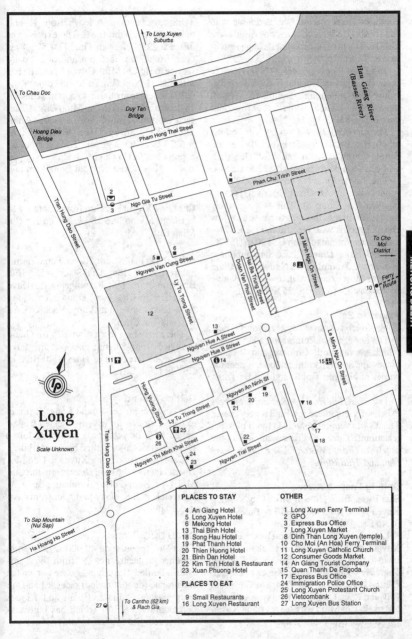

Long Xuyen

Scale Unknown

MEKONG DELTA

PLACES TO STAY

4 An Giang Hotel
5 Long Xuyen Hotel
6 Mekong Hotel
13 Thai Binh Hotel
18 Song Hau Hotel
19 Phat Thanh Hotel
20 Thien Huong Hotel
21 Binh Dan Hotel
22 Kim Tinh Hotel & Restaurant
23 Xuan Phuong Hotel

PLACES TO EAT

9 Small Restaurants
16 Long Xuyen Restaurant

OTHER

1 Long Xuyen Ferry Terminal
2 GPO
3 Express Bus Office
7 Long Xuyen Market
8 Dinh Than Long Xuyen (temple)
10 Cho Moi (An Hoa) Ferry Terminal
11 Long Xuyen Catholic Church
12 Consumer Goods Market
14 An Giang Tourist Company
15 Quan Thanh De Pagoda
17 Express Bus Office
24 Immigration Police Office
25 Long Xuyen Protestant Church
26 Vietcombank
27 Long Xuyen Bus Station

conditions here are not bad. A double with fan costs US$6 and air-con rooms are US$10. The hotel is proud of its huge restaurant and karaoke.

The *Xuan Phuong Hotel* (☎ 52041), at the corner of Nguyen Trai and Hung Vuong Sts, is also pleasant enough. Double rooms with air-con cost US$15, while a room for four people is US$20.

The *An Giang Hotel* (☎ 52297; 16 rooms) at 40 Hai Ba Trung St is not bad at all. Singles/doubles with fan cost US$8/12, while air-con doubles are US$13 to US$14.

The *Long Xuyen Hotel* (☎ 52927; 39 rooms), run by An Giang Tourism, is at 17 Nguyen Van Cung St. This is a relatively upmarket place though there are a few cheaper rooms with electric fan for US$16. Air-con rooms range from US$20 to US$26.

The *Mekong Hotel* (Khach San Cuu Long; ☎ 52365; 20 rooms) at 15 Nguyen Van Cung St is the most expensive in town with double rooms costing from US$25 to US$30.

Places to Eat
Long Xuyen is known for its flavourful rice.

The *Long Xuyen Restaurant*, a large place which serves both Chinese and Western dishes and specialises in seafood, is near the corner of Nguyen Trai St and Hai Ba Trung St.

The *Kim Tinh Hotel & Restaurant* serves excellent Vietnamese food and is very cheap. The *Xuan Phuong Hotel* also has a pleasant restaurant. There are also restaurants in the hotels *An Giang*, *Mekong*, *Long Xuyen*, *Song Hau* and *Thai Binh*.

Getting There & Away
Bus Buses from Ho Chi Minh City to Long Xuyen leave from the Mien Tay Bus Station in An Lac.

Long Xuyen Bus Station (Ben Xe Long Xuyen; ☎ 52125) is at the southern end of town opposite 96/3B Tran Hung Dao St. There are buses from Long Xuyen to Camau, Cantho, Chau Doc, Ha Tien, Ho Chi Minh City and Rach Gia (three hours). An express bus to Ho Chi Minh City leaves Long Xuyen Bus Station every day at 4 am.

Express buses also leave from several other places around town. The express bus office at 225/4 Nguyen Trai St (☎ 52238) is open from 7 am to 5 pm and offers daily service to Ho Chi Minh City at 3 am. The bus office at 11 Ngo Gia Tu St (in front of the GPO), open from 8 am to 5 pm, sends an 18-seat minibus to Ho Chi Minh City at 2 am each morning. The Tourist Services Company (Xi Nghiep Dich Vu Du Lich; ☎ 52277) at 93 Nguyen Trai St runs an express bus to Ho Chi Minh City every day at 4 am; bus tickets are sold from 7 am to 9 pm.

Car Long Xuyen is 62 km from Cantho, 126 km from Mytho and 189 km from Ho Chi Minh City.

Boat To get to the Long Xuyen Ferry Terminal from Pham Hong Thai St, cross Duy Tan Bridge and turn right. Passenger ferries leave from here to Cho Vam, Dong Tien, Hong Ngu, Kien Luong, Lai Vung, Rach Gia, Sa Dec and Tan Chau.

There may be a ferry service to An Giang Province from Saigon; check at the ferry dock at the river end of Ham Nghi Blvd in Ho Chi Minh City.

Getting Around
The best way to get around Long Xuyen is to take a *xe dap loi* (a two-wheeled wagon pulled by a bicycle) or a xe Honda loi (a two-wheeled wagon pulled by a motorbike).

Car ferries from Long Xuyen to Cho Moi District (across the river) leave from the Cho Moi (An Hoa) Ferry Terminal near 17/4 Nguyen Hue B St every half hour from 4 am to 6.30 pm.

CHAU DOC
Chau Doc (population 40,000) is a riverine commercial centre not far from the Cambodian border. The city was once known for its pirogue (dugout canoe) races. Chau Doc has sizeable Chinese, Cham and Khmer communities, each of which has built distinctive temples that are worth visiting.

Orientation

Chau Doc stretches along the bank of the Hau Giang River. The road closest to the water bears several names and is called (from north to south) Tran Hung Dao St, Gia Long St, Le Loi St and Lien Tinh Lo 10. Lien Tinh Lo 10 leads to Long Xuyen.

Information

Post Office The GPO (☎ 94550) is on the corner of Bao Ho Thoai and Gia Long Sts.

Chau Phu Temple

Chau Phu Temple (Dinh Than Chau Phu), at the corner of Bao Ho Thoai and Gia Long Sts, was built in 1926 to worship Thoai Ngoc Hau (1761-1829), who is buried at Sam Mountain. The structure is decorated with both Vietnamese and Chinese motifs. Inside are funeral tablets bearing the names of the deceased and biographical information about them.

Chau Doc Church

This small Catholic church, constructed in 1920, is across the street from 459 Lien Tinh Lo 10 and is not far from FB Phu Hiep Ferry Terminal. There are masses every day at 5 am and 5 pm; on Sunday, masses are held at 7 am and 4 pm.

Mosques

The domed and arched Chau Giang Mosque, which serves the local Cham Muslim community, is in the hamlet of Chau Giang. To get there, take the car ferry from Chau Giang Ferry Terminal in Chau Doc across the Hau Giang River. From the landing, go away from the river for 30 metres, turn left and walk 50 metres.

The Mubarak Mosque (Thanh Duong Hoi Giao) is also on the river bank opposite Chau Doc. In this mosque, children study the Koran in Arabic script. Visitors are permitted, but you should avoid entering during the calls to prayer (five times daily) unless you are a Muslim.

There are other small mosques in the Chau Doc area. These are reachable by boat, but you'll probably need a local guide to find them all.

Floating Houses

These houses, whose floats consist of empty metal drums, provide both a place to live and a livelihood for their residents. Under each house, fish are raised in suspended metal nets: the fish flourish in their natural river habitat, the family can feed them whatever scraps of biological matter it has handy, and catching the fish does not require all the exertions of fishing. Such houses have become all the rage of late and many new ones are being constructed.

Places to Stay

The *Nha Khach 44* (☎ 66540; 19 rooms) is a decent budget hotel. Singles/doubles/triples cost US$6/8/10. The hotel is at the corner of Doc Phu Thu and Phan Dinh Phung Sts.

The *Chau Doc Hotel* (☎ 66484; 36 rooms) is a large place at 17 Doc Phu Thu St. It's livable, but not great. Double rooms with fan cost US$5 and air-con costs US$9 to US$10.

The *My Loc Hotel* (☎ 66455; 20 rooms) is at 51 B Bao Ho Thoai St. This popular place has double rooms with ceiling fan and private bath for US$8. Air-con doubles are US$10. A four-person room costs US$20. Breakfast is included, but coffee costs extra.

Without a doubt, the fanciest place in town is the *Hang Chau Hotel* (☎ 66196, 66197, 66198). This hotel, right on the riverfront near the Chau Giang ferry terminal, was obviously built to catch the expected tourist trade when the Cambodian border in this area opens to foreigners. Unfortunately, this border is still not open and perhaps never will be, but the hotel is pulling in tour groups making the pilgrimage to Sam Mountain. The hotel boasts a swimming pool and piano bar. All rooms have air-con and cost US$15 to US$30. There are also two-person bungalows for rent costing US$20.

There are two hotels in town which used to accept foreigners but no longer do because they're such dumps. Possibly they will be renovated and reopened to foreigners, so

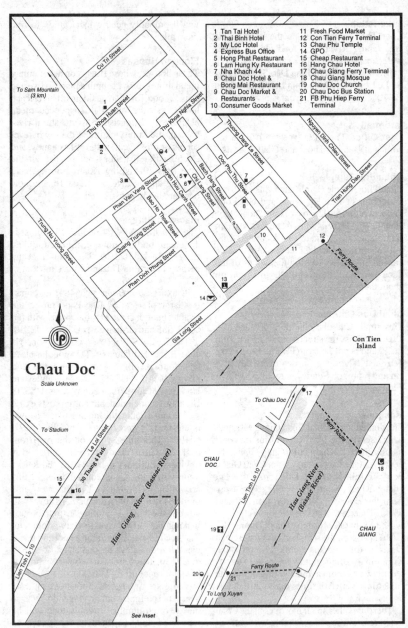

1 Tan Tai Hotel
2 Thai Binh Hotel
3 My Loc Hotel
4 Express Bus Office
5 Hong Phat Restaurant
6 Lam Hung Ky Restaurant
7 Nha Khach 44
8 Chau Doc Hotel &
   Bong Mai Restaurant
9 Chau Doc Market &
   Restaurants
10 Consumer Goods Market

11 Fresh Food Market
12 Con Tien Ferry Terminal
13 Chau Phu Temple
14 GPO
15 Cheap Restaurant
16 Hang Chau Hotel
17 Chau Giang Ferry Terminal
18 Chau Giang Mosque
19 Chau Doc Church
20 Chau Doc Bus Station
21 FB Phu Hiep Ferry
   Terminal

MEKONG DELTA

Chau Doc

Scale Unknown

Con Tien
Island

To Sam Mountain
(3 km)

To Stadium

CHAU
DOC

CHAU
GIANG

To Chau Doc

To Long Xuyen

See Inset

check these out if you're stuck for a place to stay. The two hotels in question are the *Tan Tai Hotel* (☎ 66563; 11 rooms), 273 Thu Khoa Huan St, and the *Thai Binh Hotel* (☎ 66221; 15 rooms), 37 Bao Ho Thoai St.

Places to Eat
The market in the centre of town is the cheapest place to eat and a number of the food stalls here serve the local specialities, which include *kho ca loc, mam thai, mam ruot ca, kho ca tra* and *kho ca su*.

Lam Hung Ky Restaurant at 71 Chi Lang St serves some of the best Chinese and Vietnamese food in town. Nearby, *Hong Phat Restaurant* at 79 Chi Lang St also has excellent Chinese and Vietnamese dishes. The prices at both places are very reasonable. *Bong Mai Restaurant* is on the corner of Doc Phu Thu and Phan Dinh Phung Sts; this place has a limited selection of Western-style dishes.

Cheap Vietnamese food is available in Chau Doc Market, which is spread out along Bach Dang St and nearby streets.

The chic *Hang Chau Hotel* has an excellent restaurant – you can eat while being entertained by live music. Directly opposite the hotel on the other side of the street is a cheap and excellent Vietnamese restaurant.

Getting There & Away
Bus Buses from Ho Chi Minh City to Chau Doc leave from the Mien Tay Bus Station in An Lac; the express bus is said to take six hours.

The Chau Doc Bus Station (Ben Xe Chau Doc), which is south-east of town towards Long Xuyen, is opposite 214 Lien Tinh Lo 10 St. There are nonexpress buses from Chau Doc to Camau (every other day at 8 am), Cantho, Ho Chi Minh City (at 3.30 am and in the afternoon), Long Xuyen, Soc Trang (at 10 am), Tien Giang (every other day at 5 am) and Tra Vinh (daily at 4.30 am).

An express bus to Ho Chi Minh City leaves from the Chau Doc Hotel. Express buses to Ho Chi Minh City (overnight) leave from an office on Nguyen Huu Canh St

between Thu Khoa Nghia and Phan Van Vang Sts; it is open from 7.30 am to 5 pm.

Car Chau Doc is 117 km from Cantho, 181 km from Mytho and 245 km from Ho Chi Minh City.

Boat Boats run between Chau Doc and Vinh Long, as well as between Chau Doc and Ha Tien. The big problem is that a travel permit is needed for the Chau Doc-Ha Tien run because the canal skirts the Cambodian border. Most travellers will not bother.

Getting Around
Land Transport The main forms of land transport in Chau Doc are the xe dap loi and the xe Honda loi.

Boat Boats to Chau Giang District (across the Hau Giang River) leave from two docks: vehicle ferries depart from Chau Giang Ferry Terminal (Ben Pha Chau Giang), which is opposite 419 Le Loi St; smaller, more frequent boats leave from FB Phu Hiep Ferry Terminal (Ben Pha FB Phu Hiep). To get to the latter from the centre of town, head south-east along Gia Long St (which becomes Le Loi St) and turn left at 349 Lien Tinh Lo 10. Take an immediate right and continue on for 200 metres. The prices of both ferries double at night.

Vehicle ferries to Con Tien Island depart from the Con Tien Ferry Terminal (Ben Pha Con Tien), which is off Gia Long St at the river end of Thuong Dang Le St; prices double at night.

AROUND CHAU DOC
Tan Chau District
Tan Chau District is famous all over southern Vietnam for its traditional industry, silk making. The area is also known for its wealth, which is apparent in the proliferation of TV antennas and the widespread ownership of luxury goods (eg, electric fans, high-quality cloth) imported from Thailand via Cambodia. The marketplace in Tan Chau has a selection of competitively priced Thai and Cambodian goods.

To get to Tan Chau District from Chau Doc, take a boat across the Hau Giang River from the FB Phu Hiep Ferry Terminal. Then catch a ride on the back of a *Honda om* for the 18-km trip from Chau Giang District to Tan Chau District.

Sam Mountain

There are dozens of pagodas and temples, many of them set in caves, around Sam Mountain (Nui Sam), which is about three km south-west of Chau Doc out on Bao Ho Thoai St. The Chinese influence is obvious, and this is a favourite spot for ethnic-Chinese pilgrims from Ho Chi Minh City and ethnic-Chinese tourists from Hong Kong and Taiwan.

Climbing the peak is of course the highlight of a visit to Sam Mountain. The views from the top are spectacular (weather permitting) and you can easily look into Cambodia. There is a military outpost on the summit, a legacy of the days when the Khmer Rouge made cross-border raids and massacred Vietnamese civilians. The outpost is still functional, but the soldiers are quite used to tourists taking photos now. However, you may have to ask permission and ply the soldiers with cigarettes before taking photos of them or anything that could be considered militarily sensitive.

Walking down is easier than walking up, so if you want to cheat you can have a motorbike bring you to the summit. The road to the top is on the south-west side of the mountain, so you can walk down along a peaceful, traffic-free trail on the north side which will bring you to the main temple area. The summit road has recently been decorated with amusement-park ceramic dinosaurs and the like, perhaps a sign of abominations to come. But there are also some small shrines and pavilions, which add a bit of charm and remind you that this is indeed Vietnam and not Disneyland.

Tay An Pagoda Tay An Pagoda (Chua Tay An), on the left as you arrive at Sam Mountain, is renowned for the fine carving of its hundreds of religious figures, most of which are made of wood. Aspects of the building's architecture reflect Hindu and Islamic influences. The first chief monk of Tay An Pagoda, which was founded in 1847, came from Giac Lam Pagoda in Ho Chi Minh City. Tay An Pagoda was last rebuilt in 1958.

The main gate is of traditional Vietnamese design. Above the bi-level roof there are figures of lions and two dragons fighting for possession of pearls, chrysanthemums, apricot trees and lotus blossoms. Nearby is a statue of Quan Am Thi Kinh, the Guardian Spirit of Mother & Child (for her legend, see the section on the Jade Emperor Pagoda in the Ho Chi Minh City chapter).

In front of the pagoda are statues of a black elephant with two tusks and a white elephant with six tusks. Around the pagoda there are various monks' tombs.

Temple of Lady Chua Xu The Temple of Lady Chua Xu (Mieu Ba Chua Xu), founded in the 1820s, stands facing Sam Mountain not far from Tay An Pagoda. The first building here was made of bamboo and leaves; the last reconstruction took place in 1972.

According to legend, the statue of Lady Chua Xu used to stand at the summit of Sam Mountain. In the early 19th century, Siamese troops invaded the area and, impressed with the statue, decided to take it back to Thailand with them. But as they carried the statue down the hill, it became heavier and heavier, and they were forced to abandon it by the side of the path.

One day, villagers out cutting wood came upon the statue and decided to bring it back to their village in order to build a temple for it; but it weighed too much for them to budge. Suddenly, there appeared a girl who, possessed by a spirit, declared herself to be Lady Chua Xu. She announced that 40 virgins were to be brought and that they would be able to transport the statue down the mountainside. The 40 virgins were summoned and carried the statue down the slope, but when they reached the plain, it became too heavy and they had to set it down. The people concluded that the site where the virgins halted had been selected by Lady

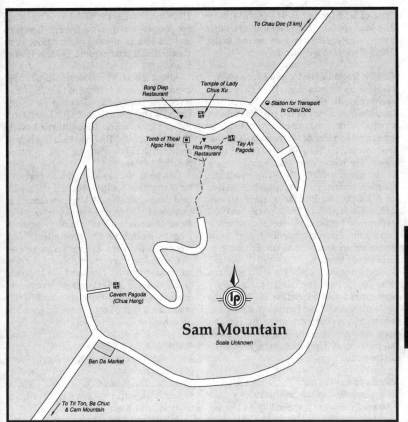

To Chau Doc (3 km)

Bong Diep
Restaurant

Temple of Lady
Chua Xu

Station for Transport
to Chau Doc

Tomb of Thoai
Ngoc Hau

Hoa Phuong
Restaurant

Tay An
Pagoda

Cavern Pagoda
(Chua Hang)

Sam Mountain

Scale Unknown

Ben Da Market

To Tri Ton, Ba Chuc
& Cam Mountain

Chua Xu for the construction of a temple, and it is at that place that the Temple of Lady Chua Xu stands to this day.

Another story relates that the wife of Thoai Ngoc Hau, builder of the Vinh Te Canal, swore to erect a temple when the canal, whose construction claimed many lives, was completed. She died before being able to carry through on her oath, but Thoai Ngoc Hau implemented her plans by building the Temple of Lady Chua Xu.

The temple's most important festival is held from the 23rd to the 26th of the fourth lunar month. During this time, pilgrims flock here, sleeping on mats in the large rooms of the two-storey rest house next to the temple.

Tomb of Thoai Ngoc Hau Thoai Ngoc Hau (1761-1829) was a high-ranking official who served the Nguyen Lords and, later, the Nguyen Dynasty. In early 1829, Thoai Ngoc Hau ordered that a tomb be constructed for himself at the foot of Sam Mountain. The site he chose is not far from Tay An Pagoda.

The steps are made of red 'beehive' (*da ong*) stone brought from the eastern part of southern Vietnam. In the middle of the platform is the Tomb of Thoai Ngoc Hau and those of his wives, Chau Thi Te and Truong Thi Miet. Nearby are several dozen other tombs where officials who served under Thoai Ngoc Hau are buried.

Cavern Pagoda The Cavern Pagoda (Chua Hang, also known as Phuoc Dien Tu) is about halfway up the western side of Sam Mountain. The lower part of the pagoda includes monks' quarters and two hexagonal tombs in which the founder of the pagoda, a female tailor named Le Thi Tho, and a former head monk, Thich Hue Thien, are buried.

The upper section consists of two parts: the main sanctuary, in which there are statues of A Di Da (the Buddha of the Past) and Thich Ca Buddha (Sakyamuni), and the cavern. At the back of the cave, which is behind the sanctuary building, is a shrine dedicated to Quan The Am Bo Tat (the Goddess of Mercy).

According to legend, Le Thi Tho came from Tay An Pagoda to this site half a century ago to lead a quiet, meditative life. When she arrived, she found two enormous snakes, one white and the other dark green. Le Thi Tho soon converted the snakes, who thereafter led pious lives. Upon her death, the snakes disappeared.

Places to Eat For tasty Vietnamese specialities (including cobra and turtle) try *Hoa Phuong Restaurant* between Tay An Pagoda and the Tomb of Thoai Ngoc Hau. This place has a huge garden. *Bong Diep Restaurant* is across from the Tomb of Thoai Ngoc Hau; the selection here is similar to Hoa Phuong Restaurant but the food is not as good.

BA CHUC

Close to the Cambodian border but just within Vietnam is Ba Chuc, otherwise known as the 'Bone Pagoda'. The pagoda stands as a grisly reminder of the horrors perpetrated by the genocidal Khmer Rouge. Between 1975 and 1978, Khmer Rouge guerillas regularly crossed the border into Vietnam and slaughtered innocent civilians. The Vietnamese might have had other motives for invading Cambodia at the end of

1978, but certainly the slaughter of Vietnamese peasants was a reasonable justification – and this is to say nothing of the million or so Cambodians exterminated by the Khmer Rouge.

About 3000 Vietnamese were killed around Ba Chuc sometime in 1978. Ba Chuc resembles Cambodia's Choeung Ek killing fields, where thousands of skulls of Khmer Rouge victims are on display. Like Choeung Ek, travellers find Ba Chuc both fascinating and horrifying – you do need a strong stomach to visit.

Getting to the pagoda will also require a bit of intestinal fortitude because the road is in dismal condition. A high-clearance van might make it during the dry season, but for much of the year the road turns to muck. A jeep or motorbike are generally recommended. If the Vietnamese government ever recognises the tourist potential of this place, the road might be improved. That would probably be the only reason for improving it, because most Vietnamese are afraid of this place and it is unlikely to develop for some time to come.

RACH GIA

Rach Gia, the capital of Kien Giang Province, is a booming port-city on the Gulf of Thailand. The population of about 120,000 includes significant numbers of ethnic-Chinese and Khmers.

Fishing and agriculture have made the town reasonably prosperous. Access to the sea and closeness to Cambodia and Thailand have also made smuggling a profitable business here. The Rach Gia area was once famous as the source of large feathers used to make ceremonial fans for the Imperial Court, but this is one industry that has little chance of reviving despite the recent economic liberalisation.

The main interest that foreigners have in Rach Gia is to use it as an overnight stop on the way to Phu Quoc Island.

Orientation

To get into town from the bus station, head north on Nguyen Trung Truc St, which becomes Le Loi St when you cross the channel. The heart of the city, where most of the hotels and restaurants are found, is between Le Loi St and Tran Phu St on the island.

Information
Tourist Office Kien Giang Tourism (Cong Ty Du Lich Kien Giang; ☎ 63824) – the provincial tourism authority – is at 12 Ly Tu Trong St.

Money Vietcombank (Ngan Hang Ngoai Thuong Viet Nam; ☎ 63427) is at 1 Huynh Man Dat St, Vinh Thanh District.

Post & Telecommunications The GPO is across the channel from the intersection of Tu Duc and Bach Dang Sts.

Pagodas & Temples
Nguyen Trung Truc Temple This temple is dedicated to Nguyen Trung Truc, a leader of the Vietnamese resistance campaign of the 1860s against the newly arrived French. Among other exploits, he led the raid that resulted in the burning of the French warship *Espérance*. Despite repeated attempts to capture him, Nguyen Trung Truc continued to fight until 1868, when the French took his mother and a number of civilians hostage and threatened to kill them if he did not surrender. Nguyen Trung Truc turned himself in and was executed by the French in the marketplace of Rach Gia on 27 October 1868.

The first temple structure was a simple building with a thatched roof; over the years it has been enlarged and rebuilt several times. The last reconstruction took place between 1964 and 1970. In the centre of the main hall on an altar is a portrait of Nguyen Trung Truc.

Nguyen Trung Truc Temple is at 18 Nguyen Cong Tru St and is open from 7 am to 6 pm.

Phat Lon Pagoda This large Cambodian Hinayana Buddhist pagoda, whose name means Big Buddha, was founded about two centuries ago. Though all of the three dozen monks who live here are ethnic-Khmers, ethnic-Vietnamese also frequent the pagoda. Prayers are held daily from 4 to 6 am and from 5 to 7 pm. The pagoda, off Quang Trung St, is open from 4 am to 5 pm during the seventh, eighth and ninth lunar months (the summer season), but guests are welcome year round.

Inside the sanctuary *(vihara)*, the figures of Sakyamuni, the historical Buddha, all wear Cambodian and Thai-style pointed hats. Around the exterior of the main hall are eight small altars. The two towers near the main entrance are used to cremate the bodies of deceased monks. Near the pagoda are the tombs of about two dozen monks.

Ong Bac De Pagoda Ong Bac De Pagoda is in the centre of town at 14 Nguyen Du St. It was built by Rach Gia's Chinese community about a century ago. On the central altar is a statue of Ong Bac De, a reincarnation of the Jade Emperor. To the left is Ong Bon, Guardian Spirit of Happiness and Virtue; to the right is Quan Cong (in Chinese, Guangong).

Pho Minh Pagoda Two Buddhist nuns live at Pho Minh Pagoda, which is at the corner of Co Bac and Nguyen Van Cu Sts. This small pagoda was built in 1967 and contains a large Thai-style Thich Ca Buddha (Sakyamuni) donated in 1971 by a Buddhist organisation in Thailand. Nearby is a Vietnamese-style Thich Ca Buddha. The nuns live in a building behind the main hall. The pagoda is open to visitors from 6 am to 10 pm; prayers are held daily from 3.30 to 4.30 am and 6.30 to 7.30 pm.

Tam Bao Pagoda Tam Bao Pagoda, which dates from the early 19th century, is near the corner of Thich Thien An and Tran Phu Sts; it was last rebuilt in 1913. The garden contains numerous trees sculpted as dragons, deer and other animals. The pagoda is open from 6 am to 8 pm; prayers are held from 4.30 to 5.30 am and 5.30 to 6.30 pm.

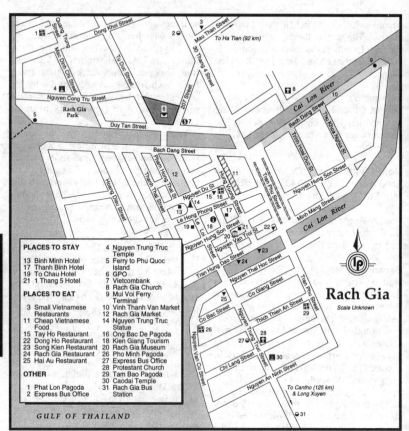

MEKONG DELTA

Caodai Temple There is a small Caodai Temple, constructed in 1969, at 189 Nguyen Trung Truc St, which is not far from Rach Gia Bus Station.

Churches
Rach Gia Church Rach Gia Church (Nha Tho Chanh Toa Rach Gia), a red brick structure built in 1918, is in Vinh Thanh Van subdistrict, across the channel from Vinh Thanh Van Market. Weekday masses are held from 5 to 6 am and 5 to 6 pm; Sunday masses are from 5 to 6 am, 7 to 8 am, 4 to 5 pm and 5 to 6 pm.

Protestant Church Services are held every Sunday from 10 am to noon at the Protestant Church, built in 1972. The church is located at 133 Nguyen Trung Truc St.

Rach Gia Museum
The refurbished Rach Gia Museum is at 21 Nguyen Van Troi St.

Vinh Thanh Van Market
Vinh Thanh Van Market, Rach Gia's main market area, stretches along Bach Dang, Trinh Hoai Duc and Thu Khoa Nghia Sts east of Tran Phu St.

The luxury goods market is between Hoang Hoa Tham and Pham Hong Thai Sts.

Places to Stay

The *Thanh Binh Hotel* (☎ 63053; 14 rooms) is an OK place though nothing to write home about. All rooms have fan and private bath. Singles/doubles cost US$4. The hotel is at 11 Ly Tu Trong St.

Somewhat better is the *Binh Minh Hotel* (☎ 62154; 20 rooms) at 48 Pham Hong Thai St. Double rooms with fan cost US$6 and US$7, while air-conditioned rooms are US$9 and US$13.

The very comfortable *1 Thang 5 Hotel* (☎ 62103; 18 rooms) is at 39 Nguyen Hung Son St. This place is also known as Khach San 1.5, though foreigners like to call it the '1½ Hotel'. Singles and doubles are priced from US$9 to US$18.

The *To Chau Hotel* (☎ 63718; 29 rooms), the best in town, is at 4F Le Loi St (next to the Thang Loi Cinema). If you're arriving by rented car, your driver will much appreciate the fact that the hotel has a garage. There are just two rooms costing US$7, otherwise it's US$9 to US$27.

Places to Eat

Rach Gia is known for its seafood, dried cuttlefish, *ca thieu* (dried fish slices), *nuoc mam* (fish sauce) and black pepper.

The restaurant in the *Binh Minh Hotel* is a favourite venue for eating snake. Choose your cobra from a cage and watch it massacred before your eyes – then you'll also be presented with a cup of the snake's blood to drink. Can you think of a more interesting way to spend an evening in Rach Gia?

The *Tay Ho Restaurant* at 16 Nguyen Du St serves good Chinese and Vietnamese food. The *Dong Ho Restaurant* at 124 Tran Phu St has Chinese, Vietnamese and Western dishes. Other places you might try are the *Rach Gia Restaurant*, on the water at the intersection of Ly Tu Trong and Tran Hung Dao Sts, and the *Song Kien Restaurant*, which is a block away at the intersection of Tran Hung Dao and Hung Vuong Sts. The

Hai Au Restaurant is at the corner of Nguyen Trung Truc and Nguyen Van Cu Sts.

Cheap, tasty Vietnamese food is sold along Hung Vuong St between Bach Dang and Le Hong Phong Sts. There are several small Vietnamese restaurants on Mau Thanh St near the intersection of 30 Thanh 4 St.

There are restaurants in the *To Chau Hotel* and the *1 Thang 5 Hotel*.

Getting There & Away

Air Rach Gia has an airport, but at the time of writing there were no regularly scheduled flights. Vietnam Airlines has contemplated the possibility of chartered flights.

Bus Buses from Ho Chi Minh City to Rach Gia leave from the Mien Tay Bus Station in An Lac; the express bus takes six to seven hours. An express minibus from Ho Chi Minh City to Rach Gia departs from an office (☎ 93318) at 83 Cach Mang Thang Tam St (half a block from the Immigration Police Office) once every three days; the trip, which begins at 4 am, costs US$2.25.

The Rach Gia Bus Station (Ben Xe Kien Giang; ☎ 3430, 2185) is south of the city on Nguyen Trung Truc St (towards Long Xuyen and Cantho). Nonexpress buses link Rach Gia with Cantho, Dong Thap (departs once a day at 7 am), Ha Tien, Ho Chi Minh City and Long Xuyen. There are daily express buses to Ho Chi Minh City (departs at 4.30 am) and Ha Tien (leaves at 2.30 am). Bus services to rural areas near Rach Gia operate between 3.30 am and 4.30 pm. Destinations include Duong Xuong, Giong Rieng, Go Quao, Hon Chong, Kien Luong, Soc Xoai, Tan Hiep, Tri Ton and Vinh Thuan.

There is an express bus office at 33, 30 Thang 4 St offering daily express service to Cantho (departs at 5 am), Ha Tien (leaves at 4.30 am) and Ho Chi Minh City (departs at 3.45 am). Another express bus to Ho Chi Minh City leaves every morning at 4 am from Trung Tam Du Lich Thanh Nien, which is at 78 Nguyen Trung Truc St.

Car Rach Gia is 92 km from Ha Tien, 125

MEKONG DELTA

km from Cantho and 248 km from Ho Chi Minh City.

Boat Rach Gia Park, at the western end of Nguyen Cong Tru St, is where you can catch ferries to Phu Quoc Island. There are departures every evening, but the time varies, so make local inquiries. The fare is US$3.

Mui Voi Ferry Terminal (*mui* means nose and *voi* means elephant – so named because of the shape of the island) is at the northeastern end of Bach Dang St. Boats from here make daily trips to Chau Doc (at 5.30 pm), Long Xuyen (at 12.30 pm) and Tan Chau (at 4.30 pm).

Getting Around
The main forms of ground transport in Rach Gia are cyclos and xe dap lois.

AROUND RACH GIA
Ancient City of Oc-Eo
Oc-Eo was a major trading city during the 1st to 6th centuries AD, when this area (along with the rest of southern Vietnam, much of southern Cambodia and the Malay Peninsula) was ruled by the Indianised empire of Funan. Much of what is known about Funan, which reached its height in the 5th century AD, comes from contemporary Chinese sources (eg, the accounts of Chinese emissaries and travellers) and the archaeological excavations at Oc-Eo, which have uncovered evidence of significant contact between Oc-Eo and what is now Thailand, Malaysia, Indonesia, Persia and even the Roman Empire.

An elaborate system of canals around Oc-Eo was used for both irrigation and transportation, prompting Chinese travellers of the time to write about 'sailing across Funan' on their way to the Malay Peninsula. Most of the buildings of Oc-Eo were built on piles, and pieces of these structures indicate the high degree of refinement achieved by Funanese civilisation. Artefacts found at Oc-Eo are on display in Ho Chi Minh City at the History Museum and the Art Museum and in Hanoi at the History Museum.

The remains of Oc-Eo are not far from Rach Gia. The site itself, a hill 11 km inland littered with potsherds and shells, is near Vong The village, which can be reached by jeep from Hue Duc village, a distance of about eight km. Oc-Eo is most easily accessible during the dry season. Special permission may be required to visit; for more information, contact Kien Giang Tourism.

HA TIEN
Ha Tien (population 80,000) is on the Gulf of Thailand eight km from the Cambodian border. The area, famous for its nearby white-sand beaches and fishing villages, is also known for its production of seafood, black pepper and items made from the shells of sea turtles. All around the area are lovely towering limestone formations that give this place a very different appearance from the rest of the Mekong Delta region. The rock formations support a network of caves, many of which have been turned into cave temples. Plantations of black-pepper trees cling to the hillsides in places where it's not too steep. On a clear day, Phu Quoc Island is visible across the water to the west.

Ha Tien was a province of Cambodia until 1708, when, in the face of attacks by the Thais, the Khmer-appointed governor, a Chinese immigrant named Mac Cuu, turned to the Vietnamese for protection and assistance. Mac Cuu thereafter governed this area as a fiefdom under the protection of the Nguyen Lords. He was succeeded as ruler by his son, Mac Thien Tu. During the 18th century, the area was invaded and pillaged several times by the Thais. Rach Gia and the southern tip of the Mekong Delta came under direct Nguyen rule in 1798.

During the rule of the genocidal Khmer Rouge regime in Cambodia (1975-79), Khmer Rouge forces repeatedly attacked Vietnamese territory and massacred hundreds of civilians. The entire populations of Ha Tien and nearby villages – tens of thousands of people – fled their homes. During this period, areas north of Ha Tien (along the Cambodian border) were sown with mines and booby-traps, which have yet to be cleared.

Orientation
The main drag is Ben Tran Hau St, which runs along the To Chau River; it turns northward just north-east of the floating toll bridge. The city's fresh produce market and general marketplace are between Ben Tran Hau St and the To Chau River. Few of Ha Tien's buildings are numbered.

Pagodas & Temples
Tombs of the Mac Cuu Family The Tombs of the Family of Mac Cuu (Lang Mac Cuu) are on a low ridge not far from town. They are known locally simply as Nui Lang, the Hill of the Tombs. Several dozen relatives of Mac Cuu, Chinese émigré and 18th-century ruler of this area, are buried here in traditional Chinese tombs decorated with figures of dragons, phoenixes, lions and guardians.

The largest tomb is that of Mac Cuu himself; it was constructed in 1809 on the orders of Emperor Gia Long and is decorated with finely carved figures of Thanh Long (the Green Dragon) and Bach Ho (the White Tiger). The tomb of Mac Cuu's first wife is flanked by dragons and phoenixes. At the bottom of the ridge is a shrine dedicated to the Mac family.

Tam Bao Pagoda Tam Bao Pagoda, also known as Sac Tu Tam Bao Tu, was founded by Mac Cuu in 1730. It is now home to seven Buddhist nuns. In front of the pagoda is a statue of Quan The Am Bo Tat (the Goddess of Mercy) standing on a lotus blossom in the middle of a pond. Inside the sanctuary, the largest statue on the dais is of A Di Da Buddha, the Buddha of the Past. It is made of bronze but has been painted. Outside the building are the tombs of 16 monks.

Near Tam Bao Pagoda is a section of the city wall dating from the early 18th century.

Tam Bao Pagoda is at 328 Phuong Thanh St and is open from 7 am to 9 pm; prayers are held from 8 to 9 am and 2 to 3 pm. From the 15th day of the fourth lunar month to the 15th day of the seventh lunar month (roughly from May to August) prayers are held six times a day.

Phu Dung Pagoda Phu Dung Pagoda, also called Phu Cu Am Tu, was founded in the mid-18th century by Mac Cuu's second wife, Nguyen Thi Xuan. It is now home to one monk.

In the middle of the main hall is a peculiar statue of nine dragons embracing newly born Thich Ca Buddha (Sakyamuni, born Siddhartha Gautama). The most interesting statue on the main dais is a bronze Thich Ca Buddha brought from China; it is kept in a glass case. On the hillside behind the main hall are the tombs of Nguyen Thi Xuan and one of her female servants; nearby are four monks' tombs.

Behind the main hall is a small temple, Dien Ngoc Hoang, dedicated to the Taoist Jade Emperor. The figures inside are of Ngoc Hoang flanked by Nam Tao, the Taoist God of the Southern Polar Star and the God of Happiness (on the right), and Bac Dao, the Taoist God of the Northern Polar Star and the God of Longevity (on the left). The statues are made of papier-mâché moulded over bamboo frames.

Phu Dung Pagoda is open from 6 am to 10 pm; prayers are held from 4 to 5 am and 7 to 8 pm. To get to Phu Dung Pagoda, turn off Phuong Thanh St next to number 374.

Thach Dong Thach Dong, the Stone Cavern, also known as Chua Thanh Van, is a subterranean Vietnamese Buddhist temple 3.5 km from town on Mac Tu Hoang St.

To the left of the entrance is the Stele of Hatred (Bia Cam Thu) commemorating the massacre of 130 people here by the forces of Khmer Rouge leader Pol Pot on 14 March 1979.

Several chambers of the grotto contain funerary tablets and altars to Ngoc Hoang (the Jade Emperor), Quan The Am Bo Tat and the two Buddhist monks who founded the temples of Thach Dong. The wind creates extraordinary sounds as it blows through the grotto's passageways. Openings in several branches of the cave afford views of nearby Cambodia.

Dong Ho
Dong Ho (*dong* means east; *ho* means lake)

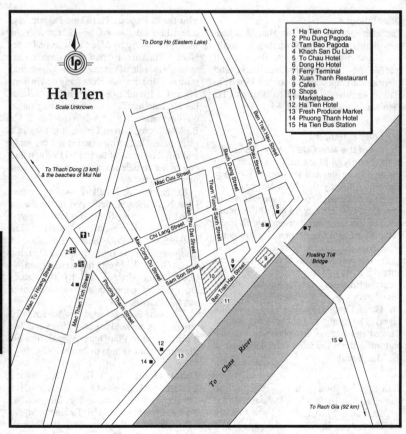

Ha Tien

Scale Unknown

To Dong Ho (Eastern Lake)

To Thach Dong (3 km) & the beaches of Mui Nai

1 Ha Tien Church
2 Phu Dung Pagoda
3 Tam Bao Pagoda
4 Khach San Du Lich
5 To Chau Hotel
6 Dong Ho Hotel
7 Ferry Terminal
8 Xuan Thanh Restaurant
9 Cafes
10 Shops
11 Marketplace
12 Ha Tien Hotel
13 Fresh Produce Market
14 Phuong Thanh Hotel
15 Ha Tien Bus Station

Mac Cuu Street
Ben Tran Hau Street
Bach Dang Street
To Chau Street
Tham Tuong Sanh Street
Tuan Phu Dat Street
Chi Lang Street
Mac Cong Du Street
Sam Son Street
Phuong Thanh Street
Mac Thien Tich Street
Mac Tu Hoang Street
Ben Tran Hau Street

Floating Toll Bridge

To Chau River

To Rach Gia (92 km)

MEKONG DELTA

is in fact not a lake at all but an inlet of the sea. The 'lake' is just east of Ha Tien on Ben Tran Hau St, and bound on the east by a chain of granite hills known at the Ngu Ho (five tigers) and on the west by hills known as To Chan. Dong Ho is said to be most beautiful on nights when there is a full or almost-full moon. According to legend, it is on such nights that fairies dance here in the moonlight.

Ha Tien Market

Ha Tien has an excellent market along the To Chau River. It's well worth your while to

stop in here – many of the goods are imported (smuggled?) from Thailand and Cambodia, and prices are lower than you can find in Ho Chi Minh City. Cigarette smuggling is a particularly big business.

Places to Stay

The *To Chau Hotel* on To Chau St is Ha Tien's bottom-end accommodation with eight rooms all costing US$5. You get what you pay for – the bath and toilet are outside and some rooms lack ceiling fans.

The *Dong Ho Hotel* (☎ 52141; 18 rooms) is simple but acceptable. Rooms cost US$6.

The bath is attached but the toilet is outside the rooms. The hotel is near the floating bridge at the corner of Ben Tran Hau and To Chau Sts.

The *Ha Tien Hotel* is at the corner of Ben Tran Hau and Phuong Thanh Sts. All rooms have the toilet outside but a basic attached washroom. Rooms with fan cost US$3, or you can pay US$6 for air-conditioning.

The *Phuong Thanh Hotel* (☎ 52152) has rooms with fan for US$5. The toilets are outside.

Most foreigners stay at the *Khach San Du Lich* (☎ 8644) on Mac Thien Tich St. Large echo-chamber rooms cost US$10 and can sleep up to four persons. The smaller rooms go for US$7. This is the only place in town where rooms have an attached bath and toilet. There are good ceiling fans but no air-conditioning.

Places to Eat
Ha Tien's speciality is an unusual variety of coconut which grows only in this area. Restaurants all around the Ha Tien area serve the coconut milk in a glass with ice, sugar and strips of coconut meat.

The *Xuan Thanh Restaurant* is opposite the market at the corner of Ben Tran Hau and Tham Tuong Sanh Sts. This place has the best food in town and the most salubrious surroundings.

There is a whole collection of small cafes on Ben Tran Hau St adjacent to the floating bridge. These places can do the usual noodle and rice dishes.

The *Khach San Du Lich* has a basic restaurant but it is not especially recommended.

Getting There & Away
Bus Buses from Ho Chi Minh City to Ha Tien leave from the Mien Tay Bus Station in An Lac; the trip takes nine to 10 hours.

Ha Tien Bus Station (Ben Xe Ha Tien) is on the other side of the floating toll bridge from the centre of town. Buses leave from here to An Giang Province, Cantho (at 5.50 am and 9.10 am), Vinh Long Province, Ho Chi Minh City (at 2 am) and Rach Gia (five times a day). The bus trip from Rach Gia to Ha Tien takes about five hours.

Car Ha Tien is 92 km from Rach Gia, 95 km from Chau Doc, 206 km from Cantho, 338 km from Ho Chi Minh City and 225 km from Phnom Penh (via Kampot). The road between Rach Gia and Ha Tien is now undergoing repairs and should be in decent shape by the time you read this. Travelling along this route you pass the largest cement factory in Vietnam at Kien Luong, though the new one being built at nearby Hon Chong might be even larger.

Boat Passenger ferries dock at the Ferry Terminal, which is not far from the To Chau Hotel next to the floating bridge. Daily ferries depart for Chau Doc at 6 am and for Tinh Bien (Cambodian border) at 11 am and noon. You can travel by boat all the way from Ho Chi Minh City to Ha Tien with a change of boats in Chau Doc, but it's a long journey and the boats are anything but luxurious. Furthermore, you need a travel permit to do the run between Ha Tien and Chau Doc because the canal straddles the Cambodian border and is thus militarily sensitive.

It may be possible to travel between Rach Gia and Ha Tien by scheduled or chartered boat; for more information, ask around each town's quay.

Getting Around
The tolls for the floating bridge across the To Chau River are US$0.03 for a person, half that for a bicycle and US$0.50 for a motorbike.

The main form of local transport is the xe dap loi.

AROUND HA TIEN
Beaches Near Town
The beaches in this part of Vietnam face the Gulf of Thailand. The water is incredibly warm and calm, like a placid lake. They're good for bathing and diving but hopeless for surfing.

Mui Nai (Stag's Head Peninsula) is four km west of Ha Tien; it is said to resemble the head of a stag with its mouth pointing upward. On top is a lighthouse; there are sand beaches on both sides of the peninsula. Mui Nai is accessible by road from both the town of Ha Tien and from Thach Dong.

No Beach (Bai No), lined with coconut palms, is several kilometres west of Ha Tien near a fishing village. Bang Beach (Bai Bang) is a long stretch of dark sand shaded by *bang* trees.

Mo So Grotto

About 17 km towards Rach Gia from Ha Tien and three km from the road, Mo So Grotto consists of three large rooms and a labyrinth of tunnels. The cave is accessible on foot during the dry season and by small boat during the wet season. Visitors should have torches (flashlights) and a local guide.

Hang Tien Grotto

Hang Tien Grotto, 25 km towards Rach Gia from Ha Tien, served as a hide-out for Nguyen Anh (later Emperor Gia Long) in 1784, when he was being pursued by the Tay Son Rebels. His fighters found zinc coins buried here, a discovery which gave the cave its name, which means Coin Grotto. Hang Tien Grotto is accessible by boat.

Hon Giang Island

Hon Giang Island, which is about 15 km from Ha Tien and can be reached by small boat, has a lovely, secluded beach. There are numerous other islands off the coast between Rach Gia and the Cambodian border. Some local people make a living gathering precious salangane, or swifts' nests (the most important ingredient of that famous Chinese delicacy, bird's-nest soup), on the islands' rocky cliffs.

HON CHONG

This small and secluded beach resort has the most attractive stretch of coastline in the Mekong Delta region. The big attractions here are Chua Hang Grotto, Duong Beach and Nghe Island.

Given the fact that this is the only real beach resort in the entire delta area, you

would think that nobody would even consider wrecking it with a horrible industrial development project. Unfortunately, that is exactly what is about to happen. We are saddened to report that a new cement factory was being constructed just one km from the beach at the time of our last visit. Although no doubt those responsible for this fiasco will deny that the factory will impact on the beach, it's hard to see how tourists won't notice the billowing cloud of cement dust and the rumble of cement trucks.

All of which means you should probably hurry up to see this lovely spot while it's still worth visiting. The great pity is that it would have been little trouble to locate the cement factory close to the existing one at Kien Luong, thus leaving the rest of the area unspoiled.

Chua Hang Grotto

The grotto is entered through a Buddhist temple set against the base of a hill. The temple is called Hai Son Tu (Sea Mountain Temple). Visitors light joss sticks and offer prayers here before entering the grotto itself, whose entrance is behind the altar. Inside is a plaster statue of Quan The Am Bo Tat (the Goddess of Mercy). The thick stalactites are hollow and resonate like bells when tapped.

Duong Beach

The beach (Bai Duong) is next to Chua Hang Grotto and is named for its *duong* trees. Although easily the prettiest beach in the Mekong Delta, don't expect powdery white sand. The waters around the delta contain heavy sentiment, so the beach tends to be hard packed. Still, the water is reasonably clear here and this is the only beach south of Saigon (excluding those on Phu Quoc Island) that looks appealing for swimming. The beach is known for its spectacular sunsets.

From the southern end of the beach (near Chua Hang Grotto), you can see Father & Son Isle (Hon Phu Tu) several hundred metres offshore; it is said to be shaped like a father embracing his son. The island, a column of stone, is perched on a 'foot' worn away by the pounding of the waves; the foot is most fully exposed at low tide.

Nghe Island

If the cement plant is allowed to open and proves to be the horror that we anticipate, your only real escape will be a boat trip to Nghe Island. This is the most beautiful island in the area, and is a favourite pilgrimage spot for Buddhists. The island contains a cave temple (Chua Hang) next to a large statue of Quan The Am Bo Tat which faces the sea. The area where you'll find the cave temple and statue is called Doc Lau Chuong.

Finding a boat to the island is not too difficult, though it will be much cheaper if you can round up a group to accompany you. Ngha Nhi Hon Tren, one of the hotels at Duong Beach, can arrange a boat trip. This cost US$40 for the full day, and the boat can accommodate 10 persons. The boat ride to the island takes approximately one to two hours.

Places to Stay There are two hotels here and one was just recently built, which is hard to fathom seeing how the beach is about to be destroyed by the aforementioned cement factory. If there is anything still worth seeing by the time you read this, consider staying at the *Nha Nghi Hon Tren* (☎ 54331; 12 rooms). This place is right on the beach and features rooms in a large beach bungalow for US$6. The staff can prepare meals on request, and the manager speaks English.

A reasonably comfortable hotel closer to the cement plant is *Nha Nghi Binh An* (☎ 54332; fax 54338; 16 rooms). It's a very quiet place in a large compound surrounded by a wall with gardens inside. Doubles with fan cost US$6, while air-conditioning raises the ante to US$11.

Places to Eat Aside from special orders prepared at your hotel, there are food stalls just by the entrance of Chua Hang Grotto. For a few dollars, you can point to one of their live chickens, which will be summarily executed and barbecued right on the spot. This is also a good place to sample the delicious Ha Tien coconuts, which grow only in this part of Vietnam.

Getting There & Away Chua Hang Grotto and Duong Beach are about 32 km towards Rach Gia from Ha Tien down a side road. This road branches off the Rach Gia-Ha Tien highway at the small town of Ba Hon, which is just west of the cement factory at Kien Luong. Buses can drop you off at Ba Hon, from where you can hire a motorbike.

PHU QUOC ISLAND

Mountainous and forested Phu Quoc Island (population 18,000) is in the Gulf of Thailand, 45 km west of Ha Tien and 15 km south of the coast of Cambodia. The tear-shaped island, which is 48 km long and has an area of 1320 sq km, is ringed with beautiful unspoiled beaches. There are fantastic views of underwater marine life through the transparent blue-green waters off some of the beaches around the southern part of the island. A number of small islands near Phu Quoc are great for fishing and swimming.

Phu Quoc is claimed by Cambodia; its Khmer name is usually rendered Ko Tral. Needless to say, the Vietnamese view it differently, and to this end have built a substantial military base at the southern end of the island. Phu Quoc is governed as a district of Vietnam's Kien Giang Province.

Phu Quoc Island served as a base of operations for the French missionary Pigneau de Behaine from the 1760s to the 1780s. Prince Nguyen Anh, later Emperor Gia Long, was sheltered here by Behaine when he was being hunted by the Tay Son Rebels.

Phu Quoc is not really part of the Mekong Delta, and doesn't share the delta's extraordinary ability to produce rice. The islanders have traditionally earned their living from the sea. Phu Quoc is known for its production of high-quality nuoc mam (fish sauce). The island's fishing fleet is based in Duong Dong town.

The island has tremendous tourism potential, so far mostly undeveloped. Transport difficulties, lack of hotel space and fear of attacks by the Khmer Rouge have kept visi-

MEKONG DELTA

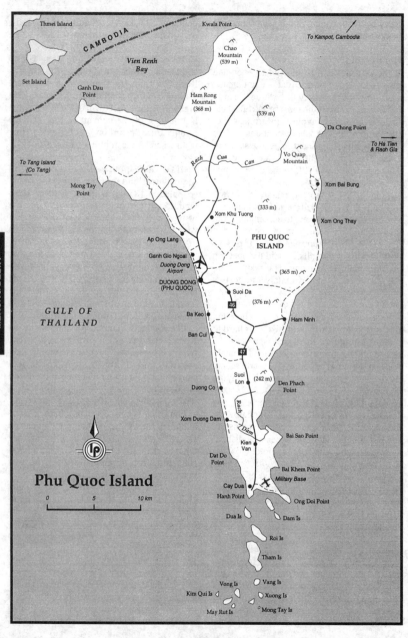

MEKONG DELTA

Phu Quoc Island

0   5   10 km

tors away. A minor problem is that the military occupies some of the best beach sites on the island. Nevertheless, recent improvements in Vietnam's economy and the flood of foreign tourists into the country will surely bring more development to this isolated backwater, for better or worse.

Beaches

The most easily accessible beaches are on the west side of the island near the town of Duong Dong. At the southern end of the island is the military base, and there is actually a public beach within the base itself. However, this one is open to civilians only on Sundays and you must leave your passport with the military receptionist while you're using the beach.

The most spectacular white sand beach of all is in a cove at the south-east part of the island between Ong Doi Point and Bai Khem Point. This beach is totally undeveloped because it's a military area, but civilians are permitted to enter. It's nearly 30 km from Duong Dong, so you'll almost certainly have to go there by motorbike unless you bring your own mountain bike to the island. You'll have to leave your motorbike near the road and walk the last 300 metres to the beach. You should lock your bike, though you'll probably find that the area is totally deserted.

Places to Stay

There are only two hotels on the island. Both are spartan, so if you're looking for Club Med, then look elsewhere.

The only place accepting foreigners at the moment is the *Khach San Huong Bien* (☎ 46113) in beautiful downtown Duong Dong. The hotel's name means 'fragrant sea'. Rooms here cost US$10, US$15 and US$20.

Getting There & Away

Air Vietnam Airlines offers on-again off-again service between Ho Chi Minh City and Duong Dong, Phu Quoc's main town. According to the official timetable, the schedule is five flights weekly but you need to check to see if these are currently running.

Boat There are ferries every evening (time varies) from Rach Gia to Duong Dong (on the west coast), a 140 km trip. The fare is US$3 and the ride takes up to 10 hours. Some boats might make a brief stop at the military base at the southern end of the island, but don't get off there, because the hotel is in Duong Dong. Perhaps some day it will be possible to reach Phu Quoc from Cambodia, but at the present time this is prohibited.

PHUNG HIEP

This small town 20 km from Cantho is notable for its floating market, which takes place every morning from around 6 to 11 am. There are perhaps bigger or better floating markets in the Mekong Delta, but this one has the good fortune of being positioned directly under a large bridge. The advantage for travellers is that the bridge makes a perfect platform for photo opportunities. As a result, this is perhaps the most photographed spot in the entire delta region.

Part of the market is also on dry land, and you can wander around and photograph at will – the friendly locals have apparently grown quite accustomed to tourists. Needless to say, the vendors would be happier if you bought something – if you'd like to get your morning snake soup or pickled turtles with fish sauce, this is the place to do it.

The town is right on National Highway 1, which means it's conceivable to reach it by public transport. However, most buses passing through Phung Hiep will make only a brief stop (if at all) and coordinating your arrival time with the market's opening could be tricky. In other words, private transport of one sort or another is preferred. Most travellers spend the night in nearby Cantho and make the morning journey to the market by motorbike, taxi or minibus.

SOC TRANG

The town itself doesn't look like much, but it has a large Khmer population that has built some very impressive temples. Furthermore, there is a very colourful annual festival, and if you're in the vicinity at the right time then it's very much worth your while to catch it.

MEKONG DELTA

Information
Tourist Office Soc Trang Tourist Company
(☎ 21498, 22015; fax 21993) is located at
131 Nguyen Chi Thanh St, adjacent to the
Tay Nam Hotel.

Kh'leng Pagoda
This stunning pagoda (Chua Kh'leng) looks
like it's been transported straight out of Cambodia. Originally built from bamboo in
1533, it had a complete rebuild in 1905 (this
time using concrete). There are seven religious festivals held here every year (worth
seeing!) – people come from all outlying
areas of the province and gather here for
these events. Even at non-festival times,
Khmer people drop in regularly to bring
donations and pray.

At the time of this writing, 12 monks were
residing in the pagoda. This place also serves
as Soc Trang's College of Buddhist Education, which at present serves 95 student
monks. The monks are friendly and happy to
show you around the pagoda and discuss
Buddhism.

Khmer Museum
This museum is dedicated to the history and
culture of Vietnam's Khmer minority.
Indeed, it serves as a sort of cultural centre,
and traditional dance and music shows are
periodically staged here. You'll have to make
inquiries about performances, because there
is no regular schedule. However, there's no
doubt that something could be arranged for
a group if a little advance notice is given.

The Khmer Museum is just opposite the
Kh'leng Pagoda.

Dat Set Pagoda
This old pagoda is unusual in that it's made
entirely of clay, rather than the brick and
concrete which are the currently fashionable
building materials in Vietnam. Just how this
pagoda manages to stay in one piece is a
mystery, but it certainly helps that the
Mekong Delta does not have earthquakes.

The Dat Set Pagoda is a few blocks east
from the Kh'leng Pagoda.

Oc Bom Boc Festival
This is a Khmer name so don't bother trying
to look it up in your Vietnamese dictionary.
Once a year, the Khmer community turns out
for longboat races on the Soc Trang River,
an event which attracts visitors from all over
Vietnam and even Cambodia. First prize is
US$1500, so it's not difficult to see why
competition is so fierce.

The races are held according to the lunar
calendar on the 15th day of the 10th moon,
which roughly means December. The races
start at noontime, but things get jumping in
Soc Trang the evening before. Not surprisingly, hotel space is at a premium during the
festival, and foreigners without a prepaid
hotel reservation will probably have to sleep
in a car or minibus.

Places to Stay
The *Tay Nam Hotel* (☎ 21757) at 133
Nguyen Chi Thanh is an OK place to stay,
but we were not pleased to find our passports
lying on the counter unattended – the staff
had gone off to dinner and simply left our
valuable documents lying around where
anybody could have walked off with them.
Aside from this very irritating incident, the
rooms were OK. A double with fan/air-con
costs US$10/14.

A bottom-end budget place is the *Ministry
of Trade Guesthouse* (☎ 21974), or Nha
Khach So Thuong Mai in Vietnamese.
Rooms with fan/air-con are US$3/7.

The *Phong Lan Hotel* (☎ 21619; 20 rooms)
is near the river at 124 Dong Khoi St. It's
pricey by Soc Trang standards – rooms with
fan are US$14, while air-con is US$16 with
cold water bath and US$21 with hot water.

The *Dong Tien Hotel* (☎ 21888; 22
rooms) is run by the military and doesn't get
many foreign visitors – the sleepy staff were
surprised to see us! It's at 2 Duong Trung
Tien, down an obscure dirt track where you
wouldn't expect to find a hotel. Room rates
are reasonable: US$6 for a room with fan and
outside bath, US$8 for fan and attached bath
and US$10 with air-con.

The newest and fanciest place by far in Soc
Trang is the *Khanh Hung Hotel* (☎ 21027; 55

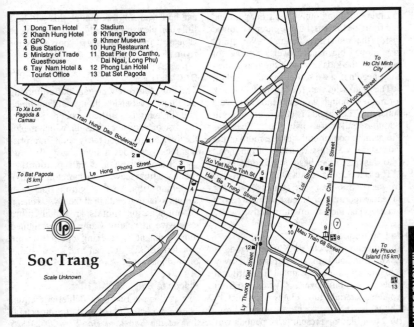

1 Dong Tien Hotel
2 Khanh Hung Hotel
3 GPO
4 Bus Station
5 Ministry of Trade
  Guesthouse
6 Tay Nam Hotel &
  Tourist Office
7 Stadium
8 Kh'leng Pagoda
9 Khmer Museum
10 Hung Restaurant
11 Boat Pier (to Cantho,
   Dai Ngai, Long Phu)
12 Phong Lan Hotel
13 Dat Set Pagoda

To Xa Lon
Pagoda &
Camau

Tran Hung Dao Boulevard

To Bat Pagoda
(5 km)

Le Hong Phong Street

Xo Viet Nghe Tinh St

Hai Ba Trung Street

To
Ho Chi Minh
City

Hung Vuong Street

Le Loi Street

Nguyen Chi Thanh Street

Mau Than 68 Street

Ly Thuong Kiet Street

To
My Phuoc
Island (15 km)

Soc Trang

Scale Unknown

MEKONG DELTA

rooms). It's at 15 Tran Hung Dao Blvd and boasts a large cafe with outdoor tables. A room with fan and attached toilet costs US$5. Air-conditioned rooms range from US$10 to US$22.

Places to Eat

The best place in town is the excellent *Hung Restaurant* (☎ 22268) at 74-76 Mau Tham 68 St. It's open from breakfast time until late into the evening and always seems to be busy.

AROUND SOC TRANG
Bat Pagoda

This is one of the Mekong Delta's most unusual sights, and now has become a favourite stopoff for both foreign and domestic tourists. The pagoda is situated just inside a large monastery compound. You enter through an archway, and almost immediately you can hear the eerie screeching from the large colony of fruit bats which reside here. There are literally thousands of these creatures hanging from the fruit trees. The largest bats weigh about one kg but have a wing span of about 1½ metres.

Fruit bats make plenty of noise – it probably has something to do with their sonar system. The noise in the morning is incredible, and so are the smells. The bats are not toilet trained, so watch out when standing under a tree or bring an umbrella. In the evening, the bats spread their wings and fly out to invade orchards all over the Mekong Delta, much to the consternation of local farmers. The farmers are known to trap the bats and eat them. Inside the monastery the creatures are protected and the bats seem to know this, which is why they stay.

Locals tend to show excessive zeal in shaking the trees to make the bats fly around so that foreigners can take photos – it's probably better to leave the poor things in peace, as you can easily take good photos of the bats hanging off the branches.

Little kids hang out by the front gate and beg from the tourists, but they aren't allowed inside the monastery grounds. We didn't give money but handed over a package of biscuits – the kids devoured them as if they hadn't eaten in a week. Perhaps they hadn't.

The monks are very friendly and don't ask for money, though it doesn't hurt to leave a donation. The pagoda is decorated with gilt Buddhas, and murals paid for by Overseas Vietnamese contributors. In one room of the monastery is a life-size statue of the monk who was the former head of the complex.

The Bat Pagoda (Chua Doi) is about five km west of Soc Trang. Best times for visiting are early morning or at least an hour before sunset, when the bats are most active.

Xa Lon Pagoda

This magnificent, classic Khmer pagoda is 12 km from Soc Trang on National Highway 1 in the direction of Camau. The original structure was built over 200 years ago from wooden materials. In 1923 it was completely rebuilt, but proved to be too small. From 1969 to 1985, the present large pagoda was slowly built as funds trickled in from donations.

Like at other pagodas, the monks lead an austere life. They eat breakfast at 6 am, and beg for contributions until 11 am, when they hold a one-hour worship. They eat again at noon and study in the afternoon – they do not eat dinner.

At the present time, 27 monks reside here. The pagoda also operates a school for the study of Buddhism and Sanskrit. The purpose of studying Sanskrit, as the monks explained, is because all original books about Buddhism were written in this ancient language.

My Phuoc Island

A 15-km journey to the north-east of Soc Trang brings you to the Hau River (a branch of the Mekong). From there it's a short boat ride to My Phuoc Island. It's an isolated spot but very suitable for growing fruit. The local government tourist agency likes to bring foreigners here for tours of the orchards. You can do it yourself too, though this will be a little complex strategically since you'll need at least a motorbike to get yourself to the riverside.

BAC LIEU

The town has a few elegant but crumbling old French colonial buildings and not much else. Farming is a difficult occupation here because of saltwater intrusion, which means the town has remained fairly poor. Enterprising locals eke out a living from fishing, oyster collection and salt production (obtained from seawater evaporating ponds).

Perhaps it's worth visiting Bac Lieu simply to take advantage of the town's cheap accommodation (hotels are much more expensive in nearby Camau). Determined tourists intent on seeking out the scenic wonders of Bac Lieu can find a few things of mild interest.

Places to Stay

Cheap living is Bac Lieu's chief attraction. There's no better place to start your search than at the *Bac Lieu Hotel* (☎ 22621; 26 rooms) at 4 Hoang Van Thu St. Basic rooms with shared toilet are US$5 to US$7. A double room with fan and attached bath is US$7 to US$10. Air-con doubles are US$20 to US$15.

In case there is a convention in town and the Bac Lieu Hotel is full, you can check out its adjacent neighbour, the *Rang Dong Hotel* (☎ 22437; 31 rooms) at 6 Hoang Van Thu St. Prices are the same as next door, though this one looks grottier.

AROUND BAC LIEU
Bird Sanctuary

Five km from town is the Bird Sanctuary (San Chim), considered Bac Lieu's greatest scenic wonder. Unfortunately, the birds have slowly been abandoning the place in recent years. No one is quite sure of the reason, but suspicion falls heavily on some sort of environmental degradation (use of pesticides, shrimp farming, encroaching human habitation, etc). In other words, the Bird Sanctuary is now something of an oxymoron.

Xiem Can Khmer Pagoda

Following the same road that takes you to the aforementioned Bird Sanctuary, you drive seven km from Bac Lieu to reach this pagoda. As Khmer pagodas go, it's OK but you can definitely see better ones in Tra Vinh or Soc Trang (not to mention Cambodia).

Bac Lieu Beach

The same road to the Bird Sanctuary and Xiem Can Khmer Pagoda eventually terminates 10 km from Bac Lieu at this beach (Bai Bien Bac Lieu). Don't expect white sand – it's basically hard-packed Mekong Delta mud. However, quite a few shellfish and other slimy and probably poisonous things crawl around where the muck meets the sea. Tidal pool enthusiasts might be impressed. Locals may be willing to take you for a walk on the mucky tidal flats where they harvest oysters.

Moi Hoa Binh Pagoda

Actually, there is something worthwhile to visit in the Bac Lieu area, though it's actually 13 km south of town along National Highway 1 (look to your left while going to Camau).

This Khmer pagoda (Chua Moi Hoa Binh) is uniquely designed, and chances are good that the monastery's enormous tower will catch your eye even if you're not looking for it. As pagodas in Vietnam go, it's relatively young, having first been built in 1952. The tower was added in 1990, though it is not entirely finished yet due to lack of funds. The tower is used to store bones of the deceased. There is a large and impressive meeting hall in front of the tower.

Most Khmer people in Minh Hai Province head for monastery schools in Soc Trang to receive a Khmer education. Therefore, very few study at the Moi Hoa Binh Pagoda outside of the small contingent of student monks.

CAMAU

Built on the swampy shores of the Ganh Hao River, Camau is the capital and largest city in Minh Hai Province, which occupies the southern tip of the Camau Peninsula. The peninsula includes all of Minh Hai Province and parts of Kien Giang and Soc Trang provinces.

Camau lies in the middle of Vietnam's largest swamp. The area is known for mosquitoes the size of hummingbirds – during the rainy season you might need a shotgun to keep them at bay. The mosquitoes come out in force just after dark and some travellers find that they need to sit under their mosquito net just to eat dinner. One traveller reported that his hotel room had the 'mother of all black spiderwebs' in one corner.

The population of Camau includes many ethnic-Khmers. Due to the boggy terrain, this area has the lowest population density in southern Vietnam.

Camau has developed rapidly in recent years, but the town itself is rather dull. The main attractions here are the nearby swamps and forests, which can be explored by boat. Birdwatchers and aspiring botanists are reportedly most enthralled with the area. Unfortunately, ridiculously high hotel prices, the distance from Saigon and the vampire mosquitoes all conspire to keep the number of foreign tourists to a minimum.

Information

Tourist Office Minh Hai Tourist Company (Cong Ty Du Lich Minh Hai; ☎ 31828) is at 17 Nguyen Van Hai St. This seems to be one of the best organised provincial tourism authorities in Vietnam – they even book international air tickets! Other services on offer include foreign currency exchange, boat rentals and visa extensions.

Money Vietcombank (☎ 33398) is at 2-3 Ly Bon St.

Zoo

Officially labelled the 19th May Forest Park, Camau's zoo shelters a poorly maintained collection of miserable animals. In the grounds of the zoo, along with a few noisy cafes, is a 'botanic garden', which looks rather like a half-acre patch of weeds. In short, there is nothing particularly inviting to see or do here.

Fish, Snake & Turtle Market

Try not to get this place confused with the zoo. This is actually a wholesale market, not a place for housewives to do their shopping. Except for the snakes, the animal life on display here is cleaned, packed into crates, frozen and shipped off to Saigon by truck.

Connoisseurs of snake meat insist that it be served fresh, which means they want to see the creature sacrificed right at the dinner table. Drinking the fresh blood is also part of the ritual, and obviously this doesn't work with frozen blood. All of which explains why the snakes are packed into wire cages and shipped off live to restaurants which specialise in this delicacy.

Even if you're vegetarian, this market is interesting to wander around – it certainly looks different from the supermarkets at home. However, animal rights activists might not be pleased.

Caodai Temple

Though not as large as the one in Tay Ninh, Camau's Caodai Temple is still a charming place staffed by friendly monks. This temple was built in 1966 and seems to be fairly active.

Places to Stay

When you see Camau's hotels, you don't know whether to laugh or cry. In a word, 'overpriced'. Figure on paying at least three times what you did in Ho Chi Minh City.

Probably the best deal overall is the *Minh Hai Trade Union Hotel* (Khach San Cong Doan; ☎ 33245; 21 rooms). It's at 9 Luu Tan Tai St, almost opposite the Caodai Temple. Although there is a fair amount of noise radiating up from the street, the rooms with fan are a bargain (by Camau standards), costing US$15 for a triple. The air-conditioned rooms are not such a good deal, priced at US$35 for a double. Rooms in the centre of the building have all their fresh air blocked by an idiotic glass enclosure – check the

balcony to make sure your room is not one of these sweat boxes.

There is some hope of getting a reasonably priced room next to the bus station, 2.5 km outside town in the direction of Ho Chi Minh City. There are a number of mini-hotels here.

The *Sao Mai Hotel* (☎ 31035, 34913), 38-40 Phan Ngoc Hien St, is a bad joke. On the plus side, all rooms have air-conditioning. On the downside, you get to pay US$15 for a windowless box with *shared* bath. A windowless box with private toilet is US$20, and rooms with a window are US$30.

Living conditions are somewhat better at the *Camau Hotel* (☎ 31165, 34401; 60 rooms), 20 Phan Ngoc Hien St, but many rooms here have the toilet outside. That's no fun when you have to dodge malarial mosquitoes chasing you all the way down the hall. Doubles with fan/air-conditioning cost US$15/20 if the toilet is outside, or US$30 to US$50 for a room with attached bath.

There is also the *Bong Hong Hotel* at 12 Quang Trung St. Rooms with fan/air-con cost US$15/20.

Another option is the *Tan Hung Hotel* at 11 Nguyen Van Hai St. All rooms cost US$30.

The *Phuong Nam Hotel* (☎ 32129, 31752; 90 rooms) at 41 Phan Dinh Phong St is expensive, but the most luxurious in Camau. Rooms with fan cost US$20, and air-con doubles are US$35 to US$55. The top-end rooms come equipped with satellite TV.

Places to Eat

Shrimp is Camau's speciality, all of which is raised in nearby ponds and mangrove swamps. Camau is also the best place in Vietnam to satisfy any sudden cravings for cobra stew.

The *Thanh Thanh Restaurant* (☎ 31076), 9 Phan Ngoc Hien St, is excellent. The restaurant is owned by Minh Hai Tourist Company, which also owns the Phuong Nam Hotel just across the street. Like everything else this government-owned company does, they do it well but not cheaply.

There is a cluster of small roadside restaurants on Ly Bon St at the entrance to the

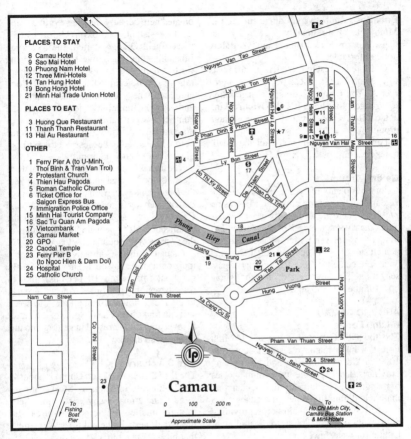

PLACES TO STAY

8 Camau Hotel
9 Sao Mai Hotel
10 Phuong Nam Hotel
12 Three Mini-Hotels
14 Tan Hung Hotel
19 Bong Hong Hotel
21 Minh Hai Trade Union Hotel

PLACES TO EAT

3 Huong Que Restaurant
11 Thanh Thanh Restaurant
13 Hai Au Restaurant

OTHER

1 Ferry Pier A (to U-Minh,
Thoi Binh & Tran Van Troi)
2 Protestant Church
4 Thien Hau Pagoda
5 Roman Catholic Church
7 Ticket Office for
Saigon Express Bus
9 Immigration Police Office
15 Minh Hai Tourist Company
16 Sac Tu Quan Am Pagoda
17 Vietcombank
18 Camau Market
20 GPO
22 Caodai Temple
23 Ferry Pier B
(to Ngoc Hien & Dam Doi)
24 Hospital
25 Catholic Church

Camau

MEKONG DELTA

market. They are very cheap and the food is OK.

The friendly outdoor restaurant in the *Minh Hai Trade Union Hotel* is not bad, and certainly more aesthetic than eating in the market.

Getting There & Away

Bus Buses from Ho Chi Minh City to Camau leave from Mien Tay Bus Station in An Lac. The trip takes 12 hours by regular bus and 10 hours by express bus. The express buses depart at least twice daily, at 5 am and 9 am.

The Camau Bus Station is 2.5 km from the centre, along National Highway 1 in the direction of Ho Chi Minh City.

Car Camau is the 'end of the line' for National Highway 1, the southernmost point in Vietnam reachable by car and bus. Drivers boldly attempting to drive the 'highway' south of Camau will soon find their vehicles sinking into a quagmire of mud and mangroves.

Camau is 179 km from Cantho (three hours by car) and 348 km from Ho Chi Minh City (seven hours).

Boat Boats run between Camau and Ho Chi Minh City approximately once every four days. The trip takes 30 hours and is certainly not comfortable.

Of more interest to travellers are the boats to U-Minh Forest. These depart from Ferry Pier A. You'll have to do some negotiation to arrange a tour here. It's also worth asking at the hotels since they may arrange a whole group.

Ferry Pier B is where you catch the speedboats heading south to Ngoc Hien.

Getting Around

Camau has plenty of cyclos, motorbikes and xe dap lois, so getting around on land is no problem. There are also plenty of water taxis along the river at the back of the market. For longer trips upriver, larger longboats collect at a cluster of jetties just outside the market area. You can either join the throngs of passengers going downriver or hire the whole boat for about US$5 an hour.

AROUND CAMAU
U-Minh Forest

The town of Camau borders the U-Minh Forest, a huge mangrove swamp covering 1000 sq km of Minh Hai and Kien Giang provinces. Local people use certain species of mangrove as a source of timber, charcoal, thatch and tannin. When the mangroves flower, bees feed on the blossoms, providing both honey and wax. The area is an important habitat for waterfowl.

The U-Minh Forest, which is the largest mangrove swamp in the world outside of the Amazon basin, was a favourite hideout for the Viet Cong during the Vietnam War. American patrol boats were frequently ambushed here and the VC regularly planted mines in the canals. The Americans responded with chemical defoliation, which made their enemy more visible but did enormous damage to the forests. Replanting efforts at first failed because the soil was so toxic, but gradually the heavy rainfall has washed the dioxin out to sea (where it no doubt poisons fish) and the forest is returning. Many eucalyptus trees have also been planted here because they have proved relatively resistant to dioxin. Unfortunately, what Agent Orange started, the locals are finishing – the mangrove forests are being further damaged by clearing for shrimp-raising ponds, charcoal making and wood chipping. The government has stepped in and tried to limit these activities, but the conflict between nature and human developers continues. And the conflict will get worse before it gets better, because Vietnam's population is still growing rapidly.

The area is known for its bird life, but these creatures too have taken a beating along with the forest ecology. Nevertheless, ornithologists derive much joy from taking boat trips around Camau. However, don't expect to find the swarms of birds to be nearly as ubiquitous as the swarms of mosquitoes.

Camau Tourist Company offers all-day tours of the forest by boat. They ask US$135 per boat (maximum 10 persons), though some bargaining is in order. You can also talk to the locals down at Ferry Pier A to see if you can find a better deal. Some of the hotels in town are also interested in getting into this business, so inquire.

Bird Sanctuary

The Bird Sanctuary (Vuon Chim) is about 45 km south-east of Camau. Storks are the largest and most easily seen birds here, though smaller feathered creatures also make their nests in the tall trees. Remember that birds will be birds – they don't particularly like humans to get close to them, and they leave their nests early in the morning in search of food. Thus, your chances of being able to get up close and have them hop onto your finger for a photo session are rather slim.

Camau Tourist Company has a full-day tour by boat to the Bird Sanctuary for US$120 (one to 10 persons).

NGOC HIEN

Except for a minuscule fishing hamlet (Tran De) and an offshore island (Hon Khoai), Ngoc Hien stakes its claim as the southernmost town in Vietnam. Few tourists come to this isolated community, which survives mainly from the shrimp-raising industry.

At the very southern tip of the delta is the Camau Nature Reserve, sometimes referred to as the Ngoc Hien Bird Sanctuary. It's one of the least developed and most protected parts of the Mekong Delta region. In this area, shrimp farming is prohibited. Access is only by boat.

At the southern end of the reserve is the tiny fishing village at Tran De. A public ferry connects Tran De to Ngoc Hien. Tran De can rightly claim to be the southernmost town in Vietnam, at least if you exclude the military base at nearby Hon Khoai Island.

If you really are obsessed with reaching Vietnam's southern tip, you'll have to take a boat from Tran De to Hon Khoai Island. Unfortunately, this is a military base and a travel permit is required to make a visit.

If you're looking to visit another remote spot, you can hire a boat to take you to Dat Mui (Cape Camau), the south-western tip of Vietnam. Rather few people find this worthwhile.

Places to Stay

There is only one hotel in Ngoc Hien, so you'll have little choice unless you plan on camping. The *Nam Can Hotel* (☎ 77039) has rooms costing US$15 to US$40 for foreigners.

Getting There & Away

A road connecting Camau to Ngoc Hien is shown on most maps of Vietnam, but it's little more than wishful thinking. Basically, it's a muddy track which is underwater most of the time, though some have attempted it by motorbike.

The trip to Ngoc Hien is best done by speedboat. These boats are readily available in Camau and take approximately four hours to do the journey. From Ngoc Hien south to Tran De takes another four hours.

HON KHOAI ISLAND

This island, 25 km south of the southern tip of the Mekong Delta, is the southernmost point in Vietnam. Unlike the delta, which is pancake flat and intensively cultivated, Hon Khoai Island is rocky, hilly and forested. Unfortunately, getting there is fraught with hassles and few people bother. To begin with, the island is a military base, so a travel permit is needed. To get this, apply in Camau at either the police station or through Camau Tourist. More than likely, the police will refuse you anyway and you'll be referred to Camau Tourist, which will of course charge for their services.

From Camau, you need to get yourself to Ngoc Hien, where you change boats for Tran De (the fishing village at the southern tip of the Mekong Delta). And from Tran De you catch a fishing boat to Hon Khoai Island.

The only place to stay in Hon Khoai Island is the military guesthouse.

Central Highlands

The Central Highlands cover the southern part of the Truong Son Mountain Range (Annamite Cordillera) and include the provinces of Lam Dong, Dac Lac (Dak Lak), Gia Lai and Kon Tum. The region, which is home to many ethno-linguistic minority groups (Montagnards), is renowned for its cool climate, beautiful mountain scenery and innumerable streams, lakes and waterfalls.

Though the population of the Central Highlands is only about two million, the area has always been considered strategically important. During the Vietnam War, considerable fighting took place around Buon Ma Thuot, Pleiku and Kon Tum.

With the exception of Lam Dong Province (in which Dalat is located), the Central Highlands was, until recently, closed to foreigners. Even Westerners with legitimate business in the area were arrested and sent back to Ho Chi Minh City. This extreme sensitivity stemmed partly from the limited nature of central government control of remote areas, as well as a concern that secret 're-education camps' (rumoured to be hidden in the region) would be discovered and publicised.

Southern Highlands

NAM CAT TIEN NATIONAL PARK

Straddling the border of three provinces – Lam Dong, Dong Nai and Song Be – this new national park is only 240 km from Ho Chi Minh City. Nam Cat Tien was hit hard with defoliants during the Vietnam War, but the large old-growth trees survived and the smaller plants have recovered. Just as important, the wildlife has made a comeback. The area is said to be the home of the Javan rhino, considered the rarest mammal in existence. Another rare creature found here is a type of wild ox called gaur. The jungles here support a healthy population of monkeys and plentiful birds. On occasion, leopards can be spotted.

Elephants also live in the park, but their presence has caused some controversy. In the early 1990s, the area just outside of Nam Cat Tien was visited by a herd of 10 hungry elephants – in search of food, the creatures fell into an abandoned bomb crater left over from the Vietnam War. Local villagers took pity on the elephants and proceeded to dig a ramp to rescue them. For their efforts, 28 villagers were killed by the ungrateful beasts, who went on a rampage. They were finally removed to zoos. In the longer term, such conflicts will likely be repeated – with Vietnam's increasing population, the competition between people and wildlife for the same living space is likely to increase.

Getting There & Away

Nam Cat Tien National Park is still an undeveloped area, and access is difficult. The most common approach is from National Highway 20, which connects Dalat with Ho Chi Minh City. To reach the park, you have to follow a dirt road which branches west from Highway 20. Unfortunately, a bridge on this access road recently collapsed, making the route impassable. It's likely that the bridge will be rebuilt, perhaps by the time you read this. In the meantime, the other approach is to take a boat across Langa Lake and then hike from there. Because this region is so remote and sees so few visitors, Dalat Tourist has thus far ignored the area. In other words, at this moment in time you are free to explore on your own, though ironically this is one area in which you really should be accompanied by a guide.

The other possible approach is from Buon Ma Thuot. Unfortunately, this route puts you into Dac Lac Province, where the police control the approach road to Nam Cat Tien. For this reason you will be forced to deal with Dac Lac Tourist, Buon Ma Thuot's government tourist agency. They ask US$200 per day for a jeep, guide and driver (all three required). The 'guides' in Buon Ma Thuot often do not speak English, do not know the area and have a tendency to get totally lost.

Some travel agencies in Ho Chi Minh City are looking into the possibility of offering tours to Nam Cat Tien. Nothing was yet in operation at the time of this writing (again, due to the collapsed bridge) but the situation looks likely to improve.

LANGA LAKE
The Saigon-Dalat highway spans this reservoir, which is crossed by a new bridge. There are lots of floating houses here, all built since 1991. The whole point of living in a floating house is to harvest the fish underneath. It's a scenic spot for photography, though the local children have become very pushy beggars because foreigners have been feeding them candy.

BAO LOC
The town of Bao Loc (also known as B'Lao; elevation 850 metres) is a convenient place to break the trip between Ho Chi Minh City and Dalat. National Highway 20 is called Tran Phu St as it passes through town. Tea, mulberry leaves (for the silkworm industry) and silk are the major local industries.

Bay Tung Falls
The trail to the Bay Tung Falls (Thac Bay Tung, which means 'Seven Steps') begins seven km towards Ho Chi Minh City from the Bao Loc Hotel along National Highway 20 (and three km from the Dai Lao Bridge over the Dai Binh River). The trailhead is in Ap Dai Lao, a hamlet in the village of Xa Loc Chau, behind a refreshment shop run by Ba Hai. The shop is on the right as you travel towards Ho Chi Minh City.

Suoi Mo (the Stream of Dreaming) is 400 metres west of Ba Hai's place along a path that passes among wood and thatch houses set amid tea bushes, coffee trees and banana and pineapple plants. The path veers left at the stream and becomes tortuously slippery as it makes its way along the bamboo and fern-lined bank. The first cascade is about

FULRO

FULRO (Front Unifié de Lutte des Races Opprimées, or the United Front for the Struggle of the Oppressed Races) was for decades a continuing thorn in the side for the Vietnamese government. FULRO is a band of well-organised guerrillas who were supported by France and later by America, Thailand and China. FULRO's recruits came mainly from Montagnards, who had no love for the Vietnamese majority. Even the old South Vietnamese government suppressed the Montagnards, but the Americans recognised their valuable skills in jungle survival. As fighters, FULRO was far more effective than troops directly under the control of the Saigon government.

Needless to say, when the Communists took over they sought retribution against FULRO rather than attempting to make peace. This may have been a mistake, because FULRO guerillas did not simply lay down their weapons and submit to 're-education'. They continued their insurrection for years.

When the Communists took over in 1975, FULRO's fighters numbered around 10,000. In just four years, over 8000 were killed or captured. Some were killed by the Khmer Rouge when they crossed into Cambodia. Ironically, when Vietnam invaded Cambodia in 1979 to battle the Khmer Rouge, FULRO benefited – the Khmer Rouge started supplying FULRO with weapons and ammunition which were obtained from China.

By the mid-1980s, FULRO was considered a spent force, with most of its guerrilla bands either dead, captured, living abroad or having given up the fight. However, in 1992, a band of several hundred FULRO adherents was found to be still living in the remote north-eastern corner of Cambodia (Ratanakiri Province) and conducting raids across the border into Vietnam. At the urging of their exiled comrades, the remaining guerillas surrendered to the Vietnamese government and were flown under UN supervision to the USA.

The insurrection issue would seem to be dead and buried, but the Vietnamese government is still hyper-sensitive about FULRO. Government guides will not answer any questions about the organisation other than to assure travellers that now it's 'perfectly safe' to visit former FULRO areas. Contrary to the far north, where minorities are left alone, the government keeps a very tight grip on the Montagnards of the Central Highlands. Hanoi's policies in this region include (1) populating the highlands with ethnic-Vietnamese settlers, especially in New Economic Zones (NEZs); (2) encouraging the replacement of traditional slash-and-burn agriculture with sedentary farming; and (3) promoting Vietnamese language and culture (Vietnamisation). However, attempts to restrict the religious activities of the Montagnards, most of whom are Protestants, have been abandoned. ■

100 metres straight ahead. Several of the pools along Suoi Mo are swimmable but the water is of uncertain purity.

Bao Loc Church

Bao Loc Church is several hundred metres towards Dalat along the highway from the Bao Loc Hotel. There is an old Shell filling station across the road. Masses are held on Sundays.

Tea Factories

If you've ever wondered how tea is prepared, you might try getting someone to show you around one of Bao Loc's tea-processing plants. The largest is Nha May Che 19/5, which is two km towards Dalat from the Bao Loc Hotel. The factory, which produces tea for export, is on the top of a low hill next to a modern yellow water tower. The second-largest tea factory is named 28/3. A joint Vietnamese and Soviet concern named Vietso (formerly Bisinée) is another place where you might inquire.

Places to Stay

The *Bao Loc Hotel* (Khach San Bao Loc) is at 14 Tran Phu St. It was built in 1940 and hasn't seen any changes since then except price increases – in a word, it's a dump, and overpriced too. About 800 metres south of the Bao Loc Hotel on the main highway is the *Hong Hoang Mini-Hotel*, which is clean and new and has hot water.

Getting There & Away

Bus The bus station is two km from the Bao Loc Hotel.

Car Bao Loc is 177 km north-east of Ho Chi Minh City, 49 km west of Di Linh and 131 km south-west of Dalat.

DAMBRI FALLS

This is one of the highest (90 metres) and most magnificent waterfalls in Vietnam that is easily accessible. The views are positively breathtaking – the walk up the steep path to the top of the falls will almost certainly take your breath away.

Dambri Falls is close to Bao Loc, in an area inhabited chiefly by minorities. Near Bao Loc, you turn off the main highway and follow a dirt road for 15 km. As you're driving this road towards the falls, the high peak off to your right is May Bay Mountain.

Foreigners pay an admission fee of US$1 to visit the falls. By way of compensation, the *Dambri Restaurant*, which adjoins the car park, is cheap and good.

DI LINH

The town of Di Linh (pronounced 'Zee Ling'), also known as Djiring, is 1010 metres above sea level. The area's main product is tea, which is grown on giant plantations founded by the French and now run by the government. The Di Linh Plateau, sometimes compared to the Cameron Highlands of Malaysia, is a great place for day hikes. Only a few decades ago, the region was famous for its tiger hunting.

Bo Bla Waterfall

Thirty-two-metre-high Bo Bla Waterfall is seven km west of town.

Getting There & Away

Di Linh is 226 km north-east of Ho Chi Minh City and 82 km south-west of Dalat on the main Ho Chi Minh City-Dalat highway. The town is 96 km from Phan Thiet by a secondary road.

WATERFALLS
Pongour Falls

Pongour Falls, the largest in the Dalat area, is about 55 km towards Ho Chi Minh City from Dalat and seven km off the highway.

During the rainy season, the falls form a full semicircle.

Gougah Falls

Gougah Falls is approximately 40 km from Dalat towards Ho Chi Minh City. It is only 500 metres from the highway and is easily accessible.

Lien Khuong Falls

At Lien Khuong Falls, the Dan Nhim River, 100 metres wide at this point, drops 15 metres over an outcrop of volcanic rock. The site, which can be seen from the highway, is 35 km towards Ho Chi Minh City from Dalat. Lien Khuong Falls is not far from Lien Khuong airport.

Lien Khuong Falls is not just one, but a number of falls close to the road which are very nice to climb around in. There is a waterfall where you can crawl under the rocky outcrop. The falls are not commercialised – there's not even a sign by the road.

Per Arenmo

DAN NHIM LAKE

Dan Nhim Lake (elevation 1042 metres) was created by a dam built between 1962 and 1964 by the Japanese as part of its war reparations. The huge Dan Nhim hydroelectric project supplies electricity to much of the south.

The lake is often used by Saigon movie studios for filming romantic lakeside scenes. The lake's surface area is 9.3 sq km.

The power station is at the western edge of the coastal plain. Water drawn from Dan Nhim Lake gathers speed as it rushes almost a vertical kilometre down from Ngoan Muc Pass in two enormous pipes.

It is said that the forested hills around Dan Nhim Lake are fine for hiking, and that there is good fishing in the area. Unfortunately, the local cops may not allow you to wander around without a permit from Dalat Tourist (see the Dalat section for details about travel permits).

CENTRAL HIGHLANDS

Places to Stay

There is a hotel in Ninh Son, though currently foreigners cannot use it.

Getting There & Away

Dan Nhim Lake is about 38 km from Dalat in the Don Duong District of Lam Dong Province. As you head towards Phan Rang, the dam is about a kilometre to the left of the Dalat-Phan Rang highway. The power station is at the base of Ngoan Muc Pass near the town of Ninh Son.

NGOAN MUC PASS

Ngoan Muc Pass (altitude 980 metres), known to the French as Bellevue Pass, is about five km towards Phan Rang from Dan Nhim Lake and 64 km west of Phan Rang. On a clear day, you can see all the way across the coastal plain to the Pacific Ocean, an aerial distance of 55 km. As the highway winds down the mountain in a series of switchbacks, it passes under the two gargantuan water pipes – still guarded by armed troops in concrete fortifications – which link Dan Nhim Lake with the hydroelectric power station. To the south of the road (to the right as you face the ocean) you can see the steep tracks of the *crémaillère* (cog railway) linking Thap Cham with Dalat (see the Dalat section for details).

Sites of interest at the top of Ngoan Muc Pass include a waterfall next to the highway, pine forests and the old Bellevue Railway Station.

Dalat Area

DALAT

Dalat (elevation 1475 metres) is situated in a temperate region dotted with lakes, waterfalls, evergreen forests and gardens. The cool climate and the park-like environment make this, in some respects, one of the most delightful cities in all of Vietnam. It was once called *Le Petit Paris* – modern-day Parisians will find this either a compliment or an insult. Dalat is by far Vietnam's most popular honeymoon spot. It's also the favourite haunt of Vietnamese artists and avant-garde types who have made this their permanent home.

Local industries include growing garden vegetables and flowers, which are sold all over southern Vietnam. But the biggest contribution to the economy of Dalat is tourism (over 300,000 domestic tourists visit every year). The downside is that the Dalat People's Committee is trying to create circus-style 'tourist attractions', complete with sailboats, mini-zoos, balloons for the kiddies and Vietnamese dressed as bunny rabbits. The local government consists of people imported entirely from former North Vietnam – they don't seem to have a clue about what tourists want.

The Dalat area was once famous for its big-game hunting, and a 1950s brochure boasted that 'a two-hour drive from the town leads to several game-rich areas abounding in deer, roes, peacocks, pheasants, wild boar, black bear, wild caws, panthers, tigers, gaurs and elephants'. So successful were the hunters that all of the big game is now extinct. However, you will get a whiff of Dalat's former glory by viewing some of the 'souvenirs' about town. As one reader notes:

What will stick in my mind most is the appalling stuffed animals they seem so fond of in Dalat. These seem to have spread all over Vietnam but the Vietnamese (and the citizens of Dalat in particular) have taken taxidermy to new lows. We had a terrible fit of the giggles as we left the Ho Chi Minh Mausoleum in Hanoi when the thought surfaced of what the Dalat animal stuffers could have done with Ho Chi Minh if the stuffing contract hadn't been given to the Russians.

At least the stuffed animals are no longer suffering. It's a different situation with the live animals, as a traveller reports:

Almost opposite and slightly southwards of the stairs down to Nguyen Thi Minh Khai St is a shop dealing with live and stuffed endangered animals. When I intended to photograph, the owner became aggressive. The still-living animals were kept in tiny cages – the gibbon and langur couldn't move their arms! The law prohibits the catching and killing of protected species, but not the sale of them either stuffed or alive. The law is new and almost unknown to the locals. It's obviously not very effective for wildlife protection.

The city's population of 125,000 includes about 5000 members of ethno-linguistic minorities *(Dan Toc)*, of which there are said to be 33 distinct groups in Lam Dong Province. Members of these hill tribes – who still refer to themselves by the French word 'Montagnards', meaning 'mountain dwellers' – can often be seen in the marketplaces wearing their traditional dress. Hill-tribe women of this area carry their infants on their backs in a long piece of cloth worn over one shoulder and tied in the front.

There is a New Economic Zone (a planned rural settlement where southern refugees and people from the overcrowded north were semi-forcibly resettled after reunification) 14 km from Dalat in Lam Ha District; it has a population of about 10,000.

History
The site of Dalat was 'discovered' in 1897 by Dr Alexandre Yersin (1863-1943), a protégé of Louis Pasteur, who was the first person to identify the plague bacillus. The city itself was established in 1912 and quickly became popular with Europeans as a cool retreat from the sweltering heat of the coastal plains and the Mekong Delta. In the local Lat language, Da Lat means 'the River of the Lat Tribe'.

During the Vietnam War Dalat was, by the tacit agreement of all parties concerned, largely spared the ravages of war. Indeed, it seems that while South Vietnamese army officers were being trained at the city's Military Academy and affluent officials of the Saigon regime were relaxing in their villas, VC cadres were doing the same thing not far away in *their* villas. Dalat fell to North Vietnamese forces without a fight on 3 April 1975. There is no problem with left-over mines and ordnance in the Dalat area.

Climate
Dalat is often called the City of Eternal Spring. The average maximum daily temperature is a cool 24°C; the average minimum daily temperature is 15°C. The dry season runs from December to March. Even during the rainy season, which lasts more or less from April to November, it is sunny most of the time.

Orientation
Dalat's sights are very spread out. The city centre is around Rap 3/4 cinema (named for the date on which Dalat was 'liberated' in 1975), which is up the hill from the central market building. Xuan Huong Lake is a prominent landmark on the southern side of town.

Information
Tourist Office Dalat Tourist (☎ 22520; fax 22661), 4 Tran Quoc Toan St, is at the southwest end of Xuan Huong Lake. This is the government-run monopoly which controls travel permits and vehicle rentals for foreigners.

Warning During our visit Dalat was Vietnam's No 1 problem area for tourists. Bus drivers for private companies were not allowed to take foreigners to Dalat, most hotels were not accepting foreigners and a travel permit was needed to visit basic tourist spots around the city. However, since our visit travellers have reported a general relaxing of these police regulations. As the situation is in flux, check with one of the tourist offices in Ho Chi Minh City or Nha Trang for up-to-date information on hotels and getting to Dalat by bus.

Because the list of places requiring a travel permit seems to be changing daily, inquire at your hotel in Dalat before setting off for a day of sightseeing.

At present, police registration of guests at hotels is required – the police want both your passport *and* visa, though at the moment they are accepting photocopies. However, these regulations have been changed often.

Finally, there is the notorious 'crackdown on prostitution'. In case this sounds like a noble idea to you, please understand that cleaning up prostitution is the last thing the Dalat police want to do. What happens is that the police pull midnight raids on hotels where foreigners stay in the hopes of shaking

CENTRAL HIGHLANDS

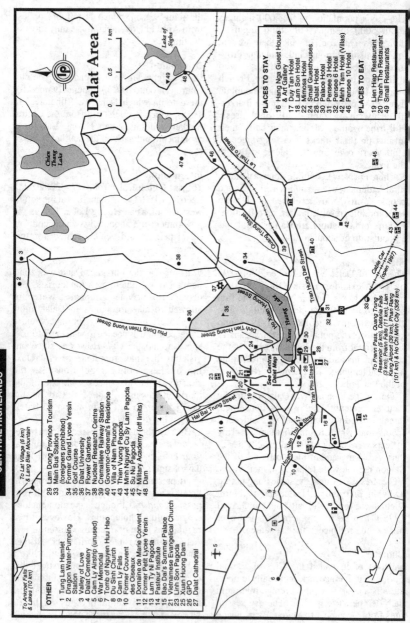

Dalat Area

To Ankroet Falls & Lakes (10 km)

To Lat Village (6 km) & Lang Bian Mountain

Chien Thang Lake

Lake of Sighs

Xuan Huong Lake

See Central Dalat Map

To Prenn Pass, Quang Trung Reservoir (5 km), Datanla Falls (3 km), Prenn Falls (11 km), Lien Kang Airport (30 km), Phan Rang (101 km) & Ho Chi Minh City (308 km)

PLACES TO STAY

16 Hang Nga Guest House & Art Gallery
17 Duy Tan Hotel
18 Lam Son Hotel
22 Anroca Hotel
24 Small Guesthouses
28 Dalat Hotel
30 Palace Hotel
31 Pensee 3 Hotel
32 Pensee 6 Hotel
42 Minh Tam Hotel (Villas)
46 Pensee 10 Hotel

PLACES TO EAT

19 Lien Hiep Restaurant
20 Thanh The Restaurant
49 Small Restaurants

OTHER

1 Tung Lam Hamlet
2 Dragon Water-Pumping Station
3 Valley of Love
4 Dalat Cemetery
5 Cam Ly Airstrip (unused)
6 Wam Ly Market
7 Tomb of Nguyen Huu Hao
8 Du Sinh Church
9 Cam Ly Falls
10 Former Couvent des Oiseaux
11 Domaine de Marie Convent
12 Former Petit Lycee Yersin
13 Lam Ty Ni Pagoda
14 Pasteur Institute
21 Bao Dai's Summer Palace
23 Vietnamese Evangelical Church
25 Linh Son Pagoda
26 Xuan Huong Dam
27 Dalat Cathedral
29 Lam Dong Province Tourism
33 Main Bus Station (foreigners prohibited)
34 Former Grand Lycee Yersin
35 Golf Course
36 Dalat University
37 Flower Gardens
38 Nuclear Research Centre
39 Cremaillere Railway Station
40 Governor General's Residence
41 Villa of Nam Phuong
43 Thien Vuong Pagoda
44 Minh Nguyet Cu Sy Lam Pagoda
45 Su Nu Pagoda
47 Military Academy (off limits)
48 Dam

down someone for a 'fine' (US$200 minimum). Attempts have been made to plant women in foreigners' hotel rooms just before raids (the women knock on your door and ask if they can come in 'for a chat'). One reason for the police registration of hotel guests is to spot foreign males staying with Vietnamese women. The problem with this is that an increasing number of expat workers in Saigon are marrying Vietnamese, and Dalat is a honeymoon resort. Newlyweds have been rousted from their beds during the night by the police – we suggest you take your honeymoon elsewhere.

Money The place to change both cash and travellers' cheques is the Agriculture Bank of Vietnam (Ngan Hang Nong Nghiep Vietnam). It's on Nguyen Van Troi St right in the central area of town.

Post & Telecommunications The GPO is across the street from the Dalat Hotel at 14 Tran Phu St. In addition to postal services, the GPO has international telegraph, telex, telephone and fax facilities.

Xuan Huong Lake

Xuan Huong Lake in the centre of Dalat was created in 1919 by a dam. It is named after a 17th-century Vietnamese poet known for her daring attacks on the hypocrisy of social conventions and the foibles of scholars, monks, mandarins, feudal lords and kings. The lake is circumnavigated by a strollable path.

Paddleboats that look like giant swans can be rented near Thanh Thuy Restaurant, which is 200 metres north-east of the dam. A golf course, which was recently refurbished with foreign money, occupies 50 hectares on the northern side of the lake near the Flower Gardens. The majestic hilltop Palace Hotel overlooks Xuan Huong Lake from the south.

Crémaillère Railway

About 500 metres to the east of Xuan Huong Lake is a railway station, and though you aren't likely to arrive in Dalat by train, the station is worth a visit. The crémaillère (cog railway) linked Dalat and Phan Rang-Thap Cham from 1928 to 1964 – it was closed in 1964 because of repeated Viet Cong attacks. The line has now been partially repaired and is operated as a tourist attraction. You can't get to anywhere useful (like Ho Chi Minh City) on this train, but you can ride eight km down the tracks to Trai Mat Village and back again. The fee for this journey is US$3 for the round trip and a platform ticket costs US$0.50.

Hang Nga Guest House & Art Gallery

Nicknamed the 'Crazy House' by locals, this is a guesthouse, cafe and art gallery all rolled into one. The architecture is something straight out of Alice in Wonderland and cannot easily be described. There are caves, giant spiderwebs made of wire, concrete 'tree trunks', one nude female statue (a rarity in Vietnam), a concrete giraffe (with a tearoom built inside) and so on. This might sound tacky, but it's not – most foreigners are absolutely astounded to find such a counter-cultural gem in Dalat.

By contrast, most Vietnamese are somewhat afraid of the place, but devoted avant-garde enthusiasts and the merely curious continue to cough up the US$0.20 admission fee to look around and take photos. The money gets ploughed back into additional art projects.

The gallery's designer, Mrs Dang Viet Nga (call her 'Hang Nga'), is from Hanoi and lived in Moscow for 14 years, where she earned a PhD in architecture. She is interesting to talk to, dresses in pure 1960s hippie garb and has something of an air of mystery about her. Hang Nga has designed a number of other buildings which dot the landscape around Dalat, including the Children's Cultural Palace and the Catholic church in Lien Khuong.

The Dalat People's Committee takes a dim view of her innovative designs. An earlier Dalat architectural masterpiece, the 'House with 100 Roofs', was torn down as a 'fire hazard' because the People's Committee thought it looked 'anti-socialist'. However, there is little chance that Hang Nga will have any trouble with the authorities – her father, President Truong Chinh, was Ho Chi Minh's successor. He served as Vietnam's second president from 1981 until his death in 1988.

Hang Nga Guest House & Art Gallery (☎ 22070) is about one km south-west of Xuan Huong Lake. The official address is 3 Huynh Thuc Khang St.

French District

The area between Rap 3/4 cinema and Phan Dinh Phung St hasn't changed much since the French departed. If, in the year 1934, someone had evacuated a provincial town in France and repopulated it with Vietnamese, this is what it would have looked like 20 years later. This is a delightful area for walking around.

Governor-General's Residence

The old French Governor-General's Residence (Dinh Toan Quyen, or Dinh 2; ☎ 22093), now used as a guesthouse and for official receptions, is a dignified building of modernist design built in 1933. The original style of furnishing has been retained in most of the structure's 25 rooms. Shoes must be taken off at the front door.

The Governor-General's Residence is about two km east of the centre of town up the hill from the intersection of Tran Hung Dao and Khoi Nghia Bac Son Sts; it is open to the public from 7 to 11 am and 1.30 to 4 pm. Entrance tickets are sold at an outbuilding (once the servants' quarters) several hundred metres from the residence itself. They may try to charge extra if you want to take photographs inside the building.

Guests can stay in the upstairs bedroom suites, with their balconies and huge bathrooms, for US$30 per person per night; for details, contact Dalat Tourist.

Bao Dai's Summer Palace

Emperor Bao Dai's Summer Palace (Biet Dien Quoc Truong, or Dinh 3) is a tan, 25-room villa constructed in 1933. The decor has not changed in decades except for

the addition of Ho Chi Minh's portrait over the fireplace. The palace, filled with artefacts from decades and governments past, is extremely interesting.

The engraved glass map of Vietnam was given to Emperor Bao Dai (born 1913; reigned 1926-45; he moved to France in the mid-'50s) in 1942 by Vietnamese students in France. In Bao Dai's office, the life-size white bust above the bookcase is of Bao Dai himself; the smaller gold and brown busts are of his father, Emperor Khai Dinh. Note the heavy brass royal seal (on the right) and military seal (on the left). The photographs over the fireplace are of (from left to right) Bao Dai, his eldest son Bao Long (in uniform) and Empress Nam Phuong, who died in 1963.

Upstairs are the royal living quarters. The room of Bao Long, who now lives in England, is decorated in yellow, the royal colour. The huge semicircular couch was used by the Emperor and Empress for family meetings, during which their three daughters were seated in the yellow chairs and their two sons in the pink chairs. Check out the ancient tan Rouathermique infra-red sauna machine near the top of the stairs.

Bao Dai's Summer Palace is set in a pine grove 500 metres south-east of the Pasteur Institute, which is on Le Hong Phong St two km south-west of the city centre. The palace is open to the public from 7 to 11 am and 1.30 to 4 pm and shoes must be removed at the door. The entry fee for foreigners is US$1 plus an extra charge for cameras and videos.

Tourists can stay here for US$30 per person per night; for more information, contact Dalat Tourist.

Flower Gardens

The Dalat Flower Gardens (Vuon Hoa Dalat; ☎ 22151) were established in 1966 by the South Vietnamese Agriculture Service and renovated in 1985. Flowers represented include hydrangeas, fuchsias and orchids (hoa lan). Most of the latter are in special shaded buildings off to the right from the entrance. The orchids are grown in blocks of coconut palm trunk and in terracotta pots with lots of ventilation holes.

Several monkeys live in cages on the grounds of the Flower Gardens – Japanese tourists like posing for photos with the animals; Vietnamese tourists enjoy tormenting the monkeys by throwing rocks and lit cigarettes, but some of the monkeys have learned to throw them back.

Near the gate you can buy *cu ly*, reddish-brown animal-shaped pieces of fern stems whose fibres are used to stop bleeding in traditional medicine. A reader says:

For kitsch, visit the Flower Gardens. I can't describe them, just go there – a marvel!

The Flower Gardens front Xuan Huong Lake at 2 Phu Dong Thien Vuong St, which leads from the lake to Dalat University; they are open from 7.30 am to 4 pm. Ticket sales are suspended for a while around noon.

Dalat University

Dalat is actually something of an educational centre. The reason for this is the climate – in the era before air-conditioning, Dalat was one of the few places in Vietnam where it was possible to study without working up a sweat. For this reason, a number of educational institutions were located there, Dalat University being the most famous.

Dalat University was founded as a Catholic university in 1957 by Hué Archbishop Ngo Dinh Thuc, older brother of President Ngo Dinh Diem (assassinated in 1963), with the help of Cardinal Spelman of New York. The university was seized from the church in 1975 and closed, but it reopened two years later as a state-run institution. There are presently over 1200 students from south-central Vietnam studying here, but they all live in off-campus boarding houses. The university library contains 10,000 books, including some in English and other Western languages.

Dalat University is at 1 Phu Dong Thien Vuong St (corner Dinh Tien Hoang St). The 38-hectare campus can easily be identified by the red-star-topped triangular tower. The

Young Montagnard girl, Dalat

red star is stuck over a cross which was originally erected by the church. The fact that the cross was never actually removed has led some to speculate that the church may some day get the campus returned to it.

Foreign visitors have to pay a fee to enter the campus. The fee is waved, of course, for the several foreign teachers employed here. They teach everything from French and English to accounting and business management.

Nuclear Research Centre

Dalat's Nuclear Research Centre uses its American-built Triga Mark II reactor for radioactive medicine to train scientists and to analyse samples collected for geological and agricultural research. The centre, financed under the US Atoms for Peace programme, was formally dedicated in 1963 by

President Ngo Dinh Diem (who was assassinated four days later) and US Ambassador Henry Cabot Lodge. In 1975, as the South was collapsing, the USA spirited away the reactor's nuclear fuel elements; the centre was reopened in 1984.

Dalat University recently opened a Department of Nuclear Technology, and some foreign experts were hired to teach the courses. This has raised a few eyebrows, but no one as yet has accused Vietnam of harbouring ambitions of becoming a nuclear power. However, it does seem like it will be a long time before Vietnam starts building nuclear power stations. The most likely immediate possible peaceful use for nuclear technology would be in medicine.

The Nuclear Research Centre, with its tall, thin chimney, can easily be seen from the Palace Hotel as well as from the Dragon Water-Pumping Station. It is *not* open to the public.

Former Petit Lycée Yersin

The former Petit Lycée Yersin at 1 Hoang Van Thu St is now a cultural centre (☎ 22511) run by the provincial government. Lessons in electric and acoustic guitar, piano, violin, clarinet, saxophone, etc, are held here, making this a good place to meet local musicians. A new music centre is being established on Tang Bat Ho St.

Valley of Love

Named the Valley of Peace by Emperor Bao Dai, the Valley of Love (Thung Lung Tinh Yeu, or Vallée d'Amour in French) had its name changed in 1972 (the year Da Thien Lake was created) by romantically minded students from Dalat University.

The place has since taken on a carnival atmosphere; tourist buses line up to regurgitate visitors, and boats line up to accommodate them. Paddleboats cost US$0.50 per hour; 15-person canoes cost US$4 an hour; obnoxious noise-making motorboats cost US$5 for a whirlwind tour of the lake.

This is a good place to see the 'Dalat Cowboys' (no relation to the American 'Dallas Cowboys' football team). The 'cowboys' are in fact Vietnamese guides dressed as American cowboys – come back in another year and they'll have the Montagnards dressed up as Indians. We've also seen Vietnamese dressed as bears, and we imagine that Mickey Mouse and Donald Duck costumes can't be far behind. The cowboys rent horses to tourists for US$4 (and up) per hour and can take you on a guided tour around the lake. The Dalat cowboys and 'bears' hassle you for cash if you accidentally take their picture – they want about US$0.20 per photo.

Refreshments and local delicacies (jams, candied fruits, etc) are on sale at the lookout near where the buses disgorge tourists.

The Valley of Love is five km north of Xuan Huong Lake out Phu Dong Thien Vuong St. The entrance fee is US$0.20.

Cam Ly Falls

Cam Ly Falls, opened as a tourist site in 1911, is one of those must-see spots for domestic visitors. The grassy areas around the 15-metre-high cascades are the habitat of horses and Dalat cowboys. Many of the cowboys you see around here aren't guides, but tourists – for a fee you can get dressed as a cowboy and have your photo taken. The waterfall is between numbers 57 and 59 on Hoang Van Thu St; it is open from 7 am to 6 pm.

Tomb of Nguyen Huu Hao

Nguyen Huu Hao, who died in 1939, was the father of Nam Phuong, Bao Dai's wife. He was the richest person in Go Cong District of the Mekong Delta. Nguyen Huu Hao's tomb is on a hilltop 400 metres north-west of Cam Ly Falls.

Dragon Water-Pumping Station

Guarded by a fanciful cement dragon, the Dragon Water-Pumping Station was built in 1977-78. The statue of the Virgin Mary holding baby Jesus and gazing towards Dalat dates from 1974. Thong Nhat Reservoir is on top of the hill just west of the pumping station.

The Dragon Water-Pumping Station is on top of a low rise 500 metres west of the entrance to the Valley of Love.

Pagodas & Churches

Lam Ty Ni Pagoda Lam Ty Ni Pagoda, also known as Quan Am Tu, was founded in 1961. The decorative front gate was constructed by the pagoda's one monk, Vien Thuc, an industrious man who learned English, French, Khmer and Thai at Dalat University. During his 27 years here, he has built flower beds and gardens in several different styles, including a miniature Japanese garden complete with a bridge. Nearby are trellis-shaded paths decorated with hanging plants. Signs list the Chinese name of each garden. Vien Thuc also built much of the pagoda's wooden furniture.

Lam Ty Ni Pagoda is about 500 metres north of the Pasteur Institute at 2 Thien My St. A visit here can easily be combined with a stop at Bao Dai's Summer Palace.

We visited Dalat and went to the Lam Ty Ni Pagoda and met the monk, Vien Thuc. This is an experience not to be missed! Mr Thuc is very warm and friendly and gave us a tour of the pagoda and his living quarters. The gardens are a tad run down as Thuc has been busy painting pictures and writing poetry. We admired some pictures on the wall, mostly abstract black ink on white rice paper and some water colours, all quite striking. He was very pleased and embraced us and took us by the arm into his studio, where he has hundreds of pictures. We asked if we could purchase some and he said we could for only the cost of the materials. We were there for three hours and Mr Thuc never stopped talking or smiling and posed with us for many photos. We ended up taking four or five pictures each and paid about US$3 each, but we met other travellers who gave him less. I admired one of his poems and he whipped out a pot of ink and a bamboo pen and wrote it on my painting. Mr Thuc rolled up our pictures in cardboard and hung them around our necks. There were five of us and we could not stop talking about our visit for weeks.

Frank Visakay

Linh Son Pagoda Linh Son Pagoda was founded in 1938. The giant bell is said to be made of bronze with gold mixed in, its great weight making it too heavy for thieves to carry off. Behind the pagoda are coffee and tea plants tended by the 15 monks, who range in age from 20 to 80, and half-a-dozen novices.

One of the monks here has led a fascinating and tragic life, whose peculiar course reflects the vagaries of Vietnam's modern history. Born in 1926 of a Japanese father and a Vietnamese mother, he was pressed into the service of the Japanese occupation forces as a translator during WW II. He got his secondary school degree from a French-language Franciscan convent in 1959 at the age of 35. His interest later turned to American literature, in which he received a master's degree (his thesis was on William Faulkner) from Dalat University in 1975. The monk speaks half-a-dozen East Asian and European languages with fluent precision.

Linh Son Pagoda is about one km from the town centre off Phan Dinh Phung St; the address is 120 Nguyen Van Troi St.

Dalat Cathedral Dalat Cathedral, which is on Tran Phu St next to the Dalat Hotel, was built between 1931 and 1942 for use by French residents and holiday-makers. The cross on the spire is 47 metres above the ground. Inside, the stained-glass windows bring a hint of medieval Europe to Dalat. The first church built on this site (in the 1920s) is to the left of the cathedral; it has a light blue arched door.

There are three priests here. Masses are held at 5.30 am and 5.15 pm every day and on Sundays at 5.30 am, 7 am and 4 pm. The parish's three choirs (one for each Sunday mass) practise on Thursdays and Saturdays from 5 to 6 pm.

Vietnamese Evangelical Church Dalat's pink Evangelical Church, the main Protestant church in the city, was built in 1940. Until 1975, it was affiliated with the Christian & Missionary Alliance. The minister here was trained at Nha Trang Bible College.

Since reunification, Vietnam's Protestants have been persecuted even more than have Catholics, in part because many Protestant clergymen were trained by American missionaries. Although religious activities at this church are still restricted by the government, Sunday is a busy day: there is Bible study from 7 to 8 am followed by worship from 8 to 10 am; a youth service is held from 1.30 to 3.30 pm.

Most of the 25,000 Protestants in Lam Dong Province, who are served by over 100 churches, are hill-tribe people. Dalat's Vietnamese Evangelical Church is one of only six churches in the province whose membership is ethnic-Vietnamese.

The Vietnamese Evangelical Church is 300 metres from Rap 3/4 cinema at 72 Nguyen Van Troi St.

Domaine de Marie Convent The pink, tile-roofed structures of the Domaine de Marie Convent (Nha Tho Domaine), constructed between 1940 and 1942, were once home to 300 nuns. Today, the eight remaining nuns support themselves by making ginger candies and by selling the fruit grown in the orchard out the back.

Suzanne Humbert, wife of Admiral Jean Decoux, Vichy-French Governor-General of Indochina from 1940 to 1945, is buried at the base of the outside back wall of the chapel. A benefactress of the chapel, she was killed in an auto accident in 1944.

Masses are held in the large chapel every day at 5.30 am and on Sundays at 5.30 am and 4.15 pm.

The Domaine de Marie Convent is on a hilltop at 6 Ngo Quyen St, which is also called Mai Hac De St. The French-speaking nuns are pleased to show visitors around and explain about their important social work for orphans and homeless and handicapped children. A small shop sells handicrafts made by the children and nuns.

Du Sinh Church Du Sinh Church was built in 1955 by Catholic refugees from the North. The four-post Sino-Vietnamese-style steeple was constructed at the insistence of a Hué-born priest of royal lineage. The church is on a hilltop with beautiful views in all directions, making this a great place for a picnic.

To get to Du Sinh Church, go 500 metres south-west along Huyen Tran Cong Chua St from the former Couvent des Oiseaux, which is now a teachers' training high school.

Thien Vuong Pagoda Thien Vuong Pagoda, also known simply as Chua Tau (the Chinese pagoda), is popular with domestic tourists, especially ethnic-Chinese. Set on a hilltop amid pine trees, the pagoda was built by the Chaozhou Chinese Congregation. Tho Da, the monk who initiated the construction of the pagoda in 1958, emigrated to the USA; there are pictures of his 1988 visit on display. The stalls out the front are a good place to buy local candied fruit and preserves.

The pagoda itself consists of three yellow buildings made of wood. In the first building is a gilded wooden statue of Ho Phap, one of the Buddha's protectors. On the other side of Ho Phap's glass case is a gilded wooden statue of Pho Hien, a helper of A Di Da Buddha (the Buddha of the Past). Shoes should be removed before entering the third building, in which there are three four-metre-high standing Buddhas donated by a British Buddhist and brought from Hong Kong in 1960. Made of gilded sandalwood and weighing 1400 kg each, the figures – said to be the largest sandalwood statues in Vietnam – represent Thich Ca Buddha (Sakyamuni, the historical Buddha; in the centre); Quan The Am Bo Tat (Avalokiteçvara, the Goddess of Mercy; on the right); and Dai The Chi Bo Tat (an assistant of A Di Da; on the left).

Thien Vuong Pagoda is about five km south-east of the centre of town out Khe Sanh St. A cable car due to open in 1997 will connect it to the new long-distance bus station. This construction project is a Swiss-Vietnamese joint venture.

Minh Nguyet Cu Sy Lam Pagoda A second Chinese Buddhist pagoda, Minh Nguyet Cu Sy Lam Pagoda, is reached by a path beginning across the road from the gate of Thien Vuong Pagoda. It was built by the Cantonese Chinese Congregation in 1962. The main sanctuary of the pagoda is a round structure constructed on a platform representing a lotus blossom.

Inside is a painted cement statue of Quan The Am Bo Tat (Avalokiteçvara, the Goddess of Mercy) flanked by two other figures. Shoes should be removed before entering. Notice the repetition of the lotus motif in the window bars, railings, gateposts, etc. There is a giant red gourd-shaped incense oven near the main sanctuary. The pagoda is open all day long.

Su Nu Pagoda Su Nu Pagoda, also known as Chua Linh Phong, is a Buddhist nunnery built in 1952. The nuns here – who, according to Buddhist regulations, are bald – wear grey or brown robes except when praying, at which time they don saffron raiment. Men are allowed to visit, but only women live here. The nunnery is open all day, but it is considered impolite to come around lunch time, when the nuns sing their prayers a cappella before eating. Across the driveway from the pagoda's buildings and set amid tea plants is the grave-marker of Head Nun Thich Nu Dieu Huong.

Su Nu Pagoda is about one km south of Le Thai To St at 72 Hoang Hoa Tham St.

Hiking & Cycling
The best way to enjoy the forests and cultivated countryside around Dalat is either on foot, seated on horseback or pedalling a bicycle.

It's important to be aware that certain areas marked with a 'C' are off limits to foreigners. Some travellers speculate that this is to hide 'secret re-education camps' or to keep you away from bands of 'Montagnard guerrillas', while another story is that there are still armed soldiers who deserted the Vietnamese army and roam the highlands robbing tourists. The government refuses to comment. Assuming that you don't run into any of the 'C' signs, some suggested routes include:

- Heading out 3 Thang 4 St, which becomes National Highway 20, to the pine forests of Prenn Pass and Quang Trung Reservoir.
- Going via the Governor-General's Residence out Khe Sanh St to Thien Vuong Pagoda.

- Taking Phu Dong Thien Vuong St from Dalat University to the Valley of Love.
- Going out to Bao Dai's Summer Palace and from there, after stopping at Lam Ty Ni Pagoda, via Thien My St and Huyen Tran Cong Chua St to Du Sinh Church.

Golf
The Dalat People's Committee set up a joint venture with a Hong Kong company to renovate the old golf course, which was once used by Bao Dai, the last Vietnamese emperor. The renovation has now been completed and the course has been renamed Dalat Pines. Memberships (good for only 20 years) start at US$15,000 but go all the way up to US$60,000 for 'corporate memberships'. Visitors can play here for US$25 to US$35 per day.

Places to Stay
Due to its popularity with domestic travellers, Dalat has an extensive network of excellent and cheap private hotels. It's a pity then that foreigners are prohibited to use these – you must stay at the more expensive government-run hotels. Of course, government-owned hotels are not off limits to Vietnamese, and when demand is heavy (Saturday night, for instance) it may be impossible to find a place to stay. If the government-owned hotels are full, you sleep in the bus station or in the street because private hotels cannot accommodate you even if they have space. In the high season (June and July), there is simply no place for foreigners to stay because everything is chock-a-block. There is another peak season surrounding the Tet holiday (most of February).

Unless you like icy showers, make sure they have hot water before you check in. If there is a power failure, the hot water will be off too, but in that case some hotels will boil water on a gas stove and give it to you in a bucket. No hotels in Dalat have air-conditioning, though it's hard to imagine why anyone would want it!

Places to Stay – bottom end
The *Hang Nga Guest House* (☎ 22070),

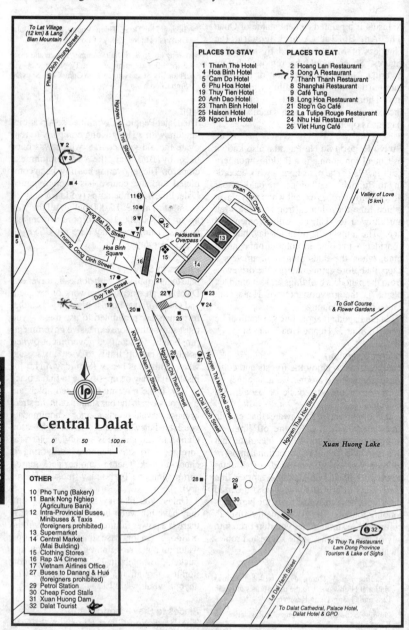

PLACES TO STAY
1 Thanh The Hotel
4 Hoa Binh Hotel
5 Cam Do Hotel
6 Phu Hoa Hotel
19 Thuy Tien Hotel
20 Anh Dao Hotel
23 Thanh Binh Hotel
25 Haison Hotel
28 Ngoc Lan Hotel

PLACES TO EAT
2 Hoang Lan Restaurant
3 Dong A Restaurant
7 Thanh Thanh Restaurant
8 Shanghai Restaurant
9 Café Tung
18 Long Hoa Restaurant
21 Stop'n Go Café
22 La Tulipe Rouge Restaurant
24 Nhu Hai Restaurant
26 Viet Hung Café

To Lat Village (12 km) & Lang Bian Mountain

Phan Dinh Phung Street

Nguyen Van Troi Street

Phan Boi Chau Street

Valley of Love (5 km)

Tang Bat Ho Street

Truong Cong Dinh Street

Hoa Binh Square

Pedestrian Overpass

Duy Tan Street

To Golf Course & Flower Gardens

Khoi Nghia Nam Ky Street

Nguyen Chi Thanh Street

Le Dai Hanh Street

Nguyen Thi Minh Khai Street

Nguyen Thai Hoc Street

Central Dalat

0   50   100 m

Xuan Huong Lake

OTHER
10 Pho Tung (Bakery)
11 Bank Nong Nghiep (Agriculture Bank)
12 Intra-Provincial Buses, Minibuses & Taxis (foreigners prohibited)
13 Supermarket
14 Central Market (Mai Building)
15 Clothing Stores
16 Rap 3/4 Cinema
17 Vietnam Airlines Office
27 Buses to Danang & Hué (foreigners prohibited)
29 Petrol Station
30 Cheap Food Stalls
31 Xuan Huong Dam
32 Dalat Tourist

To Thuy Ta Restaurant, Lam Dong Province Tourism & Lake of Sighs

Le Dai Hanh Street

To Dalat Cathedral, Palace Hotel, Dalat Hotel & GPO

CENTRAL HIGHLANDS

3 Huynh Thuc Khang, is a most amazing place, unique in Vietnam if not the world. This exotic guesthouse is actually an art gallery of sorts and a cafe. Hotel rooms are built inside of artificial tree trunks and caves. The owner is the daughter of a former president of Vietnam. Thanks to her late father's high-level political connections, Hang Nga is 'untouchable' and she is able to operate the only private hotel in Dalat that is allowed to accept foreigners. Double rooms here cost US$15 to US$35 and are worth every dong of it.

The *Hoa Binh Hotel* (☎ 22787) is dirty and has cold water only, but backpackers have long been fond of the place. The cost is set by the government at US$10 per person. The hotel is at 64 Truong Cong Dinh St.

The *Thanh The Hotel* (☎ 22180) at 118 Phan Dinh Phung St offers rooms at the requisite low-end rate of US$10 per person. Like the nearby Hoa Binh Hotel, this place catches much of the backpacker traffic.

The *Thanh Binh Hotel* (☎ 22909; 42 rooms) at 40 Nguyen Thi Minh Khai St is a good budget hotel right across the street from the central market building. Singles/doubles in backpacker-class are US$10 per person but rise to US$20/25 for first-class singles/doubles.

The *Mimosa Hotel* (☎ 22656), 170 Phan Dinh Phung St, is dirty and not recommended due to the icy manager. Minimum charge is US$10 per person.

The *Cam Do Hotel* at 81 Phan Dinh Phung St is another 'budget' place costing US$10 per person.

The *Phu Hoa Hotel* (☎ 22194), 16 Tang Bat Ho St, is an old but still reasonably pleasant place in the centre. The price is, as you guessed, US$10 per person.

The *Thuy Tien Hotel* (☎ 21731, 22482; eight rooms) is in the heart of the old French section at the corner of Duy Tan and Khoi Nghia Nam Ky Sts. At US$20 to US$32 for a double, it's hardly worth it – it looks dumpy despite the price. However, the rooms are relatively large.

The *Duy Tan Hotel* (☎ 22216; 26 rooms) at 82, 3 Thang 2 St (corner Hoang Van Thu St) is actually quite a bargain if you want to be in a quiet, out of the centre place. Travellers have complained about 'very aggressive cockroaches' here, but the fenced-in car park in front of the hotel reassures Americans and Aussies accustomed to motel-style travel. Room rates are US$10 per person.

The *Lam Son Hotel* (☎ 22362; 12 rooms) is one-half km west of the centre of town in an old French villa at 5 Hai Thuong St. This large, quiet place is good value if you don't mind the 10-minute walk from the town centre. Singles cost US$10 to US$20. The management is very friendly and travellers give it favourable comments.

VYC Travel Company is a government-owned company based in Saigon. It's the only company besides Dalat Tourist that is permitted to operate hotels for foreigners in Dalat. The standards maintained by VYC are somewhat higher than those of Dalat Tourist so you might want to take a look. Unfortunately, all the VYC hotels are too far to walk from the centre, so you'll need to take a motorbike or rent a taxi from Dalat Tourist.

VYC operates the *Pensee 6 Hotel* (☎ 22378; eight rooms), which costs US$10 per person. Nearby is the *Pensee 3 Hotel* (☎ 22286; nine rooms), 3 Ba Thang Tu St, which has plush rooms costing US$20 for either singles or doubles. There is also *Pensee 10* (☎ 22937; six rooms), 10 Phan Chu Trinh St, which costs US$15/20 for singles /doubles, but is a very long way from the centre. Near that (thus, also very far from the centre) is *Pensee 2 Hotel* (☎ 22933; 20 rooms), 2 Lu Gia St, which costs US$10. And just next to this is the three-star *Lavy Hotel* (also known as the Lam Vien VYC Hotel), which has 40 rooms costing US$30. You can make reservations in Ho Chi Minh City at VYC Travel Company (☎ 332071; fax 330399), 180 Nguyen Cu Trinh St, District 1.

Places to Stay – middle & top end

The *Anh Dao Hotel* (☎ 22384; 27 rooms) is up the hill from the central market building on Nguyen Chi Thanh St; the postal address is 50-52 Khu Hoa Binh Quarter. This hotel has some of the most beautiful rooms in Dalat and can definitely be recommended if it fits your price range. Doubles here are US$30 to US$55 and breakfast is included in the tariff.

The *Ngoc Lan Hotel* (☎ 22136; fax 24032; 33 rooms), a big place overlooking the bus station and the lake, is at 42 Nguyen Chi Thanh St. This old place has seen some recent renovation, and prices for singles/doubles/triples are US$30/36/45.

The *Haison Hotel* (☎ 22622; fax 22623) is a spiffy place at 1 Nguyen Thi Minh Khai St across the roundabout from the central market building. The hotel advertises its 'elegant and cosy dancing hall' and 'urbane service staff'. It is often filled with foreign tour groups, which might explain why it also frequently gets raided by police hoping to catch foreigners with prostitutes. Room rates here are US$25 to US$40.

The *Palace Hotel* (☎ 22203; 43 rooms) is a grand old place built between 1916 and 1922. Panoramic views of Xuan Huong Lake can be enjoyed in the hotel's expansive ground-floor public areas, where one can sit in a rattan chair sipping tea or soda while gazing out through a wall of windows. There are tennis courts nearby. A major renovation that took over three years has just been completed. Room prices have risen to an astronomical US$150 per day, making it Dalat's most expensive accommodation. The hotel's street address is 2 Tran Phu St.

Another vintage hostelry is the *Dalat Hotel* (☎ 22363; 65 rooms), built in 1907. The building, which is at 7 Tran Phu St (opposite the driveway of the Palace Hotel), has become run-down but is now undergoing renovation. The old prices were US$10 to US$20, but expect this to rise. There is a billiard room on the ground floor and a restaurant. The staff here have been traditionally unfriendly – it will be interesting to see if their attitude gets renovated too.

The *Minh Tam Hotel* (☎ 22447; 17 rooms) is three km out of town at 20A Khe Sanh St. There are nice views from here of the surrounding landscape of pine-forested hills and cultivated valleys. Formerly the magnif-

icent summer palace of Tran Le Xuan (Madame Nhu, the notorious sister-in-law of President Ngo Dinh Diem), the villa, constructed in 1936, was renovated in 1984. The unfriendly, stuck-up staff seem to have been created in Madame Nhu's image. Nevertheless, this place is a peaceful retreat, or would be were it not for the busloads of domestic tourists continually parading through the flower garden on the hotel's grounds. Double rooms in the main building cost US$50, while villas belonging to the hotel go for US$45.

Many of Dalat's 2500 chalet-style villas can be rented, but not by foreigners. If this restriction is lifted, take a look at the prime villas along the ridge south of Tran Hung Dao and Le Thai To Sts. There is a whole neighbourhood of villas near the Pasteur Institute (around Le Hong Phong St). If you don't mind the tourists tramping through, you can even stay in the old Governor-General's Residence and Bao Dai's Summer Palace for US$40 per person per night. For more information, inquire at Dalat Tourist.

Places to Eat
Local Specialities Dalat is a paradise for lovers of fresh garden vegetables, which are grown locally and sold all over the south. The abundance of just-picked peas, carrots, radishes, tomatoes, cucumbers, avocados, green peppers, lettuce, Chinese cabbage, bean sprouts, beets, green beans, potatoes, corn, bamboo shoots, garlic, spinach, squash and yams makes for meals unavailable anywhere else in the country. Persimmons and cherries are in season from November to January. Avocados are eaten for desert with either sugar or salt and pepper. Apples are known here as *bom*, after the French *pomme*. Because of fierce competition in the domestic tourism market, restaurant prices are very reasonable.

The Dalat area is justifiably famous for its strawberry jam, dried blackcurrants and candied plums and peaches, all of which can be purchased from stalls in the market area just west of Xuan Huong Lake. Other local delicacies include avocado ice cream, sweet beans *(mut dao)* and strawberry, blackberry and artichoke extracts (syrups for making drinks). The strawberry extract is great in tea. The region also produces grape, mulberry and strawberry wines. Artichoke tea, another local speciality, is made from the root of the artichoke plant. Most of these products can be purchased at the central market and at stalls in front of Thien Vuong Pagoda.

Dau hu, a type of pudding common in China, is also one of Dalat's specialities. Made from soymilk, sugar and a slice of ginger, dau hu is sold by itinerant women vendors who walk around carrying a large bowl of the stuff and a small stand suspended from either end of a bamboo pole.

Street Market The stairways down to Nguyen Thi Minh Khai St turns into a big food stall area in the late afternoon and early evening. Women sell all sorts of pre-cooked homemade dishes or prepare them on a portable charcoal stove. Prices are amazingly cheap – something like US$0.15 for noodle soup, or US$0.05 for one kg of bananas. Of course, other vendors with more permanent stalls in the marketplace sell similar things but at much higher prices. Most of the people doing business on these stairs are minority people, and one thing that should become immediately obvious is how much poorer they are than the Vietnamese. These poor sell their goods in early morning or late afternoon because during the day the police chase them away.

Restaurants The restaurants inside of Dalat's hotels are owned by the government and are notable for lousy food and rude service. Fortunately, the Dalat police still allow foreigners to eat at private restaurants (for now).

The best of the bunch in the budget range is the *Dong A Restaurant* (☎ 21033) at 82 Phan Dinh Phung St. This place dishes up Vietnamese, Chinese, Western and vegetarian cuisine. The beef steak is so good it can make you cry. The sweet'n'sour soup is also outstanding, and can be ordered vegetarian-style or with eel, pork or fish. This restaurant is open from 8 am to 10 pm.

The *Shanghai Restaurant* is on the other side of Rap 3/4 cinema from the central market building; the address is 8 Khu Hoa Binh Quarter. They serve Chinese, Vietnamese and French food from 8 am to 9.30 pm.

The *Long Hoa Restaurant* on Duy Tan St is also is in vogue with travellers and even cheaper than the Shanghai Restaurant. The *Hoang Lan Restaurant* on Phan Dinh Phung St has excellent food in the budget range.

Close to the Shanghai Restaurant is *Pho Tung,* which is not a bad restaurant but also an outstanding bakery. It's hard to resist all those delectable pastries and cakes in the windows – close your eyes as you walk by or else break out some dong and pig out.

If it's fresh Vietnamese vegetables you want, the place to find them is the *Nhu Hai Restaurant* on the traffic circle in front of the central market building.

La Tulipe Rouge Restaurant (☎ 2394) is at 1 Nguyen Thi Minh Khai St, across the square from the central market building. Operating hours are from 6 am to 9 pm. The fare includes Vietnamese, Chinese and European dishes.

Thanh Thanh Restaurant (☎ 21836) at 4 Tang Bat Ho St is possibly the most upscale eatery in Dalat, though prices are still very reasonable. Everything from the fine tablecloths to the sparkling silverware can match Europe's finest. This place does Western and Vietnamese food and is a major drawing card for French travellers. Menus are written in French and English.

There are dozens of food stalls in the market area just west of Xuan Huong Dam.

Vegetarian In addition to the Dong A Restaurant, there are vegetarian food stalls (signposted *com chay,* meaning 'vegetarian food') in the market area just west of Xuan Huong Dam. All serve delicious 100% vegetarian food prepared to resemble and taste like traditional Vietnamese meat dishes.

Cafes The coffee and cake in Dalat is the best in Vietnam, and a visit to any of the town's finer cafes should make you an instant addict. Other items worth trying are simple meals, breakfast, etc.

Stop'n Go Café (☎ 21512), Kiosk No 6, Hoa Binh Square, overlooks the market area. This is sort of Dalat's avant-garde hang-out. Mostly drinks are served, but you can also buy 'breakfast' anytime. Check out the book of poems and the paintings for sale.

The *Café Tung* at 6 Khu Hoa Binh St was a famous hang-out of Saigonese intellectuals during the 1950s. Old-timers swear that the place remains exactly as it was when they were young, including the 1950s prices (US$0.10 for coffee). As it did then, Café Tung serves only tea, coffee, hot cocoa, lemon soda and orange soda to the accompaniment of mellow French music. This is a marvellous place to warm up and unwind on a chilly evening.

The *Viet Hung Café* (Kem Viet Hung) specialities are ice cream and iced coffee. The cafe has entrances across from 22 Nguyen Chi Thanh St and on Le Dai Hanh St.

Entertainment

The busy market area just to the west of Xuan Huong Dam provides the main entertainment. This is where you can hang out and drink coffee and chat with the locals.

Hoa Binh Square and the adjacent central market building is the other hot spot. It's one big buy and sell, but this is one of the best places in Vietnam to pick up clothing at a good price.

Things to Buy

In the past few years, the Dalat tourist kitsch-junk market has really come into its own. Without any effort at all, you'll be able to find that special something for your loved ones at home – perhaps a battery-powered stuffed koala that sings 'Waltzing Matilda' or a lacquered alligator with a lightbulb in its mouth.

In addition to these useful items, Dalat is known for its *kim mao cau tich*, a kind of fern whose fibres are used to stop bleeding in traditional Chinese medicine. The stuff is

also known as *cu ly* (animals) because the fibrous matter is sold attached to branches pruned to resemble reddish-brown hairy animals. The tourists from Taiwan and Hong Kong go crazy for this stuff.

The hill tribes of Lam Dong Province make handicrafts for their own use only – but just wait, Dalat Tourist will get them too. Lat products include dyed rush mats and rice baskets that roll up when empty. The Koho and Chill produce the split-bamboo baskets used by all the national minorities in this area to carry things on their backs. The Chill also weave cloth, including the dark blue cotton shawls worn by some Montagnard women.

The hill-tribe people carry water in a hollow gourd with a corn-cob stopper that is sometimes wrapped in a leaf for a tighter fit. A market for such goods has not yet developed so there are no stores in town selling them. If you are interested in Montagnard handicrafts, you might ask around Lat Village, which is 12 km north of Dalat.

Getting There & Away

Air At present there are flights to and from Ho Chi Minh City on Monday, Wednesday and Saturday (US$40 one way).

Lien Khuong Airport is about 30 km south of the city. You will need to take a government taxi (about US$20) since foreigners are forbidden to ride in private cars. Another alternative is by motorbike, which should cost around US$4 to US$5.

Cam Ly Airstrip, only three km from the centre of Dalat, is not in use.

The Vietnam Airlines office in Dalat (☎ 22895) is at 5 Truong Cong Dinh St, which is across the street from Rap 3/4 cinema.

Bus At the time of our visit the local People's Committee was prohibiting foreigners from riding in cars, vans or buses – except for those belonging to Dalat Tourist. The only way for foreigners to legally enter Dalat by bus was by booking a seat on a bus owned by Dalat Tourist. This company has an office in Ho Chi Minh City and you can book seats on their bus for US$10 per person. You don't have to go to Dalat Tourist to do the booking

– other travel agents (Saigon Tourist, etc) can handle it.

To get out of Dalat, you can purchase bus tickets at the government-owned hotels.

At the time of this writing, private bus and taxi drivers in Dalat had sent a delegation to Hanoi to protest their treatment by the Dalat government. Assuming they have had some success and the curbs against foreigners have been lifted, you can travel by nonexpress buses. These depart when full, start at 6 am and link Dalat with:

Bao Loc (B'Lao), Cat Tien, Da Hoai, Da Teh, Danang, Di Linh (Djiring), Don Duong (Darang), Dong Van, Duc Trong, Hanoi (with a change of buses), Ho Chi Minh City (eight to nine hours), Nam Bang, Phan Rang, Phan Thiet, Phu Son, Quang Ngai, Qui Nhon, Tan My.

To get the latest bus information in Dalat you can talk to the drivers at the Intra-Provincial Bus Station (Ben Xe Khach Noi Thanh). It's next to the new cable car station, where you get cable cars to Thien Vuong Pagoda. The bus station is about one km due south of Xuan Huong Lake.

In Ho Chi Minh City, buses to Dalat depart from the Van Thanh Bus Station.

Car From Ho Chi Minh City, taking the inland route via Bao Loc and Di Linh is faster than the coastal route via Ngoan Muc Pass. Parts of the road between Dalat and Phan Rang are in poor condition, so a high-clearance vehicle is preferred though not mandatory. When you get close to the city limits of Dalat, it will probably be necessary for all Westerners to disembark and be carried to the centre by motorbike. Otherwise, the Dalat police may well confiscate the licence of your driver. You'll have to play the same cat and mouse game on departure.

Road distances from Dalat are:

Buon Ma Thuot	396 km
Danang	746 km
Di Linh	82 km
Ho Chi Minh City	308 km
Nha Trang	205 km
Phan Rang	101 km
Phan Thiet	247 km

Getting Around

Since private vehicles are forbidden to carry foreigners, you must rent cars or vans from Dalat Tourist. You can be sure that vehicles rented from the government will cost at least double compared with what is available on the free market.

Taxi Privately owned Peugeot 203s – all of them black with white roofs – park near Rap 3/4 cinema. Currently, only Vietnamese nationals are permitted to make use of these vehicles. If you at least look Vietnamese (or are an Overseas Vietnamese) you may be able to hire one for the day. Of course, the drivers are terrified of the police, so no way will they carry a Westerner unless the ban is lifted. The taxi office is next to the main bus station and is signposted as Xe Taxi Dalat.

Motorbike Motorbikes (Honda om), which can carry one passenger in addition to the driver, can be flagged down along Nguyen Thi Minh Khai St just south of the central market area. So far the government does not prohibit motorcyclists from carrying foreigners. This is probably only because Dalat Tourist doesn't rent motorcycles.

Cyclo Dalat is too hilly for cyclos.

AROUND DALAT
Lake of Sighs

The Lake of Sighs (Ho Than Tho) is a natural lake enlarged by a French-built dam; the forests in the area are hardly Dalat's finest. There are several small restaurants up the hill from the dam. Horses can be hired near the restaurants for US$4 an hour.

According to legend, Mai Nuong and Hoang Tung met here in 1788 while he was hunting and she was picking mushrooms. They fell in love and sought their parents' permission to marry. But at that time Vietnam was threatened by a Chinese invasion and Hoang Tung, heeding Emperor Quang Trung's call-to-arms, joined the army without waiting to tell Mai Nuong. Unaware that he was off fighting and afraid that his absence meant that he no longer loved her,

Mai Nuong sent word for him to meet her at the lake. When he did not come she was overcome with sorrow and, to prove her love, threw herself into the conveniently located lake and drowned. Thereafter, the lake has been known as the Lake of Sighs.

The Lake of Sighs is six km north-east of the centre of Dalat out Phan Chu Trinh St.

Prenn Pass

The area along National Highway 20 between Dalat and Datanla Falls is known as Prenn Pass. The hillsides support mature pine forests while the valleys are used to cultivate vegetables. This is a great area for hiking and horseback riding, but make local inquiries before heading out to be sure that there will be no problems with the police.

Quang Trung Reservoir

Quang Trung Reservoir (Tuyen Lam Lake) is an artificial lake created by a dam in 1980. It is named after Emperor Quang Trung (also known as Nguyen Hue), a leader of the Tay Son Rebellion who is considered a great hero for vanquishing a Chinese invasion force in 1789. The area is being developed for tourism; there are several cafes not far from the dam and paddleboats, rowboats and canoes are for rent nearby. The hillscape around the reservoir is covered with pine trees, most of them newly planted. There is a switchback path up the hill due south-west of the water intake tower. Minority farmers live and raise crops in the vicinity of the lake.

To get to Quang Trung Reservoir, head out of Dalat on National Highway 20. At a point five km from town turn right and continue for two km.

Datanla Falls

The nice thing about Datanla Falls is the short but pleasant walk to get there. The cascade is 350 metres from Highway 20 on a path that first passes through a forest of pines and then continues steeply down the hill into a rainforest. The other good thing about this place is the wildlife – lots of squirrels, birds and butterflies. This may have much to do with the fact that hunting is

prohibited in the area so the creatures are less scared of humans.

To get to Datanla Falls, turn off Highway 20 about 200 metres past the turn-off to Quang Trung Reservoir; the entrance fee is US$0.20. There is a second entrance to the falls several hundred metres farther down the road.

Prenn Falls

This is one of the largest and most beautiful falls in the Dalat area, but it is also starting to suffer the effects of commercial exploitation.

Prenn Falls (elevation 1124 metres) consists of a 15-metre free fall over a wide rock outcrop. A path goes under the outcrop, affording a view of the pool and surrounding rainforest through the curtain of falling water. An ominous sign of possible kitsch horrors to come are the 'Dalat Tourist Sailboats' now plying the waters of the tiny pool at the waterfall's base.

After a rainstorm the waterfall becomes a raging brown torrent (deforestation and the consequent soil erosion are responsible for the coffee colour). Refreshments are sold at kiosks near the falls. The park around the falls was dedicated by the Queen of Thailand in 1959.

The entrance to Prenn Falls is near the Prenn Restaurant, which is 13 km from Dalat towards Phan Rang; the entrance fee is US$0.20 but there is a US$0.50 camera fee.

Lat Village

The nine hamlets of Lat Village (population 6000), whose name is pronounced 'lak' by the locals, are about 12 km from Dalat at the base of Lang Bian Mountain. The inhabitants of five of the hamlets are of the Lat ethnic group; the residents of the other four are members of the Chill, Ma and Koho tribes, each of which speaks a different dialect.

Traditionally, Lat houses are built on piles with rough plank walls and a thatch roof. The people of Lat Village eke out a living growing rice, coffee, black beans and sweet potatoes. The villages have 300 hectares of land and produce one rice crop per year.

Many residents of Lat have been forced by economic circumstances into the business of producing charcoal, a lowly task often performed by members of Vietnam's minorities. Before 1975, many men from Lat worked with the Americans, as did Montagnards elsewhere in the Central Highlands.

Classes in the village's primary and secondary schools, successors of the École Franco-Koho established in Dalat in 1948, are conducted in Vietnamese rather than the tribal languages. Lat has one Catholic church and one Protestant church. A Koho-language Bible (Sra Goh) was published by Protestants in 1971; a Lat-language Bible, prepared by Catholics, appeared the following year. Both Montagnard dialects, which are quite similar to each other, are written in a Latin-based script.

Places to Eat There are no restaurants in Lat, just a few food stalls.

Getting There & Away Check in Dalat whether you need a permit to visit Lat Village. Permits were required at the time of our visit, but the requirement may have been rescinded by the time you go. You may be required to travel there in a Dalat Tourist car with a guide, but if travel restrictions have been relaxed, you may be allowed to take the bus, though this won't be comfortable. A small, usually packed bus makes two daily round trips between Dalat and Lat. Or you could have someone take you by motorbike.

To get to Lat from Dalat, head north on Xo Viet Nghe Tinh St. At Tung Lam Hamlet there is a fork in the road marked by a shot-up cement street sign. Continue straight on (that is, north-westward) rather than to the left (which leads to Suoi Vang, the Golden Stream, 14 km away). By bicycle, the 12-km trip from Dalat to Lat takes about 40 minutes. On foot, it's a two-hour walk. The road is in poor repair.

Lang Bian Mountain
Lang Bian Mountain (also called Lam Vien Mountain) has five volcanic peaks ranging in altitude from 2100 to 2400 metres. Of the two highest peaks, the eastern one is known to locals by the woman's name K'lang; the western one bears a man's name, K'biang. The upper reaches of the mountain are forested. Only half a century ago, the verdant foothills of Lang Bian Mountain, now defoliated, sheltered wild oxen, deer, boars, elephants, rhinoceroses and tigers.

The hike up to the top of Lang Bian Mountain, from where the views are truly spectacular, takes three to four hours from Lat Village. The path begins due north of Lat and is easily recognisable as a red gash in the green mountainside.

At present, you need a permit to go to Lang Bian Mountain. You may also be required to hire a guide. Check in Dalat whether this is still necessary.

Ankroët Falls & Lakes
The two Ankroët Lakes were created as part of a hydroelectric project. The waterfall (Thac Ankroët) is about 15 metres high. The Ankroët Lakes are 18 km north-west of Dalat in an area inhabited by hill tribes.

Chicken Village
This village has become popular with travellers because it's conveniently situated on the Dalat-Nha Trang highway, 17 km from Dalat.

The inhabitants belong to the Koho minority. To a certain extent the Koho have been assimilated into Vietnamese society. For example, they no longer live in stilt houses and they wear Vietnamese-style clothing (though very ragged). Nevertheless, the villagers have a lifestyle all their own, and it's certainly worth a stopover if you're heading to Nha Trang anyway.

This place takes its name from a huge concrete statue of a chicken which sits squarely in the centre of the village. We questioned the villagers extensively to learn the history behind this unusual statue, and were surprised to find that most had no idea or else refused to discuss when the statue was built or why. It certainly has no religious significance to the villagers. We finally sought out the most educated person in the village (most of the locals here are illiterate), and this was her story:

When a couple gets married here, it's the bride's family who must pay for the engagement ring and wedding party. Her family is also supposed to present the groom's family with a gift. We had a sad case many years ago where the man's family demanded a special gift, a chicken with nine fingers. No one ever seen such a chicken but there were rumours that these could be found in the mountains. So the girl went to the mountains to search for one. Unfortunately, her effort was in vain and she died in the wilderness. The villagers were stricken with grief by this senseless tragedy, and the girl was made into a hero.

There was fighting in this area during the war, and after liberation the government wanted to give the locals some sort of gift. The villagers asked if they could commemorate the brave young girl who died for love. The government officials were touched by this tragic story, and complied with the wishes of the villagers. So the concrete chicken was built.

The story does sound a bit far-fetched, and one local man had a somewhat different tale to tell. He claims that after the Communist victory in 1975, the villagers retreated to the woods and adopted nomadic slash and burn agriculture because of attempts to enforce farm collectivisation. Many of the men went into the illegal timber-harvesting business, which did quite a bit of damage to the region's forests. The government then granted them several redeeming concessions to entice them to relocate back to their permanent village site. After they returned, the government thought of building some sort of memorial, possibly a statue of Ho Chi Minh. It was finally decided that the concrete chicken would be most appropriate because it would commemorate the hard-working peasants. After all, what better way to symbolise chicken farmers than to build a statue of a chicken?

The residents of Chicken Village are extremely poor, but we were surprised to find no beggars at all. This is particularly remarkable given the large number of tourists who stop here. We'd like to suggest that you do *not* give sweets or money to the children, and thus turn them into beggars. If you want to help the villagers, there are a

couple of shops where you can buy simple things like drinks, biscuits and such. Some people also have weavings for sale, and you can buy these if you like. The weavers are not pushy – in fact, no one is the least bit aggressive in this village – so you can feel free to look around and not be pressured into buying anything. This lack of entrepreneurship and materialism certainly places Chicken Village into sharp contrast with Saigon, or even Dalat. It's a very welcome change, and probably the best reason for a visit.

Western Highlands

The western region of the Central Highlands along the border with Cambodia and Laos was, until recently, off limits to foreigners. It's now been opened, although the authorities in some places (Pleiku is notable) demand that you purchase a travel permit to visit tribal villages.

Roads in this area are in poor condition, but generally passable. A high clearance vehicle such as a minibus is preferable to a passenger car. Of course, the flights to Buon Ma Thuot and Pleiku now make this part of Vietnam more accessible.

BUON MA THUOT

Buon Ma Thuot (or Ban Me Thuot; population 65,000; elevation 451 metres) is the capital of Dac Lac (Dak Lak) Province. A large percentage of the area's population is made up of ethnic minorities. The government's policy of assimilation has had its effect in that nearly all the minorities now speak Vietnamese quite fluently.

One of the region's main crops is coffee, which is grown on plantations run by German managers who are said to be as imperiously demanding as were their French predecessors. Before WW II, the city was a centre for big-game hunting.

The road between Buon Ma Thuot and Ninh Hoa (north of Nha Trang) is very scenic with charming minority villages along the

Jugular Vein

Buon Ma Thuot occupies a militarily strategic location in the Central Highlands. The area is like a natural fortress, and the coastal plain to the east is but a thin strip. From here, an army could launch an attack and push down to the coastline, cutting off Saigon from Danang. Saigon itself is only some 150 km from the southern parts of the Highlands. The strategic significance of this was not lost on American generals, who used to refer to Buon Ma Thuot as South Vietnam's 'jugular vein'. North Vietnamese generals held a similar opinion.

In March 1975, Buon Ma Thuot briefly achieved world fame when North Vietnamese troops (who had been infiltrating via Laos and Cambodia) attacked the city. Just as the Americans had feared, the Communists 'went for the jugular'. In the weeks leading up to the attack, South Vietnamese military intelligence began to detect large numbers of men and equipment moving into the area. Just four days before the North Vietnamese assault came, former vice president and retired air force chief Nguyen Cao Ky warned the military high command that the enemy probably assembled two divisions (20,000 troops) to strike Buon Ma Thuot. In fact, the North Vietnamese had moved three divisions (30,000 troops, with tanks and artillery) into place almost undetected, a brilliant military achievement. Nonetheless, Ky's advice to reinforce Buon Ma Thuot was not heeded, perhaps because he was a political rival to President Nguyen Van Thieu.

This proved to be the final battle of the war. Communist forces hit Buon Ma Thuot on 10 March and quickly overwhelmed the 2000 or so ARVN defenders in the city. The North Vietnamese had expected a swift counterattack and fierce fight to the finish, but they could hardly believe what happened next. Rather than engage the enemy, President Thieu ordered a 'strategic withdrawal' from the Central Highlands. As the ARVN troops abandoned their positions without a fight, the North Vietnamese pursued them along Highway 7 to Tuy Hoa, inflicting heavy casualties. The whole withdrawal quickly turned into a rout. By 19 March, the Central Highlands were completely under the control of Communist forces. Broadcasts of the disaster on Vietnamese radio and the Voice of America undermined morale and caused many ARVN troops to desert. NVA troops from the north rushed across the DMZ and attacked Hué and Danang, but demoralised ARVN troops put up no significant resistance and instead fled onto ships and aircraft in a desperate attempt to reach Saigon. Danang fell on 29 March and Nha Trang was captured on 4 April. The South Vietnamese military organisation collapsed as high-ranking officials and military officers fled abroad. Some pockets of ARVN forces put up a fierce fight around Saigon (most notably, the 18th ARVN division at Xuan Loc), but by then it was too late.

The ARVN commander with responsibility for defending the Central Highlands, General Pham Van Phu, was arrested in early April on President Thieu's orders. Phu committed suicide on 30 April, the day Saigon fell.

When the North Vietnamese launched their offensive in Buon Ma Thuot, they had expected to fight for at least two years before taking Saigon. Instead, the war came to a conclusion in less than two months. ∎

way. However, the results of Agent Orange spraying and overlogging are conspicuous – you'll see plenty of deforested spots and logging trucks hauling away what is left. Landslides are common, probably due to the deforestation. Bamboo is being planted in this area because it grows fast and holds the soil together, but it makes a poor substitute for the old growth forest which is being lost.

The rainy season around Buon Ma Thuot lasts from April to November, though downpours are usually of short duration. Because of its lower elevation, Buon Ma Thuot is warmer and more humid than Dalat.

Information

Tourist Office Dac Lac Tourist (☎ 52322, 52324) – the provincial tourism authority – is at 3 Phan Chu Trinh St. Be prepared to pay high prices for guides who may speak only Vietnamese and lose their way while 'guiding' you.

Travel Permits Permits are still required to visit minority villages in the surrounding area, including Nam Cat Tien National Park. See Dac Lac Tourist to get these valuable bits of paper. You do *not* need a travel permit for Buon Ma Thuot itself, nor do you need one

PLACES TO STAY
1 Dac Lac Trade Union Hotel
9 People's Committee Guest House
10 Hong Kong Hotel
11 Thang Loi Hotel & Tourist Office
14 Bao Dai Villas
15 Hotel Tay Nguyen
16 Hoang Gia Hotel

PLACES TO EAT
3 Restaurants
7 Cafes
18 Foodstalls

OTHER
2 Bus Station
4 Church
5 Tank Monument
6 Hill Tribe Museum
8 Cultural Centre (minority dances)
12 GPO
13 Stadium (elephant races)
17 Cinema
19 Market

To Pleiku (197 km)
To Nha Trang (191 km)
Dinh Tien Hoang Street
Distance foreshortened (approx 2 km)
Hung Vuong Street
Phan Chu Trinh Street
Doc Lap Street
Hai Ba Trung Street
Nguyen Du Street
Phan Boi Chau Street
Ly Thuong Kiet Street
Ama Trang Long Street
Quang Trung Street
Le Hong Phong Street
To Ban Don (45 km)

Buon Ma Thuot

0   100   200 m
Approximate Scale

for travel along major highways such as the roads to Saigon, Pleiku or Nha Trang.

Hill Tribe Museum

There are said to be 31 distinct ethnic groups in Dac Lac Province, and the museum is a good place to get some understanding of these disparate groups. Displays at the museum feature traditional Montagnard dress as well as agricultural implements, fishing gear, bows and arrows, weaving looms and musical instruments. The museum has a large photo collection with explanations about the historical contacts

between the minorities and the majority Vietnamese. Some of the history is true, other is pure fiction.

The Hill Tribe Museum is near the Thang Loi Hotel at 1 Me Mai St.

Tank Monument

You can hardly miss this place, as it dominates the central square of town. The tank monument commemorates the events of 10 March 1975, when Viet Cong and North Vietnamese troops 'liberated' the city. It was this battle that triggered the complete collapse of South Vietnam.

CENTRAL HIGHLANDS

Places to Stay

The nicest hotel is three km north of the centre but within walking distance of the bus station. In fact, you should definitely stay here if you arrive by bus late in the evening, because only this hotel has a night porter. The *Dac Lac Trade Union Hotel* (Nha Nghi Cong Doan Dac Lac; ☎ 52415) has a nice garden and is a quiet place with friendly staff. The complex is pavilion-style, with a simple restaurant near the entrance. From the centre, you can catch a motorbike to the hotel for around US$0.30. Rooms with fan and hot water cost US$12 to US$15. An air-conditioned room for four persons costs US$20.

Buon Ma Thuot's main tourist hotel is the *Thang Loi Hotel* (☎ 52322), 3 Phan Chu Trinh St, facing the Tank Monument in the centre of town. Rooms here cost US$24 to US$30.

Room rates and standards are good at the *People's Committee Guest House* (Nha Khach Uy Ban Nhan Dan Tinh; ☎ 52407) at 9 Hai Ba Trung St. The price range here is US$10 to US$20.

Travellers also give reasonably good ratings to the *Bao Dai Villas* (Nha Khach Biet Dien Bao Dai; ☎ 52177). Rooms with air-conditioning cost US$25.

The *Hoang Gia Hotel* (☎ 52161), 60 Le Hong Phong St, has rooms for US$12.

The *Hong Kong Hotel* (☎ 52630) is at 30 Hai Ba Trung St. Rooms come equipped with fan and cost US$8.

Hotel Tay Nguyen (☎ 52250) at 106 Ly Thuong Kiet St costs US$25 to US$35.

Places to Eat

Café Diep at 82 Dinh Tien Hoang St is distinguished less by its food than by its pleasant surroundings. The cafe has a garden of sorts decked out with statues. Local students gather here and many can speak English. The students can often give you some insights into hill-tribe culture.

Buon Ma Thuot is justifiably famous for its coffee, the best in Vietnam. However, it's strong stuff so don't drink it before bedtime or you'll be awake all night. You can sample the coffee at any restaurant or cafe in town.

If you like it enough to take home, be sure to pick up a bag at a local grocery store because the price is many times higher in Saigon or Hanoi.

Getting There & Away

Air Vietnam Airlines flies between Buon Ma Thuot and Ho Chi Minh City twice daily. There are direct Danang-Buon Ma Thuot flights daily except Monday. There are Hanoi-Buon Ma Thuot flights (via Danang) three times weekly.

Bus There is bus service to Buon Ma Thuot from Danang and Saigon. The Saigon-Buon Ma Thuot buses take 20 hours, so an 8.30 am departure gets you to your destination at 4.30 am. Departures are from Saigon's Mien Dong Bus Station.

Car The road linking the coast with Buon Ma Thuot intersects National Highway 1 at Ninh Hoa, which is 34 km north of Nha Trang.

Part of the road is unsurfaced, but still passable by ordinary cars. Land distances from Buon Ma Thuot are as follows:

Dalat	396 km
Danang	666 km
Ho Chi Minh City	352 km
Kon Tum	246 km
Nha Trang	191 km
Ninh Hoa	160 km
Phan Rang	295 km
Pleiku	197 km
Qui Nhon	223 km

AROUND BUON MA THUOT

Drai Sap Falls

Drai Sap Falls, about 12 km from Buon Ma Thuot, is in the middle of a hardwood rainforest.

Elephant Training Centre

Just outside of Buon Ma Thuot is the Elephant Training Centre, which sells and leases trained elephants for tourism and working purposes to the rest of the country. The facilities are interesting to visit, but foreigners are charged an unreasonable US$50 for a four-hour elephant ride through some beautiful

Traditional hill-tribe dwelling in the Western Highlands

forests. You must book these trips through the government-run tourist office in Buon Ma Thuot.

Tua

The Rhade (or Ede) hamlet of Tua is 13 km from Buon Ma Thuot. The people here make a living raising animals and growing manioc, sweet potatoes and maize. This village has become one of the most heavily Vietnamised, but it has earned a higher standard of living along with the loss of cultural identity.

Rhade society is matrilineal and matrilocal (centred on the household of the wife's family). Extended families live in longhouses, each section of which houses a nuclear family. Each long-house is presided over by a man, often the husband of the senior woman of the family. The property of the extended family is owned and controlled by the oldest woman in the group.

The religion of the Rhade is animistic. In the past century many Rhade have been converted to Catholicism and Protestantism.

Ban Don

The residents of Ban Don village in Ea Sup District, which is 55 km north-west of Buon Ma Thuot, are mostly M'nong, a matrilineal tribe in which the family name is passed down through the female line and children are considered members of their mother's family. Despite feminist theories to the contrary, the M'nong are known for their fiercely belligerent attitude towards other tribes in the area, as well as towards ethnic-Vietnamese. The M'nong hunt wild elephants using domesticated elephants, dozens of which live in Ban Don.

There is a 13th-century Cham tower 36 km north of Ban Don at Ya Liao.

Dac Lac Lake

Dac Lac Lake (Ho Dac Lac) is about 50 km south of Buon Ma Thuot. Emperor Bao Dai built a small palace here, but it is now a ruin. Nevertheless, the views over the lake are fantastic and well worth the climb up adjacent hills. The nearby M'nong village is very authentic and a unique experience not to be missed.

PLEIKU

Pleiku (or Playcu; elevation 785 metres) is a market town in the centre of a vast, fertile plateau whose red soil is of volcanic origin. Many of the 35,000 inhabitants of the city are members of ethnic minorities. Pleiku is 785 metres above sea level, which makes the climate cool, but not as cold as Dalat.

In February 1965, the VC shelled a US compound in Pleiku killing eight Americans. Although the USA already had over 23,000 military advisers in Vietnam, their role was supposed to be noncombatant at that time. The attack on Pleiku was used as a justification by then President Johnson to begin a relentless bombing campaign against North

Vietnam and the rapid build-up of American troops.

During the war, Pleiku had the largest military base in the Central Highlands. When American troops departed in 1973, the South Vietnamese continued to keep Pleiku as their main combat base in the area. This may have been a mistake as it concentrated their resources far away from more strategic areas farther south. Because Pleiku was so heavily fortified, the Communists chose to strike against Buon Ma Thuot and quickly occupied a large part of the Central Highlands. When President Thieu ordered his troops at Pleiku to withdraw, the whole civilian population of Pleiku and nearby Kon Tum fled with them. The stampede to the coastline involved over 100,000 people, but tens of thousands died along the way due to VC attacks and lack of simple necessities such as food and drinking water. Many of the civilians – travelling on foot and bicycle – were also run over by tanks and military trucks during the panicked withdrawal.

The departing soldiers torched Pleiku in an effort to destroy anything that could be of use to the Communists. The city was rebuilt in the 1980s with assistance from the Soviet Union. As a result, the city has a large collection of ugly Russian-style buildings and lacks much of the colour and quaintness you find in other Vietnamese towns. Hopefully, the recent inflow of tourist dollars will bring some badly needed improvements to the architecture as well as the local economy, but for now Pleiku is a pretty monotonous town.

The Zarai minority live in the Pleiku area and have an unusual burial custom. Each deceased gets a portrait carved from wood and for years relatives bring them food. The grave is set up as a miniature village with several people buried in one graveyard. Then after seven years, the grave is abandoned.

Information

Tourist Office Gia Lai Tourism Company (☎ 24891) is inside the Pleiku Hotel. There are some very good guides working for this company, though it's not certain they are worth the high prices you must pay for them (90% of which goes to the government).

Travel Permit While you do not need a permit to stay overnight in Pleiku itself or to travel the major highways, you do need one to visit hill-tribe villages in Gia Lai Province. The permits will cost you money (the exact amount depending on where you want to go) and you may be forced to hire a guide, car and driver in Pleiku even though you may already have your own vehicle. You can figure on all this costing something like US$50 per day, but at least you get much better guides than are available in Buon Ma Thuot. However, the high prices put off many travellers who usually just skip Pleiku entirely and head for Kon Tum, where the authorities are more hospitable.

If you want a travel permit, you need to visit the Gia Lai Tourism Company. Do *not* go to the police station – travellers who have done so have received a rather nasty reception.

Yaly Falls

Sadly, this place is probably no longer worth visiting. Yaly Falls was once the largest waterfall in the Central Highlands and a hot destination for tourists. However, a new hydro-electric scheme has sucked in most of the water and there is only a trickle left. During a heavy rain it might still look impressive, but otherwise all you are going to see is a damp cliff in the forest.

Places to Stay

The place most successful at attracting the backpacker set is *Hotel 86* (☎ 24674) at 86 Nguyen Van Troi St. Rooms here cost a mere US$6.

Also good is the *Thuan Hai Hotel* at the corner of Dinh Tien Hoang and Tran Phu Sts. Doubles with fan are US$12.

The *Movie Star Hotel* (Khach San Dien Anh; ☎ 23855), 6 Vo Thi Sau St, is Pleiku's newest accommodation. It's been a big hit with travellers who don't mind spending a little extra for their comforts. All rooms have air-conditioning, though why you would need it in Pleiku's cool climate is a mystery.

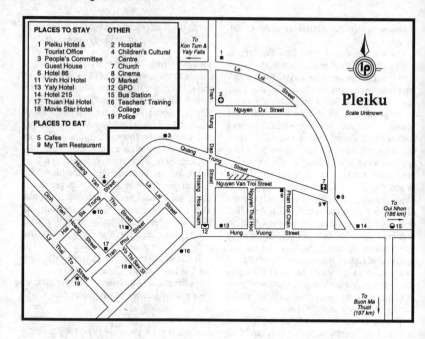

PLACES TO STAY
1 Pleiku Hotel &
  Tourist Office
3 People's Committee
  Guest House
6 Hotel 86
11 Vinh Hoi Hotel
13 Yaly Hotel
14 Hotel 215
17 Thuan Hai Hotel
18 Movie Star Hotel

PLACES TO EAT
5 Cafes
9 My Tam Restaurant

OTHER
2 Hospital
4 Children's Cultural
  Centre
7 Church
8 Cinema
10 Market
12 GPO
15 Bus Station
16 Teachers' Training
  College
19 Police

Pleiku
Scale Unknown

To Kon Tum &
Yaly Falls

To Qui Nhon
(186 km)

To Buon Ma
Thuot
(197 km)

Rooms come in three standards costing US$20, US$25 and US$30.

Also somewhat upmarket is the *Yaly Hotel* (☎ 24843), 89 Hung Vuong St. Rooms with fan cost US$15. With air-con, the range is US$20 to US$35.

The *Vinh Hoi Hotel* on Tran Phu St is dirty and the staff seemed unsure just how much to charge foreigners. Perhaps this place will see some renovation and improvement in management – keep your eye on this one.

Also somewhat disorganised is *Hotel 215* at 215 Hung Vuong St. But this one has the advantage (or perhaps disadvantage) of being near the bus station.

Most awful in town is the *Pleiku Hotel* (☎ 24628). It's a terrible place and overpriced, and (surprise!) is the headquarters of the government-run Gia Lai Tourism Company. Rooms here with fan/air-con cost US$18/25 and are definitely not worth it. You might want to take a look, though, to admire the Stalinist architecture.

There is also a *People's Committee Guest House* on Quang Trung St, which at the moment is not receiving foreigners, though it might in the future.

Places to Eat
The *My Tam Restaurant* on the corner of Le Loi and Quang Trung Sts is very cheap and dishes up tasty food – definitely recommended!

Another good option is the string of cheap cafes along Nguyen Van Troi St just across from Hotel 86.

Getting There & Away
Air Vietnam Airlines has flights connecting Pleiku to Ho Chi Minh City once daily. Flights to/from Hanoi have been temporarily suspended, but may be resumed. Flights to/from Danang run four times weekly.

Bus There is nonexpress bus service to Pleiku from most coastal cities between Nha Tranh and Danang.

Car Pleiku is linked by road to Buon Ma Thuot, Qui Nhon (via An Khe), Kon Tum and Cambodia's Ratanakiri Province (via Chu Nghe). There is a stretch of particularly barren land on the road from Buon Ma Thuot, probably the result of Agent Orange use and overlogging.

Road distances from Pleiku are 49 km to Kon Tum, 197 km to Buon Ma Thuot, 550 km to Ho Chi Minh City, 424 km to Nha Trang and 186 km to Qui Nhon.

KON TUM

Kon Tum (population 35,000; altitude 525 metres) is in a region inhabited primarily by ethnic minority groups, including the Bahnar, Jarai, Rengao and Sedeng.

Many travellers consider Kon Tum to be the garden spot of the Central Highlands. Some may argue that Dalat offers more to see, but Dalat is touristy. So far, Kon Tum remains largely unspoiled.

Like elsewhere in the Central Highlands, Kon Tum saw its share of combat during the war. A major battle between South Vietnamese forces and the North Vietnamese took place in and around Kon Tum in the spring of 1972 – the area was devastated by hundreds of US B-52 raids.

Minority Villages

There are quite a few of these all around the edges of Kon Tum. Minority-watching seems to be a favourite sport of travellers looking for the exotic, but please remember to treat the locals with respect. Some travellers seem to think that the hill tribes run around in their costumes for the benefit of photographers – this, of course, is not the case. In general, the local tribes welcome tourists, but only if you are not too intrusive.

Some of the small villages (or perhaps we should say 'neighbourhoods') are on the periphery of Kon Tum and you can even walk to them from the centre. On the west side of town are two villages which are home to the Bahnar tribe. The villages are simply called Lang Bana in Vietnamese.

On the east side of Kon Tum is Kon Tum Village (Lang Kon Tum). This is, in fact, the original Kon Tum before it grew up to become a small Vietnamese city.

At the time of this writing, the Kon Tum police were allowing foreigners to visit tribal villages without the need for a permit. Let us hope that this enlightened attitude continues.

Rong House

This isn't much of a tourist attraction, though it might be if you're lucky enough to arrive on an auspicious day. The Rong House is an activity centre, adjacent to a wooden church built on stilts. The Rong House (and sometimes the church) is the scene of important local events like meetings, weddings, festivals, prayer sessions and so on. If you stumble upon one of these activities in progress, it could be interesting. Of course, remember that uninvited guests are not always welcome at weddings.

The Rong House is very close to Kon Tum Village.

Nguc Kon Tum

This is an abandoned prison compound on the west side of Kon Tum. The prisoners incarcerated here were Viet Cong, and all were freed in 1975 when the war ended.

This was one of the more famous prisons run by the South Vietnamese, and VC who survived their internment here were made into heroes after liberation. Having a politically correct background was (and still is) very important in post-war Vietnam – many of the high-ranking officers who are *now* in the military were former prisoners at Nguc Kon Tum. ARVN soldiers who were prisoners of the VC have not fared so well.

Nguc Kon Tum is currently open to the public and you can wander inside and have a look. Unfortunately, no effort is being made to preserve the place, nor are there any guides available to explain the historical significance of what you are looking at. Apparently the local tourism authorities have not quite grasped the economic potential of this would-be war museum.

Dak To & Charlie Hill

This obscure outpost, 42 km north of Kon

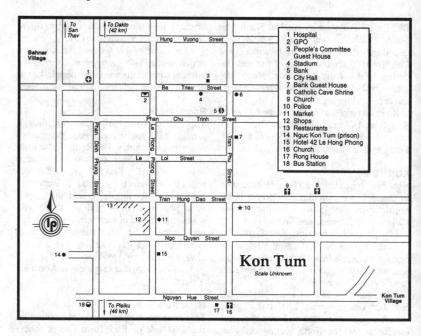

Map legend:
1 Hospital
2 GPO
3 People's Committee
   Guest House
4 Stadium
5 Bank
6 City Hall
7 Bank Guest House
8 Catholic Cave Shrine
9 Church
10 Police
11 Market
12 Shops
13 Restaurants
14 Nguc Kon Tum (prison)
15 Hotel 42 Le Hong Phong
16 Church
17 Rong House
18 Bus Station

Kon Tum
Scale Unknown

Tum, was a major battlefield during the Vietnam War. In 1972, the area was the scene of intense fighting, one of the last big battles before American troops pulled out and left the Vietnamese to fight their own war.

Dak To has become popular with visiting groups of American veterans, but you probably won't find much of interest if you're not a war buff. Perhaps more intriguingly, those few Viet Cong veterans with sufficient free time and money also like to come here to stir their memories.

About five km before reaching Dak To is Charlie Hill. At one time, the hill was a fortified ARVN stronghold before the VC tried to overrun it. The South Vietnamese officer in charge, Colonel Ngoc Minh, decided that he would neither surrender or retreat, and the battle became a fierce fight to the death. This was a prolonged battle. The VC laid siege to the hill for 1½ months before they managed to kill Colonel Minh and 150 ARVN troops who made their last stand here.

Although largely forgotten in the West, the battle is well known even now in Vietnam. The reason for this is largely because the fight was commemorated by a popular song 'The People Stayed in Charlie' (Nguoi O Lai Charlie).

Not surprisingly, the hill was heavily mined during the war and is still considered unsafe to climb.

Getting There & Away
Bus Buses connect Kon Tum to Danang, Pleiku and Buon Ma Thuot.

Car Land distances from Kon Tum are 49 km to Pleiku, 246 km to Buon Ma Thuot, 896 km to Ho Chi Minh City, 436 km to Nha Trang, 46 km to Pleiku and 198 km to Qui Nhon.

Places to Stay
Kon Tum lacks sufficient hotels to cope with the sudden demand of mass tourism, which is the main reason why many travellers

choose to stay in nearby Pleiku. However, this is expected to change.

Bottom-end accommodation in Kon Tum can be found at the *Hotel 42 Le Hong Phong* (☎ 62632). The hotel's uncreative name is the same as the address. Rooms here are US$6, and the toilet is outside and down the hall.

The *People's Committee Guest House* (Nha Khach Uy Ban Nhan Dan Tinh; ☎ 62249) on Ba Trieu St offers good and reasonably priced accommodation. Rooms cost US$20 and US$23.

The *Bank Guest House* (☎ 62610) is (no surprise) near the bank. The official address is 88 Tran Phu St. A room with three beds and air-conditioning costs US$20.

South-Central Coast

This section covers the littoral provinces of Binh Thuan, Ninh Thuan, Khanh Hoa, Phu Yen, Binh Dinh and Quang Ngai. The cities, towns, beaches and historical sites in this region, most of which are along National Highway 1, which many foreign tourists these days refer to as the 'Ho Chi Minh Trail' (the real one is farther inland), are listed from south to north.

Binh Thuan Province

PHAN THIET

Phan Thiet is best known for its nuoc mam (fish sauce) and fishing industry. The population includes descendants of the Chams, who controlled this area until 1692. During the colonial period, the Europeans lived in their own segregated ghetto, which stretched along the north bank of the Phan Thiet River, while the Vietnamese, Chams, Southern Chinese, Malays and Indonesians lived along the river's south bank.

Binh Thuan Province (at least north of Phan Thiet) is one of the most arid regions of Vietnam. The nearby plains, which are dominated by rocky, roundish mountains, support some marginal irrigated rice agriculture. The relative dryness seems to help support a large population of flies – Aussies should feel right at home.

Orientation

Phan Thiet is built along both banks of the Phan Thiet River, which is also known as the Ca Ti River and the Muong Man River. National Highway 1 runs right through town; south of the river it is known as Tran Hung Dao St while north of the river it is called Le Hong Phong St.

Information

Tourist Office The office of Binh Thuan Tourist (Cong Ty Du Lich Binh Thuan; ☎ 22494, 21394, 22894) is at 82 Trung Trac St (on the corner of Tran Hung Dao St), which is just south of the bridge over the Phan Thiet River.

Phan Thiet Beach

To get to Phan Thiet's beachfront, turn east (right if you're heading north) at Victory Monument, an arrow-shaped, concrete tower with victorious cement people at the base.

Fishing Harbour

The river flowing through the centre of town creates a small fishing harbour, which is always chock-a-block with boats. It makes for charming photography.

Mui Ne Beach

Mui Ne Beach, famous for its enormous sand dunes, is 22 km east of Phan Thiet near a fishing village at the tip of Mui Ne Peninsula. There are plans to build a hotel here. Between 8.30 am and 4 pm, a local bus makes six daily round trips between Phan Thiet Bus Station and Mui Ne.

Golf Course

A project is under way to construct a four-star hotel and golf course near the beachfront at Phan Thiet. There is no word yet on when this will be open, or on how much it will cost to play golf here. It is possible that tennis courts will be built too.

Cham Music

Performances of Cham music are sometimes held at the Vinh Thuy Hotel, which is at Phan Thiet Beach.

Places to Stay

Binh Thuan Tourist's *Phan Thiet Hotel* (☎ 2573) is at 40 Tran Hung Dao St, right in the centre of town. Double rooms with air-con and attached bath are US$15 and US$18. A triple costs US$21. The management tries to push foreigners into the more expensive rooms.

The *Vinh Thuy Hotel* (☎ 21294, 22394), built between 1985 and 1989, is along the seashore on Ton Tuc Thang St. The hotel has 66 rooms but a new wing is being added. Doubles with air-conditioning cost US$27 to US$34. To get to the Vinh Thuy Hotel, turn towards the sea (eastward) at the Victory Monument. It's an isolated place – there are no other restaurants in the area besides the one in the hotel.

The *Khach San 19-4* (☎ 2460), which is across the street from Phan Thiet Bus Station, is at 1 Tu Van Tu St (just past 217 Le Hong Phong St). It's a large place with its own restaurant and looks much like an American-style motel. The hotel overlooks a vista of salt-evaporation pools. The management is not receptive to allowing foreigners because they insist the hotel 'is not high-class enough', though it really doesn't look bad. If you insist, they will allow you to stay for US$12.

Places to Eat
There is a restaurant on the 3rd floor of the *Phan Thiet Hotel* and another at the *Vinh Thuy Hotel*. The *Khach San 19-4* also has an attached restaurant.

Getting There & Away
Bus Buses from Ho Chi Minh City to Phan Thiet depart from Mien Dong Bus Station.

Phan Thiet Bus Station (Ben Xe Binh Thuan; ☎ 2590) is on the northern outskirts of town at Tu Van Tu St, which is just past 217 Le Hong Phong St (National Highway 1). The station is open from 5.30 am to 3.30 pm; tickets should be purchased the day before departure. There are nonexpress buses from here to Bien Hoa, Ho Chi Minh City, Long Khanh, Madagoui, Mui Ne Beach, Phan Rang and Phu Cuong, as well as to other destinations within Binh Thuan Province.

Train The nearest train station to Phan Thiet is 12 km west of the town at Muong Man. The Reunification Express Train between

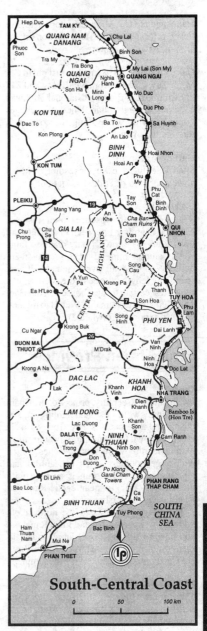

South-Central Coast

0   50   100 km

Hanoi and Ho Chi Minh City stops here. For ticket prices, see the Train section in the Getting Around chapter.

Car Phan Thiet is 198 km due east of Ho Chi Minh City, 250 km from Nha Trang and 247 km from Dalat. Because National Highway 1 passes through Phan Thiet, all vehicles going north or south along the coast pass through the town.

Getting Around
Phan Thiet has a few cyclos, some of which always seem to be at the bus station.

VINH HAO
Vinh Hao is an obscure town just off National Highway 1 between Phan Thiet and Phan Rang. The town's only claim to fame is its famous mineral waters, which are bottled and sold all over Vietnam. If you spend any length of time in the country, you are almost certain to sip a bottle of Vinh Hao. The Vietnamese claim that Vinh Hao mineral water is exported (to where?).

Ninh Thuan Province

CA NA
During the 16th century, princes of the Cham royal family would fish and hunt tigers, elephants and rhinoceroses here. Today, Ca Na is better known for its turquoise waters, lined with splendid white-sand beaches dotted with huge boulders – it's a beautiful and relaxing spot. The terrain is studded with magnificent prickly pear cacti. Rau Cau Island is visible offshore.

Tra Cang Temple is to the north about midway between Ca Na and Phan Rang, but you have to sidetrack over an abysmal dirt road to reach it. Many ethnic Chinese from Ho Chi Minh City like to visit the temple.

Places to Stay
There are two hotels in town, the *Khach San Hai Son* and *Khach San Ca Na*. Both hotels are about the same standard, charging US$10

for a large double room with electric fan and a terrace overlooking the sea. Electricity goes off at 10 pm and there are frequent power failures, so keep your torch (flashlight) handy.

Places to Eat
Both hotels have decent restaurants. Between the two hotels is the *Ca Na Restaurant*, which also has a good shop selling biscuits, film, toothpaste and other necessities.

Getting There & Away
Bus Many long-haul buses cruising National Highway 1 stop here for a break.

Car Ca Na is 114 km north of Phan Thiet and 32 km south of Phan Rang.

PHAN RANG & THAP CHAM
The twin cities of Phan Rang and Thap Cham, famous for their production of table grapes, are in a region with a semi-arid climate. The sandy soil supports scrubby vegetation; local flora includes poinciana trees and prickly pear cacti with vicious thorns. Many of the houses on the outskirts of town are decorated with Greek-style grape trellises. The area's best known sight is the group of Cham towers known as Po Klong Garai, from which Thap Cham (Cham Tower) derives its name. You can see Cham towers dotted about the countryside 20 km north of Phan Rang.

Ninh Thuan Province is home to tens of thousands of descendants of the Cham people, many of whom live in and around Phan Rang-Thap Cham.

Orientation
National Highway 1 is called Thong Nhat St as it runs through Phan Rang. Thong Nhat St is Phan Rang's main commercial street. Thap Cham, about seven km from Phan Rang, is strung out along National Highway 20, which heads west from Phan Rang towards Ninh Son and Dalat.

Information
Tourist Office The office of Ninh Thuan

Tourist (Cong Ty Du Lich Ninh Thuan; ☎ 22542) is in the Huu Nghi Hotel on Thong Nhat St in Phan Rang.

Po Klong Garai Cham Towers

Phan Rang-Thap Cham's most famous landmark is Po Klong Garai, four brick towers constructed at the end of the 13th century during the reign of the Cham monarch Jaya Simhavarman III. The towers, built as Hindu temples, stand on a brick platform at the top of Cho'k Hala, a crumbly granite hill covered with some of the most ornery cacti this side of the Rio Grande.

Over the entrance to the largest tower (the *kalan*, or sanctuary) is a carving of a dancing Shiva with six arms. Note the inscriptions on the doorposts. Inside the vestibule is a statue of the bull Nandin, symbol of the agricultural productivity of the countryside. To ensure a good crop, farmers would place an offering of fresh greens in front of Nandin's muzzle. Under the main tower is a *mukha-linga*, a

linga (a stylised phallus which symbolises maleness and creative power and which represents the Hindu god Shiva) with a painted human face on it. A wooden pyramid has been constructed above the mukha-linga.

Inside the tower opposite the entrance to the kalan you can get a good look at some of the Cham's sophisticated masonry technology. The structure attached to it was originally the main entrance to the complex.

On a nearby hill is a rock with an inscription from the year 1050 commemorating the erection of a linga by a Cham prince.

On the hill directly south of Cho'k Hala there is a concrete water tank built by the Americans in 1965. It is encircled by French pillboxes, which were built during the Franco-Viet Minh War to protect the nearby rail yards. To the north of Cho'k Hala you can see the concrete revetments of Thanh Son Airbase, used since 1975 by the Soviet-built MiGs of the Vietnamese Air Force.

Po Klong Garai is several hundred metres

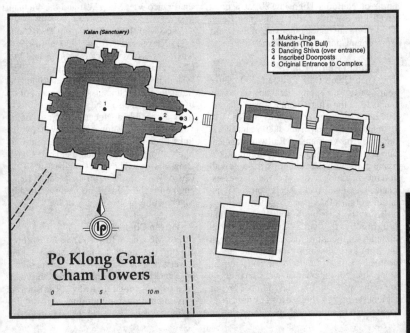

Kalan (Sanctuary)

1 Mukha-Linga
2 Nandin (The Bull)
3 Dancing Shiva (over entrance)
4 Inscribed Doorposts
5 Original Entrance to Complex

Po Klong Garai Cham Towers

0   5   10 m

Po Klong Garai Cham Towers, Phan Rang-Thap Cham

north of National Highway 20, at a point seven km towards Dalat from Phan Rang. The towers are on the other side of the tracks from Thap Cham Railway Station.

Thap Cham Rail Yards

The Thap Cham Rail Yards are 300 metres south-east of Po Klong Garai and across the tracks from the Thap Cham Railway Station. The main function of the yards, which were founded by the French about 80 years ago, is the repair of Vietnamese Railways' ancient one-metre-gauge engines and rolling stock. Spare parts are made either by hand or with antique machine tools and metal presses. Each pair of railroad wheels you see lying about weighs 500 kg.

It may be possible to tour the yards, but judging by the small armoury (which includes a 50-calibre machine gun!) kept at the front gate, it seems clear that the area is deemed to have a certain strategic importance. Indeed, the Vietnamese Communists are well aware of how vital railroads are for national security – that's why they used to go to so much trouble to sabotage them during the Franco-Viet Minh War and the Vietnam War.

The 86-km-long railway from Thap Cham to Dalat operated from 1930 until 1964, when it was closed because of repeated Viet Cong attacks. The line used a crémaillère system in which chains were used to pull the trains up the mountainside at a grade of up to 12 cm per metre. The steepest sections of track are visible at Ngoan Muc Pass (Bellevue Pass) from National Highway 20 (which links Phan Rang with Dalat). There are no plans at present to reopen the Thap Cham–Dalat Railway. The oldest engine at the Thap Cham Rail Yards is an inoperable steam engine for the crémaillère manufactured by Machinenfabrik Esselingen in 1929.

Po Ro Me Cham Tower

Po Ro Me Cham Tower (Thap Po Ro Me), among the newest of Vietnam's Cham towers, is about 15 km south of Phan Rang on a rocky hill five km towards the mountains from National Highway 1. The ruins are very interesting, but unfortunately very difficult to reach. The 'road' is a dirt track that can only be negotiated by motorbike or on foot.

The road to take is between Km 1566 and 1567 from National Highway 1. We did cross small Cham hamlets, which were nice to go through. Following the image of a small distant tower, we took a road that became a path, and then less than that. Even the motorcycle almost did not make it. And after about two km of the hill, that was it – not even a tiny path to follow. Our poor old bike could not survive the rocks and cactus and died (again!). We finally walked up the hill (great snakes!). That was magic. The feeling of being completely alone on that small hill, with only the distant sound of bells around a cow's neck and nobody around for many kilometres (amazing after weeks in Saigon) was indescribable. At the bottom of the tower are long stairs. The single tower was closed, but still worth the hill climb to get there. It is decorated with beautiful stone statues and there are two Nandin statues just before the entrance. Thank you for at least mentioning its existence, even if we were probably the only foreigners to reach it this year.

Genevieve Mayers

The kalan, which is decorated with paintings, has two inscribed doorposts, two stone statues of the bull Nandin, a bas-relief representing a deified king in the form of Shiva and two statues of queens, one of whom has an inscription on her chest. The towers are named after the last ruler of an independent Champa, King Po Ro Me (ruled 1629-51), who died a prisoner of the Vietnamese.

Tuan Tu Hamlet

There is a minaretless Cham mosque, which is closed to visitors, in the Cham hamlet of Tuan Tu (population 1000). This Muslim community is governed by elected religious leaders *(Thay Mun)*, who can easily be identified by their traditional costume, which includes a white robe and an elaborate white turban with red tassels. In keeping with Islamic precepts governing modesty, Cham women often wear head coverings and skirts. The Chams, like other ethnic minorities in Vietnam, suffer from discrimination and are even poorer than their ethnic-Vietnamese neighbours.

To get to Tuan Tu Hamlet, head south from town along National Highway 1. Go 250 metres

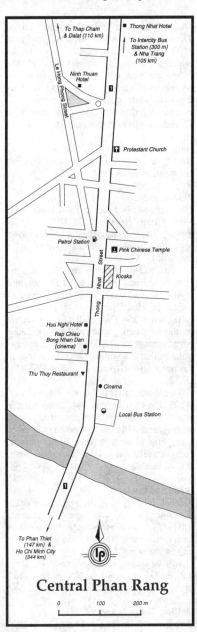

Central Phan Rang

0   100   200 m

south of the large bridge to a small bridge. Cross it and turn left (to the south-east) onto a dirt track. At the market (just past the Buddhist pagoda on the right), turn right and follow the road, part of which is lined with hedgerows of cacti, for about two km, crossing two white concrete footbridges. Ask villagers for directions along the way. Tuan Tu is three km from National Highway 1.

Ninh Chu Beach
Ninh Chu Beach (Bai Tam Ninh Chu) is five km south of Phan Rang.

Places to Stay
The main tourist hotel in Phan Rang is the *Ninh Thuan Hotel* (☎ 27100, 22142; 24 rooms). The hotel is on the north side of town opposite a small park. Rooms here are in the range of US$15 to US$35.

Also catering to the foreign market is the *Huu Nghi Hotel* (☎ 22606; 21 rooms), also known as the Phan Rang Hotel and also called the Hoa Binh Hotel. Whatever you call it, it's at 354 Thong Nhat St, 150 metres south of the pink pagoda in the market area. An advantage this place has over its competition is that it's within walking distance of the bus station. Rooms here cost US$10 to US$20.

The four-storey *Thong Nhat Hotel* (☎ 22515; 16 rooms) at 164 Thong Nhat St was under renovation at the time of this writing, and will no doubt raise prices when it reopens. In the past you could get a room here for as little as US$10, but expect that to at least double.

Places to Eat
A local delicacy is roasted or baked gecko (ky nhong) served with fresh green mango.

The *Thu Thuy Restaurant* is a three-storey eatery on Thong Nhat St. *Nha Hang 426* is across the street from the bus station. *Nha Hang 404* is at 404 Thong Nhat St. For soup, try *Pho 129* at 231 Thong Nhat St (just south of the Protestant church).

Getting There & Away
Bus Buses from Ho Chi Minh City to Phan

Rang-Thap Cham depart from Mien Dong Bus Station.

Phan Rang Intercity Bus Station (Ben Xe Phan Rang) is on the northern outskirts of town opposite 64 Thong Nhat St. There is bus service from here to Ca Na Beach, Cam Ranh Bay, Dalat, Danang, Don Duong, Ho Chi Minh City, Long Huong, Nha Trang, Nhi Ha, Noi Huyen, Phan Ri, Phan Thiet, Son Hai, Song Dan and Song My.

The local bus station (Ben Xe) is at the southern end of town across the street from 426 Thong Nhat St.

Train The Thap Cham Railway Station is about six km west of National Highway 1 within sight of Po Klong Garai Cham Towers.

Car Phan Rang is 344 km from Ho Chi Minh City, 147 km from Phan Thiet, 105 km from Nha Trang and 110 km from Dalat.

Khanh Hoa Province

CAM RANH BAY
Cam Ranh Bay is an excellent natural harbour 56 km north of Phan Rang-Thap Cham. The Russian fleet of Admiral Rodjestvenski used it in 1905 at the end of the Russo-Japanese War, as did the Japanese during WW II, when the area was still considered an excellent place for tiger hunting. In the mid-1960s, the Americans constructed a vast base here, including an extensive port, ship-repair facilities and an airstrip.

After reunification, the Russians and their fleet came back, enjoying far better facilities than they had found seven decades before. For a while this became the largest Soviet naval installation outside the USSR.

Despite repeated requests from the Russians, the Vietnamese refused to grant them permanent rights to the base. In 1988, Mikhail Gorbachev offered to abandon the installation if the Americans would do the same with their six bases across the South China Sea in the Philippines. The following

GLENN BEANLAND

ROBERT STOREY

DEANNA SWANEY

ROBERT STOREY

Central Highlands

A Women washing vegetables, Dalat
B The spectacular Dambri Falls, near Bao Loc
C An early morning view over Dalat
D Floating houses on Langa Lake

ROBERT STOREY

BRENDAN McCARTHY

BRENDAN McCARTHY

SIMON ROWE

GLENN BEANLAND

A
B	C
D	E

South-Central Coast

A Hon Chong Beach, Nha Trang
B Local barber, Nha Trang
C Detail of a fishing boat, Nha Trang
D A fish market in full swing, Nha Trang
E The fishing fleet at Phan Thiet

year, however, the Vietnamese, evidently annoyed with the Soviets, appeared to offer the Americans renewed use of Cam Ranh Bay. The Soviet presence at Cam Ranh Bay was significantly reduced in 1990 as part of the Kremlin's cost-cutting measures. The Cold War ended with the collapse of the Soviet Union in 1991. Furthermore, the USA did close its bases in the Philippines in 1991 (more accurately, the Filipino Senate unceremoniously told the Americans to leave).

Subsequent economic problems have forced the Russians to vastly cut back on their overseas military facilities. However, there are still about 200 to 300 Russians still based here, but only two or three ships at any given time.

Of course, just because the USA and former USSR no longer compete for turf does not mean that there is no need for a military base at Cam Ranh Bay. The Vietnamese are growing increasingly nervous about China's intentions. The Chinese have been rapidly and relentlessly building up their naval facilities in the South China Sea – in 1988 and again in 1992, China seized several islands claimed by Vietnam. In 1995, the Chinese navy seized some more islands claimed by the Philippines. The day may soon come when the Vietnamese will want the facilities at Cam Ranh Bay for their own military use.

The Russian government has informed the Vietnamese of a willingness to permanently withdraw from the bases whenever Vietnam repays its debts. The Vietnamese owe about 30 billion roubles to the former Soviet Union. The Russians are insisting that they should be repaid at the exchange rate in effect at the time of the loans, which was one rouble to one US dollar. The Vietnamese insist that they wish to repay the loan at the present exchange rate of about 4000 roubles to the dollar. The two sides remain far apart on the issue, but until it's revolved, Cam Ranh Bay remains the last hurrah for the Soviet navy in Asia.

There are beautiful beaches around Cam Ranh Bay – indeed, Americans stationed here during the war sometimes called it Vietnam's Hawaii. However, as long as this area remains a military base, it isn't likely to develop into a tourist resort. Some American military veterans have managed to tour the facilities at Cam Ranh Bay on organised tours arranged through government-owned travel agencies.

Places to Eat

There are some terrific seafood places along National Highway 1 right beside the '63 km to Nha Trang' and '41 km to Phan Rang' marker. One such place which has become fashionable with foreign travellers is the *Ngoc Suong Seafood Restaurant* (☎ 54603). This is a favourite lunch stop on the Dalat-Nha Trang run.

NHA TRANG

Nha Trang (population 200,000), the capital of Khanh Hoa Province, has what is probably the nicest municipal beach in all of Vietnam. Club Med hasn't arrived yet and there are still no Monte Carlo-style casinos and only a couple of neon signs. Nevertheless, this area has the potential to become another flashy resort like Thailand's Pattaya Beach (dread the thought), but that will probably take a few more years.

The turquoise waters around Nha Trang are almost transparent, making for excellent fishing, snorkelling and scuba diving. The service on the beach is incredible – massage, lunch, cold beer, manicure, beauty treatments, you name it. Of late, lots of 'massage' signs have been popping up around town, a sure sign that more visitors are expected.

Nha Trang's dry season, unlike that of Ho Chi Minh City, runs from June to September. The wettest months are October and November, but rain usually falls only at night or in the morning.

The combined fishing fleet of Khanh Hoa Province and neighbouring Phu Yen Province numbers about 10,000 trawlers and junks; they are able to fish during the 250 days of calm seas per year. The area's seafood products include abalone, lobster, prawns, cuttlefish, mackerel, pomfret, scallops, shrimps, snapper and tuna. Exportable

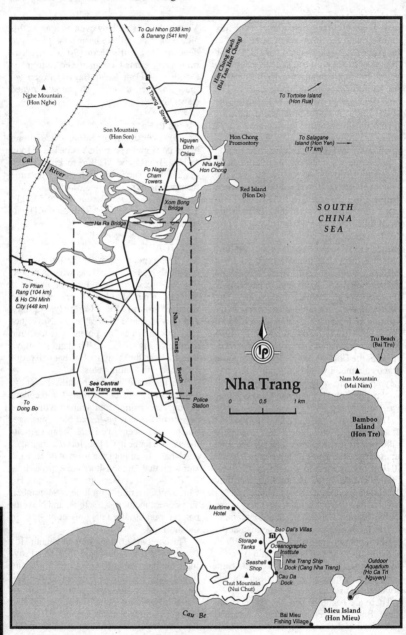

To Qui Nhon (238 km)
& Danang (541 km)

2 Thang 4 Street

Nghe Mountain
(Hon Nghe)

Hon Chong Beach
(Bai Tam Hon Chong)

To Tortoise Island
(Hon Rua)

Son Mountain
(Hon Son)

Nguyen
Dinh
Chieu

Hon Chong
Promontory

To Salagane
Island (Hon Yen)
(17 km)

Cai

River

Po Nagar
Cham
Towers

Nha Nghi
Hon Chong

Xom Bong
Bridge

Red Island
(Hon Do)

SOUTH
CHINA
SEA

Ha Ra Bridge

To Phan
Rang (104 km)
& Ho Chi Minh
City (448 km)

Nha Trang Beach

Tru Beach
(Bai Tru)

Nha Trang

Nam Mountain
(Mui Nam)

0   0.5   1 km

See Central
Nha Trang map

Police
Station

To
Dong Bo

Bamboo
Island
(Hon Tre)

Maritime
Hotel

Bao Dai's Villas

Oil
Storage
Tanks

Oceanographic
Institute

Seashell
Shop

Nha Trang Ship
Dock (Cang Nha Trang)

Outdoor
Aquarium
(Ho Ca Tri
Nguyen)

Cau Da
Dock

Chut Mountain
(Nui Chut)

Cau Be

Bai Mieu
Fishing Village

Mieu Island
(Hon Mieu)

SOUTH-CENTRAL COAST

agricultural products from the area include cashew nuts, coconuts, coffee and sesame seeds. Salt production employs 4000 people.

Orientation

Tran Phu Blvd runs along Nha Trang Beach. The centre of Nha Trang is around the Nha Trang Hotel on Thong Nhat St.

Information

Tourist Offices Khanh Hoa Tourist (Cong Ty Du Lich Khanh Hoa; ☎ 22753) is the provincial tourism authority. It can provide cars, drivers and guides and may also rent out diving and underwater fishing equipment. Their office is on the 2nd floor of a yellow two-storey building on the grounds of the Hai Yen Hotel. To get there, enter the Hai Yen Hotel through the front entrance (at 40 Tran Phu Blvd) and walk all the way through the main building. Alternatively, you can use the Hai Yen Hotel's back gate at 1 Tran Hung Dao St (next to the Hung Dao Hotel). The office is open from 7 to 11.30 am and 1.30 to 5 pm Monday to Saturday.

Nha Trang Tourism (☎ 21231), which runs various cafes and restaurants around town, has its office in the Hung Dao Hotel at 3 Tran Hung Dao St. This place also does pricey car rentals, but you can negotiate.

Money Vietcombank (Ngan Hang Ngoai Thuong; ☎ 22720) is at 17 Quang Trung St. It is open from 7 to 11.30 am and 1 to 5 pm Monday to Saturday except Thursday afternoons.

Post & Telecommunications The GPO is at 2 Tran Phu Blvd, near the northern end of Nha Trang Beach one block from the Thang Loi Hotel. It is open daily from 6.30 am to 8.30 pm. International telephone calls can be placed via Ho Chi Minh City or Hanoi. The GPO also offers fax services.

Emergency An American-built hospital, Bien Vien Tinh (☎ 22175), is on Yersin St.

Po Nagar Cham Towers

The Cham Towers of Po Nagar (The Lady of the City) were built between the 7th and 12th centuries on a site used for Hindu worship as early as the 2nd century AD. Today, both ethnic-Chinese and Vietnamese Buddhists come to Po Nagar to pray and make offerings according to their respective traditions. Out of deference to the continuing religious significance of this site, shoes should be removed before entering the towers.

There were once seven or eight towers at Po Nagar, four of which remain. All the temples face east, as did the original entrance to the complex, which is to the right as you ascend the hillock. In centuries past, a person coming to pray passed through the pillared *mandapa* (meditation hall), 10 of whose pillars can still be seen, before proceeding up the staircase to the towers.

The 23-metre-high North Tower (Thap Chinh), with its terraced pyramidal roof, vaulted interior masonry and vestibule, is a superb example of Cham architecture. It was built in 817 AD by Pangro, a minister of King Harivarman I, 43 years after the temples here

GLENN BEANLAND

Po Nagar Cham Towers, Nha Trang

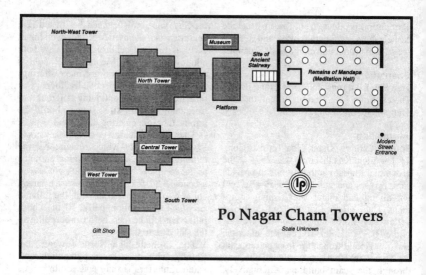

North-West Tower

Museum

Site of
Ancient
Stairway

Remains of Mandapa
(Meditation Hall)

North Tower

Platform

Modern
Street
Entrance

Central Tower

West Tower

South Tower

Po Nagar Cham Towers

Scale Unknown

Gift Shop

were sacked and burned by Malay corsairs, who probably came from Srivijaya on Sumatra. The raiders also carried off a linga made of precious metal. In 918 AD, King Indravarman III placed a gold mukha-linga in the North Tower, but it was taken by the Khmers. In 965 AD, King Jaya Indravarman I replaced the gold mukha-linga with the stone figure of Uma (a shakti of Shiva), which remains to this day.

Above the entrance to the North Tower, two musicians flank a dancing four-armed Shiva, one of whose feet is on the head of the bull Nandin. The sandstone doorposts are covered with inscriptions, as are parts of the walls of the vestibule. A gong and a drum stand under the pyramid-shaped ceiling of the antechamber. In the 28-metre-high pyramidal main chamber there is a black stone statue of the goddess Uma (in the shape of Bhagavati) with 10 arms, two of which are hidden under her vest; she is seated leaning back against some sort of monstrous animal.

The Central Tower (Thap Nam) was built partly of recycled bricks in the 12th century on the site of a structure dating from the 7th century. It is less finely constructed than the other towers and has little ornamentation; the pyramidal roof lacks terracing or pilasters. Note the inscription on the left-hand wall of the vestibule. The interior altars were once covered with silver. There is a linga inside the main chamber.

The South Tower (Mieu Dong Nam), at one time dedicated to Sandhaka (Shiva), now shelters a linga.

The richly ornamented North-West Tower (Thap Tay Bac) was originally dedicated to Ganesha. The pyramid-shaped summit of the roof of the North-West Tower has disappeared.

The West Tower, of which almost nothing remains, was constructed by King Vikrantavarman during the first half of the 9th century.

Near the North Tower is a small museum with a few mediocre examples of Cham stonework; the explanatory signs are in Vietnamese only. At one time there was a small temple on this site. If you are heading north, be sure to visit the Cham Museum in Danang, which has the finest collection of Cham statuary.

The towers of Po Nagar stand on a granite knoll two km north of Nha Trang on the left bank of the Cai River. To get there from Nha Trang, take Quang Trung St (which becomes 2 Thang 4 St) north across Ha Ra Bridge and Xom Bong Bridge, which span the mouth of the Cai River.

Hon Chong Promontory
Hon Chong is a narrow granite promontory that juts out into the turquoise waters of the South China Sea. The superb views of the mountainous coastline north of Nha Trang and nearby islands can be enjoyed while sipping something cool at one of the shaded refreshment kiosks on a bluff overlooking the promontory.

To the north-west is Nui Co Tien (Fairy Mountain), whose three summits are believed to resemble a reclining female fairy. The peak on the right is her face, which is gazing up towards the sky; the middle peak is her breasts; and the summit on the left (the highest) forms her crossed legs.

To the north-east is Hon Rua (Tortoise Island), which really does resemble a tortoise. The two islands of Hon Yen are off in the distance to the east. About 300 metres south of Hon Chong (that is, towards Nha Trang) and a few dozen metres from the beach is tiny Hon Do (Red Island), which has a Buddhist temple on top.

There is a gargantuan handprint on the massive boulder balanced at the tip of the promontory. According to local legend, it was made by a drunk male giant fairy when he fell down upon spying a female fairy bathing nude at Bai Tien (Fairy Beach), which is the point of land closest to Hon Rua. Despite the force of his fall, the giant managed to get up and eventually catch the fairy. The two began a life together but soon the gods intervened and punished the male fairy, sending him off to a 're-education camp' (this is evidently a post-1975 version of the story) for an indefinite sentence.

The love-sick female fairy waited patiently for her husband to come back, but after a very long time, despairing that he might never return, she lay down in sorrow and turned into Nui Co Tien (Fairy Mountain). When the giant male fairy finally

returned and saw what had become of his wife, he prostrated himself in grief next to the boulder with his handprint on it. He, too, turned to stone and can be seen to this day.

Hon Chong is 3.5 km from central Nha Trang. To get there from Po Nagar, head north on 2 Thang 4 St for 400 metres. Just before 15, 2 Thang 4 St, turn right onto Nguyen Dinh Chieu St and follow the road for about 700 metres. If you prefer to travel to Hon Chong by Xe Lam, catch one heading to Dong De at the Dam Market Xe Lam Station.

Beaches
Nha Trang Beach Coconut palms provide shelter for both bathers and strollers along most of Nha Trang's six km of beachfront. Beach chairs are available for rent – you can just sit all day and enjoy the drinks and light food which beach vendors have on offer. About the only time you need to move is to use the toilet or when the tide comes up. The water is remarkably clear.

Hon Chong Beach Hon Chong Beach (Bai Tam Hon Chong) is a series of beaches that begin just north of Hon Chong Promontory; fishing families live here among the coconut palms, but their refuse makes the place unsuitable for swimming or sunbathing. Behind the beaches are steep mountains whose lower reaches support crops that include mangoes and bananas.

Pasteur Institute
Nha Trang's Pasteur Institute was founded in 1895 by Dr Alexandre Yersin (1863-1943), who was – from among the tens of thousands of colonists who spent time in Vietnam – probably the Frenchman most beloved by the Vietnamese. Born in Switzerland of French and Swiss parents, Dr Yersin came to Vietnam in 1889 after working under Louis Pasteur in Paris. He spent the next four years travelling throughout the Central Highlands and recording his observations. During this period he came upon the site of what is now Dalat and recommended to the government that a hill station be established there. In

1894, in Hong Kong, he discovered the rat-borne microbe that causes bubonic plague. Dr Yersin was the first to introduce rubber and quinine-producing trees to Vietnam.

Today, the Pasteur Institute in Nha Trang coordinates vaccination and hygiene programmes for the country's southern coastal region. Despite its minuscule budget and antiquated equipment (the labs look much as they did half a century ago), the institute produces vaccines (eg, rabies, diphtheria, pertussis, typhoid) and tries to carry out research in microbiology, virology and epidemiology. Vietnam's two other Pasteur Institutes are in Ho Chi Minh City and Dalat.

Dr Yersin's library and office are now a museum; items on display include laboratory equipment (such as his astronomical instruments) and some of his personal effects. There is a picture of Dr Yersin above the door to the veranda. The model boat was given to him by local fishers with whom he spent a great deal of time. The Institute library, which is across the landing from the museum, houses many of Dr Yersin's books as well as modern scientific journals. At his request, Dr Yersin is buried near Nha Trang.

To find someone to show you the museum (Vien Bao Tang), ask around in the main building (a mauve-coloured two-storey structure) during working hours (except at lunchtime). The museum is on the 2nd floor of the back wing of the main building. To get there, go up the stairs near the sign that reads Thu Vien (Library).

Long Son Pagoda

Aside from the beach, the most impressive sight in Nha Trang is Long Son Pagoda (also known as Tinh Hoi Khanh Hoa Pagoda and An Nam Phat Hoc Hoi Pagoda). It's about 500 metres west of the railway station opposite 15, 23 Thang 10 St. The pagoda, which has resident monks, was founded in the late 19th century and has been rebuilt several times over the years. The entrance and roofs are decorated with mosaic dragons made of glass and bits of ceramic tile. The main sanctuary is an attractive hall adorned with modern interpretations of traditional motifs.

Note the ferocious nose hairs on the colourful dragons which are wrapped around the pillars on either side of the main altar.

At the top of the hill behind the pagoda is the huge white Buddha, seated on a lotus blossom, which is visible from all over the city. There are great views of Nha Trang and nearby rural areas from the platform around the 14-metre-high figure, which was built in 1963. As you approach the pagoda from the street, the 152 stone steps up the hill to the Buddha begin to the right of the structure. You should also take some time to explore off to your left, where you'll find an entrance to another impressive hall of the pagoda.

Nha Trang Cathedral

Nha Trang Cathedral, built in French Gothic style and complete with medieval-looking stained-glass windows, stands on a small hill overlooking the railway station. It was constructed of simple cement blocks between 1928 and 1933. Today, the cathedral is the seat of the bishop of Nha Trang. In 1988, a Catholic cemetery not far from the church was disinterred to make room for a new building for the railway station. The ashes were brought to the cathedral and reburied in cavities behind the wall of plaques lining the ramp up the hill.

Masses are held daily at 5 am and 4.30 pm and on Sunday at 5 am, 7 am and 4.30 pm. If the main gate on Thai Nguyen St is closed, go up the ramp opposite 17 Nguyen Trai St to the back of the building.

Oceanographic Institute

The Oceanographic Institute (Vien Nghiem Cuu Bien; ☎ 22536), founded in 1923, has an aquarium (ho ca) and specimen room open to the public; it also has a library. The ground-floor aquarium's 23 tanks are home to a variety of colourful live specimens of local marine life, including seahorses. It is open daily from 7 to 11.30 am and 1.30 to 5 pm.

Behind the main building and across the volleyball court is a large hall filled with 60,000 dead specimens of sea life, including stuffed sea birds and fish, corals and the corporeal remains of various marine creatures preserved in glass jars.

The Oceanographic Institute is six km south of Nha Trang in the port village of Cau Da (also called Cau Be). To get there, go south on Tran Phu Blvd (which becomes Tu Do St south of the airport) all the way to the end of the street. Xe Lams to Cau Da (US$0.10) leave from Dam Market Xe Lam Station.

Bao Dai's Villas (Cau Da Villas)
Between the mid-'50s and 1975, Bao Dai's Villas (☎ 22449, 21124) were used by high-ranking officials of the South Vietnamese government, including President Thieu. This all changed in 1975, when the villas were taken over for use by high-ranking Communist officials who included Prime Minister Pham Van Dong. Today, low-ranking 'capitalist tourists' can rent a room in the Villas (for details, see Places to Stay).

Bao Dai's five villas, built in the 1920s, are set on three hills with brilliant views of the South China Sea, Nha Trang Bay (to the north) and Cau Da port (to the south). Between the buildings are winding paths lined with tropical bushes and trees. Most of the villas' furnishings have not been changed in decades.

To get to Bao Dai's Villas from Nha Trang, turn left off Tran Phu Blvd just past the white cement oil storage tanks (but before reaching Cau Da village). The Villas are several hundred metres north of the Oceanographic Institute. Foreigners pay an admission fee of US$0.50.

Thung Chai Basket Boats
The two-metre-wide round baskets used by fishers to transport themselves from the shore to their boats (and between boats) are made of woven bamboo strips covered with pitch. They are known in Vietnamese as *thung chai* (*thung* means basket, *chai* means pitch). Rowed standing up, a thung chai can carry four or five people.

Nha Trang's fishing fleet operates mostly at night, spending the days in port for rest and equipment repair.

Places to Stay
Nha Trang is a trendy place for both domestic and foreign tourists, with the result that accommodation is tight despite the plethora of hotels. The situation may improve as more hotels are built, but for now it can be hard to find a room. This is particularly true if you want to stay near the beach (everybody does) and want something cheap. If you find the beachside hotels to be all full, check out the hotels nearer to the railway station. Also look into Bao Dai's Villas, which are relatively empty because they're so far from the centre of things.

Another consideration is Nha Trang's climate. Although located well within the tropical zone, Nha Trang has cool evenings and is the first place (outside the highlands) as you head north where you should try to find a hotel with hot water.

The *Royal Hotel* (☎ 22298, 22385; 44 rooms) is at 40 Thai Nguyen St, opposite the railway station. As such, it's far from the beach and not especially popular, but will probably be one place that has rooms when the beach-area hotels are full. Rooms with fan cost US$6 to US$14. Air-con doubles are US$18 to US$22.

The *Nha Trang Hotel I* (☎ 22224; 50 rooms) is a seven-storey building at 129 Thong Nhat St. It's a fine-looking hotel, the only drawback being its relatively long distance from the beach. However, that also means it will be less likely to fill up quickly. Budget rooms with fan cost US$8; air-con puts the price tag at US$12 to US$25.

Just down the block is the *Nha Trang Hotel II* (☎ 22956; 33 rooms), 21 Le Thanh Phuong St. This hotel is relatively new, which means vital things like the plumbing should be in good nick. The cheaper double rooms with fan are US$8 and US$12; air-con costs US$10 to US$15.

The tourist-class *Thang Loi Hotel* (☎ 22241; fax 21905; 57 rooms), which resembles an American-style motel, is 100 metres from the beach at 4 Pasteur St. Aside from being built on a street with a French name, the hotel also has a French nickname (Hotel La Fregate). Singles/doubles with fan

Central Nha Trang

PLACES TO STAY

6 Thang Loi Hotel
8 Post Hotel
16 Nha Trang Hotel I
17 Nha Trang Hotel II
19 Royal Hotel
25 Thong Nhat Hotel
26 Nha Khach 24
30 Nha Trang Hotel III
31 Hung Dao Hotel
32 Vien Dong Hotel
33 Hai Yen Hotel
34 Manila Hotel
37 Nha Khach 44 (Grand Hotel)
39 Nha Khach 58
41 Khatoco Hotel

PLACES TO EAT

4 Lac Canh Restaurant
5 Nha Hang 33 Le Loi
13 Ice Cream Shops
14 Restaurant Lys
15 Binh Minh Restaurant
18 Ngoc Lau Restaurant
35 Hai Yen Cafe
36 Vinagen Cafe
40 Truc Linh Restaurant

OTHER

1 Short-Haul Bus Station
2 Dam Market Xe Lam Station
3 Dam Market
7 GPO
9 Pasteur Institute & Yersin Museum
10 Youth Tourism Express Bus Station
11 Stadium
12 Vietcombank
20 Giant Seated Buddha
21 Long Son Pagoda
22 Nha Trang Railway Station
23 Nha Trang Cathedral
24 Bien Vien Tinh (hospital)
27 Vietnam Airlines
28 Church
29 Express Bus Station
38 War Memorial Obelisk

are US$6/9; with air-con and hot water they're US$20/25 to US$30/40.

Not surprisingly, the *Post Hotel* (☎ 21250; fax 24205; 24 rooms) is adjacent to the GPO. This new place has rooms in the range of US$28 to US$35.

The *Thong Nhat Hotel* (☎ 22966; 90 rooms) is at 18 Tran Phu Blvd. It's a beautiful building just across the street from the beach. Singles/doubles with electric fan

are US$9/13; with air-con and hot water they're US$15 to US$18. Triple rooms cost US$33.

The *Nha Khach 24* (☎ 22671; 68 rooms) is a government-owned beachside place at 24 Tran Phu Blvd. Built in the finest tradition of Soviet concrete-box architecture, the building is now undergoing a massive renovation. The management wasn't sure about the new prices, but estimated they would be in the range of US$20 to US$40.

The latest addition to the Nha Trang Hotel chain is the *Nha Trang Hotel III* (☎ 23933; five rooms) at 22 Tran Hung Dao St. These are in fact villas near the beach, and everyone who stays here seems to rave about the place. Doubles cost US$30.

The *Hung Dao Hotel* (☎ 27005; fax 23820; 65 rooms) is at 3 Tran Hung Dao St, next to the Vien Dong Hotel. If not full, it's a relative bargain for the good location at US$10 to US$15.

The *Vien Dong Hotel* (☎ 21606; fax 21912; 86 rooms), 1 Tran Hung Dao St, has long been a travellers' favourite though lately the price has been ramped upwards (so what else is new?). The Vien Dong (which means 'far east') has a swimming pool, rents bicycles, organises boat trips and has diving gear for hire. The cheapest singles/doubles with fan cost US$7/10, but there are only two such rooms. Better rooms with fan are US$12/16. With air-con it will set you back US$30/35 to US$35/40. According to the Vien Dong's pamphlet, 'weapons and objects with offensive smell should be kept at the reception desk'.

The *Hai Yen Hotel* (☎ 22828; fax 21902; 120 rooms), whose name means 'sea swift', faces the beach at 40 Tran Phu Blvd. The place has gone downhill in recent years, is overpriced and is not particularly recommended. While the cheapest rooms cost only US$6 to US$11, the staff claims that these are only for Vietnamese and foreigners cannot stay in them. The bottom-end rooms for foreigners with fan only are priced at US$23 to US$27 (ridiculous!), and with air-con it's US$15 (why is air-con cheaper than fan?) to US$100. The government-run

Khanh Hoa Tourist office is around the back, which just might explain things.

The *Nha Khach 44* (☎ 22445; 50 rooms) is a large place with a beach view. Also known as the Grand Hotel, it looks a bit like a former Communist Party headquarters. It's not a bad place to stay though, and prices are reasonable. Rooms with fan cost from US$9 to US$14. Air-con ups the ante to US$20 to US$45.

The 13-storey *Manila Hotel*, a Philippine joint venture, is next to Nha Khach 44. Currently under construction, this place looks like it's aimed at the upper end of the Nha Trang tourist market. No prices were available at the time of our visit.

Nha Khach 58 (☎ 26304; 40 rooms) is also known as the Hai Quan (meaning 'navy') Hotel. As you may have guessed, the address is 58 Tran Phu Blvd. Rooms with fan cost US$8 to US$12, otherwise pay US$14 to US$20 for air-con.

Khatoco Hotel (☎ 23724; fax 21925; 24 rooms) at 9 Biet Thu St is run by a tobacco company. Anti-smoking activists will perhaps want to stay elsewhere, but others will find this new hotel to be fairly plush. The price range is US$18 to US$80. Smoking in bed is not permitted.

The *Maritime Hotel* (☎ 81135; fax 81134; 62 rooms), 34 Tran Phu Blvd (southern end of Nha Trang), caters to an upmarket clientele. There are three categories of rooms here. Standard rooms are US$28 to US$29, deluxe is US$39 to US$48 and suites are US$60. The beach views from the upper floors are impressive, but it's a rather long way from the town centre.

Even farther from the town centre are *Bao Dai's Villas* (☎ 81049; fax 21906; 28 rooms), also known as Cau Da Villas. These are near Cau Da on the coast six km south of Nha Trang. In some respects, this is perhaps the classiest accommodation in the area. However, the low-end rooms are pretty basic (servants' quarters?) with the toilets outside. On the other hand, all rooms have air-conditioning and drivers and tourist guides can stay for free if accompanied by foreign tourists. Rooms with outside toilet cost US$9,

while the rest is priced from US$15 to US$35. To these prices, tack on a 10% service charge. The top-end rooms are spacious with high ceilings and enormous bathrooms. This is where Vietnam's ruling elite has rested itself since the days of French rule (including the current elite). The restaurant in an adjoining villa has good food at low prices. To get to Bao Dai's Villas from Nha Trang, go south on Tran Phu Blvd and turn left just past the white cement oil storage tanks.

The *Nha Nghi Hon Chong* (☎ 22188; 48 rooms) on Nguyen Dinh Chieu St is at the summit of a hillock 150 metres from Hon Chong Promontory. Housed in the buildings of what was, before 1975, the American-supported Protestant Theological Seminary, Nha Nghi Hon Chong no longer accepts foreigners because it's too run-down. There are some hopes for renovating it in the future. There is a huge on-site dining hall.

Places to Eat
Beach Area This might be the most aesthetically pleasing area to eat, but the restaurant selection here is surprisingly poor.

Right on the beach and opposite the Hai Yen Hotel is the huge *Hai Yen Café*. It's an outdoors place with a sun roof to offer protection from the weather. It's OK for coffee, but not much else – food is pricey, servings are stingy and the service is poor.

It's very much the same story at the *Vinagen Café*, which is adjacent to the Hai Yen Café. But the Vinagen serves only Vinagen beer (of course) and blasts continuous infernal music that often drives Western customers away.

About 100 metres north of the Hai Yen is the *Souvenir Shop*, which, despite the name, is a seaside cafe. It's generally less pretentious and cheaper than the Hai Yen or Vinagen.

One block from the beach at the southern end of town is the *Truc Linh Restaurant*. It has excellent Vietnamese food and is very cheap, but the level of English isn't too high and the menu doesn't have prices. Get it all worked out before eating. Most of the

Dragon Fruit
Nha Trang is best known for its excellent seafood, but a really exotic treat is green dragon fruit *(thanh long)*. This fruit, which is the size and shape of a small pineapple and has an almost-smooth magenta skin, grows only in the Nha Trang area. Its delicious white meat is speckled with black seeds and tastes a bit like kiwifruit. Green dragon fruit grows on a kind of creeping cactus – said to resemble a green dragon – that climbs up the trunks and branches of trees and flourishes on parched hillsides that get very little water. Thanh long is in season from May to September and can be purchased at Dam Market. It is also exported to Ho Chi Minh City and even abroad (it now fetches a high price in Taiwan), but only in Nha Trang is this fruit cheap and fresh. Locals often make a refreshing drink out of crushed green dragon fruit, ice, sugar and sweetened condensed milk. They also use it to make jam. ■

Vietnamese drivers and guides eat here, which is a pretty good recommendation.

Readers say that *Cafe des Amis* at 16 Tran Phu Blvd serves good seafood and vegetarian dishes.

Central Area One of the best restaurants in town is the *Lac Canh Restaurant*, which is a block east of Dam Market at 11 Hang Ca St. Beef, squid, giant shrimps, lobsters and the like are grilled right at your table.

Hoan Hai Restaurant at 6 Phan Chu Trinh St is near the Lac Canh and is in some ways better. The menu contains delicious marinated beef, vegetarian dishes and some of the best spring rolls in Vietnam. Friendly service too.

In the same area is the excellent *Thanh The Restaurant* (☎ 21931), 3 Phan Chu Trinh St. This place does Vietnamese, Chinese and European-style food.

The *Restaurant Lys* at 117A Hoang Van Thu St is a big, bright and energetic place with an English menu. There's also great seafood at the *Ngoc Lau Restaurant* at 37 Le Thanh Phuong St.

The *Nha Hang 33 Le Loi* at 33 Le Loi St (corner Nguyen Du St) is opposite the main gate to Dam Market. The *Nha Hang 31 Le Loi* is next door.

Then, of course, there's *Dam Market* itself, which has a collection of stalls in the covered semi-circular food pavilion. Vegetarian food can be found here too.

Some readers have raved about the vegetarian food at the *Hai Tue Restaurant* at 10 Trung Nu Buong St, near the gate to the Dam Market.

The *Binh Minh Restaurant*, founded in 1953, is at 64 Hoang Van Thu St (corner Yet Kieu St) in the centre of town; their Vietnamese dishes are excellent. However, prices are not cheap.

For ice cream, try the shops around 52 Quang Trung St (corner Ly Thanh Ton St).

Entertainment
At the Vien Dong Hotel, there are beautiful dinner performances in classical theatre (with good English commentary), classical dance or folk dance at 7.30 pm. The performances are free if you purchase dinner.

Things to Buy
There are a number of shops selling beautiful seashells (and items made from seashells) near the Oceanographic Institute in Cau Da village. As a brochure of Nha Trang Tourism put it, 'Before leaving Nha Trang, tourists had better call at Cau Da to get some souvenirs of the sea...for their dears at home'. Inexpensive guitars are on sale at 24 Hai Ba Trung St (corner Phan Chu Trinh St). The Hai Yen Hotel has a small gift shop.

Getting There & Away
Air Vietnam Airlines has flights connecting Nha Trang with Ho Chi Minh City twice daily. There are flights to/from Hanoi once daily. Flights to/from Danang fly four times a week.

Vietnam Airlines' Nha Trang office (☎ 23797) is at 12B Hoang Hoa Tham St.

Bus Express and regular buses from Ho Chi Minh City to Nha Trang depart from Mien

Dong Bus Station. By express bus, the trip takes 11 to 12 hours.

Lien Tinh Bus Station (Ben Xe Lien Tinh; ☎ 22192), Nha Trang's main intercity bus terminal, is at 23 Thang 10 St (500 metres west of the railway station). Nonexpress buses from Lien Tinh Bus Station go to:

Bao Loc, Bien Hoa (11 hours), Buon Ma Thuot (six hours), Dalat (six hours), Danang (14 hours), Di Linh, Ho Chi Minh City (12 hours), Phan Rang (2½ hours), Pleiku (10 hours), Quang Ngai, Qui Nhon (seven hours).

Express buses leave from two different stations. The Youth Tourism Express Bus Station (Du Lich Thanh Nien; ☎ 22010) is just off Yersin St at 6 Hoang Hoa Tham St; tickets are sold daily from 4 am to 6 pm. There are buses from here to:

Buon Ma Thuot (daily at 5 am; five hours), Dalat (Tuesday, Thursday and Saturday at 5 am; five hours), Danang (Monday, Wednesday and Friday at 5 am; three hours), Ho Chi Minh City (daily at 5 am and 4.30 pm; 11 hours).

The Express Bus Station (Tram Xe Toc Hanh; ☎ 22397, 22884) is about 150 metres from the Hung Dao Hotel at 46 Le Thanh Ton St; the ticket office is open every day from 6 am to 4.30 pm. Tickets for early morning buses must be purchased one to three days before departure. Tickets for most buses leaving from the Express Bus Station are also sold at Lien Tinh Bus Station. Buses depart at 5 am (unless otherwise indicated) to:

Buon Ma Thuot (5.30 am; five hours), Dalat (five hours), Danang (13 hours), Hanoi (40 hours), Ho Chi Minh City (5 am and 4.30 pm; 12 hours), Hué (15 hours), Quang Binh, Quang Ngai (10 hours), Qui Nhon (six hours), Vinh (35 hours).

The Short-Haul Bus Station (Ben Xe Noi Tinh; ☎ 22191) is opposite 111, 2 Thang 4 St. Aged Renault and De Soto omnibuses depart from here to Cam Ranh, Nhieu Giang, Ninh Hoa, Tuy Hoa, Tu Bong, Song Cau, Song Hinh, Tay Son and Van Gia.

Minibus The preferred way to go, chartered minibuses are easy to book at most of the places where travellers congregate. This includes the Hai Yen Café, Vinagen Café and Vien Dong Hotel among others. Minibuses generally go to Saigon and Hoi An – both destinations cost about US$15. Dalat-Nha Trang costs US$7.

Train The Nha Trang Railway Station (Ga Nha Trang; ☎ 22113), overlooked by the nearby cathedral, is across the street from 26 Thai Nguyen St; the ticket office is open between 7 am and 2 pm only.

This station has a separate 'Waiting Room for Foreigners and Overseas Vietnamese'. This is on the left-hand side of the main hall and has air-conditioning, fans, comfortable seats and a clean Western-style toilet – a great little oasis.

Nha Trang is well served by both express trains connecting Hanoi and Ho Chi Minh City and a daily local train between Ho Chi Minh City and Nha Trang. For ticket prices, see the Train section in the Getting Around chapter.

Car Road distances from Nha Trang are: 205 km to Buon Ma Thuot, 541 km to Danang, 448 km to Ho Chi Minh City, 104 km to Phan Rang, 424 km to Pleiku, 412 km to Quang Ngai and 238 km to Qui Nhon.

A series of roughly parallel roads head inland from near Nha Trang, linking Vietnam's deltas and coastal regions with the Central Highlands.

Getting Around
Xe Lam Dam Market Xe Lam Station (Ben Xe Lam Cho Dam) is on Nguyen Hong Son St near the corner of Nguyen Thai Hoc St. It is due north of the main building of Dam Market, which is a round modern structure several stories high. Xe Lams from Dam Market Xe Lam Station go to: Cau Da (or Cau Be, also known as Chut), where the Oceanographic Institute and the fishing boat dock are; Dong De (near Hon Chong); and Thanh (take this one to get to Dien Khanh Citadel).

Bicycle All major hotels have bicycle rentals. The cost is US$1 per day or US$0.20 per hour.

AROUND NHA TRANG
Snorkelling, Scuba Diving & Islands
Khanh Hoa Province's 71 offshore islands are renowned for the remarkably clear water surrounding them. A trip to these islands is one of the main reasons for visiting Nha Trang, so try to schedule at least one day for a boat journey.

Budget travellers looking for low-priced island tours usually book these at the Hai Yen Café or its neighbour, the Vinagen Café. These adjacent cafes are right on the beach close to the Vien Dong Hotel, which also books these trips. A one-day budget boat journey to the islands should cost around US$5. Of course, you can also pay more for a less crowded and more luxurious boat which takes you to more islands.

Khanh Hoa Tourist and Nha Trang Tourism can also make arrangements for a boat trip, but at a higher price than what you can find through the cafes and bottom-end hotels.

Boats can be hired from the aforementioned places, but you may be able to save perhaps US$1 or more (but at higher risk) on the docks at Cau Da. Snorkelling equipment can be purchased at Dam Market.

Boat trips invariably include a lunch stop at one of the fishing villages on the islands. The food is nothing short of fantastic and very cheap. If on a tour, the price of the meal might already be included in the ticket (ask first). At some islands, shallow water prevents the boats from reaching shore. In this case, you must walk perhaps several hundred metres across floats, a careful balancing act. The floats were designed for Vietnamese, and heavier Westerners might get wet – take care with your camera. Nevertheless, it's all good fun and a visit to these fishing villages is highly recommended.

The Scuba Diving Centre (☎ 23966) in Cau Da Village is a good place to hire equipment and obtain a guide who can show you the coral reefs (or what's left of them). Nev-

ertheless, always check your equipment carefully before trusting your life to it – travellers have complained of such things as air tanks half full and some dodgy Russian equipment still being used. There does not seem to be anything deliberate in this, just a case of the local standards not being quite up to foreign expectations.

Mieu Island Mieu Island (also called Tri Nguyen Island) is touted in tourist literature as the site of an 'outdoor aquarium' (Ho Ca Tri Nguyen). In fact, the 'aquarium' is an important fish-breeding farm where over 40 species of fish, crustaceans and other marine creatures are raised in three separate compartments. There is a cafe built on stilts over the water. Ask around for canoe rentals.

The main village on Mieu Island is Tri Nguyen. Bai Soai is a gravel beach on the far side of Mieu Island from Cau Da.

Most people will take some sort of boat tour booked through a hotel, cafe or Khanh Hoa Tourist. Impoverished and less hurried travellers might catch one of the regular ferries that go to Tri Nguyen village from Cau Da Dock, which is a few hundred metres south of the Oceanographic Institute.

Bamboo Island (Hon Tre) Several kilometres from the southern part of Nha Trang Beach is Bamboo Island, the largest island by far in the Nha Trang area. Tru Beach (Bai Tru) is at the northern end of the island. Ebony Island (Hon Mun), just south of Bamboo Island, is known for its snorkelling. To get to either island, you'll probably have to hire a boat.

Monkey Island (Dao Khi) The island is named for its large contingent of resident monkeys, and has become a big hit with foreign visitors. Most of the monkeys have grown quite accustomed to receiving handouts from the tourists, so there is little problem getting close enough to take a memorable photo if you bring some food. If you offer it to them, the monkeys will take the food directly from your hand. However, these are wild monkeys, not zoo animals –

you should not make any attempt to pet them, shake hands or pick them up. Some travellers have been scratched and bitten when they attempted to embrace their new-found friends.

Aside from being unwilling to cuddle, the monkeys are materialistic. They will grab the sunglasses off your face or snatch a pen from your shirt pocket and run off. So far, we haven't heard of monkeys slitting open travellers' handbags with a razor blade, but you do need to be almost as careful with your valuables here as you do in Saigon!

Monkey Island is 12 km north of Bamboo Island, and one-day boat tours can easily be arranged in Nha Trang. A faster way to get there is to take a motorbike or car 12 km north of Nha Trang – near a pagoda is a place where boats will ferry you to the island for US$1. Bring some corn or beans to feed the monkeys.

Salangane Island (Hon Yen) The name Salangane Island is actually applied to two lump-shaped islands visible in the distance from Nha Trang Beach. Salangane Island and other islands off Khanh Hoa Province are the source of Vietnam's finest salangane (swift) nests. The nests are used in birds' nest soup as well as in traditional medicine, and are considered an aphrodisiac. It is said that Emperor Minh Mang, who ruled Vietnam from 1820 to 1840, derived his extraordinary virility from the consumption of salangane nests.

The nests, which the salanganes build out of their silk-like salivary secretions, are semi-oval and about five to eight cm in diameter. They are usually harvested twice a year. Red nests are the most highly prized. Annual production in Khanh Hoa and Phu Yen provinces is about 1000 kg. At present, salangane nests fetch US$2000 per kg in the international marketplace!

There is a small, secluded beach at Salangane Island. The 17-km trip out to the islands takes three to four hours by small boat.

Dien Khanh Citadel
The citadel dates from the 17th-century

Trinh Dynasty. It was rebuilt by Prince Nguyen Anh (later Emperor Gia Long) in 1793 during his successful offensive against the Tay Son Rebels. Only a few sections of the walls and gates are extant. Dien Khanh Citadel is 11 km west of Nha Trang near the villages of Dien Toan and Dien Thanh. The best way to get to Dien Khanh Citadel is to take a Xe Lam to Thanh from Dam Market Xe Lam Station.

Ba Ho Falls
Ba Ho Falls, with its three waterfalls and three pools, is in a forested area 19 km north of Nha Trang and about one km from the road; it is a great place for a picnic. Ba Ho Falls is near Ninh Ich Xa in Vinh Xuong District and not far from Phu Huu village. To get there, take the bus to Ninh Hoa from the Short-Haul Bus Station.

Fairy Spring
The enchanting little Fairy Spring (Suoi Tien) seems to pop out of nowhere as you approach it. Like a small oasis, the spring is decorated with its own natural garden of tropical vegetation and smooth boulders.

You'll need to rent a motorbike or car to reach the spring. Driving south on National Highway 1, you come to a spot 17 km from Nha Trang where there is an archway to your left (east side of the highway). Turn off the highway here and go through the village. The road twists and winds it's way through the hills until it reaches a valley. Just as the road starts to get bad, you come upon the spring. You will probably see some other vehicles parked here as it's a popular spot with the locals.

DOC LET BEACH
Some call this the most spectacular beach in Vietnam, and it would be hard to argue with them. The beach is long and wide, with chalk-white sand and shallow water. Yet despite its beauty, Doc Let gets few visitors, though this is likely to change. From all appearances, it seems that one earlier attempt was made at tourist development, but this was abandoned and most of the buildings are

falling apart. However, there still is one functioning restaurant and guesthouse.

Doc Let Beach is on a peninsula to the north of Nha Trang. There is no public transport to this spot, so you need to hire a vehicle. To get there, drive 30 km north of Nha Trang on National Highway 1. Just north of Ninh Hoa is a petrol station and a fork in the road. Take the right fork (east) and continue for 10 km until you reach the beach.

DAI LANH BEACH

Semi-circular, casuarina-shaded Dai Lanh Beach is another beautiful spot 83 km north of Nha Trang and 153 km south of Qui Nhon on National Highway 1. At the southern end of the beach is a vast sand-dune causeway; it connects the mainland to Hon Gom, a mountainous peninsula almost 30 km in length. The main village on Hon Gom is Dam Mon (known to the French as Port Dayot), which is on a sheltered bay facing the island of Hon Lon.

At the northern end of Dai Lanh Beach is Dai Lanh Promontory (Mui Dai Lanh), named Cap Varella by the French.

Places to Stay & Eat

There is a four-storey half-completed tourist hotel just off National Highway 1, a few hundred metres south of town. Apparently, construction has been abandoned and the decaying structure is totally overgrown with weeds – makes an interesting photo. Perhaps a foreign investor will rescue the project, but if so it better happen soon before the whole thing topples over.

Just south of the abandoned hotel shell is the *Dai Lanh Restaurant*, the fanciest place in town. There are also at least a dozen small family-owned restaurants in Dai Lanh.

Getting There & Away

Dai Lanh Beach runs along National Highway 1, so any vehicle travelling along the coast between Nha Trang and Tuy Hoa (or Qui Nhon) will get you there.

Phu Yen Province

TUY HOA

Tuy Hoa, the capital of Phu Yen Province, is a nondescript little town on the coast between Dai Lanh Beach and Qui Nhon. The highway crosses a huge river on the south side of town. The river is navigable and justifies Tuy Hoa's existence – there isn't much else to the place, not even a good beach.

The main interest of Tuy Hoa to travellers is that it has good accommodation, which could be useful if you get a late start heading north or south along National Highway 1.

Information

Tourist Office Phu Yen Tourist (Cong Ty Du Lich Phu Yen; ☎ 23353) is the provincial tourist office, and can be found at 137 Le Thanh Ton St.

Places to Stay

The *Huong Sen Hotel* (☎ 23775; fax 23186; 50 rooms) and attached restaurant is a large fancy place near the centre of town. Room rates are US$15 to US$30.

SONG CAU

The village of Song Cau is an obscure place that you could easily drive past without ever noticing, but it's worth stopping if you have the time. Near the village is an immense bay, a beautiful rest stop that attracts both foreign and domestic tourists.

Foreigners doing the Nha Trang-Hoi An run often make a stopoff for brunch in Song Cau, and some visitors even spend the night.

There are two main reasons for staying overnight in Song Cau. One is to avoid spending an evening in Qui Nhon, which is much less attractive. The other reason is to take a boat trip on the bay, which the hotel restaurant (see the following Places to Stay & Eat section) can arrange for US$10. The boat can hold 10 persons.

Places to Stay & Eat

The *Nha Hang Bai Tien* (☎ 70322; 10 rooms) offers doubles with hot water for US$10. This privately run hotel and restaurant complex is built on stilts over the bay and makes for a very attractive setting. The electricity comes from a private generator, which is normally switched on from 6 pm until midnight.

Getting There & Away

Song Cau is 170 km north of Nha Trang, and 43 km south of Qui Nhon. Highway buses can drop you off and pick you up here (with luck), but most travellers will probably arrive by chartered minibus.

Binh Dinh Province

QUI NHON

Qui Nhon (or Quy Nhon; population 200,000) is the capital of Binh Dinh Province and one of Vietnam's more active second-string seaports. The beaches in the immediate vicinity of the city are nothing to write home about, but Qui Nhon is a convenient though somewhat disappointing place to break the long journey from Nha Trang to Danang. By provincial standards, however, Qui Nhon is a hopping, happening place on Sunday nights. The standard of living is fairly high, and the town is said to owe much of this prosperity to the smuggling of imported goods.

There are some Cham towers along National Highway 1 about 10 km north of the Qui Nhon turn-off.

During the Vietnam War there was considerable South Vietnamese, American, Viet Cong and South Korean military activity in the Qui Nhon area, and refugees dislocated by the fighting and counter-insurgency programmes built whole slums of tin and thatch shacks around the city. During this period, the mayor of Qui Nhon, hoping to cash in on the presence of American troops, turned his official residence into a massage parlour.

Orientation

Qui Nhon is on an east-west-oriented peninsula shaped like the nose of an anteater. The tip of the nose (the port area) is closed to the public. The Municipal Beach is on the peninsula's southern coast. The streets around Lon Market constitute Qui Nhon's town centre.

From the Municipal Beach, Cu Lao Xanh Island is visible offshore. Due east of the beach (to the left as you face the water) you can see, in the distance, an oversize statue of Tran Hung Dao erected on a promontory overlooking the fishing village of Hai Minh.

Information

Tourist Office Binh Dinh Tourism (Cong Ty Du Lich Binh Dinh; ☎ 22524, 22206, 22329) is at 10 Nguyen Hue St, just west of the Quy Nhon Hotel. They're not very helpful, so give them a miss unless you must hire a car.

Money Vietcombank (☎ 22266), or the Bank of Foreign Trade (Ngan Hang Ngoai Thuong), is at 148 Le Loi St on the corner of Tran Hung Dao St.

Post & Telecommunications The GPO is in the south-western part of town on the corner of Hai Ba Trung and Tran Phu Sts; it is open daily from 6 am to 8 pm. International telephone calls can be placed from here; telegraph services are available. There is a small post office at the corner of Phan Boi Chau and 1 Thang 4 Sts on the ground floor of Lon Market.

Emergency There is a large hospital opposite 309 Nguyen Hue St.

Long Khanh Pagoda

Long Khanh Pagoda, Qui Nhon's main pagoda, is down an alley opposite 62 Tran Cao Van St and next to 143 Tran Cao Van St. Visible from the street is a 17-metre-high Buddha (built in 1972), which presides over a lily pond strongly defended (against surprise attack?) by barbed wire. To the left of the main building is a low tower sheltering a giant drum; to the right, its twin contains an enormous bell, cast in 1970.

The main sanctuary was completed in 1946 but was damaged during the Franco-Viet Minh War; repairs were completed in 1957. In front of the large copper Thich Ca Buddha (with its multi-coloured neon halo) is a drawing of multi-armed and multi-eyed Chuan De (the Goddess of Mercy; the numerous arms and eyes means she can touch and see all). There is a colourfully painted Buddha at the edge of the raised platform. In the corridor which passes behind the main altar is a bronze bell with Chinese inscriptions; it dates from 1805.

Under the eaves of the left-hand building of the courtyard behind the sanctuary hangs a blow-up of the famous photograph of the monk Thich Quang Duc immolating himself in Saigon in June 1963 to protest the policies of the Diem regime. The 2nd level of the two-storey building behind the courtyard contains memorial plaques for deceased monks (on the middle altar) and lay people.

Long Khanh Pagoda was founded around 1700 by a Chinese merchant, Duc Son (1679-1741). The seven monks who live here preside over the religious affairs of Qui Nhon's relatively active Buddhist community. Single-sex religion classes for children are held on Sundays.

Beaches

Qui Nhon Municipal Beach, which extends along the southern side of the anteater's nose, consists of a few hundred metres of sand shaded by a coconut grove. The nicest section of beach is across from the Quy Nhon Tourist Hotel, but it has become increasingly dirty. Farther west, the shore is lined with the boats and shacks of fishing families.

A longer, quieter bathing beach begins about two km south-west of the Municipal Beach. To get there, follow Nguyen Hue St away from the tip of the peninsula westward. Part of the seafront near here is lined with industrial plants, some of which belong to the military. Ganh Rang Restaurant is at the far end of the beach.

Binh Dinh-Xiem Riep-Ratanakiri Zoo

This small seaside zoo, whose inhabitants include monkeys, crocodiles, porcupines and bears, is named for the two Cambodian provinces the animals came from. Siem Reap (Vietnamese: *Xiem Riep)* Province, where the monuments of Angkor are located, is in the north-western part of the country. Ratanakiri is in Cambodia's far north-eastern corner and borders both Laos and Vietnam. The uncharitable might classify the animals here as war booty (or prisoners of war). The zoo is at 2B Nguyen Hue St.

Lon Market

Lon Market (Cho Lon), Qui Nhon's central market, is a large modern building enclosing a courtyard in which fruits and vegetables are sold. Most goods one can reasonably expect to find in the provinces can be purchased here. Tu Hai Restaurant is on the 3rd floor facing Phan Boi Chau St.

Leper Hospital

This is not a tourist attraction, but visitors are welcome, especially if they make a small donation or purchase a few basic items from the locals. As leper hospitals go, this one is highly unusual. Rather than being a depressing place, it's a sort of model village where infected patients live together with their families in well-kept small houses. According to their abilities, the patients are working in repair-oriented businesses or small craft shops. The hospital grounds are actually so well maintained that it looks a bit like a resort.

The Leper Hospital is out on the western end of Nguyen Hue St.

Places to Stay

The *Bank Hotel* (☎ 22779; fax 21013; 20 rooms) is 300 metres from the bus station at 257 Le Hong Phong St. The rooms here have been fully renovated and this place deserves a plug. Bottom-end rooms with fan and cold-water bath are US$12. Luxuries like air-con and hot water cost US$27.

The modern *Dong Phuong Hotel* (☎ 22915; 26 rooms) at 39-41 Mai Xuan

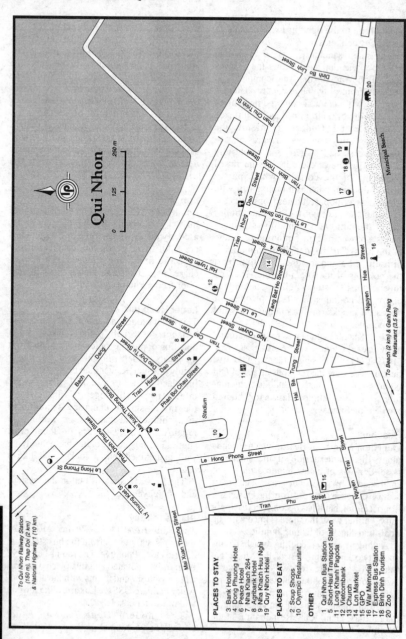

Qui Nhon

To Qui Nhon Railway Station
(150 m), Thap Doi (2 km)
& National Highway 1 (10 km)

To Beach (2 km) & Ganh Rang
Restaurant (3.5 km)

Municipal Beach

PLACES TO STAY
3   Bank Hotel
4   Dong Phuong Hotel
6   Peace Hotel
7   Nha Khach 264
8   Agribank Hotel
9   Nha Khach Huu Nghi
19 Quy Nhon Hotel

PLACES TO EAT
2   Soup Shops
10 Olympic Restaurant

OTHER
1   Qui Nhon Bus Station
5   Short-Haul Transport Station
11 Long Khanh Pagoda
12 Vietcombank
13 Church
14 Con Market
15 GPO
16 War Memorial
17 Express Bus Station
18 Binh Dinh Tourism
20 Zoo

Thuong St (near the corner of Le Hong Phong St) is perhaps the best deal in town. Singles/doubles are US$5/8 to US$6/12. Triples are US$11 to US$15. There's a good restaurant on the ground floor.

The *Nha Khach Huu Nghi* (☎ 22152; 16 rooms) at 210 Phan Boi Chau St is rather grimy but remains popular due to the low price – US$6 to US$10. There is a restaurant on the ground floor which might be OK for a bowl of noodles.

The *Peace Hotel* (Khach San Hoa Binh; ☎ 22710; 60 rooms) is at 361 Tran Hung Dao St. At US$31 to US$39, it's ridiculously overpriced for the depressing rooms.

Just across the street is the *Nha Khach 264* (☎ 21611; 12 rooms), 264 Tran Hung Dao St. Unlike its neighbour, this place is fairly priced with rooms from US$12 to US$15.

The *Agribank Hotel* (☎ 22245; fax 21073; 19 rooms) is a new, gleaming-white place obviously meant to catch the tourist traffic doing the Saigon-Hanoi sightseeing route. Rooms cost US$15 to US$25. The address is 202 Tran Hung Dao St.

The *Quy Nhon Hotel* (☎ 22401; fax 21162; 79 rooms) is at 8 Nguyen Hue St, adjacent to the city's beach. Judging from the hotel's brochures, it seems that the management believes the Qui Nhon Municipal Beach and Quy Nhon Hotel are Vietnam's answer to the French Riviera and Club Med. However, shareholders in Club Med are not exactly shaking in their boots. Room rates are US$21 to US$37, which might sound cheap until you look at what you're getting. The restaurant serves dismal food.

Places to Eat

There are only a handful of proper restaurants in Qui Nhon. One of the best is the *Olympic Restaurant*, which is on the roof of the Olympic Hotel. The hotel itself does not accept foreigners. The entrance to the Olympic Hotel is from inside the stadium.

The *Dong Phuong Restaurant* at 39-41 Mai Xuan Thuong St is on the ground floor of the Dong Phuong Hotel; it is open from 6 am to 11 pm. They have reasonably good Vietnamese food and a few Western dishes.

The *Ganh Rang Restaurant* is 3.5 km west of town along Nguyen Hue St. Built on pylons and set among palms, this privately run restaurant is right on the water at a site said to have been a favourite of Bao Dai's wife.

Getting There & Away

Air Vietnam Airlines flights link Ho Chi Minh City with Qui Nhon five times weekly. There are also flights to/from Danang three times weekly.

Phu Cat Airport is 36 km north of Qui Nhon. For airline passengers, transport to and from Phu Cat is provided by Vietnam Airlines. Small trucks to Phu Cat depart from the Short-Haul Transport Station.

In Qui Nhon, the Vietnam Airlines booking office (☎ 22953) is near the Thanh Binh Hotel in the building next to 30 Nguyen Thai Hoc St.

Bus Qui Nhon Bus Station (Ben Xe Khach Qui Nhon; ☎ 22246) is opposite 543 Tran Hung Dao St (across from where Le Hong Phong St hits Tran Hung Dao St). The non-express ticket windows are open from 5 am to 4 pm; the express ticket window (Khach Di Xe Toc Hanh), which is in the fenced-in enclosure next to the nonexpress windows, is open from 4 am to 4 pm. Tickets should be purchased the day before departure.

Express buses, all of which leave at 5 am, go to Buon Ma Thuot, Dalat, Danang, Hanoi, Ho Chi Minh City, Hué, Nha Trang, Quang Tri and Vinh.

Nonexpress buses leave from here to:

An Khe, An Lao (6 am), Bong Son (6 am), Buon Ma Thuot (5 am; eight hours), Cam Ranh, Dalat (6 am; 10 hours), Danang (6 am; six hours), Hanoi (5 am; 39 hours), Ho Chi Minh City (5 am; 16 hours), Hoi An (6 am), Hué (6 am), Kon Tum (8 am; 11 hours), Nha Trang (5 am; 5½ hours), Phu My (6 am), Pleiku (6 am; six hours), Quang Ngai (6 am; five hours), Tam Quan (6 am), Tuy Hoa, Van Canh, Vinh Thanh (6 am).

The Express Bus Station (☎ 22172) is 100 metres from the Quy Nhon Hotel at 14 Nguyen Hue St. There are express buses from here to Buon Ma Thuot, Dalat, Danang,

Dong Hoi, Hanoi, Ho Chi Minh City, Hué, Nha Trang, Ninh Binh, Quang Tri, Thanh Hoa and Vinh. All buses depart at 5 am. The ticket window (Phong Ban Ve Xe Toc Hanh Cac Tuyen Duong) is open from 6.30 to 11 am and 1.30 to 5 pm.

Vehicles to places within a 50-km radius of Qui Nhon depart from the Short-Haul Transport Station (Ben Xe 1 Thang 4), which is at the intersection of Phan Boi Chau and Mai Xuan Thuong Sts (near 280 Phan Boi Chau St and 60 Mai Xuan Thuong St). Tickets are sold in a kerbside wood and corrugated-iron kiosk. Small trucks leave from here to Binh Dinh (six km from Cha Ban), Dap Da, Dieu Tri (the railway station), Phu Cat (the airport), Tay Son (vehicles from Tay Son go to within about five km of the Quang Trung Museum), Tuy Phuoc and Vinh Thanh.

Train The city of Qui Nhon is poorly served by rail. Qui Nhon Railway Station (Ga Qui Nhon; ☎ 22036) is at the end of a 10-km spur line off the main north-south track. The station is 70 metres from Tran Hung Dao St on Hoang Hoa Tham St, which intersects Tran Hung Dao St between numbers 661 and 663.

Only two very slow local trains stop at Qui Nhon Railway Station. Train DS departs for points south at 9.45 am on even days of the month (its northward-bound twin leaves Ho Chi Minh City on odd days of the month); the trip all the way to Ho Chi Minh City takes 24 hours. Northward-bound 172 leaves at 5 am daily, arriving in Danang about 13 hours later.

The nearest the Reunification Express Train gets to Qui Nhon is Dieu Tri, 10 km from the city. Tickets for trains departing from Dieu Tri can be purchased at the Qui Nhon Railway Station, though if you arrive in Dieu Tri by train, your best bet is to purchase an onward ticket before leaving the station. For ticket prices on the Reunification Express Train, see the Train section in the Getting Around chapter. Before making the journey out to Dieu Tri it's best to check the schedule. Small trucks from Qui Nhon to Dieu Tri leave from the Short-Haul Transport Station.

Car Road distances from Qui Nhon are 677 km to Ho Chi Minh City, 238 km to Nha Trang, 186 km to Pleiku, 198 km to Kon Tum, 174 km to Quang Ngai and 303 km to Danang.

Qui Nhon is 10 km off National Highway 1. It is the nearest coastal city to Pleiku, Kon Tum and the rest of the northern section of the Central Highlands. National Highway 19 to Tay Son and Pleiku heads westward from Binh Dinh, which is 18 km north of Qui Nhon.

There is a border crossing to Cambodia's remote Ratanakiri Province about 250 km due west of Qui Nhon near the village of Chu Nghe. At present, the crossing is used by Vietnamese companies to bring Ratanakiri's forest products to the coast for export. Some day it may be possible to visit Ratanakiri, which is not accessible by land from Phnom Penh (the bridges are out), from Qui Nhon.

AROUND QUI NHON
Thap Doi
The two Cham towers of Thap Doi have curved pyramidal roofs rather than the terracing typical of Cham architecture. The larger tower, whose four granite doorways are oriented towards the cardinal directions, retains some of its ornate brickwork and remnants of the granite statuary that once graced its summit. The dismembered torsos of garudas can be seen at the corners of the roofs of both structures.

The upper reaches of the small tower are home to several flourishing trees whose creeping tendrilous roots have forced their way between the bricks, enmeshing parts of the structure in the sort of net-like tangle for which the monuments of Angkor are famous. However, the whole place is being restored, and by the time you get there it might look just like new.

Thap Doi is two km towards National Highway 1 from the Qui Nhon Bus Station. To get there, head out of town on Tran Hung Dao St and turn right between street numbers

900 and 906 onto Thap Doi St; the towers are about 100 metres from Tran Hung Dao St.

There are half a dozen or so other groups of Cham structures in the vicinity of Qui Nhon, two of which (Cha Ban and Duong Long) are described below.

Cha Ban

The ruins of the former Cham capital of Cha Ban (also known at various times as Vijaya and Qui Nhon) are 26 km north of Qui Nhon and five km from Binh Dinh. The city was built within a rectangular wall measuring 1400 metres by 1100 metres. Canh Tien Tower (Tower of Brass) stands in the centre of the enclosure. The tomb of General Vu Tinh is nearby.

Cha Ban, which served as the seat of the royal government of Champa from the year 1000 (after the loss of Indrapura, also known as Dong Duong) until 1471, was attacked and plundered repeatedly by the Vietnamese, Khmers and Chinese. In 1044, the Vietnamese prince Phat Ma occupied the city and carried off a great deal of booty as well as the Cham king's wives, harem and female dancers, musicians and singers. Cha Ban was under the control of a Khmer overseer from 1190 to 1220.

In 1377, the Vietnamese were defeated in an attempt to capture Cha Ban and their king was killed. The Vietnamese Emperor Le Thanh Ton breached the eastern gate of the city in 1471 and captured the Cham king and 50 members of the royal family. During this, the last great battle fought by the Chams, 60,000 Chams were killed and 30,000 more were taken prisoner by the Vietnamese.

During the Tay Son Rebellion, Cha Ban served as the capital of the region of central Vietnam ruled by the eldest of the three Tay Son brothers. It was attacked in 1793 by the forces of Nguyen Anh (later Emperor Gia Long) but the assault failed. In 1799, the forces of Nguyen Anh, under the command of General Vu Tinh, lay siege to the city and captured it. The Tay Son soon re-occupied the port of Thi Nai (modern-day Qui Nhon) and then lay siege to Cha Ban themselves. The siege continued for over a year, and by

June 1801, Vu Tinh's provisions were gone. Food was in short supply; all the horses and elephants had long before been eaten. Refusing to consider the ignominy of surrender, Vu Tinh had an octagonal wood tower constructed. He filled it with gunpowder and, arrayed in his ceremonial robes, went inside and blew himself up. Upon hearing the news of the death of his dedicated general, Nguyen Anh wept.

Duong Long Cham Towers

The Duong Long Cham Towers (Thap Duong Long, the Towers of Ivory) are eight km from Cha Ban. The largest of the three brick towers is embellished with granite ornamentation representing nagas (snakes) and elephants. Over the doors are bas-reliefs of women, dancers, standing lions, monsters and various animals. The corners of the structure are formed by enormous dragon heads.

Hoi Van Hot Springs

The famous hot springs of Hoi Van are north of Qui Nhon in Phu Cat District.

Quang Trung Museum

The Quang Trung Museum is dedicated to Nguyen Hue, the second-oldest of the three brothers who led the Tay Son Rebellion, who crowned himself Emperor Quang Trung in 1788. In 1789 (a few months before a Parisian mob stormed the Bastille), Quang Trung led the campaign that overwhelmingly defeated a Chinese invasion force of 200,000 troops near Hanoi. This epic battle is still celebrated as one of the greatest triumphs in Vietnamese history. Quang Trung died in 1792 at the age of 40.

During his reign, Quang Trung was something of a social reformer. He encouraged land reform, revised the system of taxation, improved the army and emphasised education, opening numerous schools and encouraging the development of Vietnamese poetry and literature. Indeed, Communist literature often portrays him as the leader of a peasant revolution whose progressive policies were crushed by the reactionary Nguyen

Dynasty, which came to power in 1802 and was overthrown by Ho Chi Minh in 1945.

The Quang Trung Museum is known for its demonstrations of *binh dinh vo*, a traditional martial art that is performed with a bamboo stick. To get there take National Highway 19 towards Pleiku. The museum, which is 48 km from Qui Nhon, is in Tay Son District five km off the highway. The Tay Son area produces a wine made of sticky rice.

Vinh Son Falls
Vinh Son Falls is 18 km off National Highway 19, which links Binh Dinh and Pleiku. To get there, you might try taking a Vinh Thanh-bound truck from the Short-Haul Transport Station in Qui Nhon and changing vehicles in Vinh Thanh.

Quang Ngai Province

SA HUYNH
Sa Huynh is a relatively prosperous little seaside town whose beautiful semi-circular beach is bordered by rice paddies and coconut palms. The town is also known for its salt marshes and salt evaporation ponds. In the vicinity of Sa Huynh, archaeologists have unearthed remains of the Dong Son Civilisation dating from the 1st century AD.

Places to Stay & Eat
Sa Huynh is a fairly pleasant place to make an overnight stop on the road trip between Nha Trang and Danang, provided the hotel has room. There is only one hotel, the small and quiet *Sa Huynh Hotel* (☎ 59208; 16 rooms), which is right on the beach. All rooms cost US$10 and are equipped with ceiling fans and attached bath, but don't expect five-star standards.

There is a respectable restaurant on the hotel grounds, but *Café Vinh* just outside the hotel gate is perhaps better.

Getting There & Away
Train Some nonexpress trains stop at the Sa Huynh Railway Station (Ga Sa Huynh), but it will be slow going.

Car Sa Huynh is on National Highway 1 about 114 km north of Qui Nhon and 60 km south of Quang Ngai.

QUANG NGAI
Quang Ngai, the capital of Quang Ngai Province, is something of a backwater. But just how much longer this will remain an undisturbed backwater is a matter of extreme speculation. In late 1994, the Vietnamese government announced plans to build an oil refinery (Vietnam's first) here, along with other industrial projects. So far, the schemes exist only on paper, but foreign financiers are said to be taking an interest. One reason for wanting to develop this region into an industrial base is that so far the area has proved to be of little interest to tourists.

Built on the south bank of the Tra Khuc River (known for its oversized waterwheels), the city is about 15 km from the coast, which is lined with beautiful beaches. The city and province of Quang Ngai are also known as Quang Nghia; the name is sometimes abbreviated as Quangai.

History
Even before WW II, Quang Ngai was an important centre of resistance to the French. During the Franco-Viet Minh War, the area was a Viet Minh stronghold. In 1962, the South Vietnamese Government introduced its ill-fated strategic hamlet programme to the area. Villagers were forcibly removed from their homes and resettled in fortified hamlets, infuriating and alienating the local population and increasing popular support for the Viet Cong. Some of the bitterest fighting of the Vietnam War took place in Quang Ngai Province.

Son My subdistrict, 14 km from Quang Ngai, was the scene of the infamous My Lai Massacre of 1968, in which hundreds of civilians were slaughtered by American soldiers. A memorial has been erected on the site of the killings.

As a result of the wars, very few bridges in Quang Ngai Province remain intact. At many river crossings, the rust-streaked concrete pylons of the old French bridges, probably destroyed by the Viet Minh, stand next to the ruins of their replacements, blown up by the VC. As it has for 15 or more years, traffic crosses the river on a third bridge, made of steel girders, of the sort that army engineering corps put up in a pinch.

Orientation
National Highway 1 is called Quang Trung St as it passes through Quang Ngai. The railway station is three km west of town out Phan Boi Chau St.

Information
Tourist Office Quang Ngai Tourism (Cong Ty Du Lich Quang Ngai; ☎ 2665, 3870) is the government's official tourist agency for Quang Ngai Province. The office is in the Song Tra Hotel.

Post & Telecommunications The GPO is 150 metres off Quang Trung St at the corner of Phan Boi Chau and Phan Dinh Phung Sts.

Places to Stay
There are four hotels in Quang Ngai but only one accepts foreigners. The *Song Tra Hotel* (☎ 22665; 38 rooms) is owned by Quang Ngai Tourism and this is where foreigners are forced to stay. The hotel is a monstrous five-storey structure on the northern outskirts of the city next to the bridge over the Tra Khuc River. There are two rooms for US$10 and four rooms for US$15, but everything else costs US$20 to US$35 and isn't worth it.

Places to Eat
A local speciality is *bo gan*, bits of beef topped with ground peanuts and eaten on pieces of giant rice crackers.

The restaurant at the *Song Tra Hotel* is where most travellers wind up eating. Alter-

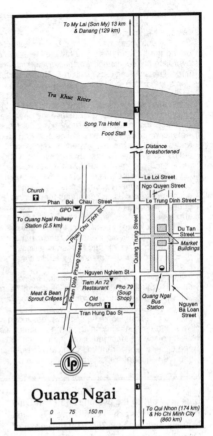

natively, there are a few food stalls right in front of the hotel where you can pick up bananas, biscuits and noodles.

If you think that you'll pick up a great meal by going into town, you'll be disappointed. As usual, you can always find some food stalls near the bus station.

Tiem An 72 Restaurant at 72 Nguyen Nghiem St is about 150 metres from the bus station, and you can at least get decent noodles here. There are cafes at numbers 47, 51 and 53 Phan Boi Chau St (near Hotel Number 2), but they don't have much to eat. Meat and bean sprout crêpes fried over open

My Lai Massacre

Son My subdistrict was the site of the most horrific war crimes committed by American troops during the Vietnam War. The My Lai Massacre consisted of a series of atrocities carried out all over Son My subdistrict, which is divided into four hamlets, one of which is named My Lai. The largest mass killing took place in Tu Cung Hamlet in Xom Lang sub-hamlet (also known as Thuan Yen sub-hamlet), where the Son My Memorial was later erected.

Son My subdistrict was a known Viet Cong stronghold, and it was widely believed that villagers in the area were providing food and shelter to the VC (if true, the villagers had little choice – the VC was known for taking cruel revenge on those who didn't 'cooperate'). Just whose idea it was to 'teach the villagers a lesson' has never been determined. What is known is that several American soldiers had been killed and wounded in the area in the days preceding the 'search-and-destroy operation' that began on the morning of 16 March 1968. The operation was carried out by Task Force Barker, which consisted of three companies of US Army infantry. At about 7.30 am – after the area around Xom Lang sub-hamlet had been bombarded with artillery and the landing zone raked with rocket and machine-gun fire from helicopter gunships – the three platoons of Charlie Company (commanded by Captain Ernest Medina) were landed by helicopter. They encountered no resistance during the 'combat-assault', nor did they come under fire at any time during the entire operation; but as soon as Charlie Company's sweep eastward began, so did the atrocities.

As the soldiers of Lieutenant William Calley's 1st Platoon moved through Xom Lang, they shot and bayoneted fleeing villagers, threw hand grenades into houses and family bomb shelters, slaughtered livestock and burned dwellings. Somewhere between 75 and 150 unarmed local people were rounded up and herded to a ditch, where they were mowed down by machine-gun fire.

In the next few hours, as command helicopters circled overhead and US Navy boats patrolled offshore, the 2nd Platoon (under Lieutenant Stephen Brooks), the 3rd Platoon (under Lieutenant Jeffrey La Cross) and the company headquarters group also committed unspeakable crimes. At least half-a-dozen groups of civilians, including women and children, were assembled and executed. Local people fleeing towards Quang Ngai along the road were machine-gunned, and wounded civilians (including young children) were summarily shot. As these massacres were taking place, at least four girls and women were raped or gang-raped by groups of soldiers. In one case, a rapist from 2nd Company is reported to have shoved the muzzle of his assault rifle into the vagina of his victim and pulled the trigger.

fires are sold in the evenings on Phan Dinh Phung St between Tran Hung Dao and Nguyen Nghiem Sts. *Pho 79* at the corner of Quang Trung and Tran Hung Dao Sts has soup.

Getting There & Away

Bus Quang Ngai Bus Station (Ben Xe Khach Quang Ngai) is opposite 32 Nguyen Nghiem St, which is about 100 metres east of Quang Trung St (National Highway 1). Buses from here go to Buon Ma Thuot (and other places in Dac Lac Province), Dalat, Danang, Ho Chi Minh City, Hoi An, Kon Tum, Pleiku, Nha Trang and Qui Nhon.

There is no express bus from Quang Ngai to Danang. Old Renault buses, which take four hours to cover the 130 km to Danang, begin their daily runs around 6 am.

Train The Quang Ngai Railway Station (Ga Quang Nghia or Ga Quang Ngai) is three km west of the centre of town. To get there, take Phan Boi Chau St west from Quang Trung St (National Highway 1) and continue going in the same direction after the street name changes to Nguyen Chanh St. At 389 Nguyen Chanh St (which you'll come to as Nguyen Chanh St curves left), continue straight on down a side street. The railway station is at the end of the street.

The Reunification Express Train stops at Quang Ngai. For ticket prices, see the Train section in the Getting Around chapter.

Car Road distances from Quang Ngai are 131 km to Danang, 860 km to Ho Chi Minh City, 412 km to Nha Trang and 174 km to Qui Nhon.

One American soldier is reported to have shot himself in the foot to get himself out of the slaughter; he was the only American casualty that day in the entire operation.

Troops who participated were ordered to keep their mouths shut about the whole incident, but several soldiers who were at Son My disobeyed orders and went public with the story after returning to the USA. When the story broke in the newspapers, it had a devastating effect on the military's morale and fuelled further public protests against the war. Unlike WW II veterans who returned home to parades and glory, American soldiers coming home from Vietnam often found themselves ostracised by their fellow citizens and taunted as 'baby killers'.

Action to cover up the atrocities was undertaken at every level of the US Army command, but eventually there were several investigations. Though a number of officers were disciplined, only one, Lieutenant Calley, was court-marshalled and found guilty of the murders of 22 unarmed civilians. He was sentenced to life imprisonment in 1971. He spent three years under house arrest at Fort Benning, Georgia, while appealing his conviction. Calley was paroled in 1974 after the US Supreme Court refused to hear his case. According to newspaper reports, he still lives in Georgia and works as a sales clerk.

Lieutenant William Calley

Calley's case still causes controversy – many have said that he was made the military's scapegoat because of his low rank, and that officers much higher up ordered the massacres. What is certain is that Calley did not act alone.

The Son My Memorial is set in a park where Xom Lang sub-hamlet once stood. Around it, among the trees and rice paddies, are the graves of some of the victims, buried in family groups. Near the memorial is a worthwhile museum opened in 1992. ■

AROUND QUANG NGAI
Son My (My Lai)

The site of the My Lai Massacre is 14 km from Quang Ngai. To get there from town, head north (towards Danang) on Quang Trung St (National Highway 1) and cross the long bridge over the Tra Khuc River. A few metres from the northern end of the bridge you will come to a triangular concrete stele indicating the way to the Son My Memorial. Turn right (eastward, parallel to the river) on the dirt road and continue for 12 km. The road to Son My passes through particularly beautiful countryside of rice paddies, manioc patches and vegetable gardens shaded by casuarinas and eucalyptus trees.

If you don't have a car, the best way to get to Son My District from Quang Ngai is to hire a motorbike (Honda om) near the bus station or along Quang Trung St.

Bien Khe Ky Beach

Bien Khe Ky Beach (Bai Bien Khe Ky) is a long, secluded beach of fine sand 17 km from Quang Ngai and several kilometres past (east of) the Son My Memorial. The beach stretches for many kilometres along a long, thin casuarina-lined spit of sand separated from the mainland by Song Kinh Giang, a body of water about 150 metres inland from the beach.

As the mass killings in and around Xom Lang were taking place a couple of kilometres to the west, another massacre was being committed by Bravo Company just east and south of the bridge across Song Kinh Giang.

This whole incident, in which up to 90 civilians may have been killed, was completely covered up, and the charges filed against Bravo Company's commanding officer, 1st Lieutenant Thomas Willingham, were eventually dismissed.

Quang Nam & Danang

The province of Quang Nam, which includes the municipality of Danang, contains Vietnam's most important Cham sites. Major Cham historical sites which have now become the stomping grounds of tourists include My Son and Simhapura (Tra Kieu).

Side trips to places like the Marble Mountains and China Beach continue to draw a steady trickle of travellers. The once-bustling city of Danang is rather quiet these days, but the Cham Museum here is top-notch.

The old port of Faifo (now called Hoi An) has a great deal of rustic charm. It's one of the best spots in Vietnam to relax and imagine what life was like in centuries past.

CHU LAI

About 30 km north of Quang Ngai, the buildings and concrete aircraft revetments of the

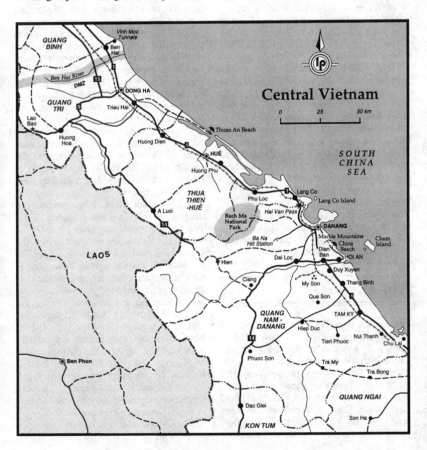

huge American base at Chu Lai stretch along several kilometres of sand to the east of National Highway 1. Despite the obvious dangers, collecting and selling scrap metal from old ordnance has become a thriving local industry. During the war, there was a huge shantytown made of packing crates and waste tin from canning factories next to the base. The inhabitants of the shantytown supported themselves by providing services to the Americans: doing laundry, selling soft drinks and engaging in prostitution.

TAM KY

Tam Ky is a nondescript town on the highway between Quang Ngai and Danang. The main point of interest are the nearby Cham Towers at Chien Dang (Chien Dang Cham).

Three Cham towers, enclosed by a wall, stand at Chien Dang, which is five km north of Tam Ky, 69 km north of Quang Ngai and 62 km south of Danang. A broken stele here dates from the 13th-century reign of King Harivarman. Many of the Cham statues you can see on display at Chien Dang were collected from other parts of the country after the Vietnam War. Many of these statues show signs of war-related damage.

Places to Stay

The *Tam Ky Hotel* (Khach San Tam Ky) is a decent place next to National Highway 1 in the centre of town. This is the only hotel in Tam Ky that accepts foreigners.

Hoi An

Hoi An is a riverside town 30 km south of Danang. Known as Faifo to early Western traders, it was one of South-East Asia's major international ports during the 17th, 18th and 19th centuries. In its heyday, Hoi An, a contemporary of Macau and Malacca, was an important port of call for Dutch, Portuguese, Chinese, Japanese and other trading vessels. Vietnamese ships and sailors based in Hoi An sailed to Thailand and Indonesia as well as to all sections of Vietnam. Today, parts of Hoi An look exactly as they did a century and a half ago. More than perhaps any other place in Vietnam, Hoi An retains the feel of centuries past, making it the sort of place that grows on you the more you explore it.

History

Recently excavated ceramic fragments from 2200 years ago constitute the earliest evidence of human habitation in the Hoi An area. They are thought to belong to the late-Iron Age Sa Huynh civilisation, which is related to the Dong Son culture of northern Vietnam.

From the 2nd to the 10th century, when this region was the heartland of the Kingdom of Champa – this is when the nearby Cham capital of Simhapura (Tra Kieu) and the temples of Indrapura (Dong Duong) and My Son were built – there was a bustling seaport at Hoi An. Persian and Arab documents from the latter part of the period mention Hoi An as a provisioning stop for trading ships. Archaeologists have uncovered the foundations of numerous Cham towers in the vicinity of Hoi An (the bricks and stones of the towers themselves were reused by later Vietnamese settlers).

In 1307, the Cham king married the daughter of a Vietnamese monarch of the Tran Dynasty, presenting Quang Nam Province to the Vietnamese as a gift. When the Cham king died, his successor refused to recognise the deal and fighting broke out; for the next century, chaos reigned. By the 15th century, peace had been restored, allowing normal commerce to resume. During the next four centuries, Chinese, Japanese, Dutch, Portuguese, Spanish, Indian, Filipino, Indonesian, Thai, French, English and American ships called at Hoi An to purchase high-grade silk (for which the area is famous), fabrics, paper, porcelain, tea, sugar, molasses, areca nuts, pepper, Chinese medicines, elephant tusks, beeswax, mother-of-pearl, lacquer, sulphur and lead.

The Chinese and Japanese traders sailed south in the spring, driven by winds out of the north-east. They would stay in Hoi An until the summer, when southerly winds would blow them home. During their four-month sojourn in Hoi An, the merchants rented waterfront houses for use as ware-houses and living quarters. Some traders began leaving full-time agents in Hoi An to take care of off-season business affairs. This is how the foreigners' colonies got started. The Japanese ceased coming to Hoi An after 1637, when the Japanese government forbade all contact with the outside world.

Hoi An was the first place in Vietnam to be exposed to Christianity. Among the 17th-century missionary visitors was the French priest Alexandre de Rhodes, who devised the Latin-based quoc ngu script for the Vietnamese language.

Hoi An was almost completely destroyed during the Tay Son Rebellion in the 1770s and 1780s but was rebuilt and continued to serve as an important port for foreign trade until the late 19th century, when the Thu Bon River (Cai River), which links Hoi An with the sea, silted up and became too shallow for navigation. During this period Danang (Tourane) began to eclipse Hoi An as a port and centre of commerce. In 1916, a rail line linking Danang with Hoi An was destroyed by a terrible storm; it was never rebuilt.

The French chose Hoi An as an administrative centre. During the American war, Hoi An remained almost completely undamaged.

Hoi An was the site of the first Chinese settlement in southern Vietnam. The town's Chinese congregational assembly halls (hoi quan) still play a special role among southern Vietnam's ethnic-Chinese, some of whom travel to Hoi An from all over the south to participate in congregation-wide celebrations. Today, 1300 of the Hoi An area's present population of about 60,000 are ethnic-Chinese. Relations between ethnic-Vietnamese and ethnic-Chinese in Hoi An are excellent, in part because the Chinese here, unlike their countryfolk elsewhere in the country, have become culturally assimilated to the point that they even speak Vietnamese among themselves.

A number of Hoi An's wooden buildings date from the first part of the 19th century or earlier, giving visitors who have just a bit of imagination the feeling that they have been transported back a couple of centuries to a time when the wharf was crowded with sailing ships, the streets teemed with porters transporting goods to and from warehouses, and traders from a dozen countries haggled in a babble of languages.

Architecture

So far, 844 structures of historical significance have been officially identified in Hoi An. These structures are of nine types:

* Houses and shops
* Wells
* Family chapels for ancestor worship
* Pagodas
* Vietnamese and Chinese temples
* Bridges
* Communal buildings
* Assembly halls (hoi quan) of various Chinese congregations
* Tombs (Vietnamese, Chinese and Japanese; no original European tombs survive)

Many of Hoi An's older structures exhibit features of traditional architecture rarely seen today. The fronts of some shops which are open during the day to display the wares are shuttered at night, as they have been for centuries, by inserting horizontal planks into grooves cut into the columns that support the roof. Some roofs are made of thousands of brick-coloured 'Yin and Yang' roof tiles, so called because of the way the alternating rows of concave and convex tiles fit together. During the rainy season, the lichens and mosses that live on the tiles spring to life, turning entire rooftops bright green.

Many of Hoi An's houses have round pieces of wood with a Yin and Yang symbol in the middle surrounded by a spiral design over the doorway. These 'watchful eyes' (mat cua) are supposed to protect the residents of the house from harm.

Every year during the rainy season, Hoi An has problems with flooding, especially near the waterfront. The greatest flood Hoi An has ever known took place in 1964, when the water reached all the way up to the roof beams of the houses.

Hoi An's historic structures are gradually being restored and there is a sincere effort being made to preserve the unique character of the city. The local government has put some thought into what is being done – the old houses must be licensed to do restoration work, and this must be done in a tasteful manner. The government certifies the historical significance of the buildings – at present, there are four categories of certificates. Many of the house owners now charge admission – as much as US$3 for a guided tour of the building – but this is negotiable. The government permits this with the idea that the funds will be used for renovation of the homes rather than towards the purchase of TVs and new motorcycles. Assistance in historical preservation is being provided to local authorities by the Archaeological Institute in Hanoi, the Japan-Vietnam Friendship Association and experts from Europe and Japan. The Old Town section of Hoi An is now closed to motor vehicles – a first in Vietnam.

Orientation
Bach Dang St runs along the Thu Bon River, which is also known as the Hoi An River and the Cai River. Many of Hoi An's most interesting sites are along Tran Phu St.

Information
Tourist Office Hoi An Tourist Company is at 12 Phan Chu Trinh St. Vehicle rentals and guides can be arranged here.

The tourist office of the Hoi An Hotel is at 6 Tran Hung Dao St and is primarily in the business of booking tours.

Money The Bank of Foreign Trade will change travellers' cheques and US dollars. The bank is 50 metres south of the GPO at 2 Hoang Dieu St. The Hoi An Hotel will exchange cash only.

Post & Telecommunications The GPO is across from 11 Tran Hung Dao St (on the north-west corner of Ngo Gia Tu and Tran Hung Dao Sts).

Emergency The hospital is opposite the GPO at 10 Tran Hung Dao St.

Japanese Covered Bridge
The Japanese Covered Bridge (Cau Nhat Ban, or Lai Vien Kieu) connects 155 Tran Phu St with 1 Nguyen Thi Minh Khai St. The first bridge on this site was constructed in 1593 by the Japanese community of Hoi An to link their neighbourhood with the Chinese quarters across the stream. The bridge was provided with a roof so it could be used as a shelter from both the rain and the sun.

The Japanese Covered Bridge is very solidly built, apparently because the original builders were afraid of earthquakes, which are common in Japan. Over the centuries, the ornamentation of the bridge has remained relatively faithful to the original Japanese design, reflecting the Japanese preference for understatement, which contrasts greatly with the Vietnamese and Chinese penchant for wild decoration. The French flattened out the roadway to make it more suitable for their motorcars but the original arched shape was restored during the major renovation work carried out in 1986.

Built into the northern side of the bridge is a small temple, Chua Cau. Over the door is written the name given to the bridge in 1719 to replace the name then in use, which meant the Japanese Bridge. The new name, Lai Vien Kieu (Bridge for Passers-by From Afar), never caught on.

According to legend, there once lived an enormous monster called Cu whose head was in India, its tail in Japan and its body in Vietnam. Whenever the monster moved, terrible disasters, such as floods and earthquakes, befell Vietnam. This bridge was built on the monster's weakest point – its 'Achilles' heel', so to speak – killing it. But the people of Hoi An took pity on the slain monster and built this temple to pray for its soul.

The two entrances to the bridge are

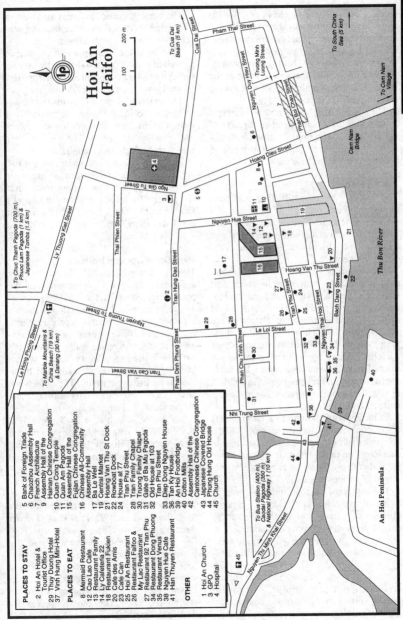

PLACES TO STAY

2   Hoi An Hotel &
    Tourist Office
29 Thuy Duong Hotel
37 Vinh Hung Mini-Hotel

PLACES TO EAT

8   Mermaid Restaurant
12 Cao Lau Cafe
13 Restaurant Family
18 Cafeteria 22
18 Restaurant Fukien
20 Cafe des Amis
23 Cafe Can
25 Hoi An Restaurant
26 Restaurant Faifoo &
    My Lac Restaurant
27 Restaurant 92 Tran Phu
34 Restaurant Dong Phuong
35 Restaurant Venus
38 Nguyen Hue Cafe
41 Han Thuyen Restaurant

OTHER

1   Hoi An Church
3   GPO
4   Hospital
5   Bank of Foreign Trade
6   Chaozhou Assembly Hall
7   French Architecture
9   Assembly Hall of the
    Hainan Chinese Congregation
10 Quan Cong Temple
11 Quan Am Pagoda
15 Assembly Hall of the
    Fujian Chinese Congregation
16 Chinese All-Community
    Assembly Hall
17 Ba Le Well
19 Central Market
21 Hoang Van Thu St Dock
22 Rowboat Dock
24 House at 77
    Tran Phu Street
28 Tran Family Chapel
30 Truong Family Chapel
31 Gate of Ba Mu Pagoda
32 Old House at 103
    Tran Thu Street
33 Diep Dong Nguyen House
39 Tan Ky House
40 An Hoi Footbridge
    Cotton Mills
42 Assembly Hall of the
    Cantonese Chinese Congregation
43 Japanese Covered Bridge
44 Phung Hung Old House
45 Church

guarded by a pair of monkeys on one side and a pair of dogs on the other. According to one story, these animals were popularly revered because many of Japan's emperors were born in years of the dog and monkey. Another tale relates that construction of the bridge was begun in the year of the monkey and finished in the year of the dog.

The stelae listing Vietnamese and Chinese contributors to a subsequent restoration of the bridge are written in Chinese characters (chu nho), the nom script not yet having become popular in these parts.

Tan Ky House

The Tan Ky House (☎ 61474) was built almost two centuries ago as the home of a well-to-do ethnic-Vietnamese merchant. The house has been lovingly preserved and today it looks almost exactly as it did in the early 19th century.

The design of the Tan Ky House shows evidence of the influence Japanese and Chinese styles had on local architecture. Japanese elements include the crabshell-shaped ceiling (in the section immediately before the courtyard), which is supported by three progressively shorter beams, one on top of the other. There are similar beams in the salon. Under the crabshell ceiling are carvings of crossed sabres enwrapped in a ribbon of silk. The sabres symbolise force; the silk represents flexibility.

Chinese poems written in inlaid mother-of-pearl are hung from a number of the columns that hold up the roof. The Chinese characters on these 150-year-old panels are formed entirely out of birds gracefully portrayed in various positions of flight.

The courtyard has four functions: to let in light; to provide ventilation; to bring a glimpse of nature into the home; and to collect rainwater and provide drainage. The stone tiles covering the patio floor were brought from Thanh Hoa Province in north-central Vietnam. The carved wooden balcony supports around the courtyard are decorated with grape leaves, a European import, further evidence of the unique mingling of cultures that took place in Hoi An.

The back of the house fronts the river. In olden times, this section of the building was rented out to foreign merchants.

That the house was a place of commerce as well as a residence is indicated by the two pulleys attached to a beam in the storage loft located just inside the front door.

The exterior of the roof is made of tiles; inside, the ceiling consists of wood. This design keeps the house cool in the summer and warm in the winter. The house's floor tiles were brought from near Hanoi.

The Tan Ky House is a private home at 101 Nguyen Thai Hoc St. It is open to visitors for a small fee. The owner, whose family has lived here for seven generations, speaks fluent French and English. The house is open every day from 8 am to noon and from 2 to 4.30 pm.

Diep Dong Nguyen House

The Diep Dong Nguyen House was built for a Chinese merchant, an ancestor of the present inhabitants, in the late 19th century. The front room on the ground floor was once a dispensary for Chinese medicines (thuoc bac), which were stored in the glass-enclosed cases lining the walls. The owner's private collection of antiques, which includes photographs, porcelain and furniture, is on display upstairs. The objects are not for sale! Two of the chairs were once lent by the family to Emperor Bao Dai.

The house, which is at 80 Nguyen Thai Hoc St (by the new numbering system) and 58 Nguyen Thai Hoc St (by the old system), is open every day from 8 am to noon and from 2 to 4.30 pm.

House at 77 Tran Phu St

This private house, which is across the street from the Restaurant 92 Tran Phu, is about three centuries old. There is some especially fine carving on the wooden walls of the rooms around the courtyard, on the roof beams and under the crabshell roof (in the salon next to the courtyard). Note the green ceramic tiles built into the railing around the courtyard balcony. The house is open to visitors for a small fee.

GLENN BEANLAND

BRENDAN McCARTHY

GREG ALFORD

GENEVIEVE WEBB

SARA JANE CLELAND

A	
B	C
D	E

Quang Nam & Danang

A The rugged coastline at Lang Co
B A market boat in Danang
C The Cham Museum in Danang

D Weathered facade in historical Hoi An
E The Japanese Covered Bridge
   in Hoi An

BRENDAN McCARTHY

BRENDAN McCARTHY

GLENN BEANLAND

GLENN BEANLAND

BRENDAN McCARTHY

A	B
	C
D	E

Hué

A A shy resident of Hué
B Nam Giao (Temple of Heaven)
C Cyclists near the Imperial Enclosure

D The walls of the Imperial Enclosure
E Gateway to Nam Giao
   (Temple of Heaven)

Assembly Hall of the Cantonese Chinese Congregation

The Assembly Hall of the Cantonese Chinese Congregation, founded in 1786, is at 176 Tran Phu St and is open daily from 6 to 7.30 am and from 1 to 5.30 pm. The main altar is dedicated to Quan Cong (Chinese: Guangong). Note the long-handled brass 'fans' to either side of the altar. The lintel and doorposts of the main entrance and a number of the columns supporting the roof are made of single blocks of granite. The other columns were carved out of the durable wood of the jackfruit tree. There are some interesting carvings on the wooden beams that support the roof in front of the main entrance.

Chinese All-Community Assembly Hall

The Chinese All-Community Assembly Hall (Chua Ba), founded in 1773, was used by all five Chinese congregations in Hoi An: Fujian, Cantonese, Hainan, Chaozhou and Hakka. The pavilions off the main courtyard incorporate 19th-century French elements.

The main entrance is on Tran Phu St opposite Hoang Van Thu St, but the only way in these days is around the back at 31 Phan Chu Trinh St.

Assembly Hall of the Fujian Chinese Congregation

The Assembly Hall of the Fujian Chinese Congregation was founded as a place to hold community meetings. Later, it was transformed into a temple for the worship of Thien Hau, Goddess of the Sea and Protector of Fishermen and Sailors, who was born in Fujian Province. The triple gate to the complex was built in 1975.

The mural near the entrance to the main hall on the right-hand wall depicts Thien Hau, her way lit by lantern light, crossing a stormy sea to rescue a foundering ship. On the wall opposite is a mural of the heads of the six Fujian families who fled from China to Hoi An in the 17th century following the overthrow of the Ming Dynasty.

The second-to-last chamber contains a statue of Thien Hau. To either side of the

BRENDAN McCARTHY

Relaxing outside one of Hoi An's many historic temples

entrance stand red-skinned Thuan Phong Nhi, who can hear for great distances, and green-skinned Thien Ly Nhan, who can see for a 1000 miles. When either sees or hears sailors in distress, they inform Thien Hau, who then sets off to effect a rescue. The replica of a Chinese boat along the right-hand wall is in 1:20 scale. The four sets of triple beams which support the roof are typically Japanese.

The central altar in the last chamber contains seated figures of the heads of the six Fujian families who immigrated to Hoi An in the 17th century. The smaller figures below them represent their successors as clan leaders. In a 30-cm-high glass dome is a figurine of Le Huu Trac, a Vietnamese physician renowned in both Vietnam and China for his curative abilities.

Behind the altar on the left is the God of Prosperity. On the right are three fairies and smaller figures representing the 12 'midwives' *(ba mu)*, each of whom teaches newborns a different skill necessary for the first year of life: smiling, sucking, lying on their stomachs and so forth. Childless couples often come here to pray for offspring. The three groups of figures in this chamber represent the elements most central to life: one's ancestors, one's children and economic wellbeing.

The middle altar of the room to the right of the courtyard commemorates deceased leaders of the Fujian congregation. On either side are lists of contributors, women on the left and men on the right. The wall panels represent the four seasons.

The Assembly Hall of the Fujian Chinese Congregation, which is opposite 35 Tran Phu St, is open from 7.30 am to noon and from 2 to 5.30 pm. It is fairly well lit and can be visited after dark. Shoes should be removed upon mounting the platform just past the naves.

Quan Cong Temple

Quan Cong Temple, also known as Chua Ong, is at 24 Tran Phu St (according to the new numbers) and 168 Tran Phu St (according to the old numbering system). Founded in 1653, this Chinese temple is dedicated to Quan Cong, whose partially gilt statue – made of papier-mâché on a wood frame – is in the central altar at the back of the sanctuary. On the left is a statue of General Chau Xuong, one of Quan Cong's guardians, striking a tough-guy pose. On the right is the rather plump administrative mandarin Quan Binh. The life-size white horse recalls a mount ridden by Quan Cong until he was given a red horse of extraordinary endurance, representations of which are common in Chinese pagodas.

Stone plaques on the walls list contributors to the construction and repair of the temple. Check out the carp-shaped rain spouts on the roof surrounding the courtyard. The carp, symbol of patience in Chinese mythology, is a popular symbol in Hoi An.

Shoes should be removed when mounting the platform in front of the statue of Quang Cong.

Assembly Hall of the Hainan Chinese Congregation

The Assembly Hall of the Hainan Chinese Congregation was built in 1883 as a memorial to 108 merchants from Hainan Island in southern China who were mistaken for pirates and killed in Quang Nam Province during the reign of Emperor Tu Duc (ruled 1848-83). The elaborate dais contains plaques in their memory. In front of the central altar is a fine gilded wood carving of Chinese court life.

The Hainan Assembly Hall is on the east end of Tran Phu St, near the corner of Hoang Dieu St.

Chaozhou Assembly Hall

The Chaozhou Chinese in Hoi An built their congregational hall in 1776. There is some outstanding woodcarving on the beams, walls and altar. On the doors in front of the altar are carvings of two Chinese girls wearing their hair in the Japanese manner.

The Chaozhou Assembly Hall is across from 157 Nguyen Duy Hieu St (near the corner of Hoang Dieu St).

Truong Family Chapel

The Truong Family Chapel (Nha Tho Toc Truong), founded about two centuries ago, is a shrine dedicated to the ancestors of this ethnic-Chinese family. Some of the memorial plaques were presented by the emperors of Vietnam to honour members of the Truong family who served as local officials and as mandarins at the imperial court. To get there, turn into the alley next to 69 Phan Chu Trinh St.

Tran Family Chapel

At 21 Le Loi St, at the intersection with Phan Chu Trinh St (north-east corner), is the Tran Family Chapel. This house for worshipping ancestors was built about 200 years ago with donations from family members. The Tran family traces its origins to China and moved to Vietnam around the year 1700. The architecture of the building reflects the influence of Chinese and Japanese styles. On the altar are wooden boxes containing the ancestors' stone tablets with Chinese characters chiselled in.

Gate of Ba Mu Pagoda

Though Ba Mu Pagoda, founded in 1628, was demolished by the South Vietnamese government during the 1960s to make room for a three-storey school building, the gate (Phat Tu) remains standing. Enormous representations of pieces of fruit form part of the wall between the two doorways.

The gate of Ba Mu Pagoda is opposite 68 Phan Chu Trinh St.

Ba Le Well

Water for the preparation of authentic *cao lau* (see Places to Eat) must be drawn from Ba Le Well and no other. The well itself, which is said to date from Cham times, is square in shape. To get there, turn down the alleyway opposite 35 Phan Chu Trinh St. Hang a right before reaching number 45/17.

French Architecture

There is a whole city block of colonnaded French buildings on Phan Boi Chau St between numbers 22 and 73.

Cotton Weaving

Hoi An is known for its production of cotton cloth. All over the city there are cotton mills with rows of fantastic wooden looms that make a rhythmic clackety-clack clackety-clack sound as a whirring cycloidal drive wheel shoots the shuttle back and forth under the watchful eyes of the machine attendant. The elegant technology used in building these domestically produced machines dates from the Industrial Revolution. Indeed, this is what mills in Victorian England must have looked like.

There are cloth mills at numbers 140 and 151 Tran Phu St.

Caodai Pagoda

Serving Hoi An's Caodai community, many of whose members live along the path out to the Japanese tombs, is the small Caodai Pagoda (built 1952) between numbers 64 and 70 Huynh Thuc Khang St (near the bus station). One priest lives here. Sugar and corn are grown in the front yard to raise some extra cash.

Hoi An Church

The only tombs of Europeans in Hoi An are in the yard of the Hoi An Church, which is at the corner of Nguyen Truong To and Le Hong Phong Sts. When this modern building was constructed to replace an earlier structure at another site, several 18th-century missionaries were reburied here.

Chuc Thanh Pagoda

Chuc Thanh Pagoda is the oldest pagoda in Hoi An. It was founded in 1454 by Minh Hai, a Buddhist monk from China. Among the antique ritual objects still in use are several bells, a stone gong two centuries old and a carp-shaped wooden gong said to be even older. Today, five elderly monks live here.

In the main sanctuary, gilt Chinese characters inscribed on a red roof beam give details of the pagoda's construction. Under a wooden canopy on the central dais sits an A Di Da Buddha flanked by two Thich Ca Buddhas (Sakyamuni). In front of them is a statue of Thich Ca as a boy flanked by his servants.

To get to Chuc Thanh Pagoda, go all the way to the end of Nguyen Truong To St and turn left. Follow the sandy path for 500 metres.

Phuoc Lam Pagoda

Phuoc Lam Pagoda was founded in the mid-17th century. Late in the century, the head monk was An Thiem, a Vietnamese prodigy who became a monk at the age of eight. When he was 18, the king drafted An Thiem's brothers into his army to put down a rebellion. An Thiem volunteered to take the places of the other men in his family and eventually rose to the rank of general. After the war, he returned to the monkhood but felt guilty about the many people he had slain. To atone for his sins, he volunteered to clean the Hoi An Market for a period of 20 years. When the 20 years were up, he was asked to come to Phuoc Lam Pagoda as head monk.

To get to Phuoc Lam Pagoda, continue past Chuc Thanh Pagoda for 350 metres. The path passes by an obelisk erected over the tomb of 13 ethnic-Chinese decapitated by the Japanese during WW II for resistance activities.

Japanese Tombs

The tombstone of the Japanese merchant Yajirobei, who died in 1647, is clearly inscribed with Japanese characters. The stele, which faces north-east towards Japan, is held in place by the tomb's original covering, which is made of an especially hard kind of cement whose ingredients include powdered seashells, the leaves of the *boi loi* tree and cane sugar. Yajirobei may have been a Christian who came to Vietnam to escape persecution in his native land.

To get to Yajirobei's tomb, go north to the end of Nguyen Truong Tu St and follow the sand path around to the left (west) for 40 metres until you get to a fork. The path that continues straight on leads to Chuc Thanh Pagoda, but you should turn right (northward). Keep going for just over one km, turning left (to the north) at the first fork and

left (to the north-west) at the second fork. When you arrive at the open fields, keep going until you cross the irrigation channel. Just on the other side of the channel turn right (south-east) onto a raised path. After going for 150 metres, turn left (north-east) into the paddies and walk 100 metres. The tomb, which is on a platform surrounded by a low stone wall, stands surrounded by rice paddies.

The tombstone of a Japanese named Masai, who died in 1629, is a few hundred metres back towards Hoi An. To get there, turn left (south-east) at a point about 100 metres towards town from the edge of the rice fields. The tombstone is on the right-hand side of the trail about 30 metres from the main path.

For help in finding the Japanese tombs, show the locals the following words: *Ma Nhat* (or *Mo Nhat)*, which means Japanese tombs.

There are other Japanese tombs in Duy Xuyen District, which is across the delta of the Thu Bon River from Hoi An.

Cua Dai Beach

The fine sands of Cua Dai Beach (Bai Tam Cua Dai) are a 20-minute bike ride from Hoi An. When there is a full moon, people come here to hang out until late at night. Changing booths are provided; refreshments are sold in the shaded kiosks.

Cham Island is 21 km offshore but can be visible on a clear day. If the weather cooperates, you may be able to see the Marble Mountains to the north-west and, behind them, the peaks around Hai Van Pass.

Cua Dai Beach is five km east of Hoi An out Cua Dai St, which is the continuation of Tran Hung Dao and Phan Dinh Phung Sts. The road passes shrimp-hatching pools built with Australian assistance.

Places to Stay

The *Hoi An Hotel* (☎ 61574; fax 61636; 130 rooms) at 6 Tran Hung Dao St is a grand colonial-style building that was a US Marine base during the Vietnam War. This is not only the largest hotel in town, it's *the* most popular hotel in Vietnam. As a practical matter, this means it's usually full by evening so you'd better get there early if you want a private room. The hotel's policy is to first fill up all the rooms, and if there are additional travellers, they will be housed in a large overflow dormitory (20 to 30 beds) costing US$3 to US$4 per person. However, backpackers looking to check into the dormitory when the hotel is not already full (morning) will be told that the dormitory doesn't exist – come back by 5 pm and it will exist, though it might be full. Regular rooms cost US$9 to US$44.

Recognising the shortage of hotel space, the local People's Committee has finally authorised private individuals to open hotels. One of the first to open was the *Thuy Duong Hotel* (☎ 61574; nine rooms) at 11 Le Loi St. This cosy little place costs US$10 to US$12.

There is also the small but plush *Vinh Hung Mini-Hotel* (☎ 61621; 14 rooms) at 143 Tran Phu St. Room rates are US$15, US$25, US$30 and US$35 with breakfast thrown in.

Places to Eat

Hoi An's contribution to Vietnamese cuisine is *cao lau*, which consists of doughy flat noodles mixed with croutons, bean sprouts and greens and topped with pork slices. It is mixed with crumbled crispy rice paper immediately before eating. Hoi An is the *only* place genuine cao lau can be made because the water used in the preparation of the authentic article must come from a particular well in town. You'll see cao lau listed on menus all over Hoi An, though perhaps not in the bakeries and French restaurants (yet).

There are heaps of new restaurants on Nguyen Hue, Tran Phu and Bach Dang Sts. Many cooking styles are available, including Western (muesli, spaghetti and pizza), Vietnamese, Chinese and vegetarian food for reasonable prices. The only negative aspect of this is that the restaurant signs are beginning to have a visual impact, sadly reminiscent of Thamel in Kathmandu and Khao San Rd in Bangkok.

Mermaid Restaurant (☎ 61527), or Nhu Y, is at 2 Tran Phu St. It dishes up great food, including late breakfasts.

Ly Cafeteria 22 (☎ 61603) at 22 Nguyen Hue St has become a Hoi An institution. Male travellers regularly fall in love with Miss Ly (is it her cooking that drives them wild?) and she has received a number of marriage proposals by mail. Nevertheless, she resolutely stays with the family and continues to churn out great food. The restaurant opens around 6.30 am, closes when empty and is always crowded (even with female travellers).

No prizes for guessing the house speciality at the *Cao Lao Café*. You can try Hoi An's famous food here at 28 Nguyen Hue St.

Restaurant Family offers real Vietnamese family cooking at 36 Tran Phu St.

Farther west on Tran Phu St is *Restaurant Fukien*. This is one of the best Chinese restaurants in town.

Restaurant 92 Tran Phu is at – you guessed it – 92 Tran Phu St. Vietnamese food is the house speciality. Just slightly farther west on the north side of Tran Phu St are the *Restaurant Faifoo* and *My Lac Restaurant*. You can also get your cao lao across the street at the *Hoi An Restaurant*.

Near the Japanese Covered Bridge you'll find the *Nguyen Hue Café* (across from 174 Tran Phu St).

Moving one block south, you hit the riverfront, which is a virtual eating arcade. The *Han Thuyen Restaurant* is also nicknamed the Floating Restaurant, though it doesn't actually float but is built on stilts over the water. Perhaps it would be better if it did float, seeing how flood-prone this river is.

Restaurant Venus at 89 Bach Dang St faces the river. *Restaurant Dong Phuong* is just next door. Farther east is *Café Can* at 74 Bach Dang St.

Cafe des Amis (☎ 61360), 52 Bach Dang St, is also along the riverside. This place gets steady rave reviews from satisfied customers. Especially recommended are the fine seafood and vegetarian cuisine.

QUANG NAM & DANANG

Things to Buy

The presence of numerous tourists has turned the fake antique business into Hoi An's major growth industry. Theoretically you could find something here that is really old, but it's hard to believe that all the genuine stuff wasn't scooped up long ago by those who came before you.

On the other hand, there is some really elegant artwork around, even if it was made only yesterday. The paintings are excellent, and prices are good (with perhaps a bit of bargaining). You'll hardly have a difficult time finding this stuff – it's everywhere and anywhere.

Getting There & Away

Bus Buses from Danang to Hoi An (via the Marble Mountains and China Beach) leave from both the Intercity Bus Station and the Short-Haul Pickup Truck Station, which has more frequent service. The ride takes an hour once the vehicle actually gets going.

The Hoi An Bus Station (Ben Quoc Doanh Xe Khach; ☎ 84) is one km west of the centre of town at 74 Huynh Thuc Khang St. Small truck-buses from here go to Dai Loc (Ai Nghia), Danang, Quang Ngai (once a day departing in the early morning), Que Son, Tam Ky and Tra My. Service to Danang begins at 5 am; the last bus to Danang departs in the late afternoon.

In October, about 30 km south of Hoi An, we were delayed at night for six hours by flooding almost a metre deep after heavy rain. Our driver slung up his hammock over the steering wheel and went to sleep. Other more determined (foolish?) drivers proceeded at a walking pace for several km behind two bus boys who waded uncomplainingly through the water. Their positions marked the edges of the road and the drivers were careful to stay between them. Wherever you looked there was the shimmer of a huge plain of water. In front of us was a line of buses and trucks whose lights sliced in two the black waters all around.

Gordon Balderston

Minibus Many hotels and cafes in Hoi An offer minibuses south to Nha Trang ($15) and north to Hué ($5).

Car There are two land routes from Danang to Hoi An. The shortest way is to drive to the Marble Mountains (11 km from Danang) and continue south along the 'Korean Highway' for another 19 km. Alternatively, you can head south from Danang on National Highway 1 and, at a signposted intersection 27 km from the city, turn left (east) for 10 km.

Boat At least a short paddle-boat trip on the Thu Bon River (the Cai River) – the largest in Quang Nam-Danang Province – is recommended. Chartered boats can be found at the Hoang Van Thu St Dock, which is across from 50 Bach Dang St. A simple boat powered by an oarswoman costs something like US$2 per hour, and for most travellers one hour will probably be enough. By motor launch it may be possible to take an all-day boat ride from Hoi An all the way to Simhapura (Tra Kieu) and the My Son area.

Small motorised ferries leave Hoi An for nearby districts and Cham Island from the Hoang Van Thu St Dock. The daily boat to Cham Island usually departs between 7 and 8 am. The daily boat to Duy Xuyen leaves at 5 am. There is also frequent service to Cam Kim Island.

Getting Around

The best way to get around Hoi An and to surrounding areas is by bicycle. You can rent bicycles opposite the Hoi An Hotel for US$1 per day or US$0.10 per hour. Some hotels rent bicycles, but of course first priority goes to their guests.

Around Hoi An

MY SON

My Son is Vietnam's most important Cham site. During the centuries when Simhapura (Tra Kieu) served as the political capital of Champa, My Son was the site of the most important Cham intellectual and religious centre and may also have served as a burial place for Cham monarchs. My Son is considered to be Champa's counterpart to the grand

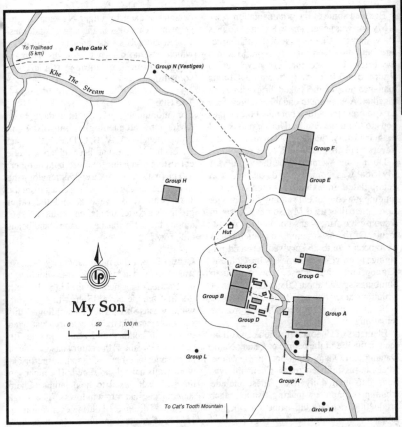

My Son

0   50   100 m

cities of South-East Asia's other Indian-influenced civilisations: Angkor (Cambodia), Bagan (Myanmar), Ayuthaya (Thailand) and Borobudur (Java).

The monuments are set in a verdant valley surrounded by hills and overlooked by massive Cat's Tooth Mountain (Hon Quap). Clear brooks (in which visitors can take a dip) run between the structures and past nearby coffee plantations. The entrance fee is US$1.25; it is used for upkeep of the site.

My Son became a religious centre under King Bhadravarman in the late 4th century. The site was occupied until the 13th century,

the longest period of development of any monument in South-East Asia (by comparison, Angkor's period of development lasted only three centuries, as did that of Pagan). Most of the temples were dedicated to Cham kings associated with divinities, especially Shiva, who was regarded as the founder and protector of Champa's dynasties.

Champa's contact with Java was extensive. Cham scholars were sent to Java to study, and there was a great deal of commerce between the two empires; Cham pottery has been found on Java. In the 12th century, the Cham king wed a Javanese wife.

Because some of the ornamentation work at My Son was never finished, archaeologists know that the Chams first built their structures and only then carved decorations into the brickwork. Researchers have yet to figure out for certain how the Chams managed to get the baked bricks to stick together. According to one theory, they used a paste prepared with a botanical oil indigenous to Central Vietnam. During one period in their history, the summits of some of the towers were covered with a layer of gold.

During the Vietnam War, the vicinity of My Son was completely devastated and depopulated in extended bitter fighting. Finding it a convenient staging ground, Viet Cong guerrillas used My Son as a base; in response the Americans bombed the monuments. Of the 68 structures of which traces have been found, 25 survived repeated pillagings in previous centuries by the Chinese, Khmer and Vietnamese. The American bombings spared about 20 of these, some of which sustained damage. Today, Vietnamese authorities are attempting to restore the remaining sites.

Elements of Cham civilisation can still be seen in the life of the people of Quang Nam-Danang and Quang Ngai provinces, whose forebears assimilated many Cham innovations into their daily lives. These include techniques for pottery making, fishing, sugar production, rice farming, irrigation, silk production and construction.

Information

Warning During the Vietnam War, the hills and valleys around the My Son site were extensively mined. When mine clearing operations were carried out in 1977, six Vietnamese sappers were killed in this vicinity. Today, grazing cows are sometimes blown up, which means that as the years pass and the poor beasts locate the mines one by one, the hills around here are becoming less and less unsafe. For your own safety, do *not* stray from marked paths.

If you are so inclined, you might try looking at the bright side: during French restoration work here in the 1930s, one person was eaten by a tiger. Nowadays, after so many years of war, the largest undomesticated animals in the area are wild pigs, which pose no danger to humans. Human-eating animals or mines…it's always something.

The Site

The monuments of My Son have been divided by archaeologists into 10 main groups, lettered A, A', B, C, D, E, F, G, H and K. Each structure has been given a name consisting of a letter followed by a number.

The first structure you encounter along the trail is the false gate K, which dates from the 11th century. Between K and the other groups is a coffee plantation begun in 1986; among the coffee bushes, peanuts and beans are grown.

Group B B1, the main sanctuary (kalan), was dedicated to Bhadresvara, which is a contraction of the name of the king who built the first temple at My Son with '-esvara,' which means Shiva. The first building on this site was erected in the 4th century, destroyed in the 6th century and rebuilt in the 7th century. Only the 11th-century base, made of large sandstone blocks, remains; the brickwork walls have disappeared. The niches in the wall were used to hold lamps (Cham sanctuaries had no windows). The linga inside was discovered during excavations in 1985 one metre beneath where it is now displayed.

B5, built in the 10th century, was used for storing sacred books and precious ritual objects, some made of gold, which were used in ceremonies performed in B1. The boat-shaped roof (the 'bow' and 'stern' have fallen off) shows the influence of Malayo-Polynesian architecture. Unlike the sanctuaries, this building has windows. The fine Cham masonry inside is all original. Over the window on the wall facing B4 is a bas-relief in brick of two elephants under a tree with two birds in it.

The ornamentation on the exterior walls of B4 is an excellent example of a Cham decorative style, typical of the 9th century,

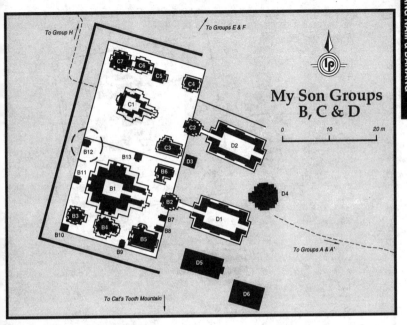

My Son Groups
B, C & D

To Group H

To Groups E & F

To Groups A & A'

To Cat's Tooth Mountain

said to resemble worms. This style is unlike anything found in other South-East Asian cultures.

B3 has an Indian-influenced pyramidal roof typical of Cham towers. Inside B6 is a bathtub-shaped basin for keeping the sacred water that was poured over the linga in B1; this basin is the only one of its kind of Cham origin known.

B2 is a gate. Around the perimeter of Group B (structures B7 through B13) are small temples dedicated to the gods of the directions of the compass (*dikpalaka*).

Group C The 8th-century sanctuary C1 was used to worship Shiva portrayed in human form (rather than in the form of a linga, as in B1). Inside is an altar where a statue of Shiva, now in the Cham Museum in Danang, used to stand. On either side of the stone doorway you can see, bored into the lintel and the floor, the holes in which two wooden doors once swung. Note the motifs, characteristic

of the 8th century, carved into the brickwork of the exterior walls.

Group D Building D1, once a mandapa (meditation house), is now used as a storeroom. It is slated to become a small museum of Cham sculpture. Objects to be displayed include a large panel of Shiva dancing on a platform above the bull Nandin: to Shiva's left is Skanda (under a tree), his son Uma, his wife and a worshipper; to Shiva's right is a dancing saint and two musicians under a tree, one with two drums, the other with a flute. The display will also include a finely carved lion – symbol of the power of the king (the lion was believed to be an incarnation of Vishnu and the protector of kings) – whose style belies Javanese influence.

Group A The path from groups B, C and D to Group A leads eastward from near D4.

Group A was almost completely destroyed by US attacks. According to locals, massive

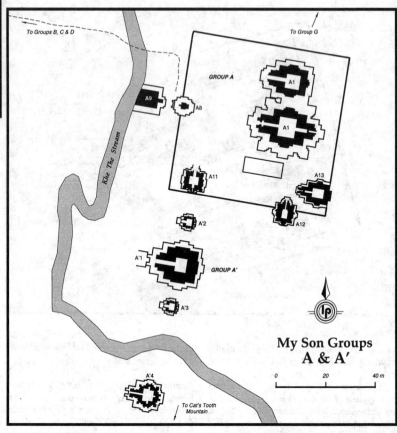

My Son Groups A & A'

A1, considered the most important monument at My Son, remained impervious to aerial bombing and was finally finished off by a helicopter-borne sapper team. All that remains of A1 today is a pile of collapsed brick walls. After the destruction of A1, Philippe Stern, an expert on Cham art and curator of the Guimet Museum in Paris, wrote a letter of protest to President Nixon, who ordered US forces to continue killing the Viet Cong but not to do any further damage to Cham monuments.

A1 was the only Cham sanctuary with two doors. One faced the east, direction of the Hindu gods; the other door faced west towards groups B, C and D and the spirits of the ancestor-kings that may have been buried there. Inside A1 is a stone altar pieced back together in 1988. Among the ruins some of the brilliant brickwork, which is of a style typical of the 10th century, is still visible. At the base of A1 on the side facing A10 (which is decorated in 9th-century style) is a carving of a worshipping figure, flanked by round columns, with a Javanese *kala-makara* (sea-monster god) above. There may be some connection between the presence of this Javanese motif and the studies in Java of a great 10th-century Cham scholar. There are plans to partially restore A1 and A10 as soon as possible.

Other Groups Group A', which dates from the 8th century, is at present overgrown and is thus inaccessible. Group E was built during the 8th to 11th centuries. Group F dates from the 8th century. Group G, which has been damaged by time rather than war, is from the 12th century. There are long-term plans to restore these monuments.

Places to Stay
Unless you have equipment to camp out at My Son, the nearest places to stay are in Hoi An and Danang.

Getting There & Away
Bus If the foregoing travel permit and car rental rule is rescinded, you might be able to get to My Son by bus, though it won't be easy. There are two daily bus runs between the Danang Intercity Bus Station and Trung Phuoc, departing Danang at 7 am and 1 pm and leaving Trung Phuoc at 7 am and 11 am. Unfortunately, Trung Phuoc is quite a way from the path to My Son. Before trying this, get definite information on exactly how close to My Son the bus will bring you. Note that there is no transport back to Danang in the afternoon.

Car The trailhead to My Son is 60 km from Danang. To get there from Danang, head south on National Highway 1. The turn-off to Hoi An is 27 km south of Danang; at a point 6.8 km south of the turn-off (and two km south of the long bridge over the Thu Bon River), turn right towards Tra Kieu. Buu Chau Hill, on which the Mountain Church sits, is 6.5 km from National Highway 1 on the left. The alleyway leading to Tra Kieu Church and its small museum is 400 metres down the road (past the marketplace).

Twelve km past Tra Kieu (and 8.6 km beyond the Chiem Son Railroad Bridge) is Kim Lam. Turn left here (going straight will lead you to a destroyed bridge). The footpath

to the My Son site is on the left-hand side of the road 6.8 km from Kim Lam.

Honda Om It's possible to get to My Son by motorbike. Ask around the Hoi An Hotel area or in the cafes.

Walking It's an appreciable hike (about five km) from the road to My Son. The trail heads south toward Cat's Tooth Mountain (Hon Quap), whose shape does in fact resemble a cat's tooth. When the dirt road is upgraded, vehicles will be able to bring visitors to a point about three km from the monuments.

About two km from the main road the path crosses the Khe The River. If you prefer to cross without swimming, take the detour which goes up the side of the hill to the left. After rejoining the main path, the trail crosses a stream fed by a spring said to have been a favourite stopping place of the famous French archaeologist Henri Parmentier.

Boat If you have lots of time and either hate walking or love boat rides, you might try hiring a small boat (ghe) to take you from Duy Phu hamlet across the Khe The reservoir (Ho Khe The) to where the Khe The River feeds into the reservoir, which is still three km from My Son. Ask the locals for a *ghe den My Son*. The ride takes about 30 minutes.

Tours Informal minibus tours are being organised by cafes in Hoi An and Danang. Ask around.

SIMHAPURA (TRA KIEU)
Simhapura (Tra Kieu), the Lion Citadel, was the first capital city of Champa, serving in that capacity from the 4th to the 8th centuries. Today, nothing remains of the city except the rectangular ramparts. A large number of artefacts, including some of the finest carvings in the Cham Museum in Danang, were found here.

You can get a good view of the city's outlines from the Mountain Church (Nha Tho Nui), which is on the top of Buu Chau Hill in Tra Kieu. This modern open-air struc-

QUANG NAM & DANANG

ture was built in 1970 to replace an earlier church destroyed by time and war. A Cham tower once stood on this spot. Simhapura is about 500 metres to the south and south-west of the hilltop.

The Mountain Church is 6.5 km from National Highway 1 and 19.5 km from the beginning of the footpath to My Son. Within Tra Kieu, it is 200 metres from the morning market (Cho Tra Kieu) and 550 metres from Tra Kieu Church.

Tra Kieu Church

Tra Kieu Church (Dia So Tra Kieu), which serves the town's Catholic population of 3000, was built a century ago (though obviously, the border of the semicircular patio, which is made of upturned artillery shells, was added later). The priest here is interested in Cham civilisation and has amassed a collection of Cham artefacts found by local people.

A 2nd-floor room in the building to the right of the church is due to open as a museum in 1990. The round ceramic objects with faces on them, which date from the 8th to the 10th century, were affixed to the ends of tile roofs. The face is that of Kala, the God of Time.

Tra Kieu Church is seven km from National Highway 1 and 19 km from the trail to My Son. It is 150 metres down an alley opposite the town's clinic of occidental medicine (Quay Thuoc Tay Y), 350 metres from the morning market (Cho Tra Kieu) and 550 metres from the Mountain Church.

INDRAPURA (DONG DUONG)

The Cham religious centre of Indrapura (Dong Duong) was the site of an important Mahayana Buddhist monastery, the Monastery of Lakshmindra-Lokeshvara, founded in 875. Indrapura served as the capital of Champa from 860 to 986, when the capital was transferred to Cha Ban (near Qui Nhon). Tragically, as a result of the devastation wrought by the French and American wars, only part of the gate to Indrapura is extant.

Indrapura is 21 km from My Son as the crow flies and 55 km from Danang.

CAM KIM ISLAND

The master woodcarvers who in previous centuries produced the fine carvings that graced the homes of Hoi An's merchants and the town's public buildings came from Kim Bong village on Cam Kim Island. These days, some of the villagers build wooden boats. To get there, catch one of the frequent boats from the Hoang Van Thu Street Dock, which is opposite 50 Bach Dang St.

CHAM ISLAND

Cham Island (Culao Cham) is in the South China Sea 21 km from Hoi An; by boat, the trip takes about two hours. The island is famous as a source of swifts' nests, which are exported to Hong Kong, Singapore and elsewhere for use in bird's nest soup.

Both foreigners and Vietnamese need authorisation to visit the island because attempts to flee the country have been disguised as excursions to Cham Island. A motorised ferry to Cham Island's two fishing villages departs from the Hoang Van Thu Street Dock at about 7 am; it returns in the afternoon.

Scuba diving is one possible form of entertainment here. You can get a permit for fishing.

Danang

Back in the heady days of the Vietnam War, Danang was often referred to as the 'Saigon of the north'. This cliche held a note of both praise and condemnation – like it's big sister to the south, Danang was notable for its booming economy, fine restaurants, busy traffic and glittering shops. 'Entertaining the military' was also a profitable business – bars and prostitutes were major service industries. As in Saigon, corruption also ran rampant. Liberation arrived in 1975, promptly putting a sizeable dent in the nightlife. However, Vietnam's recent economic liberalisation has helped Danang regain some of its former glory – and all of its vices.

Danang (population 950,000) is now Vietnam's fourth-largest city. While only of marginal interest to travellers, there are some very worthwhile sights in the surrounding area. Among the points of interest are the Marble Mountains, China Beach (Bai Non Nuoc), the Cham towers at My Son, Ba Na hill station, Hai Van Pass (Col des Nuages) and Lang Co Beach.

History

Danang, known under the French as Tourane, succeeded Hoi An (Faifo) as the most important port in central Vietnam during the 19th century.

In late March 1975 Danang, the second-largest city in South Vietnam, was the scene of utter chaos after Saigon government forces were ordered to abandon Hué and Quang Ngai had fallen to the Communists, cutting South Vietnam in two. Desperate civilians tried to flee the city as soldiers of the disintegrating South Vietnamese army engaged in an orgy of looting, pillage and rape. On 29 March 1975, two truckloads of Communist guerrillas, more than half of them women, drove into what had been the most heavily defended city in South Vietnam, and without firing a shot, declared Danang 'liberated'.

Almost the only fighting that took place as Danang fell was between South Vietnamese soldiers and civilians battling for space on flights and ships out of the city. On 27 March, the president of World Airways, Ed Daly, ignoring explicit government orders, sent two 727s from Saigon to Danang to evacuate refugees. When the first plane landed, about a thousand desperate and panicked people mobbed the tarmac. Soldiers fired assault rifles at each other and at the plane as they tried to shove their way through the rear door. As the aircraft taxied down the runway trying to take off, people climbed up into the landing-gear wells and someone threw a hand grenade, damaging the right wing.

Those who managed to fight their way aboard, kicking and punching aside anyone in their way, included over 200 soldiers, mostly members of the elite Black Panthers company. The only civilians on board were two women and one baby – and the baby was there only because it had been thrown aboard by its desperate mother, who was left on the tarmac. Several stowaways in the wheel wells couldn't hold on, and as the plane flew southward, TV cameras on the second 727 filmed them falling into the South China Sea. Upon arrival in Saigon, the Black Panthers were arrested.

Orientation

The main east-west artery in the city of Danang is known at various points along its length as Hung Vuong St (in the city centre), Ly Thai To St (near the Central Market) and Dien Bien Phu St (out around the Intercity Bus Station).

Danang is on the western bank of the Han River. Along the eastern bank, which can be reached via the Nguyen Van Troi Bridge, is a long, thin peninsula at the northern tip of which is Nui Son Tra, known as 'Monkey Mountain' to the Americans. It is now a closed military area. To the south, 11 km from the city, are the Marble Mountains. Hai Van Pass overlooks Danang from the north.

The process of bringing the names of Danang's streets in line with the sensitivities of the present government is still going on. The city's distinctive cement street signs date from the French period. Occasionally, one of the new white-on-blue metal plaques falls off, revealing the old French name.

Information

Tourist Offices Danang Tourism (Cong Ty Du Lich Da Nang; ☎ 22112, 21423; fax 21560) is the official provincial tourism authority for Quang Nam-Danang Province. The office is at 68 Bach Dang St near the GPO and is open from 7 to 11.30 am and 1 to 4.30 pm Monday to Saturday.

Vietnam Tourism (Tong Cong Ty Du Lich Viet Nam; ☎ 22990, 22999; fax 22854) is at 158 Phan Chu Trinh St.

Money Vietcombank (Ngan Hang Ngoai Thuong Viet Nam; ☎ 23784) is at 104 Le Loi

St near the corner of Hai Phong St; it is open from 7.30 to 11.30 am and 1 to 3.30 pm Monday to Saturday except Thursday and Saturday afternoons.

Post & Telecommunications The GPO (☎ 21499), which offers telex, telephone and postal services, is next to 46 Bach Dang St (corner of Le Duan St); it is open daily from 6 am to 8.30 pm.

Emergency Hospital C (Benh Vien C; ☎ 22480) is at 35 Hai Phong St.

Useful Organisations For what it's worth, you can try the Foreign Economic Relations Department of Danang at 452 Ong Ich Khiem St. There is also the Chamber of Commerce & Industry at 256 Tran Phu St.

Consulates The one particularly useful consulate is for Laos at 12 Tran Quy Cap St, almost opposite the immigration police at No 7. Tran Quy Cap St is at the northern end of town close to the Danang Hotel. Visas for Laos cost US$25 and take 24 hours to process. If you're going to exit Vietnam overland via the Lao Bao border crossing, you need to get your visa amended to indicate this. The immigration police can do this, but you must go through a travel agent rather than directly to the police themselves. Dana Tours at 3 Dong Da St is one possibility, or you can try Danang Tours near the GPO on Bach Dang St (same side).

Warning Just as it's hard to believe that Hoi An can be so good, it's hard to believe that Danang can be so bad. Danang gets the thumbs down from just about everybody. There are several reasons for this, not the least of them being the attitude of the local police. Vehicles seen carrying foreigners are stopped by the police and the occupants 'fined.'

As we left Danang we were stopped by the police and my driver had to pay them some money. It seems the police look for motorbikes with tourists, as they know the driver will have dollars. On the way back into town, we stayed behind a big lorry, I made myself as Vietnamese as we could and thus we escaped the police.

Joke Koppen

There are two major police roadblocks in town. One is on the east side of Nguyen Van Troi Bridge (the road to Hoi An) and another is west of the Intercity Bus Station (the road to Hué). Other roadblocks are moved around town (the Cham Museum entrance is a favourite spot). If you are unlucky, you may be stopped several times just trying to get across town. Some foreigners have reported being mugged by the police five times in a single day, but other travellers get through with no problem.

There shouldn't be any problem if you arrive and depart by train and travel around town by bicycle or on foot. But if you ride in a privately owned car, bus, van or even a cyclo, expect trouble and keep those dollars handy.

Cham Museum

The best sight in Danang city (and some would say the only sight) is the Cham Museum (Bao Tang Cham). The museum was founded in 1915 by the École Française d'Extrême Orient and has the finest collection of Cham sculpture in the world. Many of the sandstone carvings (altars, lingas, garudas, ganeshas and images of Shiva, Brahma and Vishnu) are absolutely stunning; this is the sort of place you can easily visit again and again. It is well worth it to get a knowledgeable guide (a scarce commodity in these parts) to show you around.

The Cham Museum is open daily from 8 to 11 am and 1 to 5 pm. Admission costs US$1 – make sure you hand over the money to an authorised member of the staff in the ticket booth, and not to some entrepreneurial gardener.

A trilingual guidebook to the museum written by its director, Tran Ky Phuong, Vietnam's most eminent scholar of Cham civilisation, gives excellent background on the art of Champa; it also includes some information on the museum's exhibits. The

Cham Museum

Entrance

Thap Mam Room

21

20

19

18

My Son Room

1

2

3

4

Tra Kieu Room

16

15

Scene D

Scene C

13

Scene A

Scene B

17

12

14

5

6

9

8

7

11

10

Dong Duong Room

1 My Son Altar; from My Son, 8th-9th century
2 Ganesha (seated elephant); from My Son, 8th-9th century
3 Birthday of Brahma; from My Son, 8th-9th century
4 Polo players; from Thach An, 7th century
5 Altar ornaments; from Khuong My, 10th century
6 The Goddess Sarasvati; from Chanh Lo, 11th century
7 Vishnu, from Tra Kieu, 10th century
8 A deity; from Dong Duong, 9th-10th century
9 A deity; from Dong Duong, 9th-10th century
10 Dong Duong Altar ornaments; from Dong Duong, 9th-10th century
11 Dong Duong Altar; from Dong Duong, 9th-10th century

12 Linga
13 Tra Kieu Altar; from Tra Kieu, 7th century
14 Dancing Shiva; from Phong Le, 10th century
15 Linga
16 Dancing female apsaras; from Quang Nam-Danang Province, 10th century
17 Altar ornaments; from Binh Dinh, 12th-14th century
18 Lions; from Thap Mam, 12th-14th century
19 Shiva; from Thap Mam, 12th-14th century
20 The elephant-lion Gajasimha; from Thap Mam, 12th-14th century
21 The sea monster Makara; from Thap Mam, 12th-14th century

booklet, entitled *Museum of Cham Sculpture – Danang* and *Bao Tang Dieu Khac Cham Da Nang* (Foreign Languages Publishing House, Hanoi, 1987), is usually on sale where you buy your entrance ticket.

Cham art can be divided into two main periods. Before the 10th century, it was very emotionally expressive, reflecting contact with seafaring cultures from Indonesia. From the 10th to the 14th century, as Champa fell into decline because of unending wars with the Vietnamese, Cham art came under Khmer influence and became more formalistic.

The museum's artefacts, which date from the 7th to 15th century, were discovered at Dong Duong (Indrapura), Khuong My, My Son, Tra Kieu (Simhapura), Thap Mam (Binh Dinh) and other sites, mostly in Quang Nam-Danang Province. The rooms in the museum are named after the localities in which the objects displayed in them were discovered.

A recurring image in Cham art is that of Uroja, the 'Mother of the Country', who gave birth to the dynasties that ruled Champa. Uroja, whose name means Woman's Breast in the Cham language, was worshipped in the form of the nipples one often sees in Cham sculpture. Also common is the linga, phallic symbol of Shiva, which came to prominence after Champa's contact with Hinduism. Cham religious beliefs (and thus Cham architecture and sculpture) were influenced by Mahayana Buddhism as early as the 4th century. In addition to its clear Indian elements, Cham art shows Javanese, Khmer and Dai Viet (Vietnamese) influences.

The four scenes carved around the base of the 7th-century Tra Kieu Altar tell part of the *Ramayana* epic in a style influenced by the Amaravati style of South India. Scene A (see diagram), in which 16 characters appear, tells the story of Prince Rama, who broke the sacred bow, Rudra, at the citadel of Videha and thus won from King Janak the right to wed his daughter, Princess Sita. Scene B, which also comprises 16 characters, shows the ambassadors sent by King Janak to

Prince Rama's father, King Dasaratha, at Ayodhya. The emissaries inform King Dasaratha of the exploits of his son, present him with gifts, and invite him to Videha to celebrate his son's wedding. In Scene C (which has 18 characters), the royal wedding ceremony (and that of three of Prince Rama's brothers, who marry three of Princess Sita's cousins) is shown. In Scene D, 11 apsaras (heavenly maidens) dance and present flowers to the newlyweds under the guidance of the two gandhara musicians who appear at the beginning of Scene A.

Former US Consulate

After reunification, the former US Consulate building was turned into Danang's Museum of American War Crimes; that's why a Huey helicopter with its door gun still attached is sitting in the courtyard. In 1975, during the chaos that reigned in the days before the Communist takeover, evacuation barges docked right across the street from the consulate. The consulate was later looted, and mobs of Vietnamese – furious at having been 'abandoned' by the Americans – tried to burn it down. Today, the brick structure is considered beyond repair and may be torn down.

The former US Consulate is on the corner of Bach Dang and Phan Dinh Phung Sts.

Danang Cathedral

Danang Cathedral (Chinh Toa Da Nang), known to locals as Con Ga Church (the Rooster Church) because of the weathercock on top of the steeple, was built for the city's French residents in 1923. Today, it serves a Catholic community of 4000. The cathedral's architecture is well worth a look, as are the medieval-style stained glass windows of various saints.

Next door to the cathedral are the offices of the diocese of Danang and the Saint Paul Convent. About 100 nuns – who, when praying, wear white habits in the summer and black habits in the winter – live here and at another convent building across the Han River.

Danang Cathedral is on Tran Phu St across from the Hai Au Hotel. If the main gate is locked, try the back entrance, which is opposite 14 Yen Bai St. Masses are held daily at 5 am and 5 pm and on Sundays at 5 am, 6.30 am and 4.30 pm.

Pagodas & Temples

Caodai Temple Danang's main Caodai Temple (Chua Cao Dai), built in 1956 and now home to six priests, is the largest such structure outside the sect's headquarters in Tay Ninh. There are 50,000 Caodais in Quang Nam-Danang Province, 20,000 in Danang itself. The temple is across the street from Hospital C (Benh Vien C), which is at 35 Hai Phong St. As at all Caodai temples, prayers are held four times a day at 6 am, noon, 6 pm and midnight.

The left-hand gate to the complex, marked 'Nu Phai', is for women; the right gate, marked 'Nam Phai', is for men. The doors to the sanctuary are also segregated: women to the left, men to the right, and priests of either sex through the central door. Behind the main altar sits an enormous globe with the 'divine eye', symbol of Caodaism, on it.

Hanging from the ceiling in front of the altar is a sign reading 'Van Giao Nhat Ly', which means 'All Religions have the same reason'. Behind the gilded letters is a picture of the founders of five of the world's great religions. From left to right they are: Mohammed; Laotse (wearing blue robes cut in the style of the Greek Orthodox); Jesus (portrayed as he is in French icons); Buddha (who has a distinctly South-East Asian appearance); and Confucius (looking as Chinese as could be).

Portraits of early Caodai leaders, dressed in turbans and white robes, are displayed in the building behind the main sanctuary. Ngo Van Chieu, founder of Caodaism, is shown standing wearing a pointed white turban and a long white robe with blue markings.*

Phap Lam Pagoda Phap Lam Pagoda (Chua Phap Lam, also known as Chua Tinh Hoi) is opposite 373 Ong Ich Khiem St (123 Ong Ich Khiem St according to the old numbering). Built in 1936, this pagoda has a brass statue of Dia Tang, the Chief of Hell,

near the entrance. Six monks live here. Thanh An Vegetarian Restaurant is just up the street.

Tam Bao Pagoda The main building of Tam Bao Pagoda (Chua Tam Bao) at 253 Phan Chu Trinh St is topped with a five-tiered tower. Only four monks live at this large pagoda, which was built in 1953.

Pho Da Pagoda Pho Da Pagoda (Pho Da Tu), which is across from 293 Phan Chu Trinh St, was built in 1923 in a traditional architectural configuration. Today, about 40 monks, most of them young, live and study here. Local lay people and their children participate actively in the pagoda's lively religious life.

Ho Chi Minh Museum

The Ho Chi Minh Museum (Bao Tang Ho Chi Minh; ☎ 5656) has three sections: a museum of military history in front of which American, Soviet and Chinese weaponry are displayed; a replica of Ho Chi Minh's house in Hanoi (complete with a small lake); and, on the other side of the pond from the house, a museum about Uncle Ho.

The museum, which is on Nguyen Van Troi St, 250 metres west of Nui Thanh St, is open Tuesday to Sunday from 7 to 11 am and 1 to 4.30 pm.

Tombs of Spanish & French Soldiers

Spanish-led Philippine and French troops attacked Danang in August 1858, ostensibly to end the mistreatment of Vietnamese Catholics and Catholic missionaries by the government of Emperor Tu Duc. The city quickly fell, but the invaders soon had to contend with cholera, dysentery, scurvy, typhus and mysterious fevers. By the summer of 1859, 20 times as many of the invaders had died of illness as had been killed in combat. Many of these soldiers are buried in a chapel (Bai Mo Phap Va Ta Ban Nha) about 15 km from the city. The names of the dead are written on the walls.

To get there, cross Nguyen Van Troi Bridge and turn left onto Ngo Quyen St.

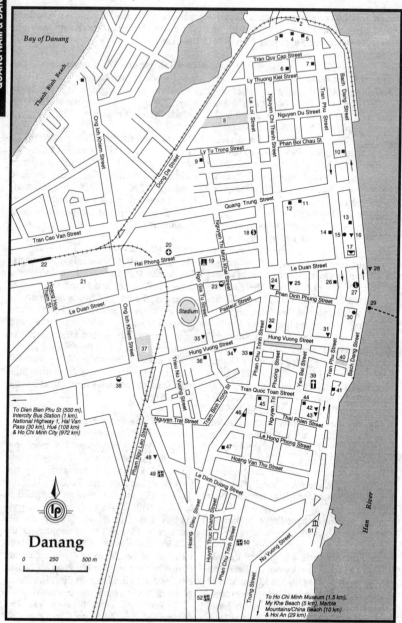

Bay of Danang

Thanh Binh Beach

Tran Quy Cap Street

Ly Thuong Kiet Street

Le Loi Street

Nguyen Chi Thanh Street

Nguyen Du Street

Bach Dang Street

Tran Phu Street

Phan Boi Chau St

Ong Ich Khiem Street

Dong Da Street

Ly Tu Trong Street

Quang Trung Street

Nguyen Thi Minh Khai Street

Tran Cao Van Street

Hoang Hoa Tham St

Hai Phong Street

Le Duan Street

Phan Dinh Phung Street

Ngo Gia Tu Street

Pasteur Street

Stadium

Le Duan Street

Hung Vuong Street

Phan Chu Trinh Street

Thuong Street

Yen Bai Street

Tran Phu Street

Bach Dang Street

Tran Quoc Toan Street

Hung Vuong Street

Nguyen Tri

Thai Phien Street

Trieu Nu Vuong Street

Tram Binh Trong St

Nguyen Trai Street

Le Hong Phong Street

Hoang Van Thu Street

Le Dinh Duong Street

Pham Ngu Lao Street

Hoang Dieu Street

Huynh Thuc Khang Street

Phan Chu Trinh Street

Nu Vuong Street

Trung Street

Han River

To Dien Bien Phu St (500 m),
Intercity Bus Station (1 km),
National Highway 1, Hai Van
Pass (30 km), Hué (108 km)
& Ho Chi Minh City (972 km)

To Ho Chi Minh Museum (1.5 km),
My Khe Beach (5 km), Marble
Mountains/China Beach (10 km)
& Hoi An (29 km)

Danang

0   250   500 m

PLACES TO STAY		PLACES TO EAT		17	GPO
				18	Vietcombank
1	Khach San Du Lich	2	Cafe Lien	19	Caodai Temple
	Thanh Binh	16	Thanh Lich Restaurant	20	Hospital C
3	Huu Nghi Hotel	24	Tuoi Hong Cafe	21	Market
4	Marble Mountains Hotel	25	Hoang Ngoc	22	Danang Railway
5	Danang Hotel		Restaurant		Station
6	Thu Bon Hotel	28	Christie's Restaurant	23	Ancient Renault
7	Peace Hotel	31	Thanh Huong		Buses
9	Hai Van Hotel		Restaurant	27	Danang Tourism &
10	Song Han Hotel	34	Dac San Restaurant		Tourist Shop
11	Ami Hotel	35	Chin Den Restaurant	29	Ferries Across the
12	Marco Polo Hotel	42	Tiem An Binh Dan		Han River
13	Bach Dang Hotel		Restaurant	30	Former US Consulate
14	Binh Duong Mini-Hotel	43	Tu Do & Kim Do	32	Municipal Theatre
26	Vinapha Hotel		Restaurants	37	Con Market
33	Thanh Thanh Hotel	48	Thanh An Vegetarian	38	Short-Haul Pickup
36	Thu Do Hotel		Restaurant		Truck Station
41	Hai Au Hotel			39	Danang Cathedral
44	Dai A Hotel	**OTHER**		40	Cho Han (market)
45	Phuong Dong Hotel			49	Phap Lam Pagoda
46	Pacific Hotel (Thai Binh	8	Market	50	Tam Bao Pagoda
	Duong Hotel)	15	Vietnam Airlines	51	Cham Museum
47	Minh Tam II Mini-Hotel		Booking Office	52	Pho Da Pagoda

Continue north to Tien Sa Port (Cang Tien Sa). The chapel, a white building, stands on the right on a low hill about half a km past the gate of the port.

Places to Stay – bottom end

Danang's ever-entrepreneurial People's Committee continues to put up new hotels in the hopes of attracting more foreign tourists. Danang's ever-entrepreneurial prostitutes are also very much in evidence. At virtually every government-run hotel, single male travellers will almost certainly be approached with an offer for a 'massage'.

One place which is privately run is the excellent *Hoai Huong Travel Shop & Guest House* (☎ 24874; fax 21279) at 105 Tran Phu St. Compared with Danang's other cell-block disasters, this hostelry is a breath of fresh air. Doubles go for US$7 per night, and there are bicycles and motorbikes for rent here.

Several large hotels are located, rather inconveniently, in the residential area at the northern tip of the peninsula on which the city of Danang is located. The *Danang Hotel* (☎ 21986; about 100 rooms) at 3 Dong Da St is popular with budget travellers. Rooms cost US$6 to US$30. The building was con-

structed in the late 1960s to house American military personnel. The Danang Hotel has an acceptable in-house restaurant.

The *Marble Mountains Hotel* (☎ 23258, 23122), 5 Dong Da St, is also known as *Khach San Ngu Hanh Son*. This place recently merged with the Danang Hotel and charges the same rates. This hotel also has a restaurant.

Next to the Danang Hotel is the *Huu Nghi Hotel* (☎ 21021, 22563; 64 rooms) at 7 Dong Da St. Rooms with fan and icy water cost US$5 to US$12. Air-con and hot water raises the premium to US$8 or US$10.

Closer to the railway station is the *Hai Van Hotel* (☎ 21300; fax 23891; 40 rooms) at 2 Nguyen Thi Minh Khai St. It's an old place but has large rooms, private bath and hot water. All rooms are equipped with both air-conditioners and ceiling fans. The toll is US$12 to US$20.

The *Thu Do Hotel* (☎ 23863; 35 rooms) at 107 Hung Vuong St is also relatively close to the railway station and just a few blocks from Con Market (Cho Con). It's one of the cheapest places in town that accepts foreigners, with rooms at US$4 to US$12. The staff were friendly during our visit and could speak surprisingly good English. However, this place is getting run-down.

The *Thanh Thanh Hotel* (☎ 21230; 50 rooms) is a friendly place but looks dingy. Rooms are priced from US$7 to US$12. The hotel is at 50 Phan Chu Trinh St.

A few blocks south at 63 Hoang Dieu St is the popular *Minh Tam II Mini-Hotel* (☎ 26687; fax 24339; 18 rooms). The price scale here is US$17 to US$35.

Another placed well favoured by the backpacker set is the *Ami Hotel* (☎ 24494; fax 25532; 16 rooms). It's at 7 Quang Trung St and has rooms for US$12 to US$26.

Dai A Hotel (☎ 27532; fax 25760; 24 rooms) is a brand-new place at 27 Yen Bai St. The range here is US$15 to US$65.

Also very new is the *Vinapha Hotel* (☎ 25072; 16 rooms) at 80 Tran Phu St. This small place has rooms for US$16 to US$18.

The *Pacific Hotel* (☎ 22137), also called the *Thai Binh Duong Hotel*, is across the street from the much pricier Phuong Dong Hotel. It's an old place but not too bad. Singles/doubles cost from US$20/23 to US$32/36.

The *Khach San Du Lich Thanh Binh* (☎ 21239; 120 rooms) at 5 Ong Ich Khiem St is right on Thanh Binh Beach, known for its crowds and polluted water. This place is reserved for Vietnamese workers on organised union vacations but they will rent to foreigners for US$10 to US$18. Few foreign travellers stay here and you'd probably be better off staying someplace else.

Places to Stay – middle & top end

At the bottom end of middle-end accommodation is the *Binh Duong Mini-Hotel* (☎ 21930; fax 27666; 12 rooms). This new hotel dishes up free breakfast and rooms for US$25 to US$35.

The *Peace Hotel* (☎ 23984; fax 23161; 25 rooms) at 3 Tran Quy Cap St is also known as the Hoa Binh Hotel. The hotel is relatively new and all rooms have air-conditioning and hot water. Rooms cost US$25 to US$50 and free breakfast is part of the package.

Just around the corner is the *Thu Bon Hotel* (☎ 21101; fax 22854; 18 rooms), 10 Ly Thuong Kiet St. It's not a bad place, but the price range is steep for this standard of accommodation. Singles are US$24 to US$27, and doubles are US$30 to US$32.

The *Song Han Hotel* (☎ 22540; 30 rooms) is along the Han River at 36 Bach Dang St. It was under renovation at the time of writing and will probably be propelled out of the budget range when it reopens.

The *Hai Au Hotel* (☎ 22722; fax 24165; 29 rooms) opened in 1989, and for a while was the best in town but has since been superseded. The hotel is conveniently located near the city centre, at 177 Tran Phu St, which is across the street from Danang Cathedral. Single and doubles cost US$40 to US$60. The hotel has a good restaurant.

The *Bach Dang Hotel* (☎ 23649; fax 21659; 91 rooms), 50 Bach Dang St, is one of the fanciest places in Danang. Rooms with all the trimmings cost US$40 to US$70. The hotel has good views of the river.

The *Phuong Dong Hotel* (☎ 21266; fax 22854; 36 rooms), 93 Phan Chu Trinh St, is a classy place with an elegant wood-panelled lobby. Recently renovated, room prices have risen through the roof. Singles are US$40 to US$46, doubles US$51 to US$57 and triples US$68.

The top of top-end accommodation in Danang has to be the all-new *Marco Polo Hotel* (☎ 23295; fax 27279; 28 rooms). This very stylish place is at 11C Quang Trung St. Singles/doubles are priced from US$50/60 to US$90/100, plus 10% surcharge.

Places to Eat

There are dozens of food stalls behind the main market building in the Con Market, and this is about the cheapest place to eat.

Prepared vegetarian food is sold on the first and 15th day of each lunar month at *Cho Han*, a vegetable market off Hung Vuong St between Bach Dang and Tran Phu Sts.

Thanh An Vegetarian Restaurant is a food stall serving vegetable dishes that resemble meat in appearance. The food here is very cheap and the restaurant is open daily from 7 am until 4 pm. This place is half a block from Phap Lam Pagoda and about one km from the city centre. The street address is 484 Ong Ich Khiem St.

The best restaurant in Danang is the *Tu Do Restaurant* (☎ 21869) at 172 Tran Phu St, 100 metres from the Hai Au Hotel; it is open from 7 am to 9 pm. The menu is extensive, the service is punctilious and the food is in fact quite good, but some of the prices are a lot higher than you'd reasonably expect to pay. Next door is the *Kim Do*, a slightly fancier place where the food is excellent but almost ridiculously expensive. Also nearby at 174 Tran Phu St is the *Tiem An Binh Dan Restaurant*, a modest place with reasonable prices.

Café Lien is directly opposite the Danang Hotel. Prices are low, the food is good and the convenient location pulls in all sorts of budget travellers. This is one place where you never know who you'll meet:

An entertaining local character is Linh, who runs a cafe opposite the Danang Hotel. She can arrange car and motorcycle hire and she will sometimes accompany you on day trips as a guide. A foreign resident with business interests in Danang told me that she was also a police informant and knew everything that was happening in the immediate vicinity of the cafe.

One evening when I was having a beer in the cafe, a blond-haired, blue-eyed and fair-skinned traveller sat down at a nearby table. I judged him to be German or Scandinavian. 'I think you are from Israel', Linh said to him. He was absolutely astonished. 'How do you know that?' he asked her. Linh first gave him a conspiratorial look, and then smiled. Finally, she whispered 'I know everything'.

Ian McVittie

Christie's Restaurant (☎ 22034) at 9 Bach Dang St has excellent food. The restaurant is suspended over the water on pilings so there are nice views of the Han River. Run by a big New Zealand man, this place dishes up continental and Vietnamese food (very nicely presented). It's a lovely place to watch the light fade on the river at night, and there is a TV and lounge area and river breezes.

The *Hoang Ngoc Restaurant* is a pleasant place, with great service and outstanding food. The lively owner, Mr Hoang, is a gem. You can try his speciality, sea slug, which tastes much better than it sounds. The restaurant is located at 106 Nguyen Chi Thanh St, near Phan Dinh Phung St.

Old woman, Danang

The *Thanh Huong Restaurant* (☎ 22101) at 40 Hung Vuong St (corner Tran Phu St) is a small, friendly place with a local clientele; it's a good place for morning soup (pho). The *Dac San Restaurant* at 95 Hung Vuong St is an OK cafe.

A breakfast of fried beef and eggs with fresh French bread and salad is available from 6 to 11 am daily at the *Chin Den Restaurant* (the name means Black Nine), which is near the stadium at 32 Ngo Gia Tu St.

The *Thanh Lich Restaurant*, near the GPO at 42 Bach Dang St, has an extensive menu in English, French and Vietnamese. This place has received good reviews from foreign business people.

For a late-evening drink, head for the extremely popular *Tuoi Hong Café* at 34 Phan Dinh Phung St (on the corner of Phan Chu Trinh St). It's the music which makes this place so popular with local young people.

Entertainment
Danang's night life is centred on Tran Phu, Hung Vuong, Le Loi and Phan Chu Trinh Sts.

The Municipal Theatre, which offers a wide variety of performances depending on which troupes are in town, is on the corner of Hung Vuong and Le Loi Sts. *Hat Tuong*, a form of classical drama, is performed by a provincial troupe that tours all around Quang Nam-Danang Province.

There are a number of cinemas along Tran Phu St near the Vietnam Airlines office. Liberation Day Cinema (Rap 29-3) is on Phan Chu Trinh St near the corner of Tran Quoc Toan St.

Things to Buy

Danang seems particularly well endowed with tailors, many of whom have shops along Hung Vuong St. For a pittance over the cost of the cloth, you can have high-quality shirts, pants, skirts, etc, tailored to fit your exact proportions. Cloth is available either from the tailor's stock or at the cloth stalls near the intersection of Hung Vuong and Yen Bai Sts. Of course, there is plenty of ready-made clothing on sale, especially along Phan Chu Trinh St.

Film and photo supplies can be purchased at 86 Phan Chu Trinh St and 136 Hung Vuong St.

Danang's central marketplace, Con Market (Cho Con) is at the intersection of Hung Vuong and Ong Ich Khiem Sts. The front section was built in 1985. Con Market has a huge selection of just about everything sold in Vietnam: household items, ceramics, fresh vegetables, stationary, cutlery, fruit, flowers, polyester clothes, etc.

Getting There & Away

Air During the Vietnam War, Danang had one of the busiest airports in the world. Dozens of American-built cement revetments, some of which are now used to house Vietnamese Air Force MiGs, still line the runways.

Vietnam Airlines flies Danang-Ho Chi Minh City direct three times daily; Danang-Hanoi three times daily; Danang-Haiphong three times a week; Danang-Pleiku four times a week; Danang-Buon Ma Thuot six times a week; Danang-Nha Trang four times a week; and Danang-Qui Nhon three times a week.

The Danang office of Vietnam Airlines (☎ 22094) is at 35 Tran Phu St.

With high hopes of attracting regular flights from abroad, Danang Airport became Danang International Airport in 1989, joining Tan Son Nhat and Noi Bai as Vietnam's third point of entry by air. There are now international flights from Danang to Bangkok, Hong Kong, Kuala Lumpur, Manila and Paris, but all these flights first stop in Ho Chi Minh City before heading abroad.

Bus The Danang Intercity Bus Station (Ben Xe Khach Da Nang; ☎ 21265) is about three km from the city centre on the thoroughfare known, at various points along its length, as Hung Vuong, Ly Thai To and Dien Bien Phu Sts. The ticket office for express buses is across the street from 200 Dien Bien Phu St; it is open from 7 to 11 am and 1 to 5 pm.

Express bus service is available to Buon Ma Thuot (17 hours), Dalat, Gia Lai, Haiphong, Hanoi (24 hours), Ho Chi Minh City (24 hours), Hong Gai, Lang Son, Nam Dinh and Nha Trang (14 hours; US$3). Tickets for nonexpress buses to Kon Tum (5 am departure), Sathay and Vinh (12 hours) are also sold here. All express buses depart at 5 am.

The nonexpress ticket office is open from 5 am until the late afternoon. There is non-express bus service from Danang Bus Station to:

Ai Nghia, Kham Duc, An Hoa, Kiem Lam, Chu Lai Quang Ngai, Dong Ha, Que Son, Giang, Qui Nhon, Giao Thuy, Tam Ky, Go Noi, Thanh My, Ha Lam, Tien Phuoc, Ha Tan, Tra My, Hoi An, Trao, Hiep Duc, Trung Mang, Hué, Trung Phuoc.

Upon arrival at the Danang Intercity Bus Station, be prepared for aggressive touting by cyclo drivers. A cyclo ride to the city centre should cost about US$0.35.

Ancient Renault buses to Cam Lam, Kim Lien, Mui Bai and Vinh Diem leave from a small local bus station about half a km from the city centre at the corner of Le Duan and Nguyen Thi Minh Khai Sts. The station is in operation from 5 am to about 6 pm.

There are now buses between Danang and Savannakhet in Laos via Dong Ha and the Lao Bao border crossing. Details are provided in the Getting There & Away chapter.

Short-Haul Pickup Truck Station Xe Lams and small passenger trucks to places in the vicinity of Danang leave from the Short-Haul Pickup Truck Station opposite 80 Hung Vuong St, which is about a block west of Con Market (Cho Con). There is service from here to Cam Le, Cau Do, Hoa Khanh, Hoi An (Faifo), Kim Lien, Nam O (there's a beach here), Non Nuoc (the Marble Mountains and China Beach), Phuoc Tuong and Son Cha. The trip to Non Nuoc takes approximately 20 minutes; the ride to Hoi An takes about one hour. Rickety vehicles leave when full (ie, packed to the roof with people). The station opens at about 5 am and closes around 5 pm.

Train The Danang Railway Station (Ga Da Nang) is about 1.5 km from the city centre on Haiphong St at the northern end of Hoang Hoa Tham St. The train ride to Hué is one of the nicest in the country (though driving up and over Hai Van Pass is also spectacular).

Northbound, the quickest ride takes about 3¼ hours to Hué. Local trains take about six hours. Watch your belongings as you pass through the pitch-black tunnels.

Danang is, of course, served by all Reunification Express trains. For ticket prices, see the Train section in the Getting Around chapter.

Car Road distances from Danang are as follows:

Hanoi	764 km
Hué	108 km
Lao Bao	
(Lao-Vietnam border)	350 km
Nha Trang	541 km
Quang Ngai	130 km
Qui Nhon	303 km
Ho Chi Minh City	972 km
Savannakhet, Laos	
(Lao-Thai border)	500 km

Getting Around

To/From the Airport By cyclo to Danang's airport only takes about 15 minutes from the centre.

Honda Om Plenty of guys with motorbikes hang around the small cafes opposite the Marble Mountains Hotel. You can arrange day trips with them to Hoi An, Marble Mountains and China Beach (US$7), My Son (US$10) and other places around Danang. Before you leave you will also probably have to pay about US$1 or so for them to fill up the tank with petrol.

Boat Ferries across the Han River depart from a dock at the foot of Phan Dinh Phung St.

Around Danang

CHINA BEACH

China Beach, made famous in the American TV serial of the same name, stretches for many kilometres north and south of the Marble Mountains. During the Vietnam War, American soldiers were airlifted here for 'rest and recreation', often including a picnic on the beach. For some, it was their last meal because they were soon returned by helicopter to combat.

Many have insisted that this isn't the real China Beach at all. The place most popular with American soldiers during the war was My Khe Beach five km to the north. The motive behind naming the current beach 'China Beach' seems to be to capitalise on the famous name so as to draw foreign tourists to the government-owned China Beach Hotel. Near the hotel, private vendors flog China Beach baseball caps, wooden carvings of Buddha, jade bracelets, new antiques and other tourist paraphernalia.

Perhaps because of its famous name, in December 1992 China Beach was the site of the first international surfing competition to be held in Vietnam.

The season for all of Danang's beaches is

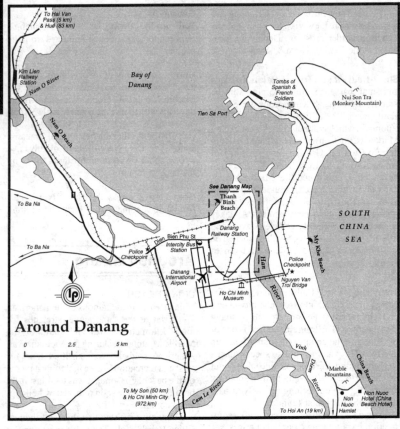

Around Danang

0   2.5   5 km

from May to July when the sea is most calm. During other times of the year the water is rough and there are usually no lifeguards on duty.

Places to Stay

The *China Beach Hotel* (☎ 36216; fax 36335; 103 rooms), also known as the Non Nuoc Seaside Resort, is right on China Beach. Singles/doubles with fan are US$12/18. Air-con rooms cost from US$34 to US$48. The hotel has two good restaurants – both charge very reasonable prices.

The staff at the hotel's car park seem to

have their own little business; when you arrive, you are sold a parking ticket for US$0.20, and when you depart the staff demands an extra dollar for 'watching the car'. But travellers have reported more serious problems here:

In Danang I hired a guy with a motorcycle (or is it a motorcycle with a guy?) to drive me to China Beach. My driver dropped me off at the gate of the China Beach Hotel from where I would walk to the coast. Immediately, he was approached by the not-too-friendly looking guards, whom he soothed by giving them cigarettes. Later he told me that they are not too keen on tourists with drivers because they prefer tourists who drive the motorcycles themselves. While you are at the beach, they replace some unit of the motorcycle with a non-working one, and when you later find out that the bike won't start, they bring you someone who can fix it. That someone places back the part which was removed and, it goes without saying, charges you handsomely for it.

As well as running a parking and motorcycle repair racket, the staff here do rent their own motorbikes for half of what the hotel charges. In view of their sordid reputation, we were in no mood to test out whether or not their rental service is reliable.

Getting There & Away

Pickup trucks to China Beach (Bai Tam Non Nuoc) depart when full from the Short-Haul Pickup Truck Station in Danang.

To get to the China Beach Hotel by car, motorcycle or bicycle, drive to the Marble Mountains (see next entry) and turn left into Non Nuoc hamlet. Follow the road past the largest Marble Mountain and keep going as it curves around to the right (almost parallel to the beach). Before you hit the sand, turn right towards the casuarina grove (and away from the beach) and follow the road around to the left.

MARBLE MOUNTAINS

The Marble Mountains consist of five stone hillocks, once islands, made of marble. Each is said to represent one of the five elements of the universe and is named accordingly: Thuy Son (water), Moc Son (wood), Hoa Son (fire), Kim So (metal or gold) and Tho Son (earth). The largest and most famous, Thuy Son, has a number of natural caves (*dong*) in which Buddhist sanctuaries have been built over the centuries. When Champa ruled this area, these same caves were used as Hindu shrines. Thuy Son is a popular pilgrimage site, especially on days of the full and sliver moons and during Tet.

A torch (flashlight) is useful inside the caves. Local children have learned that foreign tourists buy souvenirs and leave tips for unsolicited guided tours, so you are not likely to begin your visit alone. But the kids are generally good-natured, and some of the caves are difficult to find without their assistance. However, many travellers would rather enjoy the caves in peace. One traveller called it 'a hateful place that I will never visit again' and another one wrote:

I suggest stronger warnings about the children who sell souvenirs at Marble Mountain. I think that they have outgrown their cuteness and are now quite aggressive and rambunctious. My guide was a girl who could not be more than 11 but claimed to be 16. She was very informative, but obviously not very happy or well treated. I loved the scenery but found myself depressed by her and wishing very much that she would disappear. Surely something can be done about the way the souvenir shop owners exploit these children.

Keith L Rakow

But someone else said:

Marble Mountain must not be missed. The cave pagodas are the best I've seen in Asia.

Of the two paths leading up Thuy Son, the one closer to the beach (at the end of the village) makes for a better circuit once you get up the top. So unless you want to follow this entry backwards, don't go up the staircase with concrete kiosks and a black cement sign at its base. At either place, there is an admission charge of US$0.40.

At the top of the staircase (from which Cham Island is visible) is a gate, Ong Chon, which is pockmarked with bullets. Behind Ong Chon is Linh Ong Pagoda. As you enter the sanctuary, you'll see on the left a fantastic figure with a huge tongue. To the right of Linh Ong are monks' quarters and a small orchid garden.

Behind Linh Ong and to the left a path leads through two short tunnels to several caverns known as Tang Chon Dong. There are a number of concrete Buddhas and blocks of carved stone of Cham origin in these caves. Near one of the altars there is a flight of steps leading up to another cave, partially open to the sky, with two seated Buddhas in it.

To the left of the small building which is to the left of Linh Ong (ie, immediately to the left as you enter Ong Chon gate) is the main path to the rest of Thuy Son. Stairs off the main pathway lead to Vong Hai Da, a viewpoint from which a brilliant panorama of China Beach and the South China Sea is visible.

The stone-paved path continues on to the right and into a canyon. On the left is Van Thong Cave. Opposite the entrance is a cement Buddha, behind which a narrow passage leads up to a natural chimney open to the sky.

After you exit the canyon and pass through a battle-scarred masonry gate, a rocky path to the right goes to Linh Nham, a tall chimney-cave with a small altar inside. Nearby, another path leads to Hoa Nghiem, a shallow cave with a Buddha in it. But if you go down the passageway to the left of the Buddha you come to cathedral-like Huyen Khong Cave, lit by an opening to the sky. The entrance to this spectacular chamber is guarded by two administrative mandarins (to the left of the doorway) and two military mandarins (to the right).

Scattered about the cave are Buddhist and Confucian shrines; note the inscriptions carved into the stone walls. On the right a door leads to two stalactites dripping water that local legend says comes from heaven. Actually, only one stalactite drips; the other one supposedly ran dry when Emperor Tu Duc (ruled 1848-83) touched it. During the Vietnam War, this chamber was used by the VC as a field hospital. Inside is a plaque dedicated to the Women's Artillery Group, which destroyed 19 US aircraft as they sat at a base below in 1972.

Just to the left of the battle-scarred masonry gate is Tam Thai Tu, a pagoda restored by Emperor Minh Mang in 1826. A path heading obliquely to the right goes to the monks' residences, beyond which are two shrines from where a red dirt path leads to five small pagodas. Before you arrive at the monks' residences, stairs on the left-hand side of the path lead to Vong Giang Dai, which offers a fantastic 180-degree view of the other Marble Mountains and the surrounding countryside. To get to the stairway down, follow the path straight on from the masonry gate.

Non Nuoc Hamlet

Non Nuoc Hamlet is on the southern side of Thuy Son and is a few hundred metres west of China Beach. The marble carvings made here by skilled (and not-so-skilled) crafts-people would make great gifts if they didn't weigh so much. The town has been spruced up by Danang Tourism.

Getting There & Away

Short-Haul Pickup Truck Pickup trucks to the Marble Mountains (Ngu Hanh Son), Non Nuoc Hamlet and nearby China Beach (Bai Tam Non Nuoc) leave when full from the Short-Haul Pickup Truck Station in Danang. The trip takes about 20 minutes.

Car The 11-km route from Danang to the Marble Mountains passes by the remains of a two-km-long complex of former American military bases; aircraft revetments are still visible.

The Marble Mountains are 19 km north of Hoi An (Faifo) along the 'Korean Highway'.

Boat It is possible to get to the Marble Mountains from Danang by chartered boat. The 8.5-km trip up the Han River and the Vinh Diem River takes about 1¼ hours.

OTHER BEACHES

China Beach is Danang's best, but there are several other beaches scattered around the periphery of the city.

Thanh Binh Beach

Thanh Binh Beach is only a couple of kilometres from the centre of Danang. It is often crowded, notwithstanding the fact that the water is not the cleanest. To get there from Con Market, head all the way to the northern end of Ong Ich Khiem St.

My Khe Beach

My Khe Beach (Bai Tam My Khe) is about six km by road from central Danang. The beach is said to have a dangerous undertow, especially in winter. However, dangerous conditions often go hand-in-hand with large breakers which look ideal for surfing, assuming that you know what you're doing. The surf can be very good from around October to December, particularly in the morning when wind conditions are right. With this in mind, the Danang Surfers' Club was born in 1992. The club was founded by local Vietnamese who hang out at a stall called Club Kola next to the big stone gates at My Khe Beach. Board rentals are available, but you should bring some wax and a ding repair kit since neither can be purchased locally.

Many people insist that My Khe was the real China Beach of wartime fame and that the present 'China Beach' is a fake. For more discussion about this see the Around Danang section.

To get there by car, cross Nguyen Van Troi Bridge and continue straight (eastwards) across the big intersection (instead of turning right (southwards) to the Marble Mountains. If you don't have a car, try hopping on a ferry across the Han River from the foot of Phan Dinh Phung St and catching a ride southeastward to Nguyen Cong Tru St.

Nam O Beach

Nam O Beach is on the Bay of Danang about 15 km north of the city but before Hai Van Pass. The small community of Nam O has supported itself for years by producing firecrackers. However, these were banned by the government in 1995 and the community has now fallen on hard times.

North of Danang

HAI VAN PASS

Hai Van Pass, whose name means Pass of the Ocean Clouds (the French knew it as the Col des Nuages), crosses over a spur of the Truong Son Mountain Range that juts into the South China Sea. About 30 km north of Danang, National Highway 1 climbs to an elevation of 496 metres, passing south of the Ai Van Son peak (altitude 1172 metres). It's an incredibly mountainous stretch of highway with spectacular views. The railway track, with its many tunnels, goes

around the peninsula, following the shoreline to avoid the hills. Unfortunately, the buses cannot take this easy route – many break down here.

In the 15th century, Hai Van Pass formed the boundary between Vietnam and the Kingdom of Champa. Until the Vietnam War, the pass was heavily forested. At the top of the Hai Van Pass is an old French fort later used by the South Vietnamese army and the Americans. The views from near the fortress are quite spectacular. Watch out for the live mortar shells left lying about in the undergrowth!

LANG CO

Lang Co is a pretty island of palm-shaded sand with a crystal-clear turquoise blue lagoon on one side and many kilometres of beachfront facing the South China Sea on the other. It's a tranquil spot and lots of travellers make a lunch stop here and some spend the night. There are spectacular views of Lang Co, which is just north of Hai Van Pass, from both National Highway 1 and the train linking Danang and Hué.

Places to Stay & Eat

The *Lang Co Hotel* (☎ 74426; 20 rooms) is the only place in town. Singles/doubles are US$6/12 and triples/quads are US$16/22. All rooms have attached bath, and electricity is available only from about 5.30 pm until 11 pm. The hotel remains open all year round, but it's really only likely to be busy (often full) from May to July. Hotel guests can use the adjacent beach for free, but nonguests pay US$0.30 per person. On the downside, this place is in rather bad need of renovation but you get what you pay for.

Food at the hotel's restaurant is amazingly good. So good, in fact, that tour groups often stop here to eat. The speciality is, of course, seafood. The restaurant remains open from 6 am until 11 pm.

Getting There & Away

Train Lang Co Railway Station, served by nonexpress trains, is almost 10 km from the beach area. It's possible to find someone to bring you from the railway station to the beach by motorbike.

Car Lang Co is 35 km north of Danang over an extremely mountainous road. A bridge now connects the island to National Highway 1, so you no longer have to take the ferry.

BA NA HILL STATION

Ba Na, the 'Dalat of Quang Nam-Danang Province', is a hill station along the crest of Mount Ba Na (or Nui Chua), which rises 1467 metres above the coastal plain. The view in all directions is truly spectacular, and the air is fresh and cool: though it may be 36°C on the coast, the temperature is likely to be between 15° and 26°C at Ba Na. Rain often falls at altitudes of 700 to 1200 metres above sea level, but around the hill station itself the sky is usually clear. Mountain paths in the area lead to a variety of waterfalls and viewpoints.

Ba Na, founded in 1919 for use by French settlers, is not presently in any condition to welcome visitors; but the provincial government has high hopes of making Ba Na once again a magnet for tourists.

By road Ba Na is 48 km west of Danang (as the crow flies, the distance is 27 km). Until WW II, French vacationers travelled the last 20 km by sedan chair!

Hué

The most beautiful city in Vietnam, Hué (population 250,000) served as Vietnam's political capital from 1802 to 1945 under the 13 emperors of the Nguyen Dynasty. Traditionally, the city has been one of Vietnam's cultural, religious and educational centres. Today, Hué's main attractions are the splendid tombs of the Nguyen emperors, several notable pagodas and the remains of the Citadel. As locals will tell you repeatedly, the women of Hué are renowned for their beauty. Most of the city's major sights have an admission charge of US$5.

History

The citadel-city of Phu Xuan was originally built in 1687 at Bao Vinh village, five km north-east of present-day Hué. In 1744, Phu Xuan became the capital of the southern part of Vietnam, which was under the rule of the Nguyen Lords. The Tay Son Rebels occupied the city from 1786 until 1802, when it fell to Nguyen Anh. He crowned himself Emperor Gia Long, thus founding the Nguyen Dynasty, which ruled the country – at least in name – until 1945. Immediately upon his accession, Gia Long began the decades-long construction of the Citadel, the Imperial Enclosure and the Forbidden Purple City.

In 1885, when the advisers of 13-year-old Emperor Ham Nghi objected to French activities in Tonkin, French forces encircled the city. Unwisely, the outnumbered Vietnamese forces launched an attack; the French responded mercilessly. According to a contemporary French account, the French forces took three days to burn the imperial library and remove from the palace every object of value, including everything from gold and silver ornaments to mosquito nets and toothpicks. Ham Nghi fled to Laos but was eventually captured and exiled to Algeria. The French replaced him with the more pliable Dong Khanh, thus ending any pretence of genuine Vietnamese independence.

The city's present name evolved from its former name, Thanh Hoa. The word 'hoa' means 'peace' or 'harmony' in Vietnamese. The city has been called Hué for over two centuries now.

Hué was the site of the bloodiest battles of the 1968 Tet Offensive and was the only city in South Vietnam to be held by the Communists for more than a few days. While the American command was concentrating its energies on relieving the Siege of Khe Sanh, North Vietnamese and VC troops skirted the American stronghold and walked right into Hué, South Vietnam's third-largest city. When the Communists arrived, they hoisted their flag from the Citadel's flag tower, where it flew for the next 25 days; the local South Vietnamese governmental apparatus completely collapsed.

Immediately upon taking Hué, Communist political cadres implemented detailed plans to liquidate Hué's 'uncooperative' elements. Thousands of people were rounded up in extensive house-to-house searches conducted according to lists of names meticulously prepared months in advance. During the 3½ weeks Hué remained under Communist control, approximately 3000 civilians – including merchants, Buddhist monks, Catholic priests, intellectuals and a number of foreigners as well as people with ties to the South Vietnamese government – were summarily shot, clubbed to death or buried alive. The victims were buried in shallow mass graves, which were discovered around the city over the course of the next few years.

When South Vietnamese army units proved unable to dislodge the North Vietnamese and VC forces, General Westmoreland ordered US troops to recapture the city. During the next few weeks, whole neighbourhoods were levelled by VC rockets and American bombs. In 10 days of bitter combat, the VC were slowly forced to retreat from the New City. During the next two weeks, most of the area inside the

Citadel (where two-thirds of the population lived), including the Imperial Enclosure and the Forbidden Purple City, was flattened by the South Vietnamese air force, US artillery and brutal house-to-house fighting. Approximately 10,000 people died in Hué during the Tet Offensive. Thousands of VC troops, 400 South Vietnamese soldiers and 150 American Marines were among the dead, but most of those killed were civilians.

Long after the Vietnam War ended, one American veteran is said to have returned to Hué and, upon meeting a former VC officer, commented that the USA never lost a single major battle during the entire war. 'You are absolutely correct', the former officer agreed, 'but that is irrelevant, is it not?'

Orientation

Hué, 16 km inland from the South China Sea, is bisected by the Perfume River (Huong Giang or Song Huong). A Perfume River boat trip is *de rigueur* – see the Getting Around section of this chapter for details on boat rentals.

Inside the Citadel, which is on the west bank of the river, is the Imperial Enclosure, which surrounds the Forbidden Purple City, former residence of the royal family.

Dong Ba Market is near the eastern corner of the Citadel. Nearby, a commercial district stretches along the Dong Ba Canal. Across the Dong Ba Canal from Dong Ba Market are the subdistricts of Phu Cat and Phu Hiep, known for their Chinese pagodas.

On the right bank of the Perfume River is the New City, once known as the European Quarter. The Imperial Tombs are spread out over a large area to the south of the New City.

Information

Tourist Offices Try not to waste your time with the government-owned tourism authorities. Most travellers deal with DMZ Tour Office (☎ 25242) at 26 Le Loi St. This place does tours around town and beyond, puts together van rentals, etc.

The government-owned tourism authority is Thua Thien-Hué Tourism (Cong Ty Du Lich Thua Thien-Hué; ☎ 22369, 22288,

22355) at 30 Le Loi St (the building to the right as you enter the gate of the Huong Giang Hotel). Thua Thien-Hué Tourism can supply guides and cars (including 4WD). Pricey tours of the DMZ, which is in neighbouring Quang Tri Province, can be arranged here. The office is open from 7 to 11.30 am and 1.30 to 5 pm.

Hué City Tourism (Cong Ty Du Lich Thanh Pho Hué; ☎ 3577) is at 18 Le Loi St (corner Ha Noi St). It runs several tourist villas on Ly Thuong Kiet St and can rent cars and arrange traditional theatre (cai luong) and music performances. Unfortunately, service here is poor and you should probably make your arrangements elsewhere.

Warning We personally experienced no problems in Hué, and most other travellers have reported no difficulties with the police. But an occasional police roadblock appears on the east side of Phu Xuan Bridge, which we've marked on the Hué map. Another police checkpoint occasionally appears near Phu Bai Airport. Vehicles carrying foreigners are sometimes stopped at these two places, papers checked and a fine levied for an imaginary offence.

Money You can change money at the Industrial & Commercial Bank (Nhan Hang Cong Thuong; ☎ 3275) at 2A Ly Quy Don St. It's open Monday to Saturday from 7 to 11.30 am and 1.30 to 4 pm. Vietcombank (☎ 24571) is at 6 Hoang Hoa Tham St.

Post & Telecommunications International postal and telephone services are available at the GPO, 8 Hoang Hoa Tham St. It's open from 6.30 am to 9 pm.

Emergency Hué General Hospital (Benh Vien Trung Uong Hué; ☎ 2325) is at 16 Le Loi St close to the Phu Xuan Bridge.

Immigration Police Visa extensions can be done at the Immigration Police Office on Ben Nghe St. This office seems to be able to handle such matters in about 15 minutes.

Citadel

Construction of the moated Citadel (Kinh Thanh), whose perimeter is 10 km, was begun in 1804 by Emperor Gia Long on a site chosen by geomancers. The Citadel was originally made of earth, but during the first few decades of the 19th century, tens of thousands of workers laboured to cover the ramparts, built in the style of the French military architect Vauban, with a layer of bricks two metres thick.

The emperor's official functions were carried out in the Imperial Enclosure (Dai Noi, or Hoang Thanh), a citadel-within-a-citadel whose six-metre-high wall is 2.5 km in length. The Imperial Enclosure has four gates, the most famous of which is Ngo Mon Gate. Within the Imperial Enclosure is the Forbidden Purple City (Tu Cam Thanh), which was reserved for the private life of the emperor.

Three sides of the Citadel are straight; the fourth is rounded slightly to follow the curve of the river. The ramparts are encircled by a zigzag moat 30 metres across and about four metres deep. In the northern corner of the Citadel is Mang Ca fortress, once known as the French Concession, which is still used as a military base. The Citadel has 10 fortified gates, each of which is reached by a bridge across the moat.

Flag Tower The 37-metre-high Flag Tower (Cot Co), also known as the King's Knight, is Vietnam's tallest flagpole. Erected in 1809 and increased in size in 1831, a terrific typhoon (which devastated the whole city of Hué) knocked it down in 1904. The tower was rebuilt in 1915, only to be destroyed again in 1947. It was re-erected in its present form in 1949. During the VC occupation of Hué in 1968, the National Liberation Front flag flew defiantly from the tower for 3½ weeks.

Wide areas within the Citadel are now devoted to agriculture, a legacy of the destruction of 1968.

Nine Holy Cannons Located just inside the Citadel ramparts near the gates to either side of the Flag Tower, the Nine Holy Cannons, symbolic protectors of the Palace and Kingdom, were cast from brass articles captured from the Tay Son Rebels. The cannons, whose casting on the orders of Emperor Gia Long was completed in 1804, were never intended to be fired. Each is five metres long, has a bore of 23 cm and weighs about 10 tonnes. The four cannons near Ngan Gate represent the four seasons. The five cannons next to Quang Duc Gate represent the five elements: metal, wood, water, fire and soil.

Ngo Mon Gate The principal gate to the Imperial Enclosure is Ngo Mon Gate (Noon-time Gate), which faces the Flag Tower. It is open from 6.30 am to 5.30 pm; the entrance fee for foreigners is US$5.

The central passageway with its yellow doors was reserved for use by the emperor, as was the bridge across the lotus pond. Everyone else had to use the gates to either side and the paths around the lotus pond.

On top of the gate is Ngu Phung (the Belvedere of the Five Phoenixes), where the emperor appeared on important occasions, notably for the promulgation of the lunar calendar. Emperor Bao Dai ended the Nguyen Dynasty here on 30 August 1945, when he abdicated to a delegation sent by Ho Chi Minh's Provisional Revolutionary Government. The middle section of the roof is covered with yellow tiles; the roofs to either side are green.

Thai Hoa Palace Thai Hoa Palace (the Palace of Supreme Harmony), built in 1803 and moved to its present site in 1833, is a spacious hall with an ornate roof of huge timbers supported by 80 carved and lacquered columns. Reached from the Ngo Mon Gate via Trung Dao Bridge, it was used for the emperor's official receptions and other important court ceremonies, such as anniversaries and coronations. During state occasions, the king sat on his elevated throne and received homage from ranks of mandarins. Nine stelae divide the bi-level courtyard into areas for officials of each of the nine ranks in the mandarinate; administrative

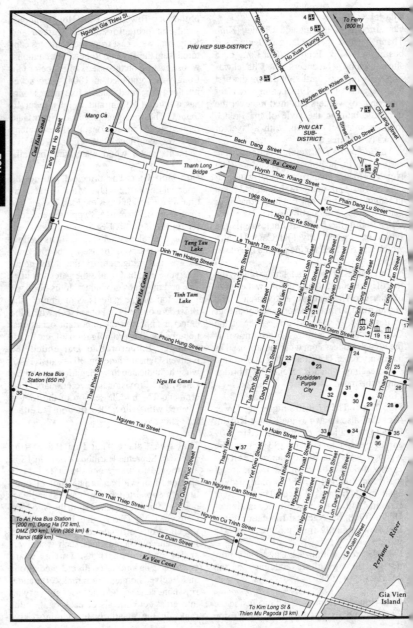

HUÉ

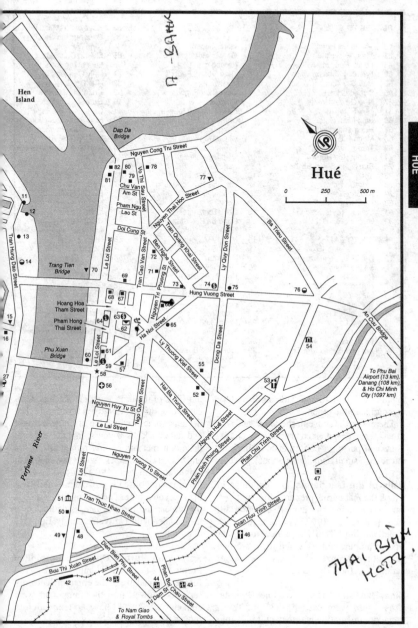

HUÉ

Hen
Island

Dap Da
Bridge

Nguyen Cong Tru Street

■ 82 80
■ 79 ● 78
81
Chu Van
Am St
Pham Ngu
Lao St
Doi Cung St

▼ 77

Hué

0   250   500 m

11
12

13

14

Trang Tien
Bridge

Tran Hung Dao Street

Le Loi Street

Vo Thi Sau Street

Nguyen Thai Hoc Street

Tran Quang Khai Street

Ben Nghe Street

Ly Quy Don Street

Ba Trieu Street

▼ 70

69

Tran Cao Van Street

71 72

Phuong St

73 ▼
74 ⊕
Hung Vuong Street
● 75
76 ⊖

68
67

Nguyen Tri Phuong St

● 66

Hoang Hoa
Tham Street

63 ⊕
64 ■ 62

Ha Noi Street

● 65

Pham Hong
Thai Street

15 ▼
16

Phu Xuan
Bridge

27

60
61
59
★ 58

⊕ 56

57

Ly Thuong Kiet Street

Dong Da Street

55
■

⌂ 54

An Cuu Bridge

To Phu Bai
Airport (13 km),
Danang (108 km),
& Ho Chi Minh
City (1097 km)

52 ■

53
⬛ i

Nguyen Huy Tu St

Ngo Quyen Street

Le Lai Street

Hai Ba Trung Street

Nguyen Truong To Street

Le Loi Street

Nguyen Hue Street

Phan Dinh Phung Street

Phan Chu Trinh Street

47 ■

51 ⌂
50 ■

Tran Thuc Nhan Street

49 ▼ ■ 48

Perfume River

Dien Bien Phu Street

Buu Thi Xuan Street

42

43 ⌂i

44
⌂i

Tu Dam St

45 ⌂i

Phan Boi Chau Street

Doan Huu Trinh Street

i 46

THAI BINH
HOTEL.

To Nam Giao
& Royal Tombs

HUÉ

PLACES TO STAY		OTHER		32	Halls of the Mandarins
				33	Chuong Duc Gate
16	Thanh Loi Hotel	1	Gate (closed)	34	Nine Dynastic Urns
21	Thanh Noi Hotel	2	Gate to military area	35	Quang Duc Gate
48	Le Loi Hué Hotel		(closed to public)	36	Five of the Nine
50	Hué City Tourism Villas	3	Tang Quang Pagoda		Holy Cannons
52	Hué City Tourism Villas		(Hinayana)	38	Nha Do Gate
55	Dongda Hotel	4	Chaozhou Pagoda	39	Chanh Tay Gate
57	Ngo Quyen Hotel	5	Chua Ba	40	Gate
61	Mini-Hotel 18	6	Hall of the Cantonese	41	Gate
66	Binh Minh Hotel		Chinese	42	Hué Railway Station
67	Hung Vuong Hotel		Congregation	43	Bao Quoc Pagoda
68	Morin Hotel	7	Chieu Ung Pagoda	44	Tu Dam Pagoda
69	Trang Tien Hotel	8	Former Indian Mosque	45	Linh Quang Pagoda
71	Thuan Hoa Hotel	9	Dieu De National		& Phan Boi Chau's
72	Ben Nghe Guest House		Pagoda		Tomb
73	Vong Canh Hotel	10	Dong Ba Gate	46	Phu Cam Cathedral
78	Kinh Do Hotel	11	Riverine Transportation	47	Tomb of Duc Duc
79	A Dong Hotel		Cooperative	51	Ho Chi Minh
80	Hoa Hong Hotel	12	Dock		Museum
81	Century Riverside Inn	13	Dong Ba Market	53	Notre Dame
82	Huong Giang Hotel	14	Dong Ba Bus Station		Cathedral
		17	Thuong Tu Gate	54	An Dinh Palace
PLACES TO EAT		18	Military Museum	56	Hué General
		19	Natural History		Hospital
15	Lac Thien Restaurant		Museum	58	Police Checkpoint
	& Lac Thanh	20	Imperial Museum	59	Hué City Tourism
	Restaurant	22	Hoa Binh Gate	60	Cercle Sportiff
27	Nguyen Hoang Bus	23	Royal Library	62	GPO
	Station & Ba Nhon	24	Hien Nhon Gate	63	Vietcombank
	Restaurant	25	Four of the Nine Holy	64	DMZ Tour Office
37	Huong Sen Restaurant		Cannons	65	Vietnam Airlines
49	Cafe 3 Le Loi	26	Ngan Gate		Booking Office
70	Song Huong Floating	28	Flag Tower	74	Industrial &
	Restaurant	29	Ngo Mon Gate		Commercial Bank
77	Am Phu Restaurant &	30	Trung Dao Bridge	75	Municipal Theatre
	Thien Duong Hotel	31	Thai Hoa Palace	76	An Cuu Bus Station

mandarins stood to one side and military mandarins to the other.

There is now a souvenir shop here, and also a music ensemble dressed in traditional outfits. They will put on a performance of imperial music for a small donation of about US$1.

Halls of the Mandarins The buildings in which the mandarins prepared for court ceremonies, held in Can Chanh Reception Hall, were restored in 1977. The structures are directly behind Thai Hoa Palace on either side of a courtyard in which there are two gargantuan bronze cauldrons (vac dong) dating from the 17th century.

Nine Dynastic Urns The Nine Dynastic Urns (dinh) were cast in 1835-36. Traditional ornamentation was then chiselled into the sides of the urns, each of which is dedicated to a different Nguyen sovereign. The designs, some of which are of Chinese origin and date back 4000 years, include the sun, the moon, meteors, clouds, mountains, rivers and various landscapes. About two metres in height and weighing 1900 to 2600 kg each, the urns symbolise the power and stability of the Nguyen throne. The central urn, which is the largest and most ornate, is dedicated to the founder of the Nguyen Dynasty, Emperor Gia Long.

Forbidden Purple City The Forbidden Purple City (Tu Cam Thanh) was reserved for the personal use of the emperor. The only servants allowed into the compound were eunuchs, who would have no temptation to molest the royal concubines.

The Forbidden Purple City was almost entirely destroyed during the Tet Offensive. The area is now given over to vegetable plots, between which touch-sensitive mimosa plants flourish. The two-storey Library (Thai Binh Lau) has been partially restored. The foundations of the Royal Theatre (Duyen Thi Duong), begun in 1826 and later home of the National Conservatory of Music, can be seen nearby.

Imperial Museum The beautiful hall which houses the Imperial Museum (formerly the Khai Dinh Museum) was built in 1845 and restored when the museum was founded in 1923. The walls are inscribed with poems written in Vietnamese nom characters. The most precious artefacts were lost during the war, but the ceramics, furniture and royal clothing that remain are well worth a look. On the left side of the hall are a royal sedan chair, a gong and a musical instrument consisting of stones hung on a bi-level rack. On the other side of the hall is the equipment for a favourite game of the emperors, the idea of which was to bounce a stick off a wooden platform and into a tall, thin jug.

The building across the street was once a former school for princes and the sons of high-ranking mandarins. Behind the school is the Military Museum, with its usual assortment of American and Soviet-made weapons, including a MiG 17. Nearby is a small natural history exhibit.

The Imperial Museum is open from 6.30 am to 5.30 pm.

Tinh Tam Lake In the middle of Tinh Tam Lake, which is 500 metres north of the Imperial Enclosure, are two islands connected by bridges. The emperors used to come here with their retinues to relax.

Tang Tau Lake An island in Tang Tau Lake, which is a few hundred metres from Tinh Tam Lake, was once the site of a royal library. It is now occupied by a small Hinayana pagoda, Ngoc Huong Pagoda.

Royal Tombs

The tombs *(lang tam)* of the Nguyen Dynasty (1802-1945) are seven to 16 km to the south of Hué. They are open from 6.30 am to 5 pm daily; the entrance fee for each tomb is US$5.

Most of the tomb complexes consist of five parts:

- A Stele Pavilion in which the accomplishments, exploits and virtues of the deceased emperor are engraved on a marble tablet. The testaments were usually written by the dead ruler's successor (though Tu Duc chose to compose his own).

- A temple for the worship of the emperor and empress. In front of each altar, on which the deceased rulers' funerary tablets were placed, is an ornate dais that once held items the emperor used every day: his tea and betelnut trays, cigarette cases, etc, most of which have disappeared.

- A sepulchre, usually inside a square or circular enclosure, where the emperor's remains are buried.

- An Honour Courtyard paved with dark-brown *bat trang* bricks along the sides of which stand stone elephants, horses and civil and military mandarins. The civil mandarins wear square hats and hold the symbol of their authority, an ivory sceptre; the military mandarins wear round hats and hold swords.

- A lotus pond surrounded by frangipani and pine trees. Almost all the tombs, which are in walled compounds, were planned by the Nguyen emperors during their lifetimes. Many of the precious ornaments once reposited in the tombs disappeared during the war.

The best way to tour the Royal Tombs is on bicycle. The quiet paved roads between the tombs pass among the solid little homes of peasants; peaceful groves of trees; rice, vegetable, manioc and sugar cane plots; and newly reafforested hills.

Nam Giao Nam Giao (Temple of Heaven) was once the most important religious site in all Vietnam. It was here that every three years the emperor solemnly offered elaborate sacrifices to the All-Highest Emperor of the August Heaven (Thuong De). The topmost esplanade, which represents Heaven, is round; the middle terrace, representing the Earth, is square, as is the lowest terrace.

HUÉ

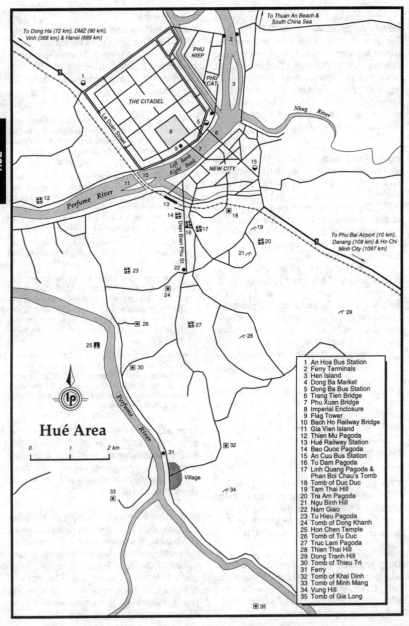

To Dong Ha (72 km), DMZ (90 km), Vinh (368 km) & Hanoi (689 km)

To Thuan An Beach & South China Sea

PHU HIEP

PHU CAT

THE CITADEL

Nhug River

Le Duan Street

Left Bank
Right Bank

NEW CITY

Perfume River

Dien Bien Phu St.

To Phu Bai Airport (10 km), Danang (108 km) & Ho Chi Minh City (1097 km)

Perfume River

Hué Area

0   1   2 km

Village

1 An Hoa Bus Station
2 Ferry Terminals
3 Hen Island
4 Dong Ba Market
5 Dong Ba Bus Station
6 Trang Tien Bridge
7 Phu Xuan Bridge
8 Imperial Enclosure
9 Flag Tower
10 Bach Ho Railway Bridge
11 Gia Vien Island
12 Thien Mu Pagoda
13 Hué Railway Station
14 Bao Quoc Pagoda
15 An Cuu Bus Station
16 Tu Dam Pagoda
17 Linh Quang Pagoda &
   Phan Boi Chau's Tomb
18 Tomb of Duc Duc
19 Tam Thai Hill
20 Tra Am Pagoda
21 Ngu Binh Hill
22 Nam Giao
23 Tu Hieu Pagoda
24 Tomb of Dong Khanh
25 Hon Chen Temple
26 Tomb of Tu Duc
27 Truc Lam Pagoda
28 Thien Thai Hill
29 Dong Tranh Hill
30 Tomb of Thieu Tri
31 Ferry
32 Tomb of Khai Dinh
33 Tomb of Minh Mang
34 Vung Hill
35 Tomb of Gia Long

After reunification, the provincial government erected – on the site where the sacrificial altar once stood – an obelisk in memory of soldiers killed in the war against the South Vietnamese government and the Americans. There was strong public sentiment in Hué against the obelisk, and the Hué Municipal People's Committee finally tore down the memorial in 1993.

Tomb of Dong Khanh Emperor Dong Khanh, nephew and adopted son of Tu Duc, was placed on the throne by the French after they captured his predecessor, Ham Nghi (who had fled after the French sacking of the royal palace in 1885), and exiled him to Algeria. Predictably, Dong Khanh proved docile; he ruled from 1886 until his death two years later.

Dong Khanh's mausoleum, the smallest of the Royal Tombs, was built in 1889. It is seven km from the city.

Tomb of Tu Duc The majestic and serene tomb of Emperor Tu Duc is set amid frangipani trees and a grove of pines. Tu Duc designed the exquisitely harmonious tomb, which was constructed between 1864 and 1867, for use both before and after his death. The enormous expense of the tomb and the forced labour used in its construction spawned a coup plot which was discovered and suppressed in 1866.

It is said that Tu Duc, who ruled from 1848 to 1883 (the longest reign of any Nguyen monarch), lived a life of truly imperial luxury: at every meal, 50 chefs prepared 50 dishes served by 50 servants; and his tea was made of drops of dew that had condensed overnight on the leaves of lotus plants. Though Tu Duc had 104 wives and countless concubines, he had no offspring. One theory has it that he became sterile after contracting smallpox.

Tu Duc's Tomb, which is surrounded by a solid octagonal wall, is entered from the east via Vu Khiem Gate. A path paved with bat trang tiles leads to Du Khiem Boat Landing, which is on the shore of Luu Khiem Lake. From the boat landing, Tinh Khiem Island,

where Tu Duc used to hunt small game, is off to the right. Across the water to the left is Xung Khiem Pavilion, where the Emperor would sit among the columns with his concubines composing or reciting poetry. The pavilion, built over the water on piles, was restored in 1986.

Across Khiem Cung Courtyard from Du Khiem Boat Landing are steps leading through a gate to Hoa Khiem Temple, where Emperor Tu Duc and Empress Hoang Le Thien Anh are worshipped. Before his death, Tu Duc used Hoa Khiem Temple as a palace, staying here during his long visits to the complex. Hoa Khiem Temple contains a number of interesting items, including a mirror used by the Emperor's concubines; a clock and other objects given to Tu Duc by the French; the Emperor and Empress's funerary tablets; and two thrones, the larger of which was for the Empress (Tu Duc was only 153 cm tall).

Minh Khiem Chamber, to the right behind Hoa Khiem Temple, was built for use as a theatre. Tu Duc's mother, the Queen Mother Tu Du, is worshipped in Luong Khiem Temple, which is directly behind Hoa Khiem Temple.

Back down at the bottom of the stairway, the brick path continues along the shore of the pond to the Honour Courtyard. Across the lake from the Honour Courtyard are the tombs of Tu Duc's adopted son, Emperor Kien Phuc, who ruled for only seven months in 1883, and the Empress Le Thien Anh, Tu Duc's wife.

After walking between the honour guard of elephants, horses and diminutive civil and military mandarins (the stone mandarins were made even shorter than the emperor), you reach the masonry Stele Pavilion, which shelters a massive stone tablet weighing about 20 tonnes. It took four years to transport the stele, the largest in Vietnam, from the area of Thanh Hoa, 500 km to the north. Tu Duc drafted the inscriptions on the stele himself in order to clarify certain aspects of his reign. He freely admitted that he had made mistakes and chose to name his tomb Khiem, which means modest. The two nearby towers symbolise the emperor's power.

Tu Duc's sepulchre, enclosed by a wall, is on the other side of a half-moon-shaped lake. In fact, Tu Duc was never actually interred here, and the site where his remains were buried along with great treasure is not known. Because of the danger of grave robbers, extreme measures were taken to keep the location secret: every one of the 200 servants who buried the king were beheaded.

Tu Duc's Tomb is seven km from Hué on Van Nien hill in Duong Xuan Thuong village.

Tomb of Thieu Tri Construction of the tomb of Thieu Tri, who ruled from 1841 to 1847, was completed in 1848. It is the only one of the Royal Tombs not enclosed by a wall. Thieu Tri's tomb, which is similar in layout to that of Minh Mang (though smaller), is about seven km from Hué.

Tomb of Khai Dinh The gaudy and crumbling tomb of Emperor Khai Dinh, who ruled from 1916 to 1925, is perhaps symptomatic of the decline of Vietnamese culture during the colonial period. Begun in 1920 and completed in 1931, the grandiose concrete structure is completely unlike Hué's other tombs. It is a synthesis of Vietnamese and European elements – even the stone faces of the mandarin honour guards are endowed with a mixture of Vietnamese and European features.

After climbing 36 steps between four dragon banisters, you get to the first courtyard, flanked by two pavilions. The Honour Courtyard, with its rows of elephants, horses and civil and military mandarins, is 26 steps farther up the hillside. In the centre of the Honour Courtyard is an octagonal Stele Pavilion.

Up three more flights of stairs is the main building, Thien Dinh, which is divided into three halls. The walls and ceiling are decorated with murals of the 'Four Seasons', the 'Eight Precious Objects', the 'Eight Fairies' and other designs made out of colourful bits of broken porcelain and glass embedded in cement. Under a graceless one-tonne concrete canopy is a gilt bronze statue of Khai Dinh in royal regalia. Behind the statue is the symbol of the sun. The Emperor's remains are interred 18 metres below the statue. Khai Dinh is worshipped in the last hall.

The Tomb of Khai Dinh is 10 km from Hué in Chau Chu village.

Tomb of Minh Mang Perhaps the most majestic of the Royal Tombs is that of Minh Mang, who ruled from 1820 to 1840. Known for the harmonious blending of its architecture with the natural surroundings, the tomb was planned during Minh Mang's lifetime and built between 1841 and 1843 by his successor.

The Honour Courtyard is reached via three gates on the eastern side of the wall: Dai Hong Mon (Great Red Gate; in the centre), Ta Hong Mon (Left Red Gate; on the left) and Huu Hong Mon (Right Red Gate; on the right). Three granite staircases lead from the Honour Courtyard to the square Stele Pavilion, Dinh Vuong. Nearby there once stood an altar on which buffaloes, horses and pigs were sacrificed.

Sung An Temple, dedicated to Minh Mang and his Empress, is reached via three terraces and Hien Duc Gate. On the other side of the temple, three stone bridges span Trung Minh Ho (The Lake of Impeccable Clarity). The central bridge, Cau Trung Dao, constructed of marble, was used only by the emperor. Minh Lau Pavilion stands on the top of three superimposed terraces representing the 'three powers': the heavens, the earth and water. Visible off to the left is the Fresh Air Pavilion; the Angling Pavilion is off to the right.

From a stone bridge across crescent-shaped Tan Nguyet Lake (Lake of the New Moon), a monumental staircase with dragon banisters leads to the sepulchre, which is surrounded by a circular wall symbolising the sun. In the middle of the enclosure, reached through a bronze door, is the Emperor's burial place, a mound of earth covered with mature pine trees and dense shrubbery.

The Tomb of Minh Mang, which is on Cam Ke hill in An Bang village, is on the left bank of the Perfume River 12 km from Hué. To get there, take a boat across the river from a point about 1.5 km south-west of Khai Dinh's tomb. Visitors have reported gross overcharging by the boat operator. Alternatively, walk along the river a bit to the north and you'll find other smaller boats and people willing to take you across for less.

Tomb of Gia Long Emperor Gia Long, who founded the Nguyen Dynasty in 1802 and ruled until 1820, ordered the construction of his tomb in 1814. According to the royal annals, the Emperor himself chose the site after scouting the area on elephant-back. The rarely visited tomb, which is presently in a state of ruin, is 14 km from Hué on the left bank of the Perfume River.

Pagodas, Temples & Churches
Thien Mu Pagoda Thien Mu Pagoda (also known as Linh Mu Pagoda), built on a hillock overlooking the Perfume River, is one of the most famous structures in all of Vietnam. Its 21-metre-high octagonal tower, seven-storey Thap Phuoc Duyen, was built by Emperor Thieu Tri in 1844 and has become the unofficial symbol of Hué. Each of the seven storeys is dedicated to a Buddha who appeared in human form *(manushi-buddha)*.

Thien Mu Pagoda was founded in 1601 by the Nguyen Lord Nguyen Hoang, governor of Thuan Hoa Province. According to legend, a Fairy Woman (Thien Mu) appeared and told the local people that a lord would come to build a pagoda for the country's prosperity. On hearing that, Nguyen Hoang ordered a pagoda to be constructed here. Over the centuries, the pagoda's buildings have been destroyed and rebuilt several times. Five monks and seven novices now live at the pagoda.

The pagoda was a hotbed of anti-government protest during the early 1960s. Surprisingly, it also became a focus of protest in the 1980s when someone was murdered near the pagoda and anti-Communist

Thien Mu Pagoda

demonstrators started here, bringing down traffic around Phu Xuan Bridge. Monks and bonzes were arrested and accused of disturbing the traffic and public order. Things have since calmed down and there are now a few nuns living at the pagoda.

To the right of the tower is a pavilion containing a stele dating from 1715. It is set on the back of a massive marble turtle, symbol of longevity. To the left of the tower is another six-sided pavilion, this one sheltering an enormous bell, Dai Hong Chung, which was cast in 1710 and weighs 2052 kg; it is said to be audible 10 km away. In the main sanctuary, in a case behind the bronze laughing Buddha, are three statues: A Di Da (pronounced 'AH-zee-dah'), the Buddha of the Past; Thich Ca (Sakyamuni), the historical Buddha; and Di Lac, the Buddha of the Future.

Behind the main sanctuary is the Austin motorcar which transported the monk Thich Quang Duc to the site in Saigon of his 1963 self-immolation, which was seen around the world in a famous photograph. Around the back are vegetable gardens in which the monks grow their own food.

Thien Mu Pagoda is on the banks of the Perfume River four km south-west of the Citadel. To get there from Dong Ba Market, head south-west (parallel to the river) on Tran Hung Dao St, which turns into Le Duan St after Phu Xuan Bridge. Cross the railway tracks and keep going on Kim Long St. Thien Mu Pagoda can also be reached by sampan.

Bao Quoc Pagoda Bao Quoc Pagoda was founded in 1670 by a Buddhist monk from China, Giac Phong. It was given its present name, which means Pagoda Which Serves the Country, in 1824 by Emperor Minh Mang, who celebrated his 40th birthday here in 1830. A school for training monks was opened at Bao Quoc Pagoda in 1940. The pagoda was last renovated in 1957.

The orchid-lined courtyard behind the sanctuary is a quiet place where students gather to study.

The central altar in the main sanctuary contains three identical statues, which represent (from left to right) Di Lac, the Buddha of the Future; Thich Ca, the historical Buddha; and A Di Da, the Buddha of the Past. Behind the three figures is a memorial room for deceased monks. Around the main building are monks' tombs, including a three-storey, red-and-grey stupa built for the pagoda's founder.

Bao Quoc Pagoda is on Ham Long Hill in Phuong Duc District. To get there, head south from Le Loi St along Dien Bien Phu St and turn right immediately after crossing the railroad tracks.

Tu Dam Pagoda Tu Dam Pagoda, which is about 600 metres south of Bao Quoc Pagoda at the corner of Dien Bien Phu and Tu Dam

Sts, is one of Vietnam's best known pagodas. Unfortunately, the present buildings were constructed in 1936 and are of little interest.

Tu Dam Pagoda was founded around 1695 by Minh Hoang Tu Dung, a Chinese monk. It was given its present name by Emperor Thieu Tri in 1841. The Unified Vietnamese Buddhist Association was established at a meeting held here in 1951. During the early 1960s, Tu Dam Pagoda was a major centre of the Buddhist anti-Diem and anti-war movement. In 1968, it was the scene of heavy fighting, scars of which remain.

Today, Tu Dam Pagoda, home to six monks, is the seat of the provincial Buddhist Association. The peculiar bronze Thich Ca Buddha in the sanctuary was cast in Hué in 1966.

Just east of the pagoda down Tu Dam St is Linh Quang Pagoda and the tomb of the scholar and anti-colonialist revolutionary Phan Boi Chau (1867-1940).

Notre Dame Cathedral Notre Dame Cathedral (Dong Chua Cuu The) at 80 Nguyen Hue St is an impressive modern building combining the functional aspects of a European cathedral with traditional Vietnamese elements, including a distinctly Oriental spire. At present, the huge cathedral, which was constructed between 1959 and 1962, has 1600 members. The two French-speaking priests hold daily masses at 5 am and 5 pm and on Sunday at 5 am, 7 am and 5 pm; children's catechism classes are conducted on Sunday mornings. Visitors who find the front gate locked should ring the bell of the yellow building next door.

Phu Cam Cathedral Phu Cam Cathedral, whose construction began in 1963 and was halted in 1975 before completion of the bell tower, is the eighth church built on this site since 1682. The Hué diocese, which is based here, hopes eventually to complete the structure if funds can be found. Phu Cam Cathedral is at 20 Doan Huu Trinh St, which is at the southern end of Nguyen Truong Tu St. Masses are held daily at 5 am and 6.45

pm and on Sundays at 5 am, 7 am, 2 pm and 7 pm.

Phu Cat & Phu Hiep Subdistricts

The island on which Phu Cat & Phu Hiep subdistricts are located can be reached by crossing the Dong Ba Canal near Dong Ba Market. The area is known for its numerous Chinese pagodas and congregational halls, many of which are along Chi Lang St.

Dieu De National Pagoda

The entrance to Dieu De National Pagoda (Quoc Tu Dieu De), built under Emperor Thieu Tri (ruled 1841-47), is along Dong Ba Canal at 102 Bach Dang St. It is one of the city's three 'national pagodas' (pagodas that were once under the direct patronage of the Emperor). Dieu De National Pagoda is famous for its four low towers, one to either side of the gate and two flanking the sanctuary. There are bells in two of the towers; the others contain a drum and a stele dedicated to the pagoda's founder.

During the regime of Ngo Dinh Diem (ruled 1955-63) and through the mid-1960s, Dieu De National Pagoda was a stronghold of Buddhist and student opposition to the South Vietnamese government and the war. In 1966, the pagoda was stormed by the police, who arrested many monks, Buddhist lay people and students and confiscated the opposition movement's radio equipment. Today, three monks live at the pagoda.

The pavilions on either side of the entrance to the main sanctuary contain the 18 La Ha, whose rank is just below that of Bodhisattva, and the eight Kim Cang, protectors of Buddha. In the back row of the main dais is Thich Ca Buddha (Sakyamuni) flanked by two assistants, Pho Hien Bo Tat (to his right) and Van Thu Bo Tat (to his left).

Former Indian Mosque

Hué's Indian Muslim community constructed the mosque at 120 Chi Lang St in 1932. The structure was used as a house of worship until 1975, when the Indian community fled. It is now a private residence.

Chieu Ung Pagoda

Chieu Ung Pagoda (Chieu Ung Tu), opposite 138 Chi Lang St, was founded by the Hainan Chinese congregation in the mid-19th century and rebuilt in 1908. It was last repaired in 1940. The sanctuary retains its original ornamentation, which is becoming faded but mercifully unaffected by the third-rate modernistic renovations that have marred other such structures. The pagoda was built as a memorial for 108 Hainan merchants who were mistaken for pirates and killed in Vietnam in 1851.

Hall of the Cantonese Chinese Congregation

The Hall of the Cantonese Chinese Congregation (Chua Quang Dong), founded almost a century ago, is opposite 154 Chi Lang St. Against the right-hand wall is a small altar holding a statue of Confucius (in Vietnamese: Khong Tu) with a gold beard. On the main altar is red-faced Quan Cong (in Chinese: Guangong) flanked by Trung Phi (on the left) and Luu Bi (on the right). On the altar to the left is Laotse with disciples to either side. On the altar to the right is Phat Ba, a female Buddha.

Chua Ba

Chua Ba, across the street from 216 Chi Lang St, was founded by the Hainan Chinese Congregation almost a century ago. It was damaged in the 1968 Tet Offensive and was subsequently reconstructed. On the central altar is Thien Hau Thanh Mau, Goddess of the Sea and Protector of Sailors. To the right is a glass case in which Quan Cong sits flanked by his usual companions, the mandarin general Chau Xuong (to his right) and the administrative mandarin Quang Binh (to his left).

Chua Ong

Chua Ong, which is opposite 224 Chi Lang St, is a large pagoda founded by the Fujian Chinese Congregation during the reign of Vietnamese Emperor Tu Duc (ruled 1848-83). The building was severely damaged during the 1968 Tet Offensive when an ammunition ship blew up nearby. A gold Buddha sits in a glass case opposite the main doors of the sanctuary. The left-hand

HUÉ

altar is dedicated to Thien Hau Thanh Mau, Goddess of the Sea and Protector of Sailors; she is flanked by her two assistants, thousand-eyed Thien Ly Nhan and red-faced Thuan Phong Nhi, who can hear for 1000 miles. On the altar to the right is Quan Cong.

Next door is a pagoda of the Chaozhou Chinese Congregation (Tieu Chau Tu).

Tang Quang Pagoda Tang Quang Pagoda (Tang Quang Tu), which is just down the road from 80 Nguyen Chi Thanh St, is the largest of the three Hinayana (Theravada, or Nam Tong) pagodas in Hué. Built in 1957, it owes its distinctive architecture to Hinayana Buddhism's historical links to Sri Lanka and India (rather than China). The pagoda's Pali name, Sangharansyarama (the Light Coming from the Buddha), is inscribed on the front of the building.

Quoc Hoc Secondary School
Quoc Hoc Secondary School (the Lycée National) is one of the most famous secondary schools in Vietnam. Founded in 1896 and run by Ngo Dinh Kha, the father of South Vietnamese President Ngo Dinh Diem, many of the school's pupils later rose to prominence in both North and South Vietnam. Numbered among Quoc Hoc Secondary School's former students are General Vo Nguyen Giap, strategist of the Viet Minh victory at Dien Bien Phu and North Vietnam's long-serving deputy premier, defence minister and commander-in-chief; Pham Van Dong, North Vietnam's Prime Minister for over a quarter of a century; and Ho Chi Minh himself, who attended the school briefly in 1908.

Next door to Quoc Hoc Secondary School, which is at 10 Le Loi St, is Hai Ba Trung Secondary School.

Neither school can be visited until after classes finish, which is about 3 pm. Otherwise, the students would have more interest in the tourists than the teachers.

Ho Chi Minh Museum
On display at the Ho Chi Minh Museum (Bao Tang Ho Chi Minh) at 9 Le Loi St are photographs, some of Ho's personal effects and documents relating to his life and accomplishments. The museum is down the block and across the street from Quoc Hoc Secondary School.

Trang Tien Bridge
The Trang Tien Bridge (formerly the Nguyen Hoang Bridge) across the Perfume River was blown up in 1968 and later repaired. The newer Phu Xuan Bridge was built in 1971.

Municipal Theatre
The Municipal Theatre (Nha Van Hoa Trung Tam) is on Huong Vuong St (corner of Ly Quy Don St).

Places to Stay – bottom end
The *Mini-Hotel 18* (☎ 23720; 12 rooms) at 18 Le Loi St is run by Hué City Tourism; doubles go for US$10 to US$12. It's a nice place and one of the better deals in the budget range.

Worth looking into is the *Hung Vuong Hotel* (☎ 23866; fax 25910; 70 rooms) at 2 Hung Vuong St. There are three standards of rooms priced at US$8, US$10 and US$40.

The *Le Loi Hué Hotel* (☎ 24668; fax 24527; 150 rooms), 2 Le Loi St, is enormous. It's also been enormously successful at attracting backpackers thanks to low prices and decent service. Singles cost US$5 to US$11, doubles US$7 to US$23 and triples US$9 to US$23. This place books bus tours, boat tours, airport taxis and so on.

Ben Nghe Guest House (☎ 23687; 18 rooms), 4 Ben Nghe St, captures a significant slice of the budget traveller market due to its low prices. Doubles cost US$6 to US$12 with attached bath and hot water.

The *Thanh Loi Hotel* (☎ 24803; fax 25344; 21 rooms), 7 Dinh Tien Hoang St, is a new place that became instantly popular after opening its doors. The ideal location on the historic west bank of Hué (near the Forbidden Purple City) is a major drawing card. The low prices also help; rooms cost US$6 to US$20.

Also in this charming neighbourhood is the *Thanh Noi* (Forbidden) *Hotel* (☎ 22478,

23438; 12 rooms) at 3 Dang Dung St. This pleasant place is in a quiet, tree-shaded compound and has its own restaurant. Rooms cost US$12 to US$17.

The *Vong Canh Hotel* (☎ 24130; fax 23424) at 25 Hung Vuong St is new place and the management is very anxious to please. Prices begin at US$15.

The *Ngo Quyen Hotel* (☎ 23278; fax 235020) at 11 Ngo Quyen St has recently been renovated. Rooms cost from US$15 to US$35.

A small family-run place is the *Binh Minh Hotel* (☎ 25526; 10 rooms) at 12 Nguyen Tri Phuong St. Rates for singles/doubles are US$10/15 to US$35/40.

The *Morin Hotel* (☎ 23526; fax 25155; 60 rooms), 30 Le Loi St, used to be *the* place for backpackers, but the rooms have become grotty. It's advisable to give this place a miss, but if nothing else is available then at least look over the room carefully before checking in. Prices are US$10 to US$30 for doubles. Overcharging in the hotel's restaurant is common.

Places to Stay – middle & top end
The *Dongda Hotel* on Ly Thuong Kiet St was under renovation at the time of this writing. Once a well-worn cheapie, don't be surprise if it jumps far upmarket.

Just next to the popular Am Phu Restaurant is the *Thien Duong Hotel* (☎ 25976; fax 28233; 25 rooms) at 33 Nguyen Thai Hoc St. The price range is US$25 to US$45.

The *Kinh Do Hotel* (☎ 23566; fax 23858; 48 rooms) is a large place that has seen recent renovation work and price rises to match. The tariff here is US$25 to US$45.

The *Thuan Hoa Hotel* (☎ 22553; fax 22470; 72 rooms), 7 Nguyen Tri Phuong St, has doubles priced from US$30 to US$50.

Some of most delightful accommodation to be had in Hué are four small houses called the *Hué City Tourism Villas* (☎ 23753). These can be found at 11, 16 and 18 Ly Thuong Kiet St and also at 5 Le Loi St. Run by Hué City Tourism, they each have a homey living room and bedroom. Rooms are priced at approximately US$25 to US$30

and can accommodate three persons. Meals are prepared on request.

A new place is the *Trang Tien Hotel* (☎ 26070; fax 26074; eight rooms), which features a few small villas. Singles are US$25 to US$45, doubles US$30 to US$50 and triples US$40 to US$60. The official address is 3 Hung Vuong St.

Also new and small is the *Hoa Hong Hotel* (☎ 24377; eight rooms) at 46C Le Loi St. This place is just opposite the enormous Century Riverside Inn. The tariff here is US$25 to US$55.

Just around the corner is the tiny *A Dong Hotel* (☎ 24148; fax 23858; nine rooms) at 1 Chu Van An St. It's priced at US$35 to US$50. Rooms here are really clean and comfortable.

The *Century Riverside Inn* (☎ 23390; fax 23399; 138 rooms), 49 Le Loi St, is a grand place on the shore of the Perfume River. Luxury like this comes at a price, in this case US$45 to US$140 plus 10% tax.

The *Huong Giang Hotel* (☎ 22122; fax 23102; 102 rooms), 51 Le Loi St, is another huge place on the river near the Dap Da Bridge. Accommodation here is priced from US$48 to US$160, and it's fair to say that you get what you pay for.

Places to Eat
West Bank The *Lac Thanh Restaurant* at 6A Dien Tien Hoang St is a fashionable gathering spot for travellers. A sign outside says 'The food is awesome' and we have to agree. See the book travellers have written in for how to order because the owner, Lac, is deaf and mute so everything is done with sign language. However, his daughter, Lan Anh, has been working hard on improving her English and can now communicate quite well.

Lac is related to the people next door at the *Lac Thien Restaurant*. And as it turns out, six of the seven children are deaf and mute! Ordering food here is pure street theatre and should not be missed. This is also the best spot in Hué to trade stories and advice with fellow travellers.

Backpackers on a tight budget should consider eating in the *Dong Ba Market*. Food here is so cheap they might as well give it away for free. Nevertheless, it's good quality. The only real problem will be finding comfortable chairs (or for that matter, any chairs) so you can sit down and enjoy your meal.

Ba Nhon Restaurant (☎ 23853), 29 Le Duan St, is actually right inside Nguyen Hoang Bus Station. It has great Vietnamese food and low prices, but so far no English menu has appeared. You can stroll into the outdoor kitchen and try pointing at what you like. Whatever you wind up with is bound to be good.

Within the Citadel, the *Huong Sen Restaurant* (☎ 3201) is at 42 Nguyen Trai St (corner of Thach Han St). This 16-sided pavilion, built on pylons in the middle of a lotus pond, is open from 9 am to midnight. The food is not necessarily the best, but you can't beat the atmosphere.

East Bank *Café 2 Le Loi* is within the grounds of the Le Loi Hué Hotel. Unusual for a hotel cafe, it's excellent. The manager speaks English and is full of useful advice.

Café 3 Le Loi is just across the street from the foregoing. Like its nearby competitor, this place dishes up fine food at cool prices and offers the opportunity to swap travellers' tales. The cafe is open daily from 6 am until midnight.

Am Phu Restaurant at 35 Nguyen Thai Hoc St has excellent Vietnamese food at reasonable prices.

The *Song Huong Floating Restaurant* is on the bank of the Perfume River just north of the Trang Tien Bridge (near the intersection of Le Loi and Hung Vuong Sts). The food here is truly awful and we are not recommending it. The nice atmosphere might make it OK for a drink though (how bad can the coffee be?).

There is a restaurant in the *Cercle Sportif*, which is on Le Loi St next to the Phu Xuan Bridge. The Cercle Sportif has tennis courts and rents paddle boats.

The restaurant on the top floor of the *Huong Giang Hotel* at 51 Le Loi St serves Vietnamese, European and vegetarian dishes. The food is excellent and the prices are surprisingly reasonable; around US$5 to US$7 for a large meal for two people.

Vegetarian Vegetarian food, which has a long tradition in Hué, is prepared at pagodas for consumption by the monks. Small groups of visitors might be invited to join the monks for a meal. Stalls in the marketplaces serve vegetarian food on the first and 15th days of the lunar month.

One good vegetarian restaurant is *Quan An Chay* (☎ 24134) at 41 Hung Vuong St. Across the street is the excellent *Nguyen Thi Gai Restaurant* at 44 Hung Vuong St.

Things to Buy
Hué is known for producing the finest conical hats in Vietnam. The city's speciality are 'poem hats', which, when held up to the light, reveal black cut-out scenes sandwiched between the layers of translucent palm leaves.

Hué also has the largest and most beautiful selection of rice paper and silk paintings in Vietnam, but prices asked are about four times the real price. You can often negotiate a 50% discount by just starting to walk away from a souvenir stall.

Dong Ba Market, which is on the left bank of the Perfume River a few hundred metres north of Trang Tien Bridge, is Hué's main market. It was rebuilt after much of the structure was destroyed by a typhoon in 1986.

Getting There & Away
Air The Vietnam Airlines Booking Office (☎ 2249) is at 12 Ha Noi St and is open Monday to Saturday from 7 to 11 am and 1.30 to 5 pm.

There are flights connecting Hué with Ho Chi Minh City (US$85 one way) and Hanoi (US$80).

Bus Hué has three main bus stations, one to destinations south (An Cuu Bus Station), another to destinations north (An Hoa Bus Station) and a short-haul bus station (Dong Ba Bus Station). A minor station is Nguyen

Hoang Bus Station, which only has buses to Quang Tri Province, though there is talk of making it into a tourist bus station.

Buses to places north of Hué depart from An Hoa Bus Station (Ben Xe An Hoa, or Ben Xe So 1; ☎ 3014), which is at the western tip of the Citadel across from 499 Le Duan St (corner Tang Bat Ho St).

Nonexpress buses from here go to Aluoi, Ba Don, Dien Sanh, Dong Ha (three hours), Dong Hoi, Hanoi, Hoan Lao, Ho Xa, Khe Sanh (twice daily; seven hours), Ky Anh, Quang Tri, Thanh Khe, Thuong Phong and Vinh.

Almost all of the buses depart at 5 or 5.30 am. Tickets for some buses (eg, to Aluoi, Ba Don, Dong Hoi, Hanoi, Hoan Lao, Thuong Phong and Vinh) can be purchased at An Cuu Bus Station.

Buses to points south of Hué leave from An Cuu Bus Station (☎ 3817), which is opposite 46 Hung Vuong St (corner Ba Trieu St); the ticket windows are open from 5 to 11 am and 1 to 6 pm.

There is daily (or more frequent) service from here to Buon Ma Thuot, Cau Hai, Danang, Ho Chi Minh City, Khe Tre, Kon Tum, Nha Trang (once every two days), Pleiku, Qui Nhon, Truoi and Vien Trinh.

Tickets for buses from An Hoa Bus Station to Aluoi, Ba Don, Dong Hoi, Hanoi, Hoan Lao, Thuong Phong and Vinh can be purchased at An Cuu Bus Station.

Vehicles to destinations in the vicinity of Hué depart from Dong Ba Bus Station (Ben Xe Dong Ba; ☎ 3055), which is on the left bank of the Perfume River between Trang Tien Bridge and Dong Ba Market. There are entrances at numbers 85 and 103 Tran Hung Dao St. Signs listing the various destinations mark the spots from which the vehicles depart.

Ancient black Citroën Traction service taxis leave for Dong Ha about every two hours between 5 am and 5 pm. Old Renaults serve La Chu, Phong Loc, Phong Son, Sia, Thuan An Beach and Vu Diem (all of which are in Huong Dien District) between 4 am and 5 pm.

Xe Lams go to An Cuu Bus Station, An Hoa Bus Station, An Lo, Bao Vinh, Cho Dinh, Cho No, Kim Long, La Chu, Phu Bai Airport, Phu Luong, Tay Loc, Thuan An Beach and Van Thanh. Dodge trucks go to Binh Dien, 30 km from Hué.

Train Hué Railway Station (Ga Hué; ☎ 2175) is on the right bank at the south-west end of Le Loi St. The ticket office is open from 7.30 am to 5 pm.

The Reunification Express Train stops in Hué. For ticket prices, see the Train section in the Getting Around chapter.

Car Ground distances from Hué are as follows:

Aluoi	60 km
Ben Hai River	94 km
Danang	108 km
Dong Ha	72 km
Dong Hoi	166 km
Hanoi	689 km
Ho Chi Minh City	1097 km
Lao Bao (Lao border)	152 km
Quang Tri	56 km
Savannakhet, Laos (Thai border)	400 km
Vinh	368 km

The road to Aluoi is negotiable only by 4WD. It may soon be possible to reach Hué by land from Thailand via Savannakhet, Lao Bao and Dong Ha.

Hitching To hitch a ride, you might try asking around the truck parking area at 1 Le Duan St (near the left-bank end of Phu Xuan Bridge).

Getting Around
To/From the Airport Hué is served by Phu Bai Airport, once an important American air base, which is 14 km south of the city centre. Taxis are typically US$8 but can be bargained (sometimes) lower. Share taxis at the airport cost as little as US$1, but don't expect a limousine (you'll get a 1975 Peugeot with no air-conditioning, for example). There have been reports of private taxis (as opposed to government-owned taxis) being

stopped near the airport by the Hué police and drivers (in reality, foreigners) being fined. Vietnam Airlines runs its own minibus from their office to the airport a couple of hours before flight time – these cost US$1 per person.

Some budget hotels (eg, the Le Loi Hué Hotel) book share taxis to the airport. Typically, this will be a car costing US$8 or less which can be shared by four persons.

Xe Lams from Dong Ba Bus Station link Hué with Phu Bai.

Car Cars with drivers can be hired from Hué City Tourism (☎ 3577) and Thua Thien-Hué Tourism (☎ 2369). The offices of Transport Company Number 3 (Cong Ty Van Tai So 3; ☎ 3922, 3622) are on Dien Bien Phu St and at the Nua Thu Hotel (☎ 3929), which the cooperative runs. The Hué City Transport Cooperative (Hop Tac O To) has offices at 1 Le Duan St (near the Citadel-side end of Phu Xuan Bridge) and on Nguyen Thai Hoc St.

Motorbike There is no set place to hire a chauffeur-driven motorbike (Honda om), which is the cheapest motor-driven way to get out to the tombs. Ask around and someone interested in earning extra cash will turn up.

Bicycle If it's not raining, the most pleasant way to tour the Hué area is by two-wheeled pedal power. Le Loi Hué Hotel at 2 Le Loi St hires out bicycles.

Boat Boat rides down the Perfume River are highly recommended – many restaurants and hotels catering to foreigners are starting to arrange these for around US$20 for a boat. Lac Thanh Restaurant and neighbouring Lac Thien Restaurant charge US$3 per person for a fantastic tour. Le Loi Hué Hotel charges US$15 per boat or you can just go to the pier opposite the railway station and book boats for US$10 which can hold around eight people. Hué City Tourism and Thua Thien-Hué Tourism can also arrange river outings but at higher cost and with poorer service. Boat tours typically take in the tombs of Tu

Duc, Thieu Tri, Minh Mang and the Thien Mu Pagoda.

Many sights in the vicinity of Hué, including Thuan An Beach, Thien Mu Pagoda and several of the Royal Tombs, can be reached by river. You might try hiring a boat behind Dong Ba Market or at the Riverine Transportation Cooperative (Van Tai Gioi Duong Song), whose office is right across Dong Ba Canal from Dong Ba Market. Boats may also be available near Dap Da Bridge, which is just east of the Huong Giang Hotel.

Around Hué

THUAN AN BEACH
Thuan An Beach (Bai Tam Thuan An), 13 km north-east of Hué, is on a splendid lagoon near the mouth of the Perfume River. Xe Lams and old Renaults from Hué to Thuan An depart from the Dong Ba Bus Station. You might also try hiring a sampan to make the trip by river. At Thuan An, you can stay at the *Tan My Hotel*.

BACH MA NATIONAL PARK
Bach Ma, a French-era hill station known for its superb weather, is 55 km south-west of Hué. Bach Ma is 1200 metres above sea level but only 20 km from Canh Duong Beach. It's location looks ideal for guarding the coastline near Hai Van Pass, and that's exactly what the Americans thought – during the war, US troops turned the area into a fortified bunker.

The national park was inaugurated in 1991. At present, there are no functioning hotels and the access road is in poor condition. There are plans to redevelop Bach Ma if the requisite capital can be found.

I tried to arrange a visit to Bach Ma from Hué. This became a time-consuming business as I was sent from tourist office, to security police, to immigration police, to Hué Prison (!) and back to the tourist office again. I was told variously that the national park did not exist, that it was too dangerous because of wild animals and bandits and that there was nothing to see but a load of trees. Finally, I just decided to turn up at the park's headquarters.

The staff at Bach Ma were surprised to see me. When an interpreter explained that I wanted to go up to the hill station, they were utterly incredulous and reluctant to do anything more. They pointed out that it was 16 km of hard walking and that today was likely to be very hot (both true). They also said that I must have a guide, which I believe is a regulation for back-country travel in all of Vietnam's national parks. However, I persevered and set off with a very nice guide who spoke very little English.

The track to Bach Ma is OK for vehicles in some places but is only passable on foot in others. To say that the access road is 'in poor condition' is an understatement. The hill station itself is a total ruin; only a few walls remain. However, I had an excellent day. The views of the forested valleys and hillsides are really splendid. I saw a couple of beautiful snakes, some wild pigs and an eagle-like bird soaring over the forest canopy. Other than that, the forest is eerily quiet in the daytime.

For the first couple of hours, I was conscious of being 'tested out' by my guide, who walked very fast and without a break. When he saw that I could keep up, he relaxed. Back at the park headquarters I asked, through my Vietnamese friend, if I could go into the park for a few days (since you tend to see more animals and birds in the mornings and evenings). This

was agreed, but I suspect only because I had proved myself. I reckon that the wardens would be unwilling to commit themselves to taking someone into the park overnight without having the measure of them first.

I returned to Bach Ma a few days later and spent three nights there with my guide. We slept in hammocks and cooked rice with fish three times a day. Unfortunately, we did not go very far into the park. This is probably because this time we were not following a clearly marked path and in case of an accident it would have been very difficult for my guide to get help or for me to find my way back again. Some of the terrain is pretty treacherous, but exciting. I also suspect that the guides are afraid of poachers, who are armed and dangerous. Going with several other visitors may ensure that you get more than one guide and they will then go further into the park.

I met the director of the national park. He expressed his desire to see more visitors to the park, used terms like 'eco-tourism' and explained that overseas interest in Vietnam's national parks programme was vital in order to raise the government's commitment. There are serious pressures from logging, poaching, agriculture, etc, which require national and provincial government assistance in overcoming. This will only happen if the park's tourist potential is seen as something worth protecting.

Tim Weisselberg

HUÉ

From 1954 to 1975, the Ben Hai River served as the demarcation line between the Republic of Vietnam (South Vietnam) and the Democratic Republic of Vietnam (North Vietnam). The Demilitarised Zone (DMZ) consisted of an area five km either side of the demarcation line.

The idea of partitioning Vietnam had its origins in a series of agreements concluded between the USA, UK and the USSR at the Potsdam Conference, which was held in Berlin in July 1945. For logistical and political reasons, the Allies decided that Japanese occupation forces to the south of the 16th parallel would surrender to the British while those to the north would surrender to the Kuomintang (Nationalist) Chinese army led by Chiang Kaishek.

In April 1954 in Geneva, Ho Chi Minh's government and the French agreed to an armistice among whose provisions was the creation of a demilitarised zone at the Ben Hai River. The agreement stated explicitly that the division of Vietnam into two zones was merely a temporary expediency and that the demarcation line did not constitute a political boundary. But when nationwide general elections planned for July 1956 were not held, Vietnam found itself divided into two states, with the Ben Hai River, which is almost exactly at the 17th parallel, as their de facto border.

During the American Vietnam War, the area just south of the DMZ was the scene of some of the bloodiest battles of the conflict. Dong Ha, Quang Tri, Con Thien, Cam Lo, Camp Carroll, the Rockpile, Khe Sanh, Lang Vay, the Ashau Valley, Hamburger Hill – these became almost household names in the USA as, year after year, TV pictures and casualty figures provided Americans with their daily evening dose of the war.

Since 1975, 5000 people have been injured or killed in and around the DMZ by mines and ordnance left over from the war. Despite the risk, impoverished peasants still dig for chunks of left-over metal to sell as scrap. The locals are paid the equivalent of US$0.03 (!) per kg of steel, US$0.38 per kg of aluminium and US$0.77 per kg of brass. Much of the metal is sold to Japan.

Orientation

The old DMZ extends from the coast westward to the Lao border; National Highway 9 (Quoc Lo 9) runs more or less parallel to the DMZ. The Ho Chi Minh Trail (Duong Truong Son), actually a series of roads, trails and paths, ran from North Vietnam southward through the Truong Son Mountains and western Laos. To prevent infiltrations and to interdict the flow of troops and matériel via the Ho Chi Minh Trail, the Americans established a line of bases along National Highway 9, including (from east to west) Cua Viet, Gio Linh, Dong Ha, Con Thien, Cam Lo, Camp Carroll, the Rockpile, Ca Lu, Khe Sanh Combat Base and Lang Vay.

The old bases along National Highway 9 (west of Dong Ha) can be visited as a day trip. The road leading south-east from the Dakrong Bridge goes to the Ashau Valley (site of the infamous Hamburger Hill) and Aluoi. With a 4WD it is possible to drive the 60 rough km from Aluoi to Hué. One traveller has described it as follows:

The area is absolutely barren – hardly a few scrubs manage to survive in the burned soil, which refuses to recover. The people make a living from scrap metal collecting, selling drinks and food to the few visitors coming here and putting entrance fees into their own pockets. The region is poverty-stricken and be prepared to have about a dozen or more people fighting between them to sell you a Coke or some fruit. Here even a 50d note can still be seen! When driving through the DMZ, countless unnamed graves are scattered about, part of Vietnam's 300,000 MIAs. Near the Doc Mieu Base there were signs of recent diggings, part of the search for US MIAs.

Information

Guides, Vehicles & Tours A good guide is required to appreciate the DMZ. After all,

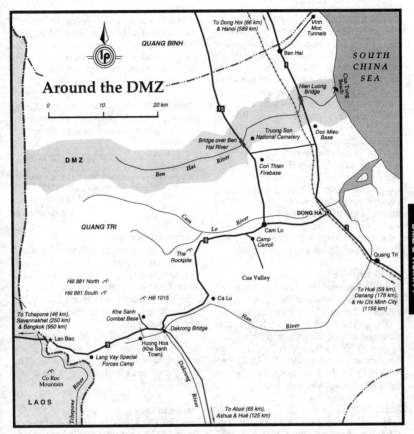

Around the DMZ

this is a historical place, but understanding the significance of each site requires some explanation. A guide is also necessary to find many of the sites since most are unmarked and it's easy to get lost in the labyrinth of dirt tracks.

Another thing you'll need is a good vehicle, preferably a 4WD jeep or a powerful motorbike which can handle rough roads. While some of the roads in the old DMZ are surfaced, many are in abysmal condition. You will need a jeep to reach the Truong Son National Cemetery, for example.

Day tours are most readily available in

Hué. The DMZ Tour Office (☎ 25242) at 26 Le Loi St gets the nod from most travellers. Alternatively, the Le Loi Hué Hotel rents jeeps with a driver and guide for US$90 per vehicle. Other hotels may offer similar deals.

Travel Permit The local government in Quang Tri Province is now requiring that foreigners secure a separate travel permit to visit any places in the DMZ off National Highway 1. The charge for the permit is US$10. You can secure these permits in the town of Dong Ha or in Hué.

Warning The war may be over but death is still fairly easy to come by in the old DMZ. At many of the places listed in this section you will find live mortar rounds, artillery projectiles and mines strewn about. As tempted as you might be to collect souvenirs, *never* touch any left-over ordnance. Watch where you step. If the locals have not carted it off for scrap, it means that even they are afraid to disturb it. White phosphorus shells – whose contents burn fiercely when exposed to air – are remarkably impervious to the effects of prolonged exposure and are likely to remain extremely dangerous for many more years. If one of these shells happens to explode while you're playing with it, your whole trip will be ruined – and don't expect a refund from Saigon Tourist.

In short, be careful. Don't become a candidate for plastic surgery – or a statistic!

DONG HA

Dong Ha, the capital of newly reconstituted Quang Tri Province, is at the intersection of National Highway 1 and National Highway 9. Dong Ha served as a US Marines command and logistics centre in 1968-69. In the spring of 1968, a division of North Vietnamese troops crossed the DMZ and attacked Dong Ha. The city was later the site of a South Vietnamese army base.

Orientation

National Highway 1 is called Le Duan St as it passes through Dong Ha. National Highway 9 (the new American-built branch), signposted as going to Lao Bao, intersects National Highway 1 next to the bus station. Tran Phu St (old National Highway 9) intersects Le Duan St 600 metres west of (towards the river from) the bus station. Tran Phu St runs south for 400 metres to the centre of town and then turns westward.

There is a market area along National Highway 1 between Tran Phu St and the river.

Information

Tourist Office Quang Tri Tourism (Cong Ty Du Lich Quang Tri) is the government-owned tourist authority for Quang Tri Province. The office is in the Dong Truong Son Hotel, three km from the city out on Tran Phu St. Cars and guides are available here, but you'd do better to arrange a guided visit to the area in Hué.

Warning Travellers just passing through have reported no problems, but those spending the night sometimes have a different tale to tell:

The friendly police in Dong Ha invited us out for beer but then held our passports they had taken from the hotel until we paid the US$50 tab. Our US$7 a night hotel also added US$20 to our bill for good measure.

Patrick Morris

French Blockhouse

The fortified French Blockhouse (Lo Khot) was used by the French and later the American and South Vietnamese armies. For a while after the war, the Blockhouse was surrounded by a display of captured American tanks and artillery pieces, thus making it a sort of quasi-museum.

These days, it's been turned into a bus station and ticket office and is scarcely recognisable for what it once was. The Blockhouse bus station is right in the centre of town.

Places to Stay

The *Nha Khach Buu Dien Tinh Buu Quang Tri* (☎ 52772; 12 rooms) is a nice, quiet place with a pleasant courtyard and friendly manager. All rooms have attached bath with hot water and can accommodate four persons. There is a security guard on duty at night. The price for foreigners is US$15 to US$20. This hotel is on the south side of town about one km from the bus station (old French Blockhouse).

Nha Nghi Du Lich Cong Doan (☎ 52744; 18 rooms) is at 4 Le Loi St, about half a km due west of the bus station. Rooms with fan and cold water cost US$9. With air-con and hot water it's US$18.

Khach San Dong Ha (☎ 52292; 18 rooms) is immediately on the north side of the bus station. Rooms with cold water cost US$10, or you can pay US$14 for the luxury of a hot bath.

The *People's Committee Guest House* (Nha Khach Uy Ban Tinh; ☎ 52361; 25 rooms) is a pleasant official guesthouse on Tran Phu St. It's just slightly north of Dong Ha Park and 400 metres to the west. Rooms with shared bath cost US$5 to US$10; private attached bath raises the tariff to US$15. Hot water is available.

Also north of the bus station by Dong Ha Park (near the ferris wheel) is the *Khach San Cong Vien* (☎ 53373; eight rooms). It's dirt-cheap accommodation at US$5 to US$7, but expect grotty rooms and cold water.

The *Dong Truong Son Hotel* (☎ 52415; 48 rooms) is three km west of the bus station on Tran Phu St. While it's not a bad place, the remote location means it's almost always empty – how it has managed to stay open for years without going bankrupt is a mystery. Room prices are from US$28 to US$30. All rooms have private bath and air-conditioning.

Places to Eat

There are a number of eateries along National Highway 1 (Le Duan St) between the bus station and Tran Phu St. These places look rather run-down but the food is pretty good because of the fierce competition for the lucrative patronage of truckers. There are more places to eat on Tran Phu St between the bus station and the People's Committee Guest House.

There is a pleasant restaurant just next door to the Nha Khach Buu Dien Tinh Buu Quang Tri (hotel). The *Huong Vinh Restaurant* is run by a married couple and their six daughters. The speciality of the house is barbecued beef cooked right at your table, served with lots of fresh vegetables. The cost for a huge meal for three people is under US$10.

The *Dong Truong Son Hotel* has its own restaurant, which – like the hotel – is usually deserted.

Getting There & Away

Bus Buses from Hué to Dong Ha depart from An Hoa Bus Station. Citroën Tractions to Dong Ha leave from Dong Ba Bus Station.

In Dong Ha, Dong Ha Bus Station (Ben Xe Khach Dong Ha; ☎ 211) is at the intersection of National Highway 1 and National Highway 9. Vehicles to Hué depart between 5 am and 5 pm. There are buses to Khe Sanh at 8 and 11 am; to get to Lao Bao, change buses in Khe Sanh. There is service every Monday and Thursday to Hanoi; the bus departs at 5 am, arriving in Vinh at 6 or 7 pm and in Hanoi at 5 am the next day. Buses also link Dong Ha with Danang, Con Thien, Cua, Dien Sanh, Hai Tri and Ho Xa, which is along National Highway 1 about 13 km west of Vinh Moc.

Train Dong Ha Railway Station (Ga Dong Ha) is a stop for the Reunification Express Train. For ticket prices, see the Train section in the Getting Around chapter.

To get to the train station from the bus station, head south-east on National Highway 1 for one km. The railway station is 150 metres across a field to the right (south-west) of the highway.

Car Road distances from Dong Ha are:

Ben Hai River	22 km
Danang	190 km
Dong Hoi	94 km
Hanoi	617 km
Ho Chi Minh City	1169 km
Hué	72 km
Khe Sanh	65 km
Lao Bao (Lao border)	80 km
Savannakhet, Laos (Thai border)	327 km
Truong Son National Cemetery	30 km
Vinh	294 km
Vinh Moc	41 km

QUANG TRI

The town of Quang Tri, 59 km north of Hué and 12.5 km south of Dong Ha Bus Station, was once an important citadel-city. In the spring of 1972, four divisions of North Vietnamese regulars backed by tanks, artillery and rockets poured across the DMZ into Quang Tri Province in what became known

DMZ & VICINITY

Peace Is Hell

Although the Americans dropped plenty of bombs and artillery shells on the north, the USA discarded plans to launch a fully fledged land invasion of North Vietnam. Ironically, the US did make ground incursions into both Laos and Cambodia to strike at enemy soldiers and supply depots, but American soldiers never crossed the DMZ. Not that it wasn't considered – some generals advocated a full-scale military assault on the North, including the use of nuclear weapons. The logic was simple – bringing the war to the North would have taken the military pressure off South Vietnam.

At least on paper, invading North Vietnam looked simple. The American generals were confident that they had sufficient firepower to smash any defences the North could hope to mount. Of course, the French had thought the same thing before they wandered into the quagmire of Dien Bien Phu.

However, the Americans had several reasons for not invading the North, most of which had little to do with the possibility of another Dien Bien Phu. One reason was that the war was becoming increasingly unpopular with the American public, and no doubt an invasion would have been costly in terms of immediate American casualties. Then there was mounting international criticism that the USA was simply engaging in imperialism, trying to subjugate Vietnam as its colony. But the main factor which caused the Americans to pause was the possibility of triggering WW III.

To this day, military buffs like to debate the issue – would an invasion of the North have changed the outcome of the war? Or would the USA have sunk even further into the morass of never-ending guerilla combat? And would China and/or Russia have entered the war on North Vietnam's behalf? And if so, would either side have dared to use nuclear weapons? As with all speculative questions, no one can truly answer, but the Americans took the nuclear threat so seriously that they didn't even declare war on North Vietnam. Throughout the entire conflict, America was officially at peace and the entire war was labelled a 'police action'. ■

as the Eastertide Offensive. They lay siege to Quang Tri City, shelling it heavily before capturing it along with the rest of the province. During the next four months, the city was almost completely obliterated by South Vietnamese artillery and massive carpet-bombing by US fighter-bombers and B-52s. The South Vietnamese army suffered 5000 casualties in the rubble-to-rubble fighting to retake Quang Tri City.

Today, there is little to see in the town of Quang Tri except a memorial and a few remains of the moat, ramparts and gates of the Citadel, once a South Vietnamese army headquarters. The Citadel is 1.6 km from National Highway 1 on Le Duan St, which runs perpendicular to National Highway 1. The ruined two-storey building between National Highway 1 and the bus station used to be a Buddhist high school.

Along National Highway 1 near the turn-off to Quang Tri is the skeleton of a church – it's definitely worth taking a look inside. It gives you the chills to see the bullet holes and know what took place here – a deadly fight between US forces and the VC.

Cua Viet Beach, once the site of an important American landing dock, is 16 km north-east of Quang Tri. Gia Dang Beach is 13 km east of town.

Getting There & Away

Bus The bus station is on Le Duan St (Quang Tri's north-south-oriented main street) 600 metres from National Highway 1. Renault buses to An Hoa Bus Station in Hué leave at 5.30 am, 6.30 am, 8 am and noon. A Citroën Traction to Dong Ba Bus Station in Hué departs daily at 6.30 am. The daily bus to Khe Sanh leaves at 8 am. There is also a service to Ho Xa.

DOC MIEU BASE

Doc Mieu Base, which is next to National Highway 1 on a low rise eight km south of the Ben Hai River, was once part of an elaborate electronic system (McNamara's Wall) intended to prevent infiltration across the DMZ. Today, it is a lunar landscape of bunkers, craters, shrapnel and live mortar rounds. Bits of cloth and decaying military boots are strewn about on the red earth. This devastation was created not by the war but by scrap-metal hunters, who have found excavations at this site particularly rewarding.

BEN HAI RIVER

Twenty-two km north of Dong Ha, National Highway 1 crosses the Ben Hai River, once the demarcation line between North and South Vietnam, over the decrepit Hien Luong Bridge. Until 1967 (when it was bombed by the Americans), the northern half of the bridge that stood on this site was painted red while the southern half was yellow. Following the signing of the Paris cease-fire agreements in 1973, the present bridge and the two flag towers were built. A typhoon knocked over the flag pole on the northern bank of the river in 1985.

CUA TUNG BEACH

Cua Tung Beach, a long, secluded stretch of sand where Vietnam's last emperor, Bao Dai, used to vacation, is just north of the mouth of the Ben Hai River. There are beaches on the southern side of the Ben Hai River as well. Every bit of land in the area not levelled for planting is pockmarked with bomb craters of all sizes. Offshore is Con Co Island, which can be reached by motorised boat; the trip takes about 2½ hours.

Getting There & Away

There are no buses to Cua Tung Beach, which can be reached by turning right (eastward) off National Highway 1 at a point 1.2 km north of the Ben Hai River. Cua Tung Beach is about seven km south of Vinh Moc via the dirt road that runs along the coast.

VINH MOC TUNNELS

The remarkable tunnels of Vinh Moc are yet another monument to the tenaciousness of North Vietnamese determination to persevere and triumph – at all costs and despite incredible difficulties – in the war against South Vietnam and the USA. A museum is being constructed on the site. A visit to the tunnels can be combined with bathing at the beautiful beaches which extend for many km north and south of Vinh Moc.

The 2.8 km of tunnels here, all of which can be visited, are the real thing, unadulterated (unlike the tunnels at Cu Chi) for viewing by tourists. It's important to realise that the underground passageways at Vinh Moc are narrower than the ones at Cu Chi. Only very slim visitors have a chance to get through the labyrinth, and if you are the least bit claustrophobic then don't even try.

Local authorities, who prefer not to lose any foreigners in the maze of forks, branches and identical weaving passageways, are adamant that visitors enter the tunnels only if accompanied by a local guide. The tunnels have been chemically treated to keep snakes away. The current entrance fee is US$9 (polite bargaining may bring it down) per group, be it one person or a dozen. Bring a torch (flashlight).

In 1966, the Americans began a massive aerial and artillery bombardment of North Vietnam. Located just north of the DMZ, Vinh Moc became one of the most heavily bombed and shelled pieces of real estate on the planet. Small family shelters could not withstand this onslaught and the villagers fled. However, the VC found it useful to have a base here and began tunnelling by hand into the red clay earth. After 18 months of work (during which the excavated earth was camouflaged to prevent its detection from the air) an enormous VC base was established underground. Civilians were employed in the digging but did not occupy the tunnels. Later, the VC were joined by North Vietnamese soldiers whose mission was to keep communications and supply lines to nearby Con Co Island open. A total of 11,500 tons of military supplies reached Con Co Island and a further 300 tons were shipped to the South thanks to the Vinh Moc tunnels.

Other villages north of the DMZ also built tunnel systems but none were as elaborate as the one at Vinh Moc. The poorly constructed tunnels of Vinh Quang village (at the mouth of the Ben Hai River) were crushed by bombs, killing everyone inside.

The tunnel network at Vinh Moc remains

essentially as it looked in 1966, though some of the 12 entrances, seven of which exit onto the palm-lined beach, have been re-timbered and others have become overgrown with foliage. The tunnels, which average 1.2 metres wide and are from 1.2 to 1.7 metres in height, were built on three levels, ranging from 15 to 26 metres below the crest of the bluff.

The tunnels were repeatedly hit by American bombs, but the only ordnance that posed a real threat was the feared 'drilling bomb'. Only once did such a bomb score a direct hit, but it failed to explode and no one was injured; the inhabitants adapted the hole for use as an air shaft. The mouths of the complex that faced the sea were sometimes hit by naval gunfire.

Offshore is Con Co Island, which during the war was an important supply depot. Today the island, which is ringed by rocky beaches, houses a small military base. The trip from Vinh Moc to Con Co takes 2½ to three hours by motorised fishing boat.

Places to Stay
There is no hotel at Vinh Moc but if you have a letter of introduction from Quang Tri Tourism you may be able to stay in a private house (a bureaucratic hassle best avoided). Basic accommodation is available at Cua Tung Beach, seven km to the south.

Getting There & Away
The turn-off to Vinh Moc from National Highway 1 is 6.5 km north of the Ben Hai River in the village of Ho Xa. Vinh Moc is 13 km from National Highway 1.

TRUONG SON NATIONAL CEMETERY
Truong Son National Cemetery is a memorial to tens of thousands of North Vietnamese soldiers from transport, construction and anti-aircraft units who were killed in the Truong Son Mountains (the Annamite Cordillera) along the Ho Chi Minh Trail. Row after row of white tombstones stretch across the hillsides in a scene eerily reminiscent of the endless lines of crosses and Stars of

David in US military cemeteries. The cemetery is maintained by disabled war veterans.

The soldiers are buried in five zones according to the part of Vietnam they came from; within each zone, the tombs are arranged by province of origin. The gravestones of five colonels (Trung Ta and Dia Ta) and seven decorated heroes, one of whom is a woman, are in a separate area. Each headstone bears the inscription 'Liet Si', which means 'martyr'. The soldiers whose remains are interred here were originally buried near where they were killed and were brought here after reunification, but many of the graves are empty, bearing the names of a small portion of Vietnam's 300,000 MIAs (soldiers 'missing in action').

On the hilltop above the sculpture garden is a three-sided stele. On one face are engraved the tributes of high-ranking Vietnamese leaders to the people who worked on the Ho Chi Minh Trail. At the bottom is a poem by the poet To Huu. Another side tells the history of the May 1959 Army Corps (Doang 5.59), which is said to have been founded on Ho Chi Minh's birthday in 1959 with the mission of constructing and maintaining a supply line to the South. The third side lists the constituent units of the May 1959 Army Corps, which eventually included five divisions. The site where the cemetery now stands was used as a base of the May 1959 Army Corps from 1972 to 1975.

Getting There & Away
The road to Truong Son National Cemetery intersects National Highway 1 some 13 km north of Dong Ha and nine km south of the Ben Hai River; the distance from the highway to the cemetery is 17 km. A rocky cart-path, passable (but just barely) by car, links Cam Lo (on National Highway 9) with Truong Son National Cemetery. The 18-km drive from Cam Lo to the cemetery passes by newly planted rubber plantations and the homes of Bru (Van Kieu) tribal people, who raise, among other crops, black pepper.

CON THIEN FIREBASE
In September 1967, North Vietnamese forces

Elderly woman near the former DMZ

backed by long-range artillery and rockets crossed the DMZ and besieged the US Marine base of Con Thien. It had been established to stop infiltrations across the DMZ and as part of McNamara's Wall (named after the US Secretary of Defense 1961-68), an abortive electronic barrier to detect infiltrators.

The Americans responded with 4000 bombing sorties (including 800 by B-52s), during which more than 40,000 tons of bombs were dropped on the North Vietnamese forces around Con Thien, transforming the gently sloping brush-covered hills that surrounded the base into a smoking moonscape of craters and ashes. As a result of the bombing the siege was lifted, but the battle had accomplished its real purpose: to divert US attention from South Vietnam's cities in preparation for the Tet Offensive.

The area around the base is still consid-ered too dangerous even for scrap-metal hunters to approach.

Getting There & Away

Con Thien Firebase is 10 km west of National Highway 1 and seven km east of Truong Son National Cemetery along the road linking National Highway 1 with the cemetery. Concrete bunkers mark the spot a few hundred metres to the south of the road where the base once stood.

Con Thien is 12 km from National Highway 9 and six km from Truong Son National Cemetery on the road that links Cam Lo with the cemetery. As you head towards the cemetery, the base is visible off to the right (east).

Six km towards National Highway 1 from Con Thien (and four km from the highway) is another US base, C-3, the rectangular ramparts of which are still visible just north of the road. It is inaccessible due to mines.

CAMP CARROLL

Established in 1966, Camp Carroll was named for a US Marine captain who was killed trying to seize a nearby ridge. The gargantuan 175-mm cannons at Camp Carroll were used to shell targets as far away as Khe Sanh. In 1972, the South Vietnamese commander of Camp Carroll, Lieutenant Colonel Ton That Dinh, surrendered and joined the North Vietnamese army; he is now a high-ranking official in Hué.

These days there is not that much to see at Camp Carroll except a few overgrown trenches and the remains of their timber roofs. Bits of military hardware and lots of rusty shell casings litter the ground. The concrete bunkers were destroyed by local people seeking to extract the steel reinforcing rods to sell as scrap; concrete chunks from the bunkers were hauled off for use in construction. Locals out prospecting for scrap metal can point out what little of the base is left.

The area around Camp Carroll now belongs to the State Pepper Enterprises (Xi Nghiep Ho Tieu Tan Lam). The pepper plants are trained so that they climb up the trunks of jackfruit trees. There are also rubber plantations nearby. The road to Camp Carroll leads on to the fertile Cua Valley, once home to a number of French settlers.

The turn-off to Camp Carroll is 11 km west of Cam Lo, 24 km east of the Dakrong Bridge and 37 km east of the Khe Sanh Bus Station. The base is three km from National Highway 9.

THE ROCKPILE

The Rockpile was named for what can only be described as a 230-metre-high pile of rocks. There was a US Marines lookout on top of the Rockpile and a base for American long-range artillery nearby. The local tribal people, who live in houses built on stilts, engage in slash-and-burn agriculture.

The Rockpile is 26 km towards Khe Sanh from Dong Ha.

DAKRONG BRIDGE

The Dakrong Bridge, 13 km east of the Khe Sanh Bus Station, was built in 1975-76 with assistance from the Cubans. The bridge crosses the Dakrong River (also known as the Ta Rin River). Hill-tribe people in the area live by slash-and-burn agriculture. Some of the tribespeople openly carry assault rifles left over from the war; this is against the law but the government seems unwilling or unable to do anything about it.

The road that heads south-east from the bridge to Aluoi was once a branch of the Ho Chi Minh Trail. Constructed with Cuban help, it passes by the stilted homes of the Bru.

ALUOI

Aluoi is approximately 65 km south-east of the Dakrong Bridge and 60 km west of Hué. There are a number of waterfalls and cascades in the area. Tribes living in the mountainous Aluoi area include the Ba Co, Ba Hy, Ca Tu and Taoi. US Army Special Forces bases in Aluoi and Ashau were overrun and abandoned in 1966; the area then became an important transshipment centre for supplies coming down the Ho Chi Minh Trail.

Among the better known military sites in the vicinity of Aluoi are landing zones Cunningham, Erskine and Razor, Hill 1175 (west of the valley) and Hill 521 (in Laos). Farther south in the Ashau Valley is 'Hamburger Hill' (Apbia Mountain). In May 1969, American forces on a search-and-destroy operation near the Lao border fought one of the fiercest engagements of the war here, suffering terrible casualties (hence the name); in less than a week of fighting, 241 American soldiers died at Hamburger Hill, a fact well publicised in the American media. A month later, after US forces withdrew from the area to continue operations elsewhere, the hill was reoccupied by the North Vietnamese.

KHE SANH COMBAT BASE

Khe Sanh Combat Base, site of the most famous siege (and one of the most controversial battles) of the American Vietnam War, sits silently on a barren plateau surrounded by vegetation-covered hills often obscured

Siege of Khe Sanh

Despite opposition from Marine Corps brass to General Westmoreland's attrition strategy (they thought it futile), the small US Army Special Forces (Green Beret) base at Khe Sanh, built to recruit and train local tribespeople, was turned into a Marine stronghold in late 1966. In April 1967, there began a series of 'Hill Fights' between the US forces and the well-dug-in North Vietnamese army infantry who held the surrounding hills. In the period of a few weeks, 155 Marines and perhaps thousands of North Vietnamese were killed. The fighting centred on hills 881 South and 881 North, both of which are about eight km north-west of Khe Sanh Combat Base.

In late 1967, American intelligence detected the movement of tens of thousands of North Vietnamese regulars armed with mortars, rockets and artillery into the hills around Khe Sanh. The commander of the US forces in Vietnam, General Westmoreland, became convinced that the North Vietnamese were planning another Dien Bien Phu, a preposterous analogy given American firepower and the proximity of Khe Sanh to supply lines and other American bases. President Johnson himself became obsessed by the spectre of Dien Bien Phu: to follow the course of the battle, he had a sand-table model of the Khe Sanh plateau constructed in the White House Situation Room, and he took the unprecedented step of requiring a written guarantee from the Joint Chiefs of Staff that Khe Sanh could be held.

Westmoreland, determined to avoid 'another Dien Bien Phu' at all costs, assembled an armada of 5000 aeroplanes and helicopters and increased the number of troops at Khe Sanh to 6000. He even ordered his staff to study the feasibility of using tactical nuclear weapons.

The 75-day Siege of Khe Sanh began on 21 January 1968 with a small-scale assault on the base perimeter. As the Marines and the South Vietnamese Rangers with them braced for a full-scale ground attack, Khe Sanh became the focus of global media attention. It was the cover story for both *Newsweek* and *Life* magazines and appeared on the front pages of countless newspapers around the world. During the next two months, the base was subject to continuous ground attacks and artillery fire. US aircraft dropped 100,000 tons of explosives on the immediate vicinity of Khe Sanh Combat Base. The expected attempt to overrun the base never came, and on 7 April 1968 after heavy fighting, US Army troops reopened National Highway 9 and linked up with the Marines, ending the siege.

It now seems clear that the Siege of Khe Sanh, in which an estimated 10,000 North Vietnamese died, was merely an enormous diversion intended to draw US forces and the attention of their commanders away from South Vietnam's population centres in preparation for the Tet Offensive, which began a week after the siege did. At the time, however, Westmoreland considered the entire Tet Offensive to be a 'diversionary effort' to distract attention from Khe Sanh!

A few days after Westmoreland's tour of duty in Vietnam ended in July 1968, American forces in the area were redeployed. Policy, it seemed, had been reassessed and holding Khe Sanh, for which so many men had died, was deemed unnecessary. After everything at Khe Sanh was buried, trucked out or blown up – nothing recognisable that could be used in a North Vietnamese propaganda film was to remain – US forces up and left Khe Sanh Combat Base under a curtain of secrecy. The American command had finally realised what a Marine officer had long before expressed this way: 'When you're at Khe Sanh, you're not really anywhere. You could lose it and you really haven't lost a damn thing'. ∎

by mist and fog. It is hard to imagine as you stand in this peaceful, verdant land, with the neat homes and vegetable plots of local tribespeople and Vietnamese settlers all around, that in this very place in early 1968 took place the bloodiest battle of the Vietnam War. Approximately 500 Americans (the official figure of 205 American dead was arrived at by statistical sleight-of-hand), some 10,000 North Vietnamese troops and uncounted civilian bystanders died amid the din of machine-guns and the fiery explosions of 1000-kg bombs, white phosphorus shells, napalm, mortars and artillery rounds of all sorts.

But little things help you to picture what the history books say happened here. The outline of the airfield remains distinct (to this day nothing will grow on it). In places, the ground is literally carpeted with bullets and rusting shell casings. And all around are little groups of local people digging holes in their relentless search for scrap metal (once, local scavengers say proudly, they unearthed an entire bulldozer!). The US MIA Team, which

Missing in Action (MIA)

An issue which continues to poison relations between the USA and Vietnam is that of US military personnel officially listed as 'missing in action'. More than two decades after US forces were withdrawn from Vietnam, there are still 2265 American soldiers whose bodies have not been found and who are therefore officially 'unaccounted for'.

The families of the missing are usually adamant – many believe that their loved ones are still alive and being held in secret prison camps somewhere in the jungles of Vietnam. POW-MIA groups in the USA continue to lobby Congress to 'do something'. It's a highly emotion-charged issue, one which is often cleverly exploited by some US politicians. 'No compromise', they insist, 'until Vietnam accounts for every one of the MIAs'.

But there are others who think that the POW-MIA groups are beating a dead horse. The figure of 2265 MIAs is almost certainly too high. About 400 flight personnel were killed when their planes crashed into the sea off the coast of Vietnam – the bodies were never recovered but they are still listed as MIAs. Many others were killed when their aircraft went down in flames over the jungle and no remains could be recovered. Still others were killed in ground combat, but the tropical jungle quickly reclaims a human corpse. Not much is said about the American MIAs from the Korean War and WW II – it was long ago assumed that all of them are dead. Nor does anyone talk about the 300,000 Vietnamese who are also MIAs.

US Senator John Kerry is the chairman of a Senate committee exploring the MIA issue. After visiting Vietnam in November 1992, he called for a reappraisal of the US body count. During a press conference, he said, 'You have certain instances in which this person was KIA (killed in action) and the body cannot be recovered...this standard has to be reviewed'.

Kerry added that in 1973, when Vietnam returned the last 590 American POWs, there were 37 soldiers believed to have been captured who were not among those released.

Could there still be some American troops being held prisoner in Vietnam? The Vietnamese government adamantly denies it. But as one observer noted, 'No one can be sure; perhaps the Vietnamese did keep some American prisoners after the war ended. But if I were them, I would have executed those prisoners long ago – keeping them around and risking discovery would be too much of an embarrassment'.

In the meantime, MIA teams continue to comb the Vietnamese countryside with little success, at a cost to American taxpayers which has now added up to over US$100 million. Many Vietnamese labourers are employed in the search teams, and 75% of their salaries go to the government. Not surprisingly, the Vietnamese government is in no hurry to see the MIA teams leave, though there is frustration with how the Americans keep raising this bogus issue in diplomatic negotiations. The fact that the MIA teams have been digging through Vietnamese cemeteries looking for American bones has also irritated many locals who would prefer to see their dead rest in peace.

On the other hand, there are plenty of Vietnamese who sense an opportunity in the MIA issue. Vietnamese civilians regularly approach the US government's representatives with fragments of bone which they claim belong to dead American MIAs. Their hope is to get some sort of cash reward, or even an immigration visa to the USA. What most do not realise is that the USA does not pay rewards for this information. Even budget travellers have been approached by the bone pedlars – some Vietnamese believe all Westerners have great influence with the US government!

Meanwhile, the whole sad saga continues to play itself out. When private POW-MIA groups started circulating photographs showing US soldiers being held prisoner in a Vietnamese camp, there was a flurry of official investigations. The photos proved to be fakes. But POW-MIA groups such as the National League of Families of American Prisoners and Missing in Southeast Asia were very effective in one regard – for a long time they frustrated the US government's attempts to establish diplomatic relations with Vietnam. ∎

is charged with finding the remains of Americans listed as 'missing-in-action', still visits the area to search for the bodies of the Americans who disappeared during the fierce battles in the surrounding hills. Most of the remains they find are Vietnamese.

Getting There & Away

To get to Khe Sanh Combat Base, turn north-westward at the triangular intersection 600 metres towards Dong Ha from Khe Sanh Bus Station. The base is on the right-hand side of the road, 2.5 km from the intersection.

KHE SANH TOWN

Set amid beautiful hills, valleys and fields at an elevation of about 600 metres, the town of Khe Sanh (Huong Hoa) is a pleasant district capital once known for its French-run coffee plantations. Many of the inhabitants are Bru tribespeople who have moved here from the surrounding hills. A popular pastime among the hill-tribe women is smoking long-stemmed pipes.

Places to Stay

The only hotel in town is *Nha Hang 17*, which costs US$5 per night. It's on the western side of Khe Sanh on the north side of the road to Lao Bao.

Getting There & Away

Khe Sanh Bus Station (Ben Xe Huong Hoa) is on National Highway 9, 600 metres south-west (towards the Lao frontier) from the triangular intersection where the road to Khe Sanh Combat Base branches off. Buses to Dong Ha depart at 7 am and around noon; the daily bus to Hué leaves at 7 am. There are two buses a day to Lao Bao; the first leaves at 6 am, the second whenever it is full. The ticket window is open from 6 to 7 am; tickets for later buses are sold on board.

If and when the border with Laos is opened for trade and travel, the public transport situation in the area is likely to improve significantly.

LANG VAY SPECIAL FORCES CAMP

In February 1968, Lang Vay (Lang Vei) Special Forces Camp, established in 1962, was attacked and overrun by North Vietnamese infantry backed by nine tanks. Of the base's 500 South Vietnamese, Bru and Montagnard defenders, 316 were killed. Ten of the 24 Americans at the base were killed; 11 of the survivors were wounded.

All that remains of dog-bone-shaped Lang Vay Base are the overgrown remains of numerous concrete bunkers. Locals can show you around.

Getting There & Away

The base is on a ridge just south-west of National Highway 9 at a point 9.2 km towards Laos from the Khe Sanh Bus Station and 7.3 km towards Khe Sanh from Lao Bao Market.

LAO BAO

Lao Bao is right on the Tchepone River (Song Xe Pon), which marks the Vietnam-Laos border. Towering above Lao Bao on the Lao side of the border is Co Roc Mountain, once a North Vietnamese artillery stronghold.

Two km from the border post is Lao Bao Market, where Thai goods smuggled through the bush from Laos to Vietnam are readily available. Merchants accept either Vietnamese dong or Lao kip.

Getting There & Away

Lao Bao is 18 km west of Khe Sanh, 80 km from Dong Ha, 152 km from Hué, 46 km east of Tchepone (Laos), 250 km east of Savannakhet, Laos (on the Thai frontier) and 950 km from Bangkok (via Ubon Ratchathani). Lao Bao may eventually become an important border crossing for trade and tourism between Thailand and central Vietnam.

DMZ & VICINITY

North-Central Vietnam

The area north of the DMZ is the former North Vietnam. While the differences between north and south have faded since reunification in 1975, there is still evidence that there were once two different countries with two different political systems.

While the south enjoyed America's largesse, which brought wartime prosperity, the north has never been anything but desperately poor – and still is. While the south was the scene of many (mostly small) land battles, it was the north that suffered from bombing – bomb craters and damaged buildings are still a feature in this part of Vietnam.

And there is also a perceptible change in attitudes – southerners see the northerners as provincial. For their part, the northerners think the southerners are money-grubbers. Both sides complain that they have trouble understanding what the other says – the two parts of Vietnam speak a sharply different, though mutually intelligible, dialect.

As a foreigner, you will probably detect some difference in attitudes as you head north of the DMZ – people are more reserved and less friendly. This is not a huge problem by any means, but it is noticeable. Most likely, the economic integration of Vietnam that is now occurring will reduce the differences between north and south, but this will take time.

DONG HOI

The fishing port of Dong Hoi is the capital of Quang Binh Province. Important archaeological finds from the Neolithic period have been made in the vicinity. During the Vietnam War, the city suffered extensive damage from US bombing. When travelling on National Highway 1 north of the DMZ, note the old French bunkers and US bomb craters lining the route; both are especially numerous near road and rail bridges. The Vietnam-Cuba Hospital is one km north of town.

Usually travellers spend the night in Dong Hoi only if they wish to visit Phong Nha Cave (see that section for details). The cave is 55 km from Dong Hoi, so it can be visited as a day trip. Some hotels in Dong Hoi (see Places to Stay) book trips to the cave.

Information
Tourist Office The Dong Hoi Tourist Office is near the Hoa Binh Hotel in the centre of town.

Beaches
Most of Quang Binh Province is lined with sand dunes and beaches. There are dozens of kilometres of beaches and dunes north of town and on a long spit of sand south of town. Nhat Le Beach is at the mouth of the Nhat Le River about 2.5 km from central Dong Hoi. Another bathing site in the region is Ly Hoa Beach.

Nhat Le River
This river flows along the east side of town and boat trips are a pleasant way to pass the time. The Phuong Dong Hotel (see Places to Stay) books boat trips for US$2.50 per hour per person, but about 10 persons are needed to make this trip economically viable.

Places to Stay
The most pleasant places to stay are on the west bank of the Nhat Le River, which is about half a kilometre east of National Highway 1.

The largest of the riverside hotels is the *Nhat Le Hotel* (☎ 22180; 46 rooms) at 16 Quach Xuan Ky St. Rooms cost US$10 to US$25.

Just to the north at 20 Quach Xuan Ky St is the *Phuong Dong Hotel* (☎ 22276; fax 22404; 34 rooms). This new place has three standards of rooms costing US$30, US$40 and US$45. This place books boat trips on the Nhat Le River, and also day trips by car or van to Phong Nha Cave.

Still on Quach Xuan Ky St but another block to the north is the *Huu Nghi Hotel*

North-Central Vietnam

0   50   100 km

(☎ 22567; 23 rooms). This place has a river view and rooms for US$20 to US$45.

Right on National Highway 1 in the centre of town is the *Hoa Binh Hotel* (☎ 22347; 18 rooms). This four-storey building (a veritable skyscraper by Dong Hoi standards) is starting to fall into disrepair, but that hasn't caused the price to come down. Rooms cost US$20 to US$25.

Getting There & Away

Bus & Car Dong Hoi is 166 km from Hué, 94 km from Dong Ha, 197 km from Vinh and 489 km from Hanoi. Dong Hoi is on National Highway 1 and sees regular bus traffic. Road traffic between Dong Ha and Dong Hoi is light, especially after the early morning.

North of the DMZ, National Highway 1 is being completely rebuilt, which means lots of gravel, dust, mud, potholes and trucks dangerously overloaded with building materials. One irony is that these heavy trucks are breaking up the existing road, even though they will help to build the new one.

There is a ferry crossing at Cua Gianh (also called Song Painh), which is 33 km north of Dong Hoi. The ferry is really just a small barge which is pushed and pulled by

---

Phong Nha Cave Expedition

In 1990 we were fortunate enough to be the first caving expedition to Vietnam. That trip was a reconnaissance, and a team of 12 returned later. Our prime objective was Phong Nha Cave. We completed the exploration. The cave is eight km long, all of which we surveyed and photographed. We explored a total of 35 km of caves in this area. All of them are spectacular river caves.

The journey to the cave includes a drive north along National Highway 1 to Bo Trach. Here you turn off to the west along a rougher, unsurfaced road which takes you to the village of Son Trach. The scenery here is very beautiful, with cone-shaped limestone hills rising from the flat valleys. Along the road from Bo Trach and in Son Trach itself there is much evidence of the war. There are bomb craters and bomb casings from unexploded shells, which are used as scrap metal or for gate posts. The journey from Dong Hoi to Son Trach takes about two hours.

The local oar-driven boats will take you up the Son River and into Phong Nha Cave. The cave was used during the war as a hospital and the impressive entrance shows effects of the attack by American war planes. Phong Nha means 'Cave of the Teeth and Wind', but unfortunately the teeth (or stalagmites) no longer remain.

Inside, the boats will take you along the large river galleries for 700 metres, where a large dry passage is found. This leads up into a decorated chamber. Nearer to the entrance the boats will land on a sandy beach, where you can walk along for 500 metres among huge stalactites and stalagmites. The cave is very beautiful and unspoilt. The ride from Son Trach into the cave and back will take two to three hours.

Howard Limbest

---

tugboats and there is often a long queue of vehicles – it can take an hour or more to get across.

Train Dong Hoi is a stop for the Reunification Express. For ticket prices, see the Train section in the Getting Around chapter.

BO TRACH

The obscure village of Bo Trach (also called Hoan Lao) is so small that it doesn't appear on many maps. Indeed, you could easily drive past without ever noticing. Aside from a pleasant beach, the real reason to come here is to visit Phong Nha Cave, 30 km to the west.

You can, of course, bypass Bo Trach entirely and most travellers do. However, Bo Trach has an upmarket hotel and quiet location, and so has carved a large niche for itself in the foreign tour group market. Independent travellers will probably find it more convenient to launch their cave explorations from Dong Hoi, which is 25 km south of Bo Trach.

Places to Stay

The *Da Nhay Hotel* (☎ 64241; 14 rooms) is a pleasant place in the countryside that rakes in the tour groups. The hotel is on the west side of National Highway 1, directly opposite a fine beach.

Inquire at the hotel about booking a vehicle to Phong Nha Cave, but be prepared to bargain because the prices quoted are definitely far higher than they should be. Perhaps some future free-market competition will change all that, but for now this hotel enjoys a local monopoly.

PHONG NHA CAVE

Phong Nha Cave is remarkable for its thousands of metres of passageways lined with a great variety of stalactites and stalagmites. The main tunnel is 1451 metres in length and has 14 halls. Travel within the cave is by boat and on foot.

The Chams utilised the grottoes of Phong Nha Cave as Buddhist sanctuaries in the 9th and 10th centuries; the remains of Cham altars and inscriptions can still be seen. Vietnamese Buddhists continue to venerate these sanctuaries, as they do other Cham religious sites.

Foreigners are charged US$6 admission fee to enter the caves.

Getting There & Away

The caves are close to the village of Son

Trach, which is about 55 km north-west of Dong Hoi. There is no public transport to Son Trach, but hotels and some travel agencies in nearby towns cater to this market.

The Phuong Dong Hotel in Dong Hoi offers transport for US$55 for 10 persons.

By contrast, the Da Nhay Hotel in Bo Trach (only 30 km from the caves) is far more expensive, charging US$120 for 12 persons. However, they also have a car which they rent for US$40 which can carry four persons.

You can travel by public bus from Dong Hoi to Bo Trach (on National Highway 1), where you will find motorcycle taxis waiting to take you to Son Trach for US$3.50. The drivers will wait for you while you visit the cave. At the office in Son Trach you can book your guide and boat – they charge US$12 per boat, which can carry up to six passengers.

DEO NGANG

Deo Ngang (Ngang Pass) is a mountainous coastal area that constitutes the easternmost section of the Hoanh Son Mountains (Transversal Range), which stretches from the Lao border to the sea along the 18th parallel. Until the 11th century, the range formed Vietnam's frontier with the Kingdom of Champa. Later, the French used it as the border between their protectorates of Annam and Tonkin; Annam Gate (Porte d'Annam) is still visible at Ngang Pass from National Highway 1.

The Hoanh Son Mountains now demarcate the border between Quang Binh Province and Ha Tinh Province. There are a number of islands offshore.

This part of Vietnam is particularly poor and has been periodically afflicted by famine. Because vehicles have to slow down when climbing Deo Ngang, the pass has long been a favourite venue for beggars. In 1992 we saw dozens of beggars here lining the highway. However, returning in 1994 we counted only five and we assume that the local economy has seen some recent improvement.

CAM XUYEN

The town of Cam Xuyen is about 150 km

north of Dong Hoi and 45 km south of Vinh. There is nothing here to see. Cam Xuyen's only significant feature is a grotty guesthouse here where you can stay if you're too tired to push on.

The *Nha Khach Cam Xuyen* (☎ 61234; five rooms), on the west side of the road, charges foreigners US$4 for Third World accommodation. It's only for the desperate, so if you're heading north then try to make it to Ha Tinh or Vinh.

HA TINH

Ha Tinh is a nondescript town on the highway between Cam Xuyen and Vinh. Most likely the only reason you'd want to stop here is if your car or bus breaks down. Foreigners zipping along National Highway 1 often spend the night here, though Vinh has a wider selection of hotels and cheaper prices.

If you need to change money, there is a branch of Vietcombank (☎ 56775) at 6 Phan Dinh Phung St.

Places to Stay

Most foreigners travelling National Highway 1 are heading north. If that describes your situation, the first hotel you see on the south side of town (and west side of the highway) is *Nha Khach Cau Phu* (☎ 56712; 22 rooms). It's a new hotel, the staff speak surprisingly good English and it's probably the second best deal in town. Rooms cost US$20 and US$25.

On the west side of Tran Phu St (National Highway 1) opposite the huge TV tower is the *Binh Minh Hotel* (☎ 56825; 21 rooms). Rooms are OK but rather pricey at US$30 and US$35.

Ha Tinh's cheapest accommodation (and not bad either) is the *Kieu Hoa Hotel* (☎ 57025; seven rooms). It's on the west side of Tran Phu St , slightly north of the TV tower. Rooms cost US$14 and the management tries (not too successfully) to speak English. However, it's a friendly place and has a small restaurant.

The worst deal in town is the *Ha Tinh Relation Hotel* (Khach San Giao Te Ha Tinh;

☎ 55589; 34 rooms), about one km east of the TV tower. It's very overpriced at US$20 to US$25 for a mediocre room with attached leaking shower. To make sure you don't oversleep, the hotel blasts military music at 5 am. The hotel is operated by the provincial tourism authority, Ha Tinh Tourism (Cong Ty Du Lich Ha Tinh).

VINH

The port city of Vinh is the capital of one of Vietnam's most populous provinces, Nghe An. While there is almost nothing of interest in the city, it is a convenient place to stop for the night if you are going overland between Hué and Hanoi.

Nghe An and neighbouring Ha Tinh provinces are endowed with poor soil and some of the worst weather in Vietnam. The area frequently suffers from floods and devastating typhoons. The locals say, 'The typhoon was born here and comes back often to visit'. The summers are very hot and dry, while during the winter the cold and rain are made all the more unpleasant by biting winds from the north.

The upland and highland regions of Nghe An, much of which is thickly forested, cover 80% of the province's territory and are home to Muong, Tai (Thai or Thay), Khmer, Meo and Tho hill-tribe people. Mountain fauna includes tigers, leopards, elephants, rhinoceroses, deer, monkeys, gibbons and flying squirrels. Nghe An's agricultural products include wet-grown rice, sugar cane, tea, mulberry leaves, areca and pomelo.

A good source of information on Nghe An and Ha Tinh provinces is *Nghe Tinh: Native Province of Ho Chi Minh*, which is volume 59 of the *Vietnamese Studies* series published in English and French in Hanoi by Xunhasaba (State Enterprise for the Export-Import of Books, Periodicals & Cultural Commodities).

Vinh's relatively harsh climate has made much of Nghe An and Ha Tinh provinces one of the most destitute regions in Vietnam.

History

Nghe An and neighbouring Ha Tinh provinces (they were once combined into a single province called Nghe Tinh) are famous for their revolutionary spirit. Both Phan Boi Chau (1867-1940) and Ho Chi Minh (1890-1969) were natives of Nghe An Province. The Nghe Tinh Uprising (1893-95) against the French was led by the scholar Phan Dinh Phung (1847-95). The Nghe Tinh Soviets Movement (1930-31) began with a series of workers' strikes and demonstrations encouraged by the newly formed Indochinese Communist Party; by the summer of 1930, peasant associations (or soviets) had seized power in some areas. The French moved swiftly to suppress the unrest, employing aircraft to attack crowds of demonstrators. The Ho Chi Minh Trail began in Nghe An Province, and much of the war matériel transported on the Ho Chi Minh Trail was shipped via the port of Vinh.

Vinh's recent history has not been the happiest. It was a pleasant citadel-city during colonial days but was destroyed in the early 1950s as a result of French aerial bombing and the Viet Minh's scorched-earth policy. Vinh was later devastated by a huge fire. To add icing on the cake, the US military obliterated the city in hundreds of air attacks and naval artillery bombardments from 1964 to 1972 which left only two buildings intact. The Americans paid a high price for the bombings – more US aircraft and pilots were shot down over Nghe An and Ha Tinh provinces than over any other part of North Vietnam. The heavy loss of planes and pilots was one reason why the US later brought in battleships to pound North Vietnam with artillery shells fired from offshore.

After the war, Vinh was rebuilt with East German financial and technical assistance, which perhaps explains why the city's grim and rapidly dilapidating buildings suffer from a uniform lack of imagination.

Vinh's one salvation is its location on National Highway 1 almost exactly midway between Hué and Hanoi. Both foreign and Vietnamese travellers use Vinh as a convenient overnight stop, which benefits the hotel and restaurant business and gives small-shop owners a chance to draw in customers.

Orientation
As National Highway 1 enters Vinh from the south, it crosses the mouth of the Lam River (Ca River), also known as Cua Hoi Estuary. Quang Trung St (which runs north-south) and Tran Phu St intersect one block north of Vinh Central Market. Street address numbers are not used in Vinh.

Information
Tourist Office The government-owned Nghe An Tourism (Cong Ty Du Lich Nghe An) is on Quang Trung St just to the north of Rap 12/9 cinema.

Money Vietcombank (Ngan Hang Ngoai Thuong Viet Nam; ☎ 2304, 2426) is at the corner of Le Loi and Nguyen Si Sach Sts.

Post & Telecommunications The post office is on Nguyen Thi Minh Khai St 300 metres north-west of Dinh Cong Trang St; it is open from 6.30 am to 9 pm.

International and domestic telephone calls can be made from the calling office (Cong Ty Dien Bao Dien Thoai), which is in a little building on Dinh Cong Trang St near the corner of Nguyen Thi Minh Khai St. The office is supposed to be open from 7 am to 9 pm. If no one is there, inquire at the cigarette stall next door or go into the telephone exchange building, which is across the field behind the calling office.

Emergency The general hospital is on the corner of Tran Phu and Le Mao Sts.

Vinh Central Market
Vinh's main marketplace, Cho Vinh, is noteworthy for the limited selection of goods offered for sale. There are food stalls around the back. Vinh Central Market is at the end of Cao Thang St, which is the southern continuation of Quang Trung St.

Veterans' Vietnam Restoration Project Clinic
A building for surgery and physical therapy was built on the grounds of Nghe Tinh Children's Hospital in the fall of 1989 by a team from the Veterans' Vietnam Restoration Project (based in Garberville, California) working alongside Vietnamese war veterans. The same group also constructed a medical clinic in Vung Tau. Nghe Tinh Children's Hospital (Benh Vien Nhi Nghe Tinh) is out Nguyen Phong Sac St (the continuation of Truong Thi St) and down a side street on the right (towards the south-east).

Birthplace of Ho Chi Minh
Kim Lien Village, where Ho Chi Minh was born in 1890, is 14 km north-west of Vinh. The house in which he was born is maintained as a sacred shrine and can be visited. Nearby is a museum.

Beaches
Vinh is 15 km from the sea. Cua Lo Beach is 20 km from the city.

Places to Stay
There are plenty of hotels in Vinh, but only 11 are authorised to accept foreigners. Fortunately, the whole price range from budget to luxurious is covered.

The *Ben Thuy Hotel* (☎ 55163; 15 rooms) is on the south side of Vinh on Nguyen Du St (National Highway 1), 1.3 km towards the centre of Vinh from the bridge over the Lam River and 1.8 km towards the bridge from the intersection of Nguyen Du and Truong Thi Sts. It's too far to walk from the railway station, but this is a very popular place with budget travellers. All rooms for foreigners cost US$14. The hotel has a small restaurant.

Also on the south side of town is the *Khach San Phuong Hoang* (☎ 42254; 26 rooms) on Nguyen Du St (National Highway 1). It's not the Hilton, but it's one of the cheapest in town at US$5 to US$9 for a room with attached bath. Only cold water is available. The management seems to be very friendly.

Another budget hotel is the *Khach San Tra Bong* (☎ 42226; 27 rooms) at the corner of Tran Phu and Le Mao Sts. All rooms have attached bath (but cold water) and cost US$5 to US$7.

Khach San Quang Trung (☎ 42265; 72

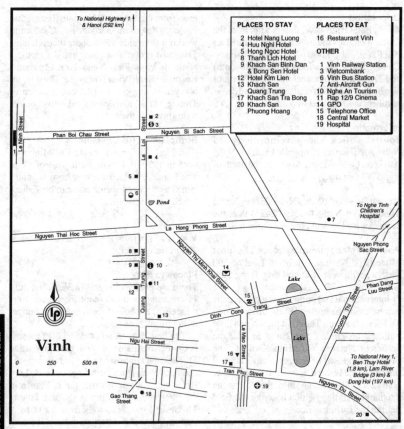

PLACES TO STAY
2 Hotel Nang Luong
4 Huu Nghi Hotel
5 Hong Ngoc Hotel
8 Thanh Lich Hotel
9 Khach San Binh Dan & Bong Sen Hotel
12 Hotel Kim Lien
13 Khach San Quang Trung
17 Khach San Tra Bong
20 Khach San Phuong Hoang

PLACES TO EAT
16 Restaurant Vinh

OTHER
1 Vinh Railway Station
3 Vietcombank
6 Vinh Bus Station
7 Anti-Aircraft Gun
10 Nghe An Tourism
11 Rap 12/9 Cinema
14 GPO
15 Telephone Office
18 Central Market
19 Hospital

Vinh

rooms) is an old apartment block converted into a hotel. It's enormous, though not especially nice. All rooms have shared bath and cost US$5.

The cheapest of the cheap is *Khach San Binh Dan* (☎ 42166; 20 rooms). When you see the rooms, you won't know whether to laugh or cry, but what do you expect for US$4?

The *Bong Sen Hotel* is a reasonable place on Quang Trung St, but it's rather disorganised. The staff didn't seem to know the hotel's phone number or address, but they did know that they have 20 rooms for rent costing between US$7 and US$12.

A truly fine place to stay is the all new *Thanh Lich Hotel* (☎ 44961; 18 rooms) at 28 Quang Trung St. Rooms are US$6 to US$25, which is certainly reasonable for what you're getting.

If you don't mind paying for a little more luxury, check out the *Hong Ngoc Hotel* (☎ 42165; fax 42129; 18 rooms). It's on Le Loi St, just north of Nguyen Thai Hoc St. It's one of those places where staff in crisp uniforms open the door to the air-conditioned lobby and say 'Good evening, please come in'. Comfortable rooms here will cost you US$25 to US$40.

The *Hotel Kim Lien* (☎ 44751; fax 43699; 76 rooms) is the largest hotel in Vinh and has everything: air-conditioning, hot water, money changer, travel agent, restaurant, massage services, the whole lot. All this luxury will cost you US$20 to US$40 for a double. The hotel is at 12 Quang Trung St in the centre of town.

The *Hotel Nang Luong* (☎ 44788; 42 rooms) is an old but friendly place at 2 Nguyen Trai St. This is the closest hotel to the railway station. Rooms all have private bath and cost US$15 to US$40.

The *Huu Nghi Hotel* (☎ 42520; fax 42813; 74 rooms) is the second-largest in town. It's a big, glittering place with air-conditioning, hot water and in-house restaurant. Rooms cost US$20 to US$50. The hotel is on Le Loi St.

Places to Eat
There are a number of small restaurants on Le Ninh St just outside the gate to the railway station. The food stalls in Vinh Central Market are behind the main building.

Restaurant Vinh (Nha Hang Vinh) has fine Vietnamese food at good prices. The worst problem is the lack of an English menu, but a little sign language and patience should do the trick.

Getting There & Away
Bus Vinh Bus Station (Ben Xe Vinh) is on Le Loi St about one km north of the Central Market; the ticket office is open from 4.30 am to 5 pm daily. Express buses to Buon Ma Thuot, Danang, Hanoi and Ho Chi Minh City depart every day at 5 am; express buses to Hanoi leave at other times of the day as well. Nonexpress buses link Vinh with:

Bahai, Huong Son (Pho Chau), Cam Xuyen, Ky Anh, Cau Giat, Lat, Con Cuong, Muong Xen, Cua, Nghia Dan, Do Luong, Phuc Son, Dung, Pleiku (Playcu), Gia Lam, Que Phong, Hanoi, Quy Chau, Ha Tinh, Quy Hop, Hoa Binh, Trung Tam, Hué, Yen Thanh.

Train Vinh Railway Station (Ga Vinh; ☎ 4924) is one km west of the intersection of Le Loi and Phan Boi Chau Sts, which is 1.5 km north of the Central Market. The Reunification Express Train stops here. For ticket prices, see the Train section in the Getting Around chapter.

Car Road distances from Vinh are as follows:

Danang	468 km
Dong Hoi	197 km
Hanoi	292 km
Hué	363 km
Lao border	97 km
Thanh Hoa	139 km

National Highway 8, which begins in Vinh, crosses into Laos at 734-metre-high Keo Nua Pass.

Getting Around
There are relatively few passenger cyclos in Vinh because the people can't afford to ride them. To get around, you might try hiring an oversize cargo cyclo.

THANH HOA
Thanh Hoa is the capital of Thanh Hoa Province; in this region, National Highway 1 is lined with bomb craters, particularly near bridges and railway stations. There is a large and attractive church on the northern outskirts of town.

Thanh Hoa Province was the site of the Lam Son Uprising (1418-28), in which Vietnamese forces led by Le Loi (later Emperor Ly Thai To) expelled the Chinese and re-established the country's independence.

Muong and Red Tai hill tribes live in the western part of the province.

Information
Thanh Hoa Tourism & Relations (Cong Ty Du Lich Va Giao Te Thanh Hoa; ☎ 52298, 52517) is the official government tourist authority for Thanh Hoa Province. The office is at 298 Quang Trung St.

Places to Stay
The *Thanh Hoa Hotel* (☎ 52517; fax 52104; 50 rooms) has the market sewn up. It's on the

west side of National Highway 1 in the centre of town. Rooms cost US$10 to US$50.

Places to Eat

Soup shops, tea shops and a few restaurants can be found along National Highway 1, especially near the southern entrance to town.

Getting There & Away

Bus & Car Thanh Hoa city is 502 km from Hué, 139 km from Vinh and 153 km from Hanoi.

Train Thanh Hoa is a stop for the Reunification Express Train. For ticket prices, see the Train section in the Getting Around chapter.

SAM SON BEACHES

The two beaches at Sam Son, among the nicest in the north, are 16 km south-east of Thanh Hoa; they are a favourite vacation spot of Hanoi residents who can afford such luxuries. Near the bridge, which the US forces repeatedly bombed, are fortifications and trenchworks. Accommodation ranges from basic bungalows to multi-storey hotels.

PHO LEN

This small community 22 km north of Thanh Hoa is home of Lotaba Tobacco Company. A tour of the cigarette factory might be possible to arrange, but don't count on it. Pho Len has one of the better cheap hotels in this part of Vietnam, and for most travellers that is the town's only real attraction.

Places to Stay

The *Lotaba Guest House* (☎ 52894; 28 rooms) is on the east side of National Highway 1. As you might have guessed, the hotel belongs to the tobacco company of the same name. Rooms with fan cost US$9, while air-con sets you back US$11. The hotel gift shop sells Lotaba cigarettes at a discount.

NINH BINH

Ninh Binh has evolved into a major travel centre in just the past couple of years. Its sudden transformation from sleepy backwa-

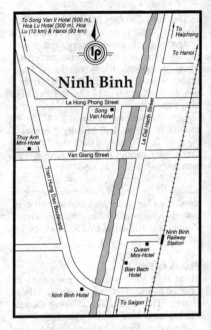

ter to tourist resort has little to do with Ninh Binh itself, but rather with its proximity to Hoa Lu (12 km from Ninh Binh). See the next section in this chapter for more information on Hoa Lu.

Although it is possible to visit Hoa Lu as a day trip from Hanoi, many travellers prefer to spend the night in Ninh Binh and thus see the sights at a more leisurely pace. Furthermore, relatively good transport facilities in Ninh Binh make the Hoa Lu area accessible to independent travellers, rather than just to tour groups.

Places to Stay

Kudos go to the *Queen Mini-Hotel* (Khach San Nu Hoang; ☎ 71874; four rooms) for being in the right place with the right price. The hotel is just 30 metres from Ninh Binh Railway Station, and rooms cost US$10 to US$15. The management even speaks English and can arrange tours to Hoa Lu. This place also rents motorbikes and bicycles if you prefer a do-it-yourself tour. The only drawback to this place is that four rooms aren't enough to satisfy demand, though the owner hopes to expand.

The *Thuy Anh Mini-Hotel* (☎ 71602; three rooms) belongs to the same family that operates the Queen Mini-Hotel. Like its big sister, this hotel does some side business renting vans, motorbikes and bicycles to Hoa Lu-bound travellers. Rooms here cost US$8 to US$20.

Right in the centre of town is the *Ninh Binh Hotel* (☎ 71337; fax 71200; 20 rooms) at 2 Tran Hung Dao St. Room rates are US$20 to US$25.

Closer to the railway station is the *Bien Bach Hotel* (☎ 71449; five rooms) at 195 Le Dai Hanh St. The price-spread here is US$15 to US$25.

The *Song Van Hotel* (☎ 71974; fax 71201; 21 rooms) is close to the river on Le Hong Phong St. Rooms come in only one standard costing US$21.

The *Song Van Hotel II* (☎ 71860; fax 71200; eight rooms) is a small place belonging to the same management. It's a bit far from things, being 500 metres north of the centre at 86 Van Giang St. The tariff here is US$10 to US$25.

The *Hoa Lu Hotel* (☎ 71217; fax 71200; 100 rooms) is by far the largest place in Ninh Binh. It's 300 metres north of town, and has singles from US$15 to US$30 and doubles costing US$20 to US$35.

Getting There & Away
Train Ninh Binh is a scheduled stop for the Reunification Express trains travelling between Hanoi and Ho Chi Minh City. For ticket prices, see the Train section in the Getting Around chapter.

Car Ninh Binh is 200 km north of Vinh, 61 km north of Thanh Hoa and 93 km south of Hanoi.

HOA LU
Known to travellers as Vietnam's 'Halong Bay without the water', Hoa Lu boasts breathtaking scenery. While Halong Bay (see the chapter in this book entitled The North) has huge rock formations jutting out of the sea, Hoa Lu has them jutting out of the rice paddies. There is a striking resemblance here to Guilin and Yangshuo, both major drawing cards in China.

Hoa Lu was the capital of Vietnam under the Dinh Dynasty (968-980) and the Early Le Dynasty (980-1009). The site was an attractive place for a capital city because of both its distance from China and the natural protection afforded by the region's bizarre landscape.

The ancient citadel of Hoa Lu, most of which has been destroyed, covered an area of about three sq km. The outer ramparts encompassed temples, shrines and the place where the king held court. The royal family lived in the inner citadel.

Today, there are two sanctuaries at Hoa Lu. Dinh Tien Hoang, restored in the 17th century, is dedicated to the Dinh Dynasty. Out the front is the stone pedestal of a royal throne; inside are bronze bells and a statue of Emperor Dinh Tien Hoang with his three sons. The second temple, Dai Hanh (or Dung Van Nga), commemorates the rulers of the Early Le Dynasty. Inside the main hall are all sorts of drums, gongs, incense burners, candle holders and weapons; to the left of the entrance is a sanctuary dedicated to Confucius.

Bich Dong Cave is in the village of Van Lam, a short boat trip away. The three sanctuaries here date from the 17th century. Another frequently visited cave is Tam Coc.

When you reach Ninh Binh, turn west for 12 km. On the right there's a hut with a bar. Pay a toll, go ahead and then you can take a tiny rowing boat (US$1) with an oarswoman. It's a beautiful landscape; high rocks, green with vegetation, rice paddies. The boat sails along a narrow canal among the fields. The silence is pure. Three times we passed grottoes. The trip may take two or more hours.

Mauro Grusovin

Places to Stay
There are currently no places to stay in Hoa Lu itself, but nearby Ninh Binh serves as the local bedroom community for travellers. Of

NORTH-CENTRAL VIETNAM

course, things might change and Hoa Lu could suddenly sprout a bunch of five-star hotels and fast-food restaurants built right into the rock formations – let's hope that it doesn't happen soon (or ever).

Getting There & Away
Train No train stops in Hoa Lu, but the Reunification Express Train stops in nearby Ninh Binh. From there, you'll need to find a car or motorbike, or have a very long walk.

Car Hoa Lu is at the southern edge of the Red River Delta in Truong Yen Village, which is in Ninh Binh Province. By car, the trip from Hanoi to Hoa Lu is 120 km due south and takes about two hours.

PHAT DIEM
Phat Diem (Kim Son) is the site of a cathedral remarkable for its vast dimensions and unique Sino-Vietnamese architecture. The vaulted ceiling is supported by massive limewood columns almost one metre in diameter and 10 metres tall. In the lateral naves, there are a number of curious wood and stone sculptures. The main altar is made of a single block of granite.

During the French era, the cathedral was an important centre of Catholicism in the north and there was a seminary here. The 1954 division of Vietnam caused Catholics to flee to the south en masse and the cathedral was closed. It is now functional again and there are also several dozen other churches in the Phat Diem district. Current estimates are that about 120,000 Catholics live in the area.

The cathedral complex comprises a number of buildings, but the main one was completed in 1891. The whole project was founded by a Vietnamese priest named Six, whose tomb is in the square fronting the cathedral. Behind the main building is a large pile of limestone boulders – Father Six piled them up for a sink test to see if the boggy ground would support his planned empire. Apparently the test was a success.

Opposite the main entrance at the back of the cathedral is the bell tower. At its base lie

two enormous stone slabs, one atop the other. Like all the other big carved stones here, these were transported from some 200 km away with only primitive gear. What's interesting about these massive stone slabs is that their sole purpose was to provide a perch for the mandarins to sit and observe (no doubt with great amusement) the rituals of the Catholics at mass. Thus did the tradition of Vietnamese 'staring squads' become firmly entrenched!

Atop the cathedral's highest tower is such an enormous bell that Quasimodo's famous chimer at Notre Dame pales in comparison. This bell and all the other heavy metal were pushed and pulled to the cathedral's top via an enormous earth ramp. After construction was completed, the dirt was spread around the church grounds to make the whole site about one metre higher than the surrounding terrain. This has, no doubt, offered important protection against the occasional flood.

Near to the main cathedral is a small chapel built of large carved stone blocks, and inside it's as cool as a cave. Also not far from the cathedral is a covered bridge dating from the late 19th century.

Getting There & Away
Phat Diem is 121 km south of Hanoi and 29 km south-east of Ninh Binh. Making the trip by motorbike from Ninh Binh is eminently feasible.

CUC PHUONG NATIONAL PARK
Cuc Phuong National Park, established in 1962, is one of Vietnam's most important nature preserves. Though wildlife has suffered a precipitous decline in Vietnam in recent decades, the park's 222 sq km of primary tropical forest remain home to an amazing variety of wildlife, including 1967 species of flora from 217 families and 749 genera; 1800 species of insects from 30 orders and 200 families; 137 species of birds; 64 species of animals; and 33 species of reptiles. Among the extraordinary variety of life forms in the park are several species discovered here, including a tree known as *Bressiaopsis Cucphuongensis* and the

endemic red-bellied squirrel *Callosciurus erythrinaceus Cucphuongensis*. The Rhesus macaque *(Macaca mullata)* can sometimes be seen in the forests. Sadly, once-common spotted deer *(Cevus nippon)* now survive only in the park's captive breeding programme.

In Con Moong Cave, one of the park's many grottoes, the stone tools of prehistoric humans have been discovered.

Cuc Phuong National Park, which is 70 km from the sea, covers an area about 25 km long and 11 km wide in the provinces of Ninh Binh, Hoa Binh and Thanh Hoa. The elevation of the highest peak in the park is 648 metres. At the park's lower elevations, the climate is subtropical.

Ho Chi Minh personally took time off from the war in 1963 to dedicate this national park, Vietnam's first. He offered a short dedication speech:

Forest is gold. If we know how to conserve it well, it will be very precious. Destruction of the forest will lead to serious effects on both life and productivity.

A guide is not mandatory, but it would be foolish and risky to attempt a trek alone through the dense jungle. There are three-day treks to Hmong villages which can be arranged through travel agencies such as Toserco in Hanoi. The rangers are very environment-conscious and enthusiastic to protect wildlife from poaching and trees from illegal logging. A few hundred metres from the park's headquarters is a breeding and research centre for spotted deer. There are now attempts being made to reintroduce them into areas from which they were previously annihilated. There is also an experiment to determine if the deer can be bred for commercial meat production.

Poaching and habitat destruction is a constant headache for the rangers. Many native species, such as the black bear, wild cats, and various birds and reptiles, have perished in the park due to human impact. In 1993, a ranger was murdered by the Hmong because he tried to stop them from logging in the park. The government responded by moving the village to another area farther from the park's boundary. However, the high birth rate among the minorities in this area assures that future conflicts are inevitable.

Places to Stay

Park headquarters charges US$10 for a few basic rooms in a Muong-style house (shared toilet and cold showers) and up to US$35 for upmarket (but sterile) rooms in their rest house.

Getting There & Away

Cuc Phuong National Park is 140 km from Hanoi (via Ninh Binh); sections of the road are in poor condition. There is no public transport, but with a car or motorbike it is possible to visit the forest as a day trip from Hanoi.

NORTH-CENTRAL VIETNAM

Hanoi

A city of lakes, shaded boulevards and verdant public parks where beggars fight over a plate of discarded noodles and prosperous shop owners exemplify Vietnam's new economic reforms – the seat of power, where absolute power corrupts absolutely.

Hanoi (population one million), capital of the Socialist Republic of Vietnam, is different things to different people. Most foreigners on a short visit find Hanoi to be slow paced, pleasant and even charming. Physically, it's a more attractive city than Ho Chi Minh City – there is less traffic, less noise, less pollution, more trees and more open space. Some have called it the Paris of the Orient – Parisians may find that either an insult or a compliment. Hanoi's centre is an architectural museum piece, its blocks of ochre buildings retaining the air of a provincial French town of the 1930s. The people of Hanoi are known for being more reserved – and at the same time more traditionally hospitable – than their southern compatriots.

Hanoi used to be notorious among travellers as a place to avoid. Many Western visitors (both backpackers and business people) were routinely harassed by the police, especially at the airport, where officials would arbitrarily detain and fine foreigners as they were trying to leave. The first author of this book, Daniel Robinson, was arrested in Hanoi and deported.

The bad reputation that Hanoi earned by harassing foreigners and resisting economic reform caused most foreign investment to flow into Ho Chi Minh City and other places in the south. Resistance to reform is strongest among ageing officials, but geriatric revolutionaries in the prime of senility are being forcibly retired. The younger generation – with no romantic attachment to the past – is only interested in the side of the bread which is buttered. Attitudes have changed remarkably fast, and the Hanoi of today is dramatically different from what it was just five years ago. The foreigners have returned as tourists, business travellers, students and expatriates. Foreign investors are now looking at Hanoi with the same enthusiasm that only a few years ago was reserved exclusively for Saigon.

The first beneficiaries of the city's recent economic resurgence have been the shop and restaurant owners. No longer is a shopping trip in Hanoi a journey to a large state department store specialising in empty shelves. The colour and liveliness has returned to the streets (and unfortunately, so has the traffic). Buildings are being repaired and foreign companies are now investing in everything from joint-venture hotels to banks and telecommunications. Hanoi, and the rest of the north, has great potential to develop export-oriented manufacturing industries – a potential now only beginning to be realised.

History

The site where Hanoi now stands has been inhabited since the Neolithic period. Emperor Ly Thai To moved his capital here in 1010 AD, renaming the site Thang Long (City of the Soaring Dragon). Hanoi served as the capital of the Later Le Dynasty, founded by Le Loi, from its establishment in 1428 until 1788, when it was overthrown by Nguyen Hué, founder of the Tay Son Dynasty. The decision by Emperor Gia Long, founder of the Nguyen Dynasty, to rule from Hué relegated Hanoi to the status of a regional capital.

Over the centuries, Hanoi has borne a variety of names, including Dong Kinh (Eastern Capital), from which the Europeans derived the name they eventually applied to all of northern Vietnam, Tonkin. The city was named Hanoi (The City in a Bend of the River) by Emperor Tu Duc in 1831. From 1902 to 1953, Hanoi served as the capital of French Indochina.

Hanoi was proclaimed the capital of Vietnam after the August Revolution of 1945, but it was not until the Geneva Accords of 1954 that the Viet Minh, driven from the city by the French in 1946, were able to return. During the Vietnam War, US bombing destroyed parts of Hanoi and killed many hundreds of civilians; almost all the damage has since been repaired.

Whatever else Ho Chi Minh may have done, he created in Hanoi and much of the north a very effective police state. For four decades, the people of Hanoi and the north have suffered under a regime characterised by the ruthless exercise of police power, anonymous denunciations by a huge network of secret informers, the detention without trial of monks, priests, landowners and anyone else seen as a potential threat to the government, and the blacklisting of dissidents and their children and their children's children. The combined legacy of human-rights violations and economic turmoil produced a steady haemorrhage of refugees, even into China despite that country's less than impressive human-rights record. Ironically, the political and economic situation has turned around so sharply in the 1990s that Vietnamese officials now worry about an invasion of refugees from China.

Orientation

Hanoi sprawls along the banks of the Red River (Song Hong), which is spanned by two bridges, the old Long Bien Bridge (now used only by non-motorised vehicles and pedestrians) and the new Chuong Duong Bridge.

The central city of Hanoi consists of four urban districts (quan): Hoan Kiem District (the centre), Ba Dinh District (the western area, which includes Ho Chi Minh's Mausoleum), Hai Ba Trung District (along the river south of Hoan Kiem District) and Dong Da District (south-west area). The southern part of the city along Giai Phong St (Hai Ba Trung District) is the tackiest part of the city, while the area around Hoan Kiem Lake (Hoan Kiem District) and West Lake (Ba Dinh District) are the most attractive.

To the north of Hoan Kiem Lake (also called the Lake of the Restored Sword and the Small Lake) is the Old Quarter (known to the French as the Cité Indigène), deline-

ated by the Citadel to the west, the old Dong Xuan Market (or what's left of it) to the north and the ramparts of the Red River to the east. The Old Quarter is characterised by narrow streets whose names change every two blocks. South and south-west of the lake is the modern city centre, known as the Ville Française to the French. The colonial-era buildings in this area house many of Hanoi's hotels, state stores and non-Socialist embassies.

Ho Chi Minh's Mausoleum is to the west of the Citadel, which is still used as a military base. In front of the mausoleum is Ba Dinh Square. Most of the city's socialist embassies are nearby in beautiful old mansions (Western latecomers had to settle for far less attractive embassy quarters elsewhere). West Lake (Ho Tay), another of Hanoi's famous lakes, is north of Ho Chi Minh's Mausoleum.

Information

Travel Agencies There are plenty of travel agencies in Hanoi, both government and private, which can provide cars, book air tickets and extend your visa. Some of these places charge the same as Vietnam Tourism, while others are only half the price. The government-run Tourism Service Company (Toserco) seems to have become a joint venture and its service has improved considerably, but you should be able to get a cheaper deal at most of the cafes – the Green Bamboo Café stands out for being the best organised. Ann's Tourist is affiliated with the Saigon company of the same name and is known for good service. Compare prices and expected standards of service before you put down the cash. The line-up of travel agencies includes:

Ann's Tourist
    26 Yet Kieu St, Hoan Kiem District (☎ 252497)
Especen
    79E Hang Trong St (☎ 258845, 266856; fax 269612)
Friendly Hanoi Tourism
    4B Duong Thanh St (☎ 267421; fax 247517)
Green Bamboo Café
    42 Nha Chung St (☎ 264949)

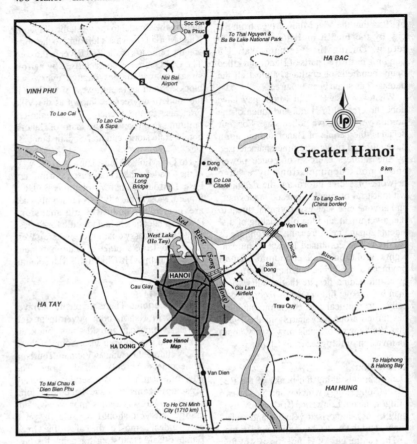

Greater Hanoi

Manfields Toserco
    102 Hang Trong St (☎ 269444; fax 269485)
OSC
    38 Yet Kieu St (☎ 264500; fax 259260)
Tourist Meeting Café
    59B Ba Trieu St (☎ 258813)
Tourist Smiling Café
    100 Cau Go St (☎ 244554)
Vietlink Trading Travel & Tour
    14A Ly Nam De St (☎ 232963; fax 237980)
Vietnam Tourism
    (Tong Cong Ty Du Lich Viet Nam) 30A Ly
    Thuong Kiet St (☎ 256916; fax 257583)
Vinatour
    54 Nguyen Du St (☎ 239190)
Vinexad
    14 Ngo Quyen St (☎ 256662; fax 255556)

Money Vietcombank is at 78 Nguyen Du St
(☎ 268035). Cash advances for Visa,
Mastercard and JCB cards are possible to
arrange for a 4% commission.

ANZ Bank (☎ 258190; fax 258188), 14
Le Thai To St, is on the western shore of
Hoan Kiem Lake. Even if you don't change
money here, take a peek inside to admire
their beautiful hand-crafted furnishings. It's
possibly the most beautiful bank in Vietnam.

Credit Lyonnais (☎ 258102; fax 260080)
at 10 Trang Thi St changes money, but
imposes a US$5 service charge unless you
change over US$200.

Other foreign or joint-venture banks with fully functioning branches (as opposed to useless representative offices) are as follows:

Banque National de Paris
    8 Tran Hung Dao St (☎ 253175; fax 266982)
Ching Fon Commercial Bank
    55 Quang Trung St (☎ 250555; fax 250566)
Indovina Bank
    88 Hai Ba Trung St (☎ 265516; fax 266320)
Societe Generale
    40 Tang Bat Ho St (☎ 259822; fax 259823)
Standard Chartered
    27 Ly Thai To St (☎ 258970; fax 258880)
VID Public Bank
    194 Tran Quang Khai St (☎ 266953; fax 266965)

Post & Telecommunications The GPO (Buu Dien Trung Vong; ☎ 257036, fax 253525), which occupies a full city block facing Hoan Kiem Lake, is at 75 Dinh Tien Hoang St (between Dinh Le and Le Thach Sts). The entrance in the middle of the block leads to the postal services windows, where you can send letters, pick up domestic packages and purchase philatelic items; the postal services section is open from 6.30 am to 8 pm.

The same entrance leads to the telex, telegram and domestic telephone office (☎ 255918), which is to the left as you enter the building. Telex and domestic telephone services are available from 6.30 am to 8 pm; telegrams can be sent 24 hours a day.

International telephone calls can be made and faxes sent from the office (☎ 252030) at the corner of Dinh Tien Hoang and Dinh Le Sts, which is open daily from 7.30 am to 9.30 pm.

Private document and parcel carriers in Hanoi include DHL (☎ 267020, 267021), which can be found at 49 Nguyen Thai Hoc St, Ba Dinh District. For rates, see the Post & Telecommunications section in the Facts for the Visitor chapter.

In Hanoi, the following special phone numbers are in use (don't count on the person who answers the phone speaking anything but Vietnamese):

Ambulance	15
Fire Brigade	14
Long-Distance Operator (Domestic)	10
Long-Distance Operator (International)	11
Police	13
Telephone Directory	16
Telephone Repairs	19
Time	17

Foreign Embassies The following list contains the addresses of foreign embassies in Hanoi:

Algeria
    12 Phan Chu Trinh St (☎ 253865)
Australia
    66 Ly Thuong Kiet St (☎ 252763, 252703)
Belgium
    10 Van Phuc St (☎ 252263, 232841)
Brazil
    15 Ngo Quyen St, Room 212 (☎ 266919)
Cambodia
    71 Tran Hung Dao St (☎ 253788, 253789)
Canada
    39 Nguyen Dinh Chieu St (☎ 265840)
China
    46 Hoang Dieu St (☎ 253736)
Cuba
    65 Ly Thuong Kiet St (☎ 252426)
Czech
    13 Chu Van An St (☎ 254131)
Denmark
    3 Van Phuc St, No 4 (☎ 231888)
Finland
    B3b Giang Vo St, F1, 2 (☎ 256754, 257096)
France
    57 Tran Hung Dao St (☎ 252719)
Germany
    29 Tran Phu St (☎ 253836)
Hungary
    47 Dien Bien Phu St (☎ 252748)
India
    58-60 Tran Hung Dao St (☎ 253406, 255975)
Indonesia
    50 Ngo Quyen St (☎ 257969)
Israel
    15 Ngo Quyen St, Room 111 ☎ 266919)
Italy
    9 Le Phung Hieu St (☎ 256246)
Japan
    Khu Trung Tu Diplomatic Quarter, E3 (☎ 257924)
Korea (South)
    29 Nguyen Dinh Chieu St (☎ 226677)
Laos
    40 Quang Trung St (☎ 268724)
Malaysia
    82 Van Phuc St (☎ 253371)
Myanmar (Burma)
    Khu Van Phuc, A3 (☎ 253369)

Hanoi

0   250   500 m

HANOI

To Dragon Hotel,
Tay Ho Hotel &
Ho Tay Villas

Nghi Tam Street

West Lake
(Ho Tay)

Thanh Nien
Street

Truc Bach
Lake

1

2
3
4
5
6

Yen Phu Street

9

Red River (Song Hong)

Long Bien
Bridge

To Gia Lam Bus
Station (2 km)

To Noi Bai Airport (30 km),
Haiphong (103 km) &
Halong Bay (165 km)

Chuong
Duong
Bridge

See Central Hanoi Map

Bach Dang Street

Hoan
Kiem
Lake

Quan Thanh Street

Phan Dinh Phung Street

Hoang Dieu Street

13

Le Duan Street

14

Dien Bien Phu Street

Hung Vuong Street

Nguyen Thai Hoc Street

Cat Linh Street

Ton Duc Thang Street

Kham Thien Street

Botanical
Gardens

Thuy – Khue Street

Hoang Hoa Tham Street

Doi Can Street

Kim Ma Street

Giang Vo Street

La Thanh Street

BA DINH
DISTRICT

Ngoc Khanh Street

See Around
Ho Chi Minh's
Mausoleum Map

Giang Vo Street

12

Lang Trung Street

To Lich River

Buoi Street

10

11

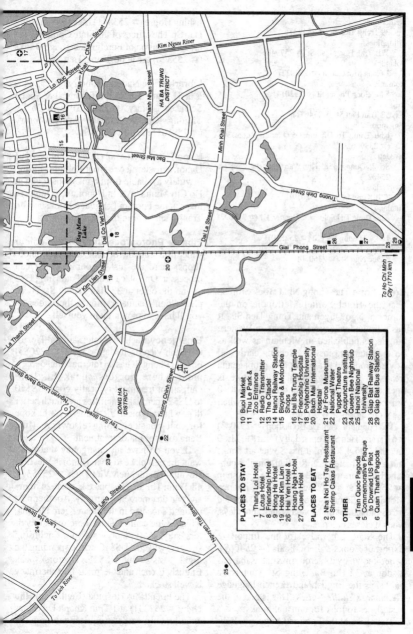

PLACES TO STAY

1 Thang Loi Hotel
7 Lotus Hotel
8 Friendship Hotel
9 Hong Ha Hotel
19 Hotel Kim Lien
26 Hai Yen Hotel &
   Hoang Nga Hotel
27 Queen Hotel

PLACES TO EAT

2 Nha Noi Ho Tay Restaurant
3 Shrimp Cakes Restaurant

OTHER

4 Tran Quoc Pagoda
5 Commemorative
   to Downed US Pilot
6 Quan Thanh Pagoda

10 Buoi Market
11 Thu Le Park &
   Zoo Entrance
12 Radio Transmitter
13 The Citadel
14 Hanoi Railway Station
15 Bicycle & Motorbike
   Shops
16 Hai Ba Trung Temple
17 Friendship Hospital
18 Polytechnic University
20 Bach Mai International
   Hospital
21 Air Force Museum
22 National Water
   Puppet Theatre
23 Acupuncture Institute
24 Queen Bee Nightclub
25 Hanoi National
   University
28 Giap Bat Railway Station
29 Giap Bat Bus Station

HANOI

Netherlands
  29 Trang Tien St (☎ 254937)
Philippines
  27B Tran Hung Dao St (☎ 257948)
Poland
  3 Chua Mot Cot St (☎ 252027)
Romania
  5 Le Hong Phong St (☎ 252014)
Russia
  58 Tran Phu St (☎ 254631)
Singapore
  Khu Trung Tu Diplomatic Quarter, Room 301
  (☎ 233966)
Sweden
  So 2, Duong 358, Khu Van Phuc (☎ 254824,
  254825)
Switzerland
  77B Kim Ma St (☎ 232019)
Thailand
  Khu Trung Tu Diplomatic Quarter, E1 (☎ 235092)
UK
  16 Ly Thuong Kiet St (☎ 252510)
USA (liaison)
  8 Doc Ngu St (☎ 236050)

Bookshops The Thong Nhat Book Store is near the Hotel Sofitel Metropole on the corner of Ngo Quyen and Trang Tien Sts. It has a limited selection of books in Western languages published in Vietnam as well as postage stamps, posters, greeting cards and Soviet-produced art books and propaganda treatises. The Thong Nhat Book Store is open daily from 8 am to noon and 1 to 8.30 pm except on Monday and Thursday, when the store closes at 4.30 pm.

The Foreign Language Bookshop (☎ 257043) at 61 Trang Tien St is open daily from 8 to 11.30 am and 2 to 4.30 pm; it has Soviet art books and a lot of material in Russian. Similar published items are available at the State Bookshop (☎ 254282) at 40 Trang Tien St. It is open Monday to Saturday from 8 to 11.30 am and 2 to 8 pm except on Mondays and Thursdays, when it closes at 5 pm.

The State Enterprise for the Import & Export of Books & Periodicals (☎ 254067), better known by its acronym Xunhasaba, has a shop at 32 Hai Ba Trung St. Xunhasaba publishes the English and French-language *Vietnamese Studies* series. This is one of the best places to look for unusual books.

The office of the Foreign Languages Publishing House (☎ 253841) is at 46 Tran Hung Dao St. The offices of the State Company for the Distribution of Foreign Language Books (☎ 255376) are at 66 Trang Tien St.

Libraries The National Library (☎ 252643) is at 31 Trang Thi St; the Technical & Social Sciences Library (☎ 252345) is at 26 Ly Thuong Kiet St; and the Army Library (☎ 258101) is on Ly Nam St.

Maps The Tourist Map *(Ban Do Du Lich)* of Hanoi, a masterpiece of four-colour printing, is widely available from bookshops (even in Ho Chi Minh City). In Hanoi itself, look for maps at the Foreign Language Bookshop on Trang Tien St or in the adjacent alleys.

Film & Photoprocessing While colour slide film can be bought in many photo shops, there are just a couple which can process it. One place is at 18 Tran Hung Dao St and the other at 33 Hang Khay St. These places don't actually mount the slides so you'll have to mount them yourself.

Emergency Bach Mai International Hospital (Benh Vien Bach Mai; ☎ 522004, 522083) on Giai Phong St has an international department where doctors speak English. Outpatient treatment typically costs US$10 to US$20 per visit. Facilities are much better than what a typical Vietnamese could hope for, but consider going elsewhere (like Bangkok) for major treatment.

If you do have an emergency that can't wait, the best place to go in Hanoi is Viet Duc Hospital (Benh Vien Viet Duc; ☎ 253531), 48 Tranh Thi St. This place is open 24 hours and can do emergency surgery. Another plus is that it's located in the Hoan Kiem District, which is the central area where most travellers stay. A typical visit (not including surgery) will cost US$10, while spending the night costs about US$25. Doctors speak English, French and German. The pharmacy is well stocked.

The Friendship Hospital (Benh Vien Huu Nghi; ☎ 252231) at 1 Tran Khanh Du St has excellent up-to-date equipment and the doctors speak English. This place does mostly diagnostic work – surgery and extensive treatment should be done elsewhere.

The Swedish Clinic (☎ 252464) on Van Phuc St is opposite the Swedish Embassy. You don't have to be Swedish to come here, but the consultation fee of US$80 will put off many travellers. However, if you have travel insurance, you might be covered. The doctor is on call 24 hours.

The French Embassy (☎ 252719), 49 Ba Trieu St, operates a 24-hour clinic for French nationals only.

Resident foreigners can contact Asia Emergency Assistance in Ho Chi Minh City (☎ 298520) or International SOS Assistance in Hanoi (☎ 226228) for information about their health plans.

Visas The Immigration Police Office is at 87 Tran Hung Dao St; it is open Monday to Saturday from 8 to 11 am and 1 to 5 pm. This office is more cooperative than the one in Ho Chi Minh City, but the reception you get is pure potluck. This is the place to go for both visa extensions and to get your visa exit point modified so you can cross by train into China. A few years ago this same office was responsible for deporting one of our Lonely Planet writers from the country.

In the majority of cases, the police will refuse to grant your visa extension directly and refer you to a travel agency. In Hanoi, it seems that government-owned agencies, such as Toserco, are more successful at getting visa extensions than the private travel agencies and cafes. In many cases, a request for a 30-day extension (which should be straightforward) is rejected and the traveller is issued only a 15-day extension.

Useful Organisations The head office of Vietcochamber (☎ 252961, 253023; fax 256446) and the Chamber of Commerce & Industry of Vietnam (☎ 266235; fax 256446) is at 33 Ba Trieu St. The Trade Service Company, which is attached to Vietcochamber, also has its offices here. It can arrange business trips, assist business people with bureaucratic formalities (visa extensions,

etc), book hotel accommodation anywhere in the country, arrange land transport of all sorts and provide translation services.

Business travellers might want to talk to the Vietnam Trade Information Centre (☎ 263227, 264038), 46 Ngo Quyen St.

The Ministry of Foreign Affairs is at 1 Ton That Dam St, near Ho Chi Minh's Mausoleum. English-speaking personnel can always be found at the North America Department (☎ 257279, 258201, ext 314 or 312). The Foreign Press Centre of the Ministry of Foreign Affairs (☎ 254697) is at 10 Le Phung Hieu St.

The International Relations Department of the Ministry of Information (☎ 253152) is at 58 Quan Su St.

Aid Organisations There are a number of foreign-aid organisations with offices in Hanoi. These include:

FAO (TC Luong Thuc Va Nong Nghiep)
  3 Nguyen Gia Thieu St (☎ 257208, 257239)
International Red Cross (UB Chu Thap Do Quoc Te)
  Hotel Sofitel Metropole, 15 Ngo Quyen St
  (☎ 254454)
UNDP (Chuong Trinh Cua LHQ Ve Phat Trien)
  27-29 Phan Boi Chau St (☎ 257495, 254254, 257318)
UNFPA (UN Fund for Population Control; Quy LHQ Ve Hoat Dong Dan So)
  Khu Giang Vo – Khoi 3 (☎ 254763)
UNHCR (Cao Uy LHQ Ve Nguoi Ti Nan)
  60 Nguyen Thai Hoc St (☎ 257871, 256785)
UNICEF (Quy Nhi Dong LHQ)
  72 Ly Thuong Kiet St (☎ 253440, 254222, 252109)
UNIDO (UN Industrial Development Organisation)
  UNDP compound, 27-29 Phan Boi Chau St
  (☎ 257495, 257318, 254254)
WFP (World Food Programme; Chuong Trinh Luong Thuc The Gioi)
  UNDP compound, 27-29 Phan Boi Chau St
  (☎ 257495, 257318, 254254)

Lakes, Temples & Pagodas

One Pillar Pagoda Hanoi's famous One Pillar Pagoda (Chua Mot Cot) was built by the Emperor Ly Thai Tong, who ruled from 1028 to 1054. According to the annals, the heirless emperor dreamed that he had met the Quan The Am Bo Tat (Goddess of Mercy),

HANOI

who, while seated on a lotus flower, handed him a male child. Ly Thai Tong then married a young peasant girl he met by chance and had a son and heir by her. To express his gratitude for this event, he constructed the One Pillar Pagoda in 1049.

The One Pillar Pagoda, built of wood on a single stone pillar 1.25 metres in diameter, is designed to resemble a lotus blossom, symbol of purity, rising out of a sea of sorrow. One of the last acts of the French before quitting Hanoi in 1954 was to destroy the One Pillar Pagoda; the structure was rebuilt by the new government. The One Pillar Pagoda is on Ong Ich Kiem St near Ho Chi Minh's Mausoleum.

Dien Huu Pagoda The entrance to Dien Huu Pagoda is a few metres from the staircase of the One Pillar Pagoda. This small pagoda, which surrounds a garden courtyard, is one of the most delightful in Hanoi. The old wood and ceramic statues on the altar are very different from those common in the south. An elderly monk can often be seen performing acupuncture on the front porch of the pagoda.

Temple of Literature The Temple of Literature (Van Mieu) is a pleasant retreat from the streets of Hanoi. It was founded in 1070 – four years after the Norman invasion of England – by Emperor Ly Thanh Tong, who dedicated it to Confucius (in Vietnamese, Khong Tu) in order to honour scholars and men of literary accomplishment.

The temple constitutes a rare example of well-preserved traditional Vietnamese architecture and is well worth a visit.

Vietnam's first university was established here in 1076 to educate the sons of mandarins. In 1484, Emperor Le Thanh Tong ordered that stelae be erected in the temple premises recording the names, places of birth and achievements of men who received doctorates *(Thai Hoc Sinh)* in each triennial examination, beginning in 1442. Though 116 examinations were held between 1442 and 1778, when the practice was discontinued, only 82 stelae are extant. In 1802,

Emperor Gia Long transferred the National University to his new capital, Hué. Major repairs were carried out here in 1920 and 1956.

The Temple of Literature consists of five courtyards divided by walls. The central pathways and gates between courtyards were reserved for the king. The walkways on one side were for the use of administrative mandarins; those on the other side were for military mandarins.

The main entrance is preceded by a gate on which an inscription requests that visitors dismount their horses before entering. Khue Van Pavilion, which is at the far side of the second courtyard, was constructed in 1802 and is considered a fine example of Vietnamese architecture. The 82 stelae, considered the most precious artefacts in the temple, are arrayed to either side of the third enclosure; each stele sits on a stone tortoise.

The Temple of Literature is two km west of Hoan Kiem Lake. The complex, which is 350 by 70 metres, is bounded by Nguyen Thai Hoc, Tong Due Thang, Quoc Tu Giam and Van Mieu Sts. Enter from Quoc Tu Giam St. It is open from 8.30 to 11.30 am and 1.30 to 4.30 pm Tuesday to Sunday; the entrance fee is US$0.50. There is a small gift shop inside the temple.

Hoan Kiem Lake Hoan Kiem Lake is an enchanting body of water right in the heart of Hanoi. Legend has it that in the mid-15th century, Heaven gave Emperor Ly Thai To (Le Loi) a magical sword, which he used to drive the Chinese out of Vietnam. One day after the war, while out boating, he came upon a giant golden tortoise swimming on the surface of the water; the creature grabbed the sword and disappeared into the depths of the lake. Since that time, the lake has been known as Ho Hoan Kiem (Lake of the Restored Sword) because the tortoise restored the sword to its divine owners.

The tiny Tortoise Pagoda, topped with a red star, is on an islet in the middle of the lake; it is often used as an emblem of Hanoi. Every morning around 6 am, local residents can be seen around Hoan Kiem Lake doing their traditional morning exercises, jogging and playing badminton.

Ngoc Son Temple Ngoc Son (Jade Mountain) Temple, founded in the 18th century, is on an island in the northern part of Hoan Kiem Lake. Surrounded by water and shaded by trees, it is a delightfully quiet place to rest. The temple is dedicated to the scholar Van Xuong, General Tran Hung Dao (who defeated the Mongols in the 13th century) and La To, patron saint of physicians.

Ngoc Son Temple is reached via wooden The Huc (Rising Sun) Bridge, painted red, which was constructed in 1885. To the left of the gate stands an obelisk whose top is shaped like a paintbrush. The temple is open daily from 8 am to 5 pm; the entrance fee is US$0.10.

West Lake Two legends explain the origins of West Lake (Ho Tay), which covers an area of five sq km. According to one, West Lake was created when the Dragon King drowned an evil nine-tailed fox in his lair, which was in a forest on this site. Another legend relates that in the 11th century, a Vietnamese Buddhist monk, Khong Lo, rendered a great service to the emperor of China, who rewarded him with a vast quantity of bronze from which he cast a huge bell. The sound of the bell could be heard all the way to China, where the Golden Buffalo Calf, mistaking the ringing for its mother's call, ran southward, trampling on the site of Ho Tay and turning it into a lake.

West Lake, also known as the Lake of Mist and the Big Lake, was once ringed with magnificent palaces and pavilions. These were destroyed in the course of various feudal wars. The circumference of West Lake is about 13 km.

Tran Quoc Pagoda is on the shore of West Lake just off Thanh Nien St, which divides West Lake from Truc Bach Lake. A stele here dating from 1639 tells the history of this site. The pagoda was rebuilt in the 15th century and again in 1842. There are a number of monks' funerary monuments in the garden.

There are already a number of luxurious villas around West Lake, and you can expect more soon. Foreign investors see this as a likely spot for hotel development and are falling over each other to sign joint-venture agreements so the facilities can be completed before the expected flood of tourists arrives.

Truc Bach Lake Truc Bach (White Silk) Lake is separated from West Lake by Thanh Nien St, which is lined with flame trees. In the 18th century, the Trinh Lords built a palace on this site; it was later turned into a reformatory for deviant royal concubines, who were condemned to weave a very fine white silk.

Quan Thanh Pagoda (also called Tran Vo Temple) is on the shore of Truc Bach Lake near the intersection of Thanh Nein and Quan Thanh Sts. The pagoda, shaded by huge trees, was established during the Ly Dynasty (ruled 1010 to 1225) and was dedicated to Tran Vo (God of the North), whose symbols of power are the tortoise and the snake. A bronze statue and bell here date from 1677.

Ambassadors' Pagoda The Ambassadors' Pagoda (Quan Su; ☎ 252427) is the official centre of Buddhism in Hanoi, attracting quite a crowd – mostly elderly women – on holidays. During the 17th century, there was a guesthouse here for the ambassadors of Buddhist countries. Today, there are about a dozen monks and nuns at the Ambassadors' Pagoda. Next to the pagoda is a store selling Buddhist ritual objects.

The Ambassadors' Pagoda is at 73 Quan Su St (between Ly Thuong Kiet and Tran Hung Dao Sts); it is open to the public every day from 7.30 to 11.30 am and 1.30 to 5.30 pm.

Hai Ba Trung Temple The Hai Ba Trung Temple, founded in 1142, is two km south of Hoan Kiem Lake on Tho Lao St. A statue here shows the two Trung sisters (1st century AD) kneeling with their arms raised, as if to address a crowd. Some people say the statue shows the sisters, who had been proclaimed queens of the Vietnamese, about to dive into a river in order to drown themselves, which they are said to have done rather than surrender following their defeat at the hands of the Chinese.

Museums

In addition to the usual two-hour lunch break, it's worth knowing that almost all of Hanoi's museums are closed on Mondays.

History Museum The History Museum (Bao Tang Lich Su), once the museum of the École Française d'Extrême Orient, is one block east of the Municipal Theatre at 1 Pham Ngu Lao St. The building, constructed of reinforced concrete, was completed in 1930.

Exhibits include artefacts from Vietnam's prehistory (Palaeolithic and Neolithic periods); proto-Vietnamese civilisations (1st and 2nd millennia BC); the Dong Son Civilisation (7th century BC to 3rd century AD); the Oc-Eo (Funan) culture of the Mekong Delta (1st to 6th century AD); the Indianised kingdom of Champa (1st to 15th century); the Khmer kingdoms; various Vietnamese dynasties and their resistance to Chinese attempts at domination; the struggle against the French; and the history of the Communist Party.

Army Museum The Army Museum (Bao Tang Quan Doi) is on Dien Bien Phu St; it is open daily except Mondays. Outside, Soviet and Chinese weaponry supplied to the North are on display alongside French and US-made weapons captured in the Franco-Viet Minh War and the Vietnam War. The centrepiece is a Soviet-built MiG-21 jet fighter triumphant amid the wreckage of French aircraft downed at Dien Bien Phu and a US F-111. The displays include scale models of various epic battles from Vietnam's long military history, including Dien Bien Phu and the capture of Saigon.

Next to the Army Museum is the hexagonal Flag Tower, which has become one of the symbols of the city. It is part of a Vauban-style citadel constructed by Emperor Gia Long (ruled 1802-19).

Air Force Museum This is one of the larger museums in Vietnam and, though seldom visited by foreigners, it's very worthwhile.

Many of the museum's exhibits are outdoors. This includes a number of Soviet MiG fighters, reconnaissance planes, helicopters and anti-aircraft equipment. Inside the museum hall are other weapons, including mortars, machine guns and some US-made bombs (hopefully defused). There is a partially truncated MiG with a ladder – you are permitted to climb up into the cockpit and have your photo taken. The museum has other war memorabilia, including paintings of obvious Soviet design and portraits of Ho Chi Minh.

The Air Force Museum is on Truong Chinh St in the Dong Da District (south-west part of the city). From the railway station it's almost five km, a rather long cyclo ride.

Ho Chi Minh Museum The museum is divided into two sections, 'Past' and 'Future'. You start in the past and move to the future by walking in a clockwise direction downwards through the museum, starting at the right-hand side once at the top of the stairs. The displays are very modern and all have a message (peace, happiness, freedom, etc).

It's probably worth taking an English-speaking guide since some of the symbolism is hard to figure out (did Ho Chi Minh have a cubist period?). The 1958 Ford Edsel bursting through the wall (an American commercial failure to symbolise America's military failure) is a knockout.

The museum is the huge cement structure next to Ho Chi Minh's Mausoleum. Photography is forbidden. Upon entering, all bags and cameras must be left at reception.

Fine Arts Museum The building housing the Fine Arts Museum (Bao Tang My Thuat; ☎ 252830) served as the Ministry of Information under the French. Here you can see some very intricate sculptures, paintings, lacquerware, ceramics and other traditional Vietnamese fine arts.

Some reproductions of antiques are on

sale here, but be sure to ask for a certificate which will clear these goods through customs when you depart Vietnam.

The Fine Arts Museum is at 66 Nguyen Thai Hoc St (corner Cao Ba Quai St), which is across the street from the back wall of the Temple of Literature; it is open from 8 am until noon and 1.30 to 4.30 pm Tuesday to Sunday.

Revolutionary Museum The Revolutionary Museum (Bao Tang Cach Mang) at 25 Tong Dan St presents the history of the Vietnamese Revolution.

Independence Museum The house at 48 Hang Ngang St (north of Hoan Kiem Lake in the Old Quarter), in which Ho Chi Minh drafted Vietnam's Declaration of Independence in 1945, has been turned into a museum.

Ho Chi Minh's Mausoleum

In the tradition of Lenin and Stalin before him and Mao after him, the final resting place of Ho Chi Minh is a glass sarcophagus set deep in the bowels of a monumental edifice that has become a site of pilgrimage. Ho Chi Minh's Mausoleum – built despite the fact that in his will Ho requested to be cremated – was constructed between 1973 and 1975 of native materials gathered from all over Vietnam; the roof and peristyle are said to evoke either a traditional communal house or a lotus flower – to many tourists it looks like a cold concrete cubicle with columns. While reviewing parades and ceremonies taking place on the grassy expanses of Ba Dinh Square, high-ranking party and government leaders stand in front of the mausoleum.

Ho Chi Minh's Mausoleum is open to the public on Tuesday, Wednesday, Thursday and Saturday mornings from 8 to 11 am; on Sundays and holidays, it is open from 7.30 to 11.30 am. The mausoleum is closed for two months a year (usually from September to early November) while Ho Chi Minh's embalmed corpse is in Russia for maintenance.

Photography is permitted outside the building but not inside. All visitors must register and check their bags and cameras at a reception hall on Chua Mot Cot St; if possible, bring your passport for identification. Soundtracks for a 20-minute video about Ho Chi Minh are available in Vietnamese, English, French, Khmer, Lao, Russian and Spanish.

Honour guards will accompany you as you march single-file from near reception to the mausoleum entrance. Inside the building, more guards wearing snowy white bleached military uniforms are stationed at intervals of five paces, giving an eerily authoritarian aspect to the macabre spectacle of the embalmed, helpless body with its wispy white hair. The whole place has a spooky 'sanitised for your protection' atmosphere.

The following rules are strictly applied to all visitors to the mausoleum:

- People wearing shorts, tank-tops, etc, will not be admitted.
- Nothing (including day packs and cameras) may be taken into the mausoleum.
- A respectful demeanour must be maintained at all times.
- For obvious reasons of decorum, photography is absolutely prohibited inside the mausoleum.
- It is forbidden to put your hands in your pockets.
- Hats must be taken off inside the mausoleum building.

Many of the visitors are groups of students, and it's interesting to watch their reactions to Ho and to discuss it with them. Most show deep respect and admiration for Ho. Though Vietnamese as a whole are mostly disappointed with communism, few (at least the younger generation) show any hostility or bitterness towards Ho himself. He is seen as the liberator of the Vietnamese people from colonialism, and Vietnam's subsequent economic and political mismanagement are viewed as the misdoings of Ho's comrades and successors. Of course, this view is reinforced by the educational system which only emphasises Ho's deeds and accomplishments.

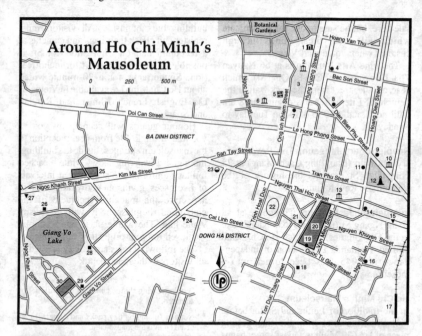

Around Ho Chi Minh's Mausoleum

0   250   500 m

PLACES TO STAY

18   Sao Mai Hotel
21   Phuong Lan Hotel
26   Giang Vo Hotel
28   Hanoi Hotel
29   Dong Do Hotel &
     Sunset Pub

PLACES TO EAT

15   Kem Tra My
     (ice cream shop)
24   Phuong Nam
     Restaurant
27   Restaurant 79

OTHER

1   Presidential
     Palace
2   Ho Chi Minh's
     Mausoleum
3   Ba Dinh Square
4   National Assembly
     Building
5   One Pillar Pagoda &
     Dien Huu Pagoda
6   Ho Chi Minh Museum
7   Reception for Ho Chi
     Minh's Mausoleum
8   Ministry of Foreign
     Affairs
9   Flag Tower
10   Army Museum

11   Chinese Embassy
12   Lenin Monument
     & Park
13   Fine Arts Museum
14   Thai Embassy
16   Market
17   Hanoi Railway
     Station
19   Entrance to Temple
     of Literature
20   Temple of
     Literature
22   Hanoi Stadium
23   Kim Ma Bus Station
25   Belgian, Malaysian,
     Myanmar &
     Swedish Embassies
30   Exhibition Hall

After exiting from the mausoleum, the tour will pass by the Presidential Palace, constructed in 1906 as the Palace of the Governor General of Indochina; it is now used for official receptions. Ho Chi Minh's house, built of the finest wooden materials in 1958, is next to a carp-filled pond. Just how much time Ho actually spent here is questionable – the house would have made a good target for US bombers had it been suspected that Ho could be found here.

Nearby are Hanoi's botanical gardens. The tour ends up at the One Pillar Pagoda (see the Lakes, Temples & Pagodas section earlier). If you're lucky, you'll catch the 'Changing of the Guard' outside Ho's Mausoleum – the amount of pomp and ceremony rivals the British equivalent at Buckingham Palace.

Old Quarter
The Old Quarter is demarcated, roughly speaking, by Hoan Kiem Lake, the Citadel, Dong Xuan Market (currently in ruins) and the ramparts of the Red River. As they have since the 15th century, the narrow streets of the Old Quarter bear names that reflect the business once conducted there: Silk St, Rice St, Paper St, Broiled Fish St, Vermicelli St, Jewellers' St, Paper Votive Objects St and so forth. This interesting area now houses a variety of small shops.

Dong Xuan Market
The three-storey Dong Xuan Market was at 1.3 km north of the northern end of Hoan Kiem Lake. We have to say 'was' rather than 'is' because the whole market went up in flames around midnight on 14 July 1994. The fire killed five people, all of whom had entered the building after the fire started to either rescue goods or steal them.

There were hundreds of stalls in the old market, and around 3000 people were employed here. The Hanoi municipal government says that the market will be rebuilt. Let us hope so, because it was certainly the most interesting and lively market in the city.

St Joseph Cathedral
Stepping inside neo-Gothic St Joseph Cathedral (inaugurated in 1886) is like being instantly transported to medieval Europe. The cathedral is noteworthy for its square towers, elaborate altar and stained-glass windows. The first Catholic mission in Hanoi was founded in 1679.

The main gate to St Joseph Cathedral is open daily from 5 to 7 am and 5 to 7 pm, the hours when masses are held. At other times of the day guests are welcome but must enter the cathedral via the compound of the Diocese of Hanoi, the entrance to which is a block away at 40 Nha Chung St. After walking through the gate, go straight and then turn right. When you reach the side door to the cathedral, ring the small bell high up to the right of the door to call the priest to let you in. Across Nha Chung St from the diocese compound is a nunnery where some elderly nuns live.

Vietnamese staring squads are alive and well in Hanoi. I went to the cathedral for midnight mass on Christmas Eve and found a number of Vietnamese and foreigners huddled on the front pews. Their presence seemed to provide great entertainment for the several thousand Vietnamese onlookers packed into the back of the building. There was a constant buzz of excitement among the rubbernecks, and a massive crush to the middle and even some pillar-scaling feats in order to get a better view. The priest interrupted the service several times to try to control the crowd. In between we were able to catch a few lines of the Vietnamese priest delivering his sermon first in Vietnamese, then French and finally English. Trilingual and very impressive, though his strong French accent made his English difficult to understand. I wasn't surprised to learn that some cathedrals in the south now only permit their congregation members to enter the building for Christmas midnight mass. Apparently, the priests issue members-only passes for the event.

Adrian Bloch

Hanoi Hilton
The 'Hanoi Hilton' is the nickname given to a prison in which US POWs – mostly aircraft crew – were held during the Vietnam War. Soon after they were captured, American pilots appeared on TV broadcasts shown around the world, confessing to their crimes and asking the US government to halt the bombing of North Vietnam. This strategy backfired – one of the pilots blinked nervously at the camera while he spoke, spelling out the word 'torture' in Morse Code.

The high walls of the forbidding triangular building, officially known as Hoa Lo Prison, are pierced by precious few barred windows. The structure, which was constructed by the French in the early 20th century, is bounded by Hai Ba Trung, Tho Nhuom and Hoa Lo Sts. Photography is forbidden.

Long Bien Bridge
The Long Bien Bridge, which crosses the Red River 600 metres north of the new

HANOI

Radio Hanoi & Jane Fonda

Hanoi's radio transmitter is nothing to see, but it's worth a historical footnote for the role it played in the war against the USA (the current transmitter is not the original one used during the war).

Those who are old enough to remember the Vietnam War will doubtless recall the radio broadcasts from Hanoi made by American film actor Jane Fonda. Ms Fonda was perhaps the most famous anti-war activist of the time. She made only one live broadcast over Radio Hanoi, her famous speech to US pilots. Subsequent broadcasts played over the radio were tape-recorded speeches and conversations made during her stay in North Vietnam.

Jane Fonda went to North Vietnam on 15 July 1972 and returned to the USA on 29 July, travelling via Paris and Beijing. She was not the only US civilian to visit Hanoi during the war, but she was certainly the most famous. In spite of the fact that a war was raging, it was never illegal for US citizens to visit North Vietnam.

That almost changed. As a direct result of Jane Fonda's visit, Representative Ichord, Chairman of the House Internal Security Committee, proposed to amend the 1950 Internal Security Act to make it illegal for any US citizen to visit a country at war with the USA. The Ichord Amendment – later known as the 'Jane Fonda Amendment' – never passed.

Her visit continues to stir emotions to this very day. After WW II, an American woman nicknamed 'Tokyo Rose' was convicted of treason (but later pardoned) for making propaganda broadcasts for the Japanese. Another American woman nicknamed 'Axis Sally' was convicted of doing the same for the Nazis. Many veterans who served in Vietnam (and some members of Congress) felt that Jane Fonda's actions were similar, but she was never prosecuted. Not that it wasn't considered – even as late as 1984 the Justice Department under the Reagan administration looked into the matter but decided that Jane Fonda's trip to North Vietnam and her public speeches did not constitute a crime.

Just as Ms Fonda has her critics, she also has her defenders. There are those who say she was simply exercising her right to freedom of speech in speaking out against a war which was morally wrong. It's also only fair to mention that she made a sincere effort to visit the captured American pilots at the nearby 'Hanoi Hilton' prison, but her request for the visit was rejected by North Vietnamese authorities (*New York Times,* 29 July 1972, page 9). On the other hand, a widely circulated photograph of Jane Fonda sitting behind an anti-aircraft gun wearing a North Vietnamese helmet particularly outraged many Americans, even those who opposed the war.

An act of treason? Or a heartfelt wish to speak out against an unjust war? You be the judge: the following public domain information is a transcript from the US Congress House Committee on Internal Security ('Travel to Hostile Areas', HR 16742, 19-25 September 1972, page 7671 – special thanks to CompuServe Military Veterans Forum):

[Radio Hanoi attributes talk on DRV visit to Jane Fonda; from Hanoi in English to American servicemen involved in the Indochina War, 1 pm GMT, 22 August 1972. Text: Here's Jane Fonda telling her impressions at the end of her visit to the Democratic Republic of Vietnam (follows recorded female voice with American accent):]

This is Jane Fonda. During my two-week visit in the Democratic Republic of Vietnam, I've had the opportunity to visit a great many places and speak to a large number of people from all walks

Chuong Duong Bridge, is a fantastic hodge-podge of repairs dating from the Vietnam War. American aircraft repeatedly bombed the strategic Long Bien Bridge (which at one time was defended by 300 anti-aircraft guns and 84 SAM missiles), yet after each attack the Vietnamese somehow managed to improvise replacement spans and return it to road and rail service. It is said that when US POWs were put to work repairing the bridge, the US military, fearing for their safety, ended the attacks.

The 1682-metre Long Bien Bridge was opened in 1902. It was once known as the Paul Doumer Bridge after the turn-of-the-century French Governor General of Indochina, Paul Doumer (1857-1932), who of life – workers, peasants, students, artists and dancers, historians, journalists, film actresses, soldiers, militia girls, members of the women's union, writers.

I visited the (Dam Xuac) agricultural coop, where the silk worms are also raised and thread is made. I visited a textile factory, a kindergarten in Hanoi. The beautiful Temple of Literature was where I saw traditional dances and heard songs of resistance. I also saw an unforgettable ballet about the guerrillas training bees in the south to attack enemy soldiers. The bees were danced by women, and they did their job well.

In the shadow of the Temple of Literature I saw Vietnamese actors and actresses perform the second act of Arthur Miller's play *All My Sons*, and this was very moving to me – the fact that artists here are translating and performing American plays while US imperialists are bombing their country.

I cherish the memory of the blushing militia girls on the roof of their factory, encouraging one of their sisters as she sang a song praising the blue sky of Vietnam – these women, who are so gentle and poetic, whose voices are so beautiful, but who, when American planes are bombing their city, become such good fighters.

I cherish the way a farmer evacuated from Hanoi, without hesitation, offered me, an American, their best individual bomb shelter while US bombs fell near by. The daughter and I, in fact, shared the shelter wrapped in each others arms, cheek against cheek. It was on the road back from Nam Dinh, where I had witnessed the systematic destruction of civilian targets – schools, hospitals, pagodas, the factories, houses, and the dike system.

As I left the United States two weeks ago, Nixon was again telling the American people that he was winding down the war, but in the rubble-strewn streets of Nam Dinh, his words echoed with sinister (words indistinct) of a true killer. And like the young Vietnamese woman I held in my arms clinging to me tightly – and I pressed my cheek against hers – I thought, this is a war against Vietnam perhaps, but the tragedy is America's.

One thing that I have learned beyond the shadow of a doubt since I've been in this country is that Nixon will never be able to break the spirit of these people; he'll never be able to turn Vietnam, north and south, into a neo-colony of the United States by bombing, by invading, by attacking in any way. One has only to go into the countryside and listen to the peasants describe the lives they led before the revolution to understand why every bomb that is dropped only strengthens their determination to resist.

I've spoken to many peasants who talked about the days when their parents had to sell themselves out to landlords as virtually slaves, when there were very few schools and much illiteracy, inadequate medical care, when they were not masters of their own lives.

But now, despite the bombs, despite the crimes being created – being committed against them by Richard Nixon, these people own their own land, build their own schools – the children learning, literacy – illiteracy is being wiped out, there is no more prostitution as there was during the time when this was a French colony. In other words, the people have taken power into their own hands, and they are controlling their own lives.

And after 4000 years of struggling against nature and foreign invaders – and the last 25 years, prior to the revolution, of struggling against French colonialism – I don't think that the people of Vietnam are about to compromise in any way, shape or form about the freedom and independence of their country, and I think Richard Nixon would do well to read Vietnamese history, particularity their poetry, and particularly the poetry written by Ho Chi Minh. [Recording ends] ∎

was assassinated a year after becoming President of France.

Government Guest House

Formerly the Palace of the Governor of Tonkin, the ornate Government Guest House (☎ 255853) was stormed during the August Revolution of 1945; the wrought-iron fence surrounding the ornate building still shows marks from bullets fired during the battle. The guesthouse, which is now used to house highly favoured official guests, is at 2 Le Thach St, across Ngo Quyen St from the Thong Nhat Hotel.

Thu Le Park & Zoo

Thu Le Park & Zoo (Bach Thu Thu Le), with its expanses of shaded grass and ponds, is six km west of Hoan Kiem Lake. The entrance is on Buoi St a few hundred metres north of Ngoc Khanh St. The zoo is open daily from 6 am to 6 pm; the entrance fee is US$0.10.

Co Loa Citadel

Co Loa Citadel (Co Loa Thanh), the first fortified citadel recorded in Vietnamese history, dates from the 3rd century BC. Only vestiges of the massive ancient ramparts, which enclosed an area of about five sq km, are extant. Co Loa again became the national capital under Ngo Quyen (reigned 939-44). In the centre of the citadel are temples dedicated to King An Duong Vuong (ruled 257-208 BC), who founded the legendary Thuc Dynasty, and his daughter My Nuong (Mi Chau). When My Nuong showed her father's magic crossbow trigger – which made the Vietnamese king invincible in battle – to her husband (who was the son of a Chinese general), he stole it and gave it to his father. With its help, the Chinese were able to defeat An Duong Vuong and his forces, depriving Vietnam of its independence.

Co Loa Citadel is 16 km north of Hanoi in Dong Anh district.

Festivals

Tet, the Vietnamese New Year, falls in late January or early February. In Hanoi, Tet is celebrated in a variety of ways. A flower market is held during the week before the beginning of Tet on Hang Luoc St. A two-week flower exhibition and competition takes place in Lenin Park beginning on the first day of the new year. Prior to 1995 (when the government banned firecrackers), there was always a firecracker festival in Dong Ky, a village three km north of Hanoi. A competition for the loudest firecracker once resulted in the building of a gargantuan firecracker 16 metres in length! On the 13th day of the first lunar month in the village of Lim in Ha Bac Province, boys and girl engage in *hat doi*, a traditional game in which groups conduct a sung dialogue with each other; other activities include chess and cock fighting. Wrestling matches are held on the 15th day of the first lunar month at Dong Da Mound, site of the uprising against Chinese invaders led by Emperor Quang Trung (Nguyen Hue) in 1788.

Vietnam's National Day, 2 September, is celebrated at Ba Dinh Square (the expanse of grass in front of Ho Chi Minh's Mausoleum) with a rally and fireworks; boat races are held on Hoan Kiem Lake.

Places to Stay

Unlike Saigon with its numerous large cheap hotels, Hanoi suffers from a serious lack of budget accommodation.

Hanoi, of course, did not enjoy the wartime economic boom that spurred hotel development in the former South Vietnam. Accommodating foreigners is a recent phenomenon in Hanoi, and the sudden invasion of backpackers since the Chinese border was opened in 1993 has resulted in a serious shortage of low-priced accommodation, especially during the peak (June through August) tourist season. To fill the gap, budding entrepreneurs have set up budget hotels each consisting of a few rooms set aside in somebody's house. These small, French-built townhouses are charming places to stay, but finding a room takes patience – you may have to walk from house to house, only to find that most are full.

On the other end of the scale are huge mansions built as official state rest and recreation centres for high-ranking Communist Party officials. These places are palatial – high ceilings, chandeliers, huge dining halls and well-tended gardens surrounded by high fences. These places are now being converted into upmarket hotels and foreign tourists with hard currency are welcomed. There has also been a recent spate of upmarket hotel construction by foreign joint ventures, but this is of little help to budget travellers.

Places to Stay – bottom end

Hoan Kiem District *Lotus Guest House* (☎ 268642) at 42V Ly Thuong Kiet St is a very friendly, quiet, clean and cheap place. Rooms begin at US$8.

The *Bodega Restaurant & Guest House* (☎ 267784; 267787; 10 rooms) at 57 Trang Tien St has good cheapish rooms even though the food is horrible. Rooms are priced here from US$20 to US$30.

The *Green Bamboo Café* (☎ 264949; four rooms) at 42 Nha Chung St is better known as a place to eat and to book tours. However, there are four rooms out back for rent, each costing US$15.

The *Queen Café* (☎ 260860) at 65 Hang Bac St has four rooms upstairs which they rent for US$5 to US$7. Not surprisingly, these fill up quickly, but the staff can often direct you elsewhere.

The *Sophia Hotel* (☎ 266848; 11 rooms) is at 6 Hang Bai St, up the stairs from the restaurant. It is adequate but barely worth it at US$20 for a double, with bathroom and hot water. The staff are friendly. If the hotel is full, they will direct you to their other place, *Sophia II*, about three km away; prices there are about the same.

The *Khach San 30-4* (☎ 252611; 29 rooms) is named after 30 April 1975, the date when the North Vietnamese entered Saigon. Not surprisingly, it's state-owned. The hotel is at 115 Tran Hung Dao St, conveniently opposite the railway station. Large echo-chamber rooms costing US$6 and US$8 have the bathroom outside, or you can pay US$35 for attached bath. This place is old and run-down, but has character and the staff proved friendly.

The *Nam Phuong Hotel* (☎ 258030; fax 258964; four rooms) is a small, pleasant place at 16 Bao Khanh St, a narrow street which leads from Hoan Kiem Lake to Hang Trong St. It costs US$15 to US$45. The staff are friendly.

The *Trang Tien Hotel* (☎ 256341; fax 251416; 46 rooms), 35 Trang Tien St, is excellent value. However, a planned renovation will probably catapult this place into the mid-range or top-end category. Double rooms cost US$8 to US$40. The location near Hoan Kiem Lake is very central.

Especen (☎ 258845, 266856; fax 269612), 79E Hang Trong St, operates nine mini-hotels around the central area of Hanoi.

There is no point in listing them all here as their office will give you a map and call ahead to book a room. The hotels all bear creative names, such as Especen-1, Especen-2, etc.

Ba Dinh District The *Hong Ha Hotel* (☎ 254911; fax 253688; 21 rooms) is at 78 Yen Phu St. This is a good place in the lower to mid-range category. Doubles cost US$20 to US$35. The hotel is close to the Long Bien Bridge, which crosses the Red River.

The *Giang Vo Hotel* (☎ 253407; 400 rooms) consists of several five-storey apartment blocks in a large compound. One entrance to the hotel, which is 3.5 km west of the city centre, faces Giang Vo Lake; there is another entrance on Ngoc Khanh St. This is *the* most popular place with Vietnamese budget travellers, but it's in a rather dull neighbourhood and foreigners prefer to give it a miss. The dumpier rooms go for US$10; rooms with air-con, fridge and hot water cost US$20.

Places to Stay – middle

Hoan Kiem District The *Phu Gia Hotel* (☎ 257512; fax 259207; 50 rooms) at 136 Hang Trong St has a pleasant location next to Hoan Kiem Lake. Not much English is spoken, but it seems to be a popular place and is often full. Double rooms cost US$25 to US$48.

The *Phung Hung Hotel* (☎ 265555, 265556) is slightly over one km north of the railway station at 2 Duong Thanh St. Though not dirt-cheap, it has become fairly popular with backpackers. The hotel has a restaurant and bicycles for rent. Rooms cost US$25.

The *Win Hotel* (☎ 233275; fax 256569; 19 rooms) at 27 Tong Duy Tan St continues to get favourable reviews from travellers. Rooms cost from US$25 to US$70.

The *Hoa Binh Hotel* (☎ 253315; fax 269818; 100 rooms), 27 Ly Thuong Kiet St, is centrally located. The old wing has a certain faded elegance to it, but the new wing is three-star standard. Prices in the old wing start at US$20 but soar to US$101 for the top-end renovated rooms. Prices in the new wing are US$120 to US$170. As for the

HANOI

Central Hanoi

HANOI

Red River (Song Hong)

To Noi Bai Airport (30 km), Haiphong (103 km), Ha Long Bay (165 km)

Chuong Duong Bridge

To West Lake (Ho Tay)

Bach Dang Street

Phuc Tan Street

Tran Nhat Duat Street

Tran Quang Kha Street

Lo Su Street

Tran N G Han Street

Hang Chieu Street

H Mam Street

H Thung Street

Ly Thai To Street

Le Lai Street

Le Thach Street

Dinh Le Street

Hang Buom Street

Hang Be Street

57

13

56

55

58

61

59

Hang Dau Street

Dao Duy Tu Street

5

Hang Bac Street

12

Cau Go Street

Dinh Tien Street

11

14

Dinh Tien Hoang Street

Hang Khai Street

H Giay Street

Hang Dao Street

10

15

Hoan Kiem Lake

OLD QUARTER

H Ngang Street

Luong V Can Street

Le Thai To Street

19

20

31

D Xuan Street

Hang Ma Street

H Duong Street

H Can Street

Hang Bo Street

6

H Quat Street

18

16

Hang Gai Street

17

Hang Trong Street

Nha Chung Street

21

22

Hang Luoc Street

Cha Ca Street

Thuoc Bac Street

7

H Thiec Street

Yen Thai Street

9

Ly Quoc Su Street

30

Hang Ga Street

Hang Vai Street

Bat Dan Street

Duong Thanh Street

Phu Doan Street

Trang Thi Street

Hoa Lo Street

8

Hang Da Street

Ngo Tram Street

23

32

25

Quan Su Street

Phung Hung Street

Hang Bong Street

24

Phan Boi Chau Street

34

33

Ly Nam De Street

35

The Citadel (military area)

To Ho Chi Minh's Mausoleum

Tran Phu Street

Dien Bien Phu Street

Nguyen Thai Hoc Street

26

27

28

29

36

37

38

0   125   250 m

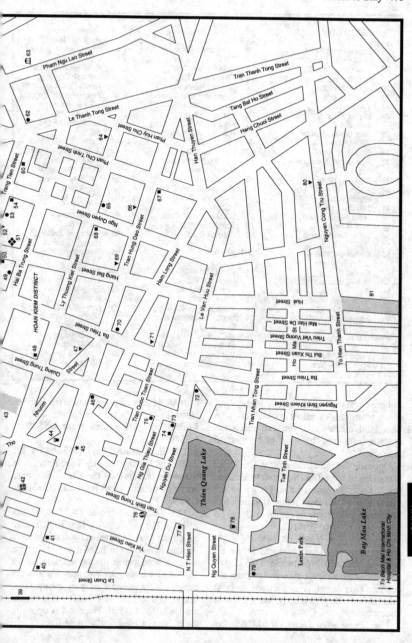

HANOI

PLACES TO STAY

8   Phung Hung Hotel
16 Nam Phuong Hotel
17 Hoa Long Hotel & Chinese Restaurant
18 Freedom Hotel
20 Phu Gia Hotel
24 Win Hotel
27 Memory Hotel & Alpo Hotel
28 Blue II Hotel & New World Hotel
29 Cuu Long Hotel
35 Rose Hotel & Saigon Hotel
36 Dong Loi Hotel
38 Mango Hotel
40 Khach San 30-4
41 Thu Do Hotel
48 Lotus Guest House
50 Sophia Hotel
54 Trang Tien Hotel
56 Dien Luc Hotel
57 Binh Minh Hotel & China Southern Airlines
58 Hotel Sofitel Metropole
60 Dan Chu Hotel
67 Hoan Kiem Hotel
68 Hoa Binh Hotel
74 Boss Hotel & VIP Club

PLACES TO EAT

2   Piano Restaurant
3   Apocalypse Now
4   Cha Ca Restaurant
5   Queen Cafe
6   Old Darling Cafe
7   Tin Tin Cafe & Bar
9   Real Darling Cafe
10 Phuc Fish & Chips
15 Thuy Ta Restaurant
22 Green Bamboo Cafe & Palace Dancehall
25 Pastry & Yogurt
26 Kem Tra My (ice cream)
37 Huong Sen Restaurant
44 Lan Anh Bar
47 The Little Italian
52 Bodega Restaurant & Guest House
59 Club Opera
64 Hué Restaurant
66 Restaurant Bistrot
69 Le Bistrot
71 Tourist Meeting Cafe
78 Top Disco Club
80 Cafe de Paris

OTHER

1   Dong Xuan Market
11 Municipal Water Puppet Theatre
12 Shoe Market
13 Minibuses to Haiphong
14 Ngoc Son Temple & The Huc Bridge
19 ANZ Bank
21 St Joeseph Cathedral
23 Viet Duc Hospital
30 National Library
31 Vietnam Airlines Booking Office
32 'Hanoi Hilton' (former prison)
33 Australian Embassy
34 German Embassy
39 Hanoi Railway Station
42 Ambassadors' Pagoda
43 19th of December Market
45 Immigration Police Office
46 Cambodian Embassy
49 Xunhasaba (books)
51 State General Department Store
53 Foreign Language Bookshop
55 GPO & Telephone Office
61 Revolutionary Museum
62 Municipal Theatre
63 History Museum
65 Thai International Airways
70 French Embassy
72 Japanese Embassy
73 Vietnam Airlines Branch Office
75 Lao Embassy Consular Section
76 Vietcombank
77 Lao Embassy
79 State Circus
81 Bicycle & Motorbike Shops

in-house restaurant, the hotel's glossy brochure promises 'excellent cook-chiefs who won gold medal' and you can reach the upstairs restaurant 'by stairs of by modern Japanese lifts'.

Opposite the railway station at 109 Trang Hung Dao St is the *Thu Do Hotel* (☎ 252288; fax 261121; 37 rooms), also known as the *Capital Hotel*. A recent renovation here has jacked up prices considerably, and rooms now cost US$56 to US$101.

The *Hai Yen Hotel* (☎ 746976; eight rooms) is at 126 Giai Phong St in the far south of Hanoi. All rooms cost US$25. It's reasonably good value though far from the centre. This hotel is a Taiwanese joint venture and, not surprisingly, has a Chinese restaurant.

The *Hoang Nga Hotel* (☎ 645165; fax 641688; 18 rooms) is adjacent to the Hai Yen Hotel and even shares the same address. Rooms here are priced from US$30 to US$40.

The *Binh Minh Hotel* (☎ 266441; fax 257725; 43 rooms), 27 Ly Thai To St, is in the same building as the China Southern Airlines office. Doubles cost US$30 to US$50.

The *Dien Luc Hotel* (☎ 250457; fax 259226; 71 rooms), 30 Ly Thai To St, is also called the *Energy Hotel*. As you might have guessed, it belongs to the Ministry of Energy, which is responsible for the frequent power blackouts which grip Vietnam. Rooms get progressively cheaper as you go upstairs. Top-floor rooms cost US$25; other rooms are US$40 to US$60. The hotel is opposite the office of China Southern Airlines.

The *Friendship Hotel* (☎ 253182; fax 259272; 38 rooms) is also known as *Khach San Huu Nghi*. There is a bar, gift shop and other amenities. Room prices here are US$40, US$47, US$57 and US$72. The hotel is a five-storey building at 23 Quan Thanh St.

The *Rose Hotel* (☎ 254438; fax 254437; 30 rooms), 20 Phan Boi Chau St, is also known as *Khach San Hoa Hong*. This attractive hotel is centrally located near the railway station and has rooms priced from US$48 to US$72.

The *Hoan Kiem Hotel* (☎ 264204; fax 268690; 20 rooms), 25 Tran Hung Dao St (corner Phan Chu Trinh St), boasts a bar, souvenir shop, sauna and restaurant. Nightly rates are US$40 to US$74.

The *Freedom Hotel* (☎ 267119; fax 243918; 11 rooms) is at 57 Hang Trong St near the west side of Hoan Kiem Lake. Rooms are on offer for US$35 to US$69.

Also near the west side of Hoan Kiem Lake is the *Hoa Long Hotel* (☎ 269319; fax 259228; eight rooms), which has rooms for US$15. This place is easy to spot thanks to the huge Chinese restaurant on the ground floor.

The old but fully remodelled *Dong Loi Hotel* (☎ 255721; fax 267999; 30 rooms) is at 94 Ly Thuong Kiet St. The door attendants wear crisp, white uniforms and greet you with 'Hello sir' or 'Good morning madam.' All this courtesy costs US$45 to US$68.

The *Mango Hotel* (☎ 243754; fax 243966; 60 rooms), 118 Le Duan St, is the newest place near the railway station. The price range here is US$25 to US$40.

The *Cuu Long Hotel* (☎ 23641; fax 247641; eight rooms) is a small place on 2 Cua Nam St, an obscure alley north of the railway station. Rooms here are US$35 to US$85.

Just up the alley from the Cuu Long Hotel is the *Blue II Hotel* (☎ 233541; fax 236393; eight rooms) at 6 Dinh Ngang St. Overnight rates are US$30 and US$80. On the same street at No 12 is the *New World Hotel* (☎ 2444163; fax 244409; 12 rooms), which costs from US$31 to US$79.

Also near the railroad tracks is the *Memory Hotel* (☎ 232668; eight rooms), 25 Nguyen Thai Hoc St. The price range is US$30 to US$50. Just a few doors down at 9 Nguyen Thai Hoc St is the *Alpo Hotel* (☎ 232770; 10 rooms), which is priced from US$30 to US$100.

Nearby to the foregoing is another mini-hotel, the *Viet My Hotel* (☎ 251046; fax 243141; six rooms) at 96B Hai Ba Trung St. There are two standards of rooms here costing US$25 and US$35. Just next door is the much more expensive (try bargaining) *Hoang Tu Hotel* which has 24 rooms priced at about US$70.

Dong Da District The *Sao Mai Hotel* (☎ 255827; fax 233887; 38 rooms), 16-18 Thong Phong Alley, Ton Duc Thang St, is a pleasant mid-sized place less than one km south of the Ho Chi Minh Mausoleum. Double rooms cost US$25 to US$35. There are many adjacent mini-hotels here – one to try is the *Phuong Lan Hotel* (☎ 231753; fax 235169; five rooms), 24 Ton Duc Thang St, which costs US$30.

The *Hotel Kim Lien* (☎ 524930; fax 524919; 48 rooms) is a former compound for Soviet workers that has gradually been built into an upmarket hotel. Rooms in Bldg 9 cost US$27 to US$54; in Bldg 5 it's US$20 to US$30; in Bldg 4 US$44 to US$109. The hotel is on the south side of Hanoi on Kim Lien St just west of the railroad tracks near Bay Mau Lake.

The *Queen Hotel* (☎ 641238; fax 641237; 32 rooms), 189 Giai Phong St, is in the tacky south side of town near the railroad tracks. All rooms are doubles and cost US$40 to US$80.

Ba Dinh District The *Lotus Hotel* (☎ 254017; fax 233232; 26 rooms) is also called the *Khach San Bong Sen*. Rooms are US$51 to US$64. The hotel is at 34 Hang Bun St in the north-eastern part of Ba Dinh District. It is located conveniently near some of Hanoi's historical sites, as the hotel's glossy brochure says: 'You have five min-

HANOI

utes only to visit to the remains of history celebrated view start from hotel.'

The *Dong Do Hotel* (☎ 343021; fax 334228; 24 rooms) is on Giang Vo St next to the Exhibition Hall (Trien Lam Giang Vo). Rooms come in three flavours costing US$35, US$89 and US$107.

West Lake Area The *Ho Tay Villas* (Khuy Biet Thu Ho Tay; ☎ 252393; fax 232126; 40 rooms) is now a tourist hotel but it previously was the Communist Party Guest House. The well-designed, spacious villas, set amid a beautifully landscaped area on West Lake, were once the exclusive preserve of top party officials; but now, visitors bearing US dollars are welcome to avail themselves of the great facilities, excellent food and friendly staff. Even if you don't stay, it's instructive to visit to see how the 'people's representatives' lived in one of Asia's poorest countries. The 5.5-km trip from downtown Hanoi to the hotel takes about half an hour by bicycle. Doubles here cost US$35 to US$90.

Places to Stay – top end
Hoan Kiem District The *Saigon Hotel* (☎ 268505; fax 266631; 44 rooms) at 80 Ly Thuong Kiet St is nice, but prices have been rising fast. The tariff here runs from US$79 to US$149.

The *Boss Hotel* (☎ 229086; fax 257634) at 60 Nguyen Du St faces Thien Quang Lake and is adjacent to a Vietnam Airlines branch booking office. Rooms cost US$71 to US$87, plus 10% surcharge. Amenities include the Blue-Diamond Restaurant and VIP Lounge.

The *Dan Chu Hotel* (☎ 254937; fax 266786; 41 rooms) is at 29 Trang Tien St. Once called the Hanoi Hotel, it was built in the late 19th century. Room rates have risen considerably since the 19th century and now range from US$65 to US$129, but breakfast is thrown in free.

The *Hotel Sofitel Metropole* (☎ 266919; fax 266920; 109 rooms), 15 Ngo Quyen St, is also known as *Khach San Thong Nhat*. This is one of the most expensive hotels in

Hanoi, considerably more costly than the luxurious villas out by West Lake. Doubles cost from US$179 to US$394, plus there is a 15% tax and service charge. The restaurant is ventilated by some three dozen ceiling fans; if they cranked them all up at once the food would get sucked into the chimney.

The *Thanh Gia Hotel* (☎ 259649; fax 229403), 24 Yet Kieu St, is near the railway station. It's a brand-new mini-hotel, and the rooms are well equipped and very comfortable. They should be at US$70 a room.

Ba Dinh District The most expensive place to stay in the capital is the *Hanoi Hotel* (☎ 254603; fax 259209; 76 rooms), D8 Giang Vo St, near Ho Chi Minh's Mausoleum. Rooms here cost a breathtaking US$130 to US$390, to which you must add 20% in the summer peak season.

West Lake Area The *Thang Loi Hotel* (☎ 268211; fax 252800; 175 rooms) is nicknamed 'the Cuban Hotel' because it was built in the mid-1970s with Cuban assistance. The floor plan of each level is said to have been copied from a one-storey Cuban building, which explains the doors that lead nowhere. Around the main building are bungalows. The hotel is built on pylons over West Lake and is surrounded by attractive landscaping. All this cushy comfort will cost you US$63 to US$127. The hotel is on Yen Phu St, 3.5 km from the city centre.

The *Tay Ho Hotel* (☎ 232380; fax 232390; 150 rooms) is in the West Lake area and offers the full range of facilities, such as a swimming pool and rental cars. Singles cost US$55 to US$80, and doubles are US$64 to US$95.

The *Dragon Hotel* (☎ 236954; fax 234745; 24 rooms), 9 Tay Ho Rd, is a small place facing the lake. Singles/doubles are US$79/89, and there are also apartments for US$158 per day. To these high prices, add 10% tax.

Places to Eat
After sampling the delectable cuisine of Ho Chi Minh City, Hanoi is disappointing. Res-

taurants in the capital tend to be more expensive than elsewhere, the food lousier and the service lethargic. This is not to say that you're going to starve, but you won't find great cheap meals on almost every street corner as you do in Saigon.

On the other hand, we can say that things have improved considerably. If you think it's lean pickings now, you should have seen it a few years ago. The large number of tourists now visiting Hanoi has created demand for good food and a supply of well-heeled customers who can afford it. Improvements in the Vietnamese domestic economy also bode well for the restaurant business. However, it will still be some years before Hanoi (and the north in general) can match the south in terms of food quality.

Cafes The budget end of the food business is dominated by a handful of small cafes preparing a variety of Vietnamese and Western dishes. Aside from the food, these are good places to meet other travellers and arrange budget tours.

The *Green Bamboo Café* (☎ 264949), 42 Nha Chung St, has it all – good food, good service, good location and low prices. This place has become a sort of unofficial travel centre – this is where you can book trips to Halong Bay, Sapa, etc, and the travel notice board here is also the best in Hanoi. The cafe operates a used book exchange.

Tin Tin Café & Bar (☎ 260326) at 14 Hang Non St is another backpacker haven. The menu includes juices, crepes, fried rice, pizza, burgers and so on, all at reasonable prices. This place is also quite a good nightlife spot.

Another favourite for backpackers are the 'two darlings' – the *Old Darling Café* at 4 Hang Quat St and the *Real Darling Café* on the same street at No 33. The two cafes have been engaged in a long-running dispute (the owners of each will give a different version of the story) over just who started the first Darling Café and who pirated the name from whom. We will give you a hint – the 'real' one is not the real one. Regardless of who you believe, both places do reasonable

Vietnamese dishes and light Western food, such as pancakes and fruit shakes. Both cafes organise bus trips to places like Halong Bay and Hoa Lu.

The *Queen Café* (☎ 260860) at 65 Hang Bac St is a small place that's been around for a while. Food is light (plenty of baguettes, fried eggs and coffee) and you can book tours here too. The situation is very similar at the *Tourist Meeting Café* (☎ 258812), 59 Ba Trieu St.

The Lonely Planet Cafe (no relation to this book!) at 33 Hang Be St in the Old Quarter has cheap food and arranges tours.

Café de Paris (☎ 212701) at 16A Nguyen Cong Tru St is an outstanding cafe proud of its Parisian atmosphere (including an accordion player on Saturday night). Homesick French travellers come here in droves.

Restaurants *The Little Italian* (☎ 258167) at 81 Tho Nhuom St is not run by an Italian, but rather by an Aussie expat. No matter, this

Food seller in Hanoi

HANOI

place does superb pizza, pasta and cocktails. It's expensive (US$8 for a pizza), but at least they accept visa cards. The restaurant offers pizza home delivery, a possible first in Hanoi.

Le Bistrot (☎ 266136), 34 Tran Hung Dao St, is notable for fine French food. Similar fare can be had at *L'Elegant* (☎ 267639) at 66 Hué St, which is open from 10 am until 11 pm.

Club Opera (☎ 268802) at 59 Le Thai To St is not a concert hall but rather an excellent Western restaurant. French travellers are most enthusiastic about the place – the decor and food will make you think you're in France rather than Vietnam. Prices here are a touch on the expensive side.

The *Hué Restaurant* is relatively unknown to foreigners (so far), but locals rave about the place. Hué is reputed to have good cuisine, and the restaurant's slogan is that their food is 'more Hué than Hué'. This place is on the east end of Ly Thuong Kiet St in the Hoan Kiem District.

The *Shrimp Cakes Restaurant* (Nha Hang Banh Tom Hotay; ☎ 257839), 1 Thanh Nien St, has a number of great dishes on the menu, including (surprise?) shrimp cakes. Weather permitting, you can sit outside and admire the view of Truc Bac Lake. The food is good and prices are moderate, but this place can be very crowded on weekends and holidays.

Restaurant Bistrot (☎ 266136) at 34 Tran Hung Dao St is an excellent French restaurant. This place has a great ambience, but has gradually moved upmarket and is no longer cheap. The menu includes squid, pigeon and other pricey delicacies. The trouble is that it has been 'discovered' by coach-loads of tourists from the Hotel Sofitel Metropole on their three-day 'Vietnam experience'.

Near the railway station, the *Huong Sen Restaurant* (☎ 252805), run by Hanoi Tourism, is at 92 Le Duan St. There are a number of other places to eat in the immediate vicinity of the railway station, including a restaurant next to the lobby of the Dong Loi Hotel. There are quite a few small restaurants around all the bus stations.

The *Cha Ca Restaurant* is an expat hangout at 14 Cha Ca St. The food is good here, but there's not much variety on the menu. The restaurant specialises in fish (in fact, cha ca means 'fried fish') and Vietnamese dishes. Cha Ca St, which is a two-block-long continuation of Luong Van Can St, begins about 500 metres north of Hoan Kiem Lake. The *Nha Thinh Restaurant* is at 28 Luong Van Can St.

At 50 Hang Vai St is the *Piano Restaurant* (☎ 232423). Chinese and Vietnamese dishes dominate the menu, but one of the specialities here is boiled crab. As the name suggests, it's a fun place with live music every evening starting at 7 pm.

The large Chinese restaurant on the ground floor of the *Hoa Long Hotel* (☎ 269319) on Hang Trong St near the west shore of Hoan Kiem Lake is well worth checking out.

Restaurant 79 is at 79 Ngoc Khanh St, which is a few hundred metres west of embassy-land in the Ba Dinh District. It caters to an expat crowd.

The excellent *Phuong Nam Restaurant* is on Giang Vo St in Block I1, which is less than 200 metres west of the Hanoi Stadium and not far from the Ho Chi Minh Mausoleum.

The *Nha Noi Ho Tay Restaurant* (☎ 257884) floats on West Lake (Ho Tay) just off Duong Thanh Nien St; it's very near Tran Quoc Pagoda. The atmosphere is very pleasant but the food is mediocre and the prices high for what you get.

Fish and chips is the latest rage to hit Hanoi. You can pay a steep premium to sample them at the *Hanoi Hotel*. More economic is *Phuc Fish & Chips* at 3 Le Thai To St.

Dog meat, a Hanoi delicacy, is available from curb-side vendors a few hundred metres north of the History Museum on Le Phung Hieu St near Tran Quang Kha St.

Ice Cream & Desserts The best ice-cream bar is inside the *Trang Tien Hotel* at 35 Trang Tien St, but it's down in the basement and is not immediately obvious.

The *Thuy Ta Restaurant* has so-so food, but the ice cream is superb. The restaurant is

GENEVIEVE WEBB

ROBERT STOREY

RICHARD EVERIST

ROBERT STOREY

SARA JANE CLELAND

RICHARD EVERIST

A	
B	C	D
E	F

Hanoi
A The tranquility of Hoan Kiem Lake
B A sculpture at the Fine Arts Museum
C French architecture near
  St Joseph Cathedral
D The Presidential Palace
E Sleeping stall holder in the
  Old Quarter
F Signs of the times in Hanoi

SARA JANE CLELAND

SARA JANE CLELAND

BRENDAN McCARTHY

Hanoi

Top Left: Elderly resident in the Old Quarter
Top Right: The imposing Ho Chi Minh Mausoleum
Bottom: The charm of Hanoi's streets

Municipal Theatre

at 1 Le Thai To St, a two-storey place over-looking Hoan Kiem Lake. Non-ice-cream dishes are limited to Vietnamese food, including what can best be described as Vietnamese chop suey.

The best ice-cream sundaes can be found at *Kem Tra My*, which is on Nguyen Thai Hoc St near Ho Chi Minh's Mausoleum.

For some of the best French pastries and coffee in Vietnam, visit the *Pastry & Yogurt Shop* (☎ 250216) at 252 Hang Bong St near the centre.

Self-Catering Many backpackers finally decide that the best way to enjoy a cheap meal is to pick up a loaf of delicious French bread, some salami, cheese and a Coke or beer, then take it back to the hotel room to enjoy it.

More determined self-caterers can buy fresh vegetables at the 19th of December Market (Cho 19-12), whose two entrances

are opposite 61 Ly Thuong Kiet St and next to 41 Hai Ba Trung St.

Entertainment

Municipal Theatre The 900-seat Municipal Theatre (☎ 254312), which faces eastward up Trang Tien St, was built in 1911 as an opera house. It was from a balcony of this building that a Viet Minh-run committee of citizens announced that it had taken over the city on 16 August 1945. These days, performances are held here in the evenings.

Pubs & Discos *Apocalypse Now* at 46 Hang Vai St in the Hoan Kiem District calls itself a 'restaurant and dive bar'. It's about as good a dive as you'll find in Hanoi. It opens at 5 pm and closes when the customers trickle away.

The *Sunset Pub* (☎ 351382) is on the top floor of the Dong Do Hotel at 10 Giang Vo St, west of Ho Chi Minh's Mausoleum.

HANOI

Pizzas and hamburgers are on the menu, and this place claims to have the longest bar in the city (16 metres). The pub is run by a Norwegian.

The *Tin Tin Café & Bar* (☎ 260326) at 14 Hang Non St is a friendly place with Western music, drinks and light snacks. It's open from 8 pm until 2 am.

There is a small pub in the upstairs portion of the Green Bamboo Café (☎ 264949) at 42 Nha Chung St. The pub boasts an open view of the stars (weather permitting). This place stays open from 6 pm to 2 am.

If Japanese culture appeals, you can have your own karaoke cubicle and sing songs to yourself at the *VIP Club* (☎ 252690). This is actually inside the Boss Hotel at 60-62 Nguyen Du St, Hai Ba Trung District. Meals can be delivered to your karaoke cubicle. There is supposed to be a 20% discount from 5 to 8 pm. The VIP Club also has slot machines and a disco with thumping music, strobe lights and large-screen video. The cover charge here is US$5 and drinks are not exactly cheap either.

Hanoi's expat community often gets together at the *Lan Anh Bar* (☎ 267552), 9A Da Tuong St. However, it's not really all that popular with short-term travellers. It is an excellent place though, and (not surprisingly) is run by an expat. This establishment also boasts French, Vietnamese and Algerian cuisine (couscous is their speciality).

The Hanoi Hotel near Giang Vo Lake is home to the *Volvo Discotheque*. This place is very expensive, so bring your visa card or a wheelbarrow full of dong.

The *Queen Bee Nightclub* on Lang Ha St is very popular, but a long way west of the centre (see Hanoi map) in the Ba Dinh District.

The *Palace Dancehall* is a popular locale on Nha Chung St (near the Green Bamboo Café). This was built on the site of the former delegation of the Apostolic Nuncio (the diplomatic representative of the Vatican) and the residence can still be seen behind the dance hall.

The *Top Disco Club* at the south-west corner of Thien Quang Lake is another spot catering to the dance market.

Water Puppets This fantastic art form is unique to Vietnam, and Hanoi is one of the best places to see it. Just on the shore of Hoan Kiem Lake is the Municipal Water Puppet Theatre (Roi Nuoc Thang Long). Performances are given from 8 to 9 pm every night except Monday. Admission is US$2, but it costs US$1 more if you bring a camera and US$5 more for video.

If your schedule permits, you'd do better to visit the National Water Puppet Theatre (Nha Hat Mua Roi Trung Uong), eight km south of the centre at 32 Truong Chinh St in the Dong Da District. There are plans (not yet realised) to build an adjacent outdoor water puppet theatre here too.

Admission here costs US$2 and photography is free, but bringing in a video camera will cost you US$5. There are four performances weekly on Tuesday, Thursday, Saturday and Sunday at 7.45 pm. Some of the cafes catering to foreigners book an inexpensive bus to the theatre, which departs central Hanoi at 6.50 pm and also brings you back.

Circus The endearingly amateurish State Circus often performs in the evening in a huge tent near the entrance to Lenin Park (Cong Vien Le Nin). Many of the performers (gymnasts, jugglers, animal trainers, etc) were trained in Eastern Europe.

Activities
Language Courses In the north, Hanoi National University (☎ 581468) has the largest market share in Vietnamese language study. The Vietnamese Language Centre is actually inside the Polytechnic University, not at the main campus of Hanoi National University at 90 Nguyen Trai St. There is a dormitory at the Polytechnic University for foreign students (Nha A-2 Bach Khoa) and this is a good place to inquire about tuition.

Hanoi's other place to study is the Hanoi

Foreign Language College, Vietnamese Language Centre (☎ 262468). The main campus is nine km from downtown, but there is a smaller campus closer to the city centre at 1 Pham Ngu Lao St. Tuition here varies depending on class size, but should be no more than US$5 per hour for individual tutoring.

Hash House Harriers Expats in Hanoi who belong to this organisation get together once weekly for a run, fun and drinking party. Hash House Harriers meets every Saturday around 4 pm. The location changes, so check for notices at the Sunset Pub, Club Opera, Lan Anh Bar and the Hotel Sofitel Metropole. There is a mandatory US$5 donation, which also gains you a free T-shirt and refreshments.

Golf King's Valley is a golf course 45 km west of Hanoi. Membership is US$5000, but the club should be open to visitors. This is the only golf course in the northern part of Vietnam.

Things to Buy

Whether or not you wish to buy anything, your first encounter will likely be with the children who sell postcards and maps. Of course, they are found all over the country, but in Hanoi there are many who are orphans and have a special card to prove it, which they will immediately show to foreigners. They are also the most notorious overchargers, asking about triple the going price. Bargaining is called for.

Bao Hung and Hai Van, at 1 and 1A Ly Quoc Su St, are great T-shirt shops; lots of Western customers seem to like the Ho Chi Minh T-shirts. Around Hang Bong/Hang Gai Sts are other T-shirt shops and places selling Viet Cong headgear. T-shirts cost US$2 to US$3.50 and either printed or embroidered ones are available. However, it might be worth keeping in mind that neither Ho Chi Minh T-shirts nor VC headgear are popular apparel with Vietnamese refugees and certain war veterans living in the West. Wearing such souvenirs while walking down a street in Los Angeles or Melbourne might offend someone, possibly endangering your relationship with the Overseas Vietnamese community, as well as your dental work.

Attractive gold-on-scarlet banners, usually given as awards for service to the Party or State, can be ordered to your specifications (with your name or date of visit, for instance) at shops at 13 and 40 Hang Bong St. Souvenir patches, sewn by hand, can also be commissioned at 13 Hang Bong St.

Hang Gai, Hang Khai and Cau Go Sts are good areas for souvenirs and antiques (real and fake). Hanoi is a good place to have informal clothes custom-tailored.

Hang Gai St and its continuation, Hang Bong St, are a good place to look for embroidered tablecloths and hangings; one shop you might try is Tan My at 109 Hang Gai St.

A good shop for silk clothing is Khai Silk (☎ 254237), 96 Hang Gai St. The proprietor is fluent in French and English, and the clothes are modern and Western in design.

Duc Loi, 76 Hang Gai St, is good for cotton and silk clothing. The staff can make whatever you want with a few days' notice. You select the fabric and design. They also knit sweaters in raw silk and you can communicate in English, French and Russian (not to mention Vietnamese).

Tien Dat at 75 Hang Gai St is another good place to get tailor-made clothing.

There is an outstanding shoe market along Hang Dau St at the north-east corner of Hoan Kiem Lake. However, it's difficult to find large sizes for big Western feet.

The government-run Vietnamese Art Association at 511 Tran Hung Dao St is where aspiring young artists display their paintings in hopes of attracting a buyer. Prices are in the US$30 to US$50 range after bargaining.

There are quite a number of stores in Hanoi offering new and antique Vietnamese handicrafts (lacquerware, mother-of-pearl inlay, ceramics, sandalwood statuettes, etc) as well as watercolours, oil paintings, prints and assorted antiques. Hanart (☎ 253045) at 43 Trang Tien St offers old ceramics, wood and stone figurines, lacquerware, mother-of-pearl inlay, ivory objects, carpets, etc. The Galerie d'Art at

HANOI

61 Thi Trang Tien St is open from 8 am to noon and 2 to 7 pm daily; its specialities include watercolours, oils, puppets and prints. My Thuat Art Gallery is at 61 Trang Tien St. Another good one is Son Ha Art Gallery (☎ 269198) at 35 Hang Than St.

Another store offering typical products of traditional Vietnamese artisanship faces Hoan Kiem Lake at 25 Hang Khai St. Studio 31, which is two stores away at 31 Hang Khai St, has a selection of paintings. There are small crafts shops at 53 and 55 Ba Trieu St. There is a souvenir shop for foreigners on the corner of Ly Thuong Kiet and Hang Bai Sts; it is open Tuesday to Sunday from 8.30 am to noon and 1.30 to 5.30 pm.

Tapes of Vietnamese music are available at Sun Ashaba at 32 Hai Ba Trung St. There is a pharmacy (Hieu Thuoc Quan Hoan Kiem; ☎ 254212) specialising in traditional medicines – including something called Gecko Elixir – at 2 Hang Bai St (corner Hang Khai St). A little farther west on Hang Khai St are several photographic shops; print film is plentiful and cheap.

For philatelic items, try the philatelic counter at the GPO (in the main postal services hall); it is run by the government philatelic corporation, Cotevina (Cong Ty Tem Viet Nam).

Hanoi's largest store is the State General Department Store (Bach Hoa Tong Hop), which is on Hang Bai St between Hai Ba Trung St and Hoan Kiem Lake. It's a good place to buy things such as lacquerware items, mother-of-pearl inlay work and silverware. It has a better selection than most shops, though prices are perhaps 10% to 30% higher than in the free market. The prices are listed alongside the items, which are encased in glass cabinets (hence there's no need to haggle), and the attendants are reasonably prompt and efficient.

Watercolour paints and brushes are available at a store at 216 Hang Bong St (corner Phung Hung St). Musical instruments can be purchased from shops at 24 and 36 Hang Gai St and 76 and 85 Hang Bong St.

Russian watches and various old (or old-looking) timepieces can be bought in several places in central Hanoi, especially along Luong Van Can and Hang Gai Sts. Formerly very cheap, watch prices are escalating rapidly.

Getting There & Away

Air Vietnam Airlines has nonstop international flights between Hanoi and Bangkok, Guangzhou (China), Nanning (China), Hong Kong, Seoul, Taipei and Vientiane. There are other international flights (via Ho Chi Minh City), including the following destinations: Amsterdam, Berlin, Dubai, Kuala Lumpur, Manila, Melbourne, Moscow, Osaka, Paris, Phnom Penh, Singapore and Sydney.

It is essential to reconfirm all reservations for flights out of the country. Even once you've gotten yourself to the airport, checked in and boarded your flight, don't uncork the champagne until the plane actually gets off the ground. Last minute 'technical problems' have been known to cause substantial delays at this airport.

Vietnam Airlines acts as sales agent for Lao Aviation (Hang Khong Lao). Domestic and international airline offices found in Hanoi are as follows:

Aeroflot
    4 Quang Thi St (☎ 252376)
Air France
    1 Ba Trieu St (☎ 253484)
Cambodia Civil Airlines
    (Hang Khong Cam Bot), A1 Van Phuc Quarters
    (☎ 264513)
Cathay Pacific
    Binh Minh Hotel, 27 Ly Thai To St (☎ 269232)
China Southern Airlines
    Binh Minh Hotel, 27 Ly Thai To St, Hoan Kiem
    District (☎ 269233, 269234)
Czech Airlines
    404 A2 Van Phuc Quarters (☎ 256512)
Malaysian Airlines System (MAS)
    15 Ngo Quyen St (☎ 268819)
Pacific Airlines
    100 Le Duan St, Dong Da District (☎ 515350,
    515356)
Singapore Airlines
    15 Ngo Quyen St (☎ 268803)
Thai International Airways
    25 Ly Thuong Kiet St (☎ 266893)
Vietnam Airlines
    Main Booking Office, 1 Quang Trung St, Hoan
    Kiem District (☎ 250888, 253577, 268913)
    Branch Office, 60 Quang Trung St (☎ 268910,
    268911)

HANOI

Pacific Airlines is the only company besides Vietnam Airlines to offer domestic flights. Both companies charge the exact same fares on domestic flights, but Pacific Airlines is cheaper on international routes. Pacific Airlines has one flight daily between Hanoi and Ho Chi Minh City.

Currently, Vietnam Airlines flies between Hanoi and the following cities in Vietnam:

Buon Ma Thuot, three times weekly; Danang, three times daily; Dien Bien Phu, three times weekly; Ho Chi Minh City, five times daily; Hué, twice daily; Na San, once weekly; Nha Trang, once daily; Pleiku, flights currently suspended.

Bus Hanoi has several main bus terminals. There are frequent minibuses throughout the day to Haiphong from Hang Thung St at the corner of Tran Quang Kha. Service begins around 5 am and the last one leaves Hanoi about 6 pm. These minibuses depart when full (and they really mean 'full'). The cost will typically be around US$2 to US$3 per person. In Haiphong, you catch the minibuses at the government-owned bus station on Nguyen Duc Canh St.

It's a rather different story for government-owned buses. You should purchase your tickets the day before departure. The so-called 'express buses' leave daily at 5 or 5.30 am. According to an incentive plan, the driver must refund 10% of the ticket price if an express bus is two hours late and 20% if the bus is three or more hours late. Most nonexpress buses depart between 4.30 and 5.30 am, though some, especially on shorter routes, leave later in the day.

Gia Lam Bus Station (Ben Xe Gia Lam) is where you catch buses to points north-east of Hanoi. This includes Halong Bay and the China border near Lang Son. The bus station is two km north-east of the centre – you have to cross the Red River to get there. Cyclos won't cross the bridge so you need to get there by motorbike or taxi.

Giap Bat Bus Station (Ben Xe Giap Bat) serves points south of Hanoi, including Saigon. The station is seven km south of the Hanoi Railway Station.

Kim Ma Bus Station (Ben Xe Kim Ma) is opposite 166 Nguyen Thai Hoc St (corner Giang Vo St). This is where you get buses to the north-west part of Vietnam, including Pho Lu and Dien Bien Phu. Tickets should be purchased the day before departure.

Train The Hanoi Railway Station (Ga Ha Noi; ☎ 253949) is opposite 115 Le Duan St at the western end of Tran Hung Dao St; the ticket office is open from 7.30 to 11.30 am and 1.30 to 3.30 pm only. There is a special counter where foreigners can purchase tickets. It's often best to buy tickets at least one day before departure to ensure a seat.

The foreigners' counter at Hanoi Station sold me a platform ticket so I could photograph the old locomotives. This cost US$5! However, with this ticket the guards unlocked the doors to the platform and I found that I had free run of the marshalling yards. Staff cheerily directed me to steam-shunting locomotives.

Roderick O'Brien

Besides the usual express and local trains linking Hanoi with Ho Chi Minh City, there are trains heading east to Haiphong (three to five hours), north-east to the Chinese border at Lang Son (six hours) and on to Beijing, and north-west to the Chinese border at Lao Cai (10 hours).

For more information on the Vietnamese train network and express train fares, see the Getting Around chapter. For information about getting to Haiphong by train, see the next chapter (The North).

Car To hire a car with a driver, contact a hotel, Vietnam Tourism or any other travel agency. A cheap Russian-built rental car can be had for about US$4 per hour, US$25 per day (under eight hours and under 100 km), or US$0.15 to US$0.25 per km. Small Japanese cars can be rented for US$5 per hour or US$35 per day or US$0.35 per km. A mini-van can carry up to 12 people and be rented for US$6 per hour or US$40 per day or US$0.40 per km.

HANOI

Road distances from Hanoi are as follows:

Ba Be Lake	240 km
Bac Giang	51 km
Bac Ninh	29 km
Bach Thong (Bac Can)	162 km
Cam Pha	190 km
Cao Bang	272 km
Da Bac (Cho Bo)	104 km
Danang	763 km
Dien Bien Phu	420 km
Ha Dong	11 km
Ha Giang	343 km
Hai Duong	58 km
Haiphong	103 km
Halong Bay (Hong Gai)	165 km
Ho Chi Minh City	1710 km
Hoa Binh	74 km
Hué	658 km
Lai Chau	490 km
Lang Son	151 km
Nam Dinh	90 km
Ninh Binh	42 km
Phat Diem	121 km
Phnom Penh, Cambodia	1964 km
Son La	308 km
Tam Dao Hill Station	85 km
Thai Binh	109 km
Thai Nguyen	80 km
Thakhek, Laos	576 km
Thanh Hoa	153 km
Tuyen Quang	165 km
Viet Tri	291 km
Yen Bai	182 km

Motorbike A long-distance journey by motorbike from Hanoi into the mountainous hinterland of the north is exciting, though slightly risky in terms of traffic accidents and definitely tiring. You probably wouldn't want to do it during the coldest months (January and February), but in midsummer you have to contend with occasionally heavy rains. Despite such annoyances, many travellers prefer motorbike travel to all other forms of transport.

Cafes in Hanoi often have bike rentals. Quality is extremely variable – some of the bikes on offer are just pure junk. The 125 cc Russian-made Minsk is probably the best overall – you will need that kind of power for the mountainous regions.

There are dozens upon dozens of motorbike shops along Hué St and this is the place to inquire about purchasing a machine. These shops also sell good-quality helmets.

Getting Around
To/From the Airport Hanoi's Noi Bai Airport is about 35 km north of the city. Road traffic from Noi Bai Airport to Hanoi crosses the Red River on the Chuong Duong Bridge, which runs parallel to the old road-and-rail Long Bien Bridge.

Buses from Hanoi to Noi Bai Airport depart from the Vietnam Airlines International Booking Office on Quang Trung St, around the corner from Trang Thi St. The schedule depends on the departure and arrival times of domestic and international flights, but in any case the buses do not go very frequently. The schedule has a not very definite departure at 4.30 am and sometimes at 6, 7, 8 and 9 am and noon as well. The trip to Noi Bai takes 50 minutes. Bus tickets are sold inside the International Booking Office and cost US$2 for buses and US$3 for minibuses. It's advisable to book at least a day in advance. As a rule, these buses are *extremely* crowded.

Vietnam Tourism charges US$20 for a taxi ride to Noi Bai Airport; the same service costs US$33 from Hanoi Tourism. With bargaining you can usually get a better price (US$12 to US$15) by hiring a private taxi; they congregate in front of the Vietnam Airlines booking office (☎ 255284) at the corner of Trang Thi and Quang Trung Sts.

Bus The better tourist map of Hanoi includes bus lines in red. Service on many of the bus routes is rather infrequent.

Tram Like Saigon, Hanoi once had an electric tram system. Hanoi's trams were kept in service longer than Saigon's, but the system finally ground to a halt around 1990. The electric cables suspended above some of the streets have been removed, and nostalgia buffs will find not a trace of this aesthetic form of public transport.

Taxi Hanoi Taxi (☎ 535252), Red Taxi (☎ 353686) and Taxi PT (☎ 535171) have entered the taxi market in the past few years and vehicles can be hailed by phone. These companies supply taxis with meters.

There is also a collection of taxis perpetually hanging around the Vietnam Airlines booking office at the corner of Trang Thi and Quang Trung Sts. These drivers of course intend to take you to the airport, but there's no reason why you couldn't pay them to take you elsewhere. There are no meters in these vehicles so advance negotiation is mandatory.

Cyclo Cyclos are slightly cheaper in Hanoi than in Ho Chi Minh City (though not if you take one you find sitting in front of a major tourist hotel). The cyclos in Hanoi are also wider than the Ho Chi Minh City variety, making it possible for two people to fit in one vehicle and share the fare.

The cyclo drivers in Hanoi are even less likely to speak English than in Ho Chi Minh City, so take a map of the city with you. And finally, some travellers have reported communication problems:

Cyclo drivers in Hanoi are far more rapacious than their Saigon counterparts. I had a fingers bargaining session with one, only to discover at the end of the ride that he was bargaining dollars and I was bargaining dong! He got 10,000d not US$10 – much to his disappointment – but I had to be very forceful to get away with it.

We should point out that these misunderstandings are sometimes sincere, not always attempts to cheat you. We know one traveller who had a vociferous argument when he tried to pay his cyclo driver 1000d rather than US$1. In fact, no one – not even a Vietnamese – can hire a cyclo for 1000d, and the price really should have been about

US$1. Bargaining with finger-language alone is perhaps not such a good idea – since you cannot possibly hold up 10,000 fingers, the best solution is to write things down.

Bicycle The best way to get around Hanoi is by bicycle. More and more hotels and cafes are now offering these for rent. Bike rentals cost about US$1 per day or even less.

If you'll be in town for more than a few days, you might consider buying a cheap Vietnamese-made bicycle, which costs only about US$35. When you leave, you can give it to someone if it hasn't been stolen by then. Ba Trieu St is the place to look for bicycle shops. If you're looking for a mountain bike or 10-speed, you might want to check out Federal Bike Shop at 1B Le Hong Phong St.

Tours There are many of these, both day tours and overnighters. The following is a list of tours supplied by a budget travel agency, so the prices should be regarded as definitely 'bottom end'. However, prices will vary according to the number of travellers and the type of accommodation desired:

Cau River, day tour, US$39 (per person)
Dien Bien Phu, five days, US$60
Halong Bay, two days, US$25
Hoa Lu, Tam Coc, Bich Dong, Cuc Phuong National Park, two days, US$49
Hoa Lu, Tam Coc, Bich Dong, day tour, US$15
Lang Son, Bang Tuong (Pinxiang, China), three days, US$98
Mai Chau, Son Da Reservoir, two days, US$35
Mai Chau, two days, US$27
Nui Coc Lake, two days, US$44
Perfume Pagoda, day tour, US$16
Sapa, four days, US$44
Tam Dao, day tour, US$15
Thay Pagoda, Tay Phuong Pagoda, day tour, US$11

HANOI

The North

Stretching from the Hoang Lien Mountains (Tonkinese Alps) eastward across the Red River Delta to the islands of Halong Bay, the northern part of Vietnam (Bac Bo), known to the French as Tonkin, includes some of the country's most spectacular scenery. The mountainous areas are home to many distinct hill-tribe groups, some of which remain relatively untouched by Vietnamese and Western influences.

Once the most tightly closed part of Vietnam, the whole north is open to all and sundry. It would even be fair to say that the north is currently more open than the south – with the exception of Haiphong, police in the north are blessedly ignoring foreigners.

Around Hanoi

PAGODAS
Perfume Pagoda

The Perfume Pagoda (Chua Huong) is southwest of Hanoi, about 60 km by road. The pagoda is one of the highlights of the Hanoi area and should not be missed. Getting to the pagoda requires a journey first by road and then by river. The return boat trip along the scenic waterways takes about three hours and is good fun.

The Perfume Pagoda itself is a complex of pagodas and Buddhist shrines built into the limestone cliffs of Huong Tich Mountain (the Mountain of the Fragrant Traces). Among the better known sites here are Thien Chu (Pagoda Leading to Heaven); Giai Oan Chu (Purgatorial Pagoda), where the faithful believe deities purify souls, cure sufferings and grant offspring to childless families; and Huong Tich Chu (Pagoda of the Perfumed Vestige).

Great numbers of Buddhist pilgrims come here during a festival that begins in the middle of the second lunar month and lasts until the last week of the third lunar month;

these dates usually end up corresponding to March and April. Pilgrims and other visitors spend their time here boating, hiking and exploring the caves. Despite the occasionally large number of visitors, this place has a peaceful and perhaps holy atmosphere.

If you want to do the river trip (highly recommended!), you need to travel from Hanoi by car for two hours to My Duc, then take a small boat rowed by two women for 1½ hours to the foot of the mountain. From where the boat lets you off, you have about a four-km (two-hour) walk up to the main pagoda area. The scenery is comparable to Halong Bay, though here you are on a river rather than by the sea. The combined fee for the boat journey and general admission ticket is US$7, and there is no way to bargain around this as the price is set by the government. The return trip to your vehicle is also by rowboat.

Some of the cafes in Hanoi book day trips to the Perfume Pagoda for US$15, which is a good deal.

Thay Pagoda

Thay Pagoda (the Master's Pagoda), also known as Thien Phuc (Heavenly Blessing), is dedicated to Thich Ca Buddha (Sakyamuni, the historical Buddha) and 18 *arhats* (monks who have attained Nirvana); the latter appear on the central altar. On the left is a statue of the 12th-century monk Tu Dao Hanh, the 'Master' after whom the pagoda is named; on the right is a statue of King Ly Nhan Tong, who is believed to be a reincarnation of Tu Dao Hanh. In front of the pagoda is a small stage built on stilts in the middle of a pond; water-puppet shows are staged here during festivals.

The pagoda's annual festival is held from the fifth to the seventh days of the third lunar month. Pilgrims and other visitors enjoy watching water-puppet shows, hiking and exploring caves in the area.

Thay Pagoda is about 40 km south-west

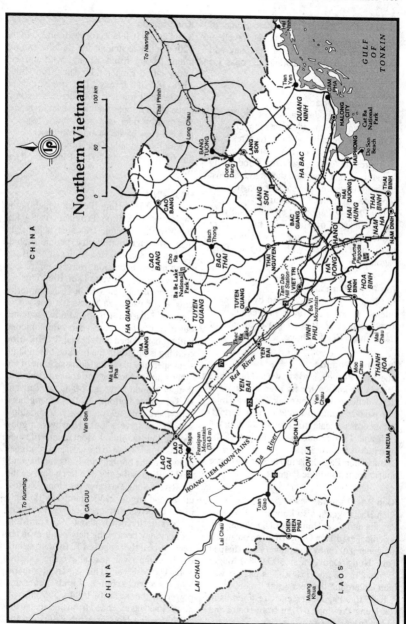

of Hanoi in Ha Tay Province. Some of Hanoi's cafes catering to budget travellers offer combined day tours of the Thay and Tay Phuong (see next listing) pagodas for US$10.

Tay Phuong Pagoda

Tay Phuong Pagoda (Pagoda of the West), also known as Sung Phuc Pagoda, consists of three parallel single-level structures built on a hillock said to resemble a buffalo. The 76 figures carved from jackfruit wood, many from the 18th century, are the pagoda's most celebrated feature. The earliest construction here dates from the 8th century.

Tay Phuong Pagoda is approximately 40 km south-west of Hanoi in Tay Phuong hamlet, Ha Tay Province. A visit here can easily be combined with a stop at Thay Pagoda.

Van Phuc Pagoda

Van Phuc Pagoda, surrounded by hills considered noteworthy for their beauty, was founded in 1037. It is 27 km north-east of Hanoi in Ha Bac Province.

Buc Thap Pagoda

Buc Thap Pagoda, also known as Ninh Phuc Pagoda, is known for its four-storey stone stupa dedicated to the monk Chuyet Cong. The pagoda's date of founding is uncertain, but records indicate that it was rebuilt in the 17th and 18th centuries; the layout of the structure is traditional.

Buc Thap Pagoda is in Ha Bac Province not far from Van Phuc Pagoda.

Kiep Bac Pagoda

Kiep Bac Pagoda, also known as Ho Quoc Pagoda and Tran Hung Dao Dai Vuong Tu, is dedicated to Tran Quoc Tuan, an outstanding general of renowned bravery who helped Tran Hung Dao defeat 300,000 Mongol invaders in the mid-1280s. The pagoda was founded around the year 1300.

Kiep Bac Pagoda, recently restored, is in Hai Hung Province 61 km from Hanoi and 32 km from Bac Ninh.

Keo Pagoda

Keo Pagoda (Chua Keo) was founded in the 12th century to honour the Buddha and the monk Khong Minh Khong, who miraculously cured Emperor Ly Than Ton (ruled 1128-38) of leprosy. The finely carved wooden bell tower is considered a masterpiece of traditional Vietnamese architecture. The nearby dike is a good place to get a general view of the pagoda complex.

Keo Pagoda is in Thai Binh Province 9.5 km from the town of Thai Binh near Thai Bac.

HOA BINH

The city of Hoa Binh (Peace), which is the capital of Hoa Binh Province, is 74 km south-west of Hanoi. This area is home to many Montagnard (hill tribe) people, including Muong and Tai. Hoa Binh can be visited on an all-day excursion from Hanoi, or as a stop on the long drive to Dien Bien Phu.

Unfortunately, Hoa Binh is the minority village for packaged tours. It's not yet as commercialised as Chiang Mai in Thailand, but give it a few more years and someone will probably open a McDonald's. Hill-tribe clothing is on sale in the market, but in large sizes specially made for tourists. Some of the other genuine Montagnard souvenirs look as if they should have a 'Made in Taiwan' sticker on the bottom. All this having been said, there's no reason why you shouldn't stop in and have a look. However, a good look at the traditional Montagnard lifestyle begins about 50 km to the west and continues right up to the border with Laos and beyond.

Hoa Binh is the site of a large dam on the Da River (Song Da), creating Song Da Reservoir, the largest in Vietnam. The flooding of the Da River displaced a large number of farmers upstream for about 200 km. More farmers may be seeking new pastures in ten years' time if the proposed Ta Bu dam is built on the same river, just above the existing Song Da Reservoir. This is part of a major hydroelectric scheme which generates power for the north. In 1994 a 500-kilovolt power line was extended from this area to the south, freeing Ho Chi Minh City from the seasonal power shortages that often blacked out the city for up to three days at a time.

BA VI MOUNTAIN

Ba Vi Mountain (elevation 1287 metres) is about 65 km west of Hanoi. There is a spectacular view of the Red River valley from the summit.

TAM DAO HILL STATION

Tam Dao Hill Station (elevation 930 metres), known to the French as the Cascade d'Argent (Silver Cascade), was founded by the French in 1907 as a place of escape from the heat of the Red River Delta.

Unfortunately, the grand colonial villas are run-down and many have been replaced by politically correct Soviet-inspired concrete-box architecture. However, there is now a belated effort being made to restore the colonial villas. The Vietnamese regard Tao Dao as the 'Dalat of the north', but foreigners often give it the thumbs down. However, one young couple wrote:

We thought this was the highlight of our trip. This place is really damp, we had to scrape the mushrooms off our sheets and clothes will stay wet. Perhaps we went at the wrong time of year, but in early April the clouds just drift right in through the open windows into your room...Tam Dao has no nightlife, but for sheer atmosphere you can't beat it. There is a grand stone staircase at the back leading up to a radio transmitter. Over towards the waterfall another path comes out on a wide area of ruins and great balustrades looking over the valley. It's like Babylon or something. The people are very friendly and there are not many tourists...We went to Tam Dao to watch birds, and it is an excellent place to do so.

Tim Woodward & Phaik Hua Tan

Our experience was decidedly less enthralling. If you're living in Hanoi and would like to find a summer weekend retreat, it might be worth coming up here for the cool weather and a change of pace. However, travellers with limited time in Vietnam will almost certainly prefer to spend their precious holidays relaxing someplace else.

The three summits of Tam Dao Mountain, all about 1400 metres in height, are visible from the hill station to the north-east. Many hill-tribe people live in the Tam Dao region, though they are largely assimilated. The best times of the year to visit Tam Dao are generally from late May to mid-September and from mid-December to February.

Dampness makes the Tam Dao area particularly rich in flora and fauna. However, logging (both legal and otherwise) has had an impact on the environment.

Remember that it is cool up in Tam Dao, and that this part of Vietnam has a distinct winter. Come prepared.

Places to Stay

The *Tam Dao Hotel* (Khach San Tam Dao; ☎ 306) is the main place for foreigners to stay.

Places to Eat

The restaurants in Tam Dao all have the same menu, written in the same handwriting. The chief items are fried or grilled deer, roast squirrel and roast silver pheasant. The latter delicacy is not yet considered an endangered species but will likely be one soon, so please don't order it!

Getting There & Away

Tam Dao Hill Station is 85 km north-west of Hanoi in Vinh Phu Province. Public transport is a problem. First, you must take a bus from Kim Ma Bus Station (west of the city centre) to Vinh Yen – the last one leaves at 1 pm. From there you must hire a motorcycle (about US$2) or taxi for the 24-km single-lane track that leads up to Tam Dao. There is a toll for using this road – about US$0.30 for motorbikes or US$1.50 for cars. In addition, you pay US$1.50 per person for an insurance policy, a very official looking thing in English (it covers you for shipping the corpse back, etc). A barrier across the road marks the toll gate, which is several km up the track.

Probably the easiest way to reach Tam Dao is to simply rent your own motorbike in Hanoi and drive yourself.

A few tour agencies in Hanoi run day trips to Tam Dao for as little as US$15 per person.

Taxi drivers typically ask something like US$45 to bring you to Tam Dao from Hanoi, and perhaps US$30 to come back and pick you up a few days later. It should be possible to bargain something cheaper.

If you're going to Ba Be Lake, you could easily arrange a stopoff in Tam Dao for a little extra money. This might be the wisest option.

North-East Vietnam

HAIPHONG

Haiphong, Vietnam's third most populous city, is the north's main industrial centre and one of the country's most important seaports. Greater Haiphong has an area of 1515 sq km and a population of 1,300,000; Haiphong proper covers 21 sq km and is home to 370,000 souls.

The French took possession of Haiphong, then a small market town, in 1874. The city soon became a major port; industrial concerns were established here in part because of the proximity of coal supplies.

One of the immediate causes of the Franco-Viet Minh War was the infamous French bombardment of the 'native quarters' of Haiphong in 1946, in which hundreds of civilians were killed and injured (a contemporary French account estimated civilian deaths at 'no more than 6000').

Haiphong came under American air and naval attacks between 1965 and 1972. In May 1972, President Nixon ordered the mining of Haiphong harbour to cut the flow of Soviet military supplies to North Vietnam. As part of the Paris Cease-Fire Agreements of 1973, the USA agreed to help clear the mines from Haiphong harbour; 10 US Navy minesweepers were involved in the effort.

Since the late 1970s, Haiphong has seen a massive outflux of refugees, including many ethnic Chinese, who have taken with them much of the city's fishing fleet.

In spite of being a major port and one of Vietnam's largest cities, Haiphong today is a sleepy place with little traffic and many dilapidated buildings. On the other hand, this port city does have the potential to develop rapidly. A Haiphong travel pamphlet has this to say about the city's aspirations for the future:

Nowadays Haiphong is one of the creative and active cities in the socialist construction and in the defence of the socialist country. The people in Haiphong are sparing no effort to build it both into a modern port city with developed industry and agriculture and a centre of import and export, tourism and attendance and at the same time an iron fortress against foreign invasion.

Orientation

It's important to keep in mind that there are two railway stations within the city limits of Haiphong. The Thuong Li Railway Station is in the west part of the city, far from the centre. The Haiphong Railway Station is right in the city centre; this is the last stop for the train coming from Hanoi and this is where you should get off.

Information

Tourist Office Vietnam Tourism (☎ 42957; fax 42974) at 12 Le Dai Hanh St is ready, willing and able to take your money if you'd like to book a trip to Cat Ba or Halong Bay. Don't expect too much in the way of information though.

Money Vietcombank (Ngan Hang Ngoai Thuong Viet Nam; ☎ 42658; fax 41117) is at 11 Hoang Dieu St, not far from the GPO.

Post & Telecommunications The GPO is at 3 Nguyen Tri Phuong St (corner Hoang Van Thu St).

Emergency If you need medical treatment, you'd do better if you get yourself to Hanoi. Otherwise, some places to try include the Traditional Medicine Hospital (Benh Vien Dong Y) on Nguyen Duc Canh St and the Vietnam-Czech Friendship Hospital (Benh Vien Viet-Tiep) on Nha Thuong St.

Warning The police have set up a permanent checkpoint on the north bank of the Cam

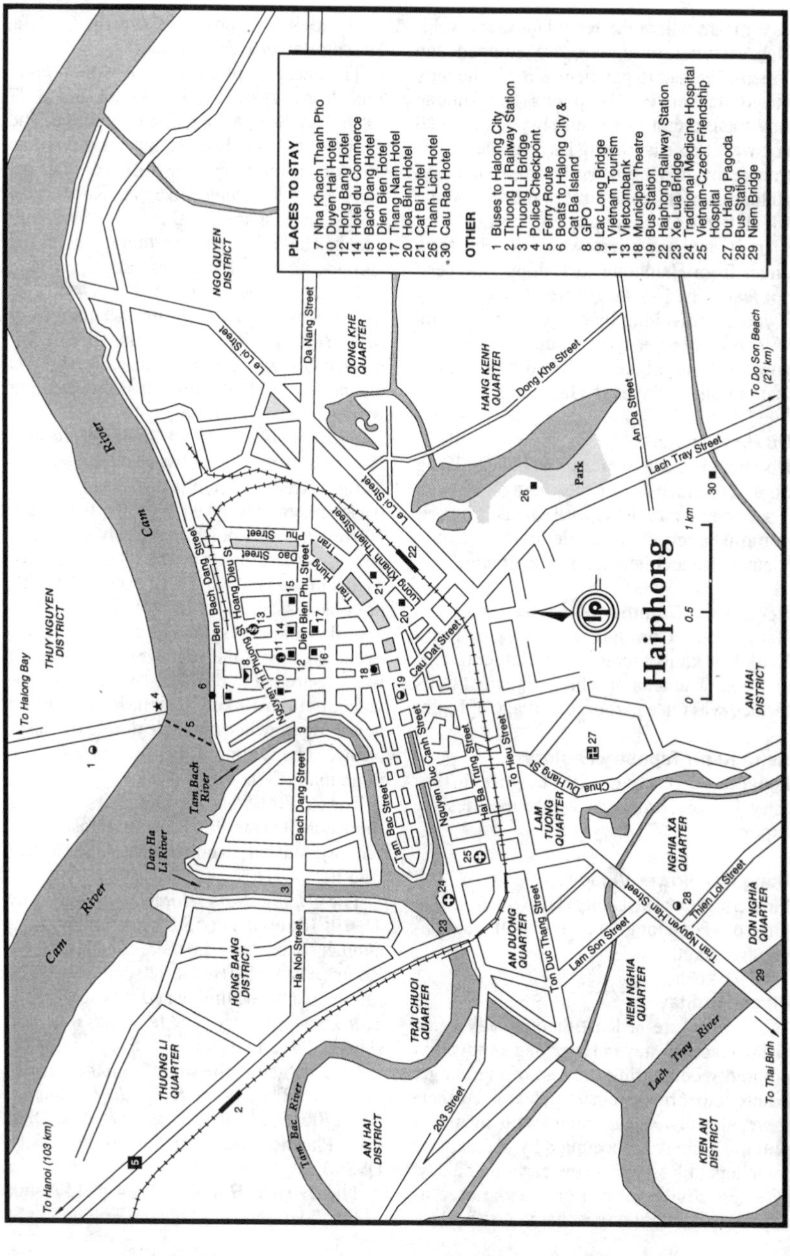

Haiphong
PLACES TO STAY
7 Nha Khach Thanh Pho
10 Duyen Hai Hotel
12 Hong Bang Hotel
14 Hotel du Commerce
15 Bach Dang Hotel
16 Dien Bien Hotel
17 Thang Nam Hotel
20 Hoa Binh Hotel
21 Cat Bi Hotel
26 Thanh Lich Hotel
30 Cau Rao Hotel
OTHER
1 Buses to Halong City
2 Thuong Li Railway Station
3 Thuong Li Bridge
4 Police Checkpoint
5 Ferry Route
6 Boats to Halong City & Cat Ba Island
8 GPO
9 Lac Long Bridge
11 Vietnam Tourism
13 Vietcombank
18 Municipal Theatre
19 Bus Station
22 Haiphong Railway Station
23 Xe Lua Bridge
24 Traditional Medicine Hospital
25 Vietnam-Czech Friendship Hospital
27 Du Hang Pagoda
28 Bus Station
29 Niem Bridge
To Halong Bay
THUY NGUYEN DISTRICT
NGO QUYEN DISTRICT
DONG KHE QUARTER
HANG KENH QUARTER
AN HAI DISTRICT
LAM TUONG QUARTER
NGHIA XA QUARTER
DON NGHIA QUARTER
NIEM NGHIA QUARTER
AN DUONG QUARTER
TRAI CHUOI QUARTER
HONG BANG DISTRICT
THUONG LI QUARTER
KIEN AN DISTRICT
Cam River
Tam Bach River
Dao Ha Li River
Lach Tray River
Park
To Hanoi (103 km)
To Thai Binh
To Do Son Beach (21 km)
0 0.5 1 km

River right where the ferry lands, and vehicles carrying foreigners are stopped and 'fined'. We had to pay here. This is the only bus route between Haiphong and Halong Bay and is therefore extremely popular. If all you want to see is Halong Bay, you can avoid trouble by driving directly from Hanoi to Halong Bay (there is a more northern route which bypasses Haiphong entirely).

Individual travellers who take the ferry direct from Haiphong to Halong Bay need not fear – the problem currently exists only if you are travelling by car, van or bus. You will *probably* not have trouble if you ride your own motorbike, but we didn't test out that option ourselves in Haiphong.

Du Hang Pagoda

Du Hang Pagoda, which is at 121 Du Hang St, was founded three centuries ago. Though it has been rebuilt several times since, it remains a good example of traditional Vietnamese architecture and sculpture.

Hang Kenh Communal House

Hang Kenh Communal House on Hang Kenh St is known for its 500 relief sculptures in wood. The area in which the structure is located was once part of the village of Kenh.

Hang Kenh Tapestry Factory

Founded 65 years ago, the Hang Kenh Tapestry Factory produces wool tapestries for export.

Dang Hai Flower Village

Flowers grown at Dang Hai, which is five km from Haiphong, are sold on the international market.

Places to Stay

While there are at least theoretically some cheap places to stay in Haiphong, renovation is rapidly converting the last of the budget hotels into pricey tourist palaces. Furthermore, the few cheap rooms still available will most likely be occupied by Vietnamese travellers unless you arrive early in the day. The best advice we can give about accommodation in Haiphong is that you should try

to avoid it – if possible, stay in Cat Ba, Halong Bay or Hanoi instead.

The cheapest place in town is the *Thanh Lich Hotel* (☎ 47361; 18 rooms). It's at 47 Lach Tray St in a park-like compound, and the only real drawback is that it's more than one km from the centre. Still, you can get there by cyclo or motorbike taxi. Rooms cost US$8 with shared bath, or US$12 with attached bath. There is a restaurant inside the compound, though it closes early.

The *Nha Khach Thanh Pho* (☎ 42524; nine rooms) is just opposite the main ferry pier on the Cam River. All rooms for foreigners cost US$25. The staff is friendly, and you can amuse or abuse yourself in the evening with a karaoke machine.

The *Hoa Binh Hotel* (☎ 46907; 19 rooms) is across from the railway station at 104 Luong Khanh Thien St. It was once a backpackers' haven, with rooms for US$6. However, it was being massively expanded during our last visit, and the total number of rooms in the new wing will exceed 100. It's possible that cheap prices will still prevail for a while in the existing old wing, but don't count on that – the manager we talked to wasn't sure if the old wing would be renovated, but most likely it will. Prices for the new wing were not available during our visit, but we'd be willing to bet that they will be more than US$6.

The *Cat Bi Hotel* (☎ 46306; fax 45181; 22 rooms) at 30 Tran Phu St is also close to the railway station. Rooms cost US$15 and US$30.

The *Thang Nam Hotel* (☎ 42818; fax 41019; 18 rooms) at 55 Dien Bien Phu St is another place that is theoretically cheap. Rooms cost US$10 to US$20, but the US$10 rooms are few in number and are usually full. Still it's worth a try. The hotel has a beauty shop and a restaurant.

Directly across the street from the foregoing is the French-era *Hotel du Commerce* (☎ 42706; fax 42560; 35 rooms) at 62 Dien Bien Phu St. The tariff here is US$25 to US$40.

The *Duyen Hai Hotel* (☎ 42157; fax 41140; 33 rooms) at 5 Nguyen Tri Phuong St has one single room costing US$23. Everything else costs US$30 to US$35.

The *Bach Dang Hotel* (☎ 42444; 21 rooms), 42 Dien Bien Phu St, has rooms covering a wide price range from US$17 to US$45.

The *Hong Bang Hotel* (☎ 42229; fax 41044; 29 rooms), 64 Dien Bien Phu St, costs US$39 for a double room equipped with bath, refrigerator and colour TV, or else pay US$65 for the deluxe rooms. The hotel has a restaurant, steam bath and massage services.

The *Dien Bien Hotel* (☎ 4..64; fax 42977; 20 rooms) is a new place at 67 Dien Bien Phu St. The hotel's name will probably not enthral French travellers, but the rooms are OK and cost US$25 to US$40.

About two km south of the centre on the highway to Do Son Beach is the *Cau Rao Hotel* (☎ 47021; fax 47586; 60 rooms). It's a quiet but pleasant place, but not much English is spoken. Doubles cost US$10 to US$40. The address is officially 460 Lach Tray St.

Places to Eat

Haiphong is noted for its excellent fresh seafood, which is available from every hotel restaurant.

Getting There & Away

Air Vietnam Airlines flies the Haiphong-Ho Chi Minh City route twice daily. There are also three flights weekly between Haiphong and Danang.

Bus You can catch Hanoi-Haiphong mini-buses throughout the day from Hang Thung St, on the corner of Tran Quang Kha St. Departures are approximately from 5 am until 6 pm, and the journey takes around 2½ hours. These minibuses depart only when full and generally will be packed to the hilt.

Buses depart Haiphong for Halong City from a bus station in the Thuy Nguyen District (north bank of the Cam River). To reach the Thuy Nguyen District, you must take a ferry (see Haiphong map).

Train Haiphong is not on the main railway line between Hanoi and Ho Chi Minh City, but there is a spur line connecting it to Hanoi. There are now four trains daily on the Hanoi-Haiphong route. Departures from Hanoi are as follows:

Depart Hanoi	Arrive Haiphong
4.30 am	8.50 am
8.35 am	11.20 am
12.10 pm	4.55 pm
2.35 pm	5.50 pm

Car Haiphong is 103 km from Hanoi on National Highway 5. There are a number of bridge crossings where motor vehicles, bicycles, pedestrians and pushcarts share the bridge with trains. The bridges are only single-lane, which means the two-way traffic has to alternate and everyone has to get off the bridge when a train comes. The result is long delays. Allow at least 2½ to three hours for the one-way Hanoi-Haiphong trip. The round-trip fare by car will be at least US$60.

Boat Being a major sea and river port, Haiphong is well connected to the rest of Vietnam by ferry. The boats tend to be slow and none too comfortable, but they certainly are cheap. You can even get to Hanoi by boat, but it's so ridiculously slow that even the poorest Vietnamese seldom travel this way. The ferries most used by travellers are the one to Halong City East and Cat Ba Island.

The boat schedule changes frequently, so it's no use presenting it here. For some destinations, boats go only once or twice weekly. A trip to Ho Chi Minh City by boat would take at least a week, possibly require a few changes of boats and could be done for as little as US$10. Some possible destinations in northern Vietnam include:

Cat Ba, Dan Tien, Do Luong, Ha Tinh, Hanoi, Hong Gai, Nam Dinh, Ninh Binh, Phu Ly, Thai Binh, Thanh Hoa, Vinh

DO SON BEACH

The palm-shaded beach at Do Son, 21 km south-east of central Haiphong, is the most popular seaside resort in the north and a favourite of Hanoi's expatriate community. The hilly four-km-long promontory ends with a string of islets. The peninsula's nine hills are known as the Cuu Long Son (Nine Dragons).

The town is famous for its ritual buffalo fights, which are held annually on the 10th day of the eighth lunar month, the date on which the leader of an 18th-century peasant rebellion here was killed.

More recently, the town has become famous for the first casino to open in Vietnam since 1975. This joint venture between the government and a Hong Kong company started operations in October 1994 and it remains to be seen just how successful it will be. Foreigners are permitted to lose their fortunes here, but Vietnamese are barred from entering the casino.

Places to Stay & Eat

The *Van Hoa Hotel* at the very tip of the peninsula offers good views but a long walk to the beach. The hotel is built in Disneyland-style decor with two turrets – you almost expect to see someone walking around in a Mickey Mouse suit. Rooms are cheap at US$10.

The *Hai Au Hotel* (☎ 61272; fax 61176) is a plush place next to the new casino. Rooms begin at US$25.

Some other places to try include the *Do Son Hotel*, *Hoa Phuong Hotel* and *Khach San Cong Doan*.

Cheap and good restaurants line the beachfront.

CAT BA NATIONAL PARK

About half of Cat Ba Island (whose total area is 354 sq km) and 90 sq km of adjacent inshore waters were declared a national park in 1986 in order to protect the island's diverse ecosystems. These include tropical evergreen forests on the hills, freshwater swamp forests at the base of the hills, coastal mangrove forests, small freshwater lakes, sandy beaches and offshore coral reefs. The main beaches are Cai Vieng, Hong Xoai Be and Hong Xoai Lon.

Cat Ba is a charming island and Vietnam's

most beautiful national park. There are numerous lakes, waterfalls and grottoes in the spectacular limestone hills, the highest of which rises 331 metres above sea level. The growth of the vegetation is stunted near the summits because of high winds. The largest permanent body of water on the island is Ech Lake, which covers an area of three hectares. Almost all of the surface streams are seasonal; most of the Cat Ba's rainwater flows into caves, following underground streams to the sea and resulting in a severe shortage of fresh water during the dry season. Though parts of the interior of the island are below sea level, most of the island is between 50 and 200 metres in elevation.

The waters off Cat Ba Island are home to 200 species of fishes, 500 species of molluscs and 400 species of arthropods. Larger marine animals in the area include seals and three species of dolphin.

Stone tools and bones left by human beings who lived between 6000 and 7000 years ago have been found at 17 sites on the island. The most thoroughly studied site is Cai Beo Cave, discovered by a French archaeologist in 1938, which is 1.5 km from Cat Ba Village.

Today, the island's human population of 12,000 is concentrated in the southern part of the island, including the town of Cat Ba. They have traditionally lived from fishing, forest exploitation and agriculture, including the growing of rice, cassava, oranges, apples and lychees. However, tourism has suddenly arrived with a bang. Lots of new hotels, restaurants, karaokes and the like are being built. This should bring the island some prosperity, though the price paid may be a loss of tranquillity (at least in the towns).

During February, March and April, Cat Ba's weather is often cold and drizzly, though the temperature rarely falls below 10°C. During the summer months, tropical storms and typhoons are frequent.

Beaches

Much to the consternation of budget travellers, you must pass through a tunnel to reach the beaches from Cat Ba Village – there is a

US$2 charge for this and you must pay *every* time you pass through the tunnel, even if you do it several times in one day. If you stay at one of the government-run hotels, you can buy a pass for US$1 which allows multiple trips through the tunnel – most unfair to the private hotel owners who cannot get this concession for their customers.

The beach itself is beautiful – nice sand and crystal clear water. At the beach there is simple food available (French bread with drinks, etc). There are also six cabins here which can be rented for US$8 per night.

The beach is in a cove. Facing out towards the water, to your left is a pathway which you can follow to yet another beach. This one has fewer people, better shade and is recommended if you want to escape from the crowds (not that Cat Ba is very crowded yet).

National Park

Cat Ba Island is home to 15 types of mammals, such as the Francois monkey *(Presbytis francoisi poliocephalus)*, wild boar *(Sus scrofa)*, deer, squirrel and hedgehog; 21 species of birds, including hawks, hornbills and cuckoos, have been sighted. Cat Ba lies on a major migration route for waterfowl (ducks, geese, shorebirds), who feed and roost in the mangrove forests and on the beaches. The 620 species of plants recorded on Cat Ba include 118 timber species and 160 plants with medicinal value. One traveller writes:

The importance of treating national park staff with respect was born out on Cat Ba Island. Here, I turned up at the park's headquarters with three others, two of whom annoyed the only available guide by their lack of deference. Feeling offended, the guide claimed it was too dangerous to go very far (the drizzle made the rocks slippery) and then said he was too tired to go and had a headache.

You pay US$1 admission to the park, and the services of a guide cost US$3 regardless of group size. A guide is not mandatory but definitely recommended – otherwise, all you are likely to see is a bunch of trees. The guide will take you on a walk through a cave, but bring a torch (flashlight).

To reach the national park there are minibuses in the morning leaving from the hotels, and the one-way trip takes 30 minutes and should cost US$0.50. It's best you negotiate directly with the minibus drivers, not with the various restaurants and hotels, which seem to overcharge for tickets. Pay for only a one-way trip and tell the driver you'll pay again for the return journey. There have been lots of complaints:

We paid US$1 per person and there was no doubt that we had paid for a return-trip ticket. But when the minibus returned in the afternoon, we were confronted by a *very* aggressive driver and his assistant. They wanted US$1 more per person. We refused, not so much because of the amount of money but because we objected to being charged double what had been previously agreed upon. We eventually found another minibus to bring us back (for US$0.50 each, of course).

Despite this unpleasantness (it's always money, money), the park *is* worth seeing and we all had a great time. I spent a week in Cat Ba and would go back in a minute.

Holger Jensen

Places to Stay

There are three hotels in Cat Ba Village. All are fairly noisy due to adjacent karaokes and the drone of generators, which operate from around 6.30 pm until 9.30 pm. Rumour has it that next year the electricity will be on for 24 hours – hopefully, this does not mean that those infernal generators will run all night! There is also a fair amount of construction going on at present, and no word on just when this might end.

One is simply called *Mini-Hotel* and costs US$3 to US$5 per night. Rooms are clean and the owner speaks good English.

Another hotel is called *Family House* and offers the same standard as the Mini-Hotel but costs US$6. This place has nice views.

The third hotel is designated the *Cat Ba Hotel*, which belongs to the government. It costs US$6.

There is a construction site where a major fourth hotel is being built. This one is supposed to be luxurious, but no word yet on room prices.

The new government hotel (a little out of town along the sea wall) may have a nice location but is run by a horrible woman and her employees are not much better. The manager even took our rented motorcycle and returned it later in the day empty of petrol!

Alfred F Hogenauer

Places to Eat

We found *Restaurant Huu Dung* to be quite all right, but it's just one of many similar places. While no restaurant in Cat Ba Village yet distinguishes itself, one recurring feature is the presence of rats on the island which invade restaurant kitchens. Many travellers have gotten sick from the food – whether this is due to contamination by rat faeces or sloppy food storage is uncertain. Either way, stick to food that is well cooked.

Getting There & Away

Cat Ba National Park is 133 km from Hanoi and 30 km east of Haiphong. A boat to Cat Ba departs from Haiphong every day at 1.30 pm and returns the next day at 6 am; the trip takes about 3½ hours and costs US$1.40. The park headquarters is at Trung Trang.

An alternative (though not recommended) way to reach Cat Ba is via the island of Cat Hai, which is closer to Haiphong. A boat departs Haiphong for Cat Hai, makes a brief stop and continues on to the port of Fulong on Cat Ba Island. A bus connects Fulong to Cat Ba Village, a distance of 30 km.

It might seem logical to hire a private boat from Halong City to drop you off in Cat Ba after you've toured Halong Bay. Unfortunately, the Haiphong sea police do not permit this because Halong Bay is in a 'rival' province.

Getting Around

Beware – there is more than one pier on the island. One is near Cat Ba Village (which is where most travellers want to go) and the other is at Fulong some 30 km away. At either pier, there should be a bus waiting to take you to Cat Ba Village, but the price will depend on which pier you are at. From the Cat Ba pier it takes approximately 30 minutes to walk the only road on the island,

though the minibus ride is recommended. From the other pier it costs US$1 for the bus. Motorbikes can take you to the pier on the morning of your departure – hopeful drivers line up their bikes at likely places near the hotels.

Russian motorbikes are available for rent in the town for US$1.50 per hour or US$5 per day.

Hotels and restaurants book boat tours around the island. You won't have to look very hard for these as the boat owners will come looking for you. You cannot get a boat from Cat Ba to take you on cruises to nearby Halong Bay. The former is in Haiphong municipality while the latter is in Quang Ninh Province – the marine police of these two jurisdictions are involved in virtual warfare and boat owners will not risk crossing the political boundary.

HALONG BAY

Magnificent Halong Bay, with its 3,000 islands rising from the clear, emerald waters of the Gulf of Tonkin, is one of the natural marvels of Vietnam. Visitors have compared the area's magical landscape of carboniferous chalk islets to Guilin, China, and Krabi in southern Thailand. These tiny islands are dotted with innumerable beaches and grottoes created by the wind and the waves.

The name Ha Long means 'Where the Dragon Descends into the Sea'. Legend has it that the islands of Halong Bay were created by a great dragon who lived in the mountains. As it ran towards the coast, its flailing tail gouged out valleys and crevasses; as it plunged into the sea, the areas dug up by the tail became filled with water, leaving only bits of high land visible.

The dragon may be legend, but sailors in the Halong Bay region have often reported sightings of a mysterious marine creature of gargantuan proportions known as the Tarasque. More paranoid elements of the military suspect it's an imperialist spy submarine, while eccentric foreigners believe they have discovered Vietnam's own version of the Loch Ness monster. Meanwhile, the monster or whatever it is continues to haunt

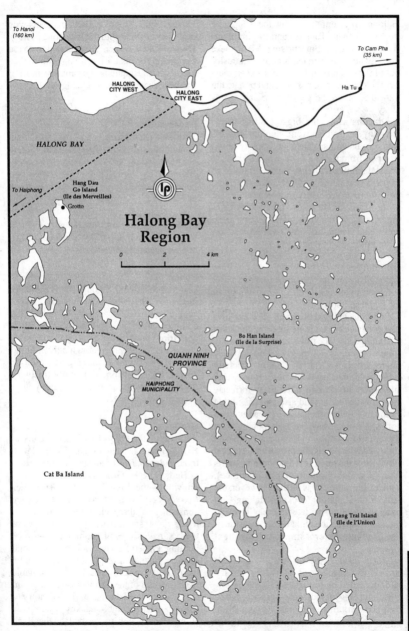

To Hanoi
(160 km)

To Cam Pha
(35 km)

HALONG
CITY WEST

HALONG
CITY EAST

Ha Tu

HALONG BAY

To Haiphong

Hang Dau
Go Island
(Ile des Merveilles)

Grotto

**Halong Bay
Region**

0   2   4 km

Bo Han Island
(Ile de la Surprise)

QUANH NINH
PROVINCE

HAIPHONG
MUNICIPALITY

Cat Ba Island

Hang Trai Island
(Ile de l'Union)

Halong Bay, unfettered by the Haiphong police, Vietnam Tourism and the Immigration authorities. Enterprising Vietnamese boat owners have made a cottage industry out of the creature, offering cash-laden tourists the chance to rent a junk and pursue the Tarasque before he gets fed up and swims away.

Dragons aside, the biggest threat to the bay may be from souvenir-hunting tourists. Rare corals and seashells are rapidly being stripped from the sea floor, while stalactites and stalagmites are being broken off from the caves. These items get turned into key rings, paperweights and ashtrays, which are on sale in the souvenir shops of Halong City. You might consider the virtue of not buying these items and spending your cash instead on postcards and silk paintings.

Orientation

Halong Bay and its numerous islands sprawl out over an area of 1500 sq km, right up to the Chinese border.

Food, accommodation and all other life-support systems are to be found in the town of Halong City. The town is bisected by a bay – the west side was formerly called Bai Chay (many still call it that) but is now officially called 'Halong City West'. A short ferry ride takes you to Halong City East, formerly known as Hon Gai (and also still called that by locals). Accommodation can be found on both sides of the bay, but Halong City West is more scenic, closer to Hanoi and more well endowed with hotels and restaurants. Halong City East is the main port district and exports coal (a major product of this province), which means the city is dirtier. However, the ferry from Haiphong docks in Halong City East, so if you arrive late you may just find it easier to spend the night on the east side of the bay before crossing over the next morning.

Much farther afield (near the Chinese border) is a beach resort at Tra Co, but it's seldom visited by foreigners.

Halong Bay straddles the border between Haiphong municipality and Quang Ninh Province. Halong City itself is safely in Quang Ninh Province (which means you don't have to deal with the Haiphong police). However, boat owners are reluctant to go too far south for fear of running into police patrols from Haiphong. Fortunately, most of the best scenery lies in Quang Ninh Province.

Information

Tourist Office There is an office of Quang Ninh Tourism (Cong Ty Du Lich Quang Ninh; ☎ 46318, 46321) on Bai Chai St in Halong City West. This agency owns two hotels and can inform you about boat tours and the like.

Money Vietcombank has plans to open a branch soon in Halong City. The location has not yet been determined.

Beach

The 'beach' around Halong City is basically mud and rock, with very calm water. It's not at all attractive for swimming. However, it's common practice to take a swim during a boat trip – the boats can take you to remote coves with clear water, though only minimal sand. If you do go swimming, it would be wise to have someone (hopefully trustworthy) watch your valuables while you're cavorting in the water.

Grottoes

Because of the type of rock the islands of Halong Bay consist of, the area is dotted with thousands of caves of all sizes and shapes.

Hang Dau Go (Grotto of Wooden Stakes), known to the French as the Grotte des Merveilles (Cave of Marvels), is a huge cave consisting of three chambers, which you reach via 90 steps. Among the stalactites of the first hall, scores of gnomes appear to be holding a meeting. The walls of the second chamber sparkle if bright light is shined on them. The cave derives its Vietnamese name from the third of the chambers, which is said to have been used during the 13th century to store the sharp bamboo stakes which Tran Hung Dao planted in the bed of the Bach

BRENDAN McCARTHY

Fishing boat in Halong Bay

Dang River to impale Kublai Khan's invasion fleet.

Drum Grotto is so named because, as the wind blows through its many stalactites and stalagmites, visitors think they hear the sound of distant drumbeats. Other well-known caves in Halong Bay include the Grotto of Bo Nau and two-km-long Hang Hanh Cave.

Islands

Some tourist boats stop at Deu (Reu) Island, which supports an unusual species of monkey distinguished by its red buttocks. A few travellers also visit Ngoc Vung Island, which has a red brick lighthouse.

Tuan Chau is another island in Halong Bay which is open to tourists. Ho Chi Minh's former summer residence is here.

Organised Tours

Vietnam Tourism in Hanoi offers rather expensive three-day tours to Halong Bay and travellers have been generally dissatisfied with these. There are heaps of private travel agencies in Hanoi which can do better – compare prices before signing on the dotted line and handing over any cash.

For budget travellers, the best deals are the tours offered through the various cafes in Hanoi. Prices for a two-day excursion (including hotel and boat trips) costs around US$25. You could hardly do it yourself for less.

However, we have also had numerous complaints about minibus tours. The complaint is basically that the minibus doesn't materialise after it's been paid for – the cafe simply books everybody onto a large bus tour with another agency and refunds are refused.

Places to Stay

Trying to do Halong Bay as a day trip from Hanoi is damn near impossible, but a few brave souls have actually done it. It's far more sensible to spend at least one night, and most people prefer two nights.

Some foreigners have reckoned that they could sleep on the boats down by the pier. However, the Halong City police object to this, both to prevent robberies and protect the hotel industry.

THE NORTH

PLACES TO STAY

8 Thanh Nien Hotel
10 Postal Hotel
12 Ngoc Mai Mini-Hotel
13 Thu Thuy Mini-Hotel
14 Phuong Vi Mini-Hotel
15 Sun Flowers Mini-Hotel
16 Van Nam Mini-Hotel
17 Hoa Binh (Peace) Hotel
18 Hai Trang Hotel
19 Thanh Lien Hotel
20 Vina Lyn Hotel
21 Suoi May Hotel
22 Rose Hotel
23 Cuu Long Hotel
24 Viet Nhat Hotel
25 Dung Tien Hotel
26 Tien Long Hotel

PLACES TO EAT

1 Binh Minh Restaurant
2 Thang Hung Restaurant
3 Hai Long Restaurant
4 Thanh Lich Restaurant
5 Thanh Huong Restaurant
6 Phuong Vi Restarant
7 Phuong Oanh Restaurant
8 Dien Bun Thit Cho
(dog restaurant)
11 Ngoc Hoa Restaurant

Halong City West

Scale Unknown

Vuon Dao Street

To Van Hai Hotel & Ferry

To Outlying Hotels & Hanoi

The majority of travellers prefer to stay in Halong City West. There are now over 30 hotels here, with a new one opening up every month or so. Keen competition keeps prices down, though you will probably have to pay more in the peak summer travel season or during Tet.

Halong City West The hotels are found in two areas. The heaviest concentration is right in the town itself. Many other hotels are strung out for two km along the highway heading west of town (towards Hanoi). The following hotels are listed from west to east, which is the direction most travellers take when approaching Halong City.

Thang Long Hotel (☎ 46458; 18 rooms), two km west of the centre. All rooms have a view of the bay. Prices are US$9 to US$13.
Hai Yen Hotel (☎ 46270; 20 rooms). All rooms here cost US$19.
Hoang Long Hotel (☎ 46234; 20 rooms). Rooms cost US$15 and US$18.

Halong Hotel (☎ 46320; fax 46318; 110 rooms). Rooms cost US$60 to US$80.
Son Long Hotel (☎ 46274; 46318; 14 rooms). Singles are US$12 to US$22 and doubles are US$15 to US$25.
Vuon Dao Hotel (☎ 46427; fax 46287; 56 rooms). Rooms cost US$35 to US$45.
Suoi Mo Hotel (☎ 46381; fax 46729; 45 rooms). Rooms cost US$30 to US$40.

The largest hotel in the town centre itself is the *Postal Hotel* (Khach San Buu Dien; ☎ 46205; fax 46226; 33 rooms). The tariff here is US$30 to US$35.

Vuon Dao St in the town centre also has a solid row of mini-hotels with little to choose between them. Prices here are the lowest in Halong City, and most budget travellers head for this area. From west to east, the hotel line-up is as follows:

Thanh Nien Hotel. Rooms cost US$12.
Ngoc Mai Mini-Hotel (☎ 46123; eight rooms). Rooms cost US$11 to US$14.

Thu Thuy Mini-Hotel (☎ 46295; five rooms). Rooms are US$6 to US$9.

Phuong Vi Mini-Hotel. There are six rooms costing from US$7 to US$9. This one looks rather basic.

Sun Flowers Mini-Hotel (Khach San Hoa Huong Duong; ☎ 46153; four rooms), 14 Vuon Dao St. Rooms cost US$8 to US$10.

Van Nam Mini-Hotel (☎ 46593; five rooms). Rooms are US$8 to US$10.

Hoa Binh Hotel (Peace Hotel; ☎ 46009; 10 rooms). All rooms cost US$12.

Hai Trang Hotel (☎ 46094; six rooms). It's US$10 for a large room with air-con and hot water.

Thanh Lien Hotel. Rooms cost US$8 to US$10.

Vina Lyn Hotel. Rooms are US$10.

Suoi May Hotel (located on a side street). Rooms are US$8 to US$10.

Rose Hotel. Rooms are US$10 to US$12.

Cuu Long Hotel. Rooms cost US$8 and US$12.

Viet Nhat Hotel. All rooms are US$10.

Dung Tien Hotel. Rooms cost US$8 and US$9.

Up on the hill overlooking the town is the large *Tien Long Hotel* (☎ 46042; 47 rooms). The going rate here is US$22.

Right near the ferry pier is the upmarket *Van Hai Hotel*, where rooms start at US$30.

Halong City East Hotels are clustered along Le Thanh Tong St, which runs in a west-east axis. Starting from the ferry pier on the west

end of town, consider the following accommodation offerings:

South Hotel (Khach San Phuong Nam; ☎ 27242; 12 rooms). Rooms cost US$13 to US$25.

Hong Ngoc Hotel (☎ 26330; fax 26103; 16 rooms), 36A Le Thanh Tong St. Rooms cost US$25 and US$27.

Viet Anh Hotel (☎ 26243; eight rooms). Rooms cost US$8 and US$12.

Queen Hotel West (☎ 25689; eight rooms), 159 Le Thanh Tong St. Rooms cost US$12 and US$15.

Nha Nghi Hoa Thuy Tien (☎ 26297; six rooms), 193 Le Thanh Tong St. Rooms are US$10 and US$12.

Queen Hotel East (☎ 26193; 11 rooms), 70 Le Thanh Tong St. Rooms are US$20 to US$25.

Van Don Muoi Hotel (☎ 26279). Rooms cost US$10 to US$12.

Huong Duong Rest House (☎ 27269; six rooms), 82 Le Thanh Tong St. Rooms cost US$11 and US$13.

Thuong Mai Hotel (☎ 27258; nine rooms), 269 Le Thanh Tong St. Rooms are US$12 and US$15.

Places to Eat

The central area of Halong City West has a solid line of cheap restaurants, all good. Choices here include the *Binh Minh*, *Thang Hung*, *Hai Long*, *Thanh Lich*, *Thanh Huong*, *Phuong Vi* and *Phuong Oanh*.

Be aware that the *Dien Bun Thit Cho* is a

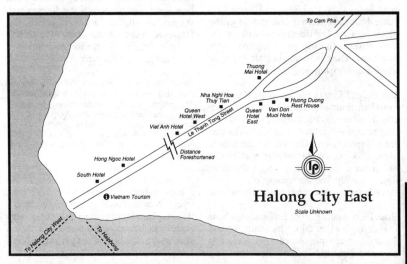

Halong City East

dogmeat restaurant. No English sign warns you of this and some travellers have unknowingly had Fido for dinner (most report that the food is good).

The *Ngoc Hao Restaurant* is relatively plush but not expensive and is recommended.

Getting There & Away

For well-heeled travellers, the usual way to get to Halong Bay is to take a car from Hanoi to Halong City, spend one night, take a boat tour the next day, spend another night in Halong City and then head back to Hanoi in the same car. Total time: three days.

For budget-minded backpackers, the usual method is to take a morning train from Hanoi to Haiphong, take the afternoon boat to Halong City (or spend the night in Haiphong), spend one night (at least) in Halong City, take a boat tour around the bay, and then take a minibus back to Hanoi or Haiphong. Minimum time: three days but usually more.

If you can find a group to share a car from Hanoi, this might be almost as economical as using public transport since you might save one night's accommodation in Haiphong.

Bus Buses from Haiphong to Halong City leave Haiphong from a bus station in the Thuy Nguyen District (north bank of the Cam River). The trip takes approximately two hours. The bus station in Halong City is about one km from the Halong Hotel.

Car Halong City is 160 km from Hanoi, 55 km from Haiphong and 45 km from Cam Pha. The one-way trip from Hanoi to Halong City by car takes at least three hours. The cost for a Hanoi-Halong City car (round-trip) is about US$100, and this price should include the driver's 'waiting time' (normally three days). Usually, you are responsible for your driver's food and accommodation expenses.

Boat Ferries depart from Haiphong harbour to Halong City East three times daily at 6 and 11 am, and at 4 pm (schedule is subject to change!). The trip takes three hours one way

and costs US$0.80. There are frequent ferries connecting Halong City East to nearby Halong City West.

Getting Around

Boat You won't see much unless you also take a boat to tour the islands and their grottoes. Cruises for a few hours up to a whole day are offered by private boat owners, travel agencies and the regional tourist office, and competition is fierce. Since the area to be cruised is large, it's advisable to have a fast boat in order to see more. The rare but romantic junks are very photogenic and can be hired as well, but are so slow on a calm day that they hardly seem to be moving.

You needn't rent a whole boat for yourself – there are plenty of other foreigners who wouldn't mind getting together a small sightseeing group and it's even possible to go with a group of Vietnamese. A mid-sized boat can hold six to 12 persons and costs around US$6 per hour. Larger boats can hold 50 to 100 persons and cost US$10 to US$20 per hour. The large boats are government-owned, while the small ones are private.

Note that there has been at least one reported pirate-style robbery from a small boat involving weapons – the foreign passengers lost all their money, passports, etc. However, most thefts are likely to be snatch-and-run style, much like the motorbikes in Saigon. One traveller reports:

Sometimes a boat approaches and offers fish and crabs, but beware – these people may be robbers! They grabbed the bag of an English guy (with passport, money and cheques) and disappeared. Our tourist boat was slow and couldn't catch that fast boat. Two travellers we met reported that the crew of their boat stole some small things while they were swimming.

Aware of the importance of tourism, the marine police in Halong City have been trying to crack down on pirates and snatch thieves. However, Halong Bay is a large place with plenty of boats, so you should keep your guard up and not put yourself in a compromising position. If your hotel has a safe where you can securely lock up your passport, you'd probably be wise to use it.

Helicopter If you've got the cash to burn, helicopters can be chartered for whirlwind tours of the bay. Of course, it's hard to imagine how you're going to get a good look at the grottoes from a helicopter unless the pilots are *really* skilled. The staff at Quang Ninh Tourism in Halong City say they can arrange this; other possible sources of helicopters include Vietnam Tourism, Toserco and Vietnam Airlines.

CAI BAU ISLAND

This large and little-visited island is 45 km north-east of Halong City. Cai Bau Island (Dao Cai Bau) is a beautiful spot and certainly unspoiled, but there do not seem to be any readily accessible sandy beaches. Local teenagers are friendly – you can play billiards with them. There is a rudimentary hotel here charging US$5.

The largest town on the island is called Cam Pha Village, and indeed the island is also sometimes referred to as Cam Pha Island (Dao Cam Pha). All this is confusing, because Cam Pha is also the name of a large town on the mainland where you catch boats to the island. If you catch a ferry, just be sure that you are indeed going to the right place. Visitors of any kind are very rare here.

LANG SON

Lang Son (elevation: 270 metres) – capital of mountainous Lang Son Province – is in an area populated largely by ethnic minorities (Tho, Nung, Man and Dao), many of whom continue their traditional way of life. There are also caves 3.5 km from Lang Son, near the village of Ky Lua.

However, the real attraction of Lang Son is neither minorities nor scenery. The town has long served as an important trading post and crossing point into China. This is one of two border crossings open to travellers wanting to enter and exit Vietnam overland from China. The opening of the border is a recent event, made possible by gradually improving relations between China and Vietnam.

It wasn't always so. True, China was a good friend of North Vietnam from 1954 (when the French departed) until the late 1970s. But China's relations with Vietnam began to sour shortly after reunification as the Vietnamese government became more and more friendly to the USSR, China's rival. There is good reason to believe that Vietnam was simply playing China and the USSR off against each other, getting aid from both.

In March 1978, when the Vietnamese government launched a campaign in the south against 'commercial opportunists', seizing private property in order to complete the country's 'socialist transformation', the campaign hit the ethnic-Chinese particularly hard. It was widely assumed that behind the Marxist-Leninist rhetoric was the ancient Vietnamese antipathy towards the Chinese. One former Chinese restaurant owner from Ho Chi Minh City described what it was like when the government seized his business in 1978:

Government officials from Hanoi came and catalogued every table, chair, chopstick, glass, plate and dish in my restaurant. Thereafter, if I broke a glass, I had to pay for it, even though everything had originally been purchased with my own money.

The anti-capitalist and anti-Chinese campaign caused as many as 500,000 of Vietnam's 1.8 million ethnic-Chinese to flee the country. Those in the north fled overland to China while those in the south left by sea. At least in the south, creating Chinese refugees proved to be a lucrative business for the government – refugees typically had to pay up to US$5000 each in 'exit fees' to be allowed to leave. In Ho Chi Minh City, Chinese entrepreneurs in 1979 had that kind of money – refugees in the north were mostly dirt-poor.

In response, China cut off all aid to Vietnam, cancelled dozens of development projects and withdrew 800 technicians. Vietnam's invasion of Cambodia in late 1978 was the icing on the cake – Beijing was

Carrying wood near Lang Son

alarmed because the Khmer Rouge were close allies of China. China's leaders – already worried by the huge build-up of Soviet military forces on the Chinese-Soviet border – became convinced that Vietnam had fallen into the Russian camp, which was trying to encircle China with hostile forces.

In February 1979, China invaded northern Vietnam 'to teach the Vietnamese a lesson'. Just what lesson the Vietnamese learned is not clear, but the Chinese learned that Vietnam's troops – hardened by years of fighting the Americans – were no easy pushover. Although China's forces were withdrawn after 17 days and the operation was officially declared a 'great success', most observers soon realised that China's People's Liberation Army (PLA) had been badly mauled by the Vietnamese. The PLA is believed to have suffered 20,000 casualties in the 2½ weeks of fighting. Ironically, China's aid to Vietnam was partially responsible for China's humiliation by the Vietnamese forces.

Officially, such past 'misunderstandings' are ancient history – trade across the Chinese-Vietnamese border is booming and both countries publicly profess to be 'good neighbours'. In practice, China and Vietnam remain highly suspicious of each other's intentions. Continued conflicts over who owns oil-drilling rights in the South China Sea is an especially sore point. China has neither forgiven nor forgotten its humiliation at the hands of the Vietnamese army, and has relentlessly been building up its military ever since. Thus, the Chinese-Vietnamese border remains militarily sensitive, though the most likely future battleground will be at sea.

Lang Son was partially destroyed in February 1979 by invading Chinese forces; the ruins of the town and the devastated frontier village of Dong Dang, 20 km to the north, were often shown to foreign journalists as evidence of Chinese aggression. If you visit China and discuss this border war, you will almost certainly be told that China acted in self-defence because the Vietnamese were pulling raids across the border and murdering innocent Chinese villagers. Virtually all Western observers from the CIA to historians consider China's version of events to be utter nonsense. The Chinese also claim they won this war – nobody outside of China believes that either.

Today, though the border region is still mined, fortified and heavily guarded, Sino-Vietnamese trade seems to be in full swing again. This has greatly benefited Lang Son, which has become a booming market town.

Information

Money Lang Son's unofficial banking system (black market) is able to exchange US dollars for dong and Chinese renminbi. In case you've still got leftover dong, it is possible to change money on the Chinese side too.

Visas Since 1992, the Vietnamese government has been permitting foreigners to exit Vietnam overland at Lang Son. If you wish to exit Vietnam via Lang Son, this must be authorised on your Vietnamese visa. If your visa shows a different exit point, you can get a change made in Hanoi or Ho Chi Minh City at the Immigration Police Office or the Foreign Ministry. Getting this change made is straightforward, though sometimes you will be told to do it through a travel agent.

Entering Vietnam overland requires a special visa. See the Visa section in the Facts for the Visitor chapter for details.

Chinese visas do not indicate an exit or entry point. You are free to enter and leave China at any official port of entry as long as your visa has not expired. Chinese visas can be arranged in Hanoi, but this can be accomplished more quickly in Hong Kong. Since Chinese visas are normally only valid for 30 days and not so easily extendable, you should clearly indicate on your visa application when you plan to enter China.

Getting There & Away

Bus Buses to Lang Son depart Hanoi's Long Bien Bus Station around 6 am. The cost is US$5 and the journey takes roughly six hours over a bone-jarring road.

There are two checkpoints along the way and locals can get searched very thoroughly, though they usually go easy with foreigners. The situation seems even worse when going the other way (towards Hanoi) – the police are known to rip luggage open with knives and confiscate 'contraband' from China. Even if you are personally spared, the searches can cause long delays and it's really a depressing sight – Vietnamese people in tears pleading with the police.

From Lang Son to the border at Dong Dang is another 20 km with yet another police checkpoint along the way. Other than walking, the cheapest way to cover this distance is to hire a motorbike for US$1. There are also army jeeps willing to take you. Make sure they take you to Huu Nghi Quan – there are a few other checkpoints but this is the only one where foreigners can cross.

Train There is one train daily departing Hanoi at 9.30 pm and arriving in Lang Son at 3.30 am. These inconvenient hours make the bus a preferred mode of transport. As with the bus, arriving by train in Lang Son leaves you 20 km from the border and you'll need to hire a motorbike.

For information on the twice-weekly train running between Hanoi and Beijing, stopping in Dong Dang, see the section on land travel in the Getting There & Away chapter.

Car The 150-km highway between Hanoi and Lang Son is in lousy condition and most passenger cars do not have sufficient high-ground clearance to negotiate this road safely. For this reason, jeeps, trucks and minibuses are the vehicles of choice. Chartering a jeep costs around US$80 to US$90. A minibus costs around US$120 but could well prove cheaper if you can get together five or six passengers to share the cost. While trucks are capable of making the journey, this seems like an uncomfortable alternative.

Despite the expense, renting a private vehicle is not a bad idea since you can be driven right to the border crossing at Dong Dang.

To/From China No matter what means of transport you use to reach the Vietnamese border, there is a walk of 600 metres from the Vietnamese border post to 'Friendship Gate' on the Chinese side. Expect to be searched thoroughly at the border – there's quite a problem with drug smuggling. After you've crossed into China and cleared all customs hassles, if you're not on the Hanoi-Beijing train you can take a bus or share taxi to Pinxiang (US$3, 20 minutes), from where you can get a train to Nanning, capital of China's Guangxi Province. Trains to Nanning depart Pinxiang at 8 am and 1.30 pm. More frequent are the buses (once every 30 minutes), which take four hours to make the journey and cost US$3.

North-Central Vietnam

CAO BANG

Cao Bang City is the capital of Cao Bang Province, many of whose inhabitants are members of the Tho, Nung, Dao and Meo national minorities. Principal products of the region include beef, pork, goats, zinc and lumber. The area is known for its waterfalls and grottoes.

Cao Bang is 272 km north of Hanoi.

BA BE LAKE NATIONAL PARK

This incredibly beautiful area boasts waterfalls, rivers, deep valleys, lakes and caves set amid towering peaks. The area is inhabited by members of the Dai minority, who live in homes built on stilts.

There are actually several lakes here, the largest of which is called Ba Be, which is about 145 metres above sea level and surrounded by steep mountains up to 1754 metres high. The 1939 Madrolle Guide to Indochina suggests getting around the area 'in a car, on horseback, or, for ladies, in a chair', meaning, of course, a sedan chair.

Ba Be (Three Bays) is the name of the southern part of a narrow body of water seven km long; the northern section of the lake, separated from Ba Be by a 100-metre-wide strip of water sandwiched between high walls of chalk rock, is called Be Kam. The Nam Nang River is navigable for 23 km between a point four km above Cho Ra and the Dau Dang Waterfall (Thac Dau Dang), which consists of a series of spectacular cascades between sheer walls of rock.

An interesting place is Puong Cave (Hang Puong). The cave is 300 metres long and passes completely through a mountain. A navigable river flows through the cave, making for an interesting boat trip. You can also organise boat trips to some nearby tribal villages. Many of the minority people are anxious to sell their home-made clothing and handicrafts to travellers.

Getting There & Away

Ba Be Lake National Park is in Cao Bang Province not far from the borders of Bac Thai Province and Tuyen Quang Province. Ba Be Lake is 240 km from Hanoi, 61 km from Bach Thong (Bac Can) and 18 km from Cho Ra.

Most visitors to the national park go from Hanoi by chartered vehicle. From Bach Thong onwards, the road gets rough and the last 50-km stretch before the park is particularly rough. This should only be attempted with a jeep, very high clearance vehicle or a powerful motorbike.

Chartering a jeep from Hanoi to the national park should cost about US$200, depending on how long you stay. One-way driving time from Hanoi to Ba Be Lake is approximately eight hours, and most travellers take three days plus two nights for the entire excursion.

At the time of this writing, nobody was offering organised tours to Ba Be Lake, but cafes and travel agencies in Hanoi were talking about the possibility. Check the noticeboards in Hanoi's cafes to see if anyone is running such trips.

Reaching this national park by public transport is possible but not easy. The way to do it is to take a bus from Hanoi to Bach Thong (Bac Can), and from there another bus to Cho Ra. In Cho Ra you will have to get a motorbike to do the last 18-km stretch of highway unless you are willing to walk (not likely).

North-West Vietnam

National Highway 6 heads slightly southwest of Hanoi before looping around the southern end of Song Da Reservoir (near Hoa Binh) and then heading north-west into the rugged mountains around Dien Bien Phu.

Getting there is half the fun. Highway 6 is mostly bitumen surface from Hanoi to Tuan Giao, but from there to Dien Bien Phu the road is still gravel. As it nears Dien Bien Phu, the highway winds through beautiful mountains and high plains inhabited by hill tribes (notably the Black Tai and Hmong) who still live as they have for generations. The Tai are most numerous in the lower lands, where they cultivate tea and fruit, and live in attractive stilt houses. In the bleaker highlands over 1000 metres elevation live the hardy Hmong.

The scenery is incredible. You pass through Hmong and Black Tai villages where they stare at you as much as you stare at them. There is not much to see at the battlefield itself but the museum presents the incredible story of Vietnamese determination. You might want to bring some food – local food consists of rice, fried pig fat and huge piles of fresh mint washed in water that made us sick. Back in Hanoi I splurged after all the bumps of the road by having a tonic water with ice at the Hotel Sofitel Metropole and then sneaking into their completely empty swimming pool.

Ingrid Muan

Of course, you needn't go the entire distance. Many travellers only go as far as Mai Chau, Moc Chau or Son La before turning back. However, they miss out on the dramatic highland scenery which is farther west. The most interesting journey of all is to head for Dien Bien Phu, then north to Lai Chau, Sapa, Lao Cai and back to Hanoi. This loop route can easily take a week but is incredibly scenic.

National Highway 6 between Hanoi and Dien Bien Phu is in reasonably good condition. A normal passenger car can make the journey, but it's much better to have a high-clearance vehicle such as a minibus. Flooding in the lowlands and valleys can be a problem during heavy rains, though the water tends to drop quickly after the storms subside. If you have a motorbike, locals with small boats can ferry you across the trouble spots.

The road between Dien Bien Phu and Lao Cai is in much poorer condition, which is why many travellers skip this route. A high-clearance vehicle is a must, but jeeps are best. A Russian-built jeep (of which there are many in Hanoi) can seat four passengers plus the driver. It's also possible to find a Russian-built military van, equipped with 4WD, which can hold more passengers than a standard jeep. Recently imported jeeps from Japan and Korea are now the vehicles of choice. A powerful motorcycle (at least 125 cc engine) should have no problem.

MAI CHAU

One of the closest places to Hanoi where you can see a real hill tribe village is Mai Chau.

It's a beautiful place, and some have called it 'another Sapa' (see the Sapa section in this chapter). Mai Chau itself is very rural with little in the way of a central area – rather, it's a collection of farms and huts spread out over a large area. The people here are ethnic Tai, though only distantly related to tribes in Thailand.

All minorities have substantial cultural autonomy. Officially the language of tuition is Vietnamese, but in fact everyone teaches the children in their own dialect. Taxes are supposed to be paid, but Hanoi is far away. It seems as long as they don't interfere with Hanoi's interests, they can do whatever they like. Police officers and members of the army in the area are often Montagnards. Unlike in the Central Highlands of the south, the Vietnamese effort to assimilate the minorities of the far north has been half-hearted and largely ineffective.

Photographing the hill tribes demands patience and the utmost respect for their feelings. Take plenty of film with you, because the minorities and the enchanting mountain scenery eat up film fast.

Places to Stay

The only official hotel in town is the *Mai Chau Hotel*, which costs US$10. However, most tours try to arrange an overnight stay in the villagers' huts, which is far more interesting.

Getting There & Away

Mai Chau is a little to the south of National Highway 6, which is the direct Hanoi-Dien Bien Phu route. So getting there requires a slight detour.

You'll be hard-pressed to find any direct public transport to Mai Chau from Hanoi. If you're not on a tour or have your own chartered vehicle, your best hope would be to take a public bus from Hanoi to Hoa Binh, followed by a motorcycle taxi to Mai Chau.

Some cafes in Hanoi (the Green Bamboo, etc) run weekly trips to Mai Chau. All transport, food and accommodation is provided for a cost as low as US$28 per person.

THE NORTH

MOC CHAU

The northern part of Vietnam produces the nation's best tea and Moc Chau is one of the prime tea-growing areas. The area also boasts a pioneer dairy industry started in the late 1970s with Australian and later UN assistance. The dairy provides the Hanoi markets with such delectable luxuries as fresh milk, sweetened condensed milk and little tooth-rotting sweet bars called 'milk cake' (banh sua). Not surprisingly, Moc Chau is a good place to sample fresh milk and yoghurt.

Moc Chau is 199 km from Hanoi along National Highway 6 and the journey takes roughly six hours by private car. Basic accommodation at the *People's Committee Guest House* (Nha Khach Uy Ban Nhan Dan Tinh) costs US$5 per person.

YEN CHAU

This small agricultural district is known for its fruits. Apart from bananas, the fruits are seasonal – mango harvesting is done in May and June, longans in July and August and custard apples in August and September.

The mangoes in particular are considered to be the best in Vietnam, though foreigners may at first find them disappointing. This is because they are small and green, rather than big, yellow and juicy, as they are in the tropical south. However, Vietnamese prefer the somewhat tart taste and aroma of the green ones. The green colour doesn't give a clue as to when the fruit is ripe, so you may need to ask a local 'expert' if the mango you're buying is ripe and ready for eating.

Yen Chau is 260 km from Hanoi and driving time is approximately eight hours by car. Yen Chau to Son La is another 60 km.

SON LA

Son La, capital of the province of the same name, makes a good overnight stop for travellers doing the run between Hanoi and Dien Bien Phu. While not one of Vietnam's highlights, the scenery isn't bad and there is certainly enough to see and do to keep you occupied for a day.

The area is populated mainly by hill tribes,

including the Black Tai, Meo, Muong and White Tai. Vietnamese influence in the area was minimal until this century; from 1959 to 1980, the region was part of the Tay Bac Autonomous Region (Khu Tay Bac Tu Tri).

Old French Prison

Son La was once the site of a French penal colony where anti-colonialist revolutionaries were held. It was destroyed by the infamous 'off-loading' of unused ammunition by American warplanes returning to base after bombing raids on Hanoi and Haiphong.

The Old French Prison (Nha Tu Cu Cua Phap) has been partially restored in the interests of historical tourism. Rebuilt turrets and watchtowers stand guard over the remains of cells, inner walls and a famous lone surviving peach tree. The tree, which blooms with the traditional Tet flowers, was planted in the compound by To Hieu, one of the former inmates of the 1940s. To Hieu has subsequently been immortalised further – there is a To Hieu St in Son La, a To Hieu Secondary School and other landmarks about town named after him.

The prison tells part of the story, but repression did not end when the French departed:

The different Meos, Black Tais, White Tais and other groups which fought during the Franco-Viet Minh War on the colonial side were afterwards treated as traitors and suffered harsh repression. Surprisingly, the French beret is still worn by many minority men. Through an interpreter I talked to a White Tai family. One of their close relatives was the friend of the Tai emperor and went with him into French exile. Until a few years ago the family was not getting any mail from France and somebody bringing a message from the family member in France was stopped by security officers and couldn't deliver the message or meet the family. Over the years they lost track of their relatives. Now the authorities have lifted all sanctions and are trying to help them to locate the person through the French embassy. A complete reversal in attitude! Similar, more dramatic stories I heard too.

Adrian Bloch

From the main highway, a maroon-coloured signpost adorned with large chains marks the entrance to the narrow road leading uphill to the prison. At the end of a road is a People's Committee office – the prison is at the back. The actual entrance to the prison is marked by a faded sign saying 'Penitentaire' above the wrought iron gates.

Hot Springs

An enjoyable few hours can be spent strolling through some Tai villages south of town, and your final reward will be a dip in the hot springs (Suoi Nuoc Nong). The communal pool is free, but you can fork out US$0.10 for a private enclosed bathtub. Although children can frolic nude in the public pool, that's less acceptable for adults, and Westerners in particular can expect to be the centre of wide-eyed attention. In other words, some sort of bathing costume is recommended.

To get there, from the signpost with the chains (same one which marks the French Prison turnoff), take the road which heads south (opposite direction of the prison). The road leads past the Party Headquarters Building, after which the pavement ends. From here it's five km to a couple of small bathing huts right beside the track and a couple of cement pools 50 metres farther on. A motorbike or high-clearance vehicle can navigate the road, but during the wet season it becomes a mud quagmire.

Lookout Tower (Cot V3)

The tower offers a sweeping overview of Son La and the surrounding area. The climb is steep and will take about 20 minutes, but the view from the top is well worth it. Photography of the scenery is permitted, but the guards will get uptight if you try to photograph the installations which serve both a telecommunications and military purpose.

Immediately to the left of the Labour Federation Guest House are the stone steps which lead up to the tower.

Forestry Research Centre

The elaborately named North-West Regional Forestry Research Centre (Trung Tam Khoa Hoc San Xuat Lam Nghiep Vung Tay Bac; ☎ 52164) was established in 1990. Travellers may (or may not) be interested in the small zoo here. The lineup of animals includes bears, civets, deer, eagles, monkeys, porcupines, squirrels and tortoises. Some of the creatures here are part of a captive breeding programme. The deer are also bred to serve a commercial purpose – the horns are periodically harvested, soaked in rice wine and sold as herbal medicine.

Regardless of your feeling about zoos, keeping some animals in captivity may be the only way to prevent them from becoming extinct. The basic problem here is deforestation, which has wiped out the native habitat of most local creatures. The expanding human population of the region and competition for agricultural land has also put the animals under stress. Poaching doesn't help the situation either.

The Forestry Research Centre is six km from Son La in the direction of Hanoi. Follow the highway east of town to a lone petrol station on the outskirts of town. Turn right onto a small unsignposted bitumen track 50 metres past the petrol station.

The Forestry Research Centre is open weekdays and Saturday from 7 to 11 am and from 1 to 5 pm. Sunday hours are from 8 to 11 am. For further inquiries, there is an office on To Hieu St.

Market

You can find a small selection of colourful woven shoulder bags, scarves and other minority crafts at Son La's market.

Tam Ta Toong Caves

There are many caves in the region, but the Tam Ta Toong Caves are the most accessible from Son La. There are actually two caves here, one dry and one which is partially flooded. The dry cave is uninteresting, but ironically has an entrance gate and requires permission and a guide. Both the permission and the guide are available and can be had for a price – inquire at hotels in town if interested.

The flooded cave is adjacent to the dry one but is more fun and no permit or guide is required. A small adjacent irrigation dam

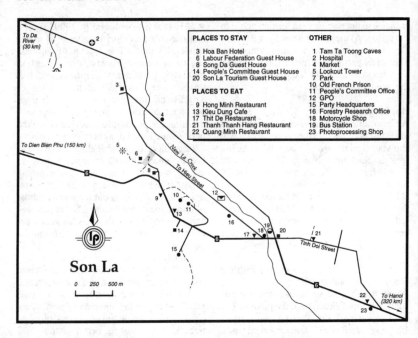

PLACES TO STAY

3 Hoa Ban Hotel
6 Labour Federation Guest House
8 Song Da Guest House
14 People's Committee Guest House
20 Son La Tourism Guest House

PLACES TO EAT

9 Hong Minh Restaurant
13 Kieu Dung Cafe
17 Thit De Restaurant
21 Thanh Thanh Hang Restaurant
22 Quang Minh Restaurant

OTHER

1 Tam Ta Toong Caves
2 Hospital
4 Market
5 Lookout Tower
7 Park
10 Old French Prison
11 People's Committee Office
12 GPO
15 Party Headquarters
16 Forestry Research Office
18 Motorcycle Shop
19 Bus Station
23 Photoprocessing Shop

Son La

0   250   500 m

supplies the water which has flooded the cave. The cave goes back about 100 metres into the hillside. You should find a raft moored at the cave entrance plus an attendant who can take you inside for a negotiable fee. Bring a torch (flashlight).

The caves are a few kilometres west of town. On the main highway towards Dien Bien Phu, a bridge crosses a creek just before the pavement ends. Turn left onto a gravel track about 20 metres before the bridge. Walk along the track by the creek (which is the outflow from the flooded cave) for about one km, crossing the creek once along the way. An aqueduct crosses the track – turn left and follow the aqueduct to the flooded cave's entrance, which is surrounded by an ugly barbed-wire fence. The dry cave is reached by following the track on the right of the flooded cave up the hill a short distance.

Places to Stay

Almost all travellers journeying between

Hanoi and Dien Bien Phu spend the night in Son La both coming and going.

At the budget end is the *Labour Federation Guest House* (Nha Khach Du Lich Lien Doan Lao Dong). The bottom-end rooms are US$3, but doubles with hot water cost US$10.

The *Song Da Guest House* (Ban Cong Tac Song Da; ☎ 52062) has rooms from US$4 to US$10. There is even a dormitory which can be booked by a small group. This place may become permanently full soon if the proposed Ta Bu hydroelectric scheme is finally approved – the hotel was built by the Da River Works Department to house the construction workers.

The *People's Committee Guest House* (Nha Khach Uy Ban Nhan Dan Tinh Son La; ☎ 52080) is poor value with mediocre rooms for US$10 to US$20.

The *Son La Tourism Guest House* (Nha Khach Du Lich Son La) attempts to be one of the town's two 'luxury' hotels. It's almost

Halong Bay, Northern Vietnam

SARA JANE CLELAND

HELEN SAVORY

HELEN SAVORY

The North

Top: Young Hmong women near Sapa
Bottom Left: A crowded local bus en route to Hanoi
Bottom Right: A Vietnamese fun park near Halong City

directly across the road from the long-distance bus station. In the unlikely event that you arrive by air, the airport bus will take you here. Room prices are US$15 to US$25.

The other upmarket establishment is the *Hoa Ban Hotel* (☎ 52395). Prices here are in the range of US$15 to US$25. The hotel is known for its good restaurant and Saturday-night disco.

Places to Eat

Thit De Restaurant dishes up Son La's special fare, goat meat. You can try the highly prized local dish *tiet canh*, a bowl of goat's blood curd dressed with a sprinkling of peanuts and vegetables. Or you can have the more conventional but tasty goat-meat steamboat.

Thanh Thanh Hang Restaurant does fish, both the freshwater and seawater variety. The menu varies by season, but you can find things like king prawns, squid and crab.

Hong Minh Restaurant is notable for its house specialty, *thit co lo* (meat with hole), which is in fact kebabs (usually called *thit nuong*). Basically, it's delicious meat grilled on a skewer.

Quang Minh Restaurant on the eastern edge of town is another good place to eat.

Kieu Dung Café is a relaxing and comfortable place to enjoy coffee. Prices are somewhat high though, at least by Son La standards.

Getting There & Away

Air Son La's airport is called Na San and is 20 km from Son La along the road towards Hanoi. Flights run only once weekly (every Thursday) and cost US$60 for a one-way ticket. There are no connecting flights between Son La and Dien Bien Phu.

In Son La, tickets can be booked at the Son La Tourism Guest House, and an airport bus runs from here.

Bus Buses take from 12 to 14 hours to travel between Hanoi and Son La, assuming there are no serious breakdowns. From Son La to Dien Bien Phu is another 10 hours.

Car Son La is 320 km from Hanoi and 150 km from Dien Bien Phu. The Hanoi-Son La run typically requires 10 hours. Son La to Dien Bien Phu is another six hours. Car rentals can be arranged in Son La. Drivers want about US$200 for the round trip to Dien Bien Phu, or US$120 for a Son La-Hanoi round trip.

TUAN GIAO

This remote town is at the junction of National Highway 6 to Dien Bien Phu (80 km, three hours) and Highway 6A to Lai Chau (90 km, four hours). Most travellers approach from the direction of Son La (75 km, three hours) and Hanoi (390 km, 13 hours). These driving times assume you are travelling by car or motorbike – for public buses, multiply travel time by 1.5 at least.

Not many people spend the night unless they are running behind schedule and can't make it to Dien Bien Phu. The *People's Committee Guest House* (Nha Khach Uy Ban Nhan Dan Tinh) can provide basic accommodation.

DIEN BIEN PHU

Dien Bien Phu was the site of that rarest of military events, a battle that can be called truly decisive. On 6 May 1954, the day before the Geneva Conference on Indochina was set to begin half a world away, Viet Minh forces overran the beleaguered French garrison at Dien Bien Phu after a 57-day siege, shattering French morale and forcing the French government to abandon its attempts to re-establish colonial control of Indochina.

Dien Bien Phu (population 10,000), capital of Dien Bien District of Lai Chau Province, is in one of the remotest parts of Vietnam. The town is 16 km from the Lao border in flat, heart-shaped Muong Thanh Valley, which is about 20 km long and five km wide and is surrounded by steep, heavily forested hills. The area is inhabited by hill-tribe people, most notably the Tai and Hmong. Ethnic Vietnamese, whom the government has been encouraging to settle in the region, currently comprise about one-third of the Muong Thanh Valley's population of 60,000.

For centuries, Dien Bien was a transit stop on the caravan route from Burma and China to northern Vietnam. Dien Bien Phu was established in 1841 by the Nguyen Dynasty to prevent raids on the Red River Delta by bandits.

In early 1954 General Henri Navarre, commander of the French forces in Indochina, sent a force of 12 battalions to occupy the Muong Thanh Valley in order to prevent the Viet Minh from crossing into Laos and threatening the Lao capital of Luang Phabang. The French units, one-third of whose members were ethnic-Vietnamese, were soon surrounded by a Viet Minh force under General Vo Nguyen Giap consisting of 33 infantry battalions, six artillery regiments and a regiment of engineers. The Viet Minh force, which outnumbered the French by five to one, was equipped with 105-mm artillery pieces and anti-aircraft guns carried by porters through jungles and across rivers in an unbelievable feat of logistics. The guns were emplaced in carefully camouflaged positions dug deep into the hills that overlooked the French positions.

A failed Viet Minh human-wave assault against the French was followed by weeks of intense artillery bombardments. Six battalions of French paratroops were parachuted into Dien Bien Phu as the situation worsened, but bad weather and the Viet Minh artillery, impervious to French air and artillery attacks, prevented sufficient reinforcements and supplies from arriving by air. An elaborate system of trenches and tunnels allowed Viet Minh soldiers to reach French positions without coming under fire. After the idea of employing American conventional bombers was rejected – as was a Pentagon proposal to use tactical atomic bombs – the French trenches and bunkers were overrun. All 13,000 men of the French garrison were either killed or taken prisoner; Viet Minh casualties are estimated at 25,000.

The site of the battle is now marked by a small museum. The headquarters of the French commander, Colonel Christian de Castries, has been recreated and nearby there are old French tanks and artillery pieces. One of the two landing strips used by the French is extant. There is a monument to Viet Minh casualties on the site of the former French position known as Eliane, where bitter fighting took place. A memorial to the 3000 French troops buried under the rice paddies was erected in 1984 on the 30th anniversary of the battle.

At present, the Vietnamese government is considering a request by French veterans of Dien Bien Phu that they be allowed to restage their paratroop drop of almost four decades ago.

History is the main attraction here, and the scenery – pleasant though it is – is just a sideshow that you can enjoy during arrival and departure overland. Dien Bien Phu seems to hold the same fascination for the French as the DMZ does for the Americans. Not surprisingly, the majority of travellers who come here now are from France.

Tourism is having quite an impact on Dien Bien Phu – the town has been transformed into one big construction site. Another reason for the boom is that Dien Bien Phu was made the capital of Lai Chau Province in 1993. This honour was bestowed upon it mainly because the old capital will be submerged underwater in a few years (see the Lai Chau section for details).

Places to Stay

The two main guesthouses are both on the main road through town. The upmarket and shining white *Mini Hotel* is highly visible to your right (coming from the direction of Hanoi). Rooms with attached bath cost US$20.

The *People's Committee Guest House* (Nha Khach Uy Ban Nhan Dan Tinh; 40 rooms) is 500 metres farther along the same road, behind a small lake. This massive facility has budget rooms from US$5 with pricier rooms currently undergoing renovation.

Getting There & Away

The overland trip to Dien Bien Phu can be more intriguing than the actual battlefield sites for which the town is so famous. Of course, you miss out on most of this if you fly.

Air Vietnam Airlines runs flights between Dien Bien Phu and Hanoi three times a week. One-way tickets cost US$60. The airport is five km from Dien Bien Phu along the road towards Lai Chau.

Bus The bus may be cheap but not really much fun – they are so packed that it's doubtful you'll get to admire the splendid scenery. Furthermore, the buses we've seen looked awfully dangerous (you need good brakes in these mountains).

Car & Motorbike The 470-km drive from Hanoi to Dien Bien Phu on National Highway 6 takes 16 hours, and it's usual to overnight in Son La. In other words, a minimum of five days is required for an overland expedition from Hanoi to Dien Bien Phu: two days to get there, a day to visit the area and two days to come back. It makes more sense to continue on from Dien Bien Phu to Lai Chau, Sapa and Lao Cai (near the Chinese border) and then back to Hanoi.

The going rate for renting a Russian car or jeep to Dien Bien Phu, Lai Chau, Sapa, Lao Cai and back to Hanoi is about US$320. It will cost more for modern Korean and Japanese vehicles. Inquire at travel agencies, cafes or your hotel about vehicle rentals.

Tours Some budget tour operators in Hanoi advertise overland trips for as little as US$60 per person. The actual price will of course depend on group size and the standard of accommodation you require.

LAI CHAU

This small town is nestled in a beautiful valley carved from spectacular mountains by the Da River (Song Da). Beneath the beauty lies a difficult existence for locals. Far from busy trade routes, normal commerce is limited and Lai Chau has been really successful only in the harvesting of particularly valuable cash crops. These include opium and timber. Needless to say, opium harvesting does not find favour with the central government. No doubt, some is exported to nearby China, Thailand and possibly even to Western countries, but a good portion of it may be supplying junkies in Saigon. The government has been trying to discourage the hill tribes from producing opium poppies.

If the opium business is falling on hard times, the same must be said for the timber industry. In recent years forest cover has been reduced and flooding has increased dramatically. Around 40 people lost their lives in 1991 in a devastating flood on the Da River which swept through the narrow valley.

It seems that floods are about to become a permanent feature of Lai Chau. The government has proposed placing a dam in the Ta Bu area (just above the current Song Da Reservoir). If this comes to pass, the only way to visit Lai Chau in the future will be by submarine. Final approval for the project is still pending, but it will almost certainly be granted.

Recognising that the town was about to go the way of Atlantis, the provincial capital was transferred from Lai Chau to Dien Bien Phu in 1993.

Places to Stay

The *People's Committee Guest House* can provide basic accommodation for US$5. Even grottier are the private dormitory-style rest houses (Nha Nghi) next to the bus station.

Getting There & Away

The shortest approach is on National Highway 6 from Tuan Giao (90 km, four hours). Most travellers will arrive from Dien Bien Phu (110 km, 4½ hours). The road from Lai Chau to Sapa and Lao Cai is in very poor condition, though some repair work is being done.

SAPA

Sapa is an old hill station built in 1922 in a beautiful valley (elevation: 1600 metres) close to the border with China. It's a spectacularly beautiful area, but getting there from Hanoi was never particularly easy because of bad roads. Other problems which prevented Sapa from becoming a slick tourist resort included WW II, the guerilla war against the French, the war with America and the border skirmish with China in 1979, not to mention Vietnam's severe economic decline in the 1980s. The old hotels built by the French were allowed to fall into disrepair, and Sapa was pretty much forgotten by nearly everyone (including the Vietnamese themselves).

Vietnam's recent tourist boom has caused a sea change in Sapa's fortunes. The bad roads are still a problem, but Sapa is now a major attraction for foreign travellers. The roads are gradually being repaired and new villas are being built, but one inconvenience which will not change quickly is the weather. If you visit off-season, don't forget your winter woollies – Sapa is known for its cold, foggy winters (down to 0°C). The chilly climate does have a few advantages though – the area boasts temperate-zone fruit trees (peaches, plums, etc) and gardens for raising medicinal herbs. The dry season for Sapa is

approximately January through June – afternoon rainshowers in the mountains are frequent.

Saturday Market

Minorities from all the surrounding villages don their most colourful costumes and head for the market on Saturday. There are some opportunities to purchase ethnic clothing and exotic hats here, but whether you buy or not the market is worth seeing. For just this reason, foreign tour groups in Hanoi usually schedule their departures so that they arrive in Sapa on Friday night.

Fansipan

Surrounding Sapa are the Hoang Lien Mountains, nicknamed the Tonkinese Alps by the French. These mountains include Fansipan, which at 3143 metres is Vietnam's highest. The summit towers above Sapa, though it is often obscured by clouds and is occasionally dusted by snow. The peak should be accessible year-round to anyone who is in good shape and properly equipped, but don't underestimate the difficulty. It is very wet and usually cold, so you must be prepared. Hiring a reputable guide is definitely recommended, but no porters are available so you must carry everything yourself. Most of the climbers are foreigners, but there are also a few adventurous Vietnamese who have the financial resources for mountaineering holidays.

Fansipan is nine km from Sapa and accessible only on foot. Despite the short distance, the round-trip walk takes nearly four days because of the rough terrain. However, no ropes or technical climbing skills are needed, just endurance. There are no mountain huts or other facilities along the way (yet), so you need to be self-sufficient. This means a sleeping bag, waterproof tent, food, stove, rainsuit or poncho, compass and other miscellaneous survival gear.

The question arises – can you rent camping equipment in Sapa? At the present time, the answer is 'no' but that may change soon. Locals in Sapa and also travel agencies

Sapa
Scale Unknown

To Lao Cai (30 km) & Hanoi (370 km)

Forestry Hotel

Old Church

Trade Union Guest House

Bank Guest House

Football Field

Steps

Steps

Steps

Steps

GPO

Trade Services Guest House

Shops

Market

Market

Cheap Restaurants

To Lai Chau (195 km)

To Fansipan (10 km)

in Hanoi have been discussing the possibility of organising trekking tours.

Other Sights
Some other well-known scenic attractions around Sapa include Thac Bac (Silver Falls) and Cau May (Cloud Bridge), which spans the Muong Hoa River.

Places to Stay
Sapa seems to have a fair bit of construction going on now to cash in on the tourist boom. Expect to find several new small guest-houses before long.

The *Bank Guest House* is just next to the football field. Rooms are equipped with hot-water washing facilities, and the cost varies from US$5 to US$7. The bank functions in the TV lounge – the friendly teller stops counting money to make you coffee.

The *Trade Services Guest House* (Nha Khach Thuong Nghiep) is next to the post office. Rooms cost US$5 to US$8, and hot water is available.

Rooms at the *Trade Union Guest House* near the old church command a sweeping view and cost US$5. This beautiful place is an old villa, but has no hot water for bathing.

The *Forestry Hotel* is on the edge of town, near the highway that heads to Lai Chau. It's the most expensive place in town, with prices varying between US$10 and US$25. How much you pay has nothing to do with the facilities – the price fluctuates according to how crowded they are. Bargaining is recommended here. The showers have a hot water heater.

Getting There & Away
Sapa's proximity to the border region makes it a possible first stop or last stop for travellers crossing between Vietnam and China.

The gateway to Sapa is Lao Cai, 30 km from Sapa. Lao Cai has a border crossing with China. Buses do make the trip (two hours) but are not reliable. They actually start out from Pho Lu and travel via Lao Cai to Sapa, and these buses wait for the train.

You can catch a ride in the back of a pickup truck. This costs around US$3 per person.

Motorbikes are available for hire in Lao Cai at US$5 per day.

Locals are also very willing to drive you up the mountain by motorbike for US$4, but travellers have reported problems with drivers taking them half way and then asking for more money to complete the journey. If you don't cough up the cash, they threaten to leave you stranded.

Driving a motorbike from Hanoi to Sapa takes two days over roads which are often muddy or flooded. The total distance between Hanoi and Sapa is 370 km.

Some of the cafes in Hanoi now offer four-day bus trips to Sapa for US$50. This is probably the most hassle-free way to do the journey.

LAO CAI
Lao Cai is also the major town at the end of the rail line and right on the Chinese border. The border crossing slammed shut during the 1979 war between China and Vietnam and remained closed until 1993. Its reopening has changed Lao Cai into a major destination for travellers journeying between Hanoi and Kunming, the capital of China's scenic Yunnan Province.

The border town on the Chinese side is called Hekou, separated from Vietnam by a river and a bridge. The bridge and border crossing is open every day from 8 am until 5 pm and you must pay a small toll to cross.

The scenery around Lao Cai is beautiful and the people very friendly.

Orientation
The border is three km from Lao Cai Railway Station. Making this journey is best accomplished on a motorbike, which costs around US$0.50.

Places to Stay
There is a horrid little no-name hotel in Lao Cai charging US$5 for a roof over your head. Local people may offer you a place to stay in their homes, but of course some sort of payment is expected. The accommodation situation will hopefully improve in the near future.

In Hekou, on the Chinese side, budget accommodation is available at the old *Hekou Hotel* or the new, relatively upmarket *Dongfeng Hotel*.

Getting There & Away

There are two trains daily in each direction on the Lao Cai-Hanoi run. One train runs during the day and the other runs at night. From Hanoi, the morning train departs at 8.20 am and arrives at Lao Cai at 7.30 pm; the evening train departs at 8.20 pm and arrives at 7.30 am. From Lao Cai, the morning train departs at 9.25 am and arrives at Hanoi at 8.45 pm; the evening train departs at 5.30 pm and arrives at 4.40 am. Tickets for foreigners cost US$7 for hard seat and US$10 for soft seat and are usually sold only on the day of departure. There is no soft sleeper. The toilets are pretty bad, so dehydrate before boarding. Once the train is under way, go to the attendant at the end of your car for a pillow and blanket – if you don't need the blanket for warmth, you can still use it as extra padding beneath your body.

Glossary

Agent Orange – a carcinogenic and mutagenic chemical herbicide used heavily during the Vietnam War
am and duong – Vietnamese equivalent of Yin and Yang
Annam – old Chinese name for Vietnam meaning 'Pacified South'
ao dai – national dress of Vietnamese women (and occasionally men)
arhat – monk who has attained nirvana
ARVN – Army of the Republic of Vietnam (the former South Vietnamese army)

bang – congregation (in the Chinese community)
bonze – Vietnamese Buddhist monk
Buu Dien – Post Office

Cai Luong – modern theatre
Caodaism – indigenous Vietnamese religious sect
can – 10-year cycle
can danh – brown (literally, 'cockroach wing')
cay son – tree from whose resin lacquer is made
Champa – Hindu kingdom dating from the late 2nd century AD
Chams – the people of Champa
chu nho – standard Chinese characters (script)
chu nom – also *nom*, Vietnamese script
Cochinchina – the southern part of Vietnam during the French colonial era
crachin – fine drizzle
cu ly – fern stems used to stop bleeding
cyclo – pedicab or bicycle rickshaw (from French)

dau – oil
dikpalata – gods of the directions of the compass
dinh – communal meeting hall
DMZ – the misnamed 'Demilitarised Zone', a strip of land which once separated North and South Vietnam

doi moi – economic restructuring or reform
DRV – Democratic Republic of Vietnam (the old North Vietnam)

flechette – experimental American weapon, an artillery shell containing thousands of darts
fu – talisman
Funan – see Oc-Eo

ghe – long, narrow rowboat
giap phep di lai – internal travel permit
gom – ceramics

hai dang – lighthouse
Han Viet – Sino-Vietnamese literature
Hat Boi – classical theatre in the south
Hat Cheo – popular theatre
Hat Tuong – classical theatre in the north
ho ca – aquarium
Ho Chi Minh Trail – route used by the NVA and VC to move supplies to guerrillas in the south
hoi – 60-year period
ho khau – a residence permit needed for everything: to attend school, seek employment, own land, register a vehicle, buy a home, start a business, etc
Honda om – motorbike taxi
huyen – rural district

Indochina – Vietnam, Cambodia and Laos. The name derives from the influence of Indian and Chinese cultures on the region.

kala-makara – sea monster god
kalan – sanctuary
khach san – hotel
Khmer – ethnic Cambodians
Kich Noi – spoken drama
Kinh – Vietnamese language
Kuomintang – or KMT, meaning 'Nationalist Party'. The KMT controlled China from around 1925 to 1949 until defeated by the Communists. The KMT still controls Taiwan.
ky – 12-year cycle

lang tam – tombs
Liberation – the 1975 takeover of the South by the North; what most foreigners call 'reunification'
Lien Xo – literally 'Soviet Union'; used to call attention to a foreigner
linga – stylised phallus which represents the Hindu god Shiva

mandapa – meditation hall
moi – derogatory word meaning 'savages', mostly used regarding hill-tribe people
mukha linga – linga with a painted human face on it (from Sanscrit)

naga – a giant snake, often depicted forming a kind of shelter over the Buddha
Nam Phai – For Men
napalm – jellied petrol (gasoline) dropped and lit from aircraft, with devastating effect
nha hang – restaurant
nha khach – hotel or guesthouse
nha nghi – guesthouse
nha thuoc – pharmacy
nha tro – dormitory
NLF – National Liberation Front; official name for the Viet Cong
nom – see chu nom
nuoc dua – coconut milk
nuoc mam – fish sauce, added to almost every dish in Vietnam
nuoc suoi – mineral water
Nu Phai – For Women
NVA – North Vietnamese Army

Oc-Eo – Indianised kingdom (also called Funan) in southern Vietnam between 1st and 6th centuries

pagoda – traditionally, an eight-sided Buddhist tower, but in Vietnam the word is commonly used to denote a temple
Phoenix Programme – or Operation Phoenix; a controversial programme run by the CIA, aimed at eliminating VC cadres by assassination, capture or defection
PRG – Provisional Revolutionary Government, the temporary Communist government set up by the Viet Cong in the South. It existed from 1969 to 1976.

quan – urban district
Quoc Am – modern Vietnamese literature
quoc ngu – Latin-based phonetic alphabet in which Vietnamese is written

rap – cinema
Revolutionary Youth League – the first Marxist group in Vietnam and predecessor of the Communist Party; founded in 1925 by Ho Chi Minh in Guangzhou (Canton), China
Roi Can – conventional puppetry
Roi Nuoc – water puppetry
ruou – wine
RVN – Republic of Vietnam (the old South Vietnam)

son then – black
SRV – Socialist Republic of Vietnam (Vietnam's current official name)
Strategic Hamlets Programme – an unsuccessful programme of the US Army and South Vietnamese government in which peasants were forcibly moved into fortified villages to deny the VC bases of support

Tet – the Vietnamese lunar new year
thanh long – dragon fruit
tinh – province
thuac bac – Chinese medicines
thung chai – gigantic round wicker baskets sealed with pitch; used as rowboats
toc hanh – express bus
Tonkin – the northern part of Vietnam during the French colonial era; also name of a body of water in the north (Tonkin Gulf)
Truyen Khan – traditional oral literature

VC – Viet Cong or Vietnamese Communists; considered a derogatory term until recently
Viet Kieu – Overseas Vietnamese
Viet Minh – League for the Independence of Vietnam, a nationalistic movement which fought the Japanese and French but later became fully communist-dominated

xang – petrol
xe dap loi – wagon pulled by bicycle
xe Honda loi – wagon pulled by a motorbike
xe Lam – three-wheeled motorised vehicle, Lambretta

Index

MAPS

TEXT

521

526

Thanks

Thanks to the many travellers who wrote in with helpful hints, useful advice and interesting and funny stories.

Anthony Abry (Jap), David Adamson (Aus), Arnold Ahlback, Jacqui Allan, Sandra Allbee (USA), Per Arenmo (S), Victor Ashe (USA), Mike Attwood, Claire Aylmer (UK), Ruth Bailey, Dana Barnett (USA), Chris Barrett (Aus), Larry Baumbach (USA), G Bell (NZ), Jon Benjamin (UK), Oliver Benn (UK), Linda Bergquist (S), Julia Bichard (UK), Martin Billington (UK), Gary Bingham (USA), David Bisbee (USA), Margaret Bishop (USA), Paul Bishop (Aus), Adrian Bloch (Nl), Tim Bourne (C), Ruth Bowen (Aus), David Boyall (Aus), Brauer (S), Fr, Sandy Brayshaw (Aus), Jane Britain (Aus), Lynda Britz (Aus), William Brown (Aus), Rachel Brun (Aus), Bruce Burger (USA), Jennifer Burns (USA), Valerie Burtin (UK), David Butler (Aus), H Cadgogan (Aus), Brendon Cantlon, Mark Carr (USA), Milton Cassidy (NZ), Philip Chappell (Aus), Rachelle Cheff (C), Benjamin Cherry (Aus), Julie Christie (UK), Chuong-Le, Sarah Clifford (HK), Jeffrey Cohen (USA), Anne Cosse, Marina Cox (Aus), Steven Crook, Paul Cummings (Aus)

Martha Dahlen (HK), Steven Dakin (Aus), Jean-Christophe Damond (F), Lindsay Davies (UK), John August Day (Jap), Dirk de Beul (B), Chris Denwood (UK), Callum Durward (NZ), Erik Duval (B), Helene Engfors (Nl), Pia Engholm (S), Daniel Eschle (CH), Caroline Falla (Jap), John Farley (USA), Ronald Fernandez (USA), Eric Fleming (Aus), Martin Franjois (F), Malcolm Fredman (Aus), Claus Fynbo (Dk), Dov & Raviv Ganchrow (Isr), Toni Gerber (CH), Bob Gibbons (UK), Fred Giovannini (USA), David Goldblum (S), Deborah Goodman (USA), Gorrit Goslinga (Nl), Germain Groll (F), Sue Grossey (UK), L R Hanson (UK), Jennifer Hardington (UK), William C Harty (USA), Anne Hastwell (Aus), Jonathon Hayssen (UK), Gerhard Heinzel (D), Mike Henderson (Aus), Frans Heuyerjans (Nl), Philip Hofmeijer (Nl), Alfred Hogenauer (A), A Hoog (Nl), Jerry Hopkins, Jo Howard (USA), Joseph Hrustinsky (Aus), Yvonne Hunziker (CH), Margaret Hussey (UK)

Holger Jensen (Dk), Max Johns (D), Matthew Jones (Aus), Hanne Jorgensen (Dk), Richard Juterbook (USA), Dr Peter Kaisser (D), Monica Kan (USA), Dave Kanler (USA), John & Heske Kannegieter (Nl), Gerhard Karl (A), Patrick Kavanagh (C), Brian Keane & Wendy Williams (USA), James Keddie (UK), John Kepski, Dr Arno Kitts (UK), Michael Kjaer (Dk), Harvey Kline (Jap), Simon Knowles (UK), Henk Kollaar (Nl), Joke Koppen (Nl), Kay & David Kos (C), C Kurz (USA), A Lachgar (F), Gwenda Lansburg (Aus), Tim Lawrence (UK), Choung-Le (V), John Leadley (UK), Hugh Levinson (UK), Jordi Llorens (Sp), David Loris, Gabriele Losch (USA), Martin Lowy (USA), John Lumley-Holmes, Martin Lykke (Dk), Brendan Lynch (Ire)

Rupert Macinnes (UK), Nguyen Thanh Mai (V), Julia Mason (UK), Genevieve Mayers (C), Tim McKnight (USA), Steve McNichols (USA), Ian McVittie (UK), Peter Mead (USA), Jane Metcalf (C), Heather Mitchell (USA), Tom Moers (Nl), Maureen Morgan (Aus), Mark Moriguchi (USA), Patrick Morris (USA), David Morrisey (NZ), Caroline Moss (UK), Stephan Mueller (CH), Alexander Muller (CH), Roger Musson (UK), Ty Van Nguyen (Aus), Henry Nilert (F), Robyn Nishimura (Aus), J North (UK), Peter Notley (Aus), Fr Roderick O'Brien (Aus), Anita O'Callaghan (Ire), Mike Olan, P A O'Neill (Aus), Dr Milton Osborne (Aus), Rainer Osterreicher (D), Yoshiaki Otsuki (Jap), Len Outram (Aus)

Sophie Perdrix (S), Magnus Persson (S), Ruth Perwani (UK), Joanne Pettit (Aus), N Thi Phu (V), Perroud Pierre-Andre (CH), Anna Pinnerup (Dk), Michael Potts (Aus), Lisa Preston (Aus), Cerian Price (Sin), June Priddle (UK), Peter Prior (Aus), Gunther Quaisser (D), Micahel Rainsbury (UK), Keith Rakow (USA), Angelina Rauschenbach (Jap), Stacy Raye (USA), Erik Reitsma (Nl), Rolf Richardson (UK), Richie Riekle (USA), Mark Riethorst (Nl), Julie Riville-Dechene (C), Abby Robinson (USA), Pete Robinson, Chris Rodway (UK), Marco Roebers (Nl), Mads Ropke (D), Ann Ryan (USA), Sandra Schenk (CH), Gerard Schlund (F), Thilo Schonfeld (D), Jason Schoonover (C), P Seller (Nl), Ronald Settle (USA), Liz Sharples (Aus), Angela Silberberg (S), Reto Sinniger (CH), P Slayer (Nl), Nicolai D Sokolinsky (B), Thierry Spanjaard (F), Peter Stoh (D), Annemette Stougaard (Dk), Nadia Stuewer (C), Harry Summers, Captain Peter Swartz (USA)

M Ten Dam (Nl), W M Tey (Sin), Ton That (V), P J Theuns (Nl), Neil Thewlis (UK), Tim & Bridget Thomas (UK), R W Timson (UK), Ho Wah Tong (Sin), Paul Trudeau (USA), Jeff Truong (USA), Michele Urbaniak (USA), John Nowell Ustick (USA), Michael Vale (UK), N C Van Beek (Nl), Henry Van Gael (B), Bernard Van Housebrouck (B), Nguyen Van Hue (V), Tran Van Le (V), Pham Van Luyen (V), Jane Vessey, Frank Visakay (USA), Ann Von Lossberg (USA), Rudiger Von Oehsen (D), Peter Von Thun (D), Philip Waldron (USA), Lynne Walkers (Aus), Inga Wallerius (S), Ian Walters (Aus), John Warburton (Aus), Gladys Watts (USA), Anne Weber (Dk), Jonas Weidow (S), Tim Weisselberg (UK), Bruce Weissman (USA), Patricia Wessels (Nl), Duncan Wetherall (UK), Kate Whitehead, Jim Whyte, Clare Williams (Aus), Robert Willis (Aus), Brigitte Wirtz (D), Julia Wood (UK), Tim Woodward, Phillip Wright (UK), Guillem Xamena (Sp), Michael Yelon (C), Erwin Zijleman (Nl)

A = Austria, Aus = Australia, B = Belgium, C = Canada, CH = Switzerland, D = Germany, Dk = Denmark, F = France, HK = Hong Kong, Ire = Ireland, Isr = Israel, Jap = Japan, Nl = The Netherlands, NZ = New Zealand, S = Sweden, Sin = Singapore, Sp = Spain, UK = United Kingdom, USA = United States of America, V = Vietnam

Dear traveller,

Prices go up, good places go bad, bad places go bankrupt...and every guidebook is inevitably outdated in places. Fortunately, many travellers write to us about their experiences, telling us when things have changed. If we reprint a book between editions, we try to include the best of this information in a Stop Press section. We also make travellers' tips immediately available on our World Wide Web Internet site (http://www.lonelyplanet.com) and in a free quarterly newsletter, *Planet Talk*.

Although much of this information has not been verified by our own first-hand research, we believe it can be very useful. We cannot vouch for its accuracy, however, so bear in mind it could be wrong.

We really enjoy hearing from people out on the road, and apart from guaranteeing that others will benefit from your good and bad experiences, we're prepared to bribe you with the offer of a free book for sending us substantial useful information.

I hope you do find this book useful – and that you let us know when it isn't. Thank you to everyone who has written.

Tony Wheeler

Introduction

The Vietnamese government is gearing up for an important Communist Party Congress in June 1996. These congresses are normally held every five or six years and publically set the Party's agenda. At this stage it is unclear the extent to which the congress will endorse the move towards a free market. There have been some worrying signs of a conservative backlash, including several arrests and a crackdown on foreign videos. In the meantime, the political hiatus can make life very difficult for the foreign businesspeople who are flocking to the country.

Embassies

Following its diplomatic recognition of Vietnam, the USA has established an embassy in Hanoi (☎ 431500), at 7 Lang Ha, Dong Da District. It's open from 8 am to 5 pm.

Visas & Permits

In late 1995, the Vietnamese authorities announced that extensions on tourist visas would no longer be granted. Business visas can still be extended but they cost more, take more time and involve more bureaucracy. As a result many travellers are making the overland run to Cambodia for a new Vietnamese visa. However, the Vietnamese immigration authorities at the Moc Bai border crossing sometimes turn away travellers trying to leave the country and send them back to Saigon if they lack a 'hotel stamp' from a hotel in Saigon on their arrival/departure card. All legal hotels in Saigon do have such a stamp and you'd be wise to get one if you plan to depart via Moc Bai. Travellers arriving at the border without a stamp have been known to get across after giving a US$20 tip to the immigration authorities.

Some travellers report that you might have problems with the Vietnamese Embassy in Bangkok. If you want to enter/exit somewhere unusual, you might find that the visa you get from that embassy is invalid, or that the embassy has ignored your request and given you standard entry/exit points.

A Vietnamese visa in Beijing costs about US$50 through a travel agency or US$25 if you do it yourself. Doing it yourself might mean very long delays, however, so the extra US$25 might be a good investment.

The phone number of the Vietnamese Embassy in Paris is ☎ 44.14.64.00.

Telephone

Vietnam is one of the world's most expensive countries from which to make international telephone calls. Making a collect call or reversing charges is impossible from a private telephone. You must do this at a post office or through a hotel operator for a charge of US$1. You should make arrangements to be called back.

All telephone numbers are changing, with an 8 added to the beginning of the number. Also, the domestic long-distance dialling prefix will be changed from 01 to 0.

Health

It's difficult to find sunscreen in Vietnam, so bring plenty.

Destinations

Dalat There's much less hassle with the authorities in Dalat these days. Foreigners are now permitted to stay at some private hotels, and hotel prices have come down. However, you still cannot hire a private taxi, and permits are still required for Lat Village and Lang Bian Mountain (these are cheaper than they were). The Mimosa Hotel is now a decent place to stay.

Danang The police roadblocks have gone, as have the arbitrary 'fines', apparently.

Hanoi There is a minibus at the airport that will take you into town for US$4 and, for an extra US$2, will drop you anywhere you want.

The train from Hanoi to Haiphong does not leave from the same place as all the other trains. The platform is just around the corner from the main station. You go left as you exit at the first main road, left again to where the road widens and becomes covered with shops selling pots and ropes. Then to the left is a narrow unpaved alley, very rough, down which you head and almost immediately to the left is the place to wait for the train.

The 'Hanoi Hilton' has been demolished.

Craft Link is a non-profit organisation linking small Vietnamese craft businesses to new markets. Craft Link holds at least three bazaars a year in Hanoi, and they are well worth visiting to see a wide variety of crafts from various regions and ethnic groups. For the date of the next bazaar, phone Craft Link

(☎ 430632) and ask for Amy Fendell or Hanh Bich Duong.

The Green Bamboo Cafe now offers an interesting day trip into suburban areas, visiting places such as Le Mat (snake village), and Van Phuc (silk village).

Ho Chi Minh City Pacific Airlines has moved to 61 Nguyen Thai St. Daily flights to Hanoi cost US$170.

The Australian Consulate (☎ 296035, fax 296031) has moved to Rooms 326-327, New World Hotel, 76 Le Lai St, District 1.

At the post office, don't get caught paying more than you should for local calls. These should be 800d, not the 10,000d the employee behind the desk might tell you.

Hoi An Twelve new hotels have opened here and there's no longer a shortage of accommodation. Prices have dropped because of the competition and some hotels are excellent value.

Nha Trang This city has changed unbelievably fast. The big party place for travellers is the Sailing Club, 72-74 Tran Phu Blvd. It's also the best place to rent watersport equipment, although for scuba gear you'll have to go elsewhere. The best place for diving is the Blue Diving Club (☎ 825390) at the Coconut Cove Resort, on the beach opposite the Hai Yen Hotel.

The Hung Dao Hotel, a favourite with budget travellers, is due to be demolished, but there are plenty of new hotels opening.

Qui Nhon The post office has moved, although the sign still hangs outside the old building, which is now some sort of military establishment. The new post office is near the short-haul transport station on Phan Boi Chau St.

Sapa Accommodation can be scarce in Sapa, so make a reservation or take your own sleeping gear.

A new road has opened north of Lao Cai, connecting the remote highland village of Bac Ha (elevation 900 metres) to the rest of the world. This area makes a good alternative to Sapa. Bac Ha is 230 km (10 hours by car) from Hanoi. Ask at the Old Darling Cafe for details about bus trips.

Getting Around

Car Rental Avis Rent A Car has set up operations in Ho Chi Minh City and Hanoi.

Travellers' Tips

We booked a minibus at Sinh Cafe from Saigon to Nha Trang. The ticket cost US$10. But it turned out to be a big bus, not a minibus, and it was almost empty. But then it stopped at every little village, picking up and discharging passengers all along the way. It took 12 hours to get to Nha Trang. So we paid US$10 for a local bus which should have cost US$2.

Christie Lee

We took the boat from Ha Tien to Chau Doc. The departure point is Tran Hung Dao St. It is probably best to take a cyclo (about 2000d) because it is difficult to find. The boat arrives about 5 am and departs about 6.30 am. Negotiate the price in advance. We finally paid a high 60,000d.

The boat has to stop at four border posts and this is a slow business. Apparently if you are the only foreigner on board the other passengers will tell you to hide in the bows because of Khmer Rouge pirates – actually it is to save them wasting time stopping for passport checks.

Peter Flegg (Aus)

I spent over two months cycling in Vietnam. I chose to go from north to south as I figured (correctly) that the weather in the north would be better in December than in February. As an unforeseen bonus, it turned out that the majority of tailwinds went my way. Also, it seemed to me (though I didn't check the passes) that the majority of passes along Highway 1 are shorter on the northern side, so the downhill runs are longer going south.

Liz Sharples (Aus)

For those inclined towards some hiking whilst in Vietnam, we strongly recommend the walk from Dac Glei to Phuoc Son. Crossing spectacular mountains covered in jungle, waterfalls and fruit plantations, and offering the privilege to view isolated hill tribes, we hiked for two days and swam in fresh water holes to complete the Central Highlands route from Buon Ma Thuot to Phuoc Son, where a local bus could be taken to Danang.

In Kontum our guide prepared us for the hike by buying us some 'snake repellent' (onions), high energy foods and enough information to fill an encyclopaedia. From Kontum a local bus takes about half a day to get to Dac Glei, where the walk commences. Aside from the odd blister, health and safety were no problem, though we kept our souvenir knives handy for tigers. The minimum equipment we recommend that you take is a tent, high-energy foods, water purification tablets and good hiking shoes.

Dorian Moro & Peter Johansen (Aus & Denmark)

Internet Info

For the latest travel information, check out the Lonely Planet web site:

http://www.lonelyplanet.com

Also useful is Journey to Vietnam:

http://maingate.net:80/vn/index.html1)

This site has FAQs about travelling to Vietnam and an archive of Reuters news reports on Vietnam.

There is also good information in the Destination Vietnam site:

http://www.well.com/user/gdisf/

This is a travel magazine by Global Directions Inc. For more links, try the Vietnam Links home page:

http://www.public.iastate.edu/~sogti/links1.html

Acknowledgments

The author, Robert Storey, supplied much of the information in this stop press after returning from a visit to Vietnam. Other reports came from: Stewart Lee Allen; Chern Sian Jye (Sin); Janine Parker (Aus); Sally Shenton (CH) and Ed van Steijn (Nl).

P.166 — MAIN ROUTE
P.172 — HITTING M → S

P 102 — syringes + needles.
— ORAL REHYDRATION SALTS

P 103 — HEART CURE

P 104 — MEDICAL KIT, + ZINC CREAM.

VEGGIE — COM CHAY

LONELY PLANET JOURNEYS

JOURNEYS is a unique collection of travellers' tales – published by the company that understands travel better than anyone else. It is a series for anyone who has ever experienced – or dreamed of – the magical moment when they encountered a strange culture or saw a place for the first time. They are tales to read while you're planning a trip, while you're on the road or while you're in an armchair, in front of a fire.

JOURNEYS books will catch the spirit of a place, illuminate a culture, recount a crazy adventure, or introduce a fascinating way of life. They will always entertain, and always enrich the experience of travel.

ISLANDS IN THE CLOUDS
Travels in the Highlands of New Guinea
Isabella Tree

This is the fascinating account of a journey to the remote and beautiful Highlands of Papua New Guinea and Irian Jaya. The author travels with a PNG Highlander who introduces her to his intriguing and complex world. *Islands in the Clouds* is a thoughtful, moving book, full of insights into a region that is rarely noticed by the rest of the world.

'One of the most accomplished travel writers to appear on the horizon for many years ... the dialogue is brilliant' – **Eric Newby**

LOST JAPAN
Alex Kerr

Lost Japan draws on the author's personal experiences of Japan over a period of 30 years. Alex Kerr takes his readers on a backstage tour: friendships with Kabuki actors, buying and selling art, studying calligraphy, exploring rarely visited temples and shrines ... The Japanese edition of this book was awarded the 1994 Shincho Gakugei Literature Prize for the best work of non-fiction.

'This deeply personal witness to Japan's wilful loss of its traditional culture is at the same time an immensely valuable evaluation of just what that culture was'
– **Donald Richie of the Japan Times**

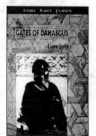

THE GATES OF DAMASCUS
Lieve Joris
Translated by Sam Garrett

This best-selling book is a beautifully drawn portrait of day-to-day life in modern Syria. Through her intimate contact with local people, Lieve Joris draws us into the fascinating world that lies behind the gates of Damascus.

'A brilliant book ... Not since Naguib Mahfouz has the everyday life of the modern Arab world been so intimately described' – **William Dalrymple**

SEAN & DAVID'S LONG DRIVE
Sean Condon

Sean and David are young townies who have rarely strayed beyond city limits. One day, for no good reason, they set out to discover their homeland, and what follows is a wildly entertaining adventure that covers half of Australia. Sean Condon has written a hilarious, offbeat road book that mixes sharp insights with deadpan humour and outright lies.

'Funny, pithy, kitsch and surreal ... This book will do for Australia what Chernobyl did for Kiev, but hey you'll laugh as the stereotypes go boom' – **Andrew Tuck, Time Out**

LONELY PLANET TRAVEL ATLASES

Lonely Planet has long been famous for the number and quality of its guidebook maps. Now we've gone one step further and in conjunction with Steinhart Katzir Publishers produced a handy companion series: Lonely Planet travel atlases – maps of a country produced in book form.

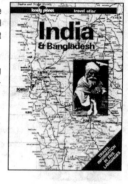

Unlike other maps, which look good but lead travellers astray, our travel atlases have been researched on the road by Lonely Planet's experienced team of writers. All details are carefully checked to ensure the atlas corresponds with the equivalent Lonely Planet guidebook.

The handy atlas format means no holes, wrinkles, torn sections or constant folding and unfolding. These atlases can survive long periods on the road, unlike cumbersome fold-out maps. The comprehensive index ensures easy reference.

- full-colour throughout
- maps researched and checked by Lonely Planet authors
- place names correspond with Lonely Planet guidebooks
  – no confusing spelling differences
- legend and travelling information in English, French, German, Japanese and Spanish
- size: 230 x 160 mm

Available now:
Thailand; India & Bangladesh; Vietnam; Zimbabwe, Botswana & Namibia

Coming soon:
Chile; Egypt; Israel; Laos; Turkey

LONELY PLANET TV SERIES & VIDEOS

Lonely Planet travel guides have been brought to life on television screens around the world. Like our guides, the programmes are based on the joy of independent travel, and look honestly at some of the most exciting, picturesque and frustrating places in the world. Each show is presented by one of three travellers from Australia, England or the USA and combines an innovative mixture of video, Super-8 film, atmospheric soundscapes and original music.

Videos of each episode – containing additional footage not shown on television – are available from good book and video shops, but the availability of individual videos varies with regional screening schedules.

Video destinations include: Alaska; Australia (Southeast); Brazil; Ecuador & the Galápagos Islands; Indonesia; Israel & the Sinai Desert; Japan; La Ruta Maya (Yucatán, Guatemala & Belize); Morocco; North India (Varanasi to the Himalaya); Pacific Islands; Vietnam; Zimbabwe, Botswana & Namibia.

Coming soon: The Arctic (Norway & Finland); Baja California; Chile & Easter Island; China (Southeast); Costa Rica; East Africa (Tanzania & Zanzibar); Great Barrier Reef (Australia); Jamaica; Papua New Guinea; the Rockies (USA); Syria & Jordan; Turkey.

The Lonely Planet TV series is produced by:
Pilot Productions
Duke of Sussex Studios
44 Uxbridge St
London W8 7TG UK

Lonely Planet videos are distributed by:
IVN Communications Inc
2246 Camino Ramon
California 94583, USA

107 Power Road, Chiswick
London W5 UK

Music from the TV series is available on CD & cassette.
For ordering information contact your nearest Lonely Planet office.

PLANET TALK

Lonely Planet's FREE quarterly newsletter

We love hearing from you and think you'd like to hear from us.
*When...*is the right time to see reindeer in Finland?
*Where...*can you hear the best palm-wine music in Ghana?
*How...*do you get from Asunción to Areguá by steam train?
*What...*is the best way to see India?

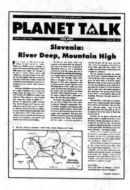

For the answer to these and many other questions read PLANET TALK.

Every issue is packed with up-to-date travel news and advice including:

*   a letter from Lonely Planet founders Tony and Maureen Wheeler
*   travel diary from a Lonely Planet author – find out what it's really like out on the road
*   feature article on an important and topical travel issue
*   a selection of recent letters from our readers
*   the latest travel news from all over the world
*   details on Lonely Planet's new and forthcoming releases

To join our mailing list contact any Lonely Planet office.

Also available: Lonely Planet T-shirts. 100% heavyweight cotton.

LONELY PLANET ONLINE

Get the latest travel information before you leave or while you're on the road

Whether you've just begun planning your next trip, or you're chasing down specific info on currency regulations or visa requirements, check out the Lonely Planet World Wide Web site for up-to-the-minute travel information.

As well as travel profiles of your favourite destinations (including interactive maps and full-colour photos), you'll find current reports from our army of researchers and other travellers, updates on health and visas, travel advisories, and the ecological and political issues you need to be aware of as you travel.

There's an online travellers' forum (the Thorn Tree) where you can share your experiences of life on the road, meet travel companions and ask other travellers for their recommendations and advice. We also have plenty of links to other Web sites useful to independent travellers.

With tens of thousands of visitors a month, the Lonely Planet Web site is one of the most popular on the Internet and has won a number of awards including GNN's Best of the Net travel award.

http://www.lonelyplanet.com

LONELY PLANET PRODUCTS

The Lonely Planet list covers every accessible part of Asia as well as Australia, the Pacific, South America, Africa, the Middle East, Europe and parts of North America. There are eight series: *travel guides* – covering a country for a range of budgets, *shoestring guides* – with compact information for low-budget travel in a major region, *walking guides*, *city guides*, *phrasebooks*, *audio packs*, *travel atlases* and *travel literature*.

EUROPE

Austria • Baltic States & Kaliningrad • Baltic States phrasebook • Britain • Central Europe on a shoestring • Central Europe phrasebook • Czech & Slovak Republics • Dublin city guide • Eastern Europe on a shoestring • Eastern Europe phrasebook • Finland • France • Greece • Greek phrasebook • Hungary • Iceland, Greenland & the Faroe Islands • Ireland • Italy • Mediterranean Europe on a shoestring • Mediterranean Europe phrasebook • Poland • Prague city guide • Russia, Ukraine & Belarus • Russian phrasebook • Scandinavian & Baltic Europe on a shoestring • Scandinavian Europe phrasebook • Slovenia • St Petersburg city guide • Switzerland • Trekking in Greece • Trekking in Spain • Vienna city guide • Walking in Switzerland • Western Europe on a shoestring • Western Europe phrasebook

NORTH AMERICA & MEXICO

Alaska • Backpacking in Alaska • California & Nevada • Canada • Hawaii • Honolulu city guide • Los Angeles city guide • Pacific Northwest USA • Rocky Mountain States • San Francisco city guide • Southwest USA • USA phrasebook

CENTRAL AMERICA & THE CARIBBEAN

Baja California • Central America on a shoestring • Costa Rica • Eastern Caribbean • Guatemala, Belize & Yucatán: La Ruta Maya • Mexico

SOUTH AMERICA

Argentina, Uruguay & Paraguay • Bolivia • Brazil • Brazilian phrasebook • Buenos Aires city guide • Chile & Easter Island • Colombia • Ecuador & the Galápagos Islands • Latin American Spanish phrasebook • Peru • Quechua phrasebook • Rio de Janeiro city guide • South America on a shoestring • Trekking in the Patagonian Andes • Venezuela

AFRICA

Arabic (Moroccan) phrasebook • Africa on a shoestring • Cape Town city guide • Central Africa • East Africa • Egypt & the Sudan • Ethiopian (Amharic) phrasebook • Kenya • Morocco • North Africa • South Africa, Lesotho & Swaziland • Swahili phrasebook • Trekking in East Africa • West Africa • Zimbabwe, Botswana & Namibia • Zimbabwe, Botswana & Namibia travel atlas

ALSO AVAILABLE:

Travel with Children • Traveller's Tales

MAIL ORDER

Lonely Planet products are distributed worldwide. They are also available by mail order from Lonely Planet, so if you have difficulty finding a title please write to us. US, Canadian and South American residents should write to Embarcadero West, 155 Filbert St, Suite 251, Oakland CA 94607, USA; European and African residents should write to 10 Barley Mow Passage, Chiswick, London W4 4PH; and residents of other countries to PO Box 617, Hawthorn, Victoria 3122, Australia.

NORTH-EAST ASIA

Beijing city guide • Cantonese phrasebook • China • Hong Kong, Macau & Canton • Japan • Japanese phrasebook • Japanese audio pack • Korea • Korean phrasebook • Mandarin phrasebook • Mongolia • Mongolian phrasebook • North-East Asia on a shoestring • Seoul city guide • Taiwan • Tibet • Tibet phrasebook • Tokyo city guide

Travel Literature: Lost Japan

INDIAN SUBCONTINENT

Bengali phrasebook • Bangladesh • Delhi city guide • Hindi/Urdu phrasebook • India • India & Bangladesh travel atlas • Karakoram Highway • Kashmir, Ladakh & Zanskar • Nepal • Nepali phrasebook • Pakistan • Sri Lanka • Sri Lanka phrasebook • Trekking in the Indian Himalaya • Trekking in the Nepal Himalaya

SOUTH-EAST ASIA

Bali & Lombok • Bangkok city guide • Burmese phrasebook • Cambodia • Ho Chi Minh city guide • Indonesia • Indonesian phrasebook • Indonesian audio pack • Jakarta city guide • Java • Laos • Lao phrasebook • Malaysia, Singapore & Brunei • Myanmar (Burma) • Philippines • Pilipino phrasebook • Singapore city guide • South-East Asia on a shoestring • Thailand • Thailand travel atlas • Thai phrasebook • Thai audio pack • Thai Hill Tribes phrasebook • Vietnam • Vietnamese phrasebook • Vietnam travel atlas

MIDDLE EAST & CENTRAL ASIA

Arab Gulf States • Arabic (Egyptian) phrasebook • Central Asia • Iran • Israel • Jordan & Syria • Middle East • Turkey • Turkish phrasebook • Trekking in Turkey • Yemen

Travel Literature: The Gates of Damascus

ISLANDS OF THE INDIAN OCEAN

Madagascar & Comoros • Maldives & Islands of the East Indian Ocean • Mauritius, Réunion & Seychelles

AUSTRALIA & THE PACIFIC

Australia • Australian phrasebook • Bushwalking in Australia • Bushwalking in Papua New Guinea • Fiji • Fijian phrasebook • Islands of Australia's Great Barrier Reef • Melbourne city guide • Micronesia • New Caledonia • New South Wales & the ACT • New Zealand • Outback Australia • Papua New Guinea • Papua New Guinea phrasebook • Queensland • Rarotonga & the Cook Islands • Samoa • Solomon Islands • Sydney city guide • Tahiti & French Polynesia • Tonga • Tramping in New Zealand • Vanuatu • Victoria • Western Australia

Travel Literature: Islands in the Clouds • Sean & David's Long Drive

THE LONELY PLANET STORY

Lonely Planet published its first book in 1973 in response to the numerous 'How did you do it?' questions Maureen and Tony Wheeler were asked after driving, bussing, hitching, sailing and railing their way from England to Australia.

Written at a kitchen table and hand collated, trimmed and stapled, *Across Asia on the Cheap* became an instant local bestseller, inspiring thoughts of another book.

Eighteen months in South-East Asia resulted in their second guide, *South-East Asia on a shoestring*, which they put together in a backstreet Chinese hotel in Singapore in 1975. The 'yellow bible' as it quickly became known to backpackers around the world, soon became *the* guide to the region. It has sold well over half a million copies and is now in its 8th edition, still retaining its familiar yellow cover.

Today there are over 180 titles, including travel guides, walking guides, language kits & phrasebooks, travel atlases and travel literature. The company is one of the largest travel publishers in the world. Although Lonely Planet initially specialised in guides to Asia, we now cover most regions of the world, including the Pacific, North America, South America, Africa, the Middle East and Europe.

The emphasis continues to be on travel for independent travellers. Tony and Maureen still travel for several months of each year and play an active part in the writing, updating and quality control of Lonely Planet's guides.

They have been joined by over 50 authors and 155 staff at our offices in Melbourne (Australia), Oakland (USA), London (UK) and Paris (France). Travellers themselves also make a valuable contribution to the guides through the feedback we receive in thousands of letters each year.

The people at Lonely Planet strongly believe that travellers can make a positive contribution to the countries they visit, both through their appreciation of the countries' culture, wildlife and natural features, and through the money they spend. In addition, the company makes a direct contribution to the countries and regions it covers. Since 1986 a percentage of the income from each book has been donated to ventures such as famine relief in Africa; aid projects in India; agricultural projects in Central America; Greenpeace's efforts to halt French nuclear testing in the Pacific; and Amnesty International.

Lonely Planet's basic travel philosophy is summed up in Tony Wheeler's comment, 'Don't worry about whether your trip will work out. Just go!'

LONELY PLANET PUBLICATIONS

Australia
PO Box 617, Hawthorn 3122, Victoria
tel: (03) 9819 1877 fax: (03) 9819 6459
e-mail: talk2us@lonelyplanet.com.au

USA
Embarcadero West, 155 Filbert St, Suite 251,
Oakland, CA 94607
tel: (510) 893 8555 TOLL FREE: 800 275-8555
fax: (510) 893 8563
e-mail: info@lonelyplanet.com

UK
10 Barley Mow Passage, Chiswick,
London W4 4PH
tel: (0181) 742 3161 fax: (0181) 742 2772
e-mail: 100413.3551@compuserve.com

France:
71 bis rue du Cardinal Lemoine, 75005 Paris
tel: 1 44 32 06 20 fax: 1 46 34 72 55
e-mail: 100560.415@compuserve.com

World Wide Web: http://www.lonelyplanet.com